Election 2001

The Official Results

Election 2001

The Official Results

Electoral **X** Commission

First published in Great Britain 2001
Politico's Publishing
8 Artillery Row
Westminster
London SW1P 1RZ

Tel 020 7931 0090
Fax 020 7828 8111
Email publishing@politicos.co.uk
Website http://www.politicos.co.uk/publishing

First published in hardback 2001

A catalogue record for this book is available from the British Library.

ISBN 1 842750 20 8

Printed and bound in Great Britain by Creative Print and Design Ltd.
Typeset by Dawn Cole, University of Plymouth.

Contents

Preface

The big drop in turnout on 7 June – down to 59.4% from 71.4% in 1997 – is surely the single most important aspect of the 2001 general election. Fewer than six out of every ten eligible voters across the United Kingdom bothered to take part in choosing the country's government for the next five years. This apparently accelerating trend away from participation in the institutions of democracy contrasts with what seems to be a growing tendency for people to make their voice heard through a variety of forms of direct action rather than through the ballot box. Politicians and commentators of all persuasions have rightly identified voter engagement as a key priority for the future.

The establishment of the Electoral Commission, on 30 November 2000, was therefore particularly timely, even if it is widely regarded as long overdue. Although the trigger for the establishment of the Commission was the need for a body to implement and monitor new controls on political party funding and campaign expenditure, our remit goes much wider to embrace modernisation of electoral process and law, and voter education. For the first time, therefore, there is a UK-wide focal point for debate and action on electoral issues. For many years we have as a nation very much taken the robust good health of our democracy for granted. The Commission's commitment is to ensure that the electoral process underpinning that democracy receives the detailed attention it deserves and has in the past often lacked. This first report on the 2001 general election seeks to identify some of the key issues on the agenda.

The Commission cannot, nor should it, seek solutions on its own. Whatever changes there may be in the future must be formulated with, and command the support of, political parties, the administrators who run elections and all those with an interest in the electoral process. Indeed, on the issue of voter turnout and engagement, it is above all the quality and persuasiveness of the policies put forward by the political parties and their ability to motivate voters that will determine future trends. Nevertheless, the Commission can play a significant role. A wide variety of causes of declining turnout at elections have been identified, matched by an equally wide variety of suggested responses. Our first priority will be a programme of research into these causes, both at a national level and among particular groups. Without that, any programme of voter education risks being well intentioned but poorly targeted. Our aim is to identify the key audiences that need to be addressed, and then to address them, not on our own, but in partnership with those organisations best placed to do so.

If initiatives designed to address declining turnout directly are for the longer term and often for others to take the lead, the Commission is determined to press forward at once with an agenda for making voting easier and more 'user friendly'. We have a statutory obligation to report on the administration of the election and our preliminary report identifies a number of key areas in which reform is urgently needed. That is not to say that the system itself is on the verge of collapse. Far from it. It is a tribute to the dedication and professionalism of those who administer our elections that public trust and confidence in the fairness and integrity of the system have been fully maintained. And there is every reason to sustain what has worked effectively for so many years, above all the independence and reputation for impartiality of local Returning Officers. Nevertheless, in consultation with Returning Officers, administrators and others, we have identified a number of key priorities.

First, although the new system of rolling voter registration is to be welcomed, the registration system needs updating in order to make it more accessible to voters, largely through the use of information technology and including considering establishing a national register. Second, we believe that we must promote the availability of means by which voters can participate without having to visit a polling station. Although we will be reporting more fully on the issue of potential and actual fraud in relation to postal voting and what further measures might be necessary to protect against it, we believe that postal votes on demand are an important benefit to the voter. Eliminating fraud is clearly critical to the all-important public trust in the electoral system. However, at the 2001 general election, the greater problems in postal voting were administrative and we will be examining how these can best be overcome. We also believe that the future lies in finding secure means of extending absent voting through use of telephones and the internet, and we will be promoting pilot schemes in these areas.

Third, and in the light of the increasing difficulties of recruiting suitably qualified and experienced staff to run elections, we plan to review the somewhat confused system of funding, with a view to rationalising it and ensuring that elections are funded in a way that is appropriate to their importance as the basis for our civil society. Fourth, we see the need to develop guidelines for electoral administrators and ensure that, through them and the development of training programmes, the practices of all match those of the best. Fifth, we will support and promote the widespread introduction of electronic systems and new technology to underpin the efficient administration of voting and counting, independently of the development of absent voting.

There are a number of other areas arising out of the election campaign, which will form part of our agenda. We will be reviewing party election broadcasts and the use of the internet in election campaigns. In the light of the experience gained in the 2001 election, in consultation with the parties we will develop and publish the Code of Practice on Campaign Expenditure indicated in the Political Parties Elections and Referendums Act 2000. On the funding and financial controls introduced under the Act, a future agenda will be identified more fully when we report on the financial aspects of the election, after the parties' and candidates' spending returns have been completed and analysed. It is already clear that we will need to review the rules as they affect small parties, in order to minimise the administrative burden on them and ensure that they are not discouraged from participation in the electoral process. We will also review the rules covering third parties, and in particular the scope of the definition of what should be regarded as 'election material'. In due course we will also review the operation of the rules on reporting large donations both to parties and to individuals, and consider the case for a cap on individual donations and for state funding of political parties.

This is an ambitious agenda for the Commission, but one which we believe must be tackled in order to bring our electoral processes up to date. The key to moving forward is not just to identify the measures we believe are needed, but to ensure that they command wide support and that in Parliament the same all-party backing that characterised the passage of the Political Parties, Elections and Referendums Act 2000 is sustained for the benefit of future generations of voters and the health of our democratic system.

Sam Younger
Chairman, Electoral Commission
July 2001

Overview

1 The General Election 2001

This is the first of the Electoral Commission's reports on the general election 2001. It provides an account of the election, including the full results of the election in each constituency, and a summary of the key facts and figures. In doing so, this publication breaks new ground. Just as importantly, it sets out an agenda for the future conduct of elections.

In the first part of this report we present an overview of the election and our preliminary assessment of the way it was administered, as well as comments on the conduct of the election campaign, media coverage, the operation of financial controls and the attitude of voters. Above all, we look at the extent to which potential voters were informed and engaged by the election campaign and how this translated into actual voting. From this overview, we draw some initial conclusions about the ways in which elections may need to change in future. We shall pursue these issues in more detail as the Commission's agenda for change. We do not attempt to predict in this report the precise outcomes of our further detailed work. However, we make clear where we believe that change is necessary and identify the main priorities for action in the immediate future. We hope that by setting out the issues that we believe warrant further examination, others will be prompted to offer their own views and suggestions and so inform our programme of work.

The second part of this report includes the official results of the election, compiled from data submitted by the Returning Officers and Acting Returning Officers of England, Wales, Scotland and Northern Ireland, and analysed by a team led by Professors Colin Rallings and Michael Thrasher at the University of Plymouth. The publication of the results in this format is in itself a break from the past. Official general election results have previously been published only as part of the Government's analysis of candidates' expenses and in recent years have not appeared until some time after the election date.

The Commission will also be publishing in spring 2002 a second volume of our report on the election, covering in detail the parties' expenditure on the campaign at local and national levels. The timing of the second volume is designed to enable us to draw on the campaign expenditure returns submitted by the main political parties, which must be with the Commission by 7 December 2001.

Facts and Figures
- In total, there were 26.4 million votes cast.
- The Labour Party secured the largest number of seats (412), winning a majority of 166. They also secured the largest number of votes, with 41% of those voting supporting them.
- Overall voter turnout was the lowest recorded for a Westminster Parliament election since the advent of universal adult suffrage. Only 59.4 % of the

44,403,238 registered voters eligible to vote in the general election chose to exercise that right. The figure for 1997 was 71.4%.

- Despite predictions that devolution might reduce the relevance of the Westminster Parliament for voters outside England, turnout in Scotland and Wales – at 58.1% and 61.4% respectively – was not significantly different from England at 59.1%. However, turnout in Northern Ireland did buck the general trend, rising by 1% over the 1997 election, reaching 68%.

- A record number of valid postal votes were cast. Preliminary data suggest a figure in excess of 1.4 million people voting by post. This compares to 738,614 valid postal votes cast at the 1997 general election. The Home Office call centre set up to deal with enquiries about postal voting received over 93,000 calls during the election period. In addition, nearly 280,000 hits were recorded on www.postalvotes.gov.uk.

- In England, Scotland and Wales, 11 registered political parties had the opportunity to present party election broadcasts. Six of these parties had broadcasts in all three nations, one had broadcasts in England and Wales, and the other four had broadcasts only in Scotland or Wales. In Northern Ireland, six parties had broadcasts.

- There were 179 parties registered with the Commission on the last day for registration, and 75 of those parties fielded candidates for the general election. There were also seven registered 'third parties'.

- Independent candidates, or candidates without description, stood in nearly 20% of all seats contested, but no 'Independent' candidate won a seat. There were also 35 registered parties who fielded candidates in only one seat, often focusing on a local issue. In Wyre Forest, the seat was won on behalf of one such party, registered as Independent Kidderminster Hospital and Health Concern.

The Electoral Commission

On 30 November 2000, following the enactment of the Political Parties, Elections and Referendums Act 2000 (PPERA), the Commission was established as an independent statutory authority covering the whole of the United Kingdom. The Commission is headed by a Chairman with five other Commissioners. The Chairman and Commissioners do not have connections to any political party, nor is the Commission accountable to the Government. It reports directly to Parliament through a committee chaired by the Speaker of the House of Commons.

The Commission is responsible for overseeing a number of aspects of electoral law, including the registration of political parties and third parties, monitoring and publication of significant donations to registered political parties and holders of elective office, and the regulation of national party spending on election campaigns. The Commission also has a role in advising those involved in elections on practice and procedure and is required to report on the administration of every major election. However, unlike many electoral commissions outside the UK, the Commission does not have responsibility for maintaining and updating electoral rolls, employing electoral services staff, or conducting parliamentary or local elections.

The Commission aims to:

- promote openness in the financial affairs of the UK's political parties
- increase public confidence in the democratic process
- promote public awareness of electoral matters and systems of government
- increase the proportion of people who vote in elections
- make an important contribution to the development of electoral processes in the UK
- become a recognised centre of expertise on electoral issues

Reviewing Elections

The Commission has a statutory responsibility to report on major UK elections. Under the terms of section 5 of PPERA, the Commission is required, following a relevant election, to "prepare and publish (in such manner as the Commission may determine) a report on the administration of the election…" In addition, section 6 of PPERA states that the Commission "shall keep under review, and from time to time submit reports to the Secretary of State on … (a) such matters relating to elections to which this section applies as the Commission may determine from time to time…(e) the registration of political parties and the regulation of their income and expenditure; (f) political advertising in the broadcast and other electronic media…" This is the first Commission report under section 5 of PPERA. However, the overview offered in this report deliberately ranges wider than the administrative issues involved in conducting an election. It highlights issues and themes that the Commission plans to return to in future in fulfilling its remit under section 6 of PPERA.

In preparing this report, the Commission has drawn on a wide range of sources. In addition to the data prepared by the University of Plymouth and included in the second part of this report, based on returns from *all* (Acting) Returning Officers, the sources used by the Commission include:

- Statistical data from the (Acting) Returning Officers in 85% of all constituencies and completed questionnaires from party election agents and Parliamentary candidates in over 90 constituencies, representing 15 different parties.
- Contributions to a seminar discussion convened by Dr David Butler, Chair of the Hansard Society, in June 2001 involving over 30 individuals from a range of interested sectors: electoral administrators, party officials, broadcasters and journalists, research and polling organisations, academics and lawyers.
- A two-part survey of voter attitudes conducted by MORI for the Commission in May and June 2001, the full results of which are available from the Commission on request or available to view at www.electoralcommission.org.uk or www.mori.com, together with an explanation of the methodology.
- Discussions and workshops with electoral administrators in Scotland, Wales, Northern Ireland and a number of regions in England.
- Responses to an invitation to comment issued by the Commission to over 60 stakeholder organisations, including broadcasters, law enforcement agencies, a range of representative bodies and registered 'third parties'.

- Visits to constituencies during the election campaign, including discussions with local media representatives, electoral administrators and party agents.
- Academic analysis provided by, amongst others, Dr Margaret Scammell at the London School of Economics, Dr Martin Harrop at the University of Newcastle-upon-Tyne and the Communications Research Centre at Loughborough University, directed by Professor Peter Golding, Professor Michael Billig and David Deacon, with Dr Dominic Wring and Dr John Downey.
- Monitoring of election-related websites and media reporting of the election.
- Public and practitioner comments, submitted to the Commission through its website and through other correspondence.

We are grateful to all those individuals and organisations that have assisted in the preparation of this report, and for responding to the tight deadlines imposed by the Commission. At this stage, because of time constraints, analysis of the information sources referred to above has been limited. The Commission intends to return to these sources, and others, in taking forward our programme of work over the next two years.

Announcing the Election

The Prime Minister announced on 8 May 2001 that the Queen had agreed to dissolve Parliament and an election for the House of Commons would be held on 7 June 2001. The Queen issued the proclamation dissolving Parliament, and declaring the calling of another, on 14 May 2001. The writs for the 2001 general election were issued the same day by the Clerk of the Crown in Chancery (the Permanent Secretary of the Lord Chancellor's Department) and the Secretary of State for Northern Ireland.

A writ is sent to the Returning Officer for each constituency, calling for the election of a Member to serve in Parliament. The Returning Officer is the senior official tasked in electoral law with managing the election process; in England and Wales, the functions of the Returning Officer are usually delegated to an Acting Returning Officer, with the Returning Officer personally playing only a ceremonial role (often including the declaration of the results). In Scotland, however, the Returning Officer will normally be the person responsible for election management. In Northern Ireland, a different set of arrangements applies because of the role of the Chief Electoral Officer in overseeing elections. The Chief Electoral Officer is the Returning Officer for all elections, but his functions are delegated to Acting Returning Officers in each constituency.

The issue of the writs officially triggered the election process. In 659 constituencies across the UK, Members of Parliament would be elected to sit in the House of Commons. Electors in 45 local authority areas in England were also able to vote in local council elections on the same date. These elections had been postponed from 3 May as a result of the foot and mouth disease outbreak in the UK. In addition, several local council by-elections took place and in Scotland there were two by-elections for vacant seats in the Scottish Parliament. The local elections in Northern Ireland, which were due on 17 May, were also postponed to 7 June.

What Was New

The legal framework for the 2001 general election was significantly different from that in place for the 1997 general election. As well as establishing the Commission, PPERA made a number of amendments to the Representation of the People Acts (RPA), and created a wide range of new obligations on political parties and others involved in election campaigns. The Election Publications Act 2001 and RPA 2000 further added to the changes made by PPERA. The following are some of the major new legal provisions affecting the 2001 general election:

* Rolling registration was introduced from 16 February 2001. There is no longer a fixed annual date of registration. Applications made early each month are now considered by Electoral Registration Officers and those eligible are added to the register at the beginning of the following month.

* From the same date, anyone on the electoral register in England, Wales or Scotland could vote by post at an election, without needing to give a reason. Postal voting could be arranged for any election during a set period, or could be requested for a specific election.

* All political parties had to be registered with the Commission by 17 May 2001 in order to use the party name on the ballot paper at the Westminster parliamentary election. Any candidate without a registered party name could appear on the ballot paper only as 'Independent' or with no description at all (save for the one seat where the Speaker was entitled to describe himself as "the Speaker standing for re-election").

* Any third party intending to spend significant sums during the election campaign (more than £10,000 in England, or more than £5,000 in any one of Scotland, Wales or Northern Ireland) on material designed to promote one or more registered parties or category of candidates was also required to register with the Commission.

* Registered political parties were required to submit weekly reports to the Commission on donations over £5000. For the first time, they were also bound by national campaign expenditure limits of £15.8 million or £24,000 per constituency contested. Registered third parties were also subject to a spending limit.

* Improvements were made in facilities for disabled voters, including large print ballot papers displayed in polling stations and the availability of a tactile voting device, both designed to assist visually impaired voters.

The second chapter of this report looks at how far these changes were understood, how effectively they were implemented and any problems that arose. It should also be noted that other legislative changes relating to electoral practice and procedure were agreed by Parliament prior to the 2001 general election, but they did not take effect before the election. These included, for example, redefining candidates' election expenses and new controls on donations to candidates.

Election Timetable and Procedures

Most of the key stages of the election timetable are fixed by law. The Representation of the People Act (RPA) 1983 sets a minimum period of 17 working days between the calling of a general election and the poll taking place. Unlike some other countries, there is no upper limit on the length of the election period. By tradition, however, the general election is called between four and six weeks ahead of polling day. The formal timetable for the 2001 general election is set out below. The main features of the timetable were largely unchanged from previous general elections, save for the new postal voting provisions.

Calendar date in 2001	Day	Stage
Tuesday 8 May	–	Trigger date for reporting party donations to the Electoral Commission
Monday 14 May	0	Proclamation summoning new Parliament, dissolution of old Parliament, issue of writ
Tuesday 15 May	1	Receipt of writ by Returning Officer
Wednesday 16 May	2	
Thursday 17 May	3	Last day for publication of notice of election (4pm) Last day for registration as a political party
Friday 18 May	4	
Monday 21 May	5	
Tuesday 22 May	6	Latest day for delivery of nomination papers, with-drawals of candidature, and appointment of election agents (4pm) Statement of persons nominated published at close of time for making objections to nomination papers (5 pm) or as soon afterwards as any objections are disposed of
Wednesday 23 May	7	
Thursday 24 May	8	
Friday 25 May	9	
Monday 28 May	–	BANK HOLIDAY
Tuesday 29 May	10	
Wednesday 30 May	11	Last day for receipt of absent (postal and proxy) voting applications (5pm)
Thursday 31 May	12	
Friday 1 June	13	
Monday 4 June	14	

cont'd . . .

Calendar date in 2001	Day	Stage
Tuesday 5 June	15	Last day for appointment of polling and counting agents
Wednesday 6 June	16	Last day for applications for spoilt or lost postal ballot papers (5pm)
Thursday 7 June	17	Polling day (7am – 10pm)
Friday 8 June	–	Ballot papers sent to the Clerk to the Crown in Chancery by the Returning Officer
Sunday 10 June	–	Deadline for return of the writs giving the name of the elected Members
Wednesday 13 June	–	Parliament reassembles
Thursday 12 July	–	Deadline for submission of candidates' election expenses to (Acting) Returning Officer
Friday 7 September	–	Deadline for submission of national campaign expenditure returns to Electoral Commission (total expenditure £250,000 *or less*)
Friday 7 December	–	Deadline for submission of national campaign expenditure returns to Electoral Commission (total expenditure *over* £250,000)

Note – In computing any period of time for the purposes of the timetable, the following days are disregarded ('*dies non*'): Saturdays, Sundays, Christmas Eve, Christmas Day, Maundy Thursday, Good Friday, bank holidays and any day appointed for public thanksgiving or mourning.

2 Election Issues

This was an election in which election process and procedure seemed, at times, to become the focus of the campaign. The Communications Research Centre at Loughborough University analysed media coverage of the election, week on week, and consistently found that around 40% of all election coverage was about the process of the election and the campaign, rather than the policies, issues or politicians' conduct. A similar pattern was evident in the 1997 election.

Even before the 2001 election was called, issues of process and constitutional propriety were raised. The possible impact of foot and mouth disease on access to candidates and polling stations and the uncertainty over the Prime Minister's preferred date for the general election both highlighted key aspects of electoral practice. During the last week of the election, stories of fraudulent postal voting became widespread, with varying degrees of accuracy or substance. The risk of large-scale public lack of interest or apathy was also a regular theme of media coverage, and an issue that all the major parties tried to address in their election campaigning.

It is also important to note that the 18 month period leading up to the general election had seen a welter of new legislation and regulations – involving more changes to electoral practice and procedure than had been experienced since the introduction of the RPA 1983, which itself was largely a consolidating measure. These changes affected not only those involved in administering elections, but those managing campaigns, the candidates and voters.

Voter Turnout

In advance of the 2001 general election, many commentators took the view that turnout was likely to fall below 70%. This was regarded as an important threshold. A survey by ICM for *BBC Radio 1* in the first week of the campaign also suggested that fewer than 20% of young people were absolutely certain to use their vote in the election. The risk of a low turnout concerned the parties, not least because of the implication for party share if particular sections of the electorate turned out to be more uninterested in the election than others. In the weeks leading up to polling day, the major political parties also focused their advertising and media messages on "getting the voters out".

In the event, the turnout was 59.4% and even lower than most commentators had dared to project. The figure is the lowest since the election in 1918, immediately following the First World War, and is the lowest ever recorded in the UK since women won the vote on equal terms with men in 1928. Equally striking is the size of the drop since the 1997 general election. This was 12 percentage points or nearly 5 million individuals. The Commission believes that identifying and addressing the causes of low turnout is a key challenge facing the UK's political system and leaders.

We provide here an initial, and therefore inconclusive, overview of the reasons why more than four in ten people were not persuaded that it was worth their while casting a vote in the 2001 general election.

Voter Participation

Although voter participation is dropping generally across Western democracies, recent UK turnout levels and trends do not compare well with other countries in Europe and beyond:

- Prior to the 2001 figures, the 1997 general election turnout of 71.4% was a new post-war low in the UK.

- The UK has the lowest turnout rates in Europe for elections to the European Parliament: 36.5% in 1994 and 24% in 1999.

- Local government elections saw a 29.6% turnout in 2000, falling from an average of 41% in the 20 years between 1976 and 1996.

- The worldwide average turnout in national elections post-1990 is 64%. The UK came 65 in a list of 163 countries ranked according to national election turnout between 1990 and 1997.

In this section, and elsewhere, we draw on the results of two surveys conducted for the Commission by MORI. The surveys were conducted by telephone at the beginning of the election campaign and during the period immediately following the election, and were designed to gauge public attitudes towards voting, elections and the political process. Phase 1 of the survey was conducted between 9 and 15 May 2001, and so began the day after the general election was called. MORI interviewed a sample of 1,801 adults aged 18+ across the UK. Phase 2 of the survey was conducted between 9 and 18 June 2001 and involved re-contacting respondents from Phase 1 who were willing to be interviewed again. MORI re-interviewed 1,162 of the original sample. Questions in Phase 2 were designed to test how the campaign influenced voters' attitudes.

This approach provided the opportunity to see how views had changed over time. However, using the same group for both phases means that there may have been an element of 'conditioning' with respondents' interest and participation in the election being boosted by taking part in the Phase 1 survey. Additionally, while those who agreed to be re-contacted are demographically similar in profile to all Phase 1 respondents, there are some attitudinal differences. For example, they are more likely to say that they are interested in politics and that they 'always' vote at general elections.

Why Vote?

The Government has not, traditionally, run voter education campaigns designed simply to encourage turnout at elections. Their focus in voter education has been registration and, in the 2001 general election, the wider availability of postal voting. From 1 July 2001, the Commission took on responsibility for voter education, but had not done so in time for the general election. Publicity to encourage voting was therefore a matter for the parties, candidates, local authorities and the media. Accordingly, the level of effort directed at persuading any particular individual to cast their vote depended largely on where they lived.

However, the reasons for low turnout go well beyond the absence of a co-ordinated national campaign to encourage voting. As we discuss later, some local newspapers, television programmes and radio stations did attempt to encourage voter participation, many electoral services teams put considerable effort into initiatives designed to maximize registration and promote flexible ways of voting, and candidates in many constituencies placed considerable emphasis on making personal contact with potential voters.

Academic analysis in the UK and elsewhere suggests that there are a number of other important factors influencing turnout: the nature of the competition between the parties, the likelihood of an individual vote making a difference to the outcome of the election (especially in areas where there is a historically large majority for one particular party), the style and content of national media coverage, and a decline in the sense of civic duty, especially among younger people. In any particular election, these factors will have varying degrees of impact.

MORI's findings reinforce the academic arguments that habit and civic duty are key motivators to voting. Civic duty and habit were among the main reasons people gave when asked by MORI at the beginning of the campaign why they said they were certain to vote on 7 June. More than one-third (36%) said they would vote because they "always vote", with one-fifth citing "civic duty/everyone should vote". Older people were more likely to mention "always voting", but "civic duty" was spontaneously mentioned equally across the age groups. One-fifth said they were "certain" to vote because "it is my right" and one in six said they would do so to "have their say" (16%). In both cases, younger people aged 18–34 were more likely to give these reasons than were older people.

These themes also came through at Phase 2; when asked why they *did* vote, 42% said "It is my civic duty/everyone should vote". Other reasons given included "I wanted to have a say" (14%), "It is my right to vote" (13%) and "I always vote" (11%). That voting is a habit is also evidenced by the fact that more than half (53%) of those who say they are "not at all interested" in politics still voted on 7 June and more than two-thirds (68%) of those "not at all interested" or "not particularly interested" in news about the election also voted.

Given the actual turnout, it is interesting to note that the overwhelming majority of people have positive attitudes towards voting. On balance, they believe it is important and they think it makes a difference. Nine in ten disagree with the proposition that "I don't think voting is very important" and three-quarters disagree *strongly*. Eight in ten disagree with the statement "I don't think voting makes much of a difference" with more than half disagreeing *strongly*. More than half (56%) of those who said they are "not at all interested" in politics still said they were likely to vote on 7 June and a similar proportion (58%) agreed that it was their duty to vote. Overall, 83% agreed that "it is my duty to vote", six times more than the 14% who disagreed. This attitude is fairly uniform among the main demographic sub-groups, but is less strongly held among 18–24 year olds. It is also relatively low among ethnic minorities, 25–34 year olds and the lower socio-economic groups. However, in each case *at least* two-thirds agree that voting is a duty and while younger people are more likely to disagree that it is a duty, they hold similar attitudes to the other groups on the importance and efficacy of voting.

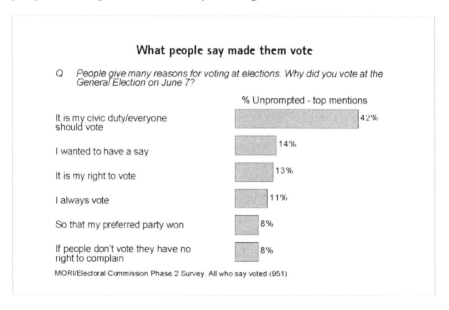

What people say made them vote

Q   *People give many reasons for voting at elections. Why did you vote at the General Election on June 7?*

% Unprompted - top mentions

Reason	%
It is my civic duty/everyone should vote	42%
I wanted to have a say	14%
It is my right to vote	13%
I always vote	11%
So that my preferred party won	8%
If people don't vote they have no right to complain	8%

MORI/Electoral Commission Phase 2 Survey, All who say voted (951)

The MORI survey conducted for the Commission at the beginning of the campaign indicated that people gave a wider range of reasons for *not* being "certain" to vote than were given by those who were "certain". It is interesting that, when pressed, a good proportion (15%) of those who were not certain conceded that they "probably would vote". The next most popular explanation for planning not to vote was "being too busy" (11%). Others felt that "there is no point in voting" or "all parties are the same" (8%), had "no interest in politics" (8%) and referred to "being away on election day" (7%). While these are fairly small percentages, they each equate to about 3% of the electorate, or 1.4 million people.

In the post-election survey, when respondents were asked why they did not vote, unprompted answers focused less on the parties and lack of interest than on practical considerations:

• One-fifth of non-voters (21%) said that they did not vote because "I couldn't get to the polling station because it was too inconvenient". Women and those *not* in full or part-time employment were most likely to give this reason, although there was little difference between urban and rural non-voters.

- One in six non-voters (16%) said they did not vote because they "were away on election day." Taken with the above, these percentages equate to significant proportions of the electorate.
- One in ten (11%) said they did not vote because they "did not receive a polling card/postal vote" and 10% said they are "not interested in politics."

In separate questioning, 15% of non-voters said they were not registered to vote, a figure rising to 29% of 18–24 year old non-voters. Looking at ethnic minority communities, 27% of black non-voters and 15% of Asian non-voters reported that they were not registered, although these figures are drawn from a small base size. However, it is instructive that only 6% of all non-voters spontaneously gave non-registration as a reason for non-voting.

In the post-election survey the percentage of respondents claiming to have voted is significantly higher than the actual turnout, in part likely to be related to the 'conditioning' effect mentioned above and the recognised tendency for some people to tell pollsters that they have voted when they have not. However, MORI's findings do suggest lower turnout among younger people, black people and those living in urban areas.

Those aged 18–34 comprise 31% of the electorate, but made up 52% of those who at the outset of the campaign expressed themselves certain not to vote or not very likely to vote on 7 June. Given the secrecy of the ballot, there is no definitive data on turnout among different age groups. MORI's estimates, based on aggregates of all its election polls, suggest that turnout fell to around 39% among 18–24 year olds. However, findings from the MORI surveys conducted for the Commission suggest that lower levels of anticipated voting and lower actual turnout among this group are not matched by different attitudes towards voting. They are just as likely as others to see voting as important and something which makes a difference. 18–24 year olds are less committed to the idea of voting as civic duty, suggesting that they need additional reasons to turn out. Moreover, 15% of 18–24 year olds cited "no interest in politics" as a reason not to vote.

In the pre-election survey, black and Asian respondents were only marginally less likely than white respondents to be "certain" or "very likely" to vote on 7 June, when looking at the two categories together. However, this masks the fact that they were less likely to be "certain" to vote (52% against 63% among whites) and more inclined to be "very likely" (20% against 13%). Also, those of black ethnic origin were markedly less likely to be "certain" voters than Asians (45% compared to 58%).

When asked what they think could be done to increase turnout, respondents to the MORI survey conducted for the Commission after the election mentioned a range of potential solutions, with the most frequent suggestion being compulsory voting. Is the answer to take away voters' choice as to whether or not they vote? The electorate itself appears to be undecided on the issue, although slightly more oppose than support making voting in elections compulsory (49% *vs* 47% according to the MORI survey conducted for the Commission at the beginning of the campaign). This represents a 4.5 point swing to opposition since the question was last asked a decade ago in 1991, when 49% supported the idea and 42% opposed it. Among those who usually or sometimes vote in general elections, opposition is higher at 60% and rises to 72% among those who never or rarely vote. The low turnout on 7 June has prompted some politicians to press for a public debate on the introduction of compulsory voting. The precedent that many point to is Australia. Peter Hain MP, for example, suggests that "Compulsory voting has worked well in Australia and Australians have never lacked any sense of liberty" (*The Times*, 9 June 2001).

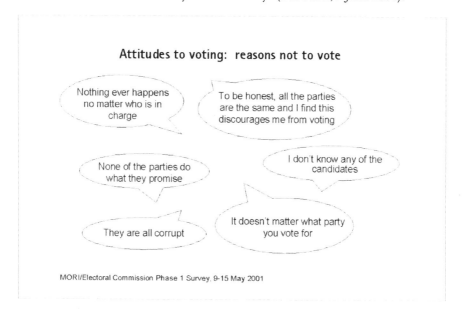

Attitudes to voting: reasons not to vote

Nothing ever happens no matter who is in charge

To be honest, all the parties are the same and I find this discourages me from voting

None of the parties do what they promise

I don't know any of the candidates

They are all corrupt

It doesn't matter what party you vote for

MORI/Electoral Commission Phase 1 Survey, 9-15 May 2001

The Commission recognises that the introduction of compulsory voting would not in itself address the underlying causes of low turnout, and in particular the apparent lack of engagement between potential voters and politics. However, the Commission believes that there is merit in opening up the question of compulsory voting for wider debate, and that it should be examined in more detail as one of a series of options which might help to contribute to higher rates of participation in elections.

The main responsibility for persuading the public of the importance of voting must rest with the politicians. For the 2001 general election, most commentators agree that the size of the Government's majority going into the election, combined with the steady message from the opinion polls that the Labour Party was significantly ahead of the other parties in popular support, created a sense of inevitability about the result. However, party campaign managers also identified an increasing mood of scepticism and cynicism amongst voters, and a sense that politics was no longer seen as relevant to voters' lives. These factors are making it increasingly difficult for the parties and candidates to engage voters during the limited period of the election campaign.

Engaging with the Campaign

In this general election, the politicians' concern to rouse the uninterested and the disenchanted was particularly evident. So did the election campaign persuade people to change their mind about whether or not to vote? In the MORI survey conducted for the Commission after the election, only 2% of those who voted had originally said that they were "certain not to vote" or "not very likely to vote". In contrast, 11% of those who had initially said they were either "certain" or "very/quite likely" to vote, ended up not voting. The main reasons given for changing from being a certain or likely voter to a non-voter included "being unwell" (11%), "having no time/being too busy" (7%) and "work commitments" (10%).

These findings certainly suggest that the campaign itself did little to persuade people that their vote mattered and the election was relevant to them, and may even have persuaded some people against voting. Most people disagreed with the suggestion that "it was an interesting election campaign" (66% against 29%). When asked for their impressions of the campaign, both favourable and unfavourable, most mentions are negative: 11% spontaneously say that it "Turned into a slanging match/not much talk about policies" and 10% thought it "Dull/boring." Non-voters are only marginally more likely to say that "It was a foregone conclusion" than voters (6% and 4%) but are much more likely to say they "Did not take any notice/not interested" (16% and 7%). Even amongst those who described themselves as *very* interested in politics at the outset of the campaign, 61% said in the post-election survey that, looking back, they did not find the election campaign interesting.

Nevertheless, it is interesting that a MORI poll for *The Times* on 29 May 2001, eight days before the day of the election, found interest in news about the election to be higher than it was in April 1997: 58% were "very" or "fairly" interested this year compared to 52% four years ago. Respondents to the MORI survey conducted for the Commission after the election also recalled being interested: 68%, more than twice the 32% who recalled being "not particularly" or "not at all interested." It is instructive that these figures are similar to the levels of interest in politics expressed by this group in the initial MORI survey conducted for the Commission (65% and 34%) suggesting that they were no less interested in the election than they are in politics generally.

These data may be regarded as evidence that declining turnout is not a function of declining interest in politics or elections but rather a failure of the campaign to connect with the electorate. This is reinforced by other findings from the MORI surveys for the Commission. On balance, people *disagreed* with the statements that "voting would not make a difference" (64% disagree to 34% agree), that "none of the parties stood for policies I would like to see" (61% to 32%) and that "there was little difference between what the main parties were offering" (58% to 38%). More crucially, non-voters were more likely to agree than disagree with these statements, with the exception of the last on which opinion is divided. It is also instructive that 27% of those who in the initial survey *disagreed* with the suggestion that "voting doesn't make much of a difference", agreed in the post-election survey that they "did not believe that voting would make much of a difference" on this occasion. In other words, a significant proportion of those who are positive about the value of voting in general were negative about it at the 2001 general election.

In this context, it is interesting to note that 24% of 18–24 year olds who had participated in the previous two or three years in activities that might broadly be described as 'active citizenship' (including presenting their views to a local or national politician, or urging someone else to, attending a political meeting, taking part in a demonstration or march, attending a meeting of an interest group, charity or organisation) did not vote. This finding reinforces the sense that young people are interested in politics and policy issues, but do not feel that a general election provides an effective route to expressing their concerns.

Non-voters were more likely than the full sample to think that the election was fought negatively (with the "parties pointing out what was wrong with the policies and personalities in other parties") than to think it was fought positively (with the "parties putting forward their own policies and personalities"). However, overall, people are less likely to think the 2001 campaign was fought negatively than was the case in both 1992 and 1997.

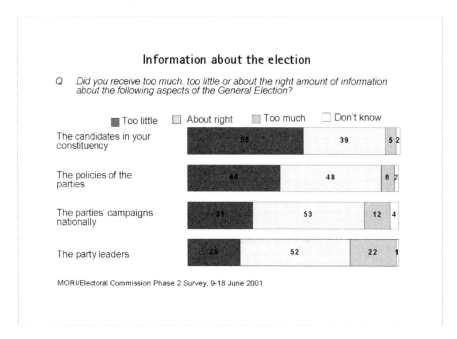

Information about the election

Q   *Did you receive too much, too little or about the right amount of information about the following aspects of the General Election?*

	Too little	About right	Too much	Don't know
The candidates in your constituency	55	39	5	2
The policies of the parties	44	48	6	2
The parties' campaigns nationally	31	53	12	4
The party leaders	25	52	22	1

MORI/Electoral Commission Phase 2 Survey, 9-18 June 2001

In this general election, in keeping with recent trends, personalities dominated election coverage. Over the course of the election campaign, the Communications Research Centre at Loughborough University calculated that Tony Blair featured in 35.4% of all election news items and William Hague in 26.4%, while Charles Kennedy took up third place. Loughborough point out that no other politician reached a double-figure rating, and conclude that the election was "highly presidential" (*The Guardian*, Golding et al, 12 June 2001). The same view is taken by the Independent Television Commission (*The ITC and the General Election 2001*, paper submitted by the ITC to the Commission, June 2001). The emphasis on party leaders in coverage of the campaign is reinforced by MORI's finding that 74% of the public felt they had the right amount of information or too much information about the party leaders. This contrasts with the 54% who felt they had enough, or too much, information about the parties' policies and 44% who were satisfied with the amount of information available to them about their local candidates.

MORI's findings suggest that information is a key driver in framing attitudes to voting and it is a particular issue among key 'hard-to-reach' groups such as young and ethnic minority voters. In the survey conducted at the beginning of the election campaign, two-thirds of young people agreed that they did not know enough about the candidates. They were also the only group more likely to agree than disagree that they did not know enough about the parties (54% to 41%).

Lack of information is also a key reason for people saying they are undecided about whom to vote for, and previous research has shown that this group is less likely actually to turn out than respondents as a whole. A MORI survey for the *The Sunday Telegraph* (13 May 2001) found that the following information-related reasons were more prevalent than those relating to scepticism or mis-trust: "Don't know enough", "Am waiting to see manifestos", "Don't know what the parties stand for" or "Don't know the candidates". While this would suggest many people think they were short of information, they are more likely than in 1997 to say that the main media – television and radio – devoted "about the right amount" of coverage to the election campaign and in judging both, fewer than 5% say that there was "too little" coverage. This suggests that if the public did not necessarily want more information *per se*, they *did* want different *types* of information, more candidate-focused and more policy-focused.

Both qualitative and quantitative research consistently finds a correlation between familiarity, with the candidate or issues, and favourability. This thesis is supported by the fact that some of the highest turnouts recorded in the 2001 general election were in areas where local issues were relevant to the campaign. The most notable was in Wyre Forest, where there was a turnout of 68% in a contest won by a local candidate standing for the Independent Kidderminster Hospital and Health Concern party, set up following a lengthy local campaign to keep the hospital open and extensive local, and national, press coverage of the issues involved. In the Brentwood and Ongar constituency the turnout was 67.3%. The election campaign here attracted considerable media and public interest, possibly because of Martin Bell's independent candidacy and the controversy surrounding the alleged involvement of a religious group in the local Conservative Association.

The other factor that plays a significant role in influencing turnout is relevance –

will my vote make a difference? In Northern Ireland, where constitutional and other issues specific to Northern Ireland dominated the political agenda, turnout was much higher than the UK average at 68%. More generally, according to research undertaken by the Electoral Reform Society (*Election 2001: Unfair and Unrepresentative*, June 2001), turnouts in the 100 most marginal seats were on average nearly 10% higher than in the 100 safest seats (63.6% as compared to 53.9%), although a larger turnout in marginal seats is not, of course, a feature unique to the 2001 election.

The National Farmers Union (NFU) also points out that, as at most general elections, voter turnout was higher than average in a number of seats of a rural and agricultural nature. Both Torridge and West Devon and Hexham, for example, had turnouts of over 70%. In such areas, the prominence of foot and mouth disease, and the politicisation of issues linked to it, may well have influenced the turnout. On the other hand, there is also evidence from the NFU that: "in many areas of the country where foot and mouth disease restrictions had all but lifted in time for the election, many farmers were relatively indifferent" (*Letter from the President of the National Farmers Union to Chairman of the Electoral Commission*, 25 June 2001).

The Commission concludes that while there were factors unique to the 2001 general election that appear to have played a particular part in depressing turnout, in particular the sense of inevitability about the result, there also appears to be a growing disconnection between the electorate and the electoral process. The task for the political parties is to re-engage with the electorate and reinvigorate national political debate to make it more relevant. This process of engagement must extend throughout the lifetime of Parliament, and not only come into play when an election is called. During election periods, the parties must also consider the implications for voter engagement of campaigning strategies which focus, as appeared to be the case in the 2001 election, on those seats where there is a good prospect of a transfer of party control, excluding a majority of the electorate from active campaigning. For some commentators, the low levels of participation in the 2001 election are evidence of a need for a move away from the 'first past the post' electoral system towards a form of proportional representation.

Such issues do not fall to the Commission to resolve. However, the Commission does have a critical role to play, through voter education and public awareness campaigns, within the terms of section 13 of PPERA. The Commission intends to examine the reasons for low turnout, looking at particular sub-groups within the wider electorate, including young people and ethnic minority communities. Building on this research, the Commission will develop, in discussion with other key stakeholders, a clearly targeted programme of voter education. The Commission also believes that it is important to assess carefully whether there are ways in which voting might be made easier and more accessible, while recognising that changes in this regard will not provide a panacea for the problems of low turnout.

Low Tech Elections

Our electoral practices and procedures are rooted in history and tradition. They reflect the circumstances of the late nineteenth century when electorates were much smaller and elections took place against a background of bribery and intimidation. One of the underlying features of the arrangements is the desire to minimise fraud. In this they have been conspicuously successful. The non-partisan nature of the UK's electoral arrangements (based on the independence of the individual constituency Returning Officer), coupled with the professionalism and dedication of the electoral administrators, have guaranteed an electoral process that is more or less universally perceived as fair. Nevertheless, as the House of Commons Public Administration Select Committee noted: "Elections and party politics have rarely been actively organised so as to encourage participation in British government" (*Public Participation, Issues and Innovation,* Public Administration Select Committee, April 2001).

A wide range of alternative voting procedures is technically possible and increasingly used in overseas administrations with very similar democratic traditions to those of the UK. In the UK itself, television companies already use telephone and internet-based voting methods for audience participation programmes. Local councils in the UK have also experimented with new ways of voting, in order to try and make the process more accessible to the electorate. These experiments suggest that improving convenience and providing greater accessibility are achievable goals. In May 2000, 32 councils ran a total of 38 experimental voting arrangements in the local government elections. The Local Government Association's (LGA) evaluation of the local pilots in May 2000 (*Elections -The 21st Century Model: An Evaluation of May 2000 Local Electoral Pilots,* November 2000) found that voters who used the new arrangements praised the councils' initiative and welcomed the arrangements.

The LGA cites the following evidence in support of new voting schemes:

"Most of those who voted by post reported [that] they found the system easy to understand and use, and would like to have it available again in the future. Postal voters in Doncaster, for example, said the system was convenient (the vote was delivered to the house, people did not have to go to a polling station and could vote on more than one day), accessible (particularly for elderly people, disabled people, those working and those with children), simple and secure. Early voting and weekend voting [were] praised for [their] added convenience and novelty. Of voters using the early voting facilities in Blackpool, approximately 25% said they would not otherwise have voted, as did a similar proportion in Chester, for example. Electors enjoying the convenience of mobile polling facilities were particularly appreciative and welcomed the sense of being more directly involved in the democratic process than they would otherwise have been. Although there were some confusions and hiccups, the majority of voters found the system of touch screen electronic voting easy to use and claimed to prefer it to the traditional way of voting. 56.1% of voters responding found the electronic voting system in Salford, for example, easier to use than the current system." (*The Way We Vote Now – Electoral Process for the 21st Century,* May 2001.)

MORI's research for the Commission indicates that there is support for reforming the mechanics of voting, but it will be important to reassure people that these are reliable and in particular that they are sufficiently fraud-proof. When prompted with a list of specific suggestions for reform and asked which would be most likely to encourage them to vote at the forthcoming election, voting using a telephone was chosen by 36%, followed by voting at a supermarket by 27%, and 24-hour voting and voting by internet both at 21%.

There are some notable differences by sub-group. 43% of 18–24 year olds say that internet voting would encourage them, whereas older people are more likely to say "don't know". Among those who rarely/never vote in general elections, 42% chose voting by telephone, six points higher than voters as a whole. Respondents were then asked whether they supported or opposed polling stations being replaced wholly with voting by other methods such as post, telephone and the internet. More than half (53%) support this, but one-third (34%) are opposed. Perhaps unsurprisingly, support is relatively low among older age groups (who are currently the most likely to vote) but is higher among younger people and those who say they rarely or never vote in general elections. When asked why they support the idea, the main reasons given relate to "convenience/ease of voting" (52%) and "will encourage people to vote" (17%). Among those who rarely or never vote and support this idea, convenience is mentioned by 63%. The main opposition is based on the idea that "people should go/prefer going", mentioned spontaneously by 46%. The other main concern focuses on "identifying fraud/hard to identify voter", which is given as a reason for opposition by 31%.

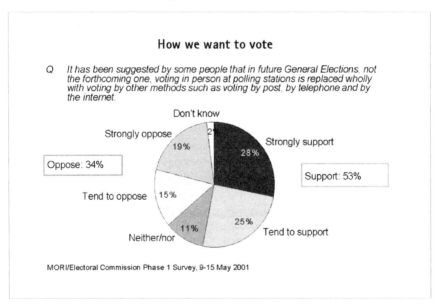

How we want to vote

Q   *It has been suggested by some people that in future General Elections, not the forthcoming one, voting in person at polling stations is replaced wholly with voting by other methods such as voting by post, by telephone and by the internet.*

Don't know

Strongly oppose   2%

19%

28%   Strongly support

Oppose: 34%

Support: 53%

Tend to oppose   15%

11%   25%

Neither/nor   Tend to support

MORI/Electoral Commission Phase 1 Survey, 9-15 May 2001

In the post-election MORI survey for the Commission, significant proportions of non-voters said that had alternative means of voting been in place on 7 June, they would have been "more likely" to have voted. This links to the finding, mentioned earlier, that many of the reasons given for non-voting relate to inconvenience and difficulties 'getting along'. Most popular of the potential new means of voting are using the telephone (including mobile phones) with 66% of non-voters saying that this would have made them more likely to vote on 7 June. It is also interesting to note that 51% of non-voters said that voting by post would have made them more likely to vote. When they were subsequently informed that this option had indeed been open to them in the election, 44% of non-voters professed to be unaware of the recent law change. This further highlights the challenge of effectively communicating reform of the mechanics of voting.

News ways of voting

In non-statutory elections, councils have been able to innovate. More detailed research is needed into the relationship between voting procedures and turnout, but a number of councils have experienced positive benefits from offering a diversity of voting schemes. Bristol conducted a local referendum on their budget in February 2001. Electors were given a choice of four budget options and three voting methods (post, telephone or internet). 40.2% of the electorate voted (7% higher than the usual local election turnout) of whom 94.18% voted by post, 3.14% by phone and 2.68% by the internet. In May 2001, the London Borough of Islington conducted a local referendum on their future council structure and the type of secondary school that should be built. Electors were offered three choices for each issue, and the same three voting methods used in Bristol. On this occasion, only 22.3% of the electorate voted – 95.2% voted by post, 2.3% by phone and 2.5% via the internet. In this case, the availability of alternative voting procedures did not lead to higher turnout by comparison with the May 1998 local elections.

It is unlikely that changing the *method* of voting can achieve major increases in voter turnout unless voters also feel that the election is relevant to them and their vote matters. However, the Commission believes that it is essential we exploit the opportunities new technologies provide and respond to new expectations. We recognise that this approach is not without problems. Electronic voting, in particular, brings with it potential difficulties in relation to authentication of the vote, the security of the system, the need to ensure privacy and, in relation to home-based internet voting, the fact that only a minority of the population has access to the internet at home.

The Commission is sponsoring, together with the LGA, Improvement and Development Agency (I&DeA) and Society of Local Authority Chief Executives (SOLACE), a major research project to explore the practicalities of full-scale remote electronic voting. The study will explore international experience and public attitudes in order to identify the conditions under which electronic voting can be successfully introduced and any barriers to implementation addressed. It will look in particular at issues of equal access and security. Electronic voting could, if introduced effectively, not only encourage voter participation but also improve the efficiency and accuracy of the administration of elections. The Commission will therefore actively encourage and, as appropriate, participate in a significant programme of pilots in this area at the 2002 local elections in England and beyond.

Foot and Mouth Disease

In March and April 2001, prior to the formal announcement of the election date, there was considerable concern about the likely adverse impact of foot and mouth disease (FMD) on the conduct and administration of the general election. By 7 June, the number of new FMD cases had reduced to five per day. In most areas, therefore, FMD did not appear significantly to affect the logistics of the campaign or the ability of farmers to participate in the election. Even in the badly hit areas, the availability of postal voting on demand meant that farmers were able to register a vote if they chose to.

However, there were some areas where the effects of the disease were felt acutely during the election period, including Cumbria and some parts of Scotland. In affected areas, electoral services teams had to find alternative sites for polling stations, and to provide disinfectant and mats. In Penrith and The Border, for example, such provision was made at every polling station. In badly hit areas, inspections and visits to polling stations during the day were cancelled and only emergency call outs were undertaken.

There were some constituencies where door-to-door canvassing and farm visits could not be attempted. Farmers in the worst affected areas also found it difficult to be involved in the election process more generally – for example, through farmers' meetings traditionally organised through the NFU. The NFU in England and Wales sought to provide an alternative mechanism for airing views by establishing *Political Candidates' Online*, an internet based system designed to allow candidates and NFU members to interact 'virtually' in the absence of live meetings. The NFU reports that take up of the scheme was relatively good, with all the main political parties in England and Wales supportive of the scheme, but "attempts by the NFU at both a local and national level were not felt able to in any way replace the human interaction that would normally occur." They conclude that "The feedback we have had from our regional offices indicates that this has been one of the quietest general election years in memory and that the agricultural electorate have felt apathetic and disinterested." (*Letter from the President of the National Farmers' Union to Chairman of the Electoral Commission*, 25 June 2001) NFU Scotland suggest that farmers' lack of interest in engaging with the election in Scotland had three root causes: the work involved in running a farm business under FMD restrictions was of greater concern than the election itself, the fact that many aspects of agricultural policy are now in the remit of the Scottish Parliament and not Westminster, and the size of the Government's majority in most Scottish seats.

Despite the adverse impact of FMD on a small number of badly hit constituencies, our overall impression is that foot and mouth did not have a significant impact on the conduct of the election. While FMD continued to be an issue for voters in rural constituencies throughout the election campaign, there was certainly no justification for earlier fears (expressed at the time when the election was expected to be held in May) that the election might not be free and fair because of foot and mouth disease restrictions.

Administration

The administration of elections tends to be a topic of little general public interest, perhaps a reflection on the invisible efficiency of the administrative machinery. The smooth running of elections is, however, vital to democracy and to public confidence in the electoral process. That much was demonstrated by the experience in the 2000 presidential election in the USA. One leading US think tank, commenting on the events of November and December 2000 in Florida, pointed out that "...for most, the striking and troubling feature of the lesson was the discovery of the underside of American Democracy – the highly decentralized, non-uniform, antiquated, confusing, error-prone, under-budgeted, poorly-staffed, arbitrary, and politicised manner that is too much part of the way that federal elections are administered" (The Brookings Institution, June 2001).

In the UK, elections are not politicised in the way experienced in the US. The generally high quality and independence of electoral staff in local authorities also ensures that errors are kept to a minimum. But in many other respects, there is much in this description that applies to the UK. This is the backdrop to the Commission's statutory duty to report on the administration of the general election, which provides an important opportunity to set an agenda for bringing the process up to date. This report discharges this duty, and these initial sections form the largest part of the report in recognition both of the statutory requirement and the intrinsic importance of the issues.

The focus here is on elections to the Westminster Parliament. However, the Commission is aware that in a number of areas there were combined elections taking place including, for example, county council elections in England. In such instances the administrative consequences can be significant. In one constituency, for example, county council elections were being held in all the district council areas included in the constituency. There was a resulting crossover of boundaries, which was in itself complicated for voters to understand and the administrators to manage. Increasing the difficulties, however, was the fact that the computer software packages used to maintain registers by the three district councils crossing the constituency were not compatible.

Voter Registration

The underpinning of any election is the register of voters. For the 2001 general election, 44,403,238 people were registered and eligible to vote, 1.3% more than in the 1997 general election. The increase is not substantial.

It is, however, interesting to note that 'rolling' registration was introduced in February

2001. This new system was designed to allow the updating of the register on a monthly basis and so increase the accuracy of the register at the point of any election. The rolling register was heralded by a Government-sponsored public awareness campaign, and there was also some local promotion of rolling registration, although this varied significantly between local authority areas. Comprehensive data is not at present available showing the extent to which rolling registration has been used, or identifying the percentage change each month to the register. However, initial soundings taken by the Commission suggest that changes to the register tend to affect between 0.1% and 0.5% of the electorate in any given month. Overall, it does not appear to have prompted any significant changes in the behaviour of those who might be expected to register.

Numbers registered to vote in UK Parliamentary elections

2001	44,403,238
1997	43,846,152
1992	43,275,316

Source: University of Plymouth

A person was eligible to vote in the 2001 general election if he or she had applied to be on the electoral roll by 5 April 2001. This was the final date for inclusion on the register published on 1 May 2001, the last published register before the closing date for candidate nominations on 17 May. This meant that by the time the election was announced on 7 May 2001, it was already too late to register. Calls and emails received by the Home Office and the Commission, as well as evidence from electoral administrators at local level, make it clear that there was a small but important minority of voters who were prompted to think of registering, or to check that they were registered, only when the election was announced. It is impossible to quantify the total number of people who were not registered to vote despite being eligible to do so (and therefore required by law to register). What is evident, however, is that understanding of how registration works is considerably less than universal.

The reasons for this are likely to be many and various. Promotion of the new rolling register may have encouraged people to think that it would be possible to register at any time up to election day. There were also some voters who had not appreciated that registration was quite separate from other processes administered by local government. In particular, there is a common assumption that by paying council tax, an individual is automatically added to the electoral roll. Others simply move home frequently and find it difficult to keep track of where they are registered. MORI's findings showed that 93% of those questioned at the beginning of the campaign believed themselves to be registered. However, only 85% of those who did not vote said that they were registered.

It is clearly unfortunate that, in an election that saw a historically low turnout, there were some prospective voters who felt that they were prevented from voting because of the current legal provisions governing registration procedures and timetables. There are some obvious potential solutions to this problem. The best of these is to ensure that as many people as possible are registered in advance of an election being called. Some local authorities have taken the initiative in promoting registration alongside other council services; for example, issuing registration forms with council tax bills. Other similar initiatives could also be pursued more widely than at present: encouraging estate agents and mortgage lenders to provide homebuyers with registration forms, undertaking awareness campaigns among groups with notably low registration rates, and appealing to self-interest. For example, some councils make a point of reminding residents that the Register of Electors is also used for checking credit references, so registering promptly at a new address could speed up loan applications.

The Commission intends to develop, in consultation with Electoral Registration Officers and their staff, a comprehensive strategy for promoting voter registration within the current legal framework. We also intend to look at ways in which the process of registration could be made easier. In some other countries, registering to vote is centralised and it is possible to register online. In the UK, managing the registration process is the responsibility of local authorities and is an exclusively paper-based process. It seems probable that a centrally administered register would increase the ease with which an individual could find out whether, and where, he or she was registered and, if not registered, set in train the process of registration.

Under a new scheme launched earlier this year, plans are already under way to link registers electronically, standardising the data and providing a centralised administration for the electronic version – although management of the register would remain locally-based. The Commission is part of the partnership, led by I&DeA, responsible for managing delivery of this new scheme. Supported by grant funding of £12 million, the project aims to provide an electronic 'one-stop-shop' providing faster, easier access to data (including search facilities) in a reliable and secure environment. This clearly provides a basis on which the register itself could, in due course, become a national register that is fully automated. A fully electronic registration system would open up considerable opportunities for improving the electoral process.

However, under the current rules there will always be some people who are not on the electoral register but who would wish to be. We therefore believe that consideration will need to be given to the current registration deadlines in relation to general and other elections. International practice provides examples of how this might be achieved. In Australia, for example, there are seven days from the announcement of a federal election for people to ensure that they are correctly enrolled before the electoral roll is closed. In the UK, one obvious cut-off point would be close of nominations, but the implications of any change to the deadline would need to be examined closely. In particular, a change of this sort would be likely to increase the workload of the electoral services staff in local authorities at a time when they are also facing the significant pressures of organising a general election.

Electoral Registration Officers already have the right to amend the register until five working days before the election if a mistake has been made. Mistakes on the electoral register are a persistent, if small-scale problem. The Commission was informed of a number of cases where errors were discovered on polling day or in the period leading up to it. In one Welsh local authority area, electoral staff reported complaints from some 50 or 60 people across three constituencies who were not on the register when it appeared they should have been. In an English constituency, a parent rang the local authority on polling day to say that their son had been refused a vote because his date of birth had been wrongly entered on the register, transposing the month and the date. Such complaints are by no means uncommon. The Commission will consider whether there is a need to grant (Acting) Returning Officers greater discretion to correct factual errors on the register that come to light up to, and including, polling day.

Dissolution of Parliament and Issue of the Writ

The timing of the announcement was a key issue in the 2001 general election. From March 2001 onwards, there was almost daily speculation in the media about the possible timing of the election. Interest in the subject was heightened significantly by the outbreak of foot and mouth disease (the first confirmed case was on 20 February 2001). Commentary was not limited to the political pages of the broadsheets. As the time drew nearer for the announcement of a possible 3 May general election, tabloid newspaper front pages were also given over to the issue. The uncertainty surrounding the timing of the general election, and the eventual postponement of the local elections planned for 3 May, inevitably focused attention on the different procedures for fixing the timing of general and local elections.

Although the Parliament Act 1911 lays down the maximum life of a Parliament as five years, there is no minimum length of a Parliament specified. In constitutional law, the timing of a general election is essentially an issue for the Royal prerogative. Formally it is the Queen who is responsible for dissolving Parliament by means of a Royal Proclamation, which also requires writs to be issued to the returning officer in each constituency. In practice, however, it is the Prime Minister who advises her to carry out these procedures, and this, under normal circumstances, gives him/her control over the date of the election. There is no law or convention that requires the Prime Minister to consult with, or seek the approval of, Parliament in setting the date of a general election. Among the various elected local, regional, national and European bodies that play a part in the UK democratic process, therefore, the House of Commons now stands alone in not being based upon the fixed-term principle.

The Prime Minister has indicated that he does not see the case for change (*BBC News Online*, 2 April 2001). Nevertheless, the introduction of several Private Members' Bills dealing with the issue, including one on 1 March introduced by Labour MP and Chairman of the Public Administration Select Committee, Tony Wright, may be indicative of growing backbench support for change. Public opinion on the issue is not straightforward to discern. MORI polls carried out in 1991 and 1995 for the Joseph Rowntree Trust showed that at least twice as many people supported the idea of fixed-term Parliaments as opposed it. A similar survey carried out by NOP in January 2001 found that nearly two-thirds of voters agreed with the statement: "It is wrong for Prime Ministers to choose when to call general elections; they should be held on fixed dates every four or five years". The MORI surveys for the Commission paint a more cautious picture, with 53% approving of fixed parliamentary terms. It is interesting that this result should come so soon after the foot and mouth disease outbreak, and the related media coverage given to the question of whether the Prime Minister should postpone the 3 May 2001 local elections and expected general election.

The arguments for and against fixed-term parliaments are complex and wide-ranging; they also touch on issues beyond the realm of electoral law and practice. Nevertheless, because of the administrative benefits of fixed-term parliaments, and the anomalous position of Westminster elections in comparison with all other elections held in the UK, the Commission plans to look further at the case for adopting fixed parliamentary terms for Westminster.

There is also another timing issue. The minimum period for a general election campaign is currently 17 working days, while for local elections it is 25 days. The disparity appears to have no basis in logic, and the tight timetable for the general election created significant problems for administrators, party agents and candidates in 2001, not least because of the changes in relation to party registration and postal voting. Where combined elections were held in England on 7 June, the different timetables created particular problems. A candidate wishing to stand for election in both local and Westminster elections could find himself in time to be nominated for one, but too late for the other. The Commission believes that the timetable for the conduct of general elections warrants further review.

Party Registration and Nomination of Candidates

For both candidates and administrators, there was an important change in nomination procedure for the 2001 general election. New rules governed the way in which candidates could describe themselves in their nomination papers and thus on the ballot paper. Since implementation of PPERA, there are effectively only three choices open to a potential candidate: belong to a registered political party, use the term 'Independent' with no further description, or provide no description at all. As a result, the only way for candidates to give the voter an indication of their views on the ballot paper was to register as a political party.

On 30 April 2001, there were 126 political parties registered in Great Britain, and 28 registered in Northern Ireland. In the eight working days between the announcement of the general election on 8 May and the deadline to register for parties intending to field candidates at the election (17 May), the Commission received 18 new applications to register, of which 17 were successful, alongside a further 8 applications approved by the deadline from parties who had submitted their applications in advance of the election being called. By the deadline, the numbers of registered parties had reached 148 for Great Britain and 31 for Northern Ireland. It is difficult to predict whether the extent of the post-announcement rush to register will be typical of future elections.

Allowing for the fact that the actual announcement of an election is likely to precipitate a number of fresh applications that would not have been made previously, these figures nevertheless suggest a lack of awareness of the new legislation regulating the description of candidates on ballot papers. There was also some confusion, for both the general and local elections, that the cut-off point for registration was the last day for publication of notice of an election rather than the close of nominations, which many individuals and parties, and some (Acting) Returning Officers, assumed was the relevant deadline. Again, this may be simply a question of teething troubles with the new legislation, but clearly requires more publicity in future elections. There was at least one constituency where the (Acting) Returning Officer took the view that there could be no more than one candidate standing with the description 'Independent'. In a further two constituencies, the (Acting) Returning Officer accepted nomination papers with unlawful descriptions attached to independent candidates, through ignorance of the new legal requirements rather than any intent to subvert the intent of the new framework. The Commission has also been notified of one case where an allegation has been made of false subscription to a nomination paper, which is a criminal offence. At the time of writing, the police are considering whether any action is appropriate in respect of the allegation.

A common complaint among parties seeking registration at the last minute was that they had been unaware, until they tried to submit their nominations, that the regulations had changed and they could not use a description other than 'Independent'. Several prospective independent candidates contacted the Commission for clarification, ultimately choosing not to register their preferred description, but expressing annoyance that they could no longer use a description that in many cases had been used at previous elections. A number of the 'parties' that registered at the last minute were very small parties, typically a candidate and one other person, which registered solely for the purposes of the election. It is too early to tell whether the regulatory framework that is integral to registration as a party will create problems for these very small parties. Two have already sought to de-register following the election. However, the controls set out under PPERA are binding until the end of the financial year after the year in which a party deregisters.

The Commission believes that there is case for reviewing the current provisions for candidate descriptions, and the linked issue of registration for 'one candidate parties', in the light of experience at this general election. It does not appear to assist either the voter or the candidate for candidates standing in one constituency on a single issue to be prevented from providing a description other than 'Independent' unless registered as a political party. There are several potential solutions to this issue including, for example, allowing independent candidates to use a description or an emblem alongside the word 'Independent' and/or operating a two-tier form of registration with lesser administrative requirements for those parties who do not meet a threshold linked to a minimum number of members. The arrangement already exists for candidates standing in parish council elections to use descriptions of not more than six words without registering with the Commission.

Despite the difficulties outlined above, in the overwhelming majority of constituencies, the new rules governing the description of candidates appeared to work well, and electoral services staff dealt sensibly and pragmatically with the requirements of the law. Initial analysis of submissions to the Commission by party agents and candidates indicates that over 80% of respondents were either satisfied or very satisfied with current nomination procedures. The smaller parties, unsurprisingly, seemed most dissatisfied with present nomination arrangements. Their main criticism was that the deposit (£500) was far too high and that it discriminated against parties with limited financial resources. Some agents from small parties favoured increasing the number of signatures required to validate a nomination (the most widely cited figure was 100), and completely doing away with the deposit. On the other hand, a few respondents from the main parties argued that the deposit level was too low and that it should be increased to £1000 in order to discourage the participation of 'frivolous candidates'. The Commission will look at these issues further, along with a range of other issues relating to the way in which smaller parties fare in general election campaigns, to identify whether there are any changes that might be made to facilitate the full participation of smaller parties.

The procedures also threw up a few practical points worthy of further consideration:

• From an administrative perspective, the changes created some pressure on the timetable for the submission of nomination papers. The process became more complex. For example, it was necessary for candidates to submit proof of authorisation to use the description of a registered party and the party's emblem.

• Some confusion has also arisen because it is permissible to include on the ballot paper a variation of the party name registered with the Commission, not exceeding six words. Some candidates used these provisions to attach a by-line such as 'the local candidate'. Such descriptions tend to reinforce the sense of unfairness felt by Independent candidates who can provide no description.

- It is not unusual, especially when dealing with first-time candidates or agents, for the nomination papers originally submitted to include errors, made without any intent to deceive. Prior checking of nomination forms should normally reveal the error early enough for it to be resubmitted correctly. Nevertheless, there may be a case for allowing a greater degree of flexibility around amendments that can be made without requiring the submission of an entirely new set of nomination papers with new subscribers.

- The requirement that a nomination must be submitted in person by the candidate or agent (or proposer or seconder) also caused a difficulty in some cases. Again, there is a case for relaxing this requirement, to allow personal delivery by anyone nominated by the candidate. More generally, it is not clear whether the continuing use of subscribers – the individuals who are required to support the candidates' nominations – serves any real value for those candidates who are members of registered parties. There is no requirement for subscribers in the European Parliament elections, and an alternative 'witness' provision applies to Scottish Parliament elections.

- Some administrators have suggested to the Commission that the rules on candidates' names should be relaxed to allow, for example, the use of a professional rather than married name and to clarify the use of prefixes such as Sir and affixes, including MEP.

- A few agents were dissatisfied with arrangements for paying the deposit. They stated that the system of requiring a banker's draft or cash was "outdated" and "awkward". A number suggested that cheques, credit cards or debit cards should be allowed for the payment of the deposit.

The Commission intends to review these aspects of nomination with a view to simplifying and streamlining the process, and allowing greater flexibility in dealing with erroneous nomination papers.

Many constituencies provide the opportunity of a formal meeting between electoral administration staff and the election agents and it is generally recognised that maintaining good informal contacts throughout the process, from the first announcement of the election to the submission of returns, is critical to efficiency and effectiveness. At the same time, electoral administrators are rightly careful not to get too close. It is the agents' responsibility to know and follow the law. Initial feedback from questionnaires distributed to party agents by the Commission suggests that most agents found the support provided by the electoral services staff useful and welcome.

Postal Voting

For the first time in a general election, electors in England, Scotland and Wales were able to apply for a postal vote without having to give any reason. Initial data analysis suggests that at least 1.4 million valid postal votes were cast in the general election, compared to 937,205 postal votes issued and 738,614 valid postal votes cast at the 1997 general election. The percentage of the electorate who were issued with a postal vote for the general election varied significantly between different constituencies, according to how proactive the Electoral Registration Officer and/or the political parties were in promoting the availability of postal voting, from less than 1% in some areas to over 30% in others. Overall, our initial data analysis suggests that the percentage of the eligible population casting a valid postal vote was around 3%. There were also significant variations in return rates, although it was exceptional for the rate to fall below 60% and most areas saw return rates in the region of 82–83%.

Postal vote return rates

	Number of postal issued	Number of postal votes cast	% cast of issued
2001*	1.7 million	1.4 million	82.3
1997	937,205	738,614	78.8
1992	835,074	692,139	82.9

Source: University of Plymouth
* Estimates based on 85% of statistical returns.

Prior to February 2001, it had only been possible to obtain a postal vote if the voter met one of several tightly defined criteria. The change in law, which applied throughout Great Britain but not Northern Ireland, reflected experience from abroad and the evidence from local authority election pilot schemes conducted in May 2000. Seven councils ran pilots in their council elections where postal voting replaced polling stations entirely. In most of these authorities, the rise in turnout was at least 50%. Turnout more than doubled where there was no requirement to provide a 'declaration of identity' (signed by the voter and a witness) along with the ballot paper. There were very few administrative problems reported as arising from the pilot projects. In passing the RPA 2000, Parliament agreed to extend the use of postal voting to any elector who requested it, but insisted on the retention of the declaration of identity.

For the 2001 general election, a number of Electoral Registration Officers conducted publicity campaigns in their council areas to promote take up of postal voting. In some areas, such as Leicester, the local media also supported postal voting through editorial material. In a number of constituencies, postal voting applications were also printed on the reverse of polling cards. Political parties publicised the availability of postal voting and other organisations, including the Royal National Institute for the Blind, the National Union of Students and trade unions, also promoted the availability of postal voting.

From central government, the Home Office ran a print media advertising campaign in England and Wales, accompanied by TV and radio advertising, encouraging take up of postal voting and inviting electors to apply for a postal ballot. In Scotland, the Scotland Office conducted a similar print and TV media advertising campaign. The advertising campaigns also promoted a telephone enquiry service for members of the public wishing to apply for a postal vote, which operated 24 hours a day, seven days a week. Over 93,000 enquiries were handled throughout the election period. Postal vote application forms were available from Electoral Registration Officers, by cutting out newspaper-based forms or visiting government websites.

Promoting postal voting

A number of local councils took a deliberately proactive approach to promoting postal voting. Cardiff County Council wrote to all 235,000 people on the register in the four Cardiff constituencies informing them of their right to apply for a postal vote. A total of 33,318 postal vote applications were received, a 700% increase on the previous year. 95% of the applicants asked for a permanent postal facility. Of the total number of applicants, 26,443 (over 79%) returned their ballot papers. Stevenage launched a campaign to encourage the take up of postal votes, including a hand-delivered leaflet and application form to all households, plus advertising in local newspapers. More than one-third of the 69,000 registered electors applied for postal votes and 74% of the postal voters returned their ballot papers. Overall turnout in Stevenage was 61%. Stevenage Borough Council estimate that without the postal vote option the turnout would have been around 55%.

The extension of postal voting also prompted a good deal of media and public interest, not always positive, initially sparked by the prospect of an election taking place against the backdrop of foot and mouth disease (and the consequent restrictions on movement for candidates and voters). At the start of the campaign, there were press reports suggesting that the wider availability of postal votes created a significant risk of fraud. Some of these claims were based on a misunderstanding about the manner in which postal votes would be provided. For example, some failed to understand that a two-stage process was involved: firstly requesting an application, which could be done several times over and without any identity checks, and secondly receiving the postal ballot paper, which would be issued only once the application forms were checked against the electoral roll and no voter would be issued with more than one. As the campaign went on, media and public understanding of how the system worked increased and more specific claims of abuses were made.

The most notable of these was the BBC's reported successful attempt to obtain the ballots papers for seven registered voters in Torbay who had recently died. Under regulations introduced by the RPA 2000, electoral administrators now have access to records kept by the Registrar of Births and Deaths. In some areas, agreement has been reached with the local Registrars for notices of deaths in the area to be automatically notified to the electoral registration team. The Commission believes that this practice should be adopted more widely. However, this will remain a risk area because of the inevitable time-keeping lag between a death notice in a newspaper and the updating of the register on receipt of notification from the Registrar.

The Torbay case highlighted the fact that, although only one postal vote would be issued to each elector, and the application would be checked against the register itself, no further checks on identity were routinely made by electoral services staff. It is important to note that the arrangements for verifying postal votes had not changed with the extension of postal voting – they were neither more nor less rigorous. Moreover, the process of verifying postal votes is no different from the way in which voting in person operates: the principal difference is that the individual is more likely to be caught attempting to vote at the same polling station several times over than in submitting several votes because of the added factor of visual recognition.   There were also concerns that political parties were collecting ballot papers and returning them to the council on behalf of voters. This practice raised concerns amongst some commentators, but there were few suggestions that it had anywhere crossed the line between a legitimate effort to encourage supporters to vote and fraud.

It would be wrong to suggest that the extension of postal voting did not bring with it risks of increased fraud. It is clear that if an individual or group is determined to perpetrate a fraud, the wider availability of postal voting provides an opportunity to do just that. The Commission regards it as essential that opportunities for fraud are minimised in the interests of maintaining public confidence in elections. The Commission has therefore requested information from all (Acting) Returning Officers in relation to the extent and nature of fraud in the 2001 election campaign, and the impact of postal voting on demand. The Commission will produce a further report on these issues, which will consider ways of reducing the scope for fraud and best practice in this regard. We will examine the experience of Northern Ireland, where electoral fraud has been recognised as an important policy issue in recent years.

However, the evidence available to us to date suggests that systematic attempts to perpetrate fraud through unlawful use of postal votes did not happen on a significant scale at the 2001 general election. One local authority (Bradford) has received allegations that a small number of individuals used intimidation to collect blank postal ballot papers from voters with a view to completing them themselves, and also collected completed ballot papers and discarded those with votes for other candidates. The Commission is also aware of other individual cases where allegations have been made that unlawful votes may have been cast. At least one individual insisted to the Commission, on receiving an application form for postal votes, that he had not asked for one. There are also cases of voters arriving at polling stations being surprised to discover that they were ineligible to vote as they were marked on the register as having applied for a postal vote, which they insist they had not. However, at the time of writing, to our knowledge only in Bradford was a full police investigation underway into suspected postal vote fraud.

At this stage, the Commission's view is that the most significant problems associated with the extension of postal voting were administrative leading, in some cases, to the effective disenfranchisement of voters. Given the scale of the increase in postal voting, electoral administrators dealt competently and diligently with the task before them. But it is clear that the sheer volume of demand which peaked as the deadline approached created its own problems. The constant stream of telephone requests for postal votes in many electoral services offices, with limited staff resources, made it difficult for election staff to deal with anything else. For example, the London Borough of Newham reported receiving 7,500 postal vote applications on the final qualifying day. It also meant that more resources had to be put into the issuing and opening of postal votes, both of which are time-consuming processes. There are a number of specific issues arising from the administration of postal voting which warrant further consideration.

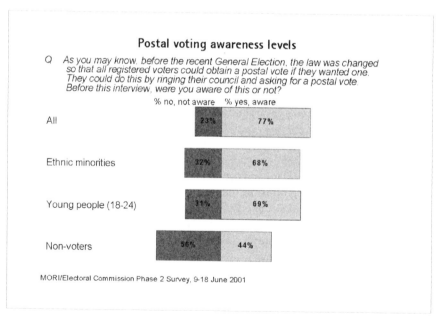

Postal voting awareness levels

Q   As you may know, before the recent General Election, the law was changed so that all registered voters could obtain a postal vote if they wanted one. They could do this by ringing their council and asking for a postal vote. Before this interview, were you aware of this or not?

% no, not aware   % yes, aware

	% no, not aware	% yes, aware
All	23%	77%
Ethnic minorities	32%	68%
Young people (18-24)	31%	69%
Non-voters	56%	44%

MORI/Electoral Commission Phase 2 Survey, 9-18 June 2001

Both electoral administrators and members of the public found the system of postal voting (two envelopes, declarations of identity) cumbersome. Where voters had failed to understand the process involved, matching declarations with ballot papers was time consuming and in some cases impossible. Where more than one election was taking place at the same time, the scope for confusion increased still further. Moreover, the scope for electoral staff, both in advance and at the count, to spot a fake witness signature was extremely limited. One administrator commented: "It was tolerable when there were low volumes, but is far too complex for a high volume operation. It is also difficult for people to understand, resulting in an unacceptably high proportion of postal votes being spoiled because voters have made some procedural mistake. We need a system which is both administratively simple and secure from abuse."

There were some members of the public who found the deadline of 30 May for applications for postal votes unacceptably rigid, finding it difficult to accept that no-one involved in the administration of the election had discretion to allow applications received after the deadline. On the other hand, many electoral administrators found that the closing date for applications for postal votes was simply too late in the process. It resulted in large numbers of applications having to be turned round within a very short space of time, many voters calling to check where their ballot papers were, and some losing their vote altogether as they had to leave the country before the postal ballot papers arrived. In a great many cases, postal ballot papers were still being sent out in the last week of the campaign, so that some voters did not receive them until polling day or even afterwards. As a result, there were instances where voters who had applied for a postal vote but had not received it turned up to vote at polling stations, and were unable to be issued with another ballot paper.

The crucial role of the Royal Mail in the operation of postal voting was emphasized by the postal strikes that occurred in many parts of England during the week before polling day. To have a strike during this period was particularly damaging. Applying for, receiving and casting a postal vote involves a series of up to five postal deliveries between the voter and the relevant electoral services team. In many cases, four of the five stages had to be completed in the space of just over a week, between the deadline for receipt of applications on 30 May and polling day on 7 June. Any votes delivered after the close of the poll were not counted. Some councils were able to agree local arrangements with the Royal Mail to ensure prompt delivery of postal ballot papers and the return of postal votes on the night of the count. Some sorting offices were willing to undertake special arrangements (for example, checking through late deliveries).

For their part, Consignia (the new name for the former Post Office Group) has told the Commission that: "we set in place a number of measures to ensure that all returned postal votes on hand were transmitted back to returning officers by close of polling. We conducted our own analysis of those votes that were handed back to returning officers after polling day. This showed that the minority had been posted before polling day, and certainly by the 5 June which we recommended to the Home Office as a guideline. The significant majority were posted on polling day itself or after…" (*Letter from Head of Westminster Affairs, Consignia, to Chairman of the Electoral Commission,* 22 June 2001.)

However, others were less positive. For example, we understand a very large number of postal votes (estimated at up to 300) for the Ynys Mon constituency were found in a sorting office on the morning of the election. They had not been delivered to voters. Some efforts were made to deliver the ballot papers on polling day, but it is inevitable that most of those applying for postal votes will not have been at home to take advantage of a ballot paper delivered on the day of the election. The significance of this particular problem is underlined by the fact that the final result in Ynys Mon involved a majority of just 800. The Commission will be making further enquiries into the events surrounding the non-delivery of postal votes in Ynys Mon.

Similar problems, although not discovered as late as polling day, were also reported in the Vale of White Horse, where an estimated 400 people experienced delays in receiving their postal ballot papers as a result of some being sent to the wrong sorting office. In another constituency, the (Acting) Returning Officer felt compelled to appear on local radio to urge local voters not to return their postal ballots by Royal Mail, but to return them in person. Some administrators have told the Commission that they would rather rely on hand delivery for postal ballots than use the Royal Mail, or use other commercial services. If postal voting on demand is to command public confidence, it will need a reliable system of delivery in order that voters may depend on it.

The Commission has also noted concerns expressed by both administrators and party election agents that there is no equivalent for postal votes of the 'marked register' used to determine which electors have actually voted. For the party officials, the lack of a marked register means that they have no means of identifying those who have yet to vote on polling day, and therefore taking action to encourage turnout, or not to send election literature to those who have already voted. Some administrators have also expressed concern that without a marked register, it is difficult to identify unusual voting patterns, for example, no votes being cast by all those registered for a postal vote in a particular area, which might suggest that postal votes had not been delivered successfully. The availability of a marked register for postal votes would also make it easier to identify any individuals seeking to vote twice by post, in cases where a replacement set of voting papers had been issued after the first set were reported 'lost'. It would, however, require a change in the law and have resource consequences for electoral administrators.

The final problem thrown up by the extension of postal voting was financial. Where large numbers were involved, the costs of processing postal votes proved to be significantly higher than processing 'ordinary' votes. Cardiff, with one of the largest postal votes in the UK, estimated on polling day that they were likely to suffer a shortfall of £7,000 in relation to their election expenditure as a result of postal voting.

The Commission regards it as essential that solutions are identified to the administrative and resourcing problems generated by the more widespread use of postal voting. These solutions may involve changes to the way in which postal voting itself operates; but they are also likely to require a comprehensive examination of the whole registration process.

Recognising that any system of 'absent' voting brings with it risks, these risks must be balanced against the potential gains in terms of improving voters' access to the poll and increasing the overall turnout. It is, of course, not possible to judge precisely what proportion of postal voters might otherwise simply have made the journey to the polling station. Evidence from the pilots conducted at the May 2000 local elections suggests that the wider availability of postal voting on demand encouraged relatively few additional voters, especially in those cases where the 'declaration of identity' was retained. However, anecdotally there is also evidence that the availability of postal voting did assist some people to vote who otherwise would not have done so and made the process more straightforward. The National Union Students, for example, concluded that: "the simplification of the process for applying for and receiving a postal vote made a great difference to many students" (*Letter from National President of the National Union of Students to Chairman of Electoral Commission*, 22 June 2001).

A number of organisations and individuals have also told the Commission that, despite the range of publicity initiatives, public awareness of the wider availability of postal voting was far from universal. MORI's findings support this conclusion, highlighting particularly low levels of awareness amongst non-voters, and significant proportions of ethnic minority respondents (32%) and young people (31%) who had not been conscious of the change.

The Commission firmly believes that there is no case for reversing the extension of postal voting secured through the RPA 2000. Indeed, if the turnout trend is to be reversed, the future is likely to bring a greater range of absent voting mechanisms. Attention must, therefore, be focused on streamlining the administration of the current postal voting arrangements to ensure that those who wish to vote are not disenfranchised without reason and to provide sufficient safeguards against fraud both in respect of current voting arrangements and any future developments.

Voting Process

At every election, there are always voters who wish to register their disapproval of all the candidates on the slate in an active way, rather than simply by not voting. The option of a positive abstention exists in some other countries, but has not won any significant level of support in Western democracies, not least because of the risk that 'None of the Above' might secure the largest proportion of the vote. While an NOP poll for *The Sunday Times* published on 20 May 2001 indicated that a significant proportion (35%) of people agreed with the statement "none of the political parties really deserves my support", there is no straightforward way to register an abstention in UK elections. The option usually used is to 'spoil' the ballot paper, but there is no ready means of distinguishing a deliberately spoilt ballot from a ballot paper completed erroneously.

At the 7 June County Council elections in Hertfordshire, a party registered as No Candidate Deserves My Vote stood a handful of candidates, its best result being 2.5% of the vote (174 votes) in St Albans South. The party takes the view that offering the opportunity of a positive abstention could assist in increasing voter turnout. The results of the MORI survey conducted for the Commission after the election offer some support for this suggestion: 12% of those asked said that being able to vote on the ballot paper for "None of the above candidates" would have made them more likely to vote, and the figure increases markedly to 33% for non-voters. However, the evidence from international practice in this regard is inconclusive. The Commission does not believe that the case is yet made out for the introduction of positive abstention within UK electoral practice, but intends to undertake a more thorough examination of the issues involved.

The Commission is also concerned to review the current design of the ballot paper. At the most basic level, it is striking that the ballot paper does not explain how to cast a vote. There is no indication as to where to place a mark or that the mark should be a cross. This information is, of course, conveyed on posters in the polling stations, but at every election there are small but significant numbers of ballot papers where it is evident that the elector has failed to understand the rules. Some of these may have had to be treated as spoilt, when they were cast with every intention of registering a vote. A further issue of concern to voters is the fact that ballot papers are issued in polling stations from 'books' of serial numbered ballot papers and the electoral number of each voter is written on the stub left in the issuing book. This raises concerns for some electors that it would be possible for electoral administrators to trace their votes and so undermine the secrecy of the ballot. The organisation Liberty argued during the 2001 election that this procedure breaches the Human Rights Act 2000, and the Home Affairs Select Committee also recommended in 1998 that the practice of numbering ballot papers, originally introduced by the Ballot Act 1872, should cease. It is important to note that the original reason for requiring the numbering of ballot papers was specifically to *allow* votes to be traced in the event of a challenge, and specifically in order to be able to prove the offence of personation. If the numbering system were to be given up, it would be necessary to identify alternative means of dealing with allegations of personation.

Administrators have also raised points with the Commission, in particular suggesting that the ballot paper should be "designed to assist counting as well as completion by the voter." There is also a significant body of opinion supporting the use of watermarked ballot papers to avoid the need for the polling clerks to use a perforating stamp to validate the paper. This would avoid the situation where a vote has to be discounted because the ballot paper has not been stamped. The absence of the official stamp on ballot papers was one of the key issues in the successful election petition in respect of the Winchester constituency following the 1997 general election. The Commission will look at all these points in reviewing the design of the ballot paper.

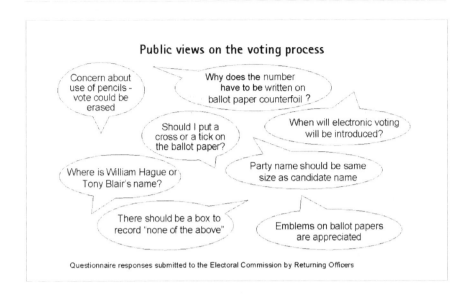

Public views on the voting process

Concern about use of pencils - vote could be erased

Why does the number have to be written on ballot paper counterfoil ?

Should I put a cross or a tick on the ballot paper?

When will electronic voting will be introduced?

Where is William Hague or Tony Blair's name?

Party name should be same size as candidate name

There should be a box to record "none of the above"

Emblems on ballot papers are appreciated

Questionnaire responses submitted to the Electoral Commission by Returning Officers

At present, the Commission has insufficient data about tendered ballots (those cases where a voter arrives at a polling station only to discover that a vote has already been cast in his or her name) to draw any conclusions about the extent to which these may indicate levels of attempted fraud. The numbers of tendered ballot papers are usually very small, but further analysis of data from Returning Officers may provide a clearer indication of the nature and extent of any problem.

Polling Stations

There were an estimated 46,500 polling stations used for this general election. Although many buildings (schools, village halls and others) are used for elections year after year, some are only ever deployed for general elections and others were used as polling stations for the first time this year. Initial indications suggest that there were a significant number of polling stations in temporary accommodation, such as portacabins. In Rhondda, for example, ten of the 72 polling stations were portacabins, two of them because it was discovered that the polling stations used on previous occasions had been demolished without notifying the electoral services team. The foot and mouth disease outbreak prior to the election also created problems in some areas, with (Acting) Returning Officers being forced, or choosing, to find alternative polling station locations. The June election also meant that some school premises were not available because of exams.

The legal requirement is to give all electors "such reasonable facilities for voting as are practicable in all the circumstances" (RPA 1983). Exactly what this means in practice varies from constituency to constituency, and security considerations must also be taken into account. It is almost impossible to meet the needs of all potential voters. Those living in rural locations may not be able to get to polling stations if there is no suitable means of public transport. Elderly and vulnerable people may not be willing to leave their homes for long periods or to travel unfamiliar routes. It is difficult to gauge the extent to which inconvenient polling station locations affect people's willingness to vote. The post-election MORI survey for the Commission found that it was the most frequently cited reason for failing to vote. 21% of those who did not vote referred to the inconvenience of the polling station. In theory, those who are unable or unwilling to travel to their nearest polling station could apply for a postal vote, but it was entirely possible that a voter would not discover the location of the polling station until the deadline for postal voting had passed. Giving electors good notice of the polling station location is increasingly important with the advent of postal voting on demand, and the use of maps and early issue of polling cards can assist in this respect.

The scope for 'bringing the election to the voter' has been explored in the UK. In local elections in Norwich in 2000, suitably equipped vehicles with polling station teams visited locations such as sheltered housing schemes, residential care homes, day centres and hospitals. In Windsor and Maidenhead, a touring polling station was taken to various locations in two large rural wards. Neither scheme made any significant impact in terms of increasing voter turnout, although the voters who used the services were appreciative. There has been no permanent change to the law regarding the location of polling stations. As long as fixed site polling stations are used, it is important that the siting of stations is given careful consideration. The Commission intends to provide best practice guidance on this point, together with advice on the internal layout of polling stations. However, we also intend to look further into moving away from fixed polling stations as the primary means of voting to provide a wider means of allowing votes to be cast.

One frequent source of complaints on election day relates to the activities of tellers outside polling stations. Tellers are volunteers, appointed by the political parties to monitor who is voting and to identify potential supporters who have not voted and so should be encouraged to turn out. Although tellers are not recognised in electoral law and have no official status, many voters, and some tellers, regard the role as semi-official. Tellers can certainly play a valuable part in encouraging voter participation, through chasing up potential voters, but it is important that their activities should not undermine public confidence in the operation of the poll and that there should be no risk of intimidation of voters.

There are a number of general provisions about control of polling stations, and access to them, which apply to tellers. Most constituencies also adopt a series of common sense principles to follow in dealing with tellers' activities. However, in numerous cases reported to the Commission, tellers sought to breach the boundaries set by the (Acting) Returning Officers. In most instances, these breaches were dealt with promptly and effectively by Presiding Officers, or a decision was taken to turn a pragmatic blind eye. The most frequent problems involve tellers seeking to operate inside polling stations (rather than outside), tellers wearing party labels instead of a simple rosette and tellers asking voters for their polling card numbers on the way in to the polling station rather than the way out. The repetition of these sorts of problems can lead to significant difficulties. In Bolton, for example, one party has registered a formal complaint with the Acting Returning Officer regarding the number of tellers from another party at polling stations. The Commission is concerned that there should be effective and consistent control of tellers' activities at polling stations, and therefore plans to assess the need for greater standardisation of practice, or regulation, in relation to the role of tellers.

The practice of appointing polling agents, nominated by the candidates or parties to attend polling stations for the purpose of identifying those attempting 'personation' (impersonating other people), has not been common practice in recent elections in Great Britain, although they play a more active role in elections in Northern Ireland. This 'rarity' factor creates problems in itself, as Presiding Officers may be unclear as to the limits of polling agents' powers and rights. It is clearly important for voters not to feel intimidated or confused by the role of the polling agent, and they must not be allowed to interfere with the conduct of the democratic process. These issues will be addressed together with the wider review of tellers' activities referred to above.

One practical issue in relation to polling hours emerged from the Commission's discussions with practitioners. While the law is clear that only those voters who have been issued with a ballot paper by 10pm may cast their votes, in practice some Presiding Officers will permit all those already inside the polling station to vote. This situation clearly needs to be regularised, so that one rule is applied in all constituencies.

Equal Access

The Commission believes that equal access to elections is an essential part of a healthy democracy and necessary to ensure high levels of voter participation. Access for disabled voters has achieved greater prominence in recent years and the vast majority of polling stations are now 'accessible' for wheelchair users, in theory at least. The entitlement to vote with the assistance of a companion has been extended to disabled voters, and the tactile voting device for visually impaired voters and large print posters are also now mandatory. However, ensuring equal access involves active effort, going beyond the requirements of the law, for a range of diverse communities.

A number of charities and other organisations representing various interests undertook promotional activity to increase awareness of the new provisions for disabled people at the 2001 election. The Royal National Institute for the Blind (RNIB), for example, provided considerable information on its website and in its newsletters. In Scotland, the Scotland Office consulted with RNIB in developing its own plans to publicise the changes introduced to assist visually impaired voters. There is clearly more that could be done in future elections to spread this type of good practice to other groups, in particular to inform those who would benefit from the extension of the use of a companion or the Presiding Officer to assist those unable to read or mark the ballot paper.

The Commission is aware of survey work looking at the accessibility of polling stations, such as that being carried out by SCOPE and the Disability Rights Commission, and will consider their conclusions. On the basis of information available to the Commission from its own observations and discussions, there does appear to be a genuine commitment on the part of electoral administrators to make elections accessible to disabled people. However, there are a number of areas where problems occurred. Occasionally, problems arose because no preliminary survey had been undertaken. At one polling station serving a large number of elderly electors, for example, a change of building led to difficulties with access. The use of temporary polling stations can also militate against providing the sort of access that might be regarded as desirable. On polling day, there is not always sufficient thought given by Presiding Officers on how best to promote and explain the availability of the new facilities; polling clerks are rarely briefed on how they can best support disabled voters. One of the consequences of limited resources is also that polling clerks and Presiding Officers do not receive training in issues such as disability awareness or customer care. This degree of support for staff is necessary to ensure true equal access.

Equal access goes beyond disability. Adults whose first language is not English form a significant number of electors in a number of cities. For these potential voters, it may be difficult to understand the voting process without the provision of explanations of the voting process in other languages. However, long-standing advice from the Home Office has discouraged the provision of information in languages other than those prescribed by statute (English and Welsh). The Commission believes that there is a possible interpretation of the law that would permit the provision of information in other languages, alongside information in the prescribed languages, and will consider this issue further with a view to providing advice to (Acting) Returning Officers at future elections.

The siting of polling stations also affects equal access. For example, at least one polling station in the 2001 election had no pedestrian street access. The Commission intends to develop best practice guidance in relation to equal access.

Staffing and Funding

The current arrangements for funding general elections are both inadequate and unnecessarily complicated. The costs of administering general elections at the local level are met by central Government. As a result, the Department of Transport, Local Government and Regions (DTLR, formerly DETR), the Scotland Office and the Northern Ireland Office are responsible for setting the rules for reimbursing costs, including the fees for most staff involved in election duties, in their respective territories (DTLR assumed these responsibilities from the Home Office in June 2001).

For the 2001 election, the fee guidelines were published by the Home Office only seven days before polling day causing considerable, and understandable, annoyance amongst electoral administrators. The administrators' grievances were further exacerbated as areas of expenditure agreed as legitimate in the past had on this occasion been excluded from permitted expenditure, for example preparing stamping instruments and transporting ballot boxes to the count. It is evident that the delay in publishing the expenditure guidance imposed an added burden on administrators already dealing with considerable pressures of recruitment. Steps must be taken to ensure that this situation does not arise in future. Action also needs to be taken to resolve the situation that applied in the 2001 general election, whereby some elements of funding are at the discretion of government after the event, and electoral services staff are not able to budget in advance for these activities.

All fees paid for election duties are subject to income tax. Rates for this election in England, Wales and Scotland were set at £135 for a Presiding Officer and £80 for a polling clerk, covering a period of over 15 hours. Increased fee rates were payable in constituencies within the London area and where combined polls were taking place. Funding for count staff was provided within a lump sum amount, set at £9,500 per constituency (rising to £10,800 where there are combined polls). In addition, there was a variety of additional payments available, including £450 for a recount, a figure which a number of administrators felt was insufficient to cover the number of staff involved. Rates were slightly lower in Northern Ireland, set at £122.28 for a Presiding Officer and £77.32 for a polling clerk. The lump sum amount from which payments to count staff was made was calculated differently, with increments made to a base of £4,460.87 according to the number of registered electors and the number of postal voters. The amount for a recount in Northern Ireland was set at £387.48.

Many constituencies found difficulty recruiting sufficient staff to undertake polling clerk and counting duties for the 2001 general election, and report that this is becoming more difficult with every successive election. Significant numbers of electoral administrators raised concerns with the Commission about the Government's decision to adopt a 'lump sum' approach to count expenses. They found that this made it difficult to pay counting assistants at a rate that was likely to attract people to turn out for a late night session. As one administrator commented to the Commission: "In general, there is a constant tension between keeping within the budget and getting enough people to do the job properly."

The initial uncertainty over the date of the election also contributed to recruitment difficulties and some of the historical sources of staff (in particular, banks and buildings societies) no longer produce significant numbers of staff with the necessary skills willing to undertake the task. A number of councils have turned to local colleges and senior school pupils to provide the necessary support on election day. Most (Acting) Returning Officers deploy a mixture of council staff and others recruited through family connections or word of mouth. Even this, however, is not without its difficulties, as there is inconsistency between councils as to whether council staff are required to take a day's annual leave in order to receive the fee.

Where the staff are not required to take leave, it is invariably easier to recruit. There is a clear need to look at the way in which elections are staffed and funded, and consider whether the current arrangements are sustainable.

It is standard practice for Presiding Officers, poll clerks and counting staff to be appointed soon after the announcement of a general election. The number of staff involved obviously varies between constituencies, but usually runs into hundreds of individuals in each constituency, none of whom is bound to take on the responsibilities involved. In most areas, the rates of pay available to staff are also a significant factor in persuading them to undertake the work. It is clearly necessary, if polling day and count arrangements are to be put in place in good time, that the expenditure framework should be in place at the earliest opportunity.

Equally important is to provide effective and timely training. Practice in this respect varies significantly, not least because there is no central funding available to support training activities. However, in the vast majority of constituencies, training or briefing meetings are provided for Presiding Officers, along with written materials. At its best, this training and the materials provided are exemplary. It is much less common for training to be provided to poll clerks. However, there are authorities where poll clerks are invited, or in the case of London Borough of Lewisham required, to attend training sessions in advance. In Lewisham, this had the double benefit of providing staff with a measure of training and establishing a level of commitment at the training stage that reduced 'drop outs' nearer to polling day.

The most significant complaint from electoral administrators in relation to funding is a far more fundamental one. Increasingly, local authorities argue that they are having effectively to subsidise elections work from budgets allocated for other responsibilities, and that recent law changes (in particular the extension of postal voting) have only exacerbated the problem. The Charges Order, laid by the Home Office, is widely considered to provide insufficient levels of funds and insufficient flexibility in use of funds, for example by effectively precluding the use of an hourly rate for payment to enumerators. As one electoral administrator commented to the Commission: "It is unacceptable that a toilet attendant at a count on double time was earning more than could be provided to counting staff." In addition, by providing for a specific election period only, administrators feel that ongoing electoral management tasks between elections are ignored. These concerns combine with the longer standing problems of securing the funds from government in a timely manner. Many authorities still await the resolution of their funding submissions from the 1997 general election. The Commission believes that a thorough review of arrangements for funding elections, including the payment and training of staff, is long overdue. This will be a key priority in our work programme.

Observers

The Commission was contacted by a number of foreign delegations during the course of the election campaign, asking to 'observe' the UK general election; many more requests went direct to the Foreign and Commonwealth Office and others involved in the administration of elections. In all cases, it was necessary to explain that there are strict legal regulations governing who can attend a polling station. Other than those entitled to vote, attendance is restricted to candidates and their election agents, polling agents and poll clerks, police officers and companions of voters with disabilities. There is also a requirement that those attending a polling station must maintain the secrecy of the ballot. On top of this is a further general prohibition on interfering with a voter when they are recording their vote, obtaining information as to voting intention or indirectly inducing a voter to display the ballot paper after it has been marked.

Despite the tight regulation, in practice some observers – including at this election members of the Commission – are permitted to visit polling stations at the discretion of the Acting Returning Officer, provided they do so without disturbing the operation of the station and comply with the general requirements of secrecy. The Commission is also aware of at least two instances where members of the press were permitted into polling stations to photograph well-known candidates casting their votes.

The formal restrictions on access to polling stations are more onerous than those applying to the count, at which it is possible for anyone permitted by the Returning Officer to attend. However, the Returning Officer can permit people other than those specified to attend only if satisfied that the official counting of the votes will not be impeded and has either consulted the election agents or thought it impracticable to do so. Every person attending the count must be given a copy in writing of the secrecy provisions of the RPA 1983.

The Organisation for Security and Co-operation in Europe (OSCE) Copenhagen Document committed the UK in 1990 to invite observers from any OSCE participating state wishing to observe elections. No action has yet been taken to give effect to this commitment. It is clear that it would be entirely inappropriate to allow unrestricted access to polling stations. However, there appears to be no reason in principle why the same rules governing access to the count should not also apply to polling stations. Northern Ireland legislation for local elections already allows anyone permitted by the Returning Officer to observe the conduct of the poll. This precedent may well provide an appropriate starting point for extending the discretion to other elections across the UK.

The Count

The count is the culmination of the work put into preparing for the election. It is also closely monitored by the candidates, and their agents, friends and families. Perhaps surprisingly, therefore, it is one of the aspects of the election process where the (Acting) Returning Officer has greatest discretion. The manner in which the verification and count are conducted, decisions as to who can have access, the provision of facilities for the media and guests, the handling of spoilt or rejected papers, the format of the result announcements and a range of other issues are all determined by the (Acting) Returning Officer, operating within a legal framework which sets certain parameters.

The discretion resting with the (Acting) Returning Officer is evident in the significant variations in the times at which results are declared. It is clear that there are a number of constituencies where the (Acting) Returning Officer makes a point of aiming to have the first declared results. The need for accuracy in the result must always be paramount, but the Commission has no evidence to suggest that constituencies declaring results early fulfilled their responsibilities anything other than diligently. Indeed, the careful exercise of discretion and judgment by (Acting) Returning Officers is one of the hallmarks of the electoral process in the UK. However, where there is scope to develop and disseminate best practice, the Commission believes that this would assist in improving efficiency across all elections. Such areas might include the opening of postal votes, procedures for verification and counting and advice on handling spoilt papers.

Fraud and Security

We have already considered the issue of postal voting fraud. However, the issue of fraud clearly goes wider than this. Both the Lord Advocate's Chambers in Scotland and the Crown Prosecution Service, covering England and Wales, told the Commission at the end of June 2001 that it was too early to know whether the general election would generate substantive claims of electoral fraud. None had been received to date, but the Crown Prosecution Services pointed out that: "These allegations…tend not to come all at once, but over a period of months following the election. Indeed, complaints are often surprisingly late" (*Letter from Director, Casework, CPS to Chairman of the Electoral Commission*, 25 June 2001).

The Association of Chief Police Officers reported to the Commission that in the majority of force areas, there had been no significant or unexpected problems at polling stations. There were a handful of allegations of postal voting abuse, but none that warranted full investigation save for Bradford, referred to earlier. Surrey police also reported that they were investigating claims from one elected MP that his posters had suffered criminal damage during the election campaign. A number of police forces also highlighted to the Commission the importance of effective communication with electoral administrators and party officials, especially in relation to the logistics of the count and policing polling stations, and the provision of security for high profile politicians visiting constituencies.

In Northern Ireland, the Director of Public Prosecution has put in place arrangements to ensure that he is informed of the number of election offences detected by the police as soon as possible after polling day. As at 20 June 2001, the Royal Ulster Constabulary had reported that three persons had been detected by police for alleged election offences. Of these, one had been charged by the police with offences of 'personation' and had appeared before the local magistrates' court. The other two persons had not been charged, but were facing allegations of possession of false identification documents. The Director of Public Prosecutions made clear to the Commission that: "This relatively small number of detections of election offences does not indicate any significant or unexpected trend in terms of electoral fraud.

Indeed, my understanding is that in the previous general election in 1997, there were no offences detected and reported to this office in regard to electoral fraud" (*Letter from Director of Public Prosecutions, Northern Ireland, to Chairman of the Electoral Commission*, 20 June 2001).

Guidance, Support and Evaluation

The range of new legislative provisions introduced in the period running up to the general election put a significant strain on the resources of the central government departments involved. There were considerable time pressures on the Home Office, Scotland Office and Northern Ireland Office in preparing the necessary secondary legislation flowing from both PPERA and the RPA 2000. There were some consequent tensions between local authority staff and those working from central government about lack of time to prepare for the implementation of new measures. One electoral administrator commented to the Commission that he had been: "showered with legislation like confetti since January."

In Scotland, government administrators made effective use of a small advisory group of experienced electoral administrators, which helped to ensure that the legislation was in a form that could be properly applied in practice. Communication between the Scotland Office and Scottish electoral administrators also appears to have been generally well managed. One exception related to the provision of guidance for polling clerks and Presiding Officers. In this instance, lack of time and resources prevented the Scotland Office from producing the type of product that would have been preferred by the electoral services staff. The Commission will explore the need for standard guidance manuals for those involved in the electoral process, to ensure that best practice is disseminated.

Guidance to Acting Returning Officers in England and Wales was published by the Home Office on 15 May 2001. While the quality of the guidance was generally agreed to be good, there was some initial disquiet among electoral administrators that the guidance was available only in electronic format, via the Home Office website, as the documentation initially available proved difficult and time-consuming to download. The Home Office responded to the criticism swiftly and produced a revised electronic text. In Scotland, the Home Office guidance was distributed without amendment due to time constraints. A UK-wide helpline for those actively involved in election management was established by the Commission to provide advice and assistance. Over 750 calls were dealt with during the election period. The Home Office and Scotland Office also dealt with significant numbers of calls. In Northern Ireland, the Electoral Office for Northern Ireland, reflecting the different arrangements applying there, fielded most queries.

One issue raised by many electoral administrators was the fact that some election stationery, traditionally prescribed by government, has not kept up with new legislation. The Commission agrees that there is a good case to be made for undertaking a comprehensive review of election stationery to ensure compliance with current practice and legislation.

In some local authorities, there is a formal process of learning from the election experience. In many areas, the Presiding Officers are also asked to complete review sheets for the benefit of the (Acting) Returning Officer. In Gateshead, for example, there is an elected member advisory group which reviews election procedures and makes recommendations. In Cardiff, there is a formal evaluation process designed to support an application for the BSI quality assurance standard. The Commission endorses the desire for formal evaluation of the general election process, as a means of identifying areas for improvement in the future as well recognising and rewarding good practice.

The Commission intends to work with electoral administrators to develop and disseminate best practice in relation to election administration among local authorities, including the development of training programmes to support it. The Commission also endorses the work of the Association of Electoral Administrators in promoting a professional qualification for those working in this field, and supports the objective of ensuring that electoral staff are able to obtain a recognised qualification.

Conduct of the Campaign

By 17 May 2001, the last date for registration of a party for the general election, 179 parties had registered with the Commission. In addition, 118 'Independent' candidates stood for election and a further 19 candidates without any description at all. For the first time, an official list of all the nominated candidates and their party affiliations was made publicly available, via the Commission's website. During the last week of the election campaign, over 130,000 hits were recorded on the website.

Campaign Strategies

It was evident from the almost static opinion polls during the election campaign that the campaign itself made little impression on the electorate. At the national level, the main parties' campaigns were highly professional, characterised by: "a narrow focus on target voters, message discipline and image management" (Drs. Margaret Scammell and Martin Harrop, *Preliminary Report for the Electoral Commission*, June 2001). The highly centralised campaigns fought by the main parties contrasted sharply with the campaigns fought by the many smaller parties and independent candidates. In terms of the policy issues, the Communications Research Centre at Loughborough University identified a convergence around a limited range of subjects, both in terms of the issues raised by the main parties and media coverage of them. Broadly, Europe dominated, with the Health Service and taxation following. In the three nations of the UK with devolved government, other issues emerged as central to the campaign – most obviously in Northern Ireland, where the progress of the peace process was the main theme.

Technology was not exploited to as great a degree as some had anticipated. At a national level, the main parties had computerised databases of electors, which were used to contact voters during the campaign. IT was also used to 'personalise' the campaign without imposing intolerable pressures on the candidates themselves. For example, during the last week of the election campaign the Labour Party sent up to 24,000 text messages to the mobile phones of supporters who had registered their details on the party website, with the aim of encouraging them to turn out and vote. E-mail was also used to support the dissemination of campaign messages within the major parties, and ensure consistency in campaign presentation. However, there was an understandable reluctance to become involved in sending unsolicited e-mail.

Securing media attention was, of course, central to all the parties' national campaigns. There were relatively few challenges from any of the parties to the national media coverage of the parties' activities. The one notable exception to this was the British National Party (BNP), which registered their concern that the BBC had unfairly denied them access to party election broadcasts and was in other ways seeking to restrict public access to information about the party, for example, through failing to provide a link to the BNP website from the BBC election website. Some independent and small party candidates also felt that the national media did not give them equal exposure, but were perhaps more resigned to this at the national rather than local level.

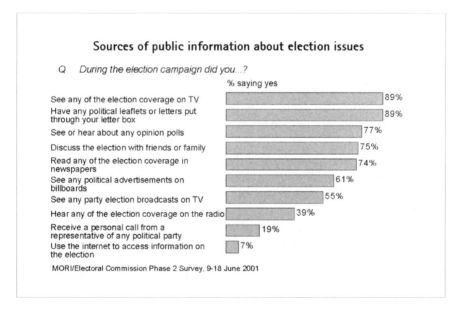

Sources of public information about election issues

Q   *During the election campaign did you...?*

% saying yes

See any of the election coverage on TV	89%
Have any political leaflets or letters put through your letter box	89%
See or hear about any opinion polls	77%
Discuss the election with friends or family	75%
Read any of the election coverage in newspapers	74%
See any political advertisements on billboards	61%
See any party election broadcasts on TV	55%
Hear any of the election coverage on the radio	39%
Receive a personal call from a representative of any political party	19%
Use the internet to access information on the election	7%

MORI/Electoral Commission Phase 2 Survey, 9-18 June 2001

At the local level, the primary campaigning tools were leafleting and public events. Traditional door-to-door canvassing remained popular with many parties and candidates, as it does with voters, although practice varied considerably from area to area. Telephone canvassing was also used, but more so by the major parties than by others. 19% of those questioned by MORI after the election recalled receiving a personal call (either on the doorstep or by phone) from a representative of a political party during the election campaign. Even for the major parties, telephone canvassing presents some problems. Access to telephone data is restricted both by the increasing numbers choosing to become ex-directory and those opting out of receiving unsolicited telephone calls through registering with the Direct Marketing Association's Telephone Preference Service.

Initial analysis of submissions to the Commission from party agents and candidates suggest that around three-quarters of campaigns used IT within the constituency. The most common uses were to send information by email to known party supporters and to communicate by email with local volunteers. Local websites were also set up in some cases to provide information about candidates and provide a contact point for electors through an email link. Some candidates did, however, have reservations about use of websites, with one choosing to suspend his site for the duration of the election: "as a precaution against incurring extra costs".

At local level, the party campaigns also relied heavily on media coverage. In some constituencies, candidates found much to praise in the local media coverage of the election. However, from the Commission's initial assessment of questionnaires returned by party election agents and candidates, a common complaint across the parties was their perception that the local media were biased towards other parties or candidates, or that they excluded coverage of local issues, concentrating exclusively on the national position. Small parties complained of almost complete lack of coverage of their candidates by the local media.

How effective were the parties' campaign strategies? MORI found that people were most likely to have seen election coverage on television or to have had political leaflets or letters through the letterbox; 89% recall these. More than half (55%) say they saw any of the party election broadcasts on television, down from 73% in 1997 and 71% in 1992. They are also thought to have had minimal influence on what people decided to do on election day; 77% say broadcasts had "not very much" influence or "none at all", similar to 1997 (74%) and significantly higher than equivalent figures for election coverage on television (50%) and in the newspapers (61%).

It appears that in many cases decisions had been made and allegiances developed over the whole four-year period leading up to the general election, or even earlier, not during the four-week campaign. Recent MORI analysis has found that three-quarters of the public say they decided which party to vote for *before* the campaign began. It may be that they were not presented with sufficient information or reasons to change those decisions or question their allegiances.

Impact of Third Parties

This general election was the first in which a person or organisation (other than a registered political party) was required by law to register as a 'third party', if intending to spend large sums in publishing material which could reasonably be regarded as intending to promote or procure electoral success of one or more registered parties or category of candidates. The provisions of PPERA 2000 make clear that it is irrelevant whether or not the material in question expressly mentions the name of any party or candidate. The breadth of these provisions created some difficulties for those organisations who wished to express a particular opinion or point of view on a matter of public interest which was likely to be perceived as placing them in support of or opposition to a particular party ideology or policy. The range of organisations registered as third parties with the Commission bears this out: Campaign for an Independent Britain, Charter 88, Democracy Movement, MSF, The Society for the Protection of the Unborn Child, The South Molton Declaration, tacticalvoter.net, UNISON, USDAW and Yes Campaign Ltd. There were fewer third party registrations than anticipated, perhaps because of reluctance to spend large sums on a campaign that was not, at least as far as the opinion polls were concerned, closely contested.

In contrast to the substantial increase in the number of applications to register as political parties following the announcement of the general election, there were just three new notifications of recognised third party status after the election was announced. Despite an advertising and promotional campaign in UK-wide print media, the Commission received fewer than 15 enquiries on its helpline for third parties. It seems that many organisations which might reasonably have been thought to be covered by the regulations took the view that they were not. There were also some apparent conflicts between charity law and the provisions concerning third party registration, which may have affected some organisations' willingness to register. The introduction of PPERA has thus not had the impact envisaged in this area. However, it remains to be seen whether organisations which should have registered under section 85 of the Act have not done so. This should come to light following the on-going compliance checks to be carried out by the Commission.

Third parties: what are they?

A third party is a person or body which campaigns on behalf of one or more registered political parties or a particular category of candidates (for example, those that hold or advocate a particular policy or opinion). PPERA restricts the amount that a third party can spend on campaigning for the electoral success of registered parties or candidates. Being registered as a recognised third party with the Commission increases a third party's spending limits. Spending in support of, or disparaging, an individual candidate is not covered by these provisions and continues to be subject to the controls set out in the RPA 1983.

During the election campaign, concerns were raised about the manner in which some registered and unregistered third parties sought to oppose individual candidates in certain constituencies. The Commission received a number of complaints about leaflets that targeted specific MPs directly, and further enquiries about the distribution of general leaflets supporting specific causes. However, there was no evidence to suggest that the organisations brought to the attention of the Commission had done anything outside the law. Moreover, initial analysis of submissions to the Commission by party agents and candidates representing over 90 constituencies suggests that overall there was little in the way of activity by registered third parties at the local level. On the whole, those activities which did take place were considered to have had very little impact on the campaign. However, it is interesting to note in this context that almost a quarter of respondents did not appear to understand the meaning of the term 'third party'. In addition to the significant proportion who admitted to not understanding the term, some took 'third party' to mean a registered political party other than the Labour and Conservative Parties, and others understood it to mean the party that came third in the ballot.

Free Facilities

By law, all nominated candidates are entitled to have a single election address, weighing no more than 60g, delivered free of charge. The election address usually takes the form of a short leaflet. If addressed to individuals, a copy of the address can be sent post free to every elector and proxy. If unaddressed, the literature can be sent post free to all households with a clearly defined address and a means of receiving the information. Responsibility for delivery rests with the Royal Mail, whose costs are reimbursed by the Government under a service level agreement. The costs of producing the leaflet itself must be met by the candidate or their party. As a result, some smaller parties and independent candidates are unable to take advantage of the free delivery, as they cannot afford the printing costs.

The Royal Mail handled the delivery of around 134 million election mailings during the 2001 election. The Royal Mail has put in place guidance notes and systems to provide advice to candidates and parties, and these central systems appeared to operate effectively. There were no significant concerns raised with the Commission about the Royal Mail's role in 'vetting' candidates' literature. In a number of cases, the Commission was also informed that local managers had been helpful to candidates and election agents. Initial analysis of submissions to the Commission from party agents and candidates suggests that two-thirds were either satisfied or very satisfied with the free leaflet delivery.

However, the Commission has also been made aware of a number of situations in which political parties were unhappy about the timeliness of the delivery, failures to deliver leaflets to properties with no other mail, the omission of some households owing to problems in matching postcodes to constituency boundaries, leaflets being delivered to the wrong constituency and, most seriously, instances where it is alleged that large numbers of election addresses from one particular party were not delivered at all. It has been suggested by several agents that there should be guaranteed delivery times for free leaflets and more checks in place to ensure that they are delivered correctly. Some suggested that the Royal Mail should be required to issue a 'completion certificate' or establish a formal monitoring system for election addresses, while others feel that responsibility for free leafleting should in future be contracted out to private companies.

For their part, Consignia has told the Commission that: "It is our belief that the vast bulk of candidates' material in the general election was delivered properly and to time. It is a common feature of the election process that there are instances where a candidate/party feels and alleges that this is not the case. In such instances, we will fully investigate the circumstances and normally, if there is any element of doubt, undertake to redeliver. However, one always needs to bear in mind that recipients' recollection of receiving this type of information is not always precise, and that other members of households can also dispose of it without informing the other residents. Having said this, we do accept that mistakes are sometimes made and we have acknowledged a number of instances of proven failure to deliver which are being investigated locally." (*Letter from Head of Westminster Affairs, Consignia, to Chairman of the Electoral Commission,* 22 June 2001). The Commission will pursue with the Royal Mail the various issues that emerged from the general election and has requested from Consignia further information about the instances of "proven failure" referred to above.

The law also provides for candidates to make free use of rooms on school premises, provided they are community, voluntary or voluntary schools, and other meeting rooms funded from the public purse. On the available evidence, such facilities are used infrequently. Indeed, some party agents responding to the Commission's questionnaire were not previously aware of these facilities. Others suggested that it would be useful to extend the free facilities to include a freephone telephone number for all candidates, perhaps reflecting the more individualised communication methods preferred by many parties. Use might also be made of local authority websites for making available information relating to candidates. The National Union of Students felt that more consistency in the way in which councils provide such information could assist those who wished to arrange public meetings or hustings with the candidates.

Broadcasting and Print Media

Is the electorate well served by media reporting of the election? After the last general election, an ITC study of television coverage concluded that most viewers thought there had been too much of the election on their screens and that the overall tenor of the coverage was negative. Most people felt that the coverage focused too much on the leaders and their personalities, and the campaign process. Women and first-time voters in particular found little to praise in the extended news programmes, special election programming and 'reports from the campaign buses'. The evident excitement of the political commentators at the once every four years treat of a general election campaign was not shared by the viewers. The ITC's analysis echoed the wider findings of the opinion pollsters that the public wanted more information on policies and what the parties stood for, and less of the political gossip, campaign tactics and personality characterisation.

Did anything change this time around? Many commentators suggest not. The media continued to spend a good deal of time and space commenting on the way the campaign itself was managed and developed. In the first week of the campaign, Loughborough University Communication Research Centre's analysis of media coverage showed that 62% of election items commented on the election process rather than policies or issues (*The Guardian*, Golding et al, 14 May 2001). By the end of the election, the picture had shifted, down to 37% of news items focusing on election process. But this figure was still 25% points higher than the new most-mentioned issue, Europe, at 9.5%. Loughborough also calculated that only 43.7% of media appearances by the three main political parties featured them presenting their own policy. The majority featured parties attacking other parties' policies, defending themselves against attacks or commenting on internal divisions (*The Guardian*, Golding et al, 12 June 2001).

It may therefore be regarded as unsurprising that the MORI survey conducted for the Commission after the election found that 51% agreed with the statement: "the election was fought by parties pointing out what was wrong with the policies and personalities in other parties", although it is interesting to note that this sentiment was less pronounced in the 2001 election than in 1997.

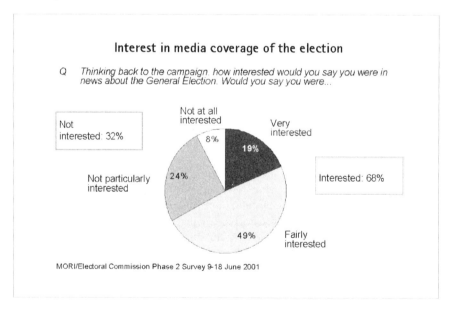

Interest in media coverage of the election

Q   Thinking back to the campaign. how interested would you say you were in
     news about the General Election. Would you say you were...

Not interested: 32%

Not at all interested 8%

Very interested 19%

Not particularly interested 24%

Interested: 68%

Fairly interested 49%

MORI/Electoral Commission Phase 2 Survey 9-18 June 2001

The BBC's Media Correspondent said at the outset of the campaign: "...you might have expected the broadcasters to have scaled back their coverage this time round. Instead they find themselves caught in a cleft stick – fearful of boring viewers and listeners but also conscious they have a duty to report the campaign as fully as they can in the interests of democracy." In fact, there was some evidence that the BBC in particular reduced the quantity of election coverage. The extended *10 O'Clock News*, for example, was shorter than the equivalent *9 O'Clock News* in 1997. However, both ITN and the BBC continued to devote substantial coverage to the election, which led the main bulletins on most nights during the campaign. Aside from the quantity of coverage, it is interesting to examine whether the 'interests of democracy' which the broadcasters felt bound to serve extended to encouraging voter turnout as well as providing information and analysis. The changing role of the print media, especially in terms of patterns of party support, also affects the way in which election coverage was presented during the 2001 election.

At a national and UK-wide level, there is considerable agreement among academics and other commentators that media coverage has changed in character and tone over recent elections. Loughborough University's Communications Research Centre point out that: "After decades of a Conservative leaning press... the endorsement in 2001 of New Labour, in circulation terms, by over 91% of the national daily press went almost without comment. Even the normally loyal *Daily Mail* could not bring itself to call explicitly for a Conservative vote, merely inviting its readers to vote against a large Labour majority. Others offered Labour support that was highly conditional, qualified and circumspect" (Loughborough University Communications Research Centre, *Paper submitted to the Electoral Commission*, 22 June 2001). Loughborough argue that a crucial consequence of this loss of partisanship among the main newspapers is a shift towards a sceptical view of all political options on offer. This is also reflected in evidence (from Dr. Margaret Scammell) that the media, especially the broadsheet newspapers, initiated more analysis and punditry than in the 1997 or 1992 elections. Although the range of issues covered was not wide, in-depth analysis of policies, 'truth watch' initiatives and the comparison of party claims all featured in the national press. One potential downside of this questioning approach is the fostering of a negative attitude among voters towards all politicians.

At a local level, it is relatively common to find journalists and news editors who regard it as part of their responsibility to encourage increased participation in elections. Some local newspapers have developed very constructive working relationships with local electoral administrators. The *Leicester Mercury*, for example, worked together with electoral services staff to provide information about postal voting. Election coverage in local newspapers is usually more substantial than their ordinary political coverage and in some cases is impressively comprehensive. In others the coverage is limited and driven principally by the presence of big name politicians in the local area. Ethnic minority media also gave considerable coverage to election issues, as well as highlighting the party leaders. The main difficulty for the ethnic minority press, however, is that most newspapers are weekly or monthly, making it impossible to provide topical election coverage.

Traditional print media are also increasingly backed up by internet sites, providing archived information and other opportunities to extend, and make more interactive, their election coverage. In Bolton, for example, the *Bolton Evening News* sponsored an on-line debate where readers could question candidates. Local radio stations, especially the BBC, provided constituency profiles and phone-in programmes with the candidates, complementing this information service with positive encouragement to vote, for example through jingles during election day encouraging voter turnout. However, there is little evidence of the extent to which the local media coverage of election issues influences, or even reaches, the voters. In interviews with the Commission, political editors from local papers and broadcast media were not confident that their readers and listeners had any great interest in the election. Many felt that the main drivers were the UK-wide and national media coverage, and that it was difficult, and not necessarily desirable, to create a local news agenda that was in any way distinct from the wider UK perspective.

Why does it matter what the media say and do? The simple answer is because most of the public get most of their information about politics and elections from the media. The MORI survey conducted for the Commission at the beginning of the campaign found that television was the most used source of information and news about politics and current issues with 88% saying they used it. This is followed by daily and Sunday newspapers, used by 74% and 54% respectively. Just under half (48%) used the radio as a source. These patterns are consistent among all groups but younger people are more likely than others to get information through family (38%) and the internet (22%), twelve and nine points higher, respectively, than the public as a whole. After the election, 49% and 38% respectively said that television and newspaper coverage had a "great deal" or "fair amount" of influence. Other potential influences (including radio, posters, leaflets, personal calls, internet coverage, opinion polls, and family and friends) were all regarded as having less impact.

The parties themselves place enormous importance on the coverage they receive, especially from the television broadcasters, and control of the agenda is all-important. One consequence of this is that discussions and disputes between parties and broadcasters can themselves become news during an election campaign. This happened most prominently in the 2001 election with media coverage of correspondence between the Labour Party General Secretary and the BBC, ITN and Sky regarding suggestions, that were denied, that the broadcasters had been "inciting and colluding with protesters at campaign visits by senior politicians".

At one stage in the election run-up, there had been speculation that a televised debate or debates between the main party leaders might go ahead for the first time in the UK. The broadcasters agreed a set of common ground rules but were unable to obtain the full support of the three main parties, and so in the end it did not happen. Where such debates occur in other countries, they appear to contribute significantly to the campaign and create a focal point, helping to engage voters in the election process. On the other hand, there are significant logistical and political issues to address, especially given the increasingly diverse political circumstances of the nations making up the UK. However, the importance of television to an election campaign cannot be doubted. The Commission believes that there would be benefit in discussing with the broadcasters and the main parties whether in future more could be done to use television as a medium to engage voters and encourage turnout. In this context a televised debate among the main party leaders, carefully set up, could play a significant role.

Public attitudes to media coverage

I think the focus should have been less on personalities and more on issues

Television is not a personal enough way of campaigning. I feel candidates should be more personal perhaps through canvassing

I prefer the old hustings rather than a TV campaign where one has contact with the politicians and can ask them questions

Image over substance. They all said the same things. Nobody spoke to me or about the things I wanted to hear

I think it was the worst campaign since 1945 - it was driven by image and not substance

I think they (politicians) are not involved enough with the public - they just talk to the media

I am a pensioner and feel people stick leaflets through your door and expect you to watch and follow the leaders. There are no meetings nowadays. You used to be able to listen to people and heckle them and ask them questions

There was too much coverage of non-issues. They failed to connect with people. People weren't really interested in it, especially young people

The coverage was superficial - all soundbites and personality and little policy

No-one is looking at what they are saying. It's not a beauty contest. Decent, honest people are derided and condemned by so-called clever interviewers. The media journalists think they are kings

I felt it was the media who helped to make it a one way ticket. No new issues expressed - there wasn't enough differences between parties

MORI/Electoral Commission Phase 2 Survey, 9-18 June 2001

Given the levels of trust placed in television by the public, the parties inevitably look for ways to get their messages across to the electorate directly through TV. Paid political advertising on television and radio is prohibited by law. Election broadcasts therefore provide one of the few opportunities for the parties to get their message across directly to the electorate *en masse*. The broadcasts appear on the five main terrestrial channels. There is no formal legal obligation on the BBC to make airtime available for party broadcasts, but it has traditionally offered unmediated airtime to the political parties via party election broadcasts. The Broadcasting Act 1990 requires the ITC to ensure that broadcasts are included in ITV, Channel 4 and Channel 5 services.

Decisions on the allocation of airtime for election broadcasts are matters for the broadcasters and broadcasting regulatory authorities: BBC, ITC, the Radio Authority and S4C in Wales. By convention, these bodies put proposals to the major parties represented in Parliament with a view to reaching consensus. They will take into account the number of candidates each party has in the election and the number of MPs it had in the previous Parliament, together with other factors affecting the strength of the parties' popular support, such as representation in devolved legislatures.

For this election, in England, Scotland and Wales, 11 registered political parties had the opportunity to present party election broadcasts. Six of these parties (Labour Party, Conservative Party, Liberal Democrats, UK Independence Party, Socialist Labour Party and the Socialist Alliance) had broadcasts in all three nations, one (Green Party) had broadcasts in England and Wales, and the other four parties (Plaid Cymru, Scottish Nationalist Party, Scottish Socialist Party and Pro-Life Alliance) had their broadcasts shown only in Scotland or Wales, all of them in accordance with the threshold criteria, by nation, of candidates standing in at least one-sixth of consistuencies. In Northern Ireland, six parties produced broadcasts. In addition, a number of election broadcasts were made on the BBC and the three national commercial radio services.

As already indicated, MORI's findings suggest that more than half the electorate (55%) saw any of the party election broadcasts on television, down from 73% in 1997 and 71% in 1992. Recall is fairly uniform across the main age and other demographic groups and 49% of non-voters say they saw at least one broadcast. Among those who did, broadcasts are on balance seen as "interesting" (51% to 33%) and "informative" (48% to 34%) but they are *not* seen as being particularly "useful" (38% to 45%). This negative approach of some of the general campaigning (referred to above) also extended, in this election campaign, to party election broadcasts.

There were a number of disputes between the parties and broadcasters during the election period. The Green Party registered its concern that, because the Scottish Green Party was registered separately from the Green Party, they were disadvantaged by the formula used to allocate broadcasts to parties. Other parties, including the BNP, were also unhappy with the allocation of airtime. The Pro-Life Alliance pursued court action against the broadcasters because of the editing required to their planned broadcast, which was eventually aired without any pictures, simply a red screen covered with the single word "censored". The Green Party also registered complaints with both the BBC and Radio Authority about its exclusion from the list of radio election broadcasts.

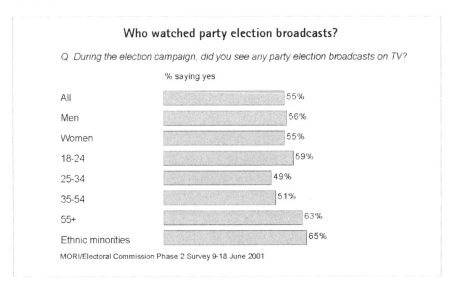

Who watched party election broadcasts?

Q During the election campaign, did you see any party election broadcasts on TV?

% saying yes

All	55%
Men	56%
Women	55%
18-24	59%
25-34	49%
35-54	51%
55+	63%
Ethnic minorities	65%

MORI/Electoral Commission Phase 2 Survey 9-18 June 2001

One of the major parties was unhappy that the broadcasters failed, in their view, to consult adequately about their plans to allocate party election broadcasts on the same basis as for the European Parliament and devolved legislature elections in 1999, rather than taking the 1997 general election allocation as their starting point. Both the Green Party and the Scottish Socialist Party also complained to the ITC that their election broadcasts would not be transmitted by Channel 4 or Channel 5 - the reason being that these channels do not split their signals for different parts of the UK and neither party qualified for a UK-wide broadcast. The ITC accepted that it was necessary to apply some sort of threshold in these situations, but agreed with the broadcasters that exceptions might be made where national parties had "significant levels of support". In practice, it was decided that only the SNP and Plaid Cymru met these criteria at the present time.

The Commission has no power to intervene in the broadcasters' decisions and would not wish to do so, although the broadcasters have an obligation under PPERA to take into account the views of the Commission. However, we plan to undertake an early review of election broadcasts, examining the role they play in the campaign and their place in a world of increasing media diversification, where satellite and cable channels do not have the same obligations. We also plan to review the consultation processes and the basis on which allocations are made.

The PPERA provided for the replacement of section 93 of the RPA 1983. Prior to the new Act, the law held that candidates could take part in an election campaign programme about their constituency only if all their rival candidates also took part or agreed that the programme might go ahead. The position now is that there is no statutory requirement for all candidates to agree on a local broadcast. Instead, the broadcasting authorities are required by law to adopt a code of practice covering this issue. In fact, the code of practice adopted by the broadcasting authorities broadly replicates the position that previously existed under the law. However, there is more flexibility. Under the new provisions, it is no longer a requirement that the consent or involvement of all candidates be secured before the broadcasting of constituency material can go ahead. The three broad conditions that do need to be satisfied are that the candidates of the three main parties (or four in Scotland, Wales and Northern Ireland) should be invited to take part, that there should be some participation of significant smaller parties and that the programme should provide viewers with a full list of candidates standing in the constituency.

The BBC's chief political adviser, and principal architect of the new code of practice, has argued (*The Guardian*, 4 June 2001) that the changes have had positive benefits: more constituency debates on local and regional programmes, more reports from constituencies on the main TV news programmes and greater use of candidates in studio discussions on key issues. The ITC also suggests that ITV regional services took significant advantage of the change, providing better and more informed coverage of constituency matters, especially in the Tyne Tees and Border areas. The Radio Authority has also reported that the national commercial radio stations warmly welcomed the change. However, enquiries to the Commission during the campaign period suggest that the changes were not universally understood by either news editors or candidates. We are also aware that both the ITV News and Channel 4 News broadcast items that effectively breached the new rules governing constituency reporting. In both cases, the ITC raised the matter with the broadcasters and appropriate action was taken. To date, the Commission does not have information from the BBC. It is also interesting to note that initial analysis of submissions from party agents and candidates suggest that a majority of respondents were not aware of the new arrangements for broadcasting local items. Of those who were aware of the changes, just under three-quarters were either satisfied or very satisfied with the new arrangements.

Internet

This election was the first in which access to the internet and email among voters had reached sufficient levels to make the use of technology a significant factor in campaign strategy. In public debates prior to the election, there was a sense that the impact of the internet could be significant, although it was never entirely clear how. It was suggested that the internet would offer political parties and candidates the opportunity to run more sophisticated and targeted campaigns, and that it could revolutionise the participation of voters themselves in the democratic process by allowing them to access information quickly and more easily. Certainly some of those involved in election planning believed that the internet was an important means of getting the message to the voters. In Northern Ireland, for example, the Democratic Unionist Party pursued an American style of campaigning using the internet and e-mail as a key tool, both within the party and externally. Some parties sought to undermine their rivals' efforts by securing website addresses in the other parties' names, while early in the campaign one party's campaigners were accused of having sent out 20,000 unsolicited e-mails masquerading as messages from a rival party. In total, it has been estimated that over £1m was spent by the main political parties on providing election websites and related material.

Primarily, the internet was seen by the parties as a medium through which they could put their message across to voters directly, without any secondary interpretation by media outlets. Yet a study of voter attitudes towards new technology during the 2001 election conducted by the Industrial Society found that only 2% of internet users said they were certain to use the internet to find out information about the election campaign. Moreover, given the choice, voters said that they did not want to access the political parties directly online. They were wary of party sites, preferring to use traditional media sites such as BBC Online (which logged over 25 million 'hits' over 7 and 8 June) or election websites set up by the broadsheet newspapers. One of the most popular of these, the Guardian Unlimited website, recorded some three million page impressions during the course of the election campaign, with one million impressions on the election night itself. A number of commentators suggested much of the online election coverage was a trial for the full-scale 'internet election' expected next time around.

MORI's findings, based on questions asked after the election, suggest that up to 7% used the internet to access information about the election at any stage in the campaign. This reflected the findings from the survey conducted at the outset of the campaign, which indicated that the internet remains a secondary source of political information for most voters. While daily newspapers and television were identified by 74% and 88%, respectively, of respondents as their main source of information about politics, only 13% used the internet to obtain information. Moreover, only 1% of respondents said that the internet was their *main* source of information. This would seem to suggest that while the internet and email are increasingly used as tools for conducting business or communication, they have yet to become a primary source of news or information about political issues, even amongst those with access to the internet.

The Commission recognises the role of the internet as a tool for mass communication, and the potential impact of internet technology on election campaigning. However, it will be important to ensure that the use of the internet in political campaigns is regulated in the same way as traditional campaigning. A recent Hansard Society report on electoral law and online campaigning noted that the internet is "famously anarchic", and argued that the exciting opportunities offered by the medium come with both risks and threats (The Hansard Society, *Electoral Law and the Internet*, March 2001). The Commission believes that the implications of online campaigning for electoral law should be assessed, and the role of the internet in future election campaigning monitored.

One way in which the internet did appear to make a difference was in facilitating the use of tactical voting. A number of websites were set up by independent organisations or individuals seeking to provide information on how tactical voting could be used to influence the outcome of the general election. Tacticalvoter.net offered a nationwide matchmaking service, pairing Labour and Liberal Democrat supporters in marginal seats, and reported 200,000 visitors and 8,000 matches during the course of the campaign. Votedorset.net provided a similar service, concentrating its efforts on three marginal Conservative seats in Dorset. The site registered 10,000 hits over seven weeks, with 300–400 comments submitted to the public discussion forum. Stophague.com encouraged broader support for the Labour candidate in the Wimbledon constituency and the Liberal Democrat in Kingston and Surbiton, and received some 4,000 visitors.

The Commission received many enquiries as to the legality of these sites, but the legal position appears to be clear. There is nothing inherently unlawful about agreeing with another elector that you will vote in a particular way. Equally, there is nothing binding in law about any such arrangement.

The actual impact of tactical voting is inevitably difficult to discern. In two seats where the incumbent party was unseated (Dorset South and Cheadle), the result could well have been influenced by tactical voting, as the total number of 'on line' pledges exceeded the size of the previous majority. However, the main trend at this election seems to have been for consolidation and protection of marginal seats. The Electoral Reform Society has identified a number of seats retained and won by the Liberal Democrats apparently with the help of Labour Party supporters and a number where Liberal Democrat supporters apparently helped to retain Labour seats (*Election 2001: Unfair and Unrepresentative*, June 2001). An interesting example was in the Kingston and Surbiton constituency, targeted by the stophague.com website, where the incumbent Liberal Democrat candidate increased his majority from 56 to 15,676 votes.

Whether or not tactical voting actually affected the outcome of the election, there was certainly an increase in media coverage and awareness of tactical voting. A number of the websites set up to promote tactical voting to influence the outcome of the general election were effective in courting media attention. The electorate also seemed to be interested in the scope for tactical voting. The MORI survey conducted for the Commission after the election also found that 15% of those who voted claimed to do so in order to keep another party out, as their own preferred party had little chance of winning. An *Observer*/ICM poll published on 3 June 2001 suggested that 66% of Labour supporters would switch to the Liberal Democrats if they were the only realistic challengers to the Conservatives, while 50% of Liberal Democrat supporters would switch to Labour.

In addition to tactical voting, there was at least one example of tactical campaigning from the main political parties. In the Wyre Forest constituency, the Liberal Democrat Party withdrew their candidate in favour of a minority party candidate, standing as part of a campaign against cutbacks at a local hospital. The Independent Kidderminster Hospital and Health Concern candidate gained votes from both Labour and Conservative supporters, and had a winning majority of 17,630.

It is also interesting to note that at least ten candidates' websites had links to tactical voting websites.

Advertising

Poster and press advertising is one of the primary means of communication for the parties, not least because it has the advantage of reaching directly to the voter. In previous general elections, posters in particular have been the source of a good deal of controversy. At the 1997 general election, for example, there was considerable attention given to the Conservative Party's poster advertising campaign projecting Tony Blair, then Leader of the Opposition, as having 'Demon Eyes'. The Advertising Standards Authority (ASA) was at that time responsible for regulating political advertising, although the relevant Codes of Practice applied only to a narrow definition of political advertising and some of the provisions of the Codes were not applied to political advertising (for example, in relation to truthful presentation). The ASA ruled against the Conservative Party's 'Demon Eyes' poster, but then found itself in the uncomfortable position of finding in favour of the Labour Party in respect of a separate claim brought by the Conservatives.

Following these events, the ASA concluded that it could do damage to the advertising industry's self-regulatory system if it were to be seen to have been deployed against one political party but not another. They also felt that they could not be expected to rule with sufficient speed and effectiveness during a brief election campaign in which the advertisers had no interest in the long-term success of the self-regulatory system. In line with these arguments, a subsequent version of the relevant Codes of Practice, which still applies today, completely exempted political advertising.

The question of how best to deal with political advertising was put to the Neill Committee on Standards in Public Life in 1998 by the Committee of Advertising Practice, the body responsible for the Codes of Practice. The Neill Committee rejected a suggestion that such responsibilities might fall to an Electoral Commission, were one to be established in the future. Instead, in their report *The Funding of Political Parties in the United Kingdom* (1998), they concluded that the best way forward was a new Code of Practice: "...we would welcome any progress which could be made in this direction by the political parties working in association with the advertising industry and we would exhort them to endeavour to formulate an agreed code." In the intervening three years, there has been no progress towards such a code.

The 2001 general election did not involve any significant controversies over advertising. There were some criticisms of the two main parties for using 'personalised' and pejorative advertisements, focusing on the party leaders' attributes. But as the ASA commented to the Commission: "we did not see anything that so blatantly breached the 'legal, decent, honest and fair' principle that we were embarrassed not to be able to intervene....We did not see any ads that, had the former [Codes] still been in place, would have been likely to result in complaints being upheld." (*Letter from the Director General of the ASA to the Chairman of the*

Commission, 22 June 2001.) The Commission agrees that the 2001 general election did not give rise to any significant problems in this area. However, the Commission is not convinced that the absence of problems in this area during the 2001 general election means that such difficulties are a thing of the past. We believe that it is appropriate to take this opportunity of the absence of controversy to review the current arrangements for monitoring political advertising.

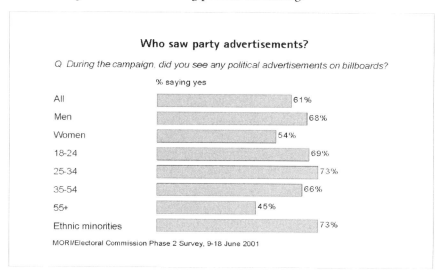

Who saw party advertisements?

Q During the campaign, did you see any political advertisements on billboards?

% saying yes

All	61%
Men	68%
Women	54%
18-24	69%
25-34	73%
35-54	66%
55+	45%
Ethnic minorities	73%

MORI/Electoral Commission Phase 2 Survey, 9-18 June 2001

Funding and Financial Controls

The PPERA introduced a raft of changes in the way that political parties are required to account for their funds. In addition to new national campaign spending limits, all parties that had not submitted a valid declaration of exemption were legally required to submit weekly donation reports to the Commission for the duration of the general election period. Parties could either make a declaration of exemption when they registered, or make a declaration of exemption to cover the general election, provided the declaration was made within one week of the announcement of a general election. This report does not seek to examine these issues in detail, as it is too early to provide any detailed analysis of the way in which this new framework has operated. In addition, those registered parties with expenditure exceeding £250,000 have six months from the end of the campaign period to submit their campaign returns to the Commission, all other parties having three months.

It is, however, possible to say that party funding did not become a significant issue in this election campaign. Whether this was a direct result of the increased transparency of donations and the limits on expenditure is impossible to judge. Certainly, press reporting on the donations was generally favourable, with most of the broadsheet papers making regular use of the information provided on the Commission's website to highlight donations to the parties and welcoming the changes that required the publication of such data.

Inevitably, there were some, especially the smaller parties, who felt that too much money was spent by the major political parties on the election, despite the caps on expenditure. On the other hand, the major parties felt that there was a good case for increasing the limits on candidates' local expenditure. The difficulty of establishing a level playing field for all parties without providing state funding of election campaigns is obvious. However, there was effective liaison between the parties and the Commission in resolving a number of legal and policy issues. The Commission advised, for example, that campaign expenditure should be calculated inclusive of VAT, whether or not this could be recovered by the party. It also advised that whilst monies payable to members of the party's staff were not campaign expenditure, any allowances or other remuneration of party workers who were not party staff, for example secondees who continued to receive a salary from their employer, should be treated as campaign expenditure.

There were some instances, mentioned earlier in this report, of third parties targeting particular constituencies. This raised issues regarding the trigger dates for expenditure controls at constituency level, and complaints about expenditure levels. In such cases, expenditure must not exceed the statutory £500 limit for third party backers or disparagers of individual candidates. Expenditure on other third party election material, for example leaflets that did not refer specifically to an individual candidate, should count towards the national controlled expenditure limits for recognised, and non-recognised, third parties. How far third parties complied with both these different limits, and the problems associated with operating within the limits, will be explored further by the Commission.

The Commission also worked closely with the political parties to ensure the smooth introduction of the new donation controls. For example, the Commission provided advice about when the release of an employee to campaign for a political party would be a donation under PPERA, and how this donation should be valued. The Commission similarly advised that any element of the price paid by the media to travel on the campaign bus in excess of the actual cost of the transport provided, should be treated as a donation to the party, and that if transport were offered free of charge to the party leader during the election campaign, this would be a donation in kind. Advice was also provided about the position of former special advisers to the Government working for parties during the campaign.

As with the quarterly donation reports submitted to the Commission, only a small number of political parties had anything to report on each occasion from among the total number of parties that had not made a valid declaration of exemption and were thus required to submit returns. There was some irritation about the weekly reports, and the requirements for nil returns, among many of the smaller parties, for whom a donation of more than £5,000 was always unlikely. A large amount of Commission time was spent chasing up the newly registered parties and smaller parties to ensure that they were aware of the requirements and to request copies of the weekly donation reports. However, as the campaign period went on, things did start to run a little more smoothly, and it remains to be seen how parties will respond to the requirements at subsequent elections when they have had time to adapt to the new legislation. Certainly the Commission would hope that by the time of the elections to the devolved legislatures in 2003, following their experiences of submitting donation reports and education initiatives, parties will be more prepared for the reporting requirements.

There was some confusion among parties and candidates regarding the imprint details that must legally be published on election material. This confusion was largely caused by the introduction and subsequent rescinding of the provision in the PPERA, which amends the imprint regulations in section 110 of the RPA 1983. Following objections from the major political parties that large stocks of election material that had been produced previously would have to be pulped, the Elections Publications Act 2001 deferred the introduction of the amendment, creating a situation in which material that complied with either the old or new section 110 would be regarded as complying with imprint regulations. Section 143 of the Act, which introduced the same imprint requirements for 'national' election material for the first time, was also suspended for the same reason. The result was that this led to confusion about exactly what imprints did comply with the law, and the Commission received several complaints about the wording and type of imprints that were used on election material. Advice was issued on the matter. The Commission urges the Government to reintroduce section 143 and the new RPA provision at the earliest opportunity, but with an implementation date designed to allow for sensible planning towards a changeover.

Devolution

As Loughborough University Communication Research Centre's analysis of media coverage highlights: "It has been another election north of the border..."(*The Guardian*, Golding et al, 4 June 2001). In Scotland, nearly 24% of all themes in election news items dealt with the constitution or devolution, while in the London-based press such issues featured in fewer than 5% of election items. Similar patterns emerge in Wales and Northern Ireland, with the constitutional issues in Northern Ireland dominating the news agenda.

This was the first general election in which there were devolved legislatures operating in three of the UK's four constituent nations. The main differences were evident in the style and content of campaigning. In Scotland, Northern Ireland and Wales, many of the core domestic policy issues of the UK-wide campaign – education, health, transport – fall within the remit of the devolved legislatures. As a result, the main political parties effectively ran different campaigns in each of the four nations, alongside the UK-wide campaigns. The campaign tactics focused not on the London-based media, but on the national media. The Labour, Conservative and Liberal Democrat parties all produced separate manifestos for Scotland and Wales. In itself, this sends an important message.

More interesting still is the fact that in these manifestos, and those for Plaid Cymru and the SNP, a good proportion of the main policy commitments related to areas of business within the control of the devolved legislatures, not Westminster. A report by the Constitution Unit at University College London ('*Devolution Literacy' and the Manifestos*, June 2001) suggests that Scottish and Welsh parties were in effect starting to fight the 2003 elections to the devolved legislatures, and so included policy commitments within the control of these legislatures in order to set out a consistent programme for the 2003 elections. The Constitution Unit report also concludes that although the Scottish and Welsh manifestos did usually acknowledge the fact of devolution, the manifestos presented in England did not. These manifestos tended to make apparently uniform commitments for the whole of the UK. The tendency, therefore, was for parties to confuse the electorate, particularly in England, about what devolution means.

In Scotland and Wales, the tone of campaigning was also slightly different. One result of proportional representation in both countries has been to encourage the creation of coalitions to run the devolved executives. These coalitions evidently made it more difficult to run campaigns for Westminster based on attacking the record of "the other side". It is interesting, however, that the MORI survey conducted after the election for the Commission showed no significant difference between the four nations of the UK in terms of voter perceptions of how 'positive' or 'negative' the campaign had been.

Northern Ireland presents a unique political environment, with candidates and parties contesting issues specific to it. While campaigning took in the conventional broad range of issues, such as health and education, the Good Friday Agreement and unresolved areas such as policing and decommissioning of weapons also raised issues for candidates and voters alike. In the North Down constituency, the pro-Agreement Alliance Party withdrew its candidate in support of the Ulster Unionist challenger to the anti-Agreement United Kingdom Unionist candidate. Although national media interest in the election campaign in Northern Ireland was limited, local coverage was wide-ranging and in-depth. There is some concern, however that the local media overplayed the constitutional issues of the election to the detriment of any discussion of other policies.

Some commentators have suggested that, following devolution, turnout was likely to be lower in Scotland and Wales than in England. MORI's findings at the outset of the election indicated that, in terms of anticipated turnout, there were no statistically significant differences between the three countries. 74% and 69% respectively said they were "certain" or "very likely" to vote in Scotland and Wales, compared to 76% in England. While the actual turnout figures were lower on 7 June, there was still little difference in the turnouts between the three nations. In Northern Ireland, by contrast, the turnout increased on 1997 figures, which may be a reflection of the importance of the political issues at stake and the fact that there were a number of seats which were known to be vulnerable to challengers.

Turnout across the UK

	UK	England	Scotland	Wales	Northern Ireland
2001	59.4	59.1	58.1	61.4	68.0
1997	71.4	71.4	71.3	73.5	67.1
1992	77.7	78.0	75.5	79.7	69.8

Source: University of Plymouth

Aside from the different campaigns, Scotland and Northern Ireland also had different administrative structures in place. In Scotland, responsibility for electoral law in relation to Westminster elections rests with the Scotland Office, while responsibility for the law and procedures for Scottish Parliament elections falls to the Scottish Executive. The infrastructure of electoral administration also differs from England and Wales, as do some of the job titles. In Northern Ireland, the role of the Chief Electoral Officer in overseeing the conduct of elections is unique in the UK. Responsibility for the administration of registration and elections lies with the staff of the Electoral Office rather than with the local authorities, and each area office reports to the Chief Electoral Officer himself. Such centralised administration offers the opportunity for coordinated management of the electoral process, and any future reform of the process may be implemented from a solid central base.

Despite these structural differences, many of the issues raised in the earlier administration section of this report apply as much to Scotland and Northern Ireland as to England and Wales. There are, however, some issues specific to the two nations.

In Scotland, there were two by-elections for Scottish Parliament seats at the same time as the Westminster elections. As there is no provision in legislation to combine elections to the Scottish Parliament with elections to the UK Parliament, these elections were run separately but in parallel. The two seats affected were Banff and Buchan, and Strathkelvin and Bearsden. The administration of the two elections in parallel also threw up some important questions, including whether the counts for Westminster and the Scottish Parliament should be on separate days or take place at the same time. It was also notable that some of the statutory provisions governing the two elections were unhelpfully inconsistent, for example in relation to polling agent notification dates. Practical issues also arose in relation to the count, including whether Westminster candidates could attend the Scottish Parliament count and the fairness of Scottish Parliament ballot boxes being opened at the Westminster count (to check for ballots papers incorrectly 'posted') when the Scottish Parliament polling agents were not permitted to attend.

Other issues emerging in Scotland related to the provision of guidance and of election forms and stationery. In comparison to the guidance and advice provided for the 1999 Scottish Parliament elections, for which resources had been available for substantial manuals and training programmes because of the new voting system, the guidance provided by the Scotland Office for this election was considered substandard by many Returning Officers. Several authorities produced their own guidance for Presiding Officers and poll clerks. In addition, one practical result of the legislative changes has been the requirement to change the text on some of the electoral forms. The Scotland Office has a commercial arrangement to produce forms and other stationery. However, the poor quality and late delivery of some of the forms for this election led to many Returning Officers producing their own forms. The Scotland Office intends to review these arrangements in consultation with Electoral Registration Officers and Returning Officers.

A further issue of particular concern to the Scottish island communities was the difficulties presented by transporting the ballot boxes to the count after the close of poll. Funding for helicopters was approved where required, but hire was not always straightforward. The Commission is aware of suggestions that legislation might need to be amended to allow for counts to take place at more than one location within a constituency, using satellite links to enable all candidates to view the proceedings. The Commission will consider this issue as part of its wider consideration of practices linked to the count.

In Northern Ireland, a different set of issues came to the fore. Prior to the election some concerns were raised that the integrity of the electoral process was in continuing danger of being undermined by the scale of abuse in Northern Ireland. Accusations were levelled by several parties that their opponents were involved in widespread electoral fraud and intimidation in a number of key seats. The postal voting facility in Northern Ireland is restricted to those unable to cast a vote in person and all applications must be attested. However, abuse of the system is widely perceived to be a significant problem, although the scale of fraud has been relatively hard to discern or prove. Large numbers of absent vote applications were received by the Electoral Office shortly before the deadline for applications, raising concerns in some quarters about whether sufficient time was left to make the appropriate checks. In relation to voting in person, voters are required to present a specified form of identity before being given a ballot paper at the polling station, a measure introduced in order to address the offence of personation. However, several of the forms of identification are less than reliable, carrying no photographic proof of identity and easy to forge.

The Commission approaches electoral issues in Northern Ireland from the perspective that confidence in the democratic process must be sustained and enhanced. The Northern Ireland Office published a Bill in June 2001 focusing on measures to combat electoral fraud. This follows on from work over the past three years, including a report of the Northern Ireland Affairs Committee on electoral malpractice and a White Paper published in March 2001. Central to policy development in this area have been issues relating to individual voter identification. The Bill has taken this agenda forward, providing for a number of anti-fraud initiatives which, taken together, represent a significant strengthening of identity verification mechanisms.

This year, for the first time, the election in Northern Ireland consisted of a synchronised poll, combining the Westminster general election with elections to the 26 district councils. Local elections, held under the single transferable vote (STV) system, have traditionally taken place on a different day than a Westminster poll, and concern was expressed that the combination would place undue pressure on the resources of the Electoral Office. Almost inevitably, the process of completing two ballot papers with separate voting systems took more time than anticipated and in some areas substantial queues built up outside polling stations. A number of spoilt ballot papers may also indicate that the combination of two electoral systems led to confusion among voters.

Despite extensive publicity, including television advertising aimed at encouraging people to vote early in the day, some Presiding Officers reported having to turn voters away at the close of poll. Frustration with these delays led to alleged reported irregularities, where voters were allowed to cast their votes after the official closing time of 10pm. In one such case, in the constituency of Fermanagh and South Tyrone, an election petition has now been brought by the defeated Ulster Unionist candidate. Concerns were also raised over the safety of staff and security of polling stations after two police officers and an elector were injured in a shooting at a polling station shortly before it closed. These comments should be viewed in the context of voting activity taking placing without problems during the morning and afternoon, and at most locations in the evening of election day.

The count for the Westminster election takes place the next day, and not overnight. This is the tradition in Northern Ireland and does not seem to be a matter of controversy.

3 An Agenda for the Future

This report provides only a preliminary overview of the key issues emerging from the 2001 general election. In the time available since 7 June, a comprehensive analysis would have been both impractical and presumptuous. The Commission is committed to undertaking further detailed work. We will draw on the views of those directly involved in the administration of electoral services and those active in political life. We also welcome the input of those who voted, and those who did not, whether through their own choice or otherwise.

Set out below are the areas of electoral practice and procedure which we have identified as our key priorities, and a number of other issues which we intend to look at in the longer term. We expect to have completed work on all the key priorities by summer 2003 and to have at least started work on the remaining areas within the same time frame. The focus of our programme is the administration of elections and voter participation, as those are the areas where the Commission has a clear statutory role and where we believe that we already have sufficient information on which to develop our programme of action. A detailed programme of review will also be produced in relation to funding and financial controls. In other areas, we recognise that there are others who must take the leading role in securing change and improvement. However, we stand ready to work with those organisations and individuals, and to be a catalyst for change where necessary.

Voter Engagement

Perhaps the single most important issue arising from the 2001 general election is the need to address, urgently and radically, the decline in public participation. Responsibility for re-engaging the electorate with the democratic process must rest in large part with the political parties. However, the Commission also has a statutory responsibility to promote public awareness of our electoral systems at both general and other elections. We are funded to carry out this work. The creation of this role within the Commission represents a major shift in our political culture. Until now, there has been no national organisation, within Government or elsewhere, responsible for encouraging or promoting public interest in elections.

Key priorities

Creating a programme of research. Examining the reasons for low turnout, looking at particular communities, including young people and ethnic minority communities. Building on this research, the Commission will develop, in discussion with other key stakeholders, a clearly targeted programme of voter education.

Identifying new ways of encouraging voting. Exploiting technology for the modernisation of our electoral systems.

Administration

The Commission believes that the efficiency and effectiveness of electoral administration is fundamental to a healthy democracy and that it has been taken for granted for too long in the UK. The funding of election management falls between local and central government, and investment in new systems and the development of best practice has not been a priority for either tier of administration in recent years. As a result, there is a dangerous dependency on goodwill at the heart of our electoral system and a lack of clarity about where investment for the future should come from. Most significantly, there has been no national strategic direction given to electoral administration. Proper funding of elections, based on clear strategic planning, is essential. The Commission also believes that it is important to recognise the role of registration as the lynchpin of the electoral system. Improvements to registration could have far wider benefits across the electoral process.

Key Priorities

Funding democracy. There is a need for a fundamental review of the funding of election management, including the resourcing of elections themselves.

Promoting best practice. Although elections are highly regulated, there is considerable diversity of practice between electoral administrators, often simply because the mechanisms for exchanging views are not in place. The Commission can play a pivotal role in developing and disseminating best practice and best value guidance and in promoting training programmes, drawing on the expertise of electoral administrators and working alongside the existing membership organisations, including the Association of Electoral Administrators, Society of Local Authority Chief Executives, the Chief Electoral Officer for Northern Ireland and the Scottish Assessors' Association.

The registration process. There is a need to identify ways in which signing up to vote can become more accessible and more automated. We intend to examine (a) how best to develop an integrated national and local strategy for registering, (b) the scope for moving the deadlines for registration prior to an election closer to polling day to maximize the numbers eligible to vote and (c) the potential benefits of creating a national electronic register.

Systems for absent voting. It is essential to assess the impact of extending postal voting, including any consequent increase in electoral fraud, and the value of the declaration of identity. As part of this review, we intend to look at the administrative issues and consider whether there is any continuing need to offer proxy votes in addition to postal votes and, if so, how to ensure that the two methods of absent voting complement each other appropriately.

Mapping the electronic future. The Commission intends to evaluate the scope for introducing information technology to our electoral system, both in relation to voting and counting of votes, whether in parallel with or as a replacement for existing methods. There is an evident need for greater flexibility about *when* and *how* we can vote. New and existing ideas will be tested through further pilot schemes as part of the local authority elections in May 2002, and the Commission will actively encourage pilots in internet and telephone voting. Research into the practicalities of introducing electronic voting is also being sponsored by the Commission, together with a consortium of other interested organisations, and is due to begin in the early autumn.

Longer Term Issues

- Review of the timetable for general elections, including an appraisal of the case for fixing the term of the Westminster Parliament.
- Codification or standardisation of statutory provisions governing the conduct of election.
- Review of ballot paper design, including the need for (and practicalities of introducing) positive abstention.
- Admission of observers to polling stations, bringing the UK into line with nearly all other major democracies, and ensuring compliance with the OSCE Copenhagen Document 1990.
- Review of the procedures for nominating candidates with a view to simplification.
- Promotion of equal access to democracy.

Conduct of Election Campaigns

The Commission is not responsible for the range of issues in relation to broadcasting, press and internet use, and party campaign activities, that may require review. However, we believe that there are some key issues where the Commission can act as an independent forum for discussion, and potentially as a generator of ideas and catalyst for change.

Key Priorities

Party election broadcasts. The Commission intends to proceed swiftly with a review of the role of broadcasts in providing voters with information to support their voting decisions, including the criteria governing their allocation. This review will take account in particular of the increasing diversification of broadcast channels, including those satellite and cable channels not bound to provide broadcasts.

Code of practice on campaign spending. The Commission is already committed to the development of a code of practice which would set out a consistent framework for the identification and categorisation of national campaign expenditure. Once in place, this code should assist in securing compliance with the national campaign expenditure limits. It will be developed in consultation with the political parties.

Longer Term Issues

• Considering again the case for a code for political advertising, in line with the recommendation of the Committee on Standards in Public Life.

• Assessing the likely future use of the internet in election campaigns, with a view to identifying any aspects that need further consideration in the context of electoral law.

• Discussing with the broadcasters and the main parties as to whether, in future, more could be done to use the medium of television to engage voters and encourage turnout, whether through a televised debate between the main party leaders or otherwise.

Funding and Financial Controls

As already indicated, the Commission takes the view that it is too early to provide detailed analysis of the way in which the new framework of PPERA has operated. In addition, registered parties have three months from the end of the campaign period to submit their campaign expenditure returns (six months for those with expenditure exceeding £250,000). However, we indicate below the areas where we believe it is already evident that further review will be necessary. This agenda will be developed as further information becomes available.

Emerging Priorities

Small parties.   The Commission intends to look into the way in which small parties, including one-candidate parties, are affected by the regulatory framework and whether there are changes which might be introduced to limit the administrative burdens on such parties without unfairly disadvantaging the larger parties.

Third parties.   Reviewing the scope of the definition of 'election material' in relation to the requirements to register as a third party.

Resolving a range of unintended consequences of the changes in the PPERA.   These include possible inconsistencies between the registration requirements on third parties and charity law.

Spending limits.   The Commission intends to look at the way in which the spending limits, at national and constituency level, operated including the trigger dates for applying the spending limits.

Longer Term Issues

• Considering the argument for a cap on political donations and state funding of political parties.

The Official Results

4 Introduction

Explanatory Notes

All constituencies in the United Kingdom are listed in alphabetical order following the practice of the Press Association and the major broadcasting organisations. Compass point references usually follow the substantive name. Thus Aberavon is number 1 and Yorkshire East number 659.

Under the name of each constituency are seven columns:

1. **Electors**: The number of electors eligible to vote on 7 June 2001.

2. **Turnout**: The number of valid votes cast expressed as a percentage of the eligible electorate.

3. **Candidate**: The surname and initials of the candidate. Those candidates who were members of the 1997–2001 Parliament are denoted by the symbol †.

4. **Party**: The party affiliation of the candidate.

5. **Vote**: The number of votes polled by the candidate.

6. **Share**: The number of votes polled by the candidate expressed as a percentage of the total valid votes cast. An asterisk indicates a forfeited deposit.

7. **Change**: The percentage change in the share of the vote for the party since the 1997 general election.

At the foot of each set of voting figures appears the majority of the successful candidate and this is also expressed as a percentage. (The rounding of percentages originally calculated to two decimal places sometimes results in the percentage majority figure differing by $\pm$ 0.1% from that obtained by subtracting the share of the first placed party from that of the second placed party.) The party that won the seat at the 1997 general election is also noted.

By-Elections

The results of by-elections held during the 1997–2001 Parliament can be found in Table 10.

Change of Party Allegiance

In a number of cases MPs changed their party allegiance following election. S. A. Woodward was elected as Conservative MP for Witney, but subsequently took the Labour whip. He was elected Labour MP for St Helens South in 2001. P. Temple-Morris was elected as Conservative MP for Leominster, but subsequently took the Labour whip. He did not contest a seat at the 2001 election. Three Labour MPs elected in 1997, D. Canavan (Falkirk West), T. Graham (Renfrewshire West), and K. R. Livingstone (Brent East), were expelled from the party during the 1997–2001 Parliament. Canavan resigned during the Parliament and none contested a seat at the 2001 election.

Electorate Statistics

Under the terms of the Representation of the People Act 2000, a system of 'rolling registration' was introduced to allow eligible persons to register to vote at any time of the year. This procedure has led to electoral registers being updated more frequently and to the numbers on the register at the time of an election differing from those 'as first published'.

The constituency electorate figures used here are as supplied by Returning Officers and have *not* been subject to the formula previously used in the *Britain Votes* series to calculate the electorate on any given date. For an explanation of that formula see Colin Rallings and Michael Thrasher (eds), *British Electoral Facts, 1832–1999* (Ashgate, 2000).

Forfeited Deposits

A candidate forfeited a deposit of £500 if he or she was not elected and did not poll more than one-twentieth of the valid votes cast.

General Election Polling Date

Polling took place on 7 June 2001.

Surnames and Initials

The surnames and initials of candidates are based on returns made to the Electoral Commission by Returning Officers. Only initials and titles that can be derived from these sources are listed.

Voting Statistics

The number of votes cast for candidates are based on returns made to the Electoral Commission by Returning Officers.

Registered Party Labels and Abbreviations

Abbrev.	*Party*	*No. of candidates*
AC	Anti-Corruption Forum	1
AL	Asian League	1
APNI	Alliance Party of Northern Ireland	10
Bean	New Millennium Bean Party	1
BNP	British National Party	33
CD	Christian Democrat	1
Ch	Peoples' Choice! Exclusively for All	1
Comm	Communist Party of Britain	6
Con	Conservative	643
Country	Countryside Party	1
CPA	Christian Peoples' Alliance	1
Cust	Direct Customer Service Party	1
DUP	Democratic Unionist Party	14
DW	Defend the Welfare State against Blairism	1
EC	Extinction Club	1
Elvis	Church of the Militant Elvis Party	1
FDP	Fancy Dress Party	1
FP	The Free Party	3
Grey	Grey Party	1
Grn	Green Party	145
Ind[1]	Independent	118
IOW	Isle of Wight Party	1
JLDP	John Lilburne Democratic Party	1
JP	Justice Party	1
JWP	Jam Wrestling Party	1
KHHC	Independent Kidderminster Hospital and Health Concern	1
LA	Left Alliance	1
Lab[2]	Labour	640
LCA	Legalise Cannabis Alliance	13
LD	Liberal Democrat	639
LE	Lower Excise Duty Party	1
Lib	Liberal Party	14
LP	Liberated Party	1
M	Muslim Party	4
Marx	Marxist Party	1
MK	Mebyon Kernow	3
MRLP	Official Monster Raving Loony Party	15

Abbrev.	*Party*	*No. of candidates*
NBP	New Britain Party	1
NF	National Front	5
NIU	Northern Ireland Unionist	2
NIWC	Northern Ireland Women's Coalition	1
Pac	Pacifist Party	1
PC	Plaid Cymru	40
PD	Progressive Democrat	1
PEC	Pro Euro Conservative Party	1
Pens	Pensioner Coalition	1
PJP	People's Justice Party	3
PL	ProLife Alliance	37
Prog U	Progressive Unionist Party	2
Ref	Reform 2000 Party	5
RM	Residents and Motorists of Great Britain	1
RRL	Rock 'N Roll Loony Party	7
RUK	Reform UK Party	1
S Alt	Socialist Alternative	2
SA	Socialist Alliance	98
Sc Ref	Scottish Freedom Referendum Party	1
SDLP	Social Democratic and Labour Party	18
SF	Sinn Fein	18
SL	Socialist Labour Party	114
SNP	Scottish National Party	72
Speaker	The Speaker seeking re-election	1
SSP	Scottish Socialist Party	72
St	Stuckist Party	1
SU	Scottish Unionist Party	2
Tatton	Tatton Group	1
Tr	Truth Party	1
TW	Third Way	2
UKI	United Kingdom Independence Party	428
UKP	United Kingdom Pathfinders	1
UKU	United Kingdom Unionist Party	1
UPP	Unrepresented People's Party	1
UU	Ulster Unionist Party	17
Vote	Vote for Yourself Party	4
WP	Workers' Party	6
WR	Wessex Regionalist Party	2
WRP	Workers Revolutionary Party	6
(no label)	candidate who gave no description	19

1. Four candidates gave descriptions which did not match with the name of a registered political party. They were:

> Dhillon, Ealing Southall
> Independent Community Candidate – Empowering Change
>
> Bhutta, Ealing Southall
> Qari
>
> Lit, Ealing Southall
> Chairman of Sunrise Radio
>
> Tutton, Aberavon
> Ratepayer

All have been coded as Independents in the results.

2. A total of 28 Labour candidates, jointly sponsored by the Co-operative Party, are described in the results as 'Lab'. The following constituencies had Lab/Co-op candidates:

Basildon	Huddersfield
Brighton Pavilion	Ilford South
Bristol North West	Islwyn
Cardiff South and Penarth	Kirkcaldy
Carrick, Cumnock and Doon Valley	Leicestershire North West
Corby	Liverpool Riverside
Dumbarton	Loughborough
Edinburgh North and Leith	Plymouth Sutton
Edmonton	Preston
Feltham and Heston	Sheffield Heeley
Glasgow Pollok	Stroud
Glasgow Rutherglen	West Bromwich West
Hemel Hempstead	Wolverhampton North East
Heywood and Middleton	Wolverhampton South East.

5 Constituency Results

Aberavon [1]

49,524	61.0	Francis, D.H.	Lab	19,063	63.1	–	8.2
		Turnbull, L.	PC	2,955	9.8	+	4.0
		Davies, C.G.	LD	2,933	9.7	–	1.6
		Miraj, M.A.	Con	2,296	7.6	–	0.3
		Tutton, A.J.	Ind	1,960	6.5		
		Beany, C.	Bean	727	2.4 ★		
		Chapman, M.	SA	256	0.8 ★		
1997: Lab				16,108	53.4		

Aberdeen Central [2]

50,190	52.7	Doran, F.†	Lab	12,025	45.5	–	4.3
		Gault, W.G.	SNP	5,379	20.4	+	4.2
		Anderson, E.	LD	4,547	17.2	+	4.0
		Whyte, S.N.G.	Con	3,761	14.2	–	5.3
		Cumbers, A.	SSP	717	2.7 ★		
1997: Lab				6,646	25.1		

Aberdeen North [3]

52,876	57.4	Savidge, M.K.†	Lab	13,157	43.3	–	4.5
		Allan, A.J.	SNP	8,708	28.7	+	6.9
		Donaldson, J.	LD	4,991	16.4	+	2.3
		Cowling, R.	Con	3,047	10.0	–	5.0
		Foreman, S.	SSP	454	1.5 ★		
1997: Lab				4,449	14.7		

Aberdeen South [4]

59,025	62.5	Begg, A.†	Lab	14,696	39.8	+	4.6
		Yuill, I.G.	LD	10,308	27.9	+	0.3
		Macdonald, M.F.	Con	7,098	19.2	–	7.1
		Angus, I.J.	SNP	4,293	11.6	+	1.9
		Watt, D.	SSP	495	1.3 ★		
1997: Lab				4,388	11.9		

Aberdeenshire W & Kincardine [5]

61,391	61.8	Smith, R.†	LD	16,507	43.5	+	2.5
		Kerr, T.	Con	11,686	30.8	–	4.1
		Hutchens, K.J.	Lab	4,669	12.3	+	3.2
		Green, J.G.	SNP	4,634	12.2	–	0.9
		Manley, A.	SSP	418	1.1 ★		
1997: LD				4,821	12.7		

Airdrie & Shotts [6]

58,349	54.4	Liddell, H.†	Lab	18,478	58.2	– 3.6
		Lindsay, A.J.	SNP	6,138	19.3	– 5.1
		Love, J.W.	LD	2,376	7.5	+ 3.3
		McIntosh, G.	Con	1,960	6.2	– 2.7
		Dempsey, M.	SU	1,439	4.5 ★	
		McGuigan, K.	SSP	1,171	3.7 ★	
		Herriot, C.	SL	174	0.5 ★	
1997: Lab				12,340	38.9	

Aldershot [7]

78,255	57.9	Howarth, J.G.D.†	Con	19,106	42.2	– 0.5
		Collett, A.P.	LD	12,512	27.6	– 2.8
		Akehurst, L.	Lab	11,394	25.2	+ 1.0
		Rumsey, D.L.	UKI	797	1.8 ★	+ 0.3
		Stacey, A.J.	Grn	630	1.4 ★	
		Pendragon, A.U.	Ind	459	1.0 ★	
		Hope, A.	MRLP	390	0.9 ★	
1997: Con				6,594	14.6	

Aldridge – Brownhills [8]

62,361	60.6	Shepherd, R.C.S.†	Con	18,974	50.2	+ 3.0
		Geary, I.D.	Lab	15,206	40.2	– 1.5
		Howes, M.	LD	3,251	8.6	– 2.6
		Rothery, J.D.	SA	379	1.0 ★	
1997: Con				3,768	10.0	

Altrincham & Sale West [9]

72,288	60.3	Brady, G.S.†	Con	20,113	46.2	+ 3.0
		Baugh, J.E.	Lab	17,172	39.4	– 0.8
		Gaskell, C.M.	LD	6,283	14.4	+ 1.8
1997: Con				2,941	6.8	

Alyn & Deeside [10]

60,478	58.6	Tami, M.R.	Lab	18,525	52.3	– 9.6
		Isherwood, M.	Con	9,303	26.3	+ 3.5
		Burnham, D.W.L.	LD	4,585	12.9	+ 3.2
		Coombs, R.	PC	1,182	3.3 ★	+ 1.6
		Armstrong-Braun, K.	Grn	881	2.5 ★	
		Crawford, W.	UKI	481	1.4 ★	
		Cooksey, M.	Ind	253	0.7 ★	
		Davies, G.	Comm	211	0.6 ★	
1997: Lab				9,222	26.0	

Amber Valley [11]

73,798	60.3	Mallaber, J.†	Lab	23,101	51.9	− 2.8
		Shaw, G.C.	Con	15,874	35.7	+ 2.2
		Smith, C.M.	LD	5,538	12.4	+ 4.7
1997: Lab				7,227	16.2	

Angus [12]

59,004	59.3	Weir, M.F.	SNP	12,347	35.3	− 13.0
		Booth, M.A.W.	Con	8,736	25.0	+ 0.3
		McFatridge, I.A.	Lab	8,183	23.4	+ 7.7
		Nield, P.J.	LD	5,015	14.3	+ 4.9
		Wallace, B.	SSP	732	2.1 ★	
1997: SNP				3,611	10.3	

Antrim East [13]

60,897	59.1	Beggs, R.†	UU	13,101	36.4	− 2.4
		Wilson, S.	DUP	12,973	36.0	+ 16.6
		Mathews, J.	APNI	4,483	12.5	− 7.7
		O'Connor, D.	SDLP	2,641	7.3	+ 2.7
		Mason, R.L.	Ind	1,092	3.0 ★	
		Graffin, J.	SF	903	2.5 ★	+ 0.9
		Greer, A.J.	Con	807	2.2 ★	− 4.6
1997: UU				128	0.4	

Antrim North [14]

74,451	66.1	Paisley, I.R.K.†	DUP	24,539	49.9	+ 3.3
		Scott, L.	UU	10,315	21.0	− 2.7
		Farren, S.	SDLP	8,283	16.8	+ 1.0
		Kelly, J.J.	SF	4,822	9.8	+ 3.5
		Dunlop, J.	APNI	1,258	2.6 ★	− 3.6
1997: DUP				14,224	28.9	

Antrim South [15]

70,651	62.5	Burnside, D.W.B.	UU	16,366	37.1	− 20.4
		McCrea, R.T.W.†	DUP	15,355	34.8	
		McKee, S.A.	SDLP	5,336	12.1	− 4.1
		Meehan, M.	SF	4,160	9.4	+ 3.9
		Ford, D.R.J.	APNI	1,969	4.5 ★	− 7.1
		Boyd, N.J.	NIU	972	2.2 ★	
1997: UU				1,011	2.3	

Argyll & Bute [16]

49,175	63.0	Reid, A.	LD	9,245	29.9	– 10.3
		Raven, H.	Lab	7,592	24.5	+ 8.9
		Petrie, D.D.	Con	6,436	20.8	+ 1.8
		Samuel, A.C.	SNP	6,433	20.8	– 2.4
		Divers, D.	SSP	1,251	4.0 ★	
1997: LD				1,653	5.3	

Arundel & South Downs [17]

70,956	64.7	Flight, H.E.†	Con	23,969	52.2	– 0.9
		Deedman, D.R.	LD	10,265	22.4	– 3.4
		Taylor, C.S.	Lab	9,488	20.7	+ 2.4
		Perrin, H.F.R.	UKI	2,167	4.7 ★	+ 1.8
1997: Con				13,704	29.9	

Ashfield [18]

73,428	53.6	Hoon, G.W.†	Lab	22,875	58.1	– 7.0
		Leigh, J.C.T.	Con	9,607	24.4	+ 4.2
		Smith, J.W.E.	LD	4,428	11.3	+ 1.6
		Harby, M.	Ind	1,471	3.7 ★	
		Watson, G.	SA	589	1.5 ★	
		Howse, K.R.	SL	380	1.0 ★	
1997: Lab				13,268	33.7	

Ashford [19]

76,699	62.5	Green, D.H.†	Con	22,739	47.4	+ 6.0
		Adams, J.P.	Lab	15,380	32.1	+ 0.4
		Fitchett, K.	LD	7,236	15.1	– 4.6
		Boden, R.T.	Grn	1,353	2.8 ★	+ 1.6
		Waller, D.L.	UKI	1,229	2.6 ★	
1997: Con				7,359	15.4	

Ashton under Lyne [20]

72,820	49.1	Heyes, D.A.	Lab	22,340	62.5	– 5.0
		Charlesworth, T.L.	Con	6,822	19.1	+ 0.1
		Fletcher, K.A.	LD	4,237	11.8	+ 2.1
		Woods, R.I.	BNP	1,617	4.5 ★	
		Rolland, N.A.	Grn	748	2.1 ★	
1997: Lab				15,518	43.4	

Aylesbury [21]

80,002	61.4	Lidington, D.R.†	Con	23,230	47.3	+ 3.1
		Jones, P.M.	LD	13,221	26.9	− 2.6
		White, K.M.	Lab	11,388	23.2	+ 1.0
		Harper, J.D.	UKI	1,248	2.5 ★	
1997: Con				10,009	20.4	

Ayr [22]

55,630	69.3	Osborne, S.†	Lab	16,801	43.6	− 4.9
		Gallie, P.	Con	14,256	37.0	+ 3.2
		Mather, J.	SNP	4,621	12.0	− 0.6
		Ritchie, S.D.	LD	2,089	5.4	+ 0.7
		Stewart, J.S.	SSP	692	1.8 ★	
		Smith, J.W.	UKI	101	0.3 ★	
1997: Lab				2,545	6.6	

Banbury [23]

84,371	61.1	Baldry, A.B.†	Con	23,271	45.2	+ 2.3
		Sibley, L.F.	Lab	18,052	35.0	+ 0.2
		Worgan, A.W.	LD	8,216	15.9	− 0.8
		Cotton, B.M.	Grn	1,281	2.5 ★	+ 1.6
		Harris, S.A.	UKI	695	1.3 ★	+ 0.7
1997: Con				5,219	10.1	

Banff & Buchan [24]

56,669	54.4	Salmond, A.E.A.†	SNP	16,710	54.2	− 1.5
		Wallace, S.	Con	6,207	20.1	− 3.7
		Harris, E.M.	Lab	4,363	14.2	+ 2.3
		Herbison, D.	LD	2,769	9.0	+ 3.0
		Rowan, A.J.G.	SSP	447	1.5 ★	
		Davidson, E.R.S.	UKI	310	1.0 ★	
1997: SNP				10,503	34.1	

Barking [25]

55,229	45.5	Hodge, M.E.†	Lab	15,302	60.9	− 4.9
		Weatherley, M.R.	Con	5,768	23.0	+ 5.4
		Keppetipola, A.K.S.	LD	2,450	9.8	+ 0.3
		Tolman, M.	BNP	1,606	6.4	
1997: Lab				9,534	37.9	

Barnsley Central [26]

60,086	45.8	Illsley, E.E.†	Lab	19,181	69.6	– 7.4
		Hartley, A.W.	LD	4,051	14.7	+ 5.2
		McCord, I.A.	Con	3,608	13.1	+ 3.3
		Rajch, H.	SA	703	2.6 ★	
1997: Lab				15,130	54.9	

Barnsley East & Mexborough [27]

65,655	49.5	Ennis, J.†	Lab	21,945	67.5	– 5.6
		Brook, S.	LD	5,156	15.9	+ 5.5
		Offord, M.J.	Con	4,024	12.4	+ 1.0
		Robinson, T.	SL	722	2.2 ★	
		Savage, G.C.	UKI	662	2.0 ★	
1997: Lab				16,789	51.6	

Barnsley West & Penistone [28]

65,291	52.9	Clapham, M.†	Lab	20,244	58.6	– 0.7
		Rowe, W.P.	Con	7,892	22.8	+ 4.5
		Crompton, M.	LD	6,428	18.6	+ 0.6
1997: Lab				12,352	35.7	

Barrow & Furness [29]

64,746	60.3	Hutton, J.M.P.†	Lab	21,724	55.7	– 1.6
		Airey, J.	Con	11,835	30.3	+ 3.1
		Rabone, B.M.	LD	4,750	12.2	+ 3.3
		Smith, J.N.	UKI	711	1.8 ★	
1997: Lab				9,889	25.3	

Basildon [30]

74,121	55.1	Smith, A.E.†	Lab	21,551	52.7	– 3.1
		Schofield, D.J.	Con	13,813	33.8	+ 3.0
		Smithard, J.	LD	3,691	9.0	+ 0.3
		Mallon, F.M.	UKI	1,397	3.4 ★	
		Duane, R.	SA	423	1.0 ★	
1997: Lab				7,738	18.9	

Basingstoke [31]

79,113	60.7	Hunter, A.R.F.†	Con	20,490	42.7	– 0.6
		Hartley, J.	Lab	19,610	40.9	+ 1.7
		Sollitt, S.R.	LD	6,693	13.9	– 3.1
		Graham, K-E.R.	UKI	1,202	2.5 ★	
1997: Con				880	1.8	

Bassetlaw [32]

68,417	56.8	Mann, J.	Lab	21,506	55.3	− 5.7
		Holley, A.S.	Con	11,758	30.2	+ 5.3
		Taylor, N.	LD	4,942	12.7	+ 2.5
		Meloy, K.J.	SL	689	1.8 ★	
1997: Lab				9,748	25.1	

Bath [33]

71,372	64.9	Foster, D.M.E.†	LD	23,372	50.5	+ 2.0
		Fox, A.P.	Con	13,478	29.1	− 2.1
		Hawkings, M.A.	Lab	7,269	15.7	− 0.7
		Boulton, M.	Grn	1,469	3.2 ★	+ 2.1
		Tettenborn, A.M.	UKI	708	1.5 ★	+ 0.9
1997: LD				9,894	21.4	

Batley & Spen [34]

63,665	60.5	Wood, M.†	Lab	19,224	49.9	+ 0.5
		Peacock, E.J.	Con	14,160	36.7	+ 0.4
		Pinnock, K.M.	LD	3,989	10.3	+ 1.5
		Lord, C.R.	Grn	595	1.5 ★	+ 0.7
		Burton, A.F.	UKI	574	1.5 ★	
1997: Lab				5,064	13.1	

Battersea [35]

67,495	54.5	Linton, M.†	Lab	18,498	50.3	− 0.5
		Shersby, L.C.A.	Con	13,445	36.5	− 2.9
		Vitelli, S.M.	LD	4,450	12.1	+ 4.7
		Barber, T.E.	Ind	411	1.1 ★	
1997: Lab				5,053	13.7	

Beaconsfield [36]

69,342	60.8	Grieve, D.C.R.†	Con	22,233	52.8	+ 3.5
		Lathrope, S.M.	Lab	9,168	21.8	+ 1.7
		Lloyd, S.A.C.	LD	9,117	21.6	+ 0.3
		Moffatt, A.	UKI	1,626	3.9 ★	+ 3.0
1997: Con				13,065	31.0	

Beckenham [37]

72,772	62.6	Lait, J.A.H.†	Con	20,618	45.3	+ 2.8
		Watts, R.F.	Lab	15,659	34.4	+ 1.0
		Feakes, A.D.	LD	7,308	16.0	- 2.1
		Moran, K.A.	Grn	961	2.1 ★	
		Pratt, C.N.	UKI	782	1.7 ★	+ 0.8
		Winfield, R.	Lib	234	0.5 ★	
1997: Con				4,959	10.9	

Bedford [38]

67,762	59.9	Hall, P.†	Lab	19,454	47.9	- 2.7
		Attenborough, C.N.	Con	13,297	32.8	- 0.9
		Headley, M.P.	LD	6,425	15.8	+ 3.5
		Rawlins, R.D.	Ind	973	2.4 ★	
		Lo Bianco, J.B.	UKI	430	1.1 ★	
1997: Lab				6,157	15.2	

Bedfordshire Mid [39]

70,794	65.9	Sayeed, J.†	Con	22,109	47.4	+ 1.4
		Valentine, J.E.	Lab	14,043	30.1	- 2.4
		Mabbutt, G.A.G.	LD	9,205	19.7	+ 2.9
		Laurence, C.G.	UKI	1,281	2.7 ★	
1997: Con				8,066	17.3	

Bedfordshire North East [40]

69,877	64.8	Burt, A.J.H.	Con	22,586	49.9	+ 5.6
		Ross, P.E.	Lab	14,009	31.0	- 1.6
		Rogerson, D.J.	LD	7,409	16.4	+ 2.1
		Hill, R.	UKI	1,242	2.7 ★	
1997: Con				8,577	19.0	

Bedfordshire South West [41]

70,666	62.1	Selous, A.E.A.	Con	18,477	42.1	+ 1.4
		Date, A.R.	Lab	17,701	40.4	- 0.1
		Pantling, M.J.	LD	6,473	14.8	+ 0.5
		Wise, T.H.	UKI	1,203	2.7 ★	+ 1.9
1997: Con				776	1.8	

Belfast East [42]

58,455	63.0	Robinson, P.D.†	DUP	15,667	42.5	– 0.1
		Lemon, T.	UU	8,550	23.2	– 2.1
		Alderdice, D.	APNI	5,832	15.8	– 8.0
		Ervine, D.W.	Prog U	3,669	10.0	
		O'Donnell, J.G.	SF	1,237	3.4 ★	+ 1.3
		Farren, C.	SDLP	880	2.4 ★	+ 0.8
		Dick, T.	Con	800	2.2 ★	– 0.2
		Bell, J.	WP	123	0.3 ★	
		Weiss, R.G.	Vote	71	0.2 ★	
1997: DUP				7,117	19.3	

Belfast North [43]

60,941	67.2	Dodds, N.A.	DUP	16,718	40.8	
		Kelly, G.	SF	10,331	25.2	+ 5.0
		Maginness, A.	SDLP	8,592	21.0	+ 0.6
		Walker, C.†	UU	4,904	12.0	– 39.8
		Delaney, M.	WP	253	0.6 ★	
		Weiss, R.G.	Vote	134	0.3 ★	
1997: UU				6,387	15.6	

Belfast South [44]

59,436	63.9	Smyth, W.M.†	UU	17,008	44.8	+ 8.8
		McDonnell, A.	SDLP	11,609	30.6	+ 6.3
		McWilliams, M.	NIWC	2,968	7.8	
		Maskey, A.	SF	2,894	7.6	+ 2.5
		Rice, G.A.	APNI	2,042	5.4	– 7.5
		Purvis, D.	Prog U	1,112	2.9 ★	
		Lynn, P.J.	WP	204	0.5 ★	
		Weiss, R.G.	Vote	115	0.3 ★	
1997: UU				5,399	14.2	

Belfast West [45]

59,617	68.7	Adams, G.†	SF	27,096	66.1	+ 10.2
		Attwood, A.	SDLP	7,754	18.9	– 19.8
		Smyth, E.	DUP	2,641	6.4	
		McGimpsey, C.	UU	2,541	6.2	+ 2.8
		Lowry, J.	WP	736	1.8 ★	
		Kerr, D.	TW	116	0.3 ★	
		Weiss, R.G.	Vote	98	0.2 ★	
1997: SF				19,342	47.2	

Berwick-upon-Tweed [46]

56,918	63.8	Beith, A.J.†	LD	18,651	51.4	+ 5.9
		Sanderson, H.G.H.	Con	10,193	28.1	+ 4.0
		Walker, M.	Lab	6,435	17.7	- 8.5
		Pearson, J.S.	UKI	1,029	2.8 ★	+ 2.0
1997: LD				8,458	23.3	

Bethnal Green & Bow [47]

76,556	50.2	King, O.T.†	Lab	19,380	50.5	+ 4.1
		Bakth, S.	Con	9,323	24.3	+ 3.2
		Ludlow, J.	LD	5,946	15.5	+ 3.5
		Bragga, A.L.	Grn	1,666	4.3 ★	+ 2.5
		Davidson, M.	BNP	1,211	3.2 ★	
		Delderfield, D.W.	NB	888	2.3 ★	
1997: Lab				10,057	26.2	

Beverley & Holderness [48]

74,741	62.0	Cran, J.D.†	Con	19,168	41.3	+ 0.2
		Langford, P.	Lab	18,387	39.6	+ 0.8
		Willie, B.S.	LD	7,356	15.9	- 2.6
		Wallis, S.J.	UKI	1,464	3.2 ★	+ 1.8
1997: Con				781	1.7	

Bexhill & Battle [49]

69,010	64.9	Barker, G.L.G.	Con	21,555	48.1	+ 0.0
		Hardy, S.P.	LD	11,052	24.7	- 0.8
		Moore-Williams, A.E.	Lab	8,702	19.4	+ 1.3
		Farage, N.P.	UKI	3,474	7.8	+ 6.2
1997: Con				10,503	23.5	

Bexleyheath & Crayford [50]

63,580	63.5	Beard, C.N.†	Lab	17,593	43.6	- 1.9
		Evennett, D.A.	Con	16,121	39.9	+ 1.5
		O'Hare, N.	LD	4,476	11.1	- 0.1
		Smith, C.	BNP	1,408	3.5 ★	
		Dunford, J.W.	UKI	780	1.9 ★	+ 1.1
1997: Lab				1,472	3.6	

Billericay [51]

78,528	58.1	Baron, J.C.	Con	21,608	47.4	+ 7.6
		Campbell, A.N.	Lab	16,595	36.4	– 0.9
		Bellard, F.	LD	6,323	13.9	– 1.9
		Yeomans, N.J.	UKI	1,072	2.4 ★	
1997: Con				5,013	11.0	

Birkenhead [52]

60,026	48.3	Field, F.†	Lab	20,418	70.5	– 0.3
		Stewart, B.J.	Con	4,827	16.7	+ 1.5
		Wood, R.J.	LD	3,722	12.8	+ 3.8
1997: Lab				15,591	53.8	

Birmingham Edgbaston [53]

67,405	56.0	Stuart, G.G.†	Lab	18,517	49.1	+ 0.5
		Hastilow, N.G.	Con	13,819	36.6	– 2.0
		Davies, N.S.	LD	4,528	12.0	+ 2.3
		Gretton, J.C.	PEC	454	1.2 ★	
		Brackenbury, S.	SL	431	1.1 ★	
1997: Lab				4,698	12.4	

Birmingham Erdington [54]

65,668	46.6	Simon, S.L.	Lab	17,375	56.8	– 2.0
		Lodge, O.A.W.	Con	7,413	24.2	– 3.3
		Johnson, S.	LD	3,602	11.8	+ 1.6
		Shore, M.P.	NF	681	2.2 ★	
		Godward, S.J.	SA	669	2.2 ★	
		Nattrass, M.	UKI	521	1.7 ★	
		Sambrook-Marshall, J.	SL	343	1.1 ★	
1997: Lab				9,962	32.6	

Birmingham Hall Green [55]

57,563	57.5	McCabe, S.J.†	Lab	18,049	54.6	+ 1.1
		White, C.M.F.	Con	11,401	34.5	+ 1.1
		Singh, P.	LD	2,926	8.8	– 0.8
		Johnson, P.F.	UKI	708	2.1 ★	
1997: Lab				6,648	20.1	

Birmingham Hodge Hill [56]

55,254	47.9	Davis, T.†	Lab	16,901	63.9	– 1.7
		Lewis, D.A.	Con	5,283	20.0	– 4.0
		Dow, C.A.	LD	2,147	8.1	– 0.4
		Windridge, L.	BNP	889	3.4 ★	
		Hussain, P.	PJP	561	2.1 ★	
		Cridge, D.	SL	284	1.1 ★	
		Vivian, H.B.	UKI	275	1.0 ★	– 0.9
		Khan, A.	M	125	0.5 ★	
1997: Lab				11,618	43.9	

Birmingham Ladywood [57]

71,113	44.3	Short, C.†	Lab	21,694	68.9	– 5.2
		Prentice, B.H.	Con	3,551	11.3	– 2.0
		Chaudhry, S.M.	LD	2,586	8.2	+ 0.3
		Ditta, A.	PJP	2,112	6.7	
		Virdee, S.P.	SL	443	1.4 ★	
		Hussain, M.	M	432	1.4 ★	
		Caffery, J.	PL	392	1.2 ★	
		Nattrass, A.	UKI	283	0.9 ★	
1997: Lab				18,143	57.6	

Birmingham Northfield [58]

55,922	52.8	Burden, R.H.†	Lab	16,528	56.0	– 1.5
		Purser, N.J.	Con	8,730	29.6	+ 1.6
		Sword, T.P.	LD	3,322	11.2	+ 0.8
		Rogers, S.L.	UKI	550	1.9 ★	
		Walder, C.R.	SA	193	0.7 ★	
		Carpenter, Z.	SL	151	0.5 ★	
		Chaffer, A.M.	Comm	60	0.2 ★	
1997: Lab				7,798	26.4	

Birmingham Perry Barr [59]

71,121	52.6	Mahmood, K.	Lab	17,415	46.5	– 16.5
		Binns, R.D.	Con	8,662	23.1	+ 1.4
		Hunt, J.P.A.	LD	8,566	22.9	+ 13.0
		Jouhl, A.S.	SL	1,544	4.1 ★	
		Johnson, C.N.	SA	465	1.2 ★	
		Nattrass, N.	UKI	352	0.9 ★	
		Roche, M.F.	Marx	221	0.6 ★	
		Davidson, R.L.	M	192	0.5 ★	
1997: Lab				8,753	23.4	

Birmingham Selly Oak [60]

71,237	56.3	Jones, L.M.†	Lab	21,015	52.4	–	3.2
		Hardeman, K.G.	Con	10,676	26.6	–	1.1
		Osborne, D.	LD	6,532	16.3	+	4.2
		Smith, B.	Grn	1,309	3.3 ★		
		Williams, S.B.	UKI	568	1.4 ★		
1997: Lab				10,339	25.8		

Birmingham Sparkbrook & Small Heath [61]

74,358	49.3	Godsiff, R.D.†	Lab	21,087	57.5	–	6.7
		Afzal, Q.H.	LD	4,841	13.2	+	3.9
		Hussain, S.	PJP	4,770	13.0		
		Hussain, I.	Con	3,948	10.8	–	6.7
		Mohammed, G.	Ind	662	1.8 ★		
		Vincent, W.	UKI	634	1.7 ★		
		Aziz, A.	M	401	1.1 ★		
		Mirza, M.S.	SA	304	0.8 ★		
1997: Lab				16,246	44.3		

Birmingham Yardley [62]

52,444	57.2	Morris, E.†	Lab	14,083	46.9	–	0.1
		Hemming, J.A.M.	LD	11,507	38.3	+	5.4
		Roberts, B.M.A.	Con	3,941	13.1	–	4.7
		Ware, A.J.	UKI	329	1.1 ★	+	0.7
		Wren, C.D.	SL	151	0.5 ★		
1997: Lab				2,576	8.6		

Bishop Auckland [63]

67,368	57.2	Foster, D.†	Lab	22,680	58.8	–	7.1
		McNish, F.P.	Con	8,754	22.7	+	2.5
		Foote Wood, C.	LD	6,073	15.7	+	6.4
		Bennett, C.D.	Grn	1,052	2.7 ★		
1997: Lab				13,926	36.1		

Blaby [64]

73,907	64.5	Robathan, A.R.G.†	Con	22,104	46.4	+	0.6
		Morgan, J.D.	Lab	15,895	33.4	–	0.4
		Welsh, G.L.	LD	8,286	17.4	+	2.5
		Scott, E.	BNP	1,357	2.8 ★		
1997: Con				6,209	13.0		

Blackburn [65]

72,611	55.5	Straw, J.W.†	Lab	21,808	54.1	− 0.9
		Cotton, J.A.	Con	12,559	31.2	+ 6.6
		Patel, I.	LD	3,264	8.1	− 2.4
		Baxter, D.	UKI	1,185	2.9 ★	
		Cullen, T.	SL	559	1.4 ★	
		Nichol, F.J.	SA	532	1.3 ★	
		Morris, P.R.	Ind	377	0.9 ★	
1997: Lab				9,249	23.0	

Blackpool North & Fleetwood [66]

74,456	57.2	Humble, J.J.†	Lab	21,610	50.8	− 1.4
		Vincent, A.T.	Con	15,889	37.3	+ 1.8
		Bate, S.	LD	4,132	9.7	+ 1.1
		Porter, J.C.	UKI	950	2.2 ★	
1997: Lab				5,721	13.4	

Blackpool South [67]

74,311	52.2	Marsden, G.†	Lab	21,060	54.3	− 2.7
		Morris, D.T.	Con	12,798	33.0	− 1.4
		Holt, D.	LD	4,115	10.6	+ 2.1
		Cowell, V.L.	UKI	819	2.1 ★	
1997: Lab				8,262	21.3	

Blaenau Gwent [68]

53,353	59.5	Smith, L.T.†	Lab	22,855	72.0	− 7.4
		Rykala, A.J.	PC	3,542	11.2	+ 5.9
		Townsend, C.E.	LD	2,945	9.3	+ 0.6
		Williams, H.B.	Con	2,383	7.5	+ 0.9
1997: Lab				19,313	60.9	

Blaydon [69]

64,574	57.4	McWilliam, J.D.†	Lab	20,340	54.8	− 5.1
		Maughan, P.J.	LD	12,531	33.8	+ 10.0
		Watson, M.A.	Con	4,215	11.4	− 1.8
1997: Lab				7,809	21.1	

Blyth Valley [70]

63,183	54.7	Campbell, R.†	Lab	20,627	59.7	− 4.5
		Reid, J.S.	LD	8,439	24.4	+ 2.0
		Daley, W.	Con	5,484	15.9	+ 2.5
1997: Lab				12,188	35.3	

Bognor Regis & Littlehampton [71]

66,903	58.2	Gibb, N.J.†	Con	17,602	45.2	+ 1.0
		O'Neill, G.K.	Lab	11,959	30.7	+ 2.2
		Peskett, P.G.	LD	6,846	17.6	- 6.4
		Stride, G.Y.	UKI	1,779	4.6 ★	+ 1.3
		Cheyne, L.R.H.	Grn	782	2.0 ★	
1997: Con				5,643	14.5	

Bolsover [72]

67,693	56.5	Skinner, D.E.†	Lab	26,249	68.6	- 5.4
		Massey, S.A.	Con	7,472	19.5	+ 2.8
		Bradley, W.M.	LD	4,550	11.9	+ 2.6
1997: Lab				18,777	49.1	

Bolton North East [73]

69,514	56.0	Crausby, D.A.†	Lab	21,166	54.3	- 1.8
		Winstanley, M.W.	Con	12,744	32.7	+ 2.3
		Perkins, T.J.	LD	4,004	10.3	+ 0.4
		McIver, K.G.	Grn	629	1.6 ★	
		Lowe, L.	SL	407	1.0 ★	
1997: Lab				8,422	21.6	

Bolton South East [74]

68,140	50.1	Iddon, B.†	Lab	21,129	61.9	- 7.0
		Rashid, H.	Con	8,258	24.2	+ 4.5
		Harasiwka, F.	LD	3,941	11.5	+ 2.8
		Kelly, W.J.	SL	826	2.4 ★	
1997: Lab				12,871	37.7	

Bolton West [75]

66,033	62.4	Kelly, R.M.†	Lab	19,381	47.0	- 2.5
		Stevens, W.J.	Con	13,863	33.6	- 1.5
		Ronson, B.O.	LD	7,573	18.4	+ 7.6
		Toomer, D.	SA	397	1.0 ★	
1997: Lab				5,518	13.4	

Bootle [76]

55,455	49.8	Benton, J.E.†	Lab	21,400	77.6	− 5.3
		Murray, J.P.	LD	2,357	8.5	+ 2.8
		Symes, J.R.	Con	2,194	8.0	− 0.5
		Flynn, D.	SL	971	3.5 ★	
		Glover, P.	SA	672	2.4 ★	
1997: Lab				19,043	69.0	

Boston & Skegness [77]

69,165	58.3	Simmonds, M.J.M.	Con	17,298	42.9	+ 0.5
		Bird, E.L.	Lab	16,783	41.6	+ 0.6
		Moffatt, D.P.	LD	4,994	12.4	− 4.2
		Wakefield, C.	UKI	717	1.8 ★	
		Harrison, M.E.R.	Grn	521	1.3 ★	
1997: Con				515	1.3	

Bosworth [78]

69,992	64.4	Tredinnick, D.A.S.†	Con	20,030	44.4	+ 3.8
		Furlong, A.C.	Lab	17,750	39.4	+ 0.7
		Ellis, J.M.H.	LD	7,326	16.2	− 1.6
1997: Con				2,280	5.1	

Bournemouth East [79]

61,520	58.2	Atkinson, D.A.†	Con	15,501	43.3	+ 1.9
		Garratt, A.C.W.	LD	12,067	33.7	+ 2.3
		Nicholson, P.M.	Lab	7,107	19.9	− 1.3
		Chamberlaine, G.F.J.	UKI	1,124	3.1 ★	+ 1.3
1997: Con				3,434	9.6	

Bournemouth West [80]

63,196	53.2	Butterfill, J.V.†	Con	14,417	42.8	+ 1.2
		Stokes, D.L.K.	Lab	9,699	28.8	+ 4.3
		Hornby, F.C.	LD	8,468	25.2	− 2.6
		Blake, C.N.	UKI	1,064	3.2 ★	+ 2.5
1997: Con				4,718	14.0	

Bracknell [81]

81,118	60.7	MacKay, A.J.†	Con	22,962	46.6	−	0.7
		Keene, J.H.	Lab	16,249	33.0	+	3.2
		Earwicker, R.W.	LD	8,428	17.1	+	1.7
		Boxall, L.J.A.	UKI	1,266	2.6 ★	+	1.6
		Roberts, D.M.	PL	324	0.7 ★		
1997: Con				6,713	13.6		

Bradford North [82]

66,443	52.7	Rooney, T.H.†	Lab	17,419	49.7	−	6.3
		Iqbal, Z.	Con	8,450	24.1	−	1.5
		Ward, D.	LD	6,924	19.8	+	5.3
		Brayshaw, J.	BNP	1,613	4.6 ★		
		Schofield, S.	Grn	611	1.7 ★		
1997: Lab				8,969	25.6		

Bradford South [83]

68,441	51.3	Sutcliffe, G.†	Lab	19,603	55.8	−	0.9
		Tennyson, G.S.G.	Con	9,941	28.3	+	0.3
		Wilson Fletcher, A.C.E.	LD	3,717	10.6	−	0.7
		North, P.	UKI	783	2.2 ★		
		Kelly, A.	SL	571	1.6 ★		
		Siddique, A.	SA	302	0.9 ★		
		Riseborough, G.F.	DW	220	0.6 ★		
1997: Lab				9,662	27.5		

Bradford West [84]

71,611	53.6	Singh, M.†	Lab	18,401	48.0	+	6.4
		Riaz, M.	Con	14,236	37.1	+	4.1
		Robinson, J.E.	Grn	2,672	7.0	+	5.1
		Khan, A.R.	LD	2,437	6.4	−	8.4
		Hussain, I.	UKI	427	1.1 ★		
		Khokhar, F.H.	AL	197	0.5 ★		
1997: Lab				4,165	10.9		

Braintree [85]

79,157	63.6	Hurst, A.A.†	Lab	21,123	42.0	−	0.7
		Newmark, B.P.V.	Con	20,765	41.3	+	1.2
		Turner, P.J.R.	LD	5,664	11.3	−	0.3
		Abbott, J.E.	Grn	1,241	2.5 ★	+	1.2
		Nolan, M.A.	LCA	774	1.5 ★		
		Cole, C.J.	UKI	748	1.5 ★		
1997: Lab				358	0.7		

Brecon & Radnorshire [86]

53,247	70.5	Williams, R.H.	LD	13,824	36.8		– 4.0
		Aubel, F.F.E.	Con	13,073	34.8		+ 5.9
		Irranca-Davies, I.H.	Lab	8,024	21.4		– 5.3
		Parri, B.	PC	1,301	3.5 ★		+ 2.0
		Mitchell, I.R.	Ind	762	2.0 ★		
		Phillips, E.F.	UKI	452	1.2 ★		
		Nicholson, R.D.	Ind	80	0.2 ★		
1997: LD				751	2.0		

Brent East [87]

55,891	51.9	Daisley, P.A.	Lab	18,325	63.2		– 4.1
		Gauke, D.M.	Con	5,278	18.2		– 4.1
		Bhatti, N.M.	LD	3,065	10.6		+ 2.8
		Aspis, S.F.	Grn	1,361	4.7 ★		
		Macken, S.	PL	392	1.4 ★		
		Cremer, I.M.J.	SL	383	1.3 ★		
		Tanna, A.	UKI	188	0.6 ★		
1997: Lab				13,047	45.0		

Brent North [88]

58,789	57.7	Gardiner, B.S.†	Lab	20,149	59.4		+ 8.7
		Allott, P.D.	Con	9,944	29.3		– 10.8
		Lorber, P.	LD	3,846	11.3		+ 3.2
1997: Lab				10,205	30.1		

Brent South [89]

55,891	51.2	Boateng, P.Y.†	Lab	20,984	73.3		+ 0.3
		Selvarajah, C.	Con	3,604	12.6		– 3.3
		Hughes, H.	LD	3,098	10.8		+ 3.1
		McDonnell, M.	SA	491	1.7 ★		
		MacStiofain, T.	RM	460	1.6 ★		
1997: Lab				17,380	60.7		

Brentford & Isleworth [90]

82,878	53.7	Keen, A.†	Lab	23,275	52.3		– 5.2
		Mack, T.K.A.	Con	12,957	29.1		– 2.6
		Hartwell, G.G.	LD	5,994	13.5		+ 5.2
		Ferriday, N.P.	Grn	1,324	3.0 ★		+ 1.8
		Ingram, G.A.	UKI	412	0.9 ★		– 0.2
		Faith, D.P.	SA	408	0.9 ★		
		Khaira, A.S.	Ind	144	0.3 ★		
1997: Lab				10,318	23.2		

Brentwood & Ongar [91]

64,693	67.3	Pickles, E.J.†	Con	16,558	38.0	– 7.4
		Bell, M.†	Ind	13,737	31.5	
		Kendall, D.J.	LD	6,772	15.6	– 10.7
		Johnson, D.R.	Lab	5,505	12.6	– 9.5
		Gulleford, K.A.	UKI	611	1.4 ★	+ 0.5
		Pryke, P.L.	Ind	239	0.5 ★	
		Bishop, D.L.	Elvis	68	0.2 ★	
		Appleton, T.		52	0.1 ★	
1997: Con				2,821	6.5	

Bridgend [92]

61,496	60.2	Griffiths, W.J.†	Lab	19,423	52.5	– 5.6
		Brisby, T.A.T.B.	Con	9,377	25.3	+ 2.5
		Barraclough, J.	LD	5,330	14.4	+ 2.9
		Mahoney, M.E.	PC	2,653	7.2	+ 3.4
		Jeremy, S.H.	PL	223	0.6 ★	
1997: Lab				10,046	27.1	

Bridgwater [93]

74,273	64.4	Liddell-Grainger, I.R.	Con	19,354	40.4	+ 3.5
		Thorn, I.L.	LD	14,367	30.0	– 3.6
		Monteith, W.J.	Lab	12,803	26.8	+ 2.0
		Gardner, V.C.	UKI	1,323	2.8 ★	
1997: Con				4,987	10.4	

Brigg & Goole [94]

64,647	63.5	Cawsey, I.A.†	Lab	20,066	48.9	– 1.3
		Stewart, D.M.	Con	16,105	39.2	+ 2.7
		Nolan, D.P.	LD	3,796	9.2	– 0.8
		Bloom, G.W.	UKI	688	1.7 ★	
		Kenny, M.A.	SL	399	1.0 ★	
1997: Lab				3,961	9.6	

Brighton Kemptown [95]

68,119	57.6	Turner, D.S.†	Lab	18,745	47.8	+ 1.3
		Theobald, G.T.	Con	13,823	35.3	– 3.6
		Marshall, J.L.	LD	4,064	10.4	+ 0.7
		Miller, H.	Grn	1,290	3.3 ★	
		Chamberlain-Webber, J.A.A.S.	UKI	543	1.4 ★	
		McLeod, J.	SL	364	0.9 ★	
		Dobbs, D.	FP	227	0.6 ★	
		Cook, E.D.	PL	147	0.4 ★	
1997: Lab				4,922	12.6	

Brighton Pavilion [96]

69,568	58.5	Lepper, D.†	Lab	19,846	48.7	− 5.9
		Gold, D.S.	Con	10,203	25.1	− 2.6
		Berry, R.	LD	5,348	13.1	+ 3.6
		Taylor, K.R.	Grn	3,806	9.3	+ 6.8
		Fyvie, I.C.	SL	573	1.4 ★	
		Dobbs, B.	FP	409	1.0 ★	
		Hutchin, S.J.	UKI	361	0.9 ★	+ 0.5
		Paragallo, M.M.	PL	177	0.4 ★	
1997: Lab				9,643	23.7	

Bristol East [97]

70,279	57.4	Corston, J.A.†	Lab	22,180	55.0	− 1.9
		Lo Presti, J.	Con	8,788	21.8	− 1.6
		Niblett, B.W.	LD	6,915	17.1	+ 2.4
		Collard, G.	Grn	1,110	2.8 ★	
		Marsh, R.C.	UKI	572	1.4 ★	
		Langley, M.P.	SL	438	1.1 ★	
		Pryor, A.M.	SA	331	0.8 ★	
1997: Lab				13,392	33.2	

Bristol North West [98]

76,903	60.4	Naysmith, J.D.†	Lab	24,236	52.1	+ 2.2
		Hansard, C.C.T.	Con	13,349	28.7	− 0.6
		Tyzack, P.L.	LD	7,387	15.9	+ 2.7
		Carr, D.M.	UKI	1,140	2.5 ★	
		Horrigan, V.M.	SL	371	0.8 ★	
1997: Lab				10,887	23.4	

Bristol South [99]

72,490	56.5	Primarolo, D.†	Lab	23,299	56.9	− 3.1
		Eddy, R.S.	Con	9,118	22.3	+ 1.1
		Main, J.R.	LD	6,078	14.8	+ 1.4
		Vowles, G.R.	Grn	1,233	3.0 ★	+ 1.6
		Drummond, B.M.A.	SA	496	1.2 ★	
		Prasad, C.	UKI	496	1.2 ★	
		Shorter, G.B.	SL	250	0.6 ★	
1997: Lab				14,181	34.6	

Bristol West [100]

84,821	65.6	Davey,V.†	Lab	20,505	36.8		+	1.6
		Williams, S.R.	LD	16,079	28.9		+	0.9
		Chesters, P.J.	Con	16,040	28.8		–	4.0
		Devaney, J.F.L.	Grn	1,961	3.5	★	+	2.2
		Kennedy, B.J.	SL	590	1.1	★		
		Muir, S.D.	UKI	490	0.9	★		
1997: Lab				4,426	8.0			

Bromley & Chislehurst [101]

67,183	64.3	Forth, E.†	Con	21,412	49.5		+	3.2
		Polydorou, S.A.	Lab	12,375	28.6		+	3.4
		Payne, G.D.S.	LD	8,180	18.9		–	4.8
		Bryant, R.M.	UKI	1,264	2.9	★	+	0.7
1997: Con				9,037	20.9			

Bromsgrove [102]

68,081	67.1	Kirkbride, J.†	Con	23,640	51.7		+	4.6
		McDonald, P.M.	Lab	15,502	33.9		–	3.9
		Rowley, A.M.	LD	5,430	11.9		+	0.0
		Gregory, I.N.	UKI	1,112	2.4	★	+	2.0
1997: Con				8,138	17.8			

Broxbourne [103]

67,987	55.7	Roe, M.A.†	Con	20,487	54.1		+	5.3
		Prendergast, D.	Lab	11,494	30.4		–	4.3
		Davies, J.M.	LD	4,158	11.0		–	0.3
		Harvey, M.	UKI	858	2.3	★		
		Cope, J.A.†	BNP	848	2.2	★		
1997: Con				8,993	23.8			

Broxtowe [104]

73,665	66.5	Palmer, N.D.†	Lab	23,836	48.6	+	1.6
		Latham, P.E.	Con	17,963	36.7	–	0.8
		Watts, D.K.	LD	7,205	14.7	+	2.8
1997: Lab				5,873	12.0		

Buckingham [105]

65,270	69.4	Bercow, J.S.†	Con	24,296	53.7	+ 3.9
		Seddon, M.A.P.	Lab	10,971	24.2	− 0.5
		Wilson, I.R.	LD	9,037	20.0	− 4.7
		Silcock, C.R.	UKI	968	2.1 ★	
1997: Con				13,325	29.4	

Burnley [106]

66,271	55.7	Pike, P.L.†	Lab	18,195	49.3	− 8.6
		Frost, R.J.J.	Con	7,697	20.9	+ 0.6
		Wright, P.R.	LD	5,975	16.2	− 1.2
		Smith, S.	BNP	4,151	11.3	
		Buttrey, R.G.	UKI	866	2.3 ★	
1997: Lab				10,498	28.5	

Burton [107]

75,259	61.7	Dean, J.E.A.†	Lab	22,783	49.0	− 2.0
		Punyer, M.A.	Con	17,934	38.6	− 0.8
		Fletcher, D.A.	LD	4,468	9.6	+ 1.1
		Crompton, I.E.	UKI	984	2.1 ★	
		Roberts, J.D.W.	PL	288	0.6 ★	
1997: Lab				4,849	10.4	

Bury North [108]

71,108	63.0	Chaytor, D.M.†	Lab	22,945	51.2	− 0.6
		Walsh, J.	Con	16,413	36.6	− 0.9
		Hackley, B.	LD	5,430	12.1	+ 3.9
1997: Lab				6,532	14.6	

Bury South [109]

67,276	58.8	Lewis, I.†	Lab	23,406	59.2	+ 2.3
		Le Page, N.L.	Con	10,634	26.9	− 5.4
		Pickstone, T.D.	LD	5,499	13.9	+ 5.5
1997: Lab				12,772	32.3	

Bury St Edmunds [110]

76,146	66.0	Ruffley, D.L.†	Con	21,850	43.5	+ 5.1
		Ereira, M.A.	Lab	19,347	38.5	+ 0.8
		Williams, A.R.	LD	6,998	13.9	− 4.3
		Howlett, J.E.	UKI	831	1.7 ★	
		Brundle, M.F.	Ind	651	1.3 ★	
		Benwell, M.C.	SL	580	1.2 ★	
1997: Con				2,503	5.0	

Caernarfon [111]

46,850	62.0	Williams, H.	PC	12,894	44.4	− 6.7
		Eaglestone, M.R.	Lab	9,383	32.3	+ 2.8
		Naish, B.	Con	4,403	15.2	+ 2.9
		Ab-Owain, E.M.	LD	1,823	6.3	+ 1.4
		Lloyd, I.D.	UKI	550	1.9 ★	
1997: PC				3,511	12.1	

Caerphilly [112]

67,300	57.7	David, W	Lab	22,597	58.2	− 9.6
		Whittle, L.G.	PC	8,172	21.0	+ 11.4
		Simmonds, D.T.	Con	4,415	11.4	+ 0.6
		Roffe, R.W.	LD	3,649	9.4	+ 1.2
1997: Lab				14,425	37.1	

Caithness, Sutherland & Easter Ross [113]

41,315	60.2	Thurso, J.A.	LD	9,041	36.4	+ 0.8
		Meighan, M.	Lab	6,297	25.3	− 2.5
		Macadam, J.H.R.	SNP	5,273	21.2	− 1.8
		Rowantree, R.I.	Con	3,513	14.1	+ 3.3
		Mabon, K.C.J.	SSP	544	2.2 ★	
		Campbell, J.G.P.	Ind	199	0.8 ★	
1997: LD				2,744	11.0	

Calder Valley [114]

75,298	63.0	McCafferty, C.†	Lab	20,244	42.7	− 3.4
		Robson-Catling, S.K.	Con	17,150	36.2	+ 1.1
		Taylor, M.F.	LD	7,596	16.0	+ 1.3
		Hutton, S.R.	Grn	1,034	2.2 ★	+ 1.3
		Nunn, J.D.	UKI	729	1.5 ★	
		Lockwood, P.D.	LCA	672	1.4 ★	
1997: Lab				3,094	6.5	

Camberwell & Peckham [115]

53,687	46.8	Harman, H.†	Lab	17,473	69.6	+ 0.1
		McCarthy, D.	LD	3,350	13.3	+ 2.1
		Morgan, J.	Con	2,740	10.9	− 0.7
		Poorun, S.	Grn	805	3.2 ★	
		Mulrenan, J.A.	SA	478	1.9 ★	
		Adams, R.W.	SL	188	0.7 ★	
		Sweeney, F.	WRP	70	0.3 ★	
1997: Lab				14,123	56.3	

Cambridge [116]

70,665	60.6	Campbell, A.†	Lab	19,316	45.1	– 8.3
		Howarth, D.R.	LD	10,737	25.1	+ 8.9
		Stuart, G.C.	Con	9,829	22.9	– 3.0
		Lawrence, S.R.	Grn	1,413	3.3 ★	+ 2.0
		Senter, H.A.	SA	716	1.7 ★	
		Baynes, A.L.	UKI	532	1.2 ★	
		Underwood, C.J.T.	PL	232	0.5 ★	
		Courtney, M.M.	WRP	61	0.1 ★	
1997: Lab				8,579	20.0	

Cambridgeshire North East [117]

79,891	60.1	Moss, M.D.†	Con	23,132	48.1	+ 5.1
		Owen, D.	Lab	16,759	34.9	+ 1.0
		Renaut, R.I.	LD	6,733	14.0	– 2.4
		Stevens, J.	UKI	1,189	2.5 ★	
		Hoey, T.A.	PL	238	0.5 ★	
1997: Con				6,373	13.3	

Cambridgeshire North West [118]

71,247	61.7	Mawhinney, B.S.†	Con	21,895	49.8	+ 1.7
		Cox, A.J.	Lab	13,794	31.4	– 0.8
		Taylor, A.S.	LD	6,957	15.8	+ 0.7
		Hudson, B.J.	UKI	881	2.0 ★	+ 1.5
		Hall, D.	Ind	429	1.0 ★	
1997: Con				8,101	18.4	

Cambridgeshire South [119]

72,095	67.1	Lansley, A.D.†	Con	21,387	44.2	+ 2.2
		Taylor, A.J.	LD	12,984	26.9	+ 1.0
		Herbert, J.	Lab	11,737	24.3	– 0.8
		Saggers, S.P.	Grn	1,182	2.4 ★	
		Davies, H.Y.	UKI	875	1.8 ★	+ 1.3
		Klepacka, B.A.	PL	176	0.4 ★	
1997: Con				8,403	17.4	

Cambridgeshire South East [120]

81,663	63.5	Paice, J.E.T.†	Con	22,927	44.2	+ 1.2
		Brinton, S.V.	LD	13,937	26.9	+ 1.8
		Inchley, A.P.	Lab	13,714	26.4	– 0.1
		Scarr, N.J.	UKI	1,308	2.5 ★	
1997: Con				8,990	17.3	

Cannock Chase [121]

74,172	55.4	Wright, A.W.†	Lab	23,049	56.1	+ 1.3
		Smithers, G.R.N.	Con	12,345	30.1	+ 2.9
		Reynolds, S.	LD	5,670	13.8	+ 5.1
1997: Lab				10,704	26.1	

Canterbury [122]

74,144	60.9	Brazier, J.W.H.†	Con	18,711	41.5	+ 2.8
		Thornberry, E.A.	Lab	16,642	36.9	+ 5.6
		Wales, P.R.	LD	8,056	17.8	- 5.9
		Dawe, H.F.	Grn	920	2.0 ★	+ 1.0
		Moore, L.D.	UKI	803	1.8 ★	+ 1.3
1997: Con				2,069	4.6	

Cardiff Central [123]

59,785	58.3	Owen Jones, J.O.†	Lab	13,451	38.6	- 5.1
		Willott, J.N.	LD	12,792	36.7	+ 11.8
		Walker, G.H.	Con	5,537	15.9	- 4.2
		Grigg, R.R.	PC	1,680	4.8 ★	+ 1.3
		Bartley, S.J.	Grn	661	1.9 ★	
		Goss, J.B.	SA	283	0.8 ★	
		Hughes, F.R.	UKI	221	0.6 ★	
		Jeremy, M.E.	PL	217	0.6 ★	
1997: Lab				659	1.9	

Cardiff North [124]

62,634	69.0	Morgan, J.†	Lab	19,845	45.9	- 4.6
		Watson, A.	Con	13,680	31.6	- 2.0
		Dixon, J.L.	LD	6,631	15.3	+ 4.4
		Jobbins, S.T.	PC	2,471	5.7	+ 3.2
		Hulston, D.E.	UKI	613	1.4 ★	
1997: Lab				6,165	14.3	

Cardiff South & Penarth [125]

62,627	57.1	Michael, A.E.†	Lab	20,094	56.2	+ 2.8
		Owen, M.K.	Con	7,807	21.8	+ 1.1
		Berman, R.S.	LD	4,572	12.8	+ 3.4
		Haines, L.E.M.	PC	1,983	5.5	+ 2.4
		Callan, J.P.	UKI	501	1.4 ★	
		Bartlett, D.C.	SA	427	1.2 ★	
		Savoury, A.	PL	367	1.0 ★	
1997: Lab				12,287	34.4	

Cardiff West [126]

58,348	58.4	Brennan, K.D.	Lab	18,594	54.6	– 5.8
		Davies, A.R.T.	Con	7,273	21.3	– 0.2
		Gasson, J.A.	LD	4,458	13.1	+ 2.2
		Bowen, D.I.	PC	3,296	9.7	+ 4.8
		Jenking, J.L.	UKI	462	1.4 ★	
1997: Lab				11,321	33.2	

Carlisle [127]

58,811	59.4	Martlew, E.A.†	Lab	17,856	51.2	– 6.3
		Mitchelson, M.R.	Con	12,154	34.8	+ 5.8
		Guest, J.M.	LD	4,076	11.7	+ 1.2
		Paisley, C.	LCA	554	1.6 ★	
		Wilcox, P.G.	SA	269	0.8 ★	
1997: Lab				5,702	16.3	

Carmarthen East & Dinefwr [128]

54,035	70.4	Price, A.	PC	16,130	42.4	+ 7.7
		Williams, A.W.†	Lab	13,540	35.6	– 7.3
		Thomas, D.N.	Con	4,912	12.9	+ 0.9
		Evans, D.D.	LD	2,815	7.4	– 0.2
		Squires, M.	UKI	656	1.7 ★	
1997: Lab				2,590	6.8	

Carmarthen West & Pembrokeshire South [129]

56,518	65.3	Ainger, N.R.†	Lab	15,349	41.6	– 7.6
		Wilson, R.	Con	10,811	29.3	+ 2.7
		Griffiths, L.H.	PC	6,893	18.7	+ 6.0
		Jeremy, W.B.R.	LD	3,248	8.8	+ 0.6
		Phillips, I.R.	UKI	537	1.5 ★	
		Turner, N.R.	Cust	78	0.2 ★	
1997: Lab				4,538	12.3	

Carrick, Cumnock & Doon Valley [130]

64,919	61.8	Foulkes, G.†	Lab	22,174	55.3	– 4.5
		Millar, G.F.	Con	7,318	18.2	+ 1.3
		Wilson, T.	SNP	6,258	15.6	– 1.1
		Rodger, R.A.	LD	2,932	7.3	+ 2.0
		McFarlane, A.J.	SSP	1,058	2.6 ★	
		McDaid, J.	SL	367	0.9 ★	
1997: Lab				14,856	37.0	

Carshalton & Wallington [131]

67,337	60.3	Brake, T.A.†	LD	18,289	45.0	+ 6.8
		Andrew, K.	Con	13,742	33.8	+ 0.3
		Cooper, M.K.	Lab	7,466	18.4	- 5.5
		Dixon, S.N.	Grn	614	1.5 ★	+ 0.7
		Haley, M.A.	UKI	501	1.2 ★	+ 0.8
1997: LD				4,547	11.2	

Castle Point [132]

68,108	58.4	Spink, R.M.	Con	17,738	44.6	+ 4.5
		Butler, C.M.†	Lab	16,753	42.1	- 0.3
		Boulton, P.A.	LD	3,116	7.8	- 1.4
		Hurrell, R.	UKI	1,273	3.2 ★	
		Roberts, D.C.	Ind	663	1.7 ★	
		Searle, N.	Tr	223	0.6 ★	
1997: Lab				985	2.5	

Ceredigion [133]

56,125	61.7	Thomas, S.†	PC	13,241	38.3	- 3.4
		Williams, M.F.	LD	9,297	26.9	+ 10.4
		Davies, P.W.	Con	6,730	19.4	+ 4.6
		Grace, D.	Lab	5,338	15.4	- 8.9
1997: PC				3,944	11.4	

Charnwood [134]

74,900	64.4	Dorrell, S.J.†	Con	23,283	48.2	+ 1.8
		Sheahan, S.D.	Lab	15,544	32.2	- 3.8
		King, S.M.	LD	7,835	16.2	+ 3.4
		Bye, J.G.	UKI	1,603	3.3 ★	
1997: Con				7,739	16.0	

Chatham & Aylesford [135]

69,759	57.0	Shaw, J.R.†	Lab	19,180	48.3	+ 5.2
		Holden, S.F.	Con	14,840	37.3	- 0.1
		Lettington, D.	LD	4,705	11.8	- 3.2
		Knopp, G.J.	UKI	1,010	2.5 ★	+ 1.5
1997: Lab				4,340	10.9	

Cheadle [136]

69,001	63.2	Calton, P.	LD	18,477	42.4	+	4.7
		Day, S.R.†	Con	18,444	42.3	–	1.4
		Dawber, H.	Lab	6,086	14.0	–	1.8
		Cavanagh, V.L.	UKI	599	1.4 ★		
1997: Con				33	0.1		

Chelmsford West [137]

78,073	61.7	Burns, S.H.M.†	Con	20,446	42.5	+	1.9
		Longden, A.	Lab	14,185	29.5	+	3.1
		Robinson, S.J.	LD	11,197	23.3	–	5.9
		Burgess, E.J.	Grn	837	1.7 ★	+	1.0
		Wedon, K.A.E.	UKI	785	1.6 ★	+	1.1
		Philbin, C.S.	LCA	693	1.4 ★		
1997: Con				6,261	13.0		

Cheltenham [138]

67,563	61.9	Jones, N.D.†	LD	19,970	47.7	–	1.7
		Garnham, R.E.	Con	14,715	35.2	–	1.1
		Erlam, A.B.	Lab	5,041	12.0	+	1.9
		Bessant, K.D.	Grn	735	1.8 ★		
		Hanks, D.K.	MRLP	513	1.2 ★		
		Carver, J.B.	UKI	482	1.2 ★	+	0.6
		Gates, A.J.	PL	272	0.7 ★		
		Everest, R.J.	Ind	107	0.3 ★		
1997: LD				5,255	12.6		

Chesham & Amersham [139]

70,021	64.7	Gillan, C.E.K.†	Con	22,867	50.5	+	0.1
		Ford, J.E.	LD	10,985	24.3	+	0.4
		Hulme, K.	Lab	8,497	18.8	–	0.9
		Harvey, I.G.H.	UKI	1,367	3.0 ★	+	1.8
		Wilkins, N.J.E.	Grn	1,114	2.5 ★		
		Duval, G.S.	PL	453	1.0 ★		
1997: Con				11,882	26.2		

City of Chester [140]

70,382	63.8	Russell, C.M.†	Lab	21,760	48.5	–	4.5
		Jones, D.I.	Con	14,866	33.1	–	1.1
		Dawson, D.A.	LD	6,589	14.7	+	5.2
		Weddell, A.A.J.	UKI	899	2.0 ★		
		Rogers, G.	Ind	763	1.7 ★		
1997: Lab				6,894	15.4		

Chesterfield [141]

73,216	60.7	Holmes, P.R.	LD	21,249	47.8	+ 8.3
		Race, D.A.R.	Lab	18,663	42.0	– 8.8
		Hitchcock, S.J.	Con	3,613	8.1	– 1.1
		Robinson, P.J.	SA	437	1.0 ★	
		Harrison, W.	SL	295	0.7 ★	
		Rawson, C.	Ind	184	0.4 ★	
1997: Lab				2,586	5.8	

Chichester [142]

77,703	63.8	Tyrie, A.G.†	Con	23,320	47.0	+ 0.6
		Ravenscroft, P.L.	LD	11,965	24.1	– 4.8
		Barlow, C.A.	Lab	10,627	21.4	+ 4.2
		Denny, D.E.	UKI	2,380	4.8 ★	+ 3.4
		Graham, G.J.E.	Grn	1,292	2.6 ★	
1997: Con				11,355	22.9	

Chingford & Woodford Green [143]

63,252	58.5	Duncan Smith, G.I.†	Con	17,834	48.2	+ 0.7
		Webb, J.L.	Lab	12,347	33.4	– 1.2
		Beanse, J.D.	LD	5,739	15.5	+ 0.0
		Griffin, J.	BNP	1,062	2.9 ★	
1997: Con				5,487	14.8	

Chipping Barnet [144]

70,239	60.4	Chapman, S.B.†	Con	19,702	46.4	+ 3.4
		Welfare, D.F.J.	Lab	17,001	40.0	– 0.9
		Hooker, S.J.	LD	5,753	13.6	+ 1.2
1997: Con				2,701	6.4	

Chorley [145]

77,036	62.2	Hoyle, L.H.†	Lab	25,088	52.3	– 0.7
		Booth, P.C.	Con	16,644	34.7	– 1.2
		Fenn, S.J.	LD	5,372	11.2	+ 2.7
		Frost, J.G.	UKI	848	1.8 ★	
1997: Lab				8,444	17.6	

Christchurch [146]

73,447	67.5	Chope, C.R.†	Con	27,306	55.1	+ 8.7
		Webb, D.J.	LD	13,762	27.8	– 14.8
		Begg, J.	Lab	7,506	15.1	+ 8.2
		Strange, M.	UKI	993	2.0 ★	+ 0.9
1997: Con				13,544	27.3	

Cities of London & Westminster [147]

71,935	47.2	Field, M.C.	Con	15,737	46.3	– 0.9
		Katz, M.D.	Lab	11,238	33.1	– 2.0
		Horwood, M.C.	LD	5,218	15.4	+ 3.1
		Charlton, H.	Grn	1,318	3.9 ★	
		Merton, C.R.	UKI	464	1.4 ★	+ 0.8
1997: Con				4,499	13.2	

Cleethorpes [148]

68,392	62.0	McIsaac, S.†	Lab	21,032	49.6	– 2.0
		Howd, S.E.J.	Con	15,412	36.3	+ 2.9
		Smith, G.	LD	5,080	12.0	+ 0.6
		Hatton, J.E.	UKI	894	2.1 ★	
1997: Lab				5,620	13.2	

Clwyd South [149]

53,680	62.4	Jones, M.D.†	Lab	17,217	51.4	– 6.7
		Biggins, T.H.	Con	8,319	24.8	+ 1.8
		Edwards, D.W.	PC	3,982	11.9	+ 5.5
		Griffiths, D.B.	LD	3,426	10.2	+ 0.9
		Theunissen, E.E.	UKI	552	1.6 ★	
1997: Lab				8,898	26.6	

Clwyd West [150]

53,962	64.1	Thomas, G.†	Lab	13,426	38.8	+ 1.7
		James, T.D.R.	Con	12,311	35.6	+ 3.1
		Williams, H.E.	PC	4,453	12.9	– 0.6
		Feeley, R.L.	LD	3,934	11.4	– 1.4
		Guest, G.M.	UKI	476	1.4 ★	
1997: Lab				1,115	3.2	

Clydebank & Milngavie [151]

51,979	62.5	Worthington, W.A.†	Lab	17,249	53.1	– 2.1
		Yuill, J.L.	SNP	6,525	20.1	– 1.1
		Ackland, R.	LD	3,909	12.0	+ 1.6
		Jardine, C.	Con	3,514	10.8	– 1.7
		Brennan, D.	SSP	1,294	4.0 ★	
1997: Lab				10,724	33.0	

Clydesdale [152]

64,423	59.3	Hood, J.†	Lab	17,822	46.6	–	5.9
		Wright, J.	SNP	10,028	26.2	+	4.1
		Newton, K.	Con	5,034	13.2	–	3.1
		Craig, M.	LD	4,111	10.8	+	2.4
		Cockshott, W.P.	SSP	974	2.5 ★		
		MacKay, D.M.	UKI	253	0.7 ★		
1997: Lab				7,794	20.4		

Coatbridge & Chryston [153]

52,178	58.1	Clarke, T.†	Lab	19,807	65.3	–	3.0
		Kearney, P.	SNP	4,493	14.8	–	2.2
		Tough, A.G.	LD	2,293	7.6	+	2.1
		Ross-Taylor, W.P.	Con	2,171	7.2	–	1.4
		Sheridan, L.	SSP	1,547	5.1		
1997: Lab				15,314	50.5		

Colchester [154]

77,958	56.1	Russell, R.E.†	LD	18,627	42.6	+	8.2
		Bentley, K.P.	Con	13,074	29.9	–	1.5
		Fegan, C.	Lab	10,925	25.0	–	5.6
		Lord, R.G.	UKI	631	1.4 ★		
		Overy-Owen, L.T.	Grey	479	1.1 ★		
1997: LD				5,553	12.7		

Colne Valley [155]

74,192	63.3	Mountford, K.C.J.†	Lab	18,967	40.4	–	0.9
		Davies, P.A.	Con	14,328	30.5	–	2.2
		Beever, G.J.	LD	11,694	24.9	+	2.3
		Plunkett, R.	Grn	1,081	2.3 ★	+	1.4
		Quarmby, A.	UKI	917	2.0 ★	+	1.1
1997: Lab				4,639	9.9		

Congleton [156]

71,941	62.7	Winterton, J.A.†	Con	20,872	46.3	+	5.1
		Flanagan, J.A.	Lab	13,738	30.5	+	2.9
		Lloyd-Griffiths, D.	LD	9,719	21.6	–	8.2
		Young, W.J.	UKI	754	1.7 ★	+	0.2
1997: Con				7,134	15.8		

Conwy [157]

54,637	62.9	Williams, B.H.†	Lab	14,366	41.8	+	6.8
		Logan, D.A.J.	Con	8,147	23.7	-	0.6
		Macdonald, V.M.	LD	5,800	16.9	-	14.3
		Owen, A.	PC	5,665	16.5	+	9.6
		Barham, A.C.	UKI	388	1.1 ★		
1997: Lab				6,219	18.1		

Copeland [158]

53,526	64.9	Cunningham, J.A.†	Lab	17,991	51.8	-	6.4
		Graham, M.	Con	13,027	37.5	+	8.3
		Gayler, M.A.	LD	3,732	10.7	+	1.5
1997: Lab				4,964	14.3		

Corby [159]

72,594	65.0	Hope, P.I.†	Lab	23,283	49.3	-	6.1
		Griffith, A.J.	Con	17,583	37.2	+	3.8
		Scudder, K.L.	LD	4,751	10.1	+	2.6
		Gillman, I.F.	UKI	855	1.8 ★	+	0.9
		Dickson, A.	SL	750	1.6 ★		
1997: Lab				5,700	12.1		

Cornwall North [160]

84,662	63.8	Tyler, P.†	LD	28,082	52.0	-	1.1
		Weller, J.	Con	18,250	33.8	+	4.3
		Goodman, M.N.	Lab	5,257	9.7	+	0.3
		Protz, G.S.	UKI	2,394	4.4 ★		
1997: LD				9,832	18.2		

Cornwall South East [161]

79,090	65.4	Breed, C.E.†	LD	23,756	45.9	-	1.2
		Gray, A.	Con	18,381	35.5	-	0.3
		Stevens, W.J.	Lab	6,429	12.4	-	0.4
		Palmer, G.G.	UKI	1,978	3.8 ★	+	1.3
		George, K.J.	MK	1,209	2.3 ★		
1997: LD				5,375	10.4		

Cotswold [162]

68,140	67.5	Clifton-Brown, G.†	Con	23,133	50.3	+	4.0
		Lawrence, A.	LD	11,150	24.2	+	1.3
		Wilkins, R.L.	Lab	10,383	22.6	-	0.1
		Stopps, J.	UKI	1,315	2.9 ★		
1997: Con				11,983	26.1		

Coventry North East [163]

74,017	50.3	Ainsworth, R.W.†	Lab	22,739	61.0	– 5.2
		Bell, G.A.	Con	6,988	18.8	– 0.6
		Sewards, G.B.	LD	4,163	11.2	+ 3.1
		Nellist, D.J.	SA	2,638	7.1	
		Sheppard, E.J.	BNP	737	2.0 ★	
1997: Lab				15,751	42.3	

Coventry North West [164]

76,673	55.5	Robinson, G.†	Lab	21,892	51.4	– 5.4
		Fairburn, A.	Con	11,018	25.9	– 0.4
		Penlington, G.N.	LD	5,832	13.7	+ 3.2
		Oddy, C.M.	Ind	3,159	7.4	
		Benson, M.E.	UKI	650	1.5 ★	
1997: Lab				10,874	25.6	

Coventry South [165]

72,570	55.3	Cunningham, J.D.†	Lab	20,125	50.2	– 0.7
		Wheeler, H.	Con	11,846	29.5	+ 0.5
		McKee, V.J.	LD	5,672	14.1	+ 4.9
		Windsor, R.P.	SA	1,475	3.7 ★	
		Rogers, I.E.	Ind	564	1.4 ★	
		Logan, T.P.	SL	414	1.0 ★	
1997: Lab				8,279	20.6	

Crawley [166]

71,629	55.2	Moffatt, L.J.†	Lab	19,488	49.3	– 5.7
		Smith, H.E.M.	Con	12,718	32.2	+ 0.4
		Seekings, L.A.	LD	5,009	12.7	+ 4.5
		Galloway, B.R.	UKI	1,137	2.9 ★	+ 2.2
		Staniford, C.J.	MRLP	383	1.0 ★	
		Khan, A.	JP	271	0.7 ★	
		Stewart, K.J.	SL	260	0.7 ★	
		Hirsch, M.J.	SA	251	0.6 ★	
1997: Lab				6,770	17.1	

Crewe & Nantwich [167]

69,040	60.2	Dunwoody, G.P.†	Lab	22,556	54.3	– 3.9
		Potter, D.R.	Con	12,650	30.4	+ 3.5
		Cannon, D.J.	LD	5,595	13.5	+ 1.7
		Croston, R.P.	UKI	746	1.8 ★	
1997: Lab				9,906	23.8	

Crosby [168]

56,610	65.1	Curtis–Thomas, C.†	Lab	20,327	55.1	+	4.1
		Collinson, R.J.	Con	11,974	32.5	–	2.3
		Drake, T.J.	LD	4,084	11.1	–	0.4
		Holt, A.M.	SL	481	1.3 ★		
1997: Lab				8,353	22.7		

Croydon Central [169]

77,568	59.1	Davies, G.R.†	Lab	21,643	47.2	+	1.6
		Congdon, D.L.	Con	17,659	38.5	–	0.1
		Booth, P.J.H.	LD	5,156	11.2	+	0.4
		Feisenberger, J.R.	UKI	545	1.2 ★	+	0.7
		Miller, L.	BNP	449	1.0 ★		
		Cartwright, J.S.	MRLP	408	0.9 ★		
1997: Lab				3,984	8.7		

Croydon North [170]

78,675	53.2	Wicks, M.H.†	Lab	26,610	63.5	+	1.4
		Allison, S.J.	Con	9,752	23.3	–	3.9
		Lawman, S.J.	LD	4,375	10.4	+	2.7
		Smith, A.G.	UKI	606	1.4 ★	+	0.7
		Madgwick, D.A.E.	SA	539	1.3 ★		
1997: Lab				16,858	40.3		

Croydon South [171]

73,372	61.4	Ottaway, R.G.J.†	Con	22,169	49.2	+	1.9
		Ryan, M.G.	Lab	13,472	29.9	+	4.6
		Gallop, A-N.	LD	8,226	18.3	–	2.9
		Garner, K.	UKI	998	2.2 ★	+	1.6
		Samuel, M.R.L.	Ch	195	0.4 ★		
1997: Con				8,697	19.3		

Cumbernauld & Kilsyth [172]

49,739	59.7	McKenna, R.†	Lab	16,144	54.4	–	4.3
		McGlashan, D.	SNP	8,624	29.0	+	1.2
		O'Donnell, J.	LD	1,934	6.5	+	2.7
		Ross, A.	Con	1,460	4.9 ★	–	1.9
		McEwan, K.	SSP	1,287	4.3 ★	+	3.3
		Taylor, T.L.	Sc Ref	250	0.8 ★		
1997: Lab				7,520	25.3		

Cunninghame North [173]

54,993	61.5	Wilson, B.†	Lab	15,571	46.0	–	4.2
		Martin, C.	SNP	7,173	21.2	+	2.8
		Wilkinson, R.	Con	6,666	19.7	–	3.7
		Chmiel, R.M.	LD	3,060	9.0	+	3.5
		Scott, S.	SSP	964	2.9 ★		
		McDaid, L.	SL	382	1.1 ★		
1997: Lab				8,398	24.8		

Cunninghame South [174]

49,982	56.2	Donohoe, B.H.†	Lab	16,424	58.4	–	4.3
		Kidd, B.	SNP	5,194	18.5	–	2.3
		Paterson, P.M.	Con	2,782	9.9	–	0.2
		Boyd, J.R.	LD	2,094	7.4	+	2.9
		Byrne, R.	SSP	1,233	4.4 ★		
		Cochrane, R.	SL	382	1.4 ★		
1997: Lab				11,230	40.0		

Cynon Valley [175]

48,639	55.4	Clwyd, A.†	Lab	17,685	65.6	–	4.1
		Cornelius, S.	PC	4,687	17.4	+	6.8
		Parry, I.H.	LD	2,541	9.4	–	0.9
		Waters, J.W.P.	Con	2,045	7.6	+	0.8
1997: Lab				12,998	48.2		

Dagenham [176]

59,340	46.5	Cruddas, J.	Lab	15,784	57.2	–	8.5
		White, M.J.	Con	7,091	25.7	+	7.2
		Gee-Turner, A.J.	LD	2,820	10.2	+	2.7
		Hill, D.	BNP	1,378	5.0 ★		
		Hamilton, B.	SA	262	0.9 ★		
		Siggins, R.J.	SL	245	0.9 ★		
1997: Lab				8,693	31.5		

Darlington [177]

64,354	62.0	Milburn, A.†	Lab	22,479	56.3	–	5.2
		Richmond, E.A.	Con	12,095	30.3	+	2.0
		Adamson, R.M.	LD	4,358	10.9	+	3.7
		Docherty, A.S.	SA	469	1.2 ★		
		Platt, C.C.	Ind	269	0.7 ★		
		Rose, A.M.	SL	229	0.6 ★		
1997: Lab				10,384	26.0		

Dartford [178]

72,241	61.9	Stoate, H.G.A.†	Lab	21,466	48.0	–	0.6
		Dunn, R.J.	Con	18,160	40.6	+	0.3
		Morgan, G.D.	LD	3,781	8.5	–	0.9
		Croucher, M.C.	UKI	989	2.2 ★		
		Davenport, K.J.	FDP	344	0.8 ★		
1997: Lab				3,306	7.4		

Daventry [179]

86,510	65.5	Boswell, T.E.†	Con	27,911	49.2	+	2.9
		Quigley, K.M.	Lab	18,262	32.2	–	2.2
		Calder, J.M.	LD	9,130	16.1	+	1.2
		Baden, P.M.	UKI	1,381	2.4 ★	+	1.7
1997: Con				9,649	17.0		

Delyn [180]

54,732	63.3	Hanson, D.G.†	Lab	17,825	51.5	–	5.7
		Brierley, P.	Con	9,220	26.6	+	0.6
		Jones, J.T.	LD	5,329	15.4	+	5.2
		Rowlinson, P.J.	PC	2,262	6.5	+	2.7
1997: Lab				8,605	24.8		

Denton & Reddish [181]

69,236	48.5	Bennett, A.F.†	Lab	21,913	65.2	–	0.2
		Newman, P.	Con	6,583	19.6	–	1.7
		Fletcher, R.	LD	4,152	12.4	–	0.9
		Cadwallender, A.	UKI	945	2.8 ★		
1997: Lab				15,330	45.6		

Derby North [182]

76,248	57.8	Laxton, R.†	Lab	22,415	50.9	–	2.3
		Holden, B.L.	Con	15,433	35.0	+	0.8
		Charlesworth, R.A.	LD	6,206	14.1	+	5.1
1997: Lab				6,982	15.8		

Derby South [183]

77,082	55.9	Beckett, M.M.†	Lab	24,310	56.4	+	0.2
		Spencer, S.A.	Con	10,455	24.3	–	0.9
		Hanson, A.P.	LD	8,310	19.3	+	4.9
1997: Lab				13,855	32.2		

Derbyshire North East [184]

71,527	58.9	Barnes, H.†	Lab	23,437	55.6	– 4.8
		Hollingsworth, J.	Con	11,179	26.5	+ 1.3
		Higginbottom, M.A.	LD	7,508	17.8	+ 3.5
1997: Lab				12,258	29.1	

Derbyshire South [185]

81,217	64.0	Todd, M.W.†	Lab	26,338	50.7	– 3.8
		Hakewill, J.C.	Con	18,487	35.6	+ 4.3
		Eagling, R.D.	LD	5,233	10.1	+ 1.1
		Blunt, J.	UKI	1,074	2.1 ★	+ 1.0
		Liversuch, P.A.	SL	564	1.1 ★	
		Taylor, J.B.	Ind	249	0.5 ★	
1997: Lab				7,851	15.1	

Derbyshire West [186]

74,651	67.8	McLoughlin, P.A.†	Con	24,280	48.0	+ 5.9
		Clamp, S.J.	Lab	16,910	33.4	– 0.1
		Beckett, J.W.R.	LD	7,922	15.7	– 1.8
		Bavester, S.D.	UKI	672	1.3 ★	+ 0.5
		Delves, N.C.E.	MRLP	472	0.9 ★	
		Goodall, R.	Ind	333	0.7 ★	
1997: Con				7,370	14.6	

Devizes [187]

82,925	64.2	Ancram, M.A.†	Con	25,159	47.2	+ 4.4
		Thorpe, J.J.	Lab	13,263	24.9	+ 0.7
		Frances, H.	LD	11,756	22.1	– 4.5
		Wood, A.S.	UKI	1,521	2.9 ★	+ 1.8
		Kennedy, L.H.C.	Ind	1,078	2.0 ★	
		Potter, V.A.	MRLP	472	0.9 ★	
1997: Con				11,896	22.3	

Devon East [188]

69,542	68.8	Swire, H.	Con	22,681	47.4	+ 4.0
		Dumper, T.R.	LD	14,486	30.3	+ 1.2
		Starr, P.	Lab	7,974	16.7	– 1.0
		Wilson, D.J.	UKI	2,696	5.6	+ 4.8
1997: Con				8,195	17.1	

Devon North [189]

72,100	68.3	Harvey, N.B.†	LD	21,784	44.2	– 6.5
		Allen, C.E.J.	Con	18,800	38.2	– 1.3
		Gale, V.G.	Lab	4,995	10.1	+ 0.4
		Knapman, R.M.	UKI	2,484	5.0	
		Bown, A.J.	Grn	1,191	2.4 ★	
1997: LD				2,984	6.1	

Devon South West [190]

70,922	66.1	Streeter, G.N.†	Con	21,970	46.8	+ 3.9
		Mavin, C.J.	Lab	14,826	31.6	+ 2.7
		Hutty, P.A.	LD	8,616	18.4	– 5.4
		Bullock, R.P..	UKI	1,492	3.2 ★	+ 2.3
1997: Con				7,144	15.2	

Devon West & Torridge [191]

78,976	70.5	Burnett, J.P.†	LD	23,474	42.2	+ 0.3
		Cox, C.G.	Con	22,280	40.0	+ 1.5
		Brenton, D.G.	Lab	5,959	10.7	– 1.7
		Edwards, R.C.	UKI	2,674	4.8 ★	+ 1.7
		Quinn, M.	Grn	1,297	2.3 ★	
1997: LD				1,194	2.1	

Dewsbury [192]

62,345	58.8	Taylor, W.A.†	Lab	18,524	50.5	+ 1.1
		Cole, R.I.G.	Con	11,075	30.2	+ 0.1
		Cuthbertson, I.M.	LD	4,382	12.0	+ 1.7
		Smith, R.A.	BNP	1,632	4.5 ★	
		Smithson, J.B.	Grn	560	1.5 ★	+ 0.6
		Peace, D.T.	UKI	478	1.3 ★	
1997: Lab				7,449	20.3	

Don Valley [193]

66,787	54.8	Flint, C.L.†	Lab	20,009	54.6	– 3.6
		Browne, J.W.	Con	10,489	28.6	+ 4.0
		Smith, P.A.	LD	4,089	11.2	+ 1.4
		Wilde, T.	Ind	800	2.2 ★	
		Cooper, D.A.	UKI	777	2.1 ★	
		Ball, N.	SL	466	1.3 ★	
1997: Lab				9,520	26.0	

Doncaster Central [194]

65,690	51.6	Winterton, R.†	Lab	20,034	59.1	–	3.0
		Meggitt, G.	Con	8,035	23.7	+	2.7
		Southcombe, M.J.	LD	4,390	12.9	+	3.5
		Gordon, D.A.	UKI	926	2.7 ★	+	1.7
		Terry, J.A.	SA	517	1.5 ★		
1997: Lab				11,999	35.4		

Doncaster North [195]

62,124	50.5	Hughes, K.M.†	Lab	19,788	63.1	–	6.7
		Kapoor, A.	Con	4,601	14.7	–	0.1
		Ross, C.A.	LD	3,323	10.6	+	2.1
		Williams, M.	Ind	2,926	9.3		
		Wallis, J.S.	UKI	725	2.3 ★		
1997: Lab				15,187	48.4		

Dorset Mid & Poole North [196]

66,675	65.6	Brooke, A.L.	LD	18,358	42.0	+	2.7
		Fraser, C.J.†	Con	17,974	41.1	+	0.4
		Selby-Bennett, J.S.	Lab	6,765	15.5	–	0.3
		Mager, J.	UKI	621	1.4 ★		
1997: Con				384	0.9		

Dorset North [197]

72,140	66.3	Walter, R.J.†	Con	22,314	46.7	+	2.4
		Gasson, E.J.	LD	18,517	38.7	–	0.4
		Wareham, M.A.	Lab	5,334	11.2	+	0.9
		Jenkins, P.	UKI	1,019	2.1 ★	+	0.6
		Duthie, J.C.M.	LE	391	0.8 ★		
		Bone, C.		246	0.5 ★		
1997: Con				3,797	7.9		

Dorset South [198]

69,223	65.5	Knight, J.	Lab	19,027	42.0	+	6.0
		Bruce, I.C.†	Con	18,874	41.6	+	5.5
		Canning, A.J.	LD	6,531	14.4	–	5.8
		Moss, L.A.W.	UKI	913	2.0 ★	+	0.3
1997: Con				153	0.3		

Dorset West [199]

71,291	69.5	Letwin, O.†	Con	22,126	44.6		+	3.5
		Green, S.	LD	20,712	41.8		+	4.1
		Hyde, R.J.	Lab	6,733	13.6		−	4.1
1997: Con				1,414	2.9			

Dover [200]

69,024	65.1	Prosser, G.M.†	Lab	21,943	48.8		−	5.7
		Watkins, P.A.	Con	16,744	37.2		+	4.4
		Hook, A.J.	LD	5,131	11.4		+	3.5
		Speakman, L.	UKI	1,142	2.5	★	+	1.7
1997: Lab				5,199	11.6			

Down North [201]

63,212	58.8	Hermon, S.	UU	20,833	56.0		+	24.9
		McCartney, R.L.†	UKU	13,509	36.3		+	1.3
		Farrell, M.	SDLP	1,275	3.4	★	−	1.0
		Robertson, J.	Con	815	2.2	★	−	2.8
		Carter, C.C.	Ind	444	1.2	★		
		McConvey, E.	SF	313	0.8	★		
1997: UKU				7,324	19.7			

Down South [202]

73,519	70.8	McGrady, E.†	SDLP	24,136	46.3		−	6.6
		Murphy, M.	SF	10,278	19.7		+	9.4
		Nesbitt, D.W.G.	UU	9,173	17.6		−	15.2
		Wells, J.H.	DUP	7,802	15.0			
		Campbell, B.	APNI	685	1.3	★	−	2.2
1997: SDLP				13,858	26.6			

Dudley North [203]

68,964	55.9	Cranston, R.F.†	Lab	20,095	52.1		+	0.9
		Griffiths, A.J.	Con	13,295	34.5		+	3.1
		Burt, R.G.	LD	3,352	8.7		+	0.5
		Darby, S.	BNP	1,822	4.7	★		
1997: Lab				6,800	17.6			

Dudley South [204]

65,579	55.4	Pearson, I.P.†	Lab	18,109	49.8	– 6.8
		Sugarman, J.A.	Con	11,292	31.1	+ 1.6
		Burt, L.J.	LD	5,421	14.9	+ 4.0
		Westwood, J.F.	UKI	859	2.4 ★	
		Thompson, A.	SA	663	1.8 ★	
1997: Lab				6,817	18.8	

Dulwich & West Norwood [205]

71,621	53.4	Jowell, T.J.†	Lab	20,999	54.9	– 6.1
		Vineall, N.E.J.	Con	8,689	22.7	– 1.5
		Pidgeon, C.V.	LD	5,805	15.2	+ 4.4
		Jones, J.	Grn	1,914	5.0	
		Kelly, B.J.	SA	839	2.2 ★	
1997: Lab				12,310	32.2	

Dumbarton [206]

55,643	61.1	McFall, J.†	Lab	16,151	47.5	– 2.1
		Robertson, I.	SNP	6,576	19.3	– 3.9
		Thompson, E.	LD	5,265	15.5	+ 7.9
		Ramsay, P.J.	Con	4,648	13.7	– 4.0
		Robertson, L.	SSP	1,354	4.0 ★	+ 3.3
1997: Lab				9,575	28.2	

Dumfries [207]

63,571	67.0	Brown, R.L.†	Lab	20,830	48.9	+ 1.4
		Charteris, J.A.	Con	11,996	28.2	+ 0.1
		Scott, J.A.R.	LD	4,955	11.6	+ 0.6
		Fisher, G.A.	SNP	4,103	9.6	– 2.4
		Dennis, J.	SSP	702	1.6 ★	
1997: Lab				8,834	20.7	

Dundee East [208]

56,535	57.3	Luke, I.	Lab	14,635	45.2	– 5.9
		Hosie, S.	SNP	10,169	31.4	+ 4.9
		Donnelly, J.A.	Con	3,900	12.0	– 3.7
		Lawrie, R.A.	LD	2,784	8.6	+ 4.5
		Duke, H.	SSP	879	2.7 ★	+ 2.1
1997: Lab				4,466	13.8	

Dundee West [209]

53,760	54.4	Ross, E.†	Lab	14,787	50.6	–	3.2
		Archer, G.	SNP	7,987	27.3	+	4.1
		Hail, I.S.	Con	2,656	9.1	–	4.1
		Dick, E.G.	LD	2,620	9.0	+	1.3
		McFarlane, J.	SSP	1,192	4.1 ★	+	3.0
1997: Lab				6,800	23.3		

Dunfermline East [210]

52,811	57.0	Brown, J.G.†	Lab	19,487	64.8	–	2.0
		Mellon, J.J.J.	SNP	4,424	14.7	–	0.8
		Randall, S.R.	Con	2,838	9.4	–	0.6
		Mainland, J.M	LD	2,281	7.6	+	1.7
		Jackson, A.	SSP	770	2.6 ★		
		Dunsmore, T.	UKI	286	1.0 ★		
1997: Lab				15,063	50.1		

Dunfermline West [211]

54,293	57.1	Squire, R.A.†	Lab	16,370	52.8	–	0.2
		Goodall, B.J.	SNP	5,390	17.4	–	1.8
		McPhate, R.	LD	4,832	15.6	+	2.0
		Mackie, J.A.	Con	3,166	10.2	–	2.4
		Stewart, C.	SSP	746	2.4 ★		
		Harper, A.D.	UKI	471	1.5 ★		
1997: Lab				10,980	35.4		

Durham North [212]

67,755	56.9	Jones, K.D.	Lab	25,920	67.2	–	3.1
		Palmer, M.R.	Con	7,237	18.8	+	4.3
		Field, C.A.	LD	5,411	14.0	+	3.0
1997: Lab				18,683	48.4		

Durham North West [213]

67,062	58.5	Armstrong, H.J.†	Lab	24,526	62.5	–	6.2
		Clouston, W.S.J.	Con	8,193	20.9	+	5.6
		Ord, A.C.	LD	5,846	14.9	+	4.1
		Hartnell, J.	SL	661	1.7 ★		
1997: Lab				16,333	41.6		

City of Durham [214]

69,610	59.6	Steinberg, G.N.†	Lab	23,254	56.1	− 7.2
		Woods, C.A.	LD	9,813	23.7	+ 8.4
		Cartmell, N.J.	Con	7,167	17.3	− 0.2
		Williamson, C.A.	UKI	1,252	3.0 ★	
1997: Lab				13,441	32.4	

Ealing Acton & Shepherd's Bush [215]

70,697	52.6	Soley, C.S.†	Lab	20,144	54.1	− 4.2
		Greening, J.	Con	9,355	25.1	− 0.7
		Tod, M.P.N.	LD	6,171	16.6	+ 5.8
		Grant, N.J.	SA	529	1.4 ★	
		Lawrie, A.J.G.	UKI	476	1.3 ★	+ 0.5
		Rule, C.J.M.	SL	301	0.8 ★	
		Ng, R.	PL	225	0.6 ★	
1997: Lab				10,789	29.0	

Ealing North [216]

77,524	58.0	Pound, S.P.†	Lab	25,022	55.7	+ 2.0
		Walker, C.A.R.	Con	13,185	29.3	− 7.9
		Fruzza, F.	LD	5,043	11.2	+ 4.2
		Seibe, A.I.	Grn	1,039	2.3 ★	+ 1.4
		Moss, D.W.	UKI	668	1.5 ★	+ 0.2
1997: Lab				11,837	26.3	

Ealing Southall [217]

82,373	56.8	Khabra, P.S.†	Lab	22,239	47.5	− 12.5
		Kawczynski, D.R.	Con	8,556	18.3	− 2.5
		Lit, A.	Ind	5,764	12.3	
		Sharma, B.K.	LD	4,680	10.0	− 0.4
		Cook, M.J.	Grn	2,119	4.5 ★	+ 2.8
		Dhillon, S.S.	Ind	1,214	2.6 ★	
		Choudhry, M.	Ind	1,166	2.5 ★	
		Brar, H.S.	SL	921	2.0 ★	
		Bhutta, M.Z.	Ind	169	0.4 ★	
1997: Lab				13,683	29.2	

Easington [218]

61,532	53.6	Cummings, J.S.†	Lab	25,360	76.8	− 3.4
		Lovel, P.F.	Con	3,411	10.3	+ 1.8
		Ord, C.J.	LD	3,408	10.3	+ 3.1
		Robinson, D.	SL	831	2.5 ★	
1997: Lab				21,949	66.5	

East Ham [219]

71,255	52.3	Timms, S.C.†	Lab	27,241	73.1	+ 8.5
		Campbell, P.J.	Con	6,209	16.7	+ 0.6
		Fox, B.	LD	2,600	7.0	+ 0.5
		Finlayson, R.	SL	783	2.1 ★	
		Pandhal, J.	UKI	444	1.2 ★	
1997: Lab				21,032	56.4	

East Kilbride [220]

66,572	62.6	Ingram, A.†	Lab	22,205	53.3	− 3.3
		Buchanan, A.	SNP	9,450	22.7	+ 1.8
		Hawthorn, E.G.	LD	4,278	10.3	+ 3.0
		McCulloch, M.	Con	4,238	10.2	− 1.8
		Stevenson, D.	SSP	1,519	3.6 ★	
1997: Lab				12,755	30.6	

East Lothian [221]

58,987	62.5	Picking, A.	Lab	17,407	47.2	− 5.5
		Mair, H.J.G.	Con	6,577	17.8	− 2.1
		Hayman, J.L.	LD	6,506	17.6	+ 7.1
		Brown, H.M.	SNP	5,381	14.6	− 1.1
		White, D.	SSP	624	1.7 ★	
		Herriot, J.H.	SL	376	1.0 ★	
1997: Lab				10,830	29.4	

Eastbourne [222]

75,170	59.6	Waterson, N.C.†	Con	19,738	44.1	+ 2.0
		Berry, C.J.	LD	17,584	39.3	+ 0.9
		Roles, G.M.	Lab	5,967	13.3	+ 0.8
		Jones, B.M.	UKI	907	2.0 ★	+ 1.5
		Williamson, M.T.	Lib	574	1.3 ★	
1997: Con				2,154	4.8	

Eastleigh [223]

74,603	63.8	Chidgey, D.W.G.†	LD	19,360	40.7	+	5.6
		Burns, C.D.	Con	16,302	34.3	+	0.6
		Jaffa, R.H.	Lab	10,426	21.9	–	4.9
		Challis, S.C.	UKI	849	1.8 ★	+	1.0
		Lyn, M.	Grn	636	1.3 ★		
1997: LD				3,058	6.4		

Eastwood [224]

68,297	70.8	Murphy, J.†	Lab	23,036	47.6	+	7.9
		Robertson, R.S.	Con	13,895	28.7	–	4.8
		Steele, A.R.M.	LD	6,239	12.9	+	1.2
		Maxwell, W.S.	SNP	4,137	8.6	–	4.5
		Murray, P.J.	SSP	814	1.7 ★		
		Tayan, M.	Ind	247	0.5 ★		
1997: Lab				9,141	18.9		

Eccles [225]

68,764	48.3	Stewart, I.†	Lab	21,395	64.5	–	2.2
		Caillard, P.J.	Con	6,867	20.7	+	2.0
		Boyd, R.D.	LD	4,920	14.8	+	4.1
1997: Lab				14,528	43.8		

Eddisbury [226]

69,181	64.2	O'Brien, S.R.†	Con	20,556	46.3	+	3.8
		Eyres, G.W.	Lab	15,988	36.0	–	4.1
		Roberts, P.D.	LD	6,975	15.7	+	2.5
		Carson, D.J.E.	UKI	868	2.0 ★		
1997: Con				4,568	10.3		

Edinburgh Central [227]

66,089	52.0	Darling, A.M.†	Lab	14,495	42.1	–	4.9
		Myles, A.	LD	6,353	18.5	+	5.4
		Orr, A.	Con	5,643	16.4	–	4.8
		McKee, I.H.	SNP	4,832	14.1	–	1.7
		Farmer, G.W.	Grn	1,809	5.3	+	3.8
		Williamson, K.	SSP	1,258	3.7 ★		
1997: Lab				8,142	23.7		

Edinburgh East & Musselburgh [228]

59,241	58.2	Strang, G.S.†	Lab	18,124	52.6	− 1.0
		Munn, R.M.	SNP	5,956	17.3	− 1.8
		Peacock, G.J.	LD	4,981	14.5	+ 3.7
		Finnie, P.W.L.	Con	3,906	11.3	− 4.1
		Durkin, D.A.M.	SSP	1,487	4.3 ★	
1997: Lab				12,168	35.3	

Edinburgh North & Leith [229]

62,731	53.0	Lazarowicz, M.J.	Lab	15,271	45.9	− 1.0
		Tombs, S.	LD	6,454	19.4	+ 6.4
		Stewart, K.	SNP	5,290	15.9	− 4.2
		Mitchell, I.G.	Con	4,626	13.9	− 3.9
		Grant, C.M.	SSP	1,334	4.0 ★	+ 3.2
		Jacobsen, D.D.	SL	259	0.8 ★	
1997: Lab				8,817	26.5	

Edinburgh Pentlands [230]

60,484	64.4	Clark, L.M.†	Lab	15,797	40.6	− 2.4
		Rifkind, M.L.	Con	14,055	36.1	+ 3.7
		Walker, D.J.	LD	4,210	10.8	+ 0.8
		Gibb, S.	SNP	4,210	10.8	− 2.2
		Mearns, J.A.	SSP	555	1.4 ★	
		McMurdo, W.	UKI	105	0.3 ★	+ 0.1
1997: Lab				1,742	4.5	

Edinburgh South [231]

64,437	57.7	Griffiths, N.†	Lab	15,671	42.2	− 4.7
		MacLaren, M.A.	LD	10,172	27.4	+ 9.7
		Buchan, G.G.C.	Con	6,172	16.6	− 4.7
		Williams, H.	SNP	3,683	9.9	− 3.0
		Fox, C.	SSP	933	2.5 ★	
		Hendry, L.M.	LCA	535	1.4 ★	
1997: Lab				5,499	14.8	

Edinburgh West [232]

62,503	63.2	Barrett, J.A.	LD	16,719	42.4	− 0.9
		Alexandra, E.	Lab	9,130	23.1	+ 4.3
		Whyte, I.	Con	8,894	22.5	− 5.4
		Smith, A.E.	SNP	4,047	10.3	+ 1.4
		Scott, B.	SSP	688	1.7 ★	
1997: LD				7,589	19.2	

Edmonton [233]

61,788	56.3	Love, A.†	Lab	20,481	58.9	–	1.4
		Burrowes, D.J.B.	Con	10,709	30.8	+	0.6
		Taylor, D.A.	LD	2,438	7.0	+	0.7
		Rolph, G.W.	UKI	406	1.2 ★	+	0.6
		Basarik, E.	Ref	344	1.0 ★		
		Medwell, H.W.	SA	296	0.9 ★		
		Saxena, R.P.	Ind	100	0.3 ★		
1997: Lab				9,772	28.1		

Ellesmere Port & Neston [234]

68,147	60.9	Miller, A.P.†	Lab	22,964	55.3	–	4.3
		Williams, G.D.	Con	12,103	29.1	+	0.1
		Kelly, S.E.	LD	4,828	11.6	+	2.7
		Crocker, H.F.	UKI	824	2.0 ★		
		Nicholls, G.L.	Grn	809	1.9 ★		
1997: Lab				10,861	26.2		

Elmet [235]

70,041	65.6	Burgon, C.†	Lab	22,038	48.0	–	4.4
		Millard, A.C.G.	Con	17,867	38.9	+	2.7
		Kirk, M.A.	LD	5,001	10.9	+	2.2
		Spence, A.M.	UKI	1,031	2.2 ★		
1997: Lab				4,171	9.1		

Eltham [236]

57,554	58.7	Efford, C.S.†	Lab	17,855	52.8	–	1.8
		Massey, S.M.	Con	10,859	32.1	+	1.0
		Morris, M.	LD	4,121	12.2	+	3.7
		Jones, T.F.	UKI	706	2.1 ★		
		Graham, A.J.	Ind	251	0.7 ★		
1997: Lab				6,996	20.7		

Enfield North [237]

67,204	57.0	Ryan, J.M.†	Lab	17,888	46.7	–	4.0
		De Bois, N.G.	Con	15,597	40.7	+	4.4
		Leighter, H.F.	LD	3,355	8.8	–	0.2
		Johns, R.P.	BNP	605	1.6 ★		
		Hall, B.J.	UKI	427	1.1 ★	+	0.1
		Akerman, M.F.	PL	241	0.6 ★		
		Course, R.		210	0.5 ★		
1997: Lab				2,291	6.0		

Enfield Southgate [238]

65,957	63.5	Twigg, S.†	Lab	21,727	51.8	+	7.6
		Flack, J.C.	Con	16,181	38.6	-	2.5
		Hoban, W.	LD	2,935	7.0	-	3.7
		Graham-Leigh, E.A.	Grn	662	1.6 ★		
		Freshwater, R.A.	UKI	298	0.7 ★		
		Malakouna, A.	Ind	105	0.3 ★		
1997: Lab				5,546	13.2		

Epping Forest [239]

72,589	58.4	Laing, E.F.†	Con	20,833	49.1	+	3.6
		Naylor, C.	Lab	12,407	29.3	-	6.3
		Heavens, M.A.C.	LD	7,884	18.6	+	5.2
		Smith, A.G.	UKI	1,290	3.0 ★		
1997: Con				8,426	19.9		

Epsom & Ewell [240]

74,266	62.8	Grayling, C.S.	Con	22,430	48.1	+	2.5
		Mansell, C.J.	Lab	12,350	26.5	+	2.1
		Vincent, J.W.	LD	10,316	22.1	-	0.7
		Webster–Gardiner, G.R.	UKI	1,547	3.3 ★	+	2.3
1997: Con				10,080	21.6		

Erewash [241]

78,484	61.9	Blackman, E.M.†	Lab	23,915	49.2	-	2.5
		Gregor MacGregor, N.A.V.	Con	16,983	34.9	-	1.6
		Garnett, M.C.	LD	5,586	11.5	+	2.9
		Smith, L.	UKI	692	1.4 ★		
		Belshaw, S.E.	BNP	591	1.2 ★		
		Seerius, R.U.	MRLP	428	0.9 ★		
		Waldock, P.A.W.	SL	401	0.8 ★		
1997: Lab				6,932	14.3		

Erith & Thamesmead [242]

66,371	50.2	Austin, J.E.†	Lab	19,769	59.3	-	2.8
		Brooks, M.J.	Con	8,602	25.8	+	5.6
		Kempton, J.	LD	3,800	11.4	-	0.6
		Dhillon, H.S.	SL	1,180	3.5 ★		
1997: Lab				11,167	33.5		

Esher & Walton [243]

73,541	61.9	Taylor, I.C.†	Con	22,296	49.0	–	0.9
		McGowan, J.	Lab	10,758	23.6	+	0.9
		Marsh, M.J.P.	LD	10,241	22.5	+	2.1
		Collignon, B.M.	UKI	2,236	4.9 ★	+	3.9
1997: Con				11,538	25.3		

Essex North [244]

71,605	62.8	Jenkin, B.C.†	Con	21,325	47.4	+	3.5
		Hawkins, P.K.	Lab	14,139	31.5	–	1.7
		Ellis, T.K.	LD	7,867	17.5	–	2.1
		Curtis, G.S.	UKI	1,613	3.6 ★	+	1.2
1997: Con				7,186	16.0		

Exeter [245]

81,946	64.2	Bradshaw, B.P.J.†	Lab	26,194	49.8	+	2.3
		Jobson, A.M.	Con	14,435	27.4	–	1.2
		Copus, R.A.A.	LD	6,512	12.4	–	5.6
		Morrish, D.J.	Lib	2,596	4.9 ★		
		Edwards, P.A.	Grn	1,240	2.4 ★	+	1.3
		Stuart, J.S.	UKI	1,109	2.1 ★	+	1.1
		Choules, F.D.	SA	530	1.0 ★		
1997: Lab				11,759	22.3		

Falkirk East [246]

58,201	57.9	Connarty, M.†	Lab	18,536	55.0	–	1.1
		Hutton, I.	SNP	7,824	23.2	–	0.7
		Stevenson, W.	Con	3,252	9.6	–	4.3
		Utting, K.	LD	2,992	8.9	+	3.7
		Weir, A.	SSP	725	2.2 ★		
		Stead, R.	SL	373	1.1 ★		
1997: Lab				10,712	31.8		

Falkirk West [247]

54,100	57.1	Joyce, E.†	Lab	16,022	51.9	–	7.5
		Kerr, D.	SNP	7,490	24.2	+	0.8
		Murray, S.	Con	2,321	7.5	–	4.6
		O'Donnell, H.	LD	2,203	7.1	+	2.0
		Buchanan, W.	Ind	1,464	4.7 ★		
		McAlpine, M.	SSP	707	2.3 ★		
		Lynch, H.	Ind	490	1.6 ★		
		Forbes, R.	SL	194	0.6 ★		
1997: Lab				8,532	27.6		

Falmouth & Camborne [248]

72,833	64.3	Atherton, C.K.†	Lab	18,532	39.6	+ 5.7
		Serpell, N.J.	Con	14,005	29.9	+ 1.1
		Brazil, J.C.M.	LD	11,453	24.5	− 0.7
		Browne, J.E.D.de la V.	UKI	1,328	2.8 ★	+ 2.2
		Wasley, H.	MK	853	1.8 ★	
		Holmes, P.T.	Lib	649	1.4 ★	
1997: Lab				4,527	9.7	

Fareham [249]

71,526	63.5	Hoban, M.G.	Con	21,389	47.1	+ 0.2
		Carr, J.W.	Lab	14,380	31.6	+ 4.7
		Pritchard, H.W.L.	LD	8,503	18.7	− 0.9
		O'Brien, W.	UKI	1,175	2.6 ★	
1997: Con				7,009	15.4	

Faversham & Kent Mid [250]

67,995	60.4	Robertson, H.	Con	18,739	45.6	+ 1.3
		Birchall, G.G.	Lab	14,556	35.5	− 0.5
		Sole, M.J.	LD	5,529	13.5	+ 1.1
		Gascoyne, J.C.	UKI	828	2.0 ★	+ 1.1
		Kemp, P.A.	Grn	799	1.9 ★	+ 1.2
		Davidson, N.A.	RRL	600	1.5 ★	
1997: Con				4,183	10.2	

Feltham & Heston [251]

73,458	49.2	Keen, A.†	Lab	21,406	59.2	− 0.5
		Mammatt, H.E.	Con	8,749	24.2	− 2.8
		Darley, A.	LD	4,998	13.8	+ 4.7
		Cheema, S.	SL	651	1.8 ★	
		Prachar, W.W.	Ind	204	0.6 ★	
		Khaira, A.S.	Ind	169	0.5 ★	
1997: Lab				12,657	35.0	

Fermanagh & South Tyrone [252]

66,640	78.0	Gildernew, M.	SF	17,739	34.1	+ 11.0
		Cooper, J.	UU	17,686	34.0	− 17.5
		Gallagher, T.	SDLP	9,706	18.7	− 4.2
		Dixon, W.J.		6,843	13.2	
1997: UU				53	0.1	

Fife Central [253]

59,597	54.6	MacDougall, J.W.	Lab	18,310	56.3	–	2.3
		Alexander, D.J.H.	SNP	8,235	25.3	+	0.3
		Riches, E.	LD	2,775	8.5	+	2.1
		Balfour, J.R.	Con	2,351	7.2	–	1.8
		Balfour, M.A.	SSP	841	2.6 ★		
1997: Lab				10,075	31.0		

Fife North East [254]

61,900	56.0	Campbell, W.M.†	LD	17,926	51.7	+	0.4
		Scott-Hayward, M.D.A.	Con	8,190	23.6	–	2.9
		Brennan, C.J	Lab	3,950	11.4	+	1.1
		Murray-Browne, K.	SNP	3,596	10.4	–	0.5
		White, K.S.	SSP	610	1.8 ★		
		Von Goetz, L.M.C.	LCA	420	1.2 ★		
1997: LD				9,736	28.1		

Finchley & Golders Green [255]

76,178	57.3	Vis, R.J.†	Lab	20,205	46.3	+	0.2
		Marshall, J.L.	Con	16,489	37.8	–	2.0
		Teather, S.L.	LD	5,266	12.1	+	0.8
		Dunn, M.J.	Grn	1,385	3.2 ★	+	2.0
		de Roeck, J.	UKI	330	0.8 ★	+	0.3
1997: Lab				3,716	8.5		

Folkestone & Hythe [256]

71,585	64.1	Howard, M.†	Con	20,645	45.0	+	6.0
		Carroll, P.D.	LD	14,738	32.1	+	5.3
		Catterall, A.M.A.	Lab	9,260	20.2	–	4.7
		Baker, J.A.	UKI	1,212	2.6 ★	+	1.9
1997: Con				5,907	12.9		

Forest of Dean [257]

66,240	67.3	Organ, D.M.†	Lab	19,350	43.4	–	4.8
		Harper, M.J.	Con	17,301	38.8	+	3.2
		Gayler, D.R.	LD	5,762	12.9	+	0.6
		Pickering, S.P.C.	Grn	1,254	2.8 ★		
		Prout, A.G.	UKI	661	1.5 ★		
		Morgan, G.R.	Ind	279	0.6 ★		
1997: Lab				2,049	4.6		

Foyle [258]

70,943	68.9	Hume, J.†	SDLP	24,538	50.2		–	2.3
		McLaughlin, M.	SF	12,988	26.6		+	2.6
		Hay, W.	DUP	7,414	15.2		–	6.4
		Davidson, A.	UU	3,360	6.9			
		Cavanagh, C.M.	APNI	579	1.2	★	–	0.5
1997: SDLP				11,550	23.6			

Fylde [259]

73,460	60.9	Jack, J.M.†	Con	23,383	52.3		+	3.4
		Stockton, J.R.	Lab	13,773	30.8		–	0.9
		Begg, J.L.	LD	6,599	14.8		+	0.1
		Brown, L.F.	UKI	982	2.2	★		
1997: Con				9,610	21.5			

Gainsborough [260]

65,870	64.2	Leigh, E.J.E.†	Con	19,555	46.2	+	3.1
		Rhodes, A.	Lab	11,484	27.1	–	1.7
		Taylor, S.C.	LD	11,280	26.7	–	1.5
1997: Con				8,071	19.1		

Galloway & Upper Nithsdale [261]

53,254	67.4	Duncan, P.J.	Con	12,222	34.0		+	3.5
		Fleming, M.G.	SNP	12,148	33.8		–	10.1
		Sloan, T.K.	Lab	7,258	20.2		+	3.9
		Wallace, N.C.	LD	3,698	10.3		+	3.9
		Harvey, A.	SSP	588	1.6	★		
1997: SNP				74	0.2			

Gateshead East & Washington West [262]

64,041	52.5	Quin, J.G.†	Lab	22,903	68.1		–	3.9
		Beadle, R.W.A.L.	LD	4,999	14.9		+	4.1
		Campbell, E.J.	Con	4,970	14.8		+	0.6
		Rouse, M.P.	UKI	743	2.2	★		
1997: Lab				17,904	53.3			

Gedling [263]

68,519	63.9	Coaker, V.R.†	Lab	22,383	51.1	+	4.3
		Bullock, J.D.	Con	16,785	38.3	–	1.2
		Gillam, A.J.	LD	4,648	10.6	+	0.7
1997: Lab				5,598	12.8		

Gillingham [264]

0,901	59.5	Clark, P.G.†	Lab	18,782	44.5		+	4.7
		Butcher, T.R.	Con	16,510	39.1		+	3.2
		Hunt, J.N.	LD	5,755	13.6		–	5.4
		Scholefield, A.J.E.	UKI	933	2.2	★	+	1.0
		Thomas, W.V.	SA	232	0.5	★		
1997: Lab				2,272	5.4			

Glasgow Anniesland [265]

53,290	50.1	Robertson, J.†	Lab	15,102	56.5		–	5.3
		Thoms, G.R.	SNP	4,048	15.1		–	2.0
		McGinty, C.P.	LD	3,244	12.1		+	4.9
		Connell, S.M.	Con	2,651	9.9		–	1.5
		McCarthy, C.	SSP	1,486	5.6		+	4.9
		McGavigan, K.	SL	191	0.7	★		
1997: Lab				11,054	41.4			

Glasgow Baillieston [266]

49,268	47.2	Wray, J.†	Lab	14,200	61.0		–	4.6
		McNeill, L.	SNP	4,361	18.7		–	0.4
		Comrie, D.	Con	1,580	6.8		–	1.0
		McVicar, J.	SSP	1,569	6.7		+	3.7
		Dundas, C.C.	LD	1,551	6.7		+	2.8
1997: Lab				9,839	42.3			

Glasgow Cathcart [267]

52,094	52.6	Harris, T.	Lab	14,902	54.4		–	3.0
		Docherty, J.	SNP	4,086	14.9		–	3.6
		Cook, R.E.	Con	3,662	13.4		+	0.6
		Henery, T.	LD	3,006	11.0		+	4.1
		Stevenson, J.R.	SSP	1,730	6.3		+	4.9
1997: Lab				10,816	39.5			

Glasgow Govan [268]

54,068	46.8	Sarwar, M.†	Lab	12,464	49.3		+	5.2
		Neary, K.	SNP	6,064	24.0		–	11.1
		Stewart, R.	LD	2,815	11.1		+	5.2
		Menzies, M.A.	Con	2,167	8.6		–	0.2
		McGartland, W.	SSP	1,531	6.1		+	3.8
		Foster, J.O.	Comm	174	0.7	★		
		Mirza, B.I.	Ind	69	0.3	★		
1997: Lab				6,400	25.3			

Glasgow Kelvin [269]

61,534	43.6	Galloway, G.†	Lab	12,014	44.8	– 6.1
		Mayberry, T.	LD	4,754	17.7	+ 3.6
		Rankin, F.A.	SNP	4,513	16.8	– 4.5
		Rankin, D.	Con	2,388	8.9	– 1.9
		Ritchie, H.	SSP	1,847	6.9	+ 5.7
		Shand, T.J.C.	Grn	1,286	4.8 ★	
1997: Lab				7,260	27.1	

Glasgow Maryhill [270]

55,431	40.1	McKechin, A.	Lab	13,420	60.4	– 4.6
		Dingwall, A.	SNP	3,532	15.9	– 1.1
		Callison, J.S.	LD	2,372	10.7	+ 3.5
		Scott, G.	SSP	1,745	7.8	+ 6.4
		Towler, G.H.W.	Con	1,162	5.2	– 0.7
1997: Lab				9,888	44.5	

Glasgow Pollok [271]

49,201	51.4	Davidson, I.G.†	Lab	15,497	61.3	+ 1.4
		Ritchie, D.	SNP	4,229	16.7	– 1.1
		Baldassara, K.R.	SSP	2,522	10.0	– 1.1
		Nelson, I.	LD	1,612	6.4	+ 2.9
		O'Brien, R.	Con	1,417	5.6	– 0.4
1997: Lab				11,268	44.6	

Glasgow Rutherglen [272]

51,855	56.3	McAvoy, T.†	Lab	16,760	57.4	– 0.1
		McLaughlin, A.	SNP	4,135	14.2	– 1.1
		Jackson, D.	LD	3,689	12.6	– 1.9
		Macaskill, M.	Con	3,301	11.3	+ 2.0
		Bonnar, W.	SSP	1,328	4.5 ★	+ 3.8
1997: Lab				12,625	43.2	

Glasgow Shettleston [273]

51,557	39.7	Marshall, D.†	Lab	13,235	64.7	– 8.5
		Byrne, J.	SNP	3,417	16.7	+ 2.7
		Kane, R.	SSP	1,396	6.8	+ 5.0
		Hutton, L.	LD	1,105	5.4	+ 1.4
		Murdoch, J.C.	Con	1,082	5.3	– 0.2
		Ritchie, M.	SL	230	1.1 ★	
1997: Lab				9,818	48.0	

Glasgow Springburn [274]

55,192	43.7	Martin, M.J.†	Speaker	16,053	66.6		
		Bain, S.	SNP	4,675	19.4	+	2.9
		Leckie, C.	SSP	1,879	7.8	+	6.5
		Houston, D.	SU	1,289	5.3		
		Silvester, R.E.W.	Ind	208	0.9 ★		
1997: Lab				11,378	47.2		

Gloucester [275]

81,207	59.4	Dhanda, P.S.	Lab	22,067	45.8	−	4.2
		James, P.S.	Con	18,187	37.7	+	2.0
		Bullamore, T.J.	LD	6,875	14.3	+	3.8
		Lines, T.	UKI	822	1.7 ★	+	0.9
		Smyth, S.J.W.	SA	272	0.6 ★		
1997: Lab				3,880	8.0		

Gordon [276]

60,059	58.3	Bruce, M.G.†	LD	15,928	45.5	+	2.9
		Milne, N.L.M.	Con	8,049	23.0	−	3.0
		Kemp, R.C.W.	SNP	5,760	16.5	−	3.5
		Thorpe, E.	Lab	4,730	13.5	+	3.2
		Sangster, J.	SSP	534	1.5 ★		
1997: LD				7,879	22.5		

Gosport [277]

69,626	57.1	Viggers, P.J.†	Con	17,364	43.6	+	0.0
		Williams, R.F.	Lab	14,743	37.1	+	6.4
		Roberts, R.D.C.	LD	6,011	15.1	−	4.5
		Bowles, J.A.	UKI	1,162	2.9 ★		
		Chetwynd, K.	SL	509	1.3 ★		
1997: Con				2,621	6.6		

Gower [278]

58,935	63.4	Caton, M.P.†	Lab	17,676	47.3	−	6.5
		Bushell, J.G.	Con	10,281	27.5	+	3.7
		Waye, S.R.	LD	4,507	12.1	−	0.9
		Caiach, S.M.	PC	3,865	10.3	+	5.2
		Shrewsbury, S.C.	Grn	607	1.6 ★		
		Hickery, D.C.	SL	417	1.1 ★		
1997: Lab				7,395	19.8		

Grantham & Stamford [279]

75,500	61.3	Davies, J.Q.†	Con	21,329	46.1	+	3.3
		Robinson, J.	Lab	16,811	36.3	-	1.4
		Carr, J.C.	LD	6,665	14.4	+	1.9
		Swain, M.J.	UKI	1,484	3.2 ★	+	2.2
1997: Con				4,518	9.8		

Gravesham [280]

69,588	62.7	Pond, C.R.†	Lab	21,773	49.9	+	0.2
		Arnold, J.A.	Con	16,911	38.8	-	0.1
		Parmenter, B.E.	LD	4,031	9.2	+	1.5
		Jenner, W.J.	UKI	924	2.1 ★		
1997: Lab				4,862	11.1		

Great Grimsby [281]

63,157	52.3	Mitchell, A.V.†	Lab	19,118	57.9	-	1.9
		Cousins, J.A.	Con	7,634	23.1	+	1.0
		De Freitas, A.	LD	6,265	19.0	+	0.9
1997: Lab				11,484	34.8		

Great Yarmouth [282]

69,194	58.3	Wright, A.D.†	Lab	20,344	50.4	-	3.0
		Reynolds, C.J.	Con	15,780	39.1	+	3.5
		Leeke, M.L.	LD	3,392	8.4	-	2.6
		Poole, B.R.	UKI	850	2.1 ★		
1997: Lab				4,564	11.3		

Greenock & Inverclyde [283]

47,884	59.3	Cairns, J.D.	Lab	14,929	52.5	-	3.6
		Brodie, C.G.	LD	5,039	17.7	+	3.9
		Murie, A.R.	SNP	4,248	14.9	-	3.6
		Haw, A.M.	Con	3,000	10.6	-	0.9
		Landels, D.W.	SSP	1,203	4.2 ★		
1997: Lab				9,890	34.8		

Greenwich & Woolwich [284]

60,114	54.1	Raynsford, W.R.N.†	Lab	19,691	60.5	-	2.9
		Forsdyke, R.J.	Con	6,258	19.2	+	0.7
		Pyne, R.D.	LD	5,082	15.6	+	3.1
		Gain, S.J.	UKI	672	2.1 ★		
		Paton, K.A.	SA	481	1.5 ★		
		Sharkey, M.M.	SL	352	1.1 ★		
1997: Lab				13,433	41.3		

Guildford [285]

76,302	62.7	Doughty, S.K.	LD	20,358	42.6	+ 8.4
		St Aubyn, N.F.†	Con	19,820	41.4	− 1.1
		Still, J.E.	Lab	6,558	13.7	− 3.8
		Porter, S.A.	UKI	736	1.5 ★	+ 0.8
		Morris, J.H.	Pac	370	0.8 ★	
1997: Con				538	1.1	

Hackney North & Stoke Newington [286]

60,444	49.0	Abbott, D.J.†	Lab	18,081	61.0	− 4.1
		Dye, P.A.R.	Con	4,430	15.0	− 2.0
		Ece, M.	LD	4,170	14.1	+ 3.9
		Chong, Y.	Grn	2,184	7.4	+ 3.1
		Chandan, S.	SL	756	2.6 ★	
1997: Lab				13,911	47.0	

Hackney South & Shoreditch [287]

63,990	47.4	Sedgemore, B.C.J.†	Lab	19,471	64.2	+ 4.8
		Vickers, A.J.M.	LD	4,422	14.6	− 0.4
		White, P.G.	Con	4,180	13.8	+ 0.5
		Prosper, C.I.	SA	1,401	4.6 ★	
		Koksal, S.	Ref	471	1.6 ★	
		Beavis, I.	Comm	259	0.9 ★	
		Rogers, W.P.	WRP	143	0.5 ★	
1997: Lab				15,049	49.6	

Halesowen & Rowley Regis [288]

65,683	59.8	Heal, S.L.†	Lab	20,804	53.0	− 1.1
		Jones, L.	Con	13,445	34.2	+ 1.4
		Harley, P.E.	LD	4,089	10.4	+ 1.9
		Sheath, A.	UKI	936	2.4 ★	
1997: Lab				7,359	18.7	

Halifax [289]

69,870	57.8	Mahon, A.†	Lab	19,800	49.0	− 5.3
		Walsh, J.R.	Con	13,671	33.8	+ 1.7
		Durkin, J.	LD	5,878	14.6	+ 2.6
		Martinek, H.E.	UKI	1,041	2.6 ★	+ 1.0
1997: Lab				6,129	15.2	

Haltemprice & Howden [290]

66,733	65.8	Davis, D.M.†	Con	18,994	43.2		– 0.8
		Neal, J.	LD	17,091	38.9		+ 10.1
		Howell, L.C.	Lab	6,898	15.7		– 7.9
		Robinson, J.	UKI	945	2.2 ★		+ 1.5
1997: Con				1,903	4.3		

Halton [291]

63,742	54.1	Twigg, J.D.†	Lab	23,841	69.2		– 1.7
		Davenport, C.H.	Con	6,413	18.6		+ 0.9
		Walker, P.J.	LD	4,216	12.2		+ 4.9
1997: Lab				17,428	50.6		

Hamilton North & Bellshill [292]

53,539	56.8	Reid, J.†	Lab	18,786	61.8		– 2.2
		Stephens, C.	SNP	5,225	17.2		– 1.9
		Frain-Bell, W.	Con	2,649	8.7		– 1.7
		Legg, K.	LD	2,360	7.8		+ 2.7
		Blackall, S.	SSP	1,189	3.9 ★		
		Mayes, S.	SL	195	0.6 ★		
1997: Lab				13,561	44.6		

Hamilton South [293]

46,665	57.3	Tynan, B.†	Lab	15,965	59.7		– 5.9
		Wilson, J.G.	SNP	5,190	19.4		+ 1.8
		Oswald, J.	LD	2,388	8.9		+ 3.8
		Richardson, N.	Con	1,876	7.0		– 1.6
		Mitchell, G.	SSP	1,187	4.4 ★		
		Murdoch, J.E.	UKI	151	0.6 ★		
1997: Lab				10,775	40.3		

Hammersmith & Fulham [294]

79,303	56.4	Coleman, I.†	Lab	19,801	44.3		– 2.5
		Carrington, M.H.M.	Con	17,786	39.8		+ 0.1
		Burden, J.	LD	5,294	11.8		+ 3.1
		Dias, D.L.	Grn	1,444	3.2 ★		+ 2.2
		Roberts, G.	UKI	375	0.8 ★		+ 0.5
1997: Lab				2,015	4.5		

Hampshire East [295]

78,229	64.3	Mates, M.J.†	Con	23,950	47.6	–	0.4
		Booker, R.A.	LD	15,060	29.9	+	1.8
		Burfoot, B.A.	Lab	9,866	19.6	+	2.5
		Coles, S.R.	UKI	1,413	2.8 ★	+	1.9
1997: Con				8,890	17.7		

Hampshire North East [296]

71,304	61.6	Arbuthnot, J.N.†	Con	23,379	53.2	+	2.3
		Plummer, M.I.	LD	10,122	23.0	+	0.3
		Jones, B.	Lab	8,744	19.9	+	3.8
		Mellstrom, G.F.C.	UKI	1,702	3.9 ★	+	3.0
1997: Con				13,257	30.2		

Hampshire North West [297]

78,044	62.3	Young, G.S.K.†	Con	24,374	50.1	+	4.9
		Mumford, M.J.	Lab	12,365	25.4	+	1.8
		Bentley, A.M.	LD	10,329	21.2	–	2.9
		Oram, S.	UKI	1,563	3.2 ★	+	0.7
1997: Con				12,009	24.7		

Hampstead & Highgate [298]

65,195	54.3	Jackson, G.M.†	Lab	16,601	46.9	–	10.5
		Mennear, K.A.	Con	8,725	24.6	–	2.6
		Simpson, J.A.	LD	7,273	20.5	+	8.1
		Cornwell, A.	Grn	1,654	4.7 ★		
		Cooper, H.B.	SA	559	1.6 ★		
		McDermott, T.B.	UKI	316	0.9 ★	+	0.6
		Xnunoftheabove, S.		144	0.4 ★		
		Teale, M.C.B.	PL	92	0.3 ★		
		Klein, A.P.		43	0.1 ★		
1997: Lab				7,876	22.2		

Harborough [299]

73,300	63.3	Garnier, E.H.†	Con	20,748	44.7	+	2.9
		Hope, J.S.	LD	15,496	33.4	+	3.9
		Jethwa, R.K.	Lab	9,271	20.0	–	5.2
		Knight, D.E.	UKI	912	2.0 ★		
1997: Con				5,252	11.3		

Harlow [300]

67,196	59.7	Rammell, W.E.†	Lab	19,169	47.8		–	6.3
		Halfon, R.H.	Con	13,941	34.8		+	2.7
		Spenceley, L.H.	LD	5,381	13.4		+	4.0
		Bennett, T.J.S.	UKI	1,223	3.0 ★		+	2.3
		Hobbs, J.M.	SA	401	1.0 ★			
1997: Lab				5,228	13.0			

Harrogate & Knaresborough [301]

65,243	64.6	Willis, G.P.†	LD	23,445	55.6		+	4.0
		Jones, A.H.	Con	14,600	34.6		–	3.8
		MacDonald, A.J.	Lab	3,101	7.4		–	1.4
		Brown, W.J.	UKI	761	1.8 ★			
		Cornforth, J.W.	PL	272	0.6 ★			
1997: LD				8,845	21.0			

Harrow East [302]

82,269	58.4	McNulty, A.J.†	Lab	26,590	55.3		+	2.8
		Wilding, P.J.	Con	15,466	32.2		–	3.3
		Kershaw, G.	LD	6,021	12.5		+	4.3
1997: Lab				11,124	23.1			

Harrow West [303]

74,083	63.0	Thomas, G.R.†	Lab	23,142	49.6		+	8.1
		Finkelstein, D.W.	Con	16,986	36.4		–	2.8
		Noyce, C.D.	LD	5,995	12.9		–	2.6
		Kefford, P.J.	UKI	525	1.1 ★			
1997: Lab				6,156	13.2			

Hartlepool [304]

68,164	55.8	Mandelson, P.B.†	Lab	22,506	59.1		–	1.6
		Robinson, A.A.	Con	7,935	20.9		–	0.5
		Boddy, N.F.H.	LD	5,717	15.0		+	1.0
		Scargill, A.	SL	912	2.4 ★			
		Cameron, I.J.H.	Ind	557	1.5 ★			
		Booth, J.R.		424	1.1 ★			
1997: Lab				14,571	38.3			

Harwich [305]

77,509	62.1	Henderson, I.J.†	Lab	21,951	45.6	+ 6.9
		Sproat, I.M.	Con	19,355	40.2	+ 3.7
		Wilcock, P.A.	LD	4,099	8.5	- 4.6
		Finnegan-Butler, A.C.	UKI	2,463	5.1	
		Lawrance, C.R.	Ind	247	0.5 ★	
1997: Lab				2,596	5.4	

Hastings & Rye [306]

70,734	58.3	Foster, M.J.†	Lab	19,402	47.1	+ 12.7
		Coote, M.S.	Con	15,094	36.6	+ 7.5
		Peters, G.	LD	4,266	10.3	- 17.6
		Coomber, A.R.	UKI	911	2.2 ★	+ 1.2
		Phillips, S.	Grn	721	1.7 ★	
		Bargery, G.E.	Ind	486	1.2 ★	
		Ord-Clarke, J.	MRLP	198	0.5 ★	
		McLean, B.R.	RRL	140	0.3 ★	
1997: Lab				4,308	10.5	

Havant [307]

70,246	57.6	Willetts, D.L.†	Con	17,769	43.9	+ 4.2
		Guthrie, P.C.	Lab	13,562	33.5	+ 1.5
		Cole, C.H.	LD	7,508	18.6	- 3.8
		Jacks, K.M.	Grn	793	2.0 ★	
		Cuell, T.J.	UKI	561	1.4 ★	
		Stanley, R.	Ind	244	0.6 ★	
1997: Con				4,207	10.4	

Hayes & Harlington [308]

57,561	56.3	McDonnell, J.M.†	Lab	21,279	65.7	+ 3.7
		McLean, R.L.	Con	7,813	24.1	- 3.1
		Boethe, N.	LD	1,958	6.0	- 1.4
		Burch, G.	BNP	705	2.2 ★	
		Kennedy, W.D.	S Alt	648	2.0 ★	
1997: Lab				13,466	41.6	

Hazel Grove [309]

65,105	59.1	Stunell, A.†	LD	20,020	52.0	- 2.5
		Bargery, N.V.	Con	11,585	30.1	- 0.4
		Miller, M.	Lab	6,230	16.2	+ 4.3
		Price, G.	UKI	643	1.7 ★	+ 1.1
1997: LD				8,435	21.9	

Hemel Hempstead [310]

73,602	62.3	McWalter, T.†	Lab	21,389	46.6	+	0.9
		Ivey, P.C.	Con	17,647	38.5	−	0.6
		Stuart, N.	LD	5,877	12.8	+	0.5
		Newton, B.	UKI	970	2.1 ★		
1997: Lab				3,742	8.2		

Hemsworth [311]

67,946	51.8	Trickett, J.H.†	Lab	23,036	65.4	−	5.2
		Truss, E.	Con	7,400	21.0	+	3.2
		Waller, E.J.	LD	3,990	11.3	+	2.5
		Turek, P.W.	SL	801	2.3 ★		
1997: Lab				15,636	44.4		

Hendon [312]

78,213	52.2	Dismore, A.H.†	Lab	21,432	52.5	+	3.1
		Evans, R.G.	Con	14,015	34.3	−	2.7
		Casey, W.J.	LD	4,724	11.6	+	0.7
		Crosbie, J.C.	UKI	409	1.0 ★	+	0.5
		Taylor, S.	WRP	164	0.4 ★		
		Stewart, M.M.	PD	107	0.3 ★		
1997: Lab				7,417	18.2		

Henley [313]

69,081	64.3	Johnson, A.B.	Con	20,466	46.1	−	0.3
		Bearder, C.Z.	LD	12,008	27.0	+	2.3
		Matthews, J.	Lab	9,367	21.1	−	1.6
		Collings, P.M.M.	UKI	1,413	3.2 ★		
		Tickell, O.T.	Grn	1,147	2.6 ★	+	1.6
1997: Con				8,458	19.0		

Hereford [314]

68,468	65.2	Keetch, P.S.†	LD	18,244	40.9	−	7.1
		Taylor, V.F.M.	Con	17,276	38.7	+	3.4
		Hallam, D.J.A.	Lab	6,739	15.1	+	2.6
		Easton, C.G.	UKI	1,184	2.7 ★		
		Gillett, D.B.	Grn	1,181	2.6 ★		
1997: LD				968	2.2		

Hertford & Stortford [315]

75,794	62.2	Prisk, M.	Con	21,074	44.7	+	0.6
		Speller, S.	Lab	15,471	32.8	+	1.4
		Goldspink, M.H.	LD	9,388	19.9	+	2.2
		Rising, S.F.	UKI	1,243	2.6 ★	+	0.4
1997: Con				5,603	11.9		

Hertfordshire North East [316]

68,718	65.0	Heald, O.†	Con	19,695	44.1	+	2.4
		Gibbons, I.A.	Lab	16,251	36.4	+	0.6
		Kingman, A.E.	LD	7,686	17.2	–	1.0
		Virgo, M.J.	UKI	1,013	2.3 ★		
1997: Con				3,444	7.7		

Hertfordshire South West [317]

73,247	64.5	Page, R.L.†	Con	20,933	44.3	–	1.7
		Dale, G.W.	Lab	12,752	27.0	–	0.9
		Featherstone, E.H.	LD	12,431	26.3	+	4.0
		Dale-Mills, C.	UKI	847	1.8 ★		
		Goffin, J.E.	PL	306	0.6 ★		
1997: Con				8,181	17.3		

Hertsmere [318]

68,853	60.3	Clappison, W.J.†	Con	19,855	47.8	+	3.5
		Broderick, H.J.	Lab	14,953	36.0	–	2.2
		Thompson, P.G.	LD	6,300	15.2	+	2.3
		Dry, J.D.	SL	397	1.0 ★		
1997: Con				4,902	11.8		

Hexham [319]

59,810	70.9	Atkinson, P.L.†	Con	18,917	44.6	+	5.8
		Brannen, P.	Lab	16,388	38.6	+	0.4
		Latham, P.R.	LD	6,380	15.0	–	2.4
		Patterson, A.H.	UKI	728	1.7 ★	–	0.8
1997: Con				2,529	6.0		

Heywood & Middleton [320]

73.005	53.1	Dobbin, J.†	Lab	22,377	57.7	–	0.0
		Hopkins, M.	Con	10,707	27.6	+	4.6
		Greenhalgh, I.	LD	4,329	11.2	–	4.5
		Burke, P.	Lib	1,021	2.6 ★		
		West, C.M.	CD	345	0.9 ★		
1997: Lab				11,670	30.1		

High Peak [321]

73,833	65.2	Levitt, T.†	Lab	22,430	46.6	− 4.2
		Chapman, S.C.	Con	17,941	37.3	+ 1.8
		Ashenden, P.J.	LD	7,743	16.1	+ 4.9
1997: Lab				4,489	9.3	

Hitchin & Harpenden [322]

67,196	66.9	Lilley, P.B.†	Con	21,271	47.3	+ 1.5
		Amos, A.T.	Lab	14,608	32.5	− 0.6
		Murphy, J.C.	LD	8,076	18.0	− 2.1
		Saunders, J.G.C.	UKI	606	1.3 ★	
		Rigby, P.E.	Ind	363	0.8 ★	
1997: Con				6,663	14.8	

Holborn & St Pancras [323]

62,722	49.6	Dobson, F.G.†	Lab	16,770	53.9	− 11.1
		Green, N.J.	LD	5,595	18.0	+ 5.5
		Serrelli, R.	Con	5,258	16.9	− 1.0
		Whitley, R.	Grn	1,875	6.0	
		Udwin, C.	SA	971	3.1 ★	
		Brar, N.	SL	359	1.2 ★	
		Nielsen, M.	UKI	301	1.0 ★	
1997: Lab				11,175	35.9	

Hornchurch [324]

61,008	58.3	Cryer, J.R.†	Lab	16,514	46.4	− 3.8
		Squire, R.C.	Con	15,032	42.3	+ 5.0
		Lea, S.	LD	2,928	8.2	+ 0.4
		Webb, L.J.	UKI	893	2.5 ★	
		Durant, D.	TW	190	0.5 ★	
1997: Lab				1,482	4.2	

Hornsey & Wood Green [325]

75,974	58.0	Roche, B.M.†	Lab	21,967	49.9	− 11.9
		Featherstone, L.C.	LD	11,353	25.8	+ 14.5
		Hollands, J.D.	Con	6,921	15.7	− 6.2
		Forbes, J.E.	Grn	2,228	5.1	+ 2.7
		Christian, L.	SA	1,106	2.5 ★	
		Rule, E.J.	SL	294	0.7 ★	
		Ataman, E.	Ref	194	0.4 ★	
1997: Lab				10,614	24.1	

Horsham [326]

79,604	63.8	Maude, F.A.A.†	Con	26,134	51.5	+	0.7
		Carr, J.H.	LD	12,468	24.6	–	0.2
		Sully, J.C.	Lab	10,267	20.2	+	1.5
		Miller, H.	UKI	1,472	2.9 ★	+	1.5
		Duggan, J.J.		429	0.8 ★		
1997: Con				13,666	26.9		

Houghton & Washington East [327]

67,946	49.5	Kemp, F.†	Lab	24,628	73.2	–	3.2
		Devenish, A.S.	Con	4,810	14.3	+	1.4
		Ormerod, R.D.	LD	4,203	12.5	+	4.8
1997: Lab				19,818	58.9		

Hove [328]

71,320	58.9	Caplin, I.K.†	Lab	19,253	45.9	+	1.3
		Langston, J.	Con	16,082	38.3	+	1.9
		De Souza, H.	LD	3,823	9.1	–	0.5
		Ballam, A.P.	Grn	1,369	3.3 ★	+	1.9
		Richards, A.K.	SA	531	1.3 ★		
		Franklin, R.K	UKI	358	0.9 ★	+	0.4
		Donovan, N.R.	Lib	316	0.8 ★		
		Dobbshead, S.	FP	196	0.5 ★		
		Major, T.S.	Ind	60	0.1 ★		
1997: Lab				3,171	7.6		

Huddersfield [329]

64,350	55.0	Sheerman, B.†	Lab	18,840	53.2	–	3.2
		Baverstock, P.A.	Con	8,794	24.9	+	3.9
		Bentley, N.D.	LD	5,300	15.0	–	2.2
		Phillips, J.L.	Grn	1,254	3.5 ★	+	1.4
		Longman, J.	UKI	613	1.7 ★		
		Hellawell, G.	SA	374	1.1 ★		
		Randall, G.M.	SL	208	0.6 ★		
1997: Lab				10,046	28.4		

Hull East [330]

66,397	46.5	Prescott, J.L.†	Lab	19,938	64.6	–	6.7
		Swinson, J.	LD	4,613	14.9	+	5.1
		Verma, S.	Con	4,276	13.8	+	0.1
		Jenkinson, J.	UKI	1,218	3.9 ★		
		Muir, L.	SL	830	2.7 ★		
1997: Lab				15,325	49.6		

Hull North [331]

62,938	45.5	McNamara, K.†	Lab	16,364	57.2	–	8.7
		Butterworth, S.	LD	5,643	19.7	+	5.1
		Charlson, P.B.	Con	4,902	17.1	+	2.1
		Robinson, T.S.	UKI	655	2.3 ★		
		Smith, R.	SA	490	1.7 ★		
		Wagner, C.A.	LCA	478	1.7 ★		
		Veasey, C.M.	Ind	101	0.4 ★		
1997: Lab				10,721	37.4		

Hull West & Hessle [332]

63,035	45.9	Johnson, A.A.†	Lab	16,880	58.4	–	0.3
		Sharp, J.C.	Con	5,929	20.5	+	2.4
		Wastling, A.E.	LD	4,364	15.1	–	3.1
		Cornforth, J.H.	UKI	878	3.0 ★		
		Harris, D.W.	Ind	512	1.8 ★		
		Skinner, D.E.	SL	353	1.2 ★		
1997: Lab				10,951	37.9		

Huntingdon [333]

80,335	61.1	Djanogly, J.S.	Con	24,507	49.9	–	5.4
		Pope, M.R.	LD	11,715	23.9	+	9.1
		Sulaiman, T.E.	Lab	11,211	22.8	–	0.6
		Norman, D.A.	UKI	1,656	3.4 ★	+	2.8
1997: Con				12,792	26.1		

Hyndburn [334]

66,533	57.5	Pope, G.J.†	Lab	20,900	54.7	–	0.9
		Britcliffe, P.	Con	12,681	33.2	+	1.3
		Greene, W.L.	LD	3,680	9.6	+	1.0
		Tomlin, J.C.	UKI	982	2.6 ★		
1997: Lab				8,219	21.5		

Ilford North [335]

68,893	58.4	Perham, L.†	Lab	18,428	45.8	–	1.6
		Bendall, V.W.H.	Con	16,313	40.5	–	0.2
		Stollar, G.P.	LD	4,717	11.7	+	1.4
		Levin, M.	UKI	776	1.9 ★		
1997: Lab				2,115	5.3		

Ilford South [336]

76,025	54.3	Gapes, M.J.†	Lab	24,619	59.6	+	1.1
		Kumar, S.	Con	10,622	25.7	–	4.4
		Scott, R.J.	LD	4,647	11.3	+	5.0
		Khan, H.	UKI	1,407	3.4 ★		
1997: Lab				13,997	33.9		

Inverness East, Nairn & Lochaber [337]

66,452	63.9	Stewart, D.J.†	Lab	15,605	36.8	+	2.9
		MacNeil, A.B.	SNP	10,889	25.6	–	3.3
		Kenton, M.P.	LD	9,420	22.2	+	4.7
		Jenkins, R.W.A.H.	Con	5,653	13.3	–	4.2
		Arnott, S.	SSP	892	2.1 ★		
1997: Lab				4,716	11.1		

Ipswich [338]

68,198	57.0	Cann, J.C.†	Lab	19,952	51.3	–	1.4
		Wild, W.E.	Con	11,871	30.5	–	0.6
		Gilbert, T.A.	LD	5,904	15.2	+	3.0
		Vinyard, W.J.	UKI	624	1.6 ★	+	1.2
		Leech, P.J.J.	SA	305	0.8 ★		
		Gratton, S.C.	SL	217	0.6 ★		
1997: Lab				8,081	20.8		

Isle of Wight [339]

104,431	60.8	Turner, A.J.	Con	25,223	39.7	+	5.7
		Brand, P.†	LD	22,397	35.3	–	7.5
		Gardiner, D.	Lab	9,676	15.2	+	2.1
		Lott, D.C.	UKI	2,106	3.3 ★	+	1.9
		Holmes, D.L.	Ind	1,423	2.2 ★		
		Scivier, P.K.	Grn	1,279	2.0 ★	+	1.3
		Murray, P.	IOW	1,164	1.8 ★		
		Spensley, J.L.	SL	214	0.3 ★		
1997: LD				2,826	4.5		

Islington North [340]

61,970	48.8	Corbyn, J.B.†	Lab	18,699	61.9	–	7.4
		Willoughby, L.	LD	5,741	19.0	+	5.4
		Rands, N.D.G.	Con	3,249	10.8	–	2.2
		Ashby, C.	Grn	1,876	6.2	+	2.0
		Cook, S.R.	SL	512	1.7 ★		
		Hassan, E.	Ref	139	0.5 ★		
1997: Lab				12,958	42.9		

Islington South & Finsbury [341]

59,516	47.4	Smith, C.R.†	Lab	15,217	53.9	− 8.6
		Sharp, K.	LD	7,937	28.1	+ 6.8
		Morgan, N.A.	Con	3,860	13.7	+ 0.7
		Booth, J.S.	SA	817	2.9 ★	
		McCarthy, T.J.	Ind	276	1.0 ★	
		Thomson, C.G.	St	108	0.4 ★	
1997: Lab				7,280	25.8	

Islwyn [342]

51,230	61.9	Touhig, J.D.†	Lab	19,505	61.5	− 12.6
		Etheridge, K.	LD	4,196	13.2	+ 4.8
		Thomas, L.	PC	3,767	11.9	+ 5.6
		Howells, P.B.	Con	2,543	8.0	+ 0.2
		Taylor, P.		1,263	4.0 ★	
		Millington, M.E.	SL	417	1.3 ★	
1997: Lab				15,309	48.3	

Jarrow [343]

62,631	55.1	Hepburn, S.†	Lab	22,777	66.1	+ 1.2
		Selby, J.	LD	5,182	15.0	+ 4.0
		Wood, D.	Con	5,056	14.7	− 0.3
		Badger, A.	UKI	716	2.1 ★	
		Le Blond, A.J.	Ind	391	1.1 ★	
		Bissett, J.		357	1.0 ★	
1997: Lab				17,595	51.0	

Keighley [344]

68,330	63.4	Cryer, C.A.†	Lab	20,888	48.2	− 2.4
		Cooke, A.S.	Con	16,883	39.0	+ 2.2
		Doyle, M.P.	LD	4,722	10.9	+ 1.1
		Cassidy, M.	UKI	840	1.9 ★	
1997: Lab				4,005	9.2	

Kensington & Chelsea [345]

64,707	43.3	Portillo, M.D.X.†	Con	15,270	54.5	+ 0.8
		Stanley, S.H.F.	Lab	6,499	23.2	− 4.8
		Falkner, K.	LD	4,416	15.8	+ 0.5
		Stephenson, J.C.	Grn	1,158	4.1 ★	
		Hockney, N.R.A.D.	UKI	416	1.5 ★	+ 0.0
		Quintavalle, J.M.	PL	179	0.6 ★	
		Crab, G.	JWP	100	0.4 ★	
1997: Con				8,771	31.3	

Kettering [346]

78,946	68.1	Sawford, P.A.†	Lab	24,034	44.7	+	1.4
		Hollobone, P.T.	Con	23,369	43.5	+	0.5
		Aron, R.J.	LD	5,469	10.2	–	0.5
		Mahoney, B.	UKI	880	1.6 ★		
1997: Lab				665	1.2		

Kilmarnock & Loudoun [347]

61,048	61.7	Browne, D.H.†	Lab	19,926	52.9	+	3.1
		Brady, J.	SNP	9,592	25.5	–	9.1
		Reece, D.H.	Con	3,943	10.5	–	0.3
		Stewart, J.D.	LD	3,177	8.4	+	4.4
		Muir, J.	SSP	1,027	2.7 ★		
1997: Lab				10,334	27.4		

Kingston & Surbiton [348]

72,687	67.5	Davey, E.J.†	LD	29,542	60.2	+23.5	
		Shaw, D.L.	Con	13,866	28.2	– 8.3	
		Woodford, P.J.	Lab	4,302	8.8	–14.3	
		Spruce, C.J.	Grn	572	1.2 ★		
		Burns, A.P.M.	UKI	438	0.9 ★	+ 0.1	
		Hayball, J.D.	SL	319	0.6 ★		
		Middleton, J.St.J.	UPP	54	0.1 ★		
1997: LD				15,676	31.9		

Kingswood [349]

81,602	64.6	Berry, R.L.†	Lab	28,903	54.9	+	1.1
		Marven, R.	Con	14,941	28.4	–	1.6
		Greenfield, C.J.	LD	7,747	14.7	+	1.9
		Smith, D.	UKI	1,085	2.1 ★		
1997: Lab				13,962	26.5		

Kirkcaldy [350]

51,559	54.6	Moonie, L.G.†	Lab	15,227	54.1	+	0.5
		Somerville, S-A.	SNP	6,264	22.2	–	0.7
		Campbell, S.	Con	3,013	10.7	–	3.0
		Weston, A.W.	LD	2,849	10.1	+	1.5
		Kinnear, D.	SSP	804	2.9 ★		
1997: Lab				8,963	31.8		

Knowsley North & Sefton East [351]

70,781	53.0	Howarth, G.E.†	Lab	25,035	66.7	− 3.2
		Chapman, K.A.	Con	6,108	16.3	− 1.0
		Roberts, R.J.	LD	5,173	13.8	+ 2.7
		Waugh, R.	SL	574	1.5 ★	
		Rossiter, T.L.	Ind	356	0.9 ★	
		Jones, D.A.	Ind	271	0.7 ★	
1997: Lab				18,927	50.4	

Knowsley South [352]

70,681	51.8	O'Hara, E.†	Lab	26,071	71.3	− 5.9
		Smithson, D.J.G.	LD	4,755	13.0	+ 4.7
		Jemetta, P.S.	Con	4,250	11.6	− 1.0
		Fogg, A.D.	SL	1,068	2.9 ★	
		McNee, M.M.	Ind	446	1.2 ★	
1997: Lab				21,316	58.3	

Lagan Valley [353]

72,671	63.2	Donaldson, J.M.†	UU	25,966	56.5	+ 1.1
		Close, S.A.	APNI	7,624	16.6	− 0.6
		Poots, E.C.	DUP	6,164	13.4	− 0.1
		Lewsley, P.	SDLP	3,462	7.5	− 0.2
		Butler, P.A.	SF	2,725	5.9	+ 3.4
1997: UU				18,342	39.9	

Lancashire West [354]

73,046	58.8	Pickthall, C.†	Lab	23,404	54.5	− 5.9
		Myers, J.	Con	13,761	32.0	+ 3.0
		Thornton, J.L.	LD	4,966	11.6	+ 4.4
		Hill, D.	Ind	523	1.2 ★	
		Braid, D.O.	Ind	317	0.7 ★	
1997: Lab				9,643	22.4	

Lancaster & Wyre [355]

79,458	65.9	Dawson, T.H.†	Lab	22,556	43.1	+ 0.3
		Barclay, S.P.	Con	22,075	42.2	+ 1.6
		Scott, E.	LD	5,383	10.3	− 1.3
		Whitelegg, J.	Grn	1,595	3.0 ★	+ 1.7
		Whittaker, J.	UKI	741	1.4 ★	+ 0.2
1997: Lab				481	0.9	

Leeds Central [356]

65,497	41.7	Benn, H.J.†	Lab	18,277	66.9	– 2.7
		Richmond, V.M.	Con	3,896	14.3	+ 0.5
		Arnold, S.D.	LD	3,607	13.2	+ 2.0
		Burgess, D.	UKI	775	2.8 ★	
		Johnston, S.	SA	751	2.8 ★	
1997: Lab				14,381	52.7	

Leeds East [357]

56,400	51.5	Mudie, G.E.†	Lab	18,290	62.9	– 4.5
		Anderson, B.J.	Con	5,647	19.4	+ 0.8
		Jennings, B.D.T.	LD	3,923	13.5	+ 3.2
		Northgreaves, R.	UKI	634	2.2 ★	
		King, M.A.	SL	419	1.4 ★	
		Socrates, P.L.B.		142	0.5 ★	
1997: Lab				12,643	43.5	

Leeds North East [358]

64,123	62.0	Hamilton, F.†	Lab	19,540	49.1	– 0.0
		Rhys, O.M.	Con	12,451	31.3	– 2.6
		Brown, J.M.	LD	6,325	15.9	+ 2.0
		Foote, C.	LA	770	1.9 ★	
		Miles, J.M.	UKI	382	1.0 ★	
		Muir, C.	SL	173	0.4 ★	
		Zaman, M.S.	Ind	132	0.3 ★	
1997: Lab				7,089	17.8	

Leeds North West [359]

72,945	58.2	Best, H.†	Lab	17,794	41.9	+ 2.0
		Pritchard, A.J.	Con	12,558	29.6	– 2.5
		Hall-Matthews, D.	LD	11,431	26.9	+ 3.3
		Jones, S.C.	UKI	668	1.6 ★	
1997: Lab				5,236	12.3	

Leeds West [360]

64,218	50.0	Battle, J.†	Lab	19,943	62.1	– 4.5
		Hopkins, K.F.	Con	5,008	15.6	– 1.9
		Finlay, D.	LD	3,350	10.4	+ 1.4
		Blackburn, D.	Grn	2,573	8.0	+ 5.8
		Finley, W.	UKI	758	2.4 ★	
		Nowosielski, N.A.B.	Lib	462	1.4 ★	
1997: Lab				14,935	46.5	

Leicester East [361]

65,526	62.1	Vaz, K.†	Lab	23,402	57.6	– 7.9
		Mugglestone, J.V.	Con	9,960	24.5	+ 0.5
		Athwal, H.	LD	4,989	12.3	+ 5.3
		Roberts, D.P.	SL	837	2.1 ★	
		Potter, C.	BNP	772	1.9 ★	
		Bennett, S.	Ind	701	1.7 ★	
1997: Lab				13,442	33.1	

Leicester South [362]

72,674	58.0	Marshall, J.†	Lab	22,958	54.5	– 3.5
		Hoile, R.D.	Con	9,715	23.1	– 0.7
		Gill, P.S.	LD	7,243	17.2	+ 3.4
		Layton, M.J.	Grn	1,217	2.9 ★	
		Gardner, A.	SL	676	1.6 ★	
		Ladwa, K.	UKI	330	0.8 ★	
1997: Lab				13,243	31.4	

Leicester West [363]

65,267	50.9	Hewitt, P.H.†	Lab	18,014	54.2	– 1.0
		Shaw, T.C.D.	Con	8,375	25.2	+ 1.5
		Vincent, A.K.	LD	5,085	15.3	+ 1.1
		Gough, M.J.C.	Grn	1,074	3.2 ★	+ 1.8
		Kirkpatrick, S.A.	SL	350	1.1 ★	
		Score, S.D.	SA	321	1.0 ★	
1997: Lab				9,639	29.0	

Leicestershire North West [364]

68,414	65.8	Taylor, D.L.†	Lab	23,431	52.1	– 4.3
		Weston, N.P.	Con	15,274	33.9	+ 3.0
		Fraser-Fleming, C.D.	LD	4,651	10.3	+ 1.7
		Nattrass, W.H.	UKI	1,021	2.3 ★	
		Nettleton, R.A.	Ind	632	1.4 ★	
1997: Lab				8,157	18.1	

Leigh [365]

71,054	49.7	Burnham, A.M.	Lab	22,783	64.5	– 4.4
		Oxley, A.J.	Con	6,421	18.2	+ 2.6
		Atkins, R.G.	LD	4,524	12.8	+ 1.6
		Kelly, W.	SL	820	2.3 ★	
		Best, C.J.H.	UKI	750	2.1 ★	
1997: Lab				16,362	46.4	

Leominster [366]

67,317	69.4	Wiggin, W.D.	Con	22,879	49.0	+ 3.7
		Downie, C.M.	LD	12,512	26.8	− 1.0
		Hart, S.J.S.	Lab	7,872	16.8	− 0.6
		Bennett, P.	Grn	1,690	3.6 ★	+ 1.5
		Kingsley, C.R.	UKI	1,590	3.4 ★	+ 2.2
		Haycock, J.B.	Ind	186	0.4 ★	
1997: Con				10,367	22.2	

Lewes [367]

66,332	68.5	Baker, N.J.†	LD	25,588	56.3	+ 13.1
		Sinnatt, S.P.R.	Con	15,878	34.9	− 5.6
		Richards, P.A.	Lab	3,317	7.3	− 3.3
		Harvey, J.S.	UKI	650	1.4 ★	+ 0.9
1997: LD				9,710	21.4	

Lewisham Deptford [368]

60,275	48.3	Ruddock, J.M.†	Lab	18,915	65.0	− 5.8
		McCartney, C.E.J.	Con	3,622	12.4	− 2.3
		Wiseman, A.D.	LD	3,409	11.7	+ 2.8
		Johnson, D.P.	Grn	1,901	6.5	
		Page, I.G.	SA	1,260	4.3 ★	
1997: Lab				15,293	52.5	

Lewisham East [369]

56,657	53.1	Prentice, B.†	Lab	16,160	53.7	− 4.6
		McInnes, D.J.	Con	7,157	23.8	− 2.1
		Buxton, D.C.	LD	4,937	16.4	+ 5.2
		Roberts, B.J.	BNP	1,005	3.3 ★	
		Kysow, J.	SA	464	1.5 ★	
		Link, M.A.J.	UKI	361	1.2 ★	
1997: Lab				9,003	29.9	

Lewisham West [370]

59,176	52.1	Dowd, J.P.†	Lab	18,816	61.1	− 0.9
		Johnson, G.A.	Con	6,896	22.4	− 1.5
		Thomas, R.K.	LD	4,146	13.5	+ 3.7
		Pearson, F.G.	UKI	485	1.6 ★	
		Long, N.	Ind	472	1.5 ★	
1997: Lab				11,920	38.7	

Leyton & Wanstead [371]

61,549	54.8	Cohen, H.M.†	Lab	19,558	58.0	– 2.8
		Heckels, E.G.	Con	6,654	19.7	– 2.5
		Wilcock, A.I.M.C.	LD	5,389	16.0	+ 0.9
		Gunstock, A.	Grn	1,030	3.1 ★	
		Labern, S.A.	SA	709	2.1 ★	
		Skaife D'Ingerthorp, M.J.	UKI	378	1.1 ★	
1997: Lab				12,904	38.3	

Lichfield [372]

63,234	65.9	Fabricant, M.L.D.†	Con	20,480	49.1	+ 6.2
		Machray, M.E.	Lab	16,054	38.5	– 3.9
		Bennion, R.P.	LD	4,462	10.7	– 0.6
		Phazey, J.J.	UKI	684	1.6 ★	
1997: Con				4,426	10.6	

Lincoln [373]

66,299	56.0	Merron, G.J.†	Lab	20,003	53.9	– 1.0
		Talbot, C–A.	Con	11,583	31.2	+ 0.2
		Gabriel, L.M.	LD	4,703	12.7	+ 1.8
		Doughty, R.W.	UKI	836	2.3 ★	
1997: Lab				8,420	22.7	

Linlithgow [374]

54,603	58.0	Dalyell, T.†	Lab	17,207	54.4	+ 0.2
		Sibbald, J.G.M.	SNP	8,078	25.5	– 1.3
		Lindhurst, G.	Con	2,836	9.0	– 3.6
		Oliver, W.M.	LD	2,628	8.3	+ 2.4
		Cornoch, E.	SSP	695	2.2 ★	
		Cronin, H.D.	RRL	211	0.7 ★	
1997: Lab				9,129	28.8	

Liverpool Garston [375]

65,094	50.2	Eagle, M.†	Lab	20,043	61.4	+ 0.1
		Keaveney, P.C.	LD	7,549	23.1	+ 4.1
		Sutton, H.C.	Con	5,059	15.5	– 0.2
1997: Lab				12,494	38.3	

Liverpool Riverside [376]

74,827	34.1	Ellman, L.J.†	Lab	18,201	71.4	+ 0.9
		Marbrow, R.D.	LD	4,251	16.7	+ 3.4
		Edwards, J.C.	Con	2,142	8.4	– 1.1
		Wilson, C.	SA	909	3.6 ★	
1997: Lab				13,950	54.7	

Liverpool Walton [377]

66,237	43.0	Kilfoyle, P.†	Lab	22,143	77.8	- 0.6
		Reid, K.J.C.	LD	4,147	14.6	+ 3.4
		Horgan, S.	Con	1,726	6.1	- 0.3
		Forrest, P.I.J.	UKI	442	1.6 ★	
1997: Lab				17,996	63.2	

Liverpool Wavertree [378]

72,555	44.3	Kennedy, J.E.†	Lab	20,155	62.7	- 1.7
		Newby, C.	LD	7,836	24.4	+ 2.8
		Allen, G.S.	Con	3,091	9.6	- 1.1
		Lane, M.J.	SL	359	1.1 ★	
		O'Brien, M.T.	SA	349	1.1 ★	
		Miney, N.L.	UKI	348	1.1 ★	
1997: Lab				12,319	38.3	

Liverpool West Derby [379]

67,921	45.5	Wareing, R.N.†	Lab	20,454	66.2	- 5.0
		Radford, S.R.	Lib	4,601	14.9	
		Moloney, P.	LD	3,366	10.9	+ 1.9
		Clare, W.G.	Con	2,486	8.0	- 0.6
1997: Lab				15,853	51.3	

Livingston [380]

64,852	55.6	Cook, R.†	Lab	19,108	53.0	- 1.9
		Sutherland, G.D.	SNP	8,492	23.6	- 3.9
		Mackenzie, G.F.	LD	3,969	11.0	+ 4.3
		Mowat, I.A.M.	Con	2,995	8.3	- 1.1
		Milne, W.M.	SSP	1,110	3.1 ★	
		Kingdon, R.M.	UKI	359	1.0 ★	
1997: Lab				10,616	29.5	

Llanelli [381]

58,148	62.3	Davies, D.J.D.†	Lab	17,586	48.6	- 9.3
		Jones, D.R.	PC	11,183	30.9	+ 11.9
		Hayes, S.A.	Con	3,442	9.5	- 2.6
		Rees, K.D.	LD	3,065	8.5	- 0.7
		Cliff, J.M.	Grn	515	1.4 ★	
		Willock, J.	SL	407	1.1 ★	
1997: Lab				6,403	17.7	

Londonderry East [382]

60,215	66.2	Campbell, G.L.	DUP	12,813	32.1	+ 6.5
		Ross, W.†	UU	10,912	27.4	- 8.2
		Dallat, J.J.	SDLP	8,298	20.8	- 0.9
		Brolly, F.R.G.	SF	6,221	15.6	+ 6.5
		Boyle, Y.	APNI	1,625	4.1 ★	- 2.3
1997: UU				1,901	4.8	

Loughborough [383]

70,078	63.1	Reed, A.J.†	Lab	22,016	49.7	+ 1.2
		Lyon, N.B.	Con	15,638	35.3	- 2.4
		Simons, J.	LD	5,667	12.8	+ 1.0
		Bigger, J.E.	UKI	933	2.1 ★	
1997: Lab				6,378	14.4	

Louth & Horncastle [384]

71,556	62.1	Tapsell, P.H.B.†	Con	21,543	48.5	+ 5.0
		Bolland, D.J.	Lab	13,989	31.5	+ 1.8
		Martin, F.M.	LD	8,928	20.1	- 4.4
1997: Con				7,554	17.0	

Ludlow [385]

63,514	67.9	Green, M.R.	LD	18,620	43.2	+ 13.5
		Taylor-Smith, M.A.	Con	16,990	39.4	- 3.0
		Knowles, N.	Lab	5,785	13.4	- 12.0
		Gaffney, J.E.	Grn	871	2.0 ★	+ 0.3
		Gutteridge, P.G.L.	UKI	858	2.0 ★	+ 1.2
1997: Con				1,630	3.8	

Luton North [386]

67,554	57.9	Hopkins, K.P.†	Lab	22,187	56.7	+ 2.1
		Sater, A.J.	Con	12,210	31.2	- 3.1
		Hoyle, B.	LD	3,795	9.7	+ 0.6
		Brown, C.D.	UKI	934	2.4 ★	+ 0.9
1997: Lab				9,977	25.5	

Luton South [387]

71,439	55.1	Moran, M.†	Lab	21,719	55.2	+	0.3
		Henderson, G.	Con	11,586	29.4	-	1.9
		Martins, R.F.	LD	4,292	10.9	+	1.3
		Scheimann, M.	Grn	798	2.0 ★	+	1.3
		Lawman, C.S.	UKI	578	1.5 ★	+	0.7
		Hearne, J.H.J.	SA	271	0.7 ★		
		Bolton, R.I.	WRP	107	0.3 ★		
1997: Lab				10,133	25.8		

Macclesfield [388]

73,123	62.3	Winterton, N.R.†	Con	22,284	48.9	-	0.7
		Carter, S.F.	Lab	15,084	33.1	-	0.6
		Flynn, F.M.	LD	8,217	18.0	+	1.3
1997: Con				7,200	15.8		

Maidenhead [389]

69,837	62.0	May, T.M.†	Con	19,506	45.0	-	4.8
		Newbound, K.D.	LD	16,222	37.4	+	11.2
		O'Farrell, J.P.	Lab	6,577	15.2	-	2.9
		Cooper, D.R.	UKI	741	1.7 ★	+	1.2
		Clarke, L.	MRLP	272	0.6 ★		
1997: Con				3,284	7.6		

Maidstone & The Weald [390]

74,002	61.6	Widdecombe, A.N.†	Con	22,621	49.6	+	5.5
		Davis, M.O.	Lab	12,303	27.0	+	0.8
		Wainman, A.J.	LD	9,064	19.9	-	2.5
		Botting, J.M.	UKI	978	2.1 ★	+	1.5
		Hunt, N.	Ind	611	1.3 ★		
1997: Con				10,318	22.6		

Makerfield [391]

68,457	50.9	McCartney, I.†	Lab	23,879	68.5	-	5.1
		Brooks, J.	Con	6,129	17.6	+	2.2
		Crowther, D.	LD	3,990	11.4	+	3.1
		Jones, M.J.	SA	858	2.5 ★		
1997: Lab				17,750	50.9		

Maldon & Chelmsford East [392]

70,252	62.8	Whittingdale, J.F.L.†	Con	21,719	49.2		+	0.6
		Kennedy, R.J.	Lab	13,257	30.1		+	1.3
		Jackson, J.M.	LD	7,002	15.9		−	3.5
		Harris, G.	UKI	1,135	2.6	★	+	0.7
		Schwarz, W.	Grn	987	2.2	★	+	0.9
1997: Con				8,462	19.2			

Manchester Blackley [393]

59,111	44.9	Stringer, G.E.†	Lab	18,285	68.9		−	1.1
		Stanbury, L.G.	Con	3,821	14.4		−	0.8
		Riding, G.A.	LD	3,015	11.4		+	0.4
		Barr, K.G.H.	SL	485	1.8	★		
		Reissmann, K.J.	SA	461	1.7	★		
		Bhatti, A.A.	AC	456	1.7	★		
1997: Lab				14,464	54.5			

Manchester Central [394]

66,268	39.1	Lloyd, A.J.†	Lab	17,812	68.7		−	2.3
		Hobson, P.A.D.	LD	4,070	15.7		+	3.4
		Powell, A.J.	Con	2,328	9.0		−	2.8
		Hall, V.	Grn	1,018	3.9	★		
		Sinclair, R.	SL	484	1.9	★		
		Brosnan, T.M.	PL	216	0.8	★		
1997: Lab				13,742	53.0			

Manchester Gorton [395]

63,834	42.7	Kaufman, G.B.†	Lab	17,099	62.8		−	2.5
		Pearcey, J.	LD	5,795	21.3		+	3.8
		Causer, C.G.	Con	2,705	9.9		−	1.8
		Bingham, B.S.	Grn	835	3.1	★	+	1.2
		Bhatti, R.A.	UKI	462	1.7	★		
		Muir, K.	SL	333	1.2	★		
1997: Lab				11,304	41.5			

Manchester Withington [396]

67,480	51.9	Bradley, K.J.C.†	Lab	19,239	54.9		−	6.7
		Zalzala, Y.	LD	7,715	22.0		+	8.4
		Samways, J.P.E.	Con	5,349	15.3		−	4.1
		Valentine, M.	Grn	1,539	4.4	★		
		Clegg, J.A.	SA	1,208	3.4	★		
1997: Lab				11,524	32.9			

Mansfield [397]

66,765	55.2	Meale, J.A.†	Lab	21,050	57.1	– 7.3
		Wellesley, W.V.	Con	10,012	27.2	+ 6.0
		Hill, T.J.	LD	5,790	15.7	+ 4.7
1997: Lab				11,038	30.0	

Medway [398]

64,934	59.5	Marshall-Andrews, R.G.†	Lab	18,914	49.0	+ 0.1
		Reckless, M.J.	Con	15,134	39.2	+ 2.3
		Juby, G.W.	LD	3,604	9.3	– 0.8
		Sinclaire, N.C.	UKI	958	2.5 ★	+ 1.6
1997: Lab				3,780	9.8	

Meirionnydd Nant Conwy [399]

32,969	63.9	Llwyd, E.†	PC	10,459	49.6	– 1.1
		Jones, D.I.	Lab	4,775	22.7	– 0.4
		Francis, E.A.	Con	3,962	18.8	+ 2.8
		Raw-Rees, D.	LD	1,872	8.9	+ 1.9
1997: PC				5,684	27.0	

Meriden [400]

73,787	60.4	Spelman, C.A.†	Con	21,246	47.7	+ 5.7
		Shawcroft, C.L.	Lab	17,462	39.2	– 1.8
		Hicks, N.S.	LD	4,941	11.1	– 1.9
		Adams, R.W.	UKI	910	2.0 ★	
1997: Con				3,784	8.5	

Merthyr Tydfil & Rhymney [401]

54,919	57.7	Havard, D.S.	Lab	19,574	61.8	– 14.9
		Hughes, R.	PC	4,651	14.7	+ 8.7
		Rogers, S.K.	LD	2,385	7.5	+ 0.1
		Cuming, R.A.	Con	2,272	7.2	+ 0.8
		Edwards, J.	Ind	1,936	6.1	
		Evans, K.	SL	692	2.2 ★	
		Lewis, A.	PL	174	0.5 ★	
1997: Lab				14,923	47.1	

Middlesbrough [402]

67,662	49.8	Bell, S.†	Lab	22,783	67.6	− 3.9
		Finn, A.W.G.G.	Con	6,453	19.1	+ 2.0
		Miller, K.	LD	3,512	10.4	+ 1.9
		Kerr-Morgan, G.	SA	577	1.7 ★	
		Andersen, K.	SL	392	1.2 ★	
1997: Lab				16,330	48.4	

Middlesbrough South & Cleveland East [403]

72,104	61.0	Kumar, A.†	Lab	24,321	55.3	+ 0.6
		Harpham, B.A.	Con	14,970	34.0	− 0.9
		Parrish, L.J.	LD	4,700	10.7	+ 3.2
1997: Lab				9,351	21.3	

Midlothian [404]

48,625	59.1	Hamilton, D.	Lab	15,145	52.7	− 0.8
		Goldie, I.R.	SNP	6,131	21.3	− 4.2
		Bell, J.D.	LD	3,686	12.8	+ 3.7
		Traquair, R.J.	Con	2,748	9.6	− 1.3
		Goupillot, R.P.	SSP	837	2.9 ★	
		Holden, T.J.E.	PL	177	0.6 ★	
1997: Lab				9,014	31.4	

Milton Keynes North East [405]

72,909	64.6	White, B.A.R.†	Lab	19,761	42.0	+ 2.5
		Rix, M.J.	Con	17,932	38.1	− 0.9
		Yeoward, D.J.	LD	8,375	17.8	+ 0.4
		Phillips, M.S.	UKI	1,026	2.2 ★	
1997: Lab				1,829	3.9	

Milton Keynes South West [406]

72,823	62.3	Starkey, P.M.†	Lab	22,484	49.5	− 4.2
		Stewart, I.A.	Con	15,506	34.2	+ 0.7
		Mohammad, N.	LD	4,828	10.6	− 1.3
		Francis, A.H.	Grn	957	2.1 ★	
		Davies, C.W.	UKI	848	1.9 ★	
		Denning, P.T.	LCA	500	1.1 ★	
		Bradbury, D.C.	SA	261	0.6 ★	
1997: Lab				6,978	15.4	

Mitcham & Morden [407]

65,671	57.8	McDonagh, S.A.†	Lab	22,936	60.4	+	2.1
		Stokes, H.A.A.	Con	9,151	24.1	−	5.6
		Harris, N.P.	LD	3,820	10.1	+	2.5
		Walsh, T.J	Grn	926	2.4 ★	+	1.6
		Tyndall, J.H.	BNP	642	1.7 ★		
		Roberts, A.K.J.	UKI	486	1.3 ★	+	1.0
1997: Lab				13,785	36.3		

Mole Valley [408]

68,316	68.9	Beresford, P.A.†	Con	23,790	50.5	+	2.5
		Savage, C.E.	LD	13,637	29.0	−	0.3
		Redford, D.	Lab	7,837	16.6	+	1.9
		Walters, R.G.	UKI	1,333	2.8 ★	+	2.0
		Newton, W.	PL	475	1.0 ★		
1997: Con				10,153	21.6		

Monmouth [409]

62,200	71.5	Edwards, H.W.E.†	Lab	19,021	42.8	−	5.0
		Evans, R.K.	Con	18,637	41.9	+	2.7
		Parker, N.M.	LD	5,080	11.4	+	1.9
		Hubbard, M.A.	PC	1,068	2.4 ★	+	1.3
		Rowlands, D.J.	UKI	656	1.5 ★		
1997: Lab				384	0.9		

Montgomeryshire [410]

44,243	65.5	Opik, L.†	LD	14,319	49.4	+	3.5
		Jones, D.R.	Con	8,085	27.9	+	1.8
		Davies, P.M.	Lab	3,443	11.9	−	7.3
		Senior, D.H.	PC	1,969	6.8	+	1.8
		Rowlands, D.W.L.	UKI	786	2.7 ★		
		Davies, R.G.	PL	210	0.7 ★		
		Taylor, R.		171	0.6 ★		
1997: LD				6,234	21.5		

Moray [411]

57,898	57.4	Robertson, A.	SNP	10,076	30.3	−	11.2
		Munro, C.M.	Lab	8,332	25.1	+	5.2
		Spencer-Nairn, C.F.	Con	7,677	23.1	−	4.5
		Gorn, L.J.	LD	5,224	15.7	+	6.8
		Anderson, N.C.	SSP	821	2.5 ★		
		Jappy, W.	Ind	802	2.4 ★		
		Kenyon, C.N.	UKI	291	0.9 ★		
1997: SNP				1,744	5.2		

Morecambe & Lunesdale [412]

68,159	61.1	Smith, G.†	Lab	20,646	49.6	+ 0.7
		Nuttall, D.J.	Con	15,554	37.3	+ 0.6
		Cotton, C.M.	LD	3,817	9.2	- 2.2
		Beaman, G.R.	UKI	935	2.2 ★	
		Adams, C.M.	Grn	703	1.7 ★	
1997: Lab				5,092	12.2	

Morley & Rothwell [413]

71,815	53.5	Challen, C.R.	Lab	21,919	57.0	- 1.5
		Schofield, D.	Con	9,829	25.6	- 0.8
		Golton, B.S.	LD	5,446	14.2	+ 3.1
		Bardsley, J.H.	UKI	1,248	3.2 ★	
1997: Lab				12,090	31.4	

Motherwell & Wishaw [414]

52,418	56.6	Roy, F.†	Lab	16,681	56.2	- 1.2
		McGuigan, J.	SNP	5,725	19.3	- 3.2
		Nolan, M.	Con	3,155	10.6	- 0.4
		Brown, I.	LD	2,791	9.4	+ 3.0
		Smellie, S.	SSP	1,260	4.2 ★	
		Watt, C.	SL	61	0.2 ★	
1997: Lab				10,956	36.9	

Neath [415]

56,001	62.5	Hain, P.G.†	Lab	21,253	60.7	- 12.8
		Llewelyn, A.	PC	6,437	18.4	+ 10.3
		Davies, D.	LD	3,335	9.5	+ 3.2
		Devine, D.W.	Con	3,310	9.5	+ 0.8
		Pudner, H.	SA	483	1.4 ★	
		Brienza, G.	PL	202	0.6 ★	
1997: Lab				14,816	42.3	

New Forest East [416]

66,723	63.2	Lewis, J.M.†	Con	17,902	42.4	- 0.5
		Dash, B.D.	LD	14,073	33.4	+ 1.1
		Goodfellow, A.G.W.	Lab	9,141	21.7	- 3.1
		Howe, W.	UKI	1,062	2.5 ★	
1997: Con				3,829	9.1	

New Forest West [417]

67,725	65.1	Swayne, D.A.†	Con	24,575	55.7	+	5.2
		Bignell, M.G.	LD	11,384	25.8	–	2.0
		Onuegbu, C.	Lab	6,481	14.7	+	0.4
		Clark, M.J.	UKI	1,647	3.7 ★	+	0.6
1997: Con				13,191	29.9		

Newark [418]

71,061	63.5	Mercer, P.J.	Con	20,983	46.5	+	7.1
		Jones, F.E.A.†	Lab	16,910	37.5	–	7.8
		Harding-Price, D.	LD	5,970	13.2	+	1.8
		Haxby, D.L.	Ind	822	1.8 ★		
		Thomson, I.	SA	462	1.0 ★		
1997: Lab				4,073	9.0		

Newbury [419]

75,487	67.3	Rendel, D.D.†	LD	24,507	48.2	–	4.7
		Benyon, R.H.R.	Con	22,092	43.5	+	5.6
		Billcliffe, S.	Lab	3,523	6.9	+	1.4
		Gray-Fisk, D.I.	UKI	685	1.3 ★	+	0.8
1997: LD				2,415	4.8		

Newcastle-under-Lyme [420]

65,739	58.8	Farrelly, C.P.	Lab	20,650	53.4	–	3.1
		Flynn, M.J.	Con	10,664	27.6	+	6.1
		Roodhouse, J.M.	LD	5,993	15.5	+	1.5
		Fyson, R.C.M.	Ind	773	2.0 ★		
		Godfrey, T.P.H.	UKI	594	1.5 ★		
1997: Lab				9,986	25.8		

Newcastle upon Tyne Central [421]

67,970	51.3	Cousins, J.M.†	Lab	19,169	55.0	–	4.2
		Psallidas, S.A.	LD	7,564	21.7	+	6.7
		Ruff, A.P.	Con	7,414	21.3	–	2.2
		Potts, G.G.	SL	723	2.1 ★		
1997: Lab				11,605	33.3		

Newcastle upon Tyne East & Wallsend [422]

61,494	53.2	Brown, N.H.†	Lab	20,642	63.1	–	8.1
		Ord, D.	LD	6,419	19.6	+	9.0
		Troman, T.D.	Con	3,873	11.8	–	2.1
		Gray, A.J.P.	Grn	651	2.0 ★		
		Narang, H.K.	Ind	563	1.7 ★		
		Carpenter, B.	SL	420	1.3 ★		
		Levy, M.R.	Comm	126	0.4 ★		
1997: Lab				14,223	43.5		

Newcastle upon Tyne North [423]

63,208	57.5	Henderson, D.J.†	Lab	21,874	60.1	–	2.0
		Smith, P.R.	Con	7,424	20.4	+	1.0
		Soult, G.A.	LD	7,070	19.4	+	4.9
1997: Lab				14,450	39.7		

Newport East [424]

57,219	54.7	Howarth, A.T.†	Lab	17,120	54.7	–	2.9
		Oakley, I.	Con	7,246	23.2	+	1.8
		Cameron, A.R.	LD	4,394	14.0	+	3.6
		Batcup, M.R.	PC	1,519	4.9 ★	+	2.9
		Screen, E.A.	SL	420	1.3 ★		
		Reynolds, N.J.	UKI	410	1.3 ★		
		Griffiths, R.D.	Comm	173	0.6 ★		
1997: Lab				9,874	31.6		

Newport West [425]

59,345	59.1	Flynn, P.P.†	Lab	18,489	52.7	–	7.8
		Morgan, W.J.	Con	9,185	26.2	+	1.8
		Watkins, V.K.	LD	4,095	11.7	+	2.0
		Salkeld, A.M.	PC	2,510	7.2	+	5.5
		Moelwyn Hughes, H.	UKI	506	1.4 ★	+	0.6
		Cavill, T.	BNP	278	0.8 ★		
1997: Lab				9,304	26.5		

Newry and Armagh [426]

72,466	76.8	Mallon, S.†	SDLP	20,784	37.4	–	5.6
		Murphy, C.T.	SF	17,209	30.9	+	9.9
		Berry, P.L.	DUP	10,795	19.4		
		McRoberts, S.	UU	6,833	12.3	–	21.5
1997: SDLP				3,575	6.4		

Norfolk Mid [427]

77,158	68.1	Simpson, K.R.†	Con	23,519	44.8	+	5.2
		Zeichner, D.S.	Lab	18,957	36.1	-	1.2
		Clifford-Jackson, V.H.	LD	7,621	14.5	-	0.5
		Agnew, J.S.	UKI	1,333	2.5 ★		
		Reeve, P.H.	Grn	1,118	2.1 ★	-	0.1
1997: Con				4,562	8.7		

Norfolk North [428]

80,061	70.2	Lamb, N.P.	LD	23,978	42.7	+	8.4
		Prior, D.G.L.†	Con	23,495	41.8	+	5.3
		Gates, M.A.	Lab	7,490	13.3	-	11.7
		Sheridan, M.P.	Grn	649	1.2 ★		
		Simison, P.C.	UKI	608	1.1 ★		
1997: Con				483	0.9		

Norfolk North West [429]

78,707	65.1	Bellingham, H.C.	Con	24,846	48.5	+	7.0
		Turner, G.†	Lab	21,361	41.7	-	2.1
		Mack, I.J.	LD	4,292	8.4	-	1.2
		Durrant, A.F.I.	UKI	704	1.4 ★		
1997: Lab				3,485	6.8		

Norfolk South [430]

82,710	67.6	Bacon, R.M.	Con	23,589	42.2	+	2.0
		Lee, A.	LD	16,696	29.9	+	1.6
		Wells, M.A.	Lab	13,719	24.5	-	1.5
		Ross-Wagenknecht, S.	Grn	1,069	1.9 ★	+	1.1
		Neal, J.W.E.	UKI	856	1.5 ★	+	0.9
1997: Con				6,893	12.3		

Norfolk South West [431]

83,903	63.1	Shephard, G.P.†	Con	27,633	52.2	+	10.2
		Hanson, A.M.	Lab	18,267	34.5	-	3.3
		Dean, G.R.	LD	5,681	10.7	-	3.2
		Smith, I.J.	UKI	1,368	2.6 ★		
1997: Con				9,366	17.7		

Normanton [432]

65,395	52.2	O'Brien, W.†	Lab	19,152	56.1	– 4.5
		Smith, G.P.	Con	9,215	27.0	+ 3.4
		Pearson, S.J.	LD	4,990	14.6	+ 2.2
		Appleyard, T.M.	SL	798	2.3 ★	
1997: Lab				9,937	29.1	

Northampton North [433]

74,124	56.0	Keeble, S.C.†	Lab	20,507	49.4	– 3.3
		Whelan, J.A.	Con	12,614	30.4	– 3.0
		Church, R.W.	LD	7,363	17.7	+ 5.0
		Torbica, D.	UKI	596	1.4 ★	+ 0.5
		White, G.	SA	414	1.0 ★	
1997: Lab				7,893	19.0	

Northampton South [434]

85,668	59.6	Clarke, A.R.†	Lab	21,882	42.9	+ 0.5
		Vara, S.L.	Con	20,997	41.1	+ 0.0
		Simpson, A.S.J.	LD	6,355	12.5	+ 1.4
		Clark, D.R.	UKI	1,237	2.4 ★	+ 0.4
		Harvey, T.L.	LP	362	0.7 ★	
		Johnson, C.D.	PL	196	0.4 ★	
1997: Lab				885	1.7	

Northavon [435]

78,840	70.7	Webb, S.J.†	LD	29,217	52.4	+ 10.0
		Ruxton, C.H.	Con	19,340	34.7	– 4.3
		Hall, R.W.	Lab	6,450	11.6	– 4.1
		Carver, C.A.	UKI	751	1.3 ★	
1997: LD				9,877	17.7	

Norwich North [436]

77,158	59.1	Gibson, I.†	Lab	21,624	47.4	– 2.3
		Mason, K.F.	Con	15,761	34.6	+ 2.1
		Toye, M.P.	LD	6,750	14.8	+ 2.2
		Tinch, R.R.T.	Grn	797	1.7 ★	
		Cheyney, G.R.S.	UKI	471	1.0 ★	
		Betts, M.C.	Ind	211	0.5 ★	
1997: Lab				5,863	12.9	

Norwich South [437]

71,276	59.8	Clarke, C.R.†	Lab	19,367	45.5	–	6.2
		French, A.J.	Con	10,551	24.8	+	1.1
		Aalders-Dunthorne, A.P.	LD	9,640	22.6	+	4.0
		Holmes, A.St.J.	Grn	1,434	3.4 ★	+	1.9
		Buffry, A.	LCA	620	1.5 ★		
		Manningham, E.D.	SA	507	1.2 ★		
		Mills, T.A.G.	UKI	473	1.1 ★		
1997: Lab				8,816	20.7		

Nottingham East [438]

65,339	45.5	Heppell, J.†	Lab	17,530	59.0	–	3.3
		Allan, R.F.	Con	7,210	24.3	+	0.8
		Ball, T.S.	LD	3,874	13.0	+	2.9
		Radcliff, P.R.	SA	1,117	3.8 ★		
1997: Lab				10,320	34.7		

Nottingham North [439]

64,281	46.7	Allen, G.W.†	Lab	19,392	64.5	–	1.2
		Wright, M.J.	Con	7,152	23.8	+	3.5
		Lee, R.A.	LD	3,177	10.6	+	2.6
		Botham, A.G.	SL	321	1.1 ★		
1997: Lab				12,240	40.7		

Nottingham South [440]

73,049	50.1	Simpson, A.J.†	Lab	19,949	54.5	–	0.8
		Manning, W.S.	Con	9,960	27.2	–	0.5
		Mulloy, K.J.V.D.	LD	6,064	16.6	+	3.7
		Bartrop, D.R.	UKI	632	1.7 ★		
1997: Lab				9,989	27.3		

Nuneaton [441]

72,101	60.1	Olner, W.J.†	Lab	22,577	52.1	–	4.1
		Lancaster, J.M.	Con	15,042	34.7	+	3.8
		Ferguson, A.D.	LD	4,820	11.1	+	2.3
		James, B.N.	UKI	873	2.0 ★	+	1.6
1997: Lab				7,535	17.4		

Ochil [442]

57,554	61.3	O'Neill, M.J.†	Lab	16,004	45.3	+	0.3
		Brown, K.J.	SNP	10,655	30.2	−	4.2
		Campbell, A.	Con	4,235	12.0	−	2.6
		Edie, P.	LD	3,253	9.2	+	4.0
		Thompson, P.N.C.	SSP	751	2.1 ★		
		Approaching, F.G.	MRLP	405	1.1 ★		
1997: Lab				5,349	15.2		

Ogmore [443]

52,185	58.2	Powell, R .†	Lab	18,833	62.0		−11.9
		Pulman, A.	PC	4,259	14.0	+	7.0
		Lewis, I.R.	LD	3,878	12.8	+	3.6
		Hill, R.J.	Con	3,383	11.1	+	1.4
1997: Lab				14,574	48.0		

Old Bexley & Sidcup [444]

67,841	62.1	Conway, D.L.	Con	19,130	45.4	+	3.4
		Dickson, J.R.C.	Lab	15,785	37.5	+	2.4
		Ford, B.J.	LD	5,792	13.7	−	2.4
		Cronin, J.	UKI	1,426	3.4 ★	+	2.4
1997: Con				3,345	7.9		

Oldham East & Saddleworth [445]

74,511	61.0	Woolas, P.J.†	Lab	17,537	38.6	−	3.1
		Sykes, H.D.	LD	14,811	32.6	−	2.8
		Heeley, C.	Con	7,304	16.1	−	3.6
		Treacy, M.	BNP	5,091	11.2		
		Little, B.A.	UKI	677	1.5 ★		
1997: Lab				2,726	6.0		

Oldham West & Royton [446]

69,409	57.6	Meacher, M.H.†	Lab	20,441	51.2	−	7.6
		Reed, D.E.S.	Con	7,076	17.7	−	5.7
		Griffin, N.J.	BNP	6,552	16.4		
		Ramsbottom, M.S.	LD	4,975	12.4	+	0.6
		Roney, J.D.	Grn	918	2.3 ★		
1997: Lab				13,365	33.4		

Orkney & Shetland [447]

31,909	52.4	Carmichael, A.	LD	6,919	41.3	- 10.6
		Mochrie, R.I.	Lab	3,444	20.6	+ 2.3
		Firth, J.L.	Con	3,121	18.7	+ 6.4
		Mowat, J.R.	SNP	2,473	14.8	+ 2.1
		Andrews, P.M.	SSP	776	4.6 ★	
1997: LD				3,475	20.8	

Orpington [448]

78,853	64.6	Horam, J.R.†	Con	22,334	43.9	+ 3.3
		Maines, C.S.	LD	22,065	43.3	+ 7.7
		Purnell, C.A.	Lab	5,517	10.8	- 7.0
		Youles, J.B.	UKI	996	2.0 ★	+ 1.1
1997: Con				269	0.5	

Oxford East [449]

71,357	55.8	Smith, A.D.†	Lab	19,681	49.4	- 7.4
		Goddard, S.H.	LD	9,337	23.4	+ 8.7
		Potter, C.	Con	7,446	18.7	- 3.3
		Singh, P.	Grn	1,501	3.8 ★	+ 1.7
		Lister, J.R.W.	SA	708	1.8 ★	
		Gardner, P.P.	UKI	570	1.4 ★	+ 0.9
		Ahmed, F.	SL	274	0.7 ★	
		Hodge, L.J.	PL	254	0.6 ★	
		Mylvaganam, P.S.	Ind	77	0.2 ★	
1997: Lab				10,344	26.0	

Oxford West & Abingdon [450]

79,915	64.5	Harris, E.L.†	LD	24,670	47.8	+ 4.9
		Matts, E.St.J.	Con	15,485	30.0	- 2.6
		Kirk, G.	Lab	9,114	17.7	- 2.5
		Woodin, M.E.	Grn	1,423	2.8 ★	+ 1.6
		Watney, M.J.A.	UKI	451	0.9 ★	+ 0.5
		Shreeve, S.B.	Ind	332	0.6 ★	
		Twigger, R.P.I.	EC	93	0.2 ★	
1997: LD				9,185	17.8	

Paisley North [451]

47,994	56.6	Adams, K.†	Lab	15,058	55.5	− 4.0
		Adam, G.	SNP	5,737	21.1	− 0.8
		Hook, J.	LD	2,709	10.0	+ 3.0
		Stevenson, C.	Con	2,404	8.9	− 0.7
		Halfpenny, J.	SSP	982	3.6 ★	
		Graham, R.	PL	263	1.0 ★	
1997: Lab				9,321	34.3	

Paisley South [452]

53,351	57.2	Alexander, D.†	Lab	17,830	58.4	+ 0.9
		Lawson, B.	SNP	5,920	19.4	− 4.0
		O'Malley, B.	LD	3,178	10.4	+ 1.0
		Cossar, A.J.	Con	2,301	7.5	− 1.1
		Curran, F.	SSP	835	2.7 ★	+ 2.3
		Graham, P.M.	PL	346	1.1 ★	
		O'Donnell, T.K.	Ind	126	0.4 ★	
1997: Lab				11,910	39.0	

Pendle [453]

62,870	63.2	Prentice, G.†	Lab	17,729	44.6	− 8.7
		Skinner, R.E.G.	Con	13,454	33.9	+ 3.6
		Whipp, D.M.B.	LD	5,479	13.8	+ 2.2
		Jackson, C.M.	BNP	1,976	5.0 ★	
		Cannon, G.G.	UKI	1,094	2.8 ★	
1997: Lab				4,275	10.8	

Penrith & The Border [454]

68,605	64.5	Maclean, D.J.†	Con	24,302	54.9	+ 7.3
		Walker, K.G.	LD	9,625	21.8	− 4.9
		Boaden, M.W.	Lab	8,177	18.5	− 3.1
		Lowther, T.S.A.	UKI	938	2.1 ★	
		Gibson, M.	LCA	870	2.0 ★	
		Moffat, J.J.	Ind	337	0.8 ★	
1997: Con				14,677	33.2	

Perth [455]

61,497	61.5	Ewing, A.	SNP	11,237	29.7	− 6.7
		Smith, E.J.	Con	11,189	29.6	+ 0.3
		Dingwall, M.	Lab	9,638	25.5	+ 0.7
		Harris, V.	LD	4,853	12.8	+ 4.8
		Byrne, F.	SSP	899	2.4 ★	
1997: SNP				48	0.1	

Peterborough [456]

64,874	61.4	Brinton, H.R.†	Lab	17,975	45.1	–	5.2
		Jackson, S.J.	Con	15,121	38.0	+	2.8
		Sandford, J.N.	LD	5,761	14.5	+	3.8
		Fairweather, J.P.	UKI	955	2.4 ★	+	1.7
1997: Lab				2,854	7.2		

Plymouth Devonport [457]

73,666	56.6	Jamieson, D.C.†	Lab	24,322	58.3	–	2.6
		Glen, J.P.	Con	11,289	27.1	+	2.9
		Baldry, K.J.	LD	4,513	10.8	+	0.1
		Parker, M.H.	UKI	958	2.3 ★	+	1.4
		Staunton, A.N.	SA	334	0.8 ★		
		Hawkins, R.J.	SL	303	0.7 ★		
1997: Lab				13,033	31.2		

Plymouth Sutton [458]

68,438	57.1	Gilroy, L.†	Lab	19,827	50.7	+	0.6
		Colvile, O.N.	Con	12,310	31.5	+	1.2
		Connett, A.M.	LD	5,605	14.3	+	0.5
		Whitton, A.D.	UKI	970	2.5 ★	+	1.4
		Leary, H.A.	SL	361	0.9 ★		
1997: Lab				7,517	19.2		

Pontefract & Castleford [459]

63,183	49.7	Cooper, Y.†	Lab	21,890	69.7	–	6.0
		Singleton, P.A.	Con	5,512	17.6	+	4.0
		Paxton, W.	LD	2,315	7.4	+	0.0
		Burdon, H.J.	UKI	739	2.4 ★		
		Bolderson, T.	SL	605	1.9 ★		
		Gill, J.	SA	330	1.1 ★		
1997: Lab				16,378	52.2		

Pontypridd [460]

71,768	53.4	Howells, K.S.†	Lab	22,963	59.9	–	3.9
		Hancock, B.W.	PC	5,279	13.8	+	7.3
		Dailey, P.M.P.	Con	5,096	13.3	+	0.4
		Brooke, E.W.	LD	4,152	10.8	–	2.6
		Warry, S.M.	UKI	603	1.6 ★		
		Biddulph, J.A.	PL	216	0.6 ★		
1997: Lab				17,684	46.2		

Poole [461]

64,644	60.7	Syms, R.A.R.†	Con	17,710	45.1	+ 3.0
		Watt, D.T.	Lab	10,544	26.9	+ 5.3
		Westbrook, N.S.E.	LD	10,011	25.5	- 5.3
		Bass, J.	UKI	968	2.5 ★	+ 1.4
1997: Con				7,166	18.3	

Poplar & Canning Town [462]

76,009	44.9	Fitzpatrick, J.†	Lab	20,866	61.2	- 2.0
		Marr, R.A.	Con	6,758	19.8	+ 4.8
		Sugden, A.E.	LD	3,795	11.1	+ 0.8
		Borg, P.	BNP	1,733	5.1	
		Boomla, K.	SA	950	2.8 ★	
1997: Lab				14,108	41.4	

Portsmouth North [463]

64,256	57.4	Rapson, S.N.J.†	Lab	18,676	50.7	+ 3.5
		Day, C.J.	Con	13,542	36.7	- 0.9
		Sanders, D.	LD	3,795	10.3	- 0.3
		McCabe, W.	UKI	559	1.5 ★	+ 0.9
		Bundy, B.	Ind	294	0.8 ★	
1997: Lab				5,134	13.9	

Portsmouth South [464]

77,095	50.9	Hancock, M.T.†	LD	17,490	44.6	+ 5.1
		Warr, P.H.	Con	11,397	29.1	- 2.1
		Heaney, G.P.	Lab	9,361	23.9	- 1.4
		Molyneux, J.T.	SA	647	1.6 ★	
		Tarrant, M.N.A.	UKI	321	0.8 ★	+ 0.5
1997: LD				6,093	15.5	

Preseli Pembrokeshire [465]

54,283	67.8	Lawrence, J.R.†	Lab	15,206	41.3	- 6.9
		Crabb, S.	Con	12,260	33.3	+ 5.6
		Sinnett, D.R.	PC	4,658	12.7	+ 6.3
		Dauncey, A.J.	LD	3,882	10.6	- 2.5
		Bowen, P.A.	SL	452	1.2 ★	
		Jones, H.W.	UKI	319	0.9 ★	
1997: Lab				2,946	8.0	

Preston [466]

73,309	49.2	Hendrick, M.P.†	Lab	20,540	57.0	– 3.8
		O'Hare, G.	Con	8,272	23.0	+ 1.0
		Chadwick, W.D.	LD	4,746	13.2	– 1.5
		Patel, B.M.	Ind	1,241	3.4 ★	
		Merrick, R.J.	Grn	1,019	2.8 ★	
		Braid, D.O.	Ind	223	0.6 ★	
1997: Lab				12,268	34.0	

Pudsey [467]

71,405	63.3	Truswell, P.A.†	Lab	21,717	48.1	– 0.0
		Procter, J.M.	Con	16,091	35.6	– 0.7
		Boddy, S.P.	LD	6,423	14.2	+ 0.2
		Sewards, D.	UKI	944	2.1 ★	
1997: Lab				5,626	12.5	

Putney [468]

60,643	56.5	Colman, A.J.†	Lab	15,911	46.5	+ 0.8
		Simpson, M.R.E.	Con	13,140	38.4	– 0.5
		Burrett, A.K.	LD	4,671	13.6	+ 2.9
		Wild, P.A.	UKI	347	1.0 ★	+ 0.5
		Windsor, Y.M.C.	PL	185	0.5 ★	
1997: Lab				2,771	8.1	

Rayleigh [469]

70,653	60.5	Francois, M.G.	Con	21,434	50.1	+ 0.4
		Clark, P.	Lab	13,144	30.7	+ 1.8
		Williams, G.	LD	6,614	15.5	– 4.3
		Morgan, C.R.	UKI	1,581	3.7 ★	
1997: Con				8,290	19.4	

Reading East [470]

74,637	58.4	Griffiths, J.P.†	Lab	19,538	44.8	+ 2.1
		Tanswell, B.J.	Con	13,943	32.0	– 3.2
		Dobrashian, T.	LD	8,078	18.5	– 0.0
		Kennet, M.F.	Grn	1,053	2.4 ★	
		Thornton, A.L.	UKI	525	1.2 ★	+ 0.7
		Williams, D.J.	SA	394	0.9 ★	
		Hammerson, P.R.	Ind	94	0.2 ★	
1997: Lab				5,595	12.8	

Reading West [471]

71,089	59.1	Salter, M.J.†	Lab	22,300	53.1	+	8.0
		Reid, S.H.	Con	13,451	32.0	-	6.9
		Martin, P.	LD	5,387	12.8	+	0.1
		Black, D.M.	UKI	848	2.0 ★	+	1.5
1997: Lab				8,849	21.1		

Redcar [472]

67,798	56.3	Baird, V.	Lab	23,026	60.3	-	7.1
		Main, C.D.R.	Con	9,583	25.1	+	2.0
		Wilson, S.W.	LD	4,817	12.6	+	3.1
		Taylor, J.R.	SL	772	2.0 ★		
1997: Lab				13,443	35.2		

Redditch [473]

62,565	59.2	Smith, J.J.†	Lab	16,899	45.6	-	4.2
		Lumley, K.E.	Con	14,415	38.9	+	2.8
		Ashall, M.R.	LD	3,808	10.3	-	0.7
		Flynn, G.S.	UKI	1,259	3.4 ★		
		Armstrong, R.K.	Grn	651	1.8 ★		
1997: Lab				2,484	6.7		

Regent's Park & Kensington North [474]

75,886	48.8	Buck, K.P.†	Lab	20,247	54.6	-	5.3
		Wilson, P.D.	Con	9,981	26.9	-	2.0
		Boyle, D.C.	LD	4,669	12.6	+	4.1
		Miller, P.A.	Grn	1,268	3.4 ★		
		Mieville, C.	SA	459	1.2 ★		
		Crisp, A.G.	UKI	354	1.0 ★		
		Regan, C.E.		74	0.2 ★		
1997: Lab				10,266	27.7		

Reigate [475]

65,618	60.2	Blunt, C.J.R.†	Con	18,875	47.8	+	4.0
		Charleton, S.P.	Lab	10,850	27.5	-	0.3
		Kulka, J.N.	LD	8,330	21.1	+	1.1
		Smith, S.P.	UKI	1,062	2.7 ★	+	2.1
		Green, H.S.	RUK	357	0.9 ★		
1997: Con				8,025	20.3		

Renfrewshire West [476]

52,889	63.3	Sheridan, J.	Lab	15,720	46.9	+	0.4
		Puthucheary, C.	SNP	7,145	21.3	–	5.2
		Sharpe, D.J.	Con	5,522	16.5	–	2.1
		Hamblen, C.A.	LD	4,185	12.5	+	4.8
		Nunnery, A.	SSP	925	2.8 ★		
1997: Lab				8,575	25.6		

Rhondda [477]

56,121	60.6	Bryant, C.J.	Lab	23,230	68.3	–	6.1
		Wood, L.	PC	7,183	21.1	+	7.8
		Hobbins, P.J.	Con	1,557	4.6 ★	+	0.8
		Cox, G.C.	LD	1,525	4.5 ★	–	1.2
		Summers, G.J.	Ind	507	1.5 ★		
1997: Lab				16,047	47.2		

Ribble South [478]

73,794	62.5	Borrow, D.S.†	Lab	21,386	46.4	–	0.4
		Owens, A.E.	Con	17,584	38.1	+	0.5
		Alcock, M.L.	LD	7,150	15.5	+	4.9
1997: Lab				3,802	8.2		

Ribble Valley [479]

74,319	66.2	Evans, N.M.†	Con	25,308	51.5	+	4.8
		Carr, M.	LD	14,070	28.6	–	6.4
		Johnstone, M.	Lab	9,793	19.9	+	4.2
1997: Con				11,238	22.9		

Richmond (Yorks) [480]

65,360	67.4	Hague, W.J.†	Con	25,951	58.9	+	10.1
		Tinnion, F.	Lab	9,632	21.9	–	5.9
		Forth, T.E.	LD	7,890	17.9	–	0.5
		Staniforth, M.E.	MRLP	561	1.3 ★		
1997: Con				16,319	37.1		

Richmond Park [481]

72,251	68.0	Tonge, J.L.†	LD	23,444	47.7	+	3.0
		Harris, T.O.C.	Con	18,480	37.6	–	1.9
		Langford, B.F.	Lab	5,541	11.3	–	1.3
		Page, J.R.	Grn	1,223	2.5 ★		
		St. John Howe, P.	UKI	348	0.7 ★		
		Perrin, R.A.	Ind	115	0.2 ★		
1997: LD				4,964	10.1		

Rochdale [482]

69,506	56.7	Fitzsimons, L.†	Lab	19,406	49.2	- 0.2
		Rowen, P.	LD	13,751	34.9	- 5.1
		Cohen, E.	Con	5,274	13.4	+ 4.6
		Harvey, N.A.L.	Grn	728	1.8 ★	
		Salim, M.		253	0.6 ★	
1997: Lab				5,655	14.3	

Rochford & Southend East [483]

71,005	52.7	Taylor, E.M.†	Con	20,058	53.6	+ 4.8
		Dandridge, C.R.	Lab	13,024	34.8	- 4.9
		Newton, S.C.	LD	2,780	7.4	- 2.0
		Hedges, A.J.	Grn	990	2.6 ★	
		Lynch, B.T.	Lib	600	1.6 ★	
1997: Con				7,034	18.8	

Romford [484]

59,893	59.6	Rosindell, A.R.	Con	18,931	53.0	+11.4
		Gordon, E.†	Lab	12,954	36.3	- 6.9
		Meyer, N.L.	LD	2,869	8.0	+ 0.1
		Ward, S.P.	UKI	533	1.5 ★	
		McAllister, F.	BNP	414	1.2 ★	
1997: Lab				5,977	16.7	

Romsey [485]

72,128	67.2	Gidley, S.J.†	LD	22,756	47.0	+17.5
		Raynes, P.J.E.	Con	20,386	42.1	- 3.9
		Roberts, S.J.	Lab	3,986	8.2	-10.3
		McCabe, A.M.	UKI	730	1.5 ★	- 2.0
		Large, D.G.	LCA	601	1.2 ★	
1997: Con				2,370	4.9	

Ross, Skye & Inverness West [486]

55,915	62.3	Kennedy, C.P.†	LD	18,832	54.1	+15.4
		Crichton, D.F.	Lab	5,880	16.9	-11.8
		Urquhart, J.	SNP	4,901	14.1	- 5.5
		Laing, A.W.	Con	3,096	8.9	- 2.0
		Scott, E.R.	Grn	699	2.0 ★	+ 1.2
		Topp, S.L.	SSP	683	2.0 ★	
		Anderson, P.A.	UKI	456	1.3 ★	
		Crawford, J.	Country	265	0.8 ★	
1997: LD				12,952	37.2	

Rossendale & Darwen [487]

70,884	58.7	Anderson, J.†	Lab	20,251	48.7	– 5.0
		Lee, G.A.	Con	15,281	36.7	+ 4.5
		Dunning, B.F.	LD	6,079	14.6	+ 4.0
1997: Lab				4,970	11.9	

Rother Valley [488]

69,174	53.2	Barron, K.J.†	Lab	22,851	62.1	– 5.5
		Duddridge, J.P.	Con	7,969	21.7	+ 5.0
		Knight, W.I.	LD	4,603	12.5	+ 0.9
		Cutts, D.	UKI	1,380	3.7 ★	
1997: Lab				14,882	40.4	

Rotherham [489]

57,931	50.7	MacShane, D.†	Lab	18,759	63.9	– 7.4
		Powell, R.	Con	5,682	19.4	+ 5.1
		Hall, A.C.	LD	3,117	10.6	+ 0.2
		Griffith, P.C.	UKI	730	2.5 ★	
		Penycate, R.W.	Grn	577	2.0 ★	
		Smith, F.	SA	352	1.2 ★	
		Bartholomew, G.C.	JLDP	137	0.5 ★	
1997: Lab				13,077	44.5	

Roxburgh & Berwickshire [490]

47,515	60.6	Kirkwood, A.J.†	LD	14,044	48.8	+ 2.3
		Turnbull, G.P.	Con	6,533	22.7	– 1.2
		Maxwell Stuart, C.	Lab	4,498	15.6	+ 0.7
		Campbell, R.A.M.	SNP	2,806	9.7	– 1.6
		Millar, A.J.	SSP	463	1.6 ★	
		Neilson, P.T.	UKI	453	1.6 ★	+ 1.0
1997: LD				7,511	26.1	

Rugby & Kenilworth [491]

79,764	67.4	King, A.†	Lab	24,221	45.0	+ 2.0
		Martin, D.J.P.	Con	21,344	39.7	– 2.6
		Fairweather, G.	LD	7,444	13.8	– 0.4
		Garratt, P.J.	UKI	787	1.5 ★	
1997: Lab				2,877	5.3	

Ruislip Northwood [492]

60,788	61.1	Wilkinson, J.A.D.†	Con	18,115	48.8	–	1.5
		Travers, G.M.	Lab	10,578	28.5	–	4.4
		Cox, M.F.	LD	7,177	19.3	+	3.1
		Lee, G.J.	Grn	724	1.9 ★		
		Edward, I.	BNP	547	1.5 ★		
1997: Con				7,537	20.3		

Runnymede & Weybridge [493]

75,569	56.1	Hammond, P.†	Con	20,646	48.7	+	0.1
		Briginshaw, J.R.	Lab	12,286	29.0	–	0.5
		Bushill, C.S.	LD	6,924	16.3	+	0.0
		Browne, C.A.	UKI	1,332	3.1 ★	+	1.9
		Gilman, C.E.L.	Grn	1,238	2.9 ★		
1997: Con				8,360	19.7		

Rushcliffe [494]

81,847	66.5	Clarke, K.H.†	Con	25,869	47.5	+	3.1
		Fallon, P.J.	Lab	18,512	34.0	–	2.2
		Hargreaves, J.A.	LD	7,395	13.6	–	0.7
		Browne, J.K.	UKI	1,434	2.6 ★	+	2.0
		Baxter, A.J.	Grn	1,236	2.3 ★		
1997: Con				7,357	13.5		

Rutland & Melton [495]

73,264	64.2	Duncan, A.J.C.†	Con	22,621	48.1	+	2.3
		O'Callaghan, M.	Lab	14,009	29.8	+	0.8
		Lee, K.	LD	8,386	17.8	–	1.4
		Baker, P.C.J.	UKI	1,223	2.6 ★	+	1.0
		Davies, C.J.	Grn	817	1.7 ★		
1997: Con				8,612	18.3		

Ryedale [496]

66,849	65.7	Greenway, J.R.†	Con	20,711	47.2	+	3.4
		Orrell, J.K.	LD	15,836	36.1	+	2.7
		Ellis, D.B.	Lab	6,470	14.7	–	3.2
		Feaster, S.	UKI	882	2.0 ★	+	0.1
1997: Con				4,875	11.1		

Saffron Walden [497]

76,724	65.2	Haselhurst, A.G.B.†	Con	24,485	48.9	+ 3.6
		Tealby-Watson, E.D.S.	LD	12,481	24.9	− 1.9
		Rogers, T.	Lab	11,305	22.6	+ 1.1
		Glover, R.	UKI	1,769	3.5 ★	+ 2.4
1997: Con				12,004	24.0	

St Albans [498]

66,040	66.3	Pollard, K.P.†	Lab	19,889	45.4	+ 3.4
		Elphicke, C.B.A.	Con	15,423	35.2	+ 2.0
		Rijke, N.D.	LD	7,847	17.9	− 3.1
		Sherwin, C.A.	UKI	602	1.4 ★	
1997: Lab				4,466	10.2	

St Helens North [499]

71,313	52.7	Watts, D.L.†	Lab	22,977	61.1	− 3.8
		Pearce, S.N.C.	Con	7,076	18.8	+ 1.5
		Beirne, J.	LD	6,609	17.6	+ 4.8
		Whatham, S.J.	SL	939	2.5 ★	
1997: Lab				15,901	42.3	

St Helens South [500]

65,741	51.4	Woodward, S.A.†	Lab	16,799	49.7	− 18.9
		Spencer, B.T.	LD	7,814	23.1	+ 9.7
		Rotherham, L.S.	Con	4,675	13.8	− 1.1
		Thompson, N.	SA	2,325	6.9	
		Perry, M.R.	SL	1,504	4.4 ★	
		Slater, B.H.	UKI	336	1.0 ★	
		Murphy, M.A.	Ind	271	0.8 ★	
		Braid, D.O.	Ind	80	0.2 ★	
1997: Lab				8,985	26.6	

St Ives [501]

74,256	66.3	George, A.H.†	LD	25,413	51.6	+ 7.1
		Richardson, J.M.	Con	15,360	31.2	+ 0.0
		Morris, W.	Lab	6,567	13.3	− 1.9
		Faulkner, M.P.	UKI	1,926	3.9 ★	+ 2.9
1997: LD				10,053	20.4	

Salford [502]

54,152	41.6	Blears, H.A.†	Lab	14,649	65.1	– 3.9
		Owen, N.	LD	3,637	16.2	+ 5.9
		King, C.J.	Con	3,446	15.3	– 2.1
		Grant, P.M.	SA	414	1.8 ★	
		Wallace, S.H.	Ind	216	1.0 ★	
		Masterson, R.	Ind	152	0.7 ★	
1997: Lab				11,012	48.9	

Salisbury [503]

80,527	65.3	Key, S.R.†	Con	24,527	46.6	+ 3.7
		Emmerson-Peirce, Y.L.	LD	15,824	30.1	– 2.1
		Mallory, S.	Lab	9,199	17.5	– 0.1
		Wood, C.M.	UKI	1,958	3.7 ★	– 2.0
		Soutar, H.D.	Grn	1,095	2.1 ★	+ 1.0
1997: Con				8,703	16.5	

Scarborough & Whitby [504]

75,213	63.2	Quinn, L.W.†	Lab	22,426	47.2	+ 1.6
		Sykes, J.D.	Con	18,841	39.6	+ 3.4
		Pearce, T.H.	LD	3,977	8.4	– 5.8
		Dixon, J.M.	Grn	1,049	2.2 ★	
		Jacob, J.H.	UKI	970	2.0 ★	
		Murray, T.B.	PL	260	0.5 ★	
1997: Lab				3,585	7.5	

Scunthorpe [505]

59,367	56.6	Morley, E.A.†	Lab	20,096	59.8	– 0.6
		Theobald, B.A.	Con	9,724	28.9	+ 2.6
		Tress, R.D.	LD	3,156	9.4	+ 1.0
		Cliff, M.J.W.		347	1.0 ★	
		Patterson, D.A.	Ind	302	0.9 ★	
1997: Lab				10,372	30.8	

Sedgefield [506]

64,925	62.0	Blair, A.C.L..†	Lab	26,110	64.9	– 6.3
		Carswell, J.D.W.	Con	8,397	20.9	+ 3.1
		Duffield, A.J.R.	LD	3,624	9.0	+ 2.5
		Spence, A.	UKI	974	2.4 ★	
		Gibson, B.	SL	518	1.3 ★	
		Driver, C.A.P.	RRL	375	0.9 ★	
		John, H.	Ind	260	0.6 ★	
1997: Lab				17,713	44.0	

Selby [507]

77,391	65.0	Grogan, J.†	Lab	22,652	45.1	– 0.8
		Mitchell, A.M.	Con	20,514	40.8	+ 1.7
		Wilcock, J.D.	LD	5,569	11.1	– 1.0
		Kenwright, H.M.N.	Grn	902	1.8 ★	
		Lewis, G.B.	UKI	635	1.3 ★	+ 0.3
1997: Lab				2,138	4.3	

Sevenoaks [508]

66,648	63.9	Fallon, M.C.†	Con	21,052	49.4	+ 4.0
		Humphreys, C.	Lab	10,898	25.6	+ 1.0
		Gray, C.J.	LD	9,214	21.6	– 2.5
		Hawkins, L.	UKI	1,155	2.7 ★	
		Ellis, M.C.	UKP	295	0.7 ★	
1997: Con				10,154	23.8	

Sheffield Attercliffe [509]

67,697	52.9	Betts, C.J.C.†	Lab	24,287	67.8	+ 2.5
		Perry, J.	Con	5,443	15.2	– 0.9
		Smith, G.	LD	5,092	14.2	– 1.5
		Arnott, P.E.	UKI	1,002	2.8 ★	
1997: Lab				18,844	52.6	

Sheffield Brightside [510]

54,134	47.2	Blunkett, D.†	Lab	19,650	76.9	+ 3.4
		Wilson, M.G.	Con	2,601	10.2	+ 1.8
		Firth, A.P.	LD	2,238	8.8	– 5.8
		Wilson, B.	SA	361	1.4 ★	
		Morris, R.J.	SL	354	1.4 ★	
		Suter, M.A.	UKI	348	1.4 ★	
1997: Lab				17,049	66.7	

Sheffield Central [511]

60,765	49.5	Caborn, R.G.†	Lab	18,477	61.4	– 2.2
		Qadar, A.	LD	5,933	19.7	+ 2.5
		Brelsford, N.	Con	3,289	10.9	– 1.0
		Little, B.	Grn	1,008	3.4 ★	+ 0.7
		Riley, N.	SA	754	2.5 ★	
		Hadfield, D.	SL	289	1.0 ★	
		Schofield, C.E.	UKI	257	0.9 ★	
		Driver, M.R.	WRP	62	0.2 ★	
1997: Lab				12,544	41.7	

Sheffield Hallam [512]

58,982	64.8	Allan, R.B.†	LD	21,203	55.4	+	4.1
		Harthman, J.P.	Con	11,856	31.0	−	2.1
		Furniss, G.	Lab	4,758	12.4	−	1.1
		Arnott, L.G.	UKI	429	1.1 ★		
1997: LD				9,347	24.4		

Sheffield Heeley [513]

61,949	55.1	Munn, M.P.	Lab	19,452	57.0	−	3.7
		Willis, D.G.	LD	7,748	22.7	+	1.4
		Abbott, C.	Con	4,864	14.2	−	1.4
		Unwin, R.D.	Grn	774	2.3 ★		
		Fischer, B.B.	SL	667	2.0 ★		
		Dunn, D.	UKI	634	1.9 ★		
1997: Lab				11,704	34.3		

Sheffield Hillsborough [514]

74,180	57.3	Jackson, H.M.†	Lab	24,170	56.8	−	0.0
		Commons, J.P.B.	LD	9,601	22.6	−	3.3
		King, G.	Con	7,801	18.3	+	3.8
		Webb, P.	UKI	964	2.3 ★		
1997: Lab				14,569	34.3		

Sherwood [515]

75,558	60.7	Tipping, S.P.†	Lab	24,900	54.2	−	4.3
		Lewis, B.K.	Con	15,527	33.8	+	5.1
		Harris, P.R.B.	LD	5,473	11.9	+	3.3
1997: Lab				9,373	20.4		

Shipley [516]

69,564	66.2	Leslie, C.M.†	Lab	20,243	44.0	+	0.6
		Senior, D.N.	Con	18,815	40.9	+	3.1
		Wright, H.	LD	4,996	10.9	−	4.2
		Love, M.J.	Grn	1,386	3.0 ★		
		Whitaker, W.	UKI	580	1.3 ★		
1997: Lab				1,428	3.1		

Shrewsbury & Atcham [517]

74,964	66.6	Marsden, P.W.B.†	Lab	22,253	44.6	+ 7.6
		McIntyre, A.E.J.	Con	18,674	37.4	+ 3.4
		Rule, J.D.	LD	6,173	12.4	- 12.6
		Curteis, H.M.T.	UKI	1,620	3.2 ★	+ 2.4
		Bullard, E.C.M.	Grn	931	1.9 ★	
		Gollins, J.G.	Ind	258	0.5 ★	
1997: Lab				3,579	7.2	

Shropshire North [518]

73,716	63.1	Paterson, O.W.†	Con	22,631	48.6	+ 8.4
		Ion, M.G.	Lab	16,390	35.2	- 0.7
		Jephcott, B.J.A.	LD	5,945	12.8	- 7.6
		Trevanion, D.H.	UKI	1,165	2.5 ★	
		Maxfield, R.	Ind	389	0.8 ★	
1997: Con				6,241	13.4	

Sittingbourne & Sheppey [519]

65,824	57.5	Wyatt, D.M.†	Lab	17,340	45.8	+ 5.2
		Lee, A.H.	Con	13,831	36.5	+ 0.2
		Lowe, E.H.	LD	5,353	14.1	- 4.2
		Young, M.J.	RRL	673	1.8 ★	
		Oakley, R.N.	UKI	661	1.7 ★	+ 0.7
1997: Lab				3,509	9.3	

Skipton & Ripon [520]

74,326	66.1	Curry, D.M.†	Con	25,736	52.4	+ 5.8
		Bateman, B.A.	LD	12,806	26.1	+ 0.9
		Dugher, M.V.	Lab	8,543	17.4	- 5.0
		Holdsworth, N.	UKI	2,041	4.2 ★	
1997: Con				12,930	26.3	

Sleaford & North Hykeham [521]

75,061	64.9	Hogg, D.M.†	Con	24,190	49.7	+ 5.7
		Donnelly, E.A.	Lab	15,568	32.0	- 2.3
		Arbon, R.	LD	7,894	16.2	+ 1.0
		Ward-Barrow, M.R.	UKI	1,067	2.2 ★	
1997: Con				8,622	17.7	

Slough [522]

73,008	53.4	Mactaggart, F.M.†	Lab	22,718	58.3	+	1.6
		Coad, D.V.	Con	10,210	26.2	-	3.1
		Kerr, K.K.K.	LD	4,109	10.5	+	3.2
		Haines, M.A.	Ind	859	2.2 ★		
		Lane, J.W.	UKI	738	1.9 ★		
		Nazir, C.S.	Ind	364	0.9 ★		
1997: Lab				12,508	32.1		

Solihull [523]

76,298	63.3	Taylor, J.M.†	Con	21,935	45.4	+	0.8
		Byron, J.M.	LD	12,528	26.0	+	0.7
		O'Brien, B.M.	Lab	12,373	25.6	+	1.3
		Moore, A.	UKI	1,061	2.2 ★		
		Pyne, S.M.	PL	374	0.8 ★		
1997: Con				9,407	19.5		

Somerton & Frome [524]

75,977	69.3	Heath, D.W.St.J.†	LD	22,983	43.6	+	4.1
		Marland, J.P.	Con	22,315	42.4	+	3.1
		Perkins, A.M.	Lab	6,113	11.6	-	4.7
		Bridgwood, P.J.	UKI	919	1.7 ★	+	1.2
		Pollock, J.	Lib	354	0.7 ★		
1997: LD				668	1.3		

South Holland & The Deepings [525]

74,390	62.1	Hayes, J.H.†	Con	25,611	55.4	+	6.2
		Walker, G.E.	Lab	14,512	31.4	-	1.9
		Hill, G.	LD	4,761	10.3	-	5.3
		Charlesworth, M.	UKI	1,318	2.9 ★		
1997: Con				11,099	24.0		

South Shields [526]

61,285	49.7	Miliband, D.W.	Lab	19,230	63.2	-	8.3
		Gardner, J.M.	Con	5,140	16.9	+	2.3
		Grainger, H.M.	LD	5,127	16.8	+	8.0
		Hardy, A.	UKI	689	2.3 ★		
		Nettleship, R.	Ind	262	0.9 ★		
1997: Lab				14,090	46.3		

Southampton Itchen [527]

76,557	54.0	Denham, J.Y.†	Lab	22,553	54.5	– 0.3
		Nokes, C.F.E.	Con	11,330	27.4	– 1.0
		Cooper, M.G.	LD	6,195	15.0	+ 3.3
		Rose, K.	UKI	829	2.0 ★	+ 1.7
		Marsh, G.L.C.A.	SA	241	0.6 ★	
		Holmes, M.A.	SL	225	0.5 ★	
1997: Lab				11,223	27.1	

Southampton Test [528]

73,840	56.3	Whitehead, A.P.V.†	Lab	21,824	52.5	– 1.7
		Gueterbock, R.S.	Con	10,617	25.5	– 2.5
		Shaw, J.D.	LD	7,522	18.1	+ 4.4
		Rankin-Moore, G.E.	UKI	792	1.9 ★	+ 1.5
		Abel, M.F.	SA	442	1.1 ★	
		Bahia, P.S.	SL	378	0.9 ★	
1997: Lab				11,207	27.0	

Southend West [529]

64,461	58.0	Amess, D.A.A.†	Con	17,313	46.3	+ 7.6
		Fisher, P.S.L.	Lab	9,372	25.1	+ 2.3
		De Ste Croix, R.	LD	9,319	24.9	– 8.2
		Lee, R.B.	UKI	1,371	3.7 ★	+ 2.3
1997: Con				7,941	21.2	

Southport [530]

70,202	58.6	Pugh, J.D.	LD	18,011	43.8	– 4.3
		Jones, L.C.	Con	15,004	36.5	+ 0.5
		Brant, P.D.	Lab	6,816	16.6	+ 4.4
		Green, D.W.	Lib	767	1.9 ★	
		Kelley, G.D.	UKI	555	1.3 ★	
1997: LD				3,007	7.3	

Southwark North & Bermondsey [531]

73,529	50.1	Hughes, S.H.W.†	LD	20,991	56.9	+ 8.3
		Abrams, K.J.	Lab	11,359	30.8	– 9.5
		Wallace, E.	Con	2,800	7.6	+ 0.6
		Jenkins, R.G.	Grn	752	2.0 ★	
		Shore, L.	NF	612	1.7 ★	
		McWhirter, R.	UKI	271	0.7 ★	
		Davies, J.P.		77	0.2 ★	
1997: LD				9,632	26.1	

Spelthorne [532]

68,731	60.8	Wilshire, D.†	Con	18,851	45.1	+	0.2
		Shaw, A.M.	Lab	15,589	37.3	-	0.9
		Rimmer, M.E.	LD	6,156	14.7	+	1.6
		Squire, R.P.F.	UKI	1,198	2.9 ★	+	2.0
1997: Con				3,262	7.8		

Stafford [533]

67,934	65.3	Kidney, D.N.†	Lab	21,285	48.0	+	0.4
		Cochrane, P.A.	Con	16,253	36.6	-	2.6
		Pinkerton, J.	LD	4,205	9.5	-	1.1
		Bradford, R.T.O.	UKI	2,315	5.2		
		Hames, M.D.	RRL	308	0.7 ★		
1997: Lab				5,032	11.3		

Staffordshire Moorlands [534]

66,760	63.9	Atkins, C.†	Lab	20,904	49.0	-	3.2
		Hayes, M.D.	Con	15,066	35.3	+	2.8
		Redfern, J.P.	LD	5,928	13.9	+	1.8
		Gilbert, P.	UKI	760	1.8 ★		
1997: Lab				5,838	13.7		

Staffordshire South [535]

69,959	60.3	Cormack, P.T.†	Con	21,295	50.5	+	0.5
		Kalinauckas, P.	Lab	14,414	34.2	-	0.5
		Harrison, J.K.	LD	4,891	11.6	+	0.3
		Lynch, M.J.	UKI	1,580	3.7 ★		
1997: Con				6,881	16.3		

Stalybridge & Hyde [536]

66,265	48.4	Purnell, J.M.D.	Lab	17,781	55.5	-	3.4
		Reid, A.R.	Con	8,922	27.8	+	3.3
		Jones, B.	LD	4,327	13.5	+	1.5
		Bennett, F.	UKI	1,016	3.2 ★		
1997: Lab				8,859	27.6		

Stevenage [537]

69,897	60.7	Follett, D.B.†	Lab	22,025	51.9	–	3.5
		Quar, G.B.	Con	13,459	31.7	–	1.1
		Davies, H.	LD	6,027	14.2	+	5.3
		Glennon, S.	SA	449	1.1 ★		
		Losonczi, A.	Ind	320	0.8 ★		
		Bell, S.T.A.	PL	173	0.4 ★		
1997: Lab				8,566	20.2		

Stirling [538]

53,097	67.7	McGuire, A.†	Lab	15,175	42.2	–	5.2
		Mawdsley, G.	Con	8,901	24.8	–	7.7
		Macaulay, F.E.	SNP	5,877	16.4	+	3.0
		Freeman, C.E.	LD	4,208	11.7	+	5.5
		Mullen, C.C.	SSP	1,012	2.8 ★		
		Ruskell, M.C.	Grn	757	2.1 ★		
1997: Lab				6,274	17.5		

Stockport [539]

66,395	53.3	Coffey, A.†	Lab	20,731	58.6	–	4.3
		Allen, J.A.	Con	9,162	25.9	+	3.6
		Hunter, M.J.	LD	5,490	15.5	+	4.9
1997: Lab				11,569	32.7		

Stockton North [540]

64,629	54.8	Cook, F.†	Lab	22,470	63.4	–	3.4
		Vigar, A.A.	Con	7,823	22.1	+	3.3
		Wallace, M.	LD	4,208	11.9	+	1.0
		Wennington, W.	Grn	926	2.6 ★		
1997: Lab				14,647	41.3		

Stockton South [541]

70,337	62.9	Taylor, D.J.†	Lab	23,414	53.0	–	2.3
		Devlin, T.R.	Con	14,328	32.4	–	0.6
		Fletcher, S.	LD	6,012	13.6	+	4.5
		Coombs, L.W.	SA	455	1.0 ★		
1997: Lab				9,086	20.6		

Stoke-on-Trent Central [542]

59,750	47.4	Fisher, M.†	Lab	17,170	60.6	–	5.6
		Clark, J.M.	Con	5,352	18.9	+	2.2
		Webb, G.G.	LD	4,148	14.6	+	2.7
		Wise, R.	Ind	1,657	5.8		
1997: Lab				11,818	41.7		

Stoke-on-Trent North [543]

57,998	51.9	Walley, J.L.†	Lab	17,460	58.0	− 7.2
		Browning, B.A.V.	Con	5,676	18.8	− 1.3
		Jebb, H.W.G.	LD	3,580	11.9	+ 1.2
		Wanger, C.L.	Ind	3,399	11.3	
1997: Lab				11,784	39.1	

Stoke-on-Trent South [544]

70,032	51.4	Stevenson, G.W.†	Lab	19,366	53.8	− 8.2
		Bastiman, P.D.	Con	8,877	24.6	+ 2.3
		Coleman, C.F.	LD	4,724	13.1	+ 2.9
		Knapper, A.M.	Ind	1,703	4.7 ★	
		Batkin, S.R.	BNP	1,358	3.8 ★	
1997: Lab				10,489	29.1	

Stone [545]

68,847	66.3	Cash, W.N.P.†	Con	22,395	49.1	+ 2.2
		Palfreyman, J.	Lab	16,359	35.8	− 3.8
		McKeown, B.	LD	6,888	15.1	+ 3.0
1997: Con				6,036	13.2	

Stourbridge [546]

64,610	61.8	Shipley, D.A.†	Lab	18,823	47.1	− 0.0
		Eyre, S.J.A.	Con	15,011	37.6	+ 1.8
		Bramall, C.	LD	4,833	12.1	− 2.2
		Knotts, J.M.	UKI	763	1.9 ★	
		Atherton, M.R.	SL	494	1.2 ★	
1997: Lab				3,812	9.5	

Strangford [547]

72,192	59.9	Robinson, I.	DUP	18,532	42.8	+ 12.6
		McNarry, D.	UU	17,422	40.3	− 4.0
		McCarthy, K.	APNI	2,902	6.7	− 6.4
		McCarthy, D.T.	SDLP	2,646	6.1	− 0.6
		Johnston, L.P.M.	SF	930	2.2 ★	+ 0.9
		Wilson, C.	NIU	822	1.9 ★	
1997: UU				1,110	2.6	

Stratford-on-Avon [548]

84,219	65.2	Maples, J.C.†	Con	27,606	50.3	+ 2.0
		Juned, S.A.	LD	15,804	28.8	+ 3.2
		Hussain, M.	Lab	9,164	16.7	− 3.9
		Mole, R.A.	UKI	1,184	2.2 ★	+ 1.3
		Davies, M.E.	Grn	1,156	2.1 ★	
1997: Con				11,802	21.5	

Strathkelvin & Bearsden [549]

62,869	66.0	Lyons, J.	Lab	19,250	46.4	− 6.5
		Macdonald, G.F.	LD	7,533	18.2	+ 8.4
		Smith, C.	SNP	6,675	16.1	− 0.2
		Roxburgh, W.M.	Con	6,635	16.0	− 4.1
		Telfer, W.	SSP	1,393	3.4 ★	
1997: Lab				11,717	28.2	

Streatham [550]

76,021	49.1	Hill, K.†	Lab	21,401	57.3	− 5.5
		O'Brien, R.	LD	6,771	18.1	+ 4.6
		Hocking, S.J.	Con	6,639	17.8	− 4.0
		Sajid, M.	Grn	1,641	4.4 ★	
		Tucker, G.	SA	906	2.4 ★	
1997: Lab				14,630	39.2	

Stretford & Urmston [551]

71,222	54.8	Hughes, B.J.†	Lab	23,836	61.1	+ 2.6
		Mackie, J.D.	Con	10,565	27.1	− 3.4
		Bridges, J.R.	LD	3,891	10.0	+ 1.8
		Price, K.	Ind	713	1.8 ★	
1997: Lab				13,271	34.0	

Stroud [552]

78,818	70.0	Drew, D.E.†	Lab	25,685	46.6	+ 3.9
		Carmichael, N.	Con	20,646	37.4	− 0.5
		Beasley, J.J.	LD	6,036	10.9	− 4.5
		Cranston, K.D.	Grn	1,913	3.5 ★	− 0.5
		Blake, A.G.	UKI	895	1.6 ★	
1997: Lab				5,039	9.1	

Suffolk Central & Ipswich North [553]

74,200	63.5	Lord, M.N.†	Con	20,924	44.4	+	1.8
		Jones, C.E.	Lab	17,455	37.1	+	1.2
		Elvin, A.M.	LD	7,593	16.1	–	4.5
		Wright, J.P.	UKI	1,132	2.4 ★		
1997: Con				3,469	7.4		

Suffolk Coastal [554]

76,823	65.6	Gummer, J.S.†	Con	21,847	43.3	+	4.8
		Gardner, N.R.	Lab	17,521	34.8	+	2.0
		Schur, A.E.	LD	9,192	18.2	–	3.2
		Burn, M.R.	UKI	1,847	3.7 ★		
1997: Con				4,326	8.6		

Suffolk South [555]

68,456	66.2	Yeo, T.S.K.†	Con	18,748	41.4	+	4.1
		Young, M.C.	Lab	13,667	30.2	+	0.9
		Munt, T.J.	LD	11,296	24.9	–	2.8
		Allen, D.C.	UKI	1,582	3.5 ★		
1997: Con				5,081	11.2		

Suffolk West [556]

70,129	60.5	Spring, R.J.G.†	Con	20,201	47.6	+	6.7
		Jefferys, M.J.	Lab	15,906	37.5	+	0.4
		Martlew, R.B.	LD	5,017	11.8	–	2.2
		Burrows, W.	UKI	1,321	3.1 ★		
1997: Con				4,295	10.1		

Sunderland North [557]

60,846	49.0	Etherington, W.†	Lab	18,685	62.7	–	5.6
		Harris, M.R.	Con	5,331	17.9	+	1.2
		Lennox, J.A.	LD	3,599	12.1	+	1.7
		Herron, N.A.	Ind	1,518	5.1		
		Guynan, D.E.	BNP	687	2.3 ★		
1997: Lab				13,354	44.8		

Sunderland South [558]

64,577	48.3	Mullin, C.J.†	Lab	19,921	63.9	– 4.2
		Boyd, J.W.M.	Con	6,254	20.1	+ 1.2
		Greenfield, M.	LD	3,675	11.8	+ 0.2
		Dobbie, J.	BNP	576	1.8 ★	
		Moore, J.D.	UKI	470	1.5 ★	– 0.0
		Warner, R.	MRLP	291	0.9 ★	
1997: Lab				13,667	43.8	

Surrey East [559]

74,338	63.3	Ainsworth, P.M.†	Con	24,706	52.5	+ 2.4
		Pursehouse, J.	LD	11,503	24.4	+ 2.0
		Tanner, J.	Lab	8,994	19.1	– 2.1
		Stone, A.B.	UKI	1,846	3.9 ★	+ 2.9
1997: Con				13,203	28.1	

Surrey Heath [560]

75,858	59.5	Hawkins, N.J.†	Con	22,401	49.7	– 1.9
		Lelliott, M.P.	LD	11,582	25.7	+ 3.9
		Norman, J.A.	Lab	9,640	21.4	+ 0.3
		Hunt, N.J.	UKI	1,479	3.3 ★	+ 2.1
1997: Con				10,819	24.0	

Surrey South West [561]

70,570	70.3	Bottomley, V.H.B.M.†	Con	22,462	45.3	+ 0.7
		Cordon, S.R.	LD	21,601	43.6	+ 3.8
		Whelton, M.J.	Lab	4,321	8.7	– 0.7
		Clark, T.R.	UKI	1,208	2.4 ★	+ 1.7
1997: Con				861	1.7	

Sussex Mid [562]

70,623	64.9	Soames, A.N.W.†	Con	21,150	46.2	+ 2.7
		Wilkins, I.L.	LD	14,252	31.1	+ 0.5
		Mitchell, P.N.J.	Lab	8,693	19.0	+ 0.3
		Holdsworth, P.A.	UKI	1,126	2.5 ★	+ 1.3
		Berry, P.B.	MRLP	601	1.3 ★	
1997: Con				6,898	15.1	

Sutton & Cheam [563]

63,648	62.4	Burstow, P.K.†	LD	19,382	48.8	+ 6.5
		Maitland, O.H.	Con	15,078	38.0	+ 0.1
		Homan, L.F.	Lab	5,263	13.2	− 2.2
1997: LD				4,304	10.8	

Sutton Coldfield [564]

71,856	60.5	Mitchell, A.J.B.	Con	21,909	50.4	− 1.8
		Pocock, R.L.	Lab	11,805	27.2	+ 3.3
		Turner, M.M.	LD	8,268	19.0	− 0.3
		Nattrass, M.	UKI	1,186	2.7 ★	
		Robinson, I.R.	Ind	284	0.7 ★	
1997: Con				10,104	23.3	

Swansea East [565]

57,520	52.3	Anderson, D.†	Lab	19,612	65.2	−10.2
		Ball, J.G.	PC	3,464	11.5	+ 8.1
		Speht, R.	LD	3,064	10.2	+ 1.3
		Morris, P.R.	Con	3,026	10.1	+ 0.8
		Young, J.A.	Grn	463	1.5 ★	
		Jenkins, T.C.	UKI	443	1.5 ★	
1997: Lab				19,149	63.7	

Swansea West [566]

57,493	55.8	Williams, A.J.†	Lab	15,644	48.7	− 7.5
		Harper, M.M.	Con	6,094	19.0	− 1.5
		Day, A.M.	LD	5,313	16.6	+ 2.0
		Titherington, I.R.	PC	3,404	10.6	+ 4.0
		Lewis, R.D.	UKI	653	2.0 ★	
		Shrewsbury, M.J.	Grn	626	2.0 ★	
		Thraves, A.	SA	366	1.1 ★	
1997: Lab				9,550	29.8	

Swindon North [567]

69,355	61.0	Wills, M.D.†	Lab	22,371	52.9	+ 3.1
		Martin, N.D.	Con	14,266	33.7	− 0.1
		Nation, D.J.	LD	4,891	11.6	− 1.4
		Lloyd, B.E.	UKI	800	1.9 ★	
1997: Lab				8,105	19.1	

Swindon South [568]

71,080	61.0	Drown, J.K.†	Lab	22,260	51.3	+ 4.5
		Coombs, S.C.	Con	14,919	34.4	− 1.4
		Brewer, G.C.	LD	5,165	11.9	− 2.5
		Sharp, P.V.D.	UKI	713	1.6 ★	
		Gillard, C.R.	RRL	327	0.8 ★	
1997: Lab				7,341	16.9	

Tamworth [569]

69,596	57.8	Jenkins, B.D.†	Lab	19,722	49.0	− 2.8
		Gunter, L.V.M.	Con	15,124	37.6	+ 0.8
		Pinkett, J.	LD	4,721	11.7	+ 3.7
		Sootheran, P.B.	UKI	683	1.7 ★	+ 1.0
1997: Lab				4,598	11.4	

Tatton [570]

64,954	63.5	Osborne, G.G.O.	Con	19,860	48.1	+ 10.7
		Conquest, S.G.	Lab	11,249	27.3	
		Ash, M.	LD	7,685	18.6	
		Sheppard, M.B.B.	UKI	769	1.9 ★	
		Sharratt, P.N.	Ind	734	1.8 ★	
		Allinson, V.C.	Tatton	505	1.2 ★	
		Batchelor, W.J.	Ind	322	0.8 ★	
		Hunt, J.B.	Ind	154	0.4 ★	
1997: Ind				8,611	20.9	

Taunton [571]

81,651	67.6	Flook, A.J.	Con	23,033	41.7	+ 3.0
		Ballard, J.M.†	LD	22,798	41.3	− 1.4
		Govier, A.J.	Lab	8,254	14.9	+ 1.4
		Canton, M.H.	UKI	1,140	2.1 ★	
1997: LD				235	0.4	

Tayside North [572]

61,645	62.5	Wishart, P.	SNP	15,441	40.1	− 4.8
		Fraser, M.M.	Con	12,158	31.6	− 4.2
		Docherty, T.	Lab	5,715	14.8	+ 3.6
		Robertson, J.M.	LD	4,365	11.3	+ 3.2
		Adams, R.	SSP	620	1.6 ★	
		Macdonald, T.		220	0.6 ★	
1997: SNP				3,283	8.5	

Teignbridge [573]

85,533	69.3	Younger-Ross, R.	LD	26,343	44.4	+	5.7
		Nicholls, P.C.M.†	Con	23,332	39.3	+	0.1
		Bain, C.D.	Lab	7,366	12.4	-	5.6
		Exmouth, P.E.	UKI	2,269	3.8 ★	+	1.3
1997: Con				3,011	5.1		

Telford [574]

59,431	52.0	Wright, D.	Lab	16,854	54.6	-	3.2
		Henderson, A.D.	Con	8,471	27.4	+	0.0
		Wiggin, S.	LD	3,983	12.9	+	1.1
		Brookes, N.	UKI	1,098	3.6 ★		
		Jeffries, M.P.	SA	469	1.5 ★		
1997: Lab				8,383	27.2		

Tewkesbury [575]

70,930	63.7	Robertson, L.A.†	Con	20,830	46.1	+	0.3
		Dhillon, K.	Lab	12,167	26.9	+	0.7
		Martin, S.	LD	11,863	26.2	-	1.8
		Vernall, C.D.		335	0.7 ★		
1997: Con				8,663	19.2		

Thanet North [576]

71,012	59.0	Gale, R.J.†	Con	21,050	50.3	+	6.2
		Laing, J.S.	Lab	14,400	34.4	-	4.0
		Proctor, S.	LD	4,603	11.0	-	0.4
		Moore, J.D.	UKI	980	2.3 ★	+	1.4
		Shortt, D.J.S.	Ind	440	1.1 ★		
		Holmes, T.F.	NF	395	0.9 ★		
1997: Con				6,650	15.9		

Thanet South [577]

61,680	63.9	Ladyman, S.J.†	Lab	18,002	45.7	-	0.5
		Macgregor, M.C.	Con	16,210	41.1	+	1.3
		Voizey, G.S.B.	LD	3,706	9.4	-	2.3
		Baldwin, W.	Ind	770	2.0 ★		
		Eccott, T.A.	UKI	502	1.3 ★	-	0.1
		Franklin, B.F.	NF	242	0.6 ★		
1997: Lab				1,792	4.5		

Thurrock [578]

76,180	49.0	Mackinlay, A.†	Lab	21,121	56.5	– 6.8
		Penning, M.A.	Con	11,124	29.8	+ 3.0
		Lathan, J.B.	LD	3,846	10.3	+ 2.2
		Sheppard, C.	UKI	1,271	3.4 ★	+ 1.6
1997: Lab				9,997	26.8	

Tiverton & Honiton [579]

80,646	69.2	Browning, A.F.†	Con	26,258	47.1	+ 5.7
		Barnard, J.A.W.	LD	19,974	35.8	– 2.7
		Owen, I.M.	Lab	6,647	11.9	– 0.9
		Langmaid, A.	UKI	1,281	2.3 ★	
		Burgess, M.P.	Grn	1,030	1.8 ★	+ 1.0
		Roach, J.	Lib	594	1.1 ★	
1997: Con				6,284	11.3	

Tonbridge & Malling [580]

65,979	64.3	Stanley, J.P.†	Con	20,956	49.4	+ 1.4
		Hayman, V.	Lab	12,706	29.9	+ 2.7
		Canet, J.M.	LD	7,605	17.9	– 1.3
		Croucher, L.M.F.	UKI	1,169	2.8 ★	+ 1.7
1997: Con				8,250	19.4	

Tooting [581]

68,447	54.9	Cox, T.M.†	Lab	20,332	54.1	– 5.6
		Nicoll, A.J.M.	Con	9,932	26.4	– 0.7
		James, S.A.	LD	5,583	14.9	+ 5.5
		Ledbury, M.	Grn	1,744	4.6 ★	+ 3.5
1997: Lab				10,400	27.7	

Torbay [582]

76,072	62.5	Sanders, A.M.†	LD	24,015	50.5	+ 10.9
		Sweeting, C.St.J.	Con	17,307	36.4	– 3.2
		McKay, J.R.	Lab	4,484	9.4	– 5.4
		Booth, G.H.	UKI	1,512	3.2 ★	– 0.5
		Neale, P.W.	Ind	251	0.5 ★	
1997: LD				6,708	14.1	

Torfaen [583]

61,115	57.7	Murphy, P.P.†	Lab	21,883	62.1	–	7.0
		Evans, J.P.	Con	5,603	15.9	+	3.6
		Masters, A.	LD	3,936	11.2	–	1.0
		Smith, S.P.	PC	2,720	7.7	+	5.3
		Vipass, B.M.	UKI	657	1.9 ★		
		Bell, S.	SA	443	1.3 ★		
1997: Lab				16,280	46.2		

Totnes [584]

72,548	67.9	Steen, A.D.†	Con	21,914	44.5	+	8.0
		Oliver, R.C.	LD	18,317	37.2	+	2.3
		Wildy, T.T.	Lab	6,005	12.2	–	4.2
		Mackinlay, C.	UKI	3,010	6.1	+	4.3
1997: Con				3,597	7.3		

Tottenham [585]

65,568	48.2	Lammy, D.L.†	Lab	21,317	67.5	–	1.8
		Fernandes, U.	Con	4,401	13.9	–	1.8
		Khan, M.	LD	3,008	9.5	–	1.3
		Budge, P.	Grn	1,443	4.6 ★	+	1.8
		Bennett, W.E.	SA	1,162	3.7 ★		
		Shefki, U.T.	Ref	270	0.9 ★		
1997: Lab				16,916	53.5		

Truro & St Austell [586]

79,219	63.5	Taylor, M.O.J.†	LD	24,296	48.3	–	0.2
		Bonner, T.P.C.	Con	16,231	32.3	+	5.8
		Phillips, D.M.	Lab	6,889	13.7	–	1.6
		Wonnacott, J.A.	UKI	1,664	3.3 ★	+	2.3
		Jenkin, C.J.T.	MK	1,137	2.3 ★		
		Lee, J.W.		78	0.2 ★		
1997: LD				8,065	16.0		

Tunbridge Wells [587]

64,534	62.3	Norman, A.J.†	Con	19,643	48.9	+	3.7
		Brown, K.J.	LD	9,913	24.7	–	5.0
		Carvell, I.P.	Lab	9,332	23.2	+	2.8
		Webb, V.C.	UKI	1,313	3.3 ★	+	2.7
1997: Con				9,730	24.2		

Tweeddale, Ettrick & Lauderdale [588]

52,430	63.4	Moore, M.K.†	LD	14,035	42.3	+ 11.0
		Geddes, K.	Lab	8,878	26.7	− 0.7
		Brocklehurst, A.	Con	5,118	15.4	− 6.7
		Thomson, R.G.	SNP	4,108	12.4	− 4.7
		Lockhart, N.P.M.	SSP	695	2.1 ★	
		Hein, J.	Lib	383	1.2 ★	
1997: LD				5,157	15.5	

Twickenham [589]

75,225	66.4	Cable, J.V.†	LD	24,344	48.7	+ 3.6
		Longworth, N.R.S.	Con	16,689	33.4	− 4.3
		Rogers, D.P.	Lab	6,903	13.8	− 1.8
		Maciejowska, J.S.	Grn	1,423	2.8 ★	
		Hollebone, R.T.	UKI	579	1.2 ★	
1997: LD				7,655	15.3	

Tyne Bridge [590]

58,900	44.2	Clelland, D.G.†	Lab	18,345	70.5	− 6.3
		Cook, J.S.	Con	3,456	13.3	+ 2.2
		Wallace, J.C.	LD	3,213	12.3	+ 4.4
		Fitzpatrick, J.	SL	533	2.0 ★	
		Robson, S.J.	SA	485	1.9 ★	
1997: Lab				14,889	57.2	

Tynemouth [591]

65,184	67.4	Campbell, A.†	Lab	23,364	53.2	− 2.1
		Poulsen, K.	Con	14,686	33.5	+ 0.1
		Reid, P.A.	LD	5,108	11.6	+ 2.8
		Rollings, M.G.	UKI	745	1.7 ★	+ 0.8
1997: Lab				8,678	19.8	

Tyneside North [592]

64,914	57.7	Byers, S.J.†	Lab	26,027	69.5	− 3.3
		Ruffell, M.B.	Con	5,459	14.6	+ 0.9
		Reed, S.L.	LD	4,649	12.4	+ 1.9
		Taylor, A.F.	UKI	770	2.1 ★	
		Burnett, W.P.H	SA	324	0.9 ★	
		Capstick, W.K.	SL	240	0.6 ★	
1997: Lab				20,568	54.9	

Tyrone West [593]

60,739	79.9	Doherty, P.	SF	19,814	40.8	+ 10.0
		Thompson, W.J.†	UU	14,774	30.4	- 4.1
		Rodgers, B.	SDLP	13,942	28.7	- 3.3
1997: UU				5,040	10.4	

Ulster Mid [594]

61,390	81.3	McGuinness, M.†	SF	25,502	51.1	+ 11.0
		McCrea, R.W.I.	DUP	15,549	31.1	- 5.2
		Haughey, E.	SDLP	8,376	16.8	- 5.3
		Donnelly, F.	WP	509	1.0 ★	
1997: SF				9,953	19.9	

Upminster [595]

56,829	59.6	Watkinson, A.E.	Con	15,410	45.5	+ 6.0
		Darvill, K.E.†	Lab	14,169	41.9	- 4.3
		Truesdale, P.J.	LD	3,183	9.4	- 0.1
		Murray, T.P.	UKI	1,089	3.2 ★	
1997: Lab				1,241	3.7	

Upper Bann [596]

72,574	70.3	Trimble, D.†	UU	17,095	33.5	- 10.1
		Simpson, D.	DUP	15,037	29.5	+ 18.0
		O'Hagan, D.M.	SF	10,771	21.1	+ 9.0
		Kelly, D.	SDLP	7,607	14.9	- 9.3
		French, T.	WP	527	1.0 ★	
1997: UU				2,058	4.0	

Uxbridge [597]

58,068	57.5	Randall, A.J.†	Con	15,751	47.1	+ 3.6
		Salisbury-Jones, D.N.	Lab	13,653	40.9	- 1.0
		Royce, C.M.	LD	3,426	10.3	- 0.6
		Cannons, P.R.	UKI	588	1.8 ★	
1997: Con				2,098	6.3	

Vale of Clwyd [598]

50,842	63.6	Ruane, C.S.†	Lab	16,179	50.0	- 2.7
		Murphy, B.	Con	10,418	32.2	+ 2.4
		Rees, G.	LD	3,058	9.5	+ 0.7
		Williams, J.	PC	2,300	7.1	+ 1.2
		Campbell, W.D.M.	UKI	391	1.2 ★	+ 0.5
1997: Lab				5,761	17.8	

Vale of Glamorgan [599]

67,774	66.7	Smith, J.W.P.†	Lab	20,524	45.4	– 8.5
		Inkin, S.L.	Con	15,824	35.0	+ 0.7
		Smith, D.H.	LD	5,521	12.2	+ 3.0
		Franks, C.P.	PC	2,867	6.3	+ 3.8
		Warry, T.N.	UKI	448	1.0 ★	
1997: Lab				4,700	10.4	

Vale of York [600]

73,335	66.1	McIntosh, A.C.B.†	Con	25,033	51.6	+ 6.9
		Jukes, C.J.	Lab	12,516	25.8	– 0.6
		Stone, G.M.	LD	9,799	20.2	– 3.6
		Thornber, P.M.	UKI	1,142	2.4 ★	
1997: Con				12,517	25.8	

Vauxhall [601]

74,474	44.8	Hoey, C.L.†	Lab	19,738	59.1	– 4.7
		Bottrall, A.F.	LD	6,720	20.1	+ 4.1
		Compton, G.F.T.	Con	4,489	13.4	– 1.8
		Collins, W.S.B.	Grn	1,485	4.4 ★	+ 2.2
		Bennett, T.C.	SA	853	2.6 ★	
		Boyd, M.N.	Ind	107	0.3 ★	
1997: Lab				13,018	39.0	

Wakefield [602]

75,750	54.5	Hinchliffe, D.M.†	Lab	20,592	49.9	– 7.5
		Karran, T.	Con	12,638	30.6	+ 2.2
		Dale, D.	LD	5,097	12.4	+ 1.2
		Greenwood, S.F.	Grn	1,075	2.6 ★	
		Cannon, J.	UKI	677	1.6 ★	
		Aziz, A.	SL	634	1.5 ★	
		Griffiths, M.	SA	541	1.3 ★	
1997: Lab				7,954	19.3	

Wallasey [603]

64,889	57.6	Eagle, A.†	Lab	22,718	60.8	– 3.8
		Rennie, L.	Con	10,442	28.0	+ 4.1
		Reisdorf, P.T.C.	LD	4,186	11.2	+ 2.9
1997: Lab				12,276	32.9	

Walsall North [604]

65,981	49.0	Winnick, D.J.†	Lab	18,779	58.1	+ 1.5
		Pitt, M.G.	Con	9,388	29.1	+ 1.5
		Heap, M.A.	LD	2,923	9.0	- 0.3
		Mayo, J.D.	UKI	812	2.5 ★	
		Church, D.J.	SA	410	1.3 ★	
1997: Lab				9,391	29.1	

Walsall South [605]

62,626	55.7	George, B.T.†	Lab	20,574	59.0	+ 1.1
		Bird, M.A.	Con	10,643	30.5	- 1.2
		Tomlinson, W.L.	LD	2,365	6.8	+ 0.5
		Bennett, D.	UKI	974	2.8 ★	
		Smith, P.E.	SA	343	1.0 ★	
1997: Lab				9,931	28.5	

Walthamstow [606]

64,403	53.5	Gerrard, N.F.†	Lab	21,402	62.2	- 1.0
		Boys Smith, N.J.	Con	6,221	18.1	- 2.2
		Dunphy, P.G.	LD	5,024	14.6	+ 0.9
		Donovan, S.P.	S Alt	806	2.3 ★	
		Phillips, W.	BNP	389	1.1 ★	
		Mayer, G.K.	UKI	298	0.9 ★	
		Duffy, B.Z.	PL	289	0.8 ★	
1997: Lab				15,181	44.1	

Wansbeck [607]

63,132	59.3	Murphy, D.†	Lab	21,617	57.8	- 7.7
		Thompson, J.A.	LD	8,516	22.8	+ 6.8
		Lake, R.I.	Con	4,774	12.8	- 1.2
		Kirkup, M.R.	Ind	1,076	2.9 ★	
		Best, N.F.	Grn	954	2.5 ★	+ 0.4
		Attwell, G.W.H.	UKI	482	1.3 ★	
1997: Lab				13,101	35.0	

Wansdyke [608]

70,850	69.9	Norris, D.†	Lab	23,206	46.8	+ 2.8
		Watt, C.D.	Con	17,593	35.5	+ 0.2
		Coleshill, G.M.	LD	7,135	14.4	- 2.4
		Hayden, F.E.	Grn	958	1.9 ★	
		Sandell, P.G.	UKI	655	1.3 ★	+ 0.5
1997: Lab				5,613	11.3	

Wantage [609]

76,129	64.5	Jackson, R.V.†	Con	19,475	39.6	–	0.2
		Beer, S.	Lab	13,875	28.2	–	0.7
		Fawcett, N.M.	LD	13,776	28.0	+	1.5
		Brooks-Saxl, D.	Grn	1,062	2.2 ★	+	1.0
		Tolstoy, N.	UKI	941	1.9 ★	+	1.1
1997: Con				5,600	11.4		

Warley [610]

58,065	54.1	Spellar, J.F.†	Lab	19,007	60.5	–	3.3
		Pritchard, M.A.	Con	7,157	22.8	–	1.3
		Cockings, R.E.	LD	3,315	10.6	+	0.8
		Dardi, H.S.	SL	1,936	6.2		
1997: Lab				11,850	37.7		

Warrington North [611]

72,445	53.7	Jones, H.M.†	Lab	24,026	61.7	–	0.4
		Usher, J.R.	Con	8,870	22.8	–	1.2
		Smith, R.A.	LD	5,232	13.4	+	3.1
		Kirkham, J.H.	UKI	782	2.0 ★		
1997: Lab				15,156	39.0		

Warrington South [612]

74,283	61.2	Southworth, H.M.†	Lab	22,419	49.3	–	2.9
		Mosley, C.M.E.	Con	15,022	33.0	+	0.5
		Barlow, R.J.	LD	7,419	16.3	+	3.2
		Kelley, J.	UKI	637	1.4 ★		
1997: Lab				7,397	16.3		

Warwick & Leamington [613]

81,405	65.8	Plaskitt, J.A.†	Lab	26,108	48.8	+	4.3
		Bannerman, D.C.	Con	20,155	37.6	–	1.2
		Forbes, L.C.	LD	5,964	11.1	–	0.7
		Kime, A.C.	SA	664	1.2 ★		
		Warwick, G.J.G.	UKI	648	1.2 ★		
1997: Lab				5,953	11.1		

Warwickshire North [614]

73,825	60.2	O'Brien, M.†	Lab	24,023	54.1	–	4.3
		Parsons, G.P.	Con	14,384	32.4	+	1.2
		Powell, W.H.	LD	5,052	11.4	+	3.9
		Flynn, J.P.	UKI	950	2.1 ★	+	1.2
1997: Lab				9,639	21.7		

Watford [615]

75,872	61.1	Ward, C.†	Lab	20,992	45.3	–	0.0
		McManus, M.N.	Con	15,437	33.3	–	1.5
		Hames, D.	LD	8,088	17.4	+	0.7
		Kingsley, D.S.	Grn	900	1.9 ★		
		Stewart-Mole, E.	UKI	535	1.2 ★		
		Berry, J.H.	SA	420	0.9 ★		
1997: Lab				5,555	12.0		

Waveney [616]

77,613	60.8	Blizzard, B.†	Lab	23,914	50.7	–	5.3
		Scott, L.	Con	15,361	32.6	–	1.9
		Young, D.A.	LD	5,370	11.4	+	2.4
		Aylett, B.	UKI	1,097	2.3 ★		
		Elliott, G.J.	Grn	983	2.1 ★		
		Mallin, R.	SA	442	0.9 ★		
1997: Lab				8,553	18.1		

Wealden [617]

83,066	63.5	Hendry, C.	Con	26,279	49.8	+	0.0
		Murphy, S.J.	LD	12,507	23.7	–	2.0
		Fordham, K.E.	Lab	10,705	20.3	+	3.1
		Riddle, K.A.	UKI	1,539	2.9 ★	+	2.0
		Salmon, J.P.	Grn	1,273	2.4 ★		
		Thornton, C.O.	Pens	453	0.9 ★		
1997: Con				13,772	26.1		

Weaver Vale [618]

68,236	57.6	Hall, M.T.†	Lab	20,611	52.5	–	3.9
		Cross, C.R.	Con	10,974	27.9	–	0.6
		Griffiths, T.N.	LD	5,643	14.4	+	2.1
		Cooksley, M.J.	Ind	1,484	3.8 ★		
		Bradshaw, J.R.	UKI	559	1.4 ★		
1997: Lab				9,637	24.5		

Wellingborough [619]

79,549	64.1	Stinchcombe, P.D.†	Lab	23,867	46.8	+	2.6
		Bone, P.W.	Con	21,512	42.2	–	1.6
		Gaskell, P.K.	LD	4,763	9.3	–	0.0
		Ellwood, A.R.	UKI	864	1.7 ★	–	0.4
1997: Lab				2,355	4.6		

Wells [620]

74,189	69.2	Heathcoat-Amory, D.P.†	Con	22,462	43.8	+	4.4
		Oakes, G.J.	LD	19,666	38.3	–	0.1
		Merryfield, A.P.	Lab	7,915	15.4	–	2.7
		Reed, A.S.	UKI	1,104	2.2 ★		
		Bex, C.	WR	167	0.3 ★		
1997: Con				2,796	5.4		

Welwyn Hatfield [621]

67,004	63.9	Johnson, M.J.†	Lab	18,484	43.2	–	3.9
		Shapps, G.V.	Con	17,288	40.4	+	3.9
		Cooke, D.E.	LD	6,021	14.1	+	0.5
		Biggs, M.J.	UKI	798	1.9 ★		
		Pinto, F.K.	PL	230	0.5 ★		
1997: Lab				1,196	2.8		

Wentworth [622]

64,033	52.8	Healey, J.†	Lab	22,798	67.5	–	4.8
		Roberts, M.D.	Con	6,349	18.8	+	3.8
		Wildgoose, D.B.	LD	3,652	10.8	+	1.6
		Wilkinson, J.	UKI	979	2.9 ★		
1997: Lab				16,449	48.7		

West Bromwich East [623]

61,180	53.4	Watson, T.A.	Lab	18,250	55.9	–	1.3
		McFarlane, R.D.J.	Con	8,487	26.0	+	1.6
		Garrett, I.A.G.	LD	4,507	13.8	–	1.1
		Grey, S.G.	UKI	835	2.6 ★		
		Johal, S.S.	SL	585	1.8 ★		
1997: Lab				9,763	29.9		

West Bromwich West [624]

66,765	47.7	Bailey, A.E.†	Lab	19,352	60.8		
		Bissell, K.E.	Con	7,997	25.1		
		Smith, S.L.	LD	2,168	6.8		
		Salvage, J.S.	BNP	1,428	4.5 ★		
		Walker, K.R.	UKI	499	1.6 ★		
		Singh, B.	SL	396	1.2 ★		
1997: Speaker				11,355	35.7		

West Ham [625]

59,828	48.9	Banks, A.L.†	Lab	20,449	69.9	−	3.0
		Kamall, S.S.	Con	4,804	16.4	+	1.4
		Fox, P.	LD	2,166	7.4	+	0.0
		Chandler-Oatts, J.M.	Grn	1,197	4.1 ★		
		Batten, G.J.	UKI	657	2.2 ★		
1997: Lab				15,645	53.4		

Westbury [626]

76,056	66.6	Murrison, A.W.	Con	21,299	42.1	+	1.5
		Vigar, D.C.	LD	16,005	31.6	+	1.7
		Cardy, S.P.	Lab	10,847	21.4	+	0.3
		Booth-Jones, C.V.C.	UKI	1,261	2.5 ★	+	1.1
		Gledhill, B.	Grn	1,216	2.4 ★		
1997: Con				5,294	10.5		

Western Isles [627]

21,706	60.6	MacDonald, C.A.†	Lab	5,924	45.0	−	10.6
		Nicholson, A.	SNP	4,850	36.9	+	3.5
		Taylor, D.S.	Con	1,250	9.5	+	2.8
		Horne, J.	LD	849	6.5	+	3.4
		Telfer, J.L.	SSP	286	2.2 ★		
1997: Lab				1,074	8.2		

Westmorland & Lonsdale [628]

70,637	67.8	Collins, T.W.G.†	Con	22,486	46.9	+	4.7
		Farron, T.	LD	19,339	40.4	+	7.0
		Bateson, J.A.	Lab	5,234	10.9	−	9.7
		Gibson, R.	UKI	552	1.2 ★		
		Bell, T.J.	Ind	292	0.6 ★		
1997: Con				3,147	6.6		

Weston-Super-Mare [629]

74,322	62.8	Cotter, B.J.†	LD	18,424	39.5	– 0.6
		Penrose, J.D.	Con	18,086	38.7	+ 1.0
		Kraft, D.	Lab	9,235	19.8	+ 1.9
		Lukins, W.J.	UKI	650	1.4 ★	
		Peverelle, C.J.	Ind	206	0.4 ★	
		Sibley, R.S.	Ind	79	0.2 ★	
1997: LD				338	0.7	

Wigan [630]

64,040	52.5	Turner, N.†	Lab	20,739	61.7	– 6.8
		Page, M.L.	Con	6,996	20.8	+ 3.9
		Beswick, T.R.	LD	4,970	14.8	+ 4.8
		Lowe, D.	SA	886	2.6 ★	
1997: Lab				13,743	40.9	

Wiltshire North [631]

78,624	67.3	Gray, J.W.†	Con	24,090	45.5	+ 1.7
		Pym, H.R.	LD	20,212	38.2	+ 0.4
		Garton, J.	Lab	7,556	14.3	+ 0.0
		Dowdney, N.F.	UKI	1,090	2.1 ★	+ 1.4
1997: Con				3,878	7.3	

Wimbledon [632]

63,930	64.3	Casale, R.M.†	Lab	18,806	45.7	+ 3.0
		Hammond, S.W.	Con	15,062	36.6	+ 0.1
		Pierce, M.D.	LD	5,341	13.0	– 3.6
		Thacker, R.K.	Grn	1,007	2.4 ★	+ 1.5
		Glencross, R.E.	CPA	479	1.2 ★	
		Bell, M.	UKI	414	1.0 ★	
1997: Lab				3,744	9.1	

Winchester [633]

81,801	72.3	Oaten, M.†	LD	32,282	54.6	+ 12.5
		Hayes, A.R.	Con	22,648	38.3	– 3.8
		Wyeth, S.M.	Lab	3,498	5.9	– 4.6
		Martin, J.	UKI	664	1.1 ★	+ 0.4
		Rous, H.E.	WR	66	0.1 ★	
1997: LD				9,634	16.3	

Windsor [634]

73,854	57.0	Trend, M.St.J.†	Con	19,900	47.3		− 0.9
		Pinfield, P.N.	LD	11,011	26.1		− 2.5
		Muller, M.	Lab	10,137	24.1		+ 5.8
		Fagan, J.W.F.	UKI	1,062	2.5 ★		+ 1.9
1997: Con				8,889	21.1		

Wirral South [635]

60,653	65.6	Chapman, J.K.†	Lab	18,890	47.4		− 3.5
		Millard, A.P.	Con	13,841	34.8		− 1.6
		Gilchrist, P.N.	LD	7,087	17.8		+ 7.4
1997: Lab				5,049	12.7		

Wirral West [636]

62,294	65.0	Hesford, S.†	Lab	19,105	47.2		+ 2.3
		Lynch, C.J.J.	Con	15,070	37.2		− 1.8
		Holbrook, S.A.	LD	6,300	15.6		+ 2.9
1997: Lab				4,035	10.0		

Witney [637]

74,612	65.9	Cameron, D.W.D.	Con	22,153	45.0		+ 2.0
		Bartlet, M.J.G.	Lab	14,180	28.8		− 1.8
		Epps, G.D.	LD	10,000	20.3		+ 0.5
		Stevenson, M.C.	Grn	1,100	2.2 ★		+ 1.1
		Beadle, B.	Ind	1,003	2.0 ★		
		Dukes, K.	UKI	767	1.6 ★		+ 0.2
1997: Con				7,973	16.2		

Woking [638]

71,254	60.2	Malins, H.J.†	Con	19,747	46.0		+ 7.6
		Hilliar, A.R.	LD	12,988	30.3		+ 3.0
		Hussain, S.	Lab	8,714	20.3		− 0.7
		Harvey, M.J.	UKI	1,461	3.4 ★		+ 2.4
1997: Con				6,759	15.8		

Wokingham [639]

68,430	64.1	Redwood, J.A.†	Con	20,216	46.1		− 4.0
		Longton, R.E.	LD	14,222	32.4		+ 1.1
		Syed, M.P.	Lab	7,633	17.4		+ 0.6
		Carstairs, F.J.	UKI	897	2.0 ★		
		Owen, P.T.	MRLP	880	2.0 ★		
1997: Con				5,994	13.7		

Wolverhampton North East [640]

59,616	52.8	Purchase, K.†	Lab	18,984	60.3	+ 1.0
		Miller, M.F.L.	Con	9,019	28.6	+ 0.7
		Bourne, S.M.	LD	2,494	7.9	+ 2.6
		McCartney, T.P.G.	UKI	997	3.2 ★	
1997: Lab				9,965	31.6	

Wolverhampton South East [641]

53,243	51.3	Turner, D.†	Lab	18,409	67.4	+ 3.7
		Pepper, A.N.S.	Con	5,945	21.8	+ 1.6
		Wild, P.	LD	2,389	8.8	− 0.7
		Barry, J.M.	NF	554	2.0 ★	
1997: Lab				12,464	45.7	

Wolverhampton South West [642]

65,909	62.1	Marris, R.H.	Lab	19,735	48.3	− 2.1
		Chambers, D.I.R.	Con	16,248	39.7	− 0.2
		Dixon, M.D.	LD	3,425	8.4	+ 0.2
		Walker, W.A.	Grn	805	2.0 ★	
		Hope, J.D.S.	UKI	684	1.7 ★	
1997: Lab				3,487	8.5	

Woodspring [643]

71,018	68.7	Fox, L.†	Con	21,297	43.7	− 0.8
		Stevens, C.	Lab	12,499	25.6	+ 4.9
		Eldridge, C.W.	LD	11,816	24.2	− 6.1
		Shopland, D.W.	Ind	1,412	2.9 ★	
		Lawson, R.H.	Grn	1,282	2.6 ★	+ 1.4
		Crean, F.	UKI	452	0.9 ★	
1997: Con				8,798	18.0	

Worcester [644]

71,255	62.0	Foster, M.J.†	Lab	21,478	48.6	− 1.5
		Adams, R.D.	Con	15,712	35.5	− 0.2
		Chandler, P.J.	LD	5,578	12.6	+ 0.1
		Chamings, R.J.	UKI	1,442	3.3 ★	+ 1.5
1997: Lab				5,766	13.0	

Worcestershire Mid [645]

72,055	62.3	Luff, P.J.†	Con	22,937	51.1	+ 3.7
		Bannister, D.C.	Lab	12,310	27.4	- 1.5
		Browne, R.W.	LD	8,420	18.8	+ 0.1
		Eaves, A.E.	UKI	1,230	2.7 ★	+ 1.5
1997: Con				10,627	23.7	

Worcestershire West [646]

66,769	67.1	Spicer, W.M.H.†	Con	20,597	46.0	+ 0.9
		Hadley, M.P.J.	LD	15,223	34.0	- 3.3
		Azmi, W.U.	Lab	6,275	14.0	- 1.7
		Morris, I.	UKI	1,574	3.5 ★	
		Victory, M.G.	Grn	1,138	2.5 ★	+ 0.5
1997: Con				5,374	12.0	

Workington [647]

65,965	63.4	Cunningham, T.A.	Lab	23,209	55.5	- 8.7
		Stoddart, T.	Con	12,359	29.6	+ 5.1
		Francis, I.W.	LD	5,214	12.5	+ 4.4
		Peacock, J.	LCA	1,040	2.5 ★	
1997: Lab				10,850	25.9	

Worsley [648]

69,300	51.0	Lewis, T.†	Lab	20,193	57.1	- 5.1
		Ellwood, T.	Con	8,406	23.8	- 0.5
		Bleakley, R.M.	LD	6,188	17.5	+ 3.9
		Entwistle, D.E.	SL	576	1.6 ★	
1997: Lab				11,787	33.3	

Worthing East & Shoreham [649]

72,101	59.7	Loughton, T.P.†	Con	18,608	43.2	+ 2.7
		Yates, D.J.	Lab	12,469	29.0	+ 5.0
		Elgood, P.S.	LD	9,876	22.9	- 7.6
		McCulloch, J.	UKI	1,195	2.8 ★	+ 1.0
		Baldwin, C.J.	LCA	920	2.1 ★	
1997: Con				6,139	14.3	

Worthing West [650]

72,419	59.7	Bottomley, P.J.†	Con	20,508	47.5	+ 1.3
		Walsh, J.M.M.	LD	11,471	26.5	- 4.6
		Butcher, A.T.	Lab	9,270	21.5	+ 5.2
		Cross, T.P.	UKI	1,960	4.5 ★	+ 2.5
1997: Con				9,037	20.9	

The Wrekin [651]

65,781	63.1	Bradley, P.C.S.†	Lab	19,532	47.1	+ 0.1
		Rees-Mogg, J.W.	Con	15,945	38.4	− 1.8
		Jenkins, I.C.	LD	4,738	11.4	− 1.4
		Brookes, D.	UKI	1,275	3.1 ★	
1997: Lab				3,587	8.6	

Wrexham [652]

50,465	59.5	Lucas, I.C.	Lab	15,934	53.0	− 3.1
		Elphick, F.A.L.	Con	6,746	22.5	− 1.4
		Davies, R.A.	LD	5,153	17.1	+ 3.9
		Evans, M.W.	PC	1,783	5.9	+ 2.7
		Brookes, J.	UKI	432	1.4 ★	
1997: Lab				9,188	30.6	

Wycombe [653]

74,297	60.5	Goodman, P.A.C.	Con	19,064	42.4	+ 2.5
		Shafique, C.	Lab	15,896	35.3	− 0.1
		Tomlin, D.D.	LD	7,658	17.0	− 1.5
		Cooke, C.W.R.	UKI	1,059	2.4 ★	
		Laker, J.S.	Grn	1,057	2.4 ★	+ 1.0
		Fitton, D.A.H.	Ind	240	0.5 ★	
1997: Con				3,168	7.0	

Wyre Forest [654]

72,152	68.0	Taylor, R.T.	KHHC	28,487	58.1	
		Lock, D.A.†	Lab	10,857	22.1	− 26.6
		Simpson, G.M.	Con	9,350	19.1	− 17.1
		Millington, A.J.	UKI	368	0.8 ★	+ 0.2
1997: Lab				17,630	35.9	

Wythenshawe & Sale East [655]

72,127	48.6	Goggins, P.G.†	Lab	21,032	60.0	+ 1.9
		Fildes, S.F.M.	Con	8,424	24.0	− 1.1
		Tucker, V.M.	LD	4,320	12.3	− 0.1
		Crookes, L.D.	Grn	869	2.5 ★	
		Shaw, F.B.	SL	410	1.2 ★	
1997: Lab				12,608	36.0	

Yeovil [656]

74,991	64.2	Laws, D.A.	LD	21,266	44.2	− 4.6
		Forgione, M.F.	Con	17,338	36.0	+ 8.4
		Conway, P.J.A.	Lab	7,077	14.7	− 0.2
		Boxall, N.D.	UKI	1,131	2.3 ★	
		Begg, A.L.	Grn	786	1.6 ★	+ 0.3
		Prior, A.J.	Lib	534	1.1 ★	
1997: LD				3,928	8.2	

Ynys Mon [657]

53,398	63.7	Owen, A.	Lab	11,906	35.0	+ 1.8
		Williams, E.S.	PC	11,106	32.6	− 6.8
		Fox, A.	Con	7,653	22.5	+ 1.0
		Bennett, N.	LD	2,772	8.1	+ 4.3
		Wykes, F.C.	UKI	359	1.1 ★	
		Donald, N.	Ind	222	0.7 ★	
1997: PC				800	2.4	

York [658]

81,354	59.0	Bayley, H.†	Lab	25,072	52.3	− 7.7
		McIntyre, M.	Con	11,293	23.5	− 1.2
		Waller, A.M.	LD	8,519	17.8	+ 6.6
		Shaw, W.T.	Grn	1,465	3.1 ★	+ 1.5
		Ormston, F.	SA	674	1.4 ★	
		Bate, R.F.	UKI	576	1.2 ★	+ 0.7
		Cambridge, G.	MRLP	381	0.8 ★	
1997: Lab				13,779	28.7	

Yorkshire East [659]

72,052	60.1	Knight, G.	Con	19,861	45.9	+ 3.2
		Simpson-Laing, T-L.	Lab	15,179	35.0	− 0.8
		Hardy, M-R.	LD	6,300	14.5	− 4.0
		Pearson, T.J.	UKI	1,661	3.8 ★	
		Dessoy, P.W.	Ind	313	0.7 ★	
1997: Con				4,682	10.8	

6 Tables

Table 1. Full Summary Results by Country

England	Votes	Votes%	%ch	Candidates	Elected	Lost Dep.
Lab	9,056,824	41.4	-2.1	529	323	0
Con	7,705,870	35.2	1.5	529	165	0
LD	4,246,853	19.4	1.5	528	40	0
UKI	374,775	1.7	1.3	392	0	386
Grn	158,173	0.7	0.5	135	0	126
Ind	76,348	0.3		101	0	94
SA	55,295	0.3		92	0	90
SL	51,299	0.2		96	0	95
BNP	46,851	0.2		32	0	27
KHHC	28,487	0.1		1	1	0
Lib	13,302	0.1		13	0	12
LCA	7,722	0.0		11	0	11
PJP	7,443	0.0		3	0	1
PL	7,058	0.0		27	0	27
MRLP	6,250	0.0		14	0	14
(No label)	3,211	0.0		15	0	15
MK	3,199	0.0		3	0	3
NF	2,484	0.0		5	0	5
RRL	2,423	0.0		6	0	6
S Alt	1,454	0.0		2	0	2
Ref	1,418	0.0		5	0	5
IOW	1,164	0.0		1	0	1
M	1,150	0.0		4	0	4
NB	888	0.0		1	0	1
FP	832	0.0		3	0	3
LA	770	0.0		1	0	1
WRP	607	0.0		6	0	6
Tatton	505	0.0		1	0	1
CPA	479	0.0		1	0	1
Grey	479	0.0		1	0	1
RM	460	0.0		1	0	1
AC	456	0.0		1	0	1
PEC	454	0.0		1	0	1
Pens	453	0.0		1	0	1
Comm	445	0.0		3	0	3
LE	391	0.0		1	0	1
Pac	370	0.0		1	0	1
LP	362	0.0		1	0	1
RUK	357	0.0		1	0	1
CD	345	0.0		1	0	1
FDP	344	0.0		1	0	1
UKP	295	0.0		1	0	1
JP	271	0.0		1	0	1
WR	233	0.0		2	0	2
Tr	223	0.0		1	0	1
Marx	221	0.0		1	0	1
DW	220	0.0		1	0	1
AL	197	0.0		1	0	1
Ch	195	0.0		1	0	1
TW	190	0.0		1	0	1
JLDP	137	0.0		1	0	1
St	108	0.0		1	0	1

Contd./

England	Votes	Votes%	%ch	Candidates	Elected	Lost Dep.
PD	107	0.0		1	0	1
JWP	100	0.0		1	0	1
EC	93	0.0		1	0	1
Elvis	68	0.0		1	0	1
UPP	54	0.0		1	0	1
Total Vote	21,870,762			2588	529	968
Electorate	36,991,780	59.1% turnout				

Scotland	Votes	Votes%	%ch	Candidates	Elected	Lost Dep.
Lab	1,001,173	43.3	-2.3	71	55	0
SNP	464,314	20.1	-2.0	72	5	0
LD	378,034	16.3	3.4	71	10	0
Con	360,658	15.6	-1.9	71	1	1
SSP	72,516	3.1	2.8	72	0	62
Speaker	16,053	0.7		1	1	0
Grn	4,551	0.2	0.1	4	0	3
Ind	3,605	0.2		8	0	8
UKI	3,236	0.1	0.1	11	0	11
SL	3,184	0.1		12	0	12
SU	2,728	0.1		2	0	1
LCA	955	0.0		2	0	2
PL	786	0.0		3	0	3
MRLP	405	0.0		1	0	1
Lib	383	0.0		1	0	1
Country	265	0.0		1	0	1
Sc Ref	250	0.0		1	0	1
(No label)	220	0.0		1	0	1
RRL	211	0.0		1	0	1
Comm	174	0.0		1	0	1
Total Vote	2,313,701			407	72	110
Electorate	3,984,306	58.1% turnout				

Wales	Votes	Votes%	%ch	Candidates	Elected	Lost Dep.
Lab	666,956	48.6	-6.2	40	34	0
Con	288,665	21.0	1.5	40	0	1
PC	195,893	14.3	4.3	40	4	5
LD	189,434	13.8	1.5	40	2	1
UKI	12,552	0.9	0.9	25	0	25
Ind	5,720	0.4		7	0	5
Grn	3,753	0.3	0.2	6	0	6
SL	2,805	0.2		6	0	6
SA	2,258	0.2		6	0	6
PL	1,609	0.1		7	0	7
(No label)	1,434	0.1		2	0	2
Bean	727	0.1		1	0	1
Comm	384	0.0		2	0	2
BNP	278	0.0		1	0	1
Cust	78	0.0		1	0	1
Total Vote	1,372,546			224	40	69
Electorate	2,236,143	61.4% turnout				

Contd./

Northern Ireland	Votes	Votes%	%ch	Candidates	Elected	Lost Dep.
UU	216,839	26.8	-5.9	17	6	0
DUP	181,999	22.5	8.9	14	5	0
SF	175,933	21.7	5.7	18	4	4
SDLP	169,865	21.0	-3.2	18	3	2
APNI	28,999	3.6	-4.4	10	0	5
UKU	13,509	1.7	0.0	1	0	0
(No label)	6,843	0.8		1	0	0
Prog U	4,781	0.6		2	0	1
NIWC	2,968	0.4		1	0	0
Con	2,422	0.3	-0.9	3	0	3
WP	2,352	0.3		6	0	6
NIU	1,794	0.2		2	0	2
Ind	1,536	0.2		2	0	2
Vote	418	0.1		4	0	4
TW	116	0.0		1	0	1
Total Vote	810,374			100	18	30
Electorate	1,191,009	68.0% turnout				

Table 2. Full Summary Results – Great Britain

Great Britain	Votes	Votes%	%ch	Candidates	Elected	Lost Dep.
Lab	10,724,953	42.0	-2.4	640	412	0
Con	8,355,193	32.7	1.2	640	166	2
LD	4,814,321	18.8	1.6	639	52	1
SNP	464,314	1.8	-0.2	72	5	0
UKI	390,563	1.5	1.2	428	0	422
PC	195,893	0.8	0.2	40	4	5
Grn	166,477	0.7	0.4	145	0	135
Ind	85,673	0.3		116	0	107
SSP	72,516	0.3	0.3	72	0	62
SA	57,553	0.2		98	0	96
SL	57,288	0.2		114	0	113
BNP	47,129	0.2		33	0	28
KHHC	28,487	0.1		1	1	0
Speaker	16,053	0.1		1	1	0
Lib	13,685	0.1		14	0	13
PL	9,453	0.0		37	0	37
LCA	8,677	0.0		13	0	13
PJP	7,443	0.0		3	0	1
MRLP	6,655	0.0		15	0	15
(No label)	4,865	0.0		18	0	18
MK	3,199	0.0		3	0	3
SU	2,728	0.0		2	0	1
RRL	2,634	0.0		7	0	7
NF	2,484	0.0		5	0	5
S Alt	1,454	0.0		2	0	2
Ref	1,418	0.0		5	0	5
IOW	1,164	0.0		1	0	1

Contd./

Great Britain	Votes	Votes%	%ch	Candidates	Elected	Lost Dep.
M	1,150	0.0		4	0	4
Comm	1,003	0.0		6	0	6
NB	888	0.0		1	0	1
FP	832	0.0	.	3	0	3
LA	770	0.0		1	0	1
Bean	727	0.0		1	0	1
WRP	607	0.0		6	0	6
Tatton	505	0.0		1	0	1
CPA	479	0.0		1	0	1
Grey	479	0.0		1	0	1
RM	460	0.0		1	0	1
AC	456	0.0		1	0	1
PEC	454	0.0		1	0	1
Pens	453	0.0		1	0	1
LE	391	0.0		1	0	1
Pac	370	0.0		1	0	1
LP	362	0.0		1	0	1
RUK	357	0.0		1	0	1
CD	345	0.0		1	0	1
FDP	344	0.0		1	0	1
UKP	295	0.0		1	0	1
JP	271	0.0		1	0	1
Country	265	0.0		1	0	1
Sc Ref	250	0.0		1	0	1
WR	233	0.0		2	0	2
Tr	223	0.0	.	1	0	1
Marx	221	0.0		1	0	1
DW	220	0.0		1	0	1
AL	197	0.0		1	0	1
Ch	195	0.0		1	0	1
TW	190	0.0		1	0	1
JLDP	137	0.0		1	0	1
St	108	0.0		1	0	1
PD	107	0.0		1	0	1
JWP	100	0.0		1	0	1
EC	93	0.0		1	0	1
Cust	78	0.0		1	0	1
Elvis	68	0.0		1	0	1
UPP	54	0.0		1	0	1
Total Vote	25,557,009			3219	641	1147
Electorate	43,212,229	**59.1% turnout**				

Table 3. Full Summary Results – United Kingdom

United Kingdom	Votes	Votes%	%ch	Candidates	Elected	Lost Dep.
Lab	10,724,953	40.7	-2.5	640	412	0
Con	8,357,615	31.7	1.0	643	166	5
LD	4,814,321	18.3	1.5	639	52	1
SNP	464,314	1.8	-0.2	72	5	0
UKI	390,563	1.5	1.1	428	0	422
UU	216,839	0.8	0.0	17	6	0
PC	195,893	0.7	0.2	40	4	5
DUP	181,999	0.7	0.3	14	5	0
SF	175,933	0.7	0.3	18	4	4
SDLP	169,865	0.6	0.0	18	3	2
Grn	166,477	0.6	0.4	145	0	135
Ind	87,209	0.3		118	0	109
SSP	72,516	0.3	0.2	72	0	62
SA	57,553	0.2		98	0	96
SL	57,288	0.2		114	0	113
BNP	47,129	0.2		33	0	28
APNI	28,999	0.1	-0.1	10	0	5
KHHC	28,487	0.1		1	1	0
Speaker	16,053	0.1		1	1	0
Lib	13,685	0.1		14	0	13
UKU	13,509	0.1	0.0	1	0	0
(No label)	11,708	0.0		19	0	18
PL	9,453	0.0		37	0	37
LCA	8,677	0.0		13	0	13
PJP	7,443	0.0		3	0	1
MRLP	6,655	0.0		15	0	15
Prog U	4,781	0.0		2	0	1
MK	3,199	0.0		3	0	3
NIWC	2,968	0.0		1	0	0
SU	2,728	0.0		2	0	1
RRL	2,634	0.0		7	0	7
NF	2,484	0.0		5	0	5
WP	2,352	0.0		6	0	6
NIU	1,794	0.0		2	0	2
S Alt	1,454	0.0		2	0	2
Ref	1,418	0.0		5	0	5
IOW	1,164	0.0		1	0	1
M	1,150	0.0		4	0	4
Comm	1,003	0.0		6	0	6
NB	888	0.0		1	0	1
FP	832	0.0		3	0	3
LA	770	0.0		1	0	1
Bean	727	0.0		1	0	1
WRP	607	0.0		6	0	6
Tatton	505	0.0		1	0	1
CPA	479	0.0		1	0	1
Grey	479	0.0		1	0	1
RM	460	0.0		1	0	1

Contd./

United Kingdom	Votes	Votes%	%ch	Candidates	Elected	Lost Dep.
AC	456	0.0		1	0	1
PEC	454	0.0		1	0	1
Pens	453	0.0		1	0	1
Vote	418	0.0		4	0	4
LE	391	0.0		1	0	1
Pac	370	0.0		1	0	1
LP	362	0.0		1	0	1
RUK	357	0.0		1	0	1
CD	345	0.0		1	0	1
FDP	344	0.0		1	0	1
TW	306	0.0		2	0	2
UKP	295	0.0		1	0	1
JP	271	0.0		1	0	1
Country	265	0.0		1	0	1
Sc Ref	250	0.0		1	0	1
WR	233	0.0		2	0	2
Tr	223	0.0		1	0	1
Marx	221	0.0		1	0	1
DW	220	0.0		1	0	1
AL	197	0.0		1	0	1
Ch	195	0.0		1	0	1
JLDP	137	0.0		1	0	1
St	108	0.0		1	0	1
PD	107	0.0		1	0	1
JWP	100	0.0		1	0	1
EC	93	0.0		1	0	1
Cust	78	0.0		1	0	1
Elvis	68	0.0		1	0	1
UPP	54	0.0		1	0	1
Total Vote	26,367,383			3319	659	1177
Electorate	44,403,238		59.4% turnout			

Table 4. Concise Summary Results

England	Votes	Votes%	%ch	Candidates	Elected	Lost Dep.
Con	7,705,870	35.2	1.5	529	165	0
Lab	9,056,824	41.4	-2.1	529	323	0
LD	4,246,853	19.4	1.5	528	40	0
UKI	374,775	1.7	1.3	392	0	386
Grn	158,173	0.7	0.5	135	0	126
Others	328,267	1.5	-2.7	475	1	456
Total Vote	21,870,762			2588	529	968
Electorate	36,991,780	59.1**% turnout**				

Scotland	Votes	Votes%	%ch	Candidates	Elected	Lost Dep.
Con	360,658	15.6	-1.9	71	1	1
Lab	1,001,173	43.3	-2.3	71	55	0
LD	378,034	16.3	3.4	71	10	0
SNP	464,314	20.1	-2.0	72	5	0
UKI	3,236	0.1	0.1	11	0	11
Grn	4,551	0.2	0.1	4	0	3
SSP	72,516	3.1	2.8	72	0	62
Others	29,219	1.3	-0.2	35	1	33
Total Vote	2,313,701			407	72	110
Electorate	3,984,306	58.1**% turnout**				

Wales	Votes	Votes%	%ch	Candidates	Elected	Lost Dep.
Con	288,665	21.0	1.5	40	0	1
Lab	666,956	48.6	-6.2	40	34	0
LD	189,434	13.8	1.5	40	2	1
PC	195,893	14.3	4.3	40	4	5
UKI	12,552	0.9	0.9	25	0	25
Grn	3,753	0.3	0.2	6	0	6
Others	15,293	1.1	-2.1	33	0	31
Total Vote	1,372,546			224	40	69
Electorate	2,236,143	61.4**% turnout**				

Northern Ireland	Votes	Votes%	%ch	Candidates	Elected	Lost Dep.
Con	2,422	0.3	-0.9	3	0	3
UU	216,839	26.8	-5.9	17	6	0
DUP	181,999	22.5	8.9	14	5	0
UKU	13,509	1.7	0.0	1	0	0
APNI	28,999	3.6	-4.4	10	0	5
SDLP	169,865	21.0	-3.2	18	3	2
SF	175,933	21.7	5.7	18	4	4
Others	20,808	2.6	-0.1	19	0	16
Total Vote	810,374			100	18	30
Electorate	1,191,009	68.0**% turnout**				

Contd./

Great Britain	Votes	Votes%	%ch	Candidates	Elected	Lost Dep.
Con	8,210,065	32.1	0.7	633	161	2
Lab	10,626,788	41.6	-2.7	633	410	0
LD	4,751,100	18.6	1.4	632	52	1
SNP	464,314	1.8	-0.2	72	5	0
PC	195,893	0.8	0.2	40	4	5
UKI	382,421	1.5	1.1	421	0	422
Grn	163,349	0.6	0.4	142	0	135
SSP	72,516	0.3	0.3	72	0	62
Others	371,325	1.5	-2.4	539	2	520
Total Vote	25,557,009			3184	634	1147
Electorate	43,212,229	59.1**% turnout**				

United Kingdom	Votes	Votes%	%ch	Candidates	Elected	Lost Dep.
Con	8,357,615	31.7	1.0	643	166	5
Lab	10,724,953	40.7	-2.5	640	412	0
LD	4,814,321	18.3	1.5	639	52	1
SNP	464,314	1.8	-0.2	72	5	0
PC	195,893	0.7	0.2	40	4	5
UKI	390,563	1.5	1.1	428	0	422
Grn	166,477	0.6	0.4	145	0	135
Others	1,253,247	4.8	-1.7	712	20	609
Total Vote	26,367,383			3319	659	1177
Electorate	44,403,238	59.4**% turnout**				

Table 5. General Election Voting in the English Regions

East Midlands	Con	Lab	LD	Other	Total
votes	727,386	879,886	300,831	43,799	1,951,902
votes% 2001	37.3	45.1	15.4	2.2	
votes% 1997	34.9	47.8	13.6	3.7	
change 97/01	2.4	-2.8	1.8	-1.5	
seats 2001	15	28	1	0	44
seats 1997	14	30	0	0	44

Eastern	Con	Lab	LD	Other	Total
votes	1,053,197	926,344	440,405	99,105	2,519,051
votes% 2001	41.8	36.8	17.5	3.9	
votes% 1997	39.5	38.6	17.1	4.8	
change 97/01	2.3	-1.8	0.4	-0.8	
seats 2001	34	20	2	0	56
seats 1997	33	22	1	0	56

London	Con	Lab	LD	Other	Total
votes	841,751	1,307,229	482,888	128,855	2,760,723
votes% 2001	30.5	47.4	17.5	4.7	
votes% 1997	31.2	49.5	14.6	4.7	
change 97/01	-0.7	-2.1	2.9	0.0	
seats 2001	13	55	6	0	74
seats 1997	11	57	6	0	74

North East	Con	Lab	LD	Other	Total
votes	233,802	651,821	182,824	28,454	1,096,901
votes% 2001	21.3	59.4	16.7	2.6	
votes% 1997	19.8	64.0	12.6	3.6	
change 97/01	1.5	-4.6	4.1	-1.0	
seats 2001	1	28	1	0	30
seats 1997	1	28	1	0	30

North West	Con	Lab	LD	Other	Total
votes	848,899	1,469,700	485,262	95,987	2,899,848
votes% 2001	29.3	50.7	16.7	3.3	
votes% 1997	27.6	53.6	14.5	4.4	
change 97/01	1.7	-2.9	2.3	-1.1	
seats 2001	9	64	3	0	76
seats 1997	9	64	2	1	76

Contd. /

South East	Con	Lab	LD	Other	Total
votes	1,590,628	1,090,367	879,228	151,383	3,711,606
votes% 2001	42.9	29.4	23.7	4.1	
votes% 1997	41.9	29.1	23.3	5.7	
change 97/01	1.0	0.2	0.4	-1.6	
seats 2001	53	22	8	0	83
seats 1997	54	22	7	0	83

South West	Con	Lab	LD	Other	Total
votes	946,629	645,121	765,824	98,766	2,456,340
votes% 2001	38.5	26.3	31.2	4.0	
votes% 1997	36.7	26.4	31.3	5.5	
change 97/01	1.8	-0.2	-0.1	-1.5	
seats 2001	20	16	15	0	51
seats 1997	22	15	14	0	51

West Midlands	Con	Lab	LD	Other	Total
votes	818,776	1,049,242	343,929	128,459	2,340,406
votes% 2001	35.0	44.8	14.7	5.5	
votes% 1997	33.7	47.0	13.8	5.5	
change 97/01	1.2	-2.1	0.9	-0.1	
seats 2001	13	43	2	1	59
seats 1997	14	43	1	1	59

Yorks. & The Humber	Con	Lab	LD	Other	Total
votes	644,802	1,037,114	365,662	86,407	2,133,985
votes% 2001	30.2	48.6	17.1	4.0	
votes% 1997	28.0	51.9	16.0	4.1	
change 97/01	2.3	-3.3	1.1	-0.1	
seats 2001	7	47	2	0	56
seats 1997	7	47	2	0	56

Table 6. General Election Voting in the English Counties

Avon	Con	Lab	LD	Other	Total
votes	152,030	177,782	134,170	19,185	483,167
votes% 2001	31.5	36.8	27.8	4.0	
votes% 1997	32.7	36.5	26.3	4.5	
change 97/01	-1.2	0.3	1.4	-0.5	
seats 2001	1	6	3	0	10
seats 1997	1	6	3	0	10

Bedfordshire	Con	Lab	LD	Other	Total
votes	100,265	109,113	37,599	7,817	254,794
votes% 2001	39.4	42.8	14.8	3.1	
votes% 1997	38.6	44.0	12.8	4.6	
change 97/01	0.8	-1.1	1.9	-1.6	
seats 2001	3	3	0	0	6
seats 1997	3	3	0	0	6

Berkshire	Con	Lab	LD	Other	Total
votes	142,280	108,675	91,964	11,002	353,921
votes% 2001	40.2	30.7	26.0	3.1	
votes% 1997	42.2	28.5	24.6	4.7	
change 97/01	-2.0	2.2	1.4	-1.6	
seats 2001	4	3	1	0	8
seats 1997	4	3	1	0	8

Buckinghamshire	Con	Lab	LD	Other	Total
votes	145,128	98,165	63,221	12,724	319,238
votes% 2001	45.5	30.7	19.8	4.0	
votes% 1997	43.7	30.6	21.2	4.5	
change 97/01	1.8	0.1	-1.4	-0.6	
seats 2001	5	2	0	0	7
seats 1997	5	2	0	0	7

Cambridgeshire	Con	Lab	LD	Other	Total
votes	138,798	104,506	68,824	11,843	323,971
votes% 2001	42.8	32.3	21.2	3.7	
votes% 1997	42.0	34.5	17.9	5.6	
change 97/01	0.8	-2.2	3.4	-1.9	
seats 2001	5	2	0	0	7
seats 1997	5	2	0	0	7

Cheshire	Con	Lab	LD	Other	Total
votes	164,470	214,236	72,118	11,609	462,433
votes% 2001	35.6	46.3	15.6	2.5	
votes% 1997	33.4	46.5	12.3	7.8	
change 97/01	2.2	-0.2	3.3	-5.3	
seats 2001	4	7	0	0	11
seats 1997	3	7	0	1	11

Contd./

Cleveland	Con	Lab	LD	Other	Total
votes	61,092	138,520	28,966	5,015	233,593
votes% 2001	26.2	59.3	12.4	2.1	
votes% 1997	25.2	62.4	9.8	2.6	
change 97/01	1.0	-3.1	2.6	-0.5	
seats 2001	0	6	0	0	6
seats 1997	0	6	0	0	6

Cornwall	Con	Lab	LD	Other	Total
votes	82,227	43,674	113,000	13,216	252,117
votes% 2001	32.6	17.3	44.8	5.2	
votes% 1997	30.4	17.1	43.9	8.6	
change 97/01	2.3	0.2	0.9	-3.4	
seats 2001	0	1	4	0	5
seats 1997	0	1	4	0	5

Cumbria	Con	Lab	LD	Other	Total
votes	96,163	94,191	46,736	5,563	242,653
votes% 2001	39.6	38.8	19.3	2.3	
votes% 1997	33.5	45.9	16.5	4.1	
change 97/01	6.1	-7.0	2.7	-1.8	
seats 2001	2	4	0	0	6
seats 1997	2	4	0	0	6

Derbyshire	Con	Lab	LD	Other	Total
votes	141,717	227,768	79,845	6,392	455,722
votes% 2001	31.1	50.0	17.5	1.4	
votes% 1997	29.5	53.6	13.8	3.1	
change 97/01	1.6	-3.6	3.7	-1.7	
seats 2001	1	8	1	0	10
seats 1997	1	9	0	0	10

Devon	Con	Lab	LD	Other	Total
votes	212,576	128,599	173,639	30,182	544,996
votes% 2001	39.0	23.6	31.9	5.5	
votes% 1997	36.8	25.9	31.3	6.1	
change 97/01	2.2	-2.3	0.6	-0.5	
seats 2001	4	3	4	0	11
seats 1997	5	3	3	0	11

Dorset	Con	Lab	LD	Other	Total
votes	156,222	72,715	108,426	7,339	344,702
votes% 2001	45.3	21.1	31.5	2.1	
votes% 1997	41.8	18.8	34.1	5.3	
change 97/01	3.5	2.3	-2.6	-3.2	
seats 2001	6	1	1	0	8
seats 1997	8	0	0	0	8

Contd. /

Durham	Con	Lab	LD	Other	Total
votes	55,254	170,329	38,533	6,890	271,006
votes% 2001	20.4	62.9	14.2	2.5	
votes% 1997	17.6	68.5	9.7	4.2	
change 97/01	2.8	-5.7	4.5	-1.6	
seats 2001	0	7	0	0	7
seats 1997	0	7	0	0	7

East Sussex	Con	Lab	LD	Other	Total
votes	138,652	105,937	84,232	22,053	350,874
votes% 2001	39.5	30.2	24.0	6.3	
votes% 1997	39.4	29.2	24.0	7.4	
change 97/01	0.1	1.0	0.0	-1.1	
seats 2001	3	4	1	0	8
seats 1997	3	4	1	0	8

Essex	Con	Lab	LD	Other	Total
votes	315,589	255,526	122,663	42,887	736,665
votes% 2001	42.8	34.7	16.7	5.8	
votes% 1997	40.3	36.5	18.2	5.0	
change 97/01	2.5	-1.8	-1.6	0.8	
seats 2001	11	5	1	0	17
seats 1997	10	6	1	0	17

Gloucestershire	Con	Lab	LD	Other	Total
votes	114,812	94,693	61,656	9,855	281,016
votes% 2001	40.9	33.7	21.9	3.5	
votes% 1997	39.5	34.0	22.6	4.0	
change 97/01	1.4	-0.3	-0.6	-0.4	
seats 2001	2	3	1	0	6
seats 1997	2	3	1	0	6

Greater London (N.)	Con	Lab	LD	Other	Total
votes	485,220	850,441	209,312	83,849	1,628,822
votes% 2001	29.8	52.2	12.9	5.1	
votes% 1997	30.5	54.1	10.6	4.8	
change 97/01	-0.7	-1.9	2.3	0.3	
seats 2001	8	37	0	0	45
seats 1997	6	39	0	0	45

Greater London (S.)	Con	Lab	LD	Other	Total
votes	356,531	456,788	273,576	45,006	1,131,901
votes% 2001	31.5	40.4	24.2	4.0	
votes% 1997	32.2	42.8	20.5	4.5	
change 97/01	-0.7	-2.5	3.7	-0.6	
seats 2001	5	18	6	0	29
seats 1997	5	18	6	0	29

Contd. /

Greater Manchester	Con	Lab	LD	Other	Total
votes	245,361	540,982	184,334	37,573	1,008,250
votes% 2001	24.3	53.7	18.3	3.7	
votes% 1997	24.1	56.3	16.0	3.5	
change 97/01	0.2	-2.7	2.2	0.3	
seats 2001	1	25	2	0	28
seats 1997	2	25	1	0	28

Hampshire	Con	Lab	LD	Other	Total
votes	316,520	210,610	211,595	23,583	762,308
votes% 2001	41.5	27.6	27.8	3.1	
votes% 1997	41.2	28.3	25.3	5.1	
change 97/01	0.3	-0.7	2.4	-2.0	
seats 2001	10	3	4	0	17
seats 1997	11	3	3	0	17

Hereford & Worcester	Con	Lab	LD	Other	Total
votes	146,806	97,932	69,215	43,092	357,045
votes% 2001	41.1	27.4	19.4	12.1	
votes% 1997	41.0	32.6	21.9	4.5	
change 97/01	0.1	-5.2	-2.5	7.5	
seats 2001	4	2	1	1	8
seats 1997	4	3	1	0	8

Hertfordshire	Con	Lab	LD	Other	Total
votes	202,569	188,308	81,899	11,878	484,654
votes% 2001	41.8	38.9	16.9	2.5	
votes% 1997	40.6	39.7	16.0	3.7	
change 97/01	1.2	-0.8	0.9	-1.3	
seats 2001	6	5	0	0	11
seats 1997	6	5	0	0	11

Humberside	Con	Lab	LD	Other	Total
votes	122,005	173,958	63,664	12,528	372,155
votes% 2001	32.8	46.7	17.1	3.4	
votes% 1997	30.4	50.4	15.8	3.3	
change 97/01	2.4	-3.6	1.3	0.0	
seats 2001	3	7	0	0	10
seats 1997	3	7	0	0	10

Isle of Wight	Con	Lab	LD	Other	Total
votes	25,223	9,676	22,397	6,186	63,482
votes% 2001	39.7	15.2	35.3	9.7	
votes% 1997	34.0	13.2	42.7	10.1	
change 97/01	5.7	2.1	-7.5	-0.3	
seats 2001	1	0	0	0	1
seats 1997	0	0	1	0	1

Contd./

Kent	Con	Lab	LD	Other	Total
votes	314,496	272,877	112,024	24,460	723,857
votes% 2001	43.4	37.7	15.5	3.4	
votes% 1997	40.5	37.1	17.0	5.4	
change 97/01	3.0	0.6	-1.6	-2.0	
seats 2001	9	8	0	0	17
seats 1997	9	8	0	0	17

Lancashire	Con	Lab	LD	Other	Total
votes	232,940	298,739	84,827	22,618	639,124
votes% 2001	36.4	46.7	13.3	3.5	
votes% 1997	34.2	49.2	12.7	3.9	
change 97/01	2.3	-2.5	0.6	-0.4	
seats 2001	2	13	0	0	15
seats 1997	2	13	0	0	15

Leicestershire	Con	Lab	LD	Other	Total
votes	167,748	182,290	74,964	14,776	439,778
votes% 2001	38.1	41.5	17.0	3.4	
votes% 1997	36.8	43.8	15.1	4.3	
change 97/01	1.4	-2.4	1.9	-0.9	
seats 2001	5	5	0	0	10
seats 1997	5	5	0	0	10

Lincolnshire	Con	Lab	LD	Other	Total
votes	141,109	109,150	49,225	5,943	305,427
votes% 2001	46.2	35.7	16.1	1.9	
votes% 1997	42.4	36.9	17.5	3.1	
change 97/01	3.8	-1.2	-1.4	-1.2	
seats 2001	6	1	0	0	7
seats 1997	6	1	0	0	7

Merseyside	Con	Lab	LD	Other	Total
votes	109,965	321,552	97,247	18,624	547,388
votes% 2001	20.1	58.7	17.8	3.4	
votes% 1997	19.7	61.9	14.4	3.9	
change 97/01	0.3	-3.1	3.3	-0.5	
seats 2001	0	15	1	0	16
seats 1997	0	15	1	0	16

Norfolk	Con	Lab	LD	Other	Total
votes	165,174	141,129	78,050	13,068	397,421
votes% 2001	41.6	35.5	19.6	3.3	
votes% 1997	36.7	39.9	18.2	5.1	
change 97/01	4.8	-4.4	1.4	-1.9	
seats 2001	4	3	1	0	8
seats 1997	4	4	0	0	8

Contd. /

North Yorkshire	Con	Lab	LD	Other	Total
votes	162,679	110,412	87,841	12,571	373,503
votes% 2001	43.6	29.6	23.5	3.4	
votes% 1997	40.0	32.8	23.0	4.2	
change 97/01	3.6	−3.2	0.5	−0.8	
seats 2001	4	3	1	0	8
seats 1997	4	3	1	0	8

Northamptonshire	Con	Lab	LD	Other	Total
votes	123,986	131,835	37,831	7,535	301,187
votes% 2001	41.2	43.8	12.6	2.5	
votes% 1997	40.4	45.0	11.1	3.4	
change 97/01	0.8	−1.3	1.4	−0.9	
seats 2001	1	5	0	0	6
seats 1997	1	5	0	0	6

Northumberland	Con	Lab	LD	Other	Total
votes	39,368	65,067	41,986	4,269	150,690
votes% 2001	26.1	43.2	27.9	2.8	
votes% 1997	22.7	48.7	25.0	3.7	
change 97/01	3.4	−5.5	2.9	−0.8	
seats 2001	1	2	1	0	4
seats 1997	1	2	1	0	4

Nottinghamshire	Con	Lab	LD	Other	Total
votes	152,826	228,843	58,966	9,153	449,788
votes% 2001	34.0	50.9	13.1	2.0	
votes% 1997	30.6	54.3	10.9	4.3	
change 97/01	3.4	−3.5	2.3	−2.2	
seats 2001	2	9	0	0	11
seats 1997	1	10	0	0	11

Oxfordshire	Con	Lab	LD	Other	Total
votes	108,296	84,269	78,007	15,092	285,664
votes% 2001	37.9	29.5	27.3	5.3	
votes% 1997	38.0	31.7	24.7	5.6	
change 97/01	−0.1	−2.2	2.6	−0.3	
seats 2001	4	1	1	0	6
seats 1997	4	1	1	0	6

Shropshire	Con	Lab	LD	Other	Total
votes	82,711	80,814	39,459	8,934	211,918
votes% 2001	39.0	38.1	18.6	4.2	
votes% 1997	37.2	39.7	20.5	2.7	
change 97/01	1.9	−1.5	−1.9	1.6	
seats 2001	1	3	1	0	5
seats 1997	2	3	0	0	5

Contd./

Somerset	Con	Lab	LD	Other	Total
votes	104,502	42,162	101,080	7,458	255,202
votes% 2001	40.9	16.5	39.6	2.9	
votes% 1997	36.5	17.4	40.6	5.4	
change 97/01	4.4	-0.9	-1.0	-2.5	
seats 2001	3	0	2	0	5
seats 1997	2	0	3	0	5

South Yorkshire	Con	Lab	LD	Other	Total
votes	94,503	296,403	90,624	21,282	502,812
votes% 2001	18.8	58.9	18.0	4.2	
votes% 1997	16.7	62.3	16.6	4.4	
change 97/01	2.1	-3.3	1.4	-0.2	
seats 2001	0	14	1	0	15
seats 1997	0	14	1	0	15

Staffordshire	Con	Lab	LD	Other	Total
votes	171,461	229,216	59,678	17,086	477,441
votes% 2001	35.9	48.0	12.5	3.6	
votes% 1997	33.7	51.3	10.7	4.2	
change 97/01	2.2	-3.3	1.8	-0.6	
seats 2001	3	9	0	0	12
seats 1997	3	9	0	0	12

Suffolk	Con	Lab	LD	Other	Total
votes	130,802	127,762	51,370	11,612	321,546
votes% 2001	40.7	39.7	16.0	3.6	
votes% 1997	37.6	40.2	17.6	4.6	
change 97/01	3.0	-0.4	-1.6	-1.0	
seats 2001	5	2	0	0	7
seats 1997	5	2	0	0	7

Surrey	Con	Lab	LD	Other	Total
votes	236,024	107,897	133,636	17,878	495,435
votes% 2001	47.6	21.8	27.0	3.6	
votes% 1997	46.2	22.3	24.5	7.0	
change 97/01	1.4	-0.5	2.5	-3.4	
seats 2001	10	0	1	0	11
seats 1997	11	0	0	0	11

Tyne and Wear	Con	Lab	LD	Other	Total
votes	78,088	277,905	73,339	12,280	441,612
votes% 2001	17.7	62.9	16.6	2.8	
votes% 1997	17.3	67.1	11.8	3.8	
change 97/01	0.4	-4.2	4.8	-1.0	
seats 2001	0	13	0	0	13
seats 1997	0	13	0	0	13

Contd. /

Warwickshire	Con	Lab	LD	Other	Total
votes	98,531	106,093	39,084	6,262	249,970
votes% 2001	39.4	42.4	15.6	2.5	
votes% 1997	38.7	43.8	13.9	3.6	
change 97/01	0.7	-1.4	1.7	-1.1	
seats 2001	1	4	0	0	5
seats 1997	1	4	0	0	5

West Midlands	Con	Lab	LD	Other	Total
votes	319,267	535,187	136,493	53,085	1,044,032
votes% 2001	30.6	51.3	13.1	5.1	
votes% 1997	29.8	51.5	11.3	7.4	
change 97/01	0.8	-0.2	1.7	-2.3	
seats 2001	4	25	0	0	29
seats 1997	4	24	0	1	29

West Sussex	Con	Lab	LD	Other	Total
votes	164,009	92,261	82,152	18,405	356,827
votes% 2001	46.0	25.9	23.0	5.2	
votes% 1997	44.7	24.3	25.6	5.5	
change 97/01	1.3	1.6	-2.6	-0.3	
seats 2001	7	1	0	0	8
seats 1997	7	1	0	0	8

West Yorkshire	Con	Lab	LD	Other	Total
votes	265,615	456,341	123,533	40,026	885,515
votes% 2001	30.0	51.5	14.0	4.5	
votes% 1997	28.8	54.0	12.9	4.2	
change 97/01	1.2	-2.5	1.0	0.3	
seats 2001	0	23	0	0	23
seats 1997	0	23	0	0	23

Wiltshire	Con	Lab	LD	Other	Total
votes	124,260	85,496	73,853	11,531	295,140
votes% 2001	42.1	29.0	25.0	3.9	
votes% 1997	40.2	28.0	26.2	5.6	
change 97/01	1.9	1.0	-1.2	-1.7	
seats 2001	4	2	0	0	6
seats 1997	4	2	0	0	6

Table 7. General Election Voting within the Scottish Parliament Electoral Areas

Central Scotland	Con	Lab	LD	SNP	Other	Total
votes	27,025	182,550	26,792	69,751	16,410	322,528
votes% 2001	8.4	56.6	8.3	21.6	5.1	
votes% 1997	10.4	59.4	5.2	23.4	1.6	
change 97/01	-2.1	-2.8	3.1	-1.8	3.5	
seats 2001	0	10	0	0	0	10
seats 1997	0	10	0	0	0	10

Glasgow	Con	Lab	LD	SNP	Other	Total
votes	19,410	127,594	24,148	43,060	36,533	250,745
votes% 2001	7.7	50.9	9.6	17.2	14.6	
votes% 1997	8.5	60.4	7.3	19.2	4.6	
change 97/01	-0.8	-9.5	2.3	-2.0	10.0	
seats 2001	0	9	0	0	1	10
seats 1997	0	10	0	0	0	10

Highlands and Islands	Con	Lab	LD	SNP	Other	Total
votes	30,746	53,074	59,530	44,895	7,965	196,210
votes% 2001	15.7	27.0	30.3	22.9	4.1	
votes% 1997	16.2	27.0	27.7	26.7	2.4	
change 97/01	-0.6	0.0	2.7	-3.8	1.7	
seats 2001	0	2	4	1	0	7
seats 1997	0	2	4	1	0	7

Lothians	Con	Lab	LD	SNP	Other	Total
votes	51,875	139,948	59,172	50,719	12,352	314,066
votes% 2001	16.5	44.6	18.8	16.1	3.9	
votes% 1997	19.2	45.9	14.9	18.4	1.5	
change 97/01	-2.7	-1.4	3.9	-2.3	2.4	
seats 2001	0	8	1	0	0	9
seats 1997	0	8	1	0	0	9

Mid Scotland and Fife	Con	Lab	LD	SNP	Other	Total
votes	56,041	119,876	47,342	71,119	9,612	303,990
votes% 2001	18.4	39.4	15.6	23.4	3.2	
votes% 1997	21.1	40.0	12.6	25.3	1.0	
change 97/01	-2.7	-0.6	2.9	-1.9	2.2	
seats 2001	0	6	1	2	0	9
seats 1997	0	6	1	2	0	9

North East Scotland	Con	Lab	LD	SNP	Other	Total
votes	55,140	91,245	65,469	75,987	6,178	294,019
votes% 2001	18.8	31.0	22.3	25.8	2.1	
votes% 1997	22.4	30.9	18.9	26.1	1.7	
change 97/01	-3.7	0.2	3.4	-0.3	0.4	
seats 2001	0	5	2	2	0	9
seats 1997	0	5	2	2	0	9

South of Scotland	Con	Lab	LD	SNP	Other	Total
votes	71,836	132,092	54,464	54,647	9,344	322,383
votes% 2001	22.3	41.0	16.9	17.0	2.9	
votes% 1997	22.6	43.4	13.4	19.1	1.6	
change 97/01	-0.3	-2.4	3.5	-2.1	1.3	
seats 2001	1	6	2	0	0	9
seats 1997	0	6	2	1	0	9

Contd./

West of Scotland	Con	Lab	LD	SNP	Other	Total
votes	48,585	154,794	41,117	54,136	11,128	309,760
votes% 2001	15.7	50.0	13.3	17.5	3.6	
votes% 1997	18.2	51.3	9.2	19.9	1.3	
change 97/01	-2.5	-1.3	4.0	-2.4	2.3	
seats 2001	0	9	0	0	0	9
seats 1997	0	9	0	0	0	9

Table 8. General Election Voting within the Welsh Assembly Electoral Areas

Mid and West Wales	Con	Lab	LD	PC	Other	Total
votes	63,275	83,261	52,322	65,834	5,425	270,117
votes% 2001	23.4	30.8	19.4	24.4	2.0	
votes% 1997	20.7	37.8	18.4	20.1	3.0	
change 97/01	2.7	-6.9	1.0	4.3	-1.0	
seats 2001	0	3	2	3	0	8
seats 1997	0	4	2	2	0	8

North Wales	Con	Lab	LD	PC	Other	Total
votes	76,520	134,761	35,880	45,627	5,196	297,984
votes% 2001	25.7	45.2	12.0	15.3	1.7	
votes% 1997	24.2	46.9	11.7	14.1	3.0	
change 97/01	1.5	-1.7	0.3	1.2	-1.3	
seats 2001	0	8	0	1	0	9
seats 1997	0	7	0	2	0	9

South Wales Central	Con	Lab	LD	PC	Other	Total
votes	58,819	156,386	42,192	29,446	5,526	292,369
votes% 2001	20.1	53.5	14.4	10.1	1.9	
votes% 1997	20.3	58.1	11.8	5.6	4.2	
change 97/01	-0.2	-4.6	2.6	4.5	-2.3	
seats 2001	0	8	0	0	0	8
seats 1997	0	8	0	0	0	8

South Wales East	Con	Lab	LD	PC	Other	Total
votes	52,284	161,044	30,680	27,949	8,025	279,982
votes% 2001	18.7	57.5	11.0	10.0	2.9	
votes% 1997	16.7	66.1	9.4	4.2	3.6	
change 97/01	2.0	-8.6	1.6	5.8	-0.7	
seats 2001	0	8	0	0	0	8
seats 1997	0	8	0	0	0	8

South Wales West	Con	Lab	LD	PC	Other	Total
votes	37,767	131,504	28,360	27,037	7,426	232,094
votes% 2001	16.3	56.7	12.2	11.6	3.2	
votes% 1997	15.0	65.6	10.7	5.7	3.0	
change 97/01	1.3	-9.0	1.5	5.9	0.2	
seats 2001	0	7	0	0	0	7
seats 1997	0	7	0	0	0	7

Table 9. Seats That Changed Hands 1997-2001

Conservative gains (9)

From Labour	*From Liberal Democrat*	*From Ind*	*From SNP*
Castle Point	Isle of Wight	Tatton	Galloway & Upper
Norfolk North West	Newark	Taunton	Nithsdale
Romford			
Upminster			

Labour gains (3)

From Conservative	*From Plaid Cymru*	*From Speaker*
Dorset South	Ynys Mon	West Bromwich West

Liberal Democrat gains (8)

From Conservative	*From Labour*
Cheadle	Chesterfield
Dorset Mid & Poole North	
Guildford	
Ludlow	
Norfolk North	
Romsey	
Teignbridge	

Plaid Cymru gain
From Labour
Carmarthen East & Dinefwr

Independent Kidderminster Hospital and Health Concern gain
From Labour
Wyre Forest

Speaker gain
From Labour
Glasgow Springburn

DUP gains (3)
From Ulster Unionist
Belfast North
Londonderry East
Strangford

SF gains (2)
From Ulster Unionist
Fermanagh & South Tyrone
Tyrone West

UU gain
From United Kingdom Unionist
Down North

Table 10. By-election Results 1997-2001

1. Uxbridge - 31 July 1997
(Death of Michael Shersby on 8 May 1997)

57,446	55.5	Randall, A.J.	Con	16,288	51.1	+	7.6
		Slaughter, A.F.	Lab	12,522	39.3	−	2.5
		Kerr, K.K.K.	LD	1,792	5.6	−	5.3
		Sutch, D.	MRLP	396	1.2 ★		
		Leonard, J.A.	Ind	259	0.8 ★	−	0.2
		Taylor, F.	BNP	205	0.6 ★		
		Anderson, I.H.M.	ND	157	0.5 ★		
		McAuley, J.C.	NF	110	0.3 ★		
		Middleton, H.	Orig Lib	69	0.2 ★		
		Feisenberger, J.R.	UKI	39	0.1 ★		
		Carroll, R.	Ind	30	0.1 ★		
1997:Con				3,766	11.8		

Leonard stood as 'Socialist'
ND is an abbreviation for National Democrat
Carroll stood as 'Emerald Rainbow Islands Dream Ticket'

2. Paisley South - 6 November 1997
(Death of Gordon McMaster on 28 July 1997)

54,386	43.1	Alexander, D.G.	Lab	10,346	44.1	−	13.4
		Blackford, I.	SNP	7,615	32.5	+	9.1
		McCartin, E.	LD	2,582	11.0	+	1.6
		Laidlaw, S.G.	Con	1,643	7.0	−	1.7
		Deighan, J.A.	PL	578	2.5 ★		
		Curran, F.	SSA	306	1.3 ★	+	0.9
		McLauchlan, C.W.	S. Ind Lab	155	0.7 ★		
		Herriot, C.	SL	153	0.7 ★		
		Blair, K.R.	NL	57	0.2 ★		
1997: Lab				2,731	11.7		

Curran stood as 'Scottish Socialist Alliance - Fighting Corruption'
McLauchlan stood as 'Scottish Independent Labour - Justified and Ancient'
NL is an abbreviation for Natural Law Party

3. Beckenham - 20 November 1997
(Resignation of Piers Merchant on 21 October 1997)

73,232	43.6	Lait, J.A.H.	Con	13,162	41.2	−	1.2
		Hughes R.N.	Lab	11,935	37.4	+	4.0
		Vetterlein, R.E.	LD	5,864	18.4	+	0.2
		Rimmer, P.H.	Lib	330	1.0 ★	−	3.1
		McAuley, J.C.	NF	267	0.8 ★		
		Mead, L.F.	NBR	237	0.7 ★		
		Campion, T.J.	Soc F	69	0.2 ★		
		Small, J.D.	NL	44	0.1 ★		
1997: Con				1,227	3.8		

Mead stood as 'New Britain, Referendum'
Campion stood as 'Social Foundation'

Contd. /

4. Winchester – 20 November 1997
(General Election result challenged, Election Petition, writ moved on 28 October 1997)

79,116	68.7	Oaten, M.	LD	37,006	68.0	+ 26.0
		Malone, G.	Con	15,450	28.4	– 13.6
		Davies, P.	Lab	944	1.7 ★	– 8.8
		Page, R.	UKI	521	1.0 ★	+ 0.2
		Sutch, D.	MRLP	316	0.6 ★	+ 0.1
		Huggett, R.J.	Ind	59	0.1 ★	
		Barry, R.	NL	48	0.1 ★	
		Everest, R.J.	Ind	40	0.1 ★	
1997: LD				21,556	39.6	

Huggett stood as 'Literal Democrat Mark Here to Win'
Everest stood as 'Euro Conservative'

5. Leeds Central – 10 June 1999
(Death of Derek Fatchett on 9 May 1999)

67,280	19.6	Benn, H.J.	Lab	6,361	48.2	– 21.4
		Wild, P.	LD	4,068	30.8	+ 19.6
		Wild, W.E.	Con	1,618	12.3	– 1.4
		Blackburn, D.	Grn	478	3.6 ★	
		Northgreaves, R.	UKI	353	2.7 ★	
		Hill, C.	Ind	258	2.0 ★	
		Fitzgerald, J.	Ind	51	0.4 ★	
1997: Lab				2,293	17.4	

Hill stood as 'Left Alliance'
Fitzgerald stood as 'Equal Parenting Campaign'

6. Eddisbury – 22 July 1999
(Resignation of Alastair Goodlad on 28 June 1999)

67,086	51.4	O'Brien, S.R.	Con	15,465	44.8	+ 2.3
		Hanson, M.R.	Lab	13,859	40.2	+ 0.0
		Roberts, P.D.	LD	4,757	13.8	+ 0.6
		Hope, A.	MRLP	238	0.7 ★	
		Grice, D.	NL	98	0.3 ★	
		Everest, R.J.	Ind	80	0.2 ★	
1997: Con				1,606	4.7	

Everest stood as 'Euro Conservative'

Contd. /

7. Hamilton South – 23 September 1999
(Elevation to peerage of George Robertson on 24 August 1999)

47,081	41.3	Tynan, B.	Lab	7,172	36.9		– 28.7
		Ewing, A.	SNP	6,616	34.0		+ 16.4
		Blackall, S.	SSP	1,847	9.5		
		Ferguson, C.	Con	1,406	7.2		– 1.4
		Mungall, S.A.	HAWA	1,075	5.5		
		MacLaren, M.A.	LD	634	3.3 ★		– 1.9
		Burns, M.	PL	257	1.3 ★		– 0.8
		Dewar, T.	SL	238	1.2 ★		
		Reid, J.W.	SU	113	0.6 ★		
		McConnachie, A.D.	UKI	61	0.3 ★		
		Stidolph, G.W.	NL	18	0.1 ★		
		Drummond Moray, J.S.H.	Ind	17	0.1 ★		
1997: Lab				556	2.9		

Mungall stood as 'Hamilton Accies Home, Watson Away'
Drummond Moray stood as 'Status Quo'

8. Wigan – 23 September 1999
(Death of Roger Stott on 8 August 1999)

64,775	25.0	Turner, N.	Lab	9,641	59.6		– 9.0
		Peet, T.	Con	2,912	18.0		+ 1.1
		Rule, J.D.	LD	2,148	13.3		+ 3.3
		Whittaker, J.	UKI	834	5.2		
		Kelly, W.	SL	240	1.5 ★		
		Maile, C.J.	Ind Grn	190	1.2 ★		
		Ebbs, S.	ND	100	0.6 ★		
		Davis, P.	NL	64	0.4 ★		+ 0.2
		Braid, D.O.	Ind	58	0.4 ★		
1997: Lab				6,729	41.6		

Contd./

9. Kensington and Chelsea – 25 November 1999

(Death of Alan Clark on 4 September 1999)

65,806	29.7	Portillo, M.D.X.	Con	11,004	56.4	+	2.8
		Atkinson, J.R.	Lab	4,298	22.0	–	5.9
		Woodthorpe Browne, R.	LD	1,831	9.4	–	5.9
		Stevens, J.C.C.	PEC	740	3.8 ★		
		Hockney, D.	UKI	450	2.3 ★	+	0.9
		Charlton, H.C.	Grn	446	2.3 ★		
		de Vere Beauclerk, C.	Ind	182	0.9 ★		
		Paisley, C.	LCA	141	0.7 ★		
		Irwin, M.	Ind	97	0.5 ★		
		Oliver, G.	Ind	75	0.4 ★		
		Scott-Fawcett, S.	Ref	57	0.3 ★		
		Hodges, L.	Ind	48	0.2 ★		
		Valente, G.	NL	35	0.2 ★	–	0.1
		Lovebucket, L.	Ind	26	0.1 ★		
		Davies, J.	Ind	24	0.1 ★		
		May, P.	Ind	24	0.1 ★		
		Hope, A.	MRLP	20	0.1 ★		
		Samuelson, T.	Ind	15	0.1 ★		
				6,706	34.4		

1997: Con

de Vere Beauclerk stood as 'Democratic Party'
Irwin stood as 'Campaign for Living Will Legislation'
Oliver stood as 'UK Pensioners'
Hodges stood as 'Daily and Sunday Sport'
Lovebucket stood as 'People's net dream ticket'
Davies stood as 'Ind Environmentalist: Stop Climatic Change'
May stood as 'Equal Parenting'
Samuelson stood as 'Stop Tobacco Companies Farming Our Children'

10. Ceredigion – 3 February 2000

(Resignation of Cynog Dafis on 10 January 2000)

55,025	45.6	Thomas, S.	PC	10,716	42.8	+	1.1
		Williams, M.F.	LD	5,768	23.0	+	6.5
		Davies, P.W.	Con	4,138	16.5	+	1.6
		Battle, M.	Lab	3,612	14.4	–	9.9
		Bufton, J.A.	UKI	487	1.9 ★		
		Berkeley Davies, J.	Ind Grn	289	1.2 ★		
		Shipton, M.J.	Ind	55	0.2 ★		
				4,948	19.7		

1997: PC

Shipton stood as '"Wales on Sunday": Match Funding Now'

Contd. /

11. Romsey – 4 May 2000
(Death of Michael Colvin on 24 February 2000)

69,701	55.5	Gidley, S.J.	LD	19,571	50.6	+ 21.1
		Palmer, T.J.	Con	16,260	42.0	– 4.0
		Howard, A.P.	Lab	1,451	3.7 ★	– 14.8
		Rankin-Moore, G.E.	UKI	901	2.3 ★	– 1.2
		Large, D.G.	LCA	417	1.1 ★	
		Lamont, T.	Ind	109	0.3 ★	
1997: Con				3,311	8.6	

12. Tottenham – 22 June 2000
(Death of Bernie Grant on 8 April 2000)

64,554	25,4	Lammy, D.L.	Lab	8,785	53.5	– 15.8
		Hames, D.J.	LD	3,139	19.1	+ 8.3
		Ellison, J.E.	Con	2,634	16.0	+ 0.3
		Bennett, W.E.	Ind	885	5.4	
		Budge, P.	Grn	606	3.7 ★	+ 0.9
		Basarik, E.	Ind	177	1.1 ★	
		Tanna, A.	UKI	136	0.8 ★	
		de Braam, D.L.D.	Ind Con	55	0.3 ★	
1997: Lab				5,646	34.4	

Bennett stood as 'London Socialist Alliance'
Basarik stood as 'Reform 2000 Anti-VAT'

13. South Antrim – 21 September 2000
(Death of Clifford Forsythe on 27 April 2000)

71,047	43.0	McCrea, R.T.W.	DUP	11,601	38.0	
		Burnside, D.W.B.	UU	10,779	35.3	– 22.2
		McClelland, S.D.	SDLP	3,496	11.4	– 4.7
		Meehan, M.	SF	2,611	8.5	+ 3.0
		Ford, D.R.J.	APNI	2,031	6.6	– 5.0
		Collins, D.H.	NL	49	0.2 ★	– 0.3
1997: UU				822	2.7	

14. Glasgow, Anniesland – 23 November 2000
(Death of Donald Dewar on 11 October 2000)

52,609	38.4	Robertson, J.	Lab	10,539	52.1	– 9.7
		Thoms, G.R.	SNP	4,202	20.8	+ 3.7
		Luckhurst, D.A.	Con	2,188	10.8	– 0.6
		McGinty, C.P.	LD	1,630	8.1	+ 0.8
		McCarthy, C.	SSP	1,441	7.1	+ 6.5
		Lyden, W.	Ind	212	1.0 ★	
1997: Lab				6,337	31.4	

Lyden stood as 'Family Action Movement'

Contd. /

15. Preston – 23 November 2000
(Death of Audrey Wise on 2 September 2000)

72,229	29.6	Hendrick, M.P.	Lab	9,765	45.7	– 15.1
		O'Hare, G.	Con	5,339	25.0	+ 3.1
		Chadwick, W.D.	LD	3,454	16.2	+ 1.5
		Cartwright, T.	Ind	1,210	5.7	
		Beaman, G.R.	UKI	458	2.1 ★	
		Merrick, R.J.	Grn	441	2.1 ★	
		Garrett, P.A.	Ind	416	1.9 ★	
		Jackson, C.M.	BNP	229	1.1 ★	
		Franklin–Braid, D.O.	Ind	51	0.2 ★	
1997: Lab				4,426	20.7	

Cartwright stood as 'Lancashire Socialist Alliance'
Garrett stood as 'Preston Alliance – Christian People's Alliance'
Franklin–Braid stood as 'Battle of Britain Christian Alliance'

16. West Bromwich West – 23 November 2000
(Resignation of Betty Boothroyd on 23 October 2000)

68,408	27.6	Bailey, A.E.	Lab	9,640	51.1	
		Bissell, K.E.	Con	6,408	33.9	
		Smith, S.L.	LD	1,791	9.5	
		Griffin, N.J.	BNP	794	4.2 ★	
		Oakton, J.P.	UKI	246	1.3 ★	
1997: Speaker				3,232	17.1	

17. Falkirk West – 21 December 2000
(Resignation of Dennis Canavan on 11 November 2000)

53,851	36.2	Joyce, E.	Lab	8,492	43.5	– 15.8
		Kerr, D.	SNP	7,787	39.9	+ 16.5
		Stevenson, C.	Con	1,621	8.3	– 3.8
		Hunter, I.G.	SSP	989	5.1	
		O'Donnell, H.	LD	615	3.2 ★	– 2.0
1997: Lab				705	3.6	

Sources: House of Commons Library;
Local Government Chronicle Elections Centre, University of Plymouth.

Table 11. Three Way Marginal Seats*

Constituency	1st	%maj 1st over 2nd	2nd	%maj 1st over 3rd	3rd
Perth	SNP	0.1	Con	4.2	Lab
Moray	SNP	5.2	Lab	7.2	Con
Bristol West	Lab	8.0	LD	8.0	Con
Argyll & Bute	LD	5.3	Lab	9.1	Con
Londonderry East	DUP	4.8	UU	11.3	SDLP
Wantage	Con	11.4	Lab	11.6	LD
Angus	SNP	10.3	Con	11.9	Lab
Tyrone West	SF	10.4	UU	12.1	SDLP
Upper Bann	UU	4.0	DUP	12.4	SF
Ynys Mon	Lab	2.4	PC	12.5	Con
Bridgwater	Con	10.4	LD	13.7	Lab
Galloway & Upper Nithsdale	Con	0.2	SNP	13.8	Lab
Inverness East, Nairn & Lochaber	Lab	11.1	SNP	14.6	LD
Leeds North West	Lab	12.3	Con	15.0	LD
Falmouth & Camborne	Lab	9.7	Con	15.1	LD
Caithness, Sutherland & Easter Ross	LD	11.0	Lab	15.2	SNP
Fermanagh & South Tyrone	SF	0.1	UU	15.5	SDLP
Brecon & Radnorshire	LD	2.0	Con	15.5	Lab
Colne Valley	Lab	9.9	Con	15.5	LD
Suffolk South	Con	11.2	Lab	16.5	LD
Aldershot	Con	14.6	LD	17.0	Lab
Colchester	LD	12.7	Con	17.6	Lab
Norfolk South	Con	12.3	LD	17.6	Lab
Bournemouth West	Con	14.0	Lab	17.7	LD
Cambridgeshire South East	Con	17.3	LD	17.8	Lab
Newry and Armagh	SDLP	6.4	SF	18.0	DUP
Hertfordshire South West	Con	17.3	Lab	18.0	LD
Eastleigh	LD	6.4	Con	18.8	Lab
Ceredigion	PC	11.4	LD	18.8	Con
Chelmsford West	Con	13.0	Lab	19.2	LD
Woodspring	Con	18.0	Lab	19.4	LD
Gainsborough	Con	19.1	Lab	19.6	LD
Poole	Con	18.3	Lab	19.6	LD
Weston-Super-Mare	LD	0.7	Con	19.7	Lab
Solihull	Con	19.5	LD	19.8	Lab
Edinburgh West	LD	19.2	Lab	19.8	Con
Tewkesbury	Con	19.2	Lab	19.8	LD
Belfast North	DUP	15.6	SF	19.9	SDLP
Cambridgeshire South	Con	17.4	LD	20.0	Lab

* Defined as seats where the winning party's margin over the third-placed party is 20% or less.

Table 12. Seats in Rank Order of %Majority

Conservative seats

Constituency	%maj	maj 2nd
1 Galloway & Upper Nithsdale	0.2	74 SNP
2 Taunton	0.4	235 LD
3 Orpington	0.5	269 LD
4 Boston & Skegness	1.3	515 Lab
5 Beverley & Holderness	1.7	781 Lab
6 Surrey South West	1.7	861 LD
7 Bedfordshire South West	1.8	776 Lab
8 Basingstoke	1.8	880 Lab
9 Castle Point	2.5	985 Lab
10 Dorset West	2.9	1414 LD
11 Upminster	3.7	1241 Lab
12 Haltemprice & Howden	4.3	1903 LD
13 Isle of Wight	4.5	2826 LD
14 Canterbury	4.6	2069 Lab
15 Eastbourne	4.8	2154 LD
16 Bury St Edmunds	5.0	2503 Lab
17 Bosworth	5.1	2280 Lab
18 Wells	5.4	2796 LD
19 Hexham	6.0	2529 Lab
20 Uxbridge	6.3	2098 Lab
21 Chipping Barnet	6.4	2701 Lab
22 Brentwood & Ongar	6.5	2821 Ind
23 Westmorland & Lonsdale	6.6	3147 LD
24 Gosport	6.6	2621 Lab
25 Altrincham & Sale West	6.8	2941 Lab
26 Norfolk North West	6.8	3485 Lab
27 Wycombe	7.0	3168 Lab
28 Totnes	7.3	3597 LD
29 Wiltshire North	7.3	3878 LD
30 Suffolk Central & Ipswich North	7.4	3469 Lab
31 Maidenhead	7.6	3284 LD
32 Hertfordshire North East	7.7	3444 Lab
33 Spelthorne	7.8	3262 Lab
34 Old Bexley & Sidcup	7.9	3345 Lab
35 Dorset North	7.9	3797 LD
36 Meriden	8.5	3784 Lab
37 Suffolk Coastal	8.6	4326 Lab
38 Norfolk Mid	8.7	4562 Lab
39 Newark	9.0	4073 Lab
40 New Forest East	9.1	3829 LD
41 Bournemouth East	9.6	3434 LD
42 Grantham & Stamford	9.8	4518 Lab
43 Aldridge – Brownhills	10.0	3768 Lab
44 Suffolk West	10.1	4295 Lab
45 Banbury	10.1	5219 Lab
46 Faversham & Kent Mid	10.2	4183 Lab
47 Eddisbury	10.3	4568 Lab
48 Havant	10.4	4207 Lab
49 Bridgwater	10.4	4987 LD
50 Westbury	10.5	5294 LD
51 Lichfield	10.6	4426 Lab
52 Yorkshire East	10.8	4682 Lab
53 Beckenham	10.9	4959 Lab
54 Billericay	11.0	5013 Lab
55 Ryedale	11.1	4875 LD
56 Suffolk South	11.2	5081 Lab
57 Tiverton & Honiton	11.3	6284 LD
58 Harborough	11.3	5252 LD
59 Wantage	11.4	5600 Lab
60 Hertsmere	11.8	4902 Lab
61 Hertford & Stortford	11.9	5603 Lab
62 Worcestershire West	12.0	5374 LD
63 Norfolk South	12.3	6893 LD
64 Folkestone & Hythe	12.9	5907 LD
65 Chelmsford West	13.0	6261 Lab
66 Blaby	13.0	6209 Lab
67 Stone	13.2	6036 Lab
68 Cities of London & Westminster	13.2	4499 Lab
69 Cambridgeshire N.E.	13.3	6373 Lab
70 Shropshire North	13.4	6241 Lab
71 Rushcliffe	13.5	7357 Lab
72 Bracknell	13.6	6713 Lab
73 Wokingham	13.7	5994 LD
74 Bournemouth West	14.0	4718 Lab
75 Worthing East & Shoreham	14.3	6139 Lab
76 Bognor Regis & Littlehampton	14.5	5643 Lab
77 Aldershot	14.6	6594 LD
78 Derbyshire West	14.6	7370 Lab
79 Hitchin & Harpenden	14.8	6663 Lab
80 Chingford & Woodford Green	14.8	5487 Lab
81 Sussex Mid	15.1	6898 LD
82 Devon South West	15.2	7144 Lab
83 Ashford	15.4	7359 Lab
84 Fareham	15.4	7009 Lab
85 Woking	15.8	6759 LD
86 Macclesfield	15.8	7200 Lab
87 Congleton	15.8	7134 Lab
88 Thanet North	15.9	6650 Lab
89 Essex North	16.0	7186 Lab
90 Charnwood	16.0	7739 Lab
91 Witney	16.2	7973 Lab
92 Staffordshire South	16.3	6881 Lab
93 Salisbury	16.5	8703 LD
94 Romford	16.7	5977 Lab
95 Louth & Horncastle	17.0	7554 Lab
96 Daventry	17.0	9649 Lab
97 Devon East	17.1	8195 LD
98 Bedfordshire Mid	17.3	8066 Lab
99 Hertfordshire South West	17.3	8181 Lab
100 Cambridgeshire S. E.	17.3	8990 LD

Contd. /

101 Cambridgeshire South	17.4	8403	LD
102 Hampshire East	17.7	8890	LD
103 Norfolk South West	17.7	9366	Lab
104 Sleaford & North Hykeham	17.7	8622	Lab
105 Bromsgrove	17.8	8138	Lab
106 Woodspring	18.0	8798	Lab
107 Poole	18.3	7166	Lab
108 Rutland & Melton	18.3	8612	Lab
109 Cambridgeshire N.W.	18.4	8101	Lab
110 Rochford & Southend E.	18.8	7034	Lab
111 Bedfordshire North East	19.0	8577	Lab
112 Henley	19.0	8458	LD
113 Gainsborough	19.1	8071	Lab
114 Tewkesbury	19.2	8663	Lab
115 Maldon & Chelmsford E.	19.2	8462	Lab
116 Croydon South	19.3	8697	Lab
117 Rayleigh	19.4	8290	Lab
118 Tonbridge & Malling	19.4	8250	Lab
119 Solihull	19.5	9407	LD
120 Runnymede & Weybridge	19.7	8360	Lab
121 Epping Forest	19.9	8426	Lab
122 Ruislip Northwood	20.3	7537	Lab
123 Reigate	20.3	8025	Lab
124 Aylesbury	20.4	10009	LD
125 Tatton	20.9	8611	Lab
126 Bromley & Chislehurst	20.9	9037	Lab
127 Worthing West	20.9	9037	LD
128 Windsor	21.1	8889	LD
129 Southend West	21.2	7941	Lab
130 Fylde	21.5	9610	LD
131 Stratford-on-Avon	21.5	11802	LD
132 Mole Valley	21.6	10153	LD
133 Epsom & Ewell	21.6	10080	Lab
134 Leominster	22.2	10367	LD
135 Devizes	22.3	11896	Lab
136 Maidstone & The Weald	22.6	10318	Lab
137 Ribble Valley	22.9	11238	LD
138 Chichester	22.9	11355	LD
139 Sutton Coldfield	23.3	10104	Lab
140 Bexhill & Battle	23.5	10503	LD
141 Worcestershire Mid	23.7	10627	Lab
142 Broxbourne	23.8	8993	Lab
143 Sevenoaks	23.8	10154	Lab
144 Surrey Heath	24.0	10819	LD
145 Saffron Walden	24.0	12004	LD
146 South Holland & The Deepings	24.0	11099	Lab
147 Tunbridge Wells	24.2	9730	LD
148 Hampshire North West	24.7	12009	Lab
149 Esher & Walton	25.3	11538	Lab
150 Vale of York	25.8	12517	Lab
151 Huntingdon	26.1	12792	LD
152 Cotswold	26.1	11983	LD
153 Wealden	26.1	13772	LD
154 Chesham & Amersham	26.2	11882	LD
155 Skipton & Ripon	26.3	12930	LD
156 Horsham	26.9	13666	LD
157 Christchurch	27.3	13544	LD
158 Surrey East	28.1	13203	LD
159 Buckingham	29.4	13325	Lab
160 Arundel & South Downs	29.9	13704	LD
161 New Forest West	29.9	13191	LD
162 Hampshire North East	30.2	13257	LD
163 Beaconsfield	31.0	13065	Lab
164 Kensington & Chelsea	31.3	8771	Lab
165 Penrith & The Border	33.2	14677	LD
166 Richmond (Yorks)	37.1	16319	Lab

Labour seats

Constituency	%maj	maj	2nd
1 Dorset South	0.3	153	Con
2 Braintree	0.7	358	Con
3 Monmouth	0.9	384	Con
4 Lancaster & Wyre	0.9	481	Con
5 Kettering	1.2	665	Con
6 Northampton South	1.7	885	Con
7 Cardiff Central	1.9	659	LD
8 Ynys Mon	2.4	800	PC
9 Welwyn Hatfield	2.8	1196	Con
10 Shipley	3.1	1428	Con
11 Clwyd West	3.2	1115	Con
12 Bexleyheath & Crayford	3.6	1472	Con
13 Milton Keynes North East	3.9	1829	Con
14 Hornchurch	4.2	1482	Con
15 Selby	4.3	2138	Con
16 Edinburgh Pentlands	4.5	1742	Con
17 Hammersmith & Fulham	4.5	2015	Con
18 Thanet South	4.5	1792	Con
19 Forest of Dean	4.6	2049	Con
20 Wellingborough	4.6	2355	Con
21 Ilford North	5.3	2115	Con
22 Rugby & Kenilworth	5.3	2877	Con
23 Gillingham	5.4	2272	Con
24 Harwich	5.4	2596	Con
25 Enfield North	6.0	2291	Con
26 Oldham East & Saddleworth	6.0	2726	LD
27 Calder Valley	6.5	3094	Con
28 Ayr	6.6	2545	Con
29 Redditch	6.7	2484	Con
30 Peterborough	7.2	2854	Con
31 Shrewsbury & Atcham	7.2	3579	Con
32 Dartford	7.4	3306	Con
33 Scarborough & Whitby	7.5	3585	Con
34 Hove	7.6	3171	Con
35 Bristol West	8.0	4426	LD
36 Preseli Pembrokeshire	8.0	2946	Con
37 Gloucester	8.0	3880	Con
38 Putney	8.1	2771	Con
39 Hemel Hempstead	8.2	3742	Con
40 Western Isles	8.2	1074	SNP
41 Ribble South	8.2	3802	Con
42 Finchley & Golders Green	8.5	3716	Con

Contd. /

43	Wolverhampton S.W.	8.5	3487 Con	98 Battersea	13.7	5053 Con
44	Birmingham Yardley	8.6	2576 LD	99 Dundee East	13.8	4466 SNP
45	The Wrekin	8.6	3587 Con	100 Portsmouth North	13.9	5134 Con
46	Croydon Central	8.7	3984 Con	101 Cardiff North	14.3	6165 Con
47	Elmet	9.1	4171 Con	102 Erewash	14.3	6932 Con
48	Wimbledon	9.1	3744 Con	103 Copeland	14.3	4964 Con
49	Stroud	9.1	5039 Con	104 Rochdale	14.3	5655 LD
50	Keighley	9.2	4005 Con	105 Loughborough	14.4	6378 Con
51	Sittingbourne & Sheppey	9.3	3509 Con	106 Bury North	14.6	6532 Con
52	High Peak	9.3	4489 Con	107 Aberdeen North	14.7	4449 SNP
53	Stourbridge	9.5	3812 Con	108 Edinburgh South	14.8	5499 LD
54	Brigg & Goole	9.6	3961 Con	109 Derbyshire South	15.1	7851 Con
55	Falmouth & Camborne	9.7	4527 Con	110 Ochil	15.2	5349 SNP
56	Medway	9.8	3780 Con	111 Bedford	15.2	6157 Con
57	Colne Valley	9.9	4639 Con	112 Halifax	15.2	6129 Con
58	Wirral West	10.0	4035 Con	113 City of Chester	15.4	6894 Con
59	St Albans	10.2	4466 Con	114 Milton Keynes S.W.	15.4	6978 Con
60	Vale of Glamorgan	10.4	4700 Con	115 Derby North	15.8	6982 Con
61	Burton	10.4	4849 Con	116 Amber Valley	16.2	7227 Con
62	Hastings & Rye	10.5	4308 Con	117 Warrington South	16.3	7397 Con
63	Pendle	10.8	4275 Con	118 Carlisle	16.3	5702 Con
64	Bradford West	10.9	4165 Con	119 Swindon South	16.9	7341 Con
65	Chatham & Aylesford	10.9	4340 Con	120 Crawley	17.1	6770 Con
66	Inverness East, Nairn &			121 Nuneaton	17.4	7535 Con
	Lochaber	11.1	4716 SNP	122 Stirling	17.5	6274 Con
67	Warwick & Leamington	11.1	5953 Con	123 Chorley	17.6	8444 Con
68	Gravesham	11.1	4862 Con	124 Dudley North	17.6	6800 Con
69	Great Yarmouth	11.3	4564 Con	125 Llanelli	17.7	6403 PC
70	Wansdyke	11.3	5613 Con	126 Vale of Clwyd	17.8	5761 Con
71	Stafford	11.3	5032 Con	127 Leeds North East	17.8	7089 Con
72	Tamworth	11.4	4598 Con	128 Conwy	18.1	6219 Con
73	Dover	11.6	5199 Con	129 Leicestershire North West	18.1	8157 Con
74	Aberdeen South	11.9	4388 LD	130 Waveney	18.1	8553 Con
75	Rossendale & Darwen	11.9	4970 Con	131 Hendon	18.2	7417 Con
76	Watford	12.0	5555 Con	132 Halesowen & Rowley		
77	Broxtowe	12.0	5873 Con	Regis	18.7	7359 Con
78	Corby	12.1	5700 Con	133 Dudley South	18.8	6817 Con
79	Morecambe & Lunesdale	12.2	5092 Con	134 Eastwood	18.9	9141 Con
80	Carmarthen West &			135 Basildon	18.9	7738 Con
	Pembrokeshire South	12.3	4538 Con	136 Northampton North	19.0	7893 Con
81	Leeds North West	12.3	5236 Con	137 Swindon North	19.1	8105 Con
82	Birmingham Edgbaston	12.4	4698 Con	138 Plymouth Sutton	19.2	7517 Con
83	Pudsey	12.5	5626 Con	139 Wakefield	19.3	7954 Con
84	Brighton Kemptown	12.6	4922 Con	140 Tynemouth	19.8	8678 Con
85	Wirral South	12.7	5049 Con	141 Gower	19.8	7395 Con
86	Gedling	12.8	5598 Con	142 Cambridge	20.0	8579 LD
87	Reading East	12.8	5595 Con	143 Birmingham Hall Green	20.1	6648 Con
88	Norwich North	12.9	5863 Con	144 Stevenage	20.2	8566 Con
89	Harlow	13.0	5228 Con	145 Dewsbury	20.3	7449 Con
90	Worcester	13.0	5766 Con	146 Clydesdale	20.4	7794 SNP
91	Batley & Spen	13.1	5064 Con	147 Sherwood	20.4	9373 Con
92	Harrow West	13.2	6156 Con	148 Stockton South	20.6	9086 Con
93	Enfield Southgate	13.2	5546 Con	149 Coventry South	20.6	8279 Con
94	Cleethorpes	13.2	5620 Con	150 Norwich South	20.7	8816 Con
95	Bolton West	13.4	5518 Con	151 Eltham	20.7	6996 Con
96	Blackpool N. & Fleetwood	13.4	5721 Con	152 Dumfries	20.7	8834 Con
97	Staffordshire Moorlands	13.7	5838 Con	153 Ipswich	20.8	8081 Con

Contd. /

154 Blaydon	21.1 7809 LD	210 Southampton Itchen	27.1 11223 Con
155 Reading West	21.1 8849 Con	211 Bridgend	27.1 10046 Con
156 Middlesbrough South &		212 Telford	27.2 8383 Con
Cleveland East	21.3 9351 Con	213 Nottingham South	27.3 9989 Con
157 Blackpool South	21.3 8262 Con	214 Kilmarnock & Loudoun	27.4 10334 SNP
158 Hyndburn	21.5 8219 Con	215 Bradford South	27.5 9662 Con
159 Bolton North East	21.6 8422 Con	216 Falkirk West	27.6 8532 SNP
160 Warwickshire North	21.7 9639 Con	217 Stalybridge & Hyde	27.6 8859 Con
161 Hampstead & Highgate	22.2 7876 Con	218 Tooting	27.7 10400 Con
162 Exeter	22.3 11759 Con	219 Regent's Park &	
163 Lancashire West	22.4 9643 Con	Kensington North	27.7 10266 Con
164 Crosby	22.7 8353 Con	220 Edmonton	28.1 9772 Con
165 Lincoln	22.7 8420 Con	221 Dumbarton	28.2 9575 SNP
166 Blackburn	23.0 9249 Con	222 Strathkelvin & Bearsden	28.2 11717 LD
167 Harrow East	23.1 11124 Con	223 Huddersfield	28.4 10046 Con
168 Brentford & Isleworth	23.2 10318 Con	224 Walsall South	28.5 9931 Con
169 Dundee West	23.3 6800 SNP	225 Burnley	28.5 10498 Con
170 Birmingham Perry Barr	23.4 8753 Con	226 York	28.7 13779 Con
171 Bristol North West	23.4 10887 Con	227 Linlithgow	28.8 9129 SNP
172 Edinburgh Central	23.7 8142 LD	228 Ealing Acton &	
173 Brighton Pavilion	23.7 9643 Con	Shepherd's Bush	29.0 10789 Con
174 Crewe & Nantwich	23.8 9906 Con	229 Leicester West	29.0 9639 Con
175 Hornsey & Wood Green	24.1 10614 LD	230 Walsall North	29.1 9391 Con
176 Weaver Vale	24.5 9637 Con	231 Normanton	29.1 9937 Con
177 Cunninghame North	24.8 8398 SNP	232 Derbyshire North East	29.1 12258 Con
178 Delyn	24.8 8605 Con	233 Stoke-on-Trent South	29.1 10489 Con
179 Bassetlaw	25.1 9748 Con	234 Ealing Southall	29.2 13683 Con
180 Aberdeen Central	25.1 6646 SNP	235 East Lothian	29.4 10830 Con
181 Glasgow Govan	25.3 6400 SNP	236 Livingston	29.5 10616 SNP
182 Cumbernauld & Kilsyth	25.3 7520 SNP	237 Swansea West	29.8 9550 Con
183 Barrow & Furness	25.3 9889 Con	238 West Bromwich East	29.9 9763 Con
184 Luton North	25.5 9977 Con	239 Lewisham East	29.9 9003 Con
185 Coventry North West	25.6 10874 Con	240 Mansfield	30.0 11038 Con
186 Renfrewshire West	25.6 8575 SNP	241 Brent North	30.1 10205 Con
187 Bradford North	25.6 8969 Con	242 Heywood & Middleton	30.1 11670 Con
188 Luton South	25.8 10133 Con	243 Wrexham	30.6 9188 Con
189 Birmingham Selly Oak	25.8 10339 Con	244 East Kilbride	30.6 12755 SNP
190 Islington S. & Finsbury	25.8 7280 LD	245 Scunthorpe	30.8 10372 Con
191 Newcastle-under-Lyme	25.8 9986 Con	246 Fife Central	31.0 10075 SNP
192 Workington	25.9 10850 Con	247 Plymouth Devonport	31.2 13033 Con
193 Oxford East	26.0 10344 LD	248 Midlothian	31.4 9014 SNP
194 Don Valley	26.0 9520 Con	249 Leicester South	31.4 13243 Con
195 Darlington	26.0 10384 Con	250 Morley & Rothwell	31.4 12090 Con
196 Alyn & Deeside	26.0 9222 Con	251 Dagenham	31.5 8693 Con
197 Cannock Chase	26.1 10704 Con	252 Newport East	31.6 9874 Con
198 Ellesmere Port & Neston	26.2 10861 Con	253 Wolverhampton N.E.	31.6 9965 Con
199 Bethnal Green & Bow	26.2 10057 Con	254 Falkirk East	31.8 10712 SNP
200 Ealing North	26.3 11837 Con	255 Kirkcaldy	31.8 8963 SNP
201 Birmingham Northfield	26.4 7798 Con	256 Slough	32.1 12508 Con
202 Kingswood	26.5 13962 Con	257 Derby South	32.2 13855 Con
203 Edinburgh N. & Leith	26.5 8817 LD	258 Dulwich & W. Norwood	32.2 12310 Con
204 Newport West	26.5 9304 Con	259 Bury South	32.3 12772 Con
205 Clwyd South	26.6 8898 Con	260 City of Durham	32.4 13441 LD
206 St Helens South	26.6 8985 LD	261 Birmingham Erdington	32.6 9962 Con
207 Thurrock	26.8 9997 Con	262 Stockport	32.7 11569 Con
208 Southampton Test	27.0 11207 Con	263 Wallasey	32.9 12276 Con
209 Glasgow Kelvin	27.1 7260 LD	264 Manchester Withington	32.9 11524 LD

Contd. /

265 Clydebank & Milngavie	33.0 10724 SNP	319 Cunninghame South	40.0 11230 SNP
266 Leicester East	33.1 13442 Con	320 Croydon North	40.3 16858 Con
267 Bristol East	33.2 13392 Con	321 Hamilton South	40.3 10775 SNP
268 Cardiff West	33.2 11321 Con	322 Rother Valley	40.4 14882 Con
269 Newcastle upon Tyne		323 Nottingham North	40.7 12240 Con
Central	33.3 11605 LD	324 Wigan	40.9 13743 Con
270 Worsley	33.3 11787 Con	325 Greenwich & Woolwich	41.3 13433 Con
271 Oldham West & Royton	33.4 13365 Con	326 Stockton North	41.3 14647 Con
272 Erith & Thamesmead	33.5 11167 Con	327 Glasgow Anniesland	41.4 11054 SNP
273 Ashfield	33.7 13268 Con	328 Poplar & Canning Town	41.4 14108 Con
274 Ilford South	33.9 13997 Con	329 Manchester Gorton	41.5 11304 LD
275 Stretford & Urmston	34.0 13271 Con	330 Hayes & Harlington	41.6 13466 Con
276 Preston	34.0 12268 Con	331 Durham North West	41.6 16333 Con
277 Sheffield Hillsborough	34.3 14569 LD	332 Sheffield Central	41.7 12544 LD
278 Sheffield Heeley	34.3 11704 LD	333 Stoke-on-Trent Central	41.7 11818 Con
279 Paisley North	34.3 9321 SNP	334 Coventry North East	42.3 15751 Con
280 Cardiff South & Penarth	34.4 12287 Con	335 St Helens North	42.3 15901 Con
281 Bristol South	34.6 14181 Con	336 Glasgow Baillieston	42.3 9839 SNP
282 Nottingham East	34.7 10320 Con	337 Neath	42.3 14816 PC
283 Great Grimsby	34.8 11484 Con	338 Islington North	42.9 12958 LD
284 Greenock & Inverclyde	34.8 9890 LD	339 Glasgow Rutherglen	43.2 12625 SNP
285 Feltham & Heston	35.0 12657 Con	340 Ashton under Lyne	43.4 15518 Con
286 Wansbeck	35.0 13101 LD	341 Newcastle upon Tyne	
287 Redcar	35.2 13443 Con	East & Wallsend	43.5 14223 LD
288 Blyth Valley	35.3 12188 LD	342 Leeds East	43.5 12643 Con
289 Edinburgh East &		343 Eccles	43.8 14528 Con
Musselburgh	35.3 12168 SNP	344 Sunderland South	43.8 13667 Con
290 Doncaster Central	35.4 11999 Con	345 Birmingham Hodge Hill	43.9 11618 Con
291 Dunfermline West	35.4 10980 SNP	346 Sedgefield	44.0 17713 Con
292 West Bromwich West	35.7 11355 Con	347 Walthamstow	44.1 15181 Con
293 Barnsley West & Penistone	35.7 12352 Con	348 Birmingham Sparkbrook	
294 Holborn & St Pancras	35.9 11175 LD	& Small Heath	44.3 16246 LD
295 Wythenshawe & Sale East	36.0 12608 Con	349 Hemsworth	44.4 15636 Con
296 Bishop Auckland	36.1 13926 Con	350 Glasgow Maryhill	44.5 9888 SNP
297 Mitcham & Morden	36.3 13785 Con	351 Rotherham	44.5 13077 Con
298 Motherwell & Wishaw	36.9 10956 SNP	352 Glasgow Pollok	44.6 11268 SNP
299 Carrick, Cumnock &		353 Hamilton North &	
Doon Valley	37.0 14856 Con	Bellshill	44.6 13561 SNP
300 Caerphilly	37.1 14425 PC	354 Sunderland North	44.8 13354 Con
301 Hull North	37.4 10721 LD	355 Brent East	45.0 13047 Con
302 Bolton South East	37.7 12871 Con	356 Denton & Reddish	45.6 15330 Con
303 Warley	37.7 11850 Con	357 Wolverhampton S.E.	45.7 12464 Con
304 Hull West & Hessle	37.9 10951 Con	358 Pontypridd	46.2 17684 PC
305 Barking	37.9 9534 Con	359 Torfaen	46.2 16280 Con
306 Liverpool Garston	38.3 12494 LD	360 South Shields	46.3 14090 Con
307 Leyton & Wanstead	38.3 12904 Con	361 Leigh	46.4 16362 Con
308 Hartlepool	38.3 14571 Con	362 Leeds West	46.5 14935 Con
309 Liverpool Wavertree	38.3 12319 LD	363 Hackney North & Stoke	
310 Lewisham West	38.7 11920 Con	Newington	47.0 13911 LD
311 Airdrie & Shotts	38.9 12340 SNP	364 Merthyr Tydfil & Rhymney	47.1 14923 PC
312 Warrington North	39.0 15156 Con	365 Rhondda	47.2 16047 PC
313 Vauxhall	39.0 13018 LD	366 Glasgow Shettleston	48.0 9818 SNP
314 Paisley South	39.0 11910 SNP	367 Ogmore	48.0 14574 PC
315 Stoke-on-Trent North	39.1 11784 Con	368 Cynon Valley	48.2 12998 PC
316 Streatham	39.2 14630 LD	369 Islwyn	48.3 15309 LD
317 Glasgow Cathcart	39.5 10816 SNP	370 Doncaster North	48.4 15187 Con
318 Newcastle upon Tyne N.	39.7 14450 Con	371 Middlesbrough	48.4 16330 Con

Contd. /

372 Durham North	48.4 18683 Con	11 Newbury	4.8 2415 Con
373 Wentworth	48.7 16449 Con	12 Romsey	4.9 2370 Con
374 Salford	48.9 11012 LD	13 Teignbridge	5.1 3011 Con
375 Bolsover	49.1 18777 Con	14 Argyll & Bute	5.3 1653 Lab
376 Hackney South &		15 Chesterfield	5.8 2586 Lab
Shoreditch	49.6 15049 LD	16 Devon North	6.1 2984 Con
377 Hull East	49.6 15325 LD	17 Eastleigh	6.4 3058 Con
378 Dunfermline East	50.1 15063 SNP	18 Southport	7.3 3007 Con
379 Knowsley N. & Sefton E.	50.4 18927 Con	19 Yeovil	8.2 3928 Con
380 Coatbridge & Chryston	50.5 15314 SNP	20 Richmond Park	10.1 4964 Con
381 Halton	50.6 17428 Con	21 Cornwall South East	10.4 5375 Con
382 Makerfield	50.9 17750 Con	22 Sutton & Cheam	10.8 4304 Con
383 Jarrow	51.0 17595 LD	23 Caithness, Sutherland &	
384 Liverpool West Derby	51.3 15853 Lib	Easter Ross	11.0 2744 Lab
385 Barnsley E. & Mexborough	51.6 16789 LD	24 Carshalton & Wallington	11.2 4547 Con
386 Pontefract & Castleford	52.2 16378 Con	25 Cheltenham	12.6 5255 Con
387 Lewisham Deptford	52.5 15293 Con	26 Colchester	12.7 5553 Con
388 Sheffield Attercliffe	52.6 18844 Con	27 Aberdeenshire W &	
389 Leeds Central	52.7 14381 Con	Kincardine	12.7 4821 Con
390 Manchester Central	53.0 13742 LD	28 Torbay	14.1 6708 Con
391 Gateshead East &		29 Twickenham	15.3 7655 Con
Washington West	53.3 17904 LD	30 Tweeddale, Ettrick &	
392 Aberavon	53.4 16108 PC	Lauderdale	15.5 5157 Lab
393 West Ham	53.4 15645 Con	31 Portsmouth South	15.5 6093 Con
394 Tottenham	53.5 16916 Con	32 Truro & St Austell	16.0 8065 Con
395 Birkenhead	53.8 15591 Con	33 Winchester	16.3 9634 Con
396 Manchester Blackley	54.5 14464 Con	34 Northavon	17.7 9877 Con
397 Liverpool Riverside	54.7 13950 LD	35 Oxford West & Abingdon	17.8 9185 Con
398 Tyneside North	54.9 20568 Con	36 Cornwall North	18.2 9832 Con
399 Barnsley Central	54.9 15130 LD	37 Edinburgh West	19.2 7589 Lab
400 Camberwell & Peckham	56.3 14123 LD	38 St Ives	20.4 10053 Con
401 East Ham	56.4 21032 Con	39 Orkney & Shetland	20.8 3475 Lab
402 Tyne Bridge	57.2 14889 Con	40 Harrogate &	
403 Birmingham Ladywood	57.6 18143 Con	Knaresborough	21.0 8845 Con
404 Knowsley South	58.3 21316 LD	41 Bath	21.4 9894 Con
405 Houghton & Washington E.	58.9 19818 Con	42 Lewes	21.4 9710 Con
406 Brent South	60.7 17380 Con	43 Montgomeryshire	21.5 6234 Con
407 Blaenau Gwent	60.9 19313 PC	44 Hazel Grove	21.9 8435 Con
408 Liverpool Walton	63.2 17996 LD	45 Gordon	22.5 7879 Con
409 Swansea East	63.7 19149 Grn	46 Berwick-upon-Tweed	23.3 8458 Con
410 Easington	66.5 21949 Con	47 Sheffield Hallam	24.4 9347 Con
411 Sheffield Brightside	66.7 17049 Con	48 Roxburgh & Berwickshire	26.1 7511 Con
412 Bootle	69.0 19043 LD	49 Southwark North &	
		Bermondsey	26.1 9632 Lab
		50 Fife North East	28.1 9736 Con

Liberal Democrat seats

Constituency	%maj	maj 2nd
1 Cheadle	0.1	33 Con
2 Weston-Super-Mare	0.7	338 Con
3 Norfolk North	0.9	483 Con
4 Dorset Mid & Poole N.	0.9	384 Con
5 Guildford	1.1	538 Con
6 Somerton & Frome	1.3	668 Con
7 Brecon & Radnorshire	2.0	751 Con
8 Devon West & Torridge	2.1	1194 Con
9 Hereford	2.2	968 Con
10 Ludlow	3.8	1630 Con

51 Kingston & Surbiton	31.9	15676 Con
52 Ross, Skye & Inverness W.	37.2	12952 Lab

Scottish National seats

Constituency	%maj	vote 2nd
1 Perth	0.1	48 Con
2 Moray	5.2	1744 Lab
3 Tayside North	8.5	3283 Con
4 Angus	10.3	3611 Con
5 Banff & Buchan	34.1	10503 Con

Contd. /

Plaid Cymru seats

Constituency	%maj	maj	2nd
1 Carmarthen E. & Dinefwr	6.8	2590	Lab
2 Ceredigion	11.4	3944	LD
3 Caernarfon	12.1	3511	Lab
4 Meirionnydd Nant Conwy	27.0	5684	Lab

KHHC seat

Constituency	%maj	maj	2nd
– Wyre Forest	35.9	17630	Lab

Ulster Unionist seats

Constituency	%maj	maj	2nd
1 Antrim East	0.4	128	DUP
2 Antrim South	2.3	1011	DUP
3 Upper Bann	4.0	2058	DUP
4 Belfast South	14.2	5399	SDLP
5 Down North	19.7	7324	UKU
6 Lagan Valley	39.9	18342	APNI

Democratic Unionist seats

Constituency	%maj	maj	2nd
1 Strangford	2.6	1110	UU
2 Londonderry East	4.8	1901	UU
3 Belfast North	15.6	6387	SF
4 Belfast East	19.3	7117	UU
5 Antrim North	28.9	14224	UU

SDLP seats

Constituency	%maj	maj	2nd
1 Newry and Armagh	6.4	3575	SF
2 Foyle	23.6	11550	SF
3 Down South	26.6	13858	SF

Sinn Fein seats

Constituency	%maj	maj	2nd
1 Fermanagh & S. Tyrone	0.1	53	UU
2 Tyrone West	10.4	5040	UU
3 Ulster Mid	19.9	9953	DUP
4 Belfast West	47.2	19342	SDLP

Table 13. Seats in Rank Order of %Majority by Region and Country

EAST MIDLANDS

Constituency	%maj	maj	2nd
Conservative seats			
4 Boston & Skegness	1.3	515	Lab
17 Bosworth	5.1	2280	Lab
39 Newark	9.0	4073	Lab
42 Grantham & Stamford	9.8	4518	Lab
58 Harborough	11.3	5252	LD
66 Blaby	13.0	6209	Lab
71 Rushcliffe	13.5	7357	Lab
78 Derbyshire West	14.6	7370	Lab
90 Charnwood	16.0	7739	Lab
95 Louth & Horncastle	17.0	7554	Lab
96 Daventry	17.0	9649	Lab
104 Sleaford & N. Hykeham	17.7	8622	Lab
108 Rutland & Melton	18.3	8612	Lab
113 Gainsborough	19.1	8071	Lab
146 South Holland & The Deepings	24.0	11099	Lab
Labour seats			
5 Kettering	1.2	665	Con
6 Northampton South	1.7	885	Con
20 Wellingborough	4.6	2355	Con
52 High Peak	9.3	4489	Con
77 Broxtowe	12.0	5873	Con
78 Corby	12.1	5700	Con
86 Gedling	12.8	5598	Con
102 Erewash	14.3	6932	Con
105 Loughborough	14.4	6378	Con
109 Derbyshire South	15.1	7851	Con
115 Derby North	15.8	6982	Con
116 Amber Valley	16.2	7227	Con
129 Leicestershire North West	18.1	8157	Con
136 Northampton North	19.0	7893	Con
147 Sherwood	20.4	9373	Con
165 Lincoln	22.7	8420	Con
179 Bassetlaw	25.1	9748	Con
213 Nottingham South	27.3	9989	Con
229 Leicester West	29.0	9639	Con
232 Derbyshire North East	29.1	12258	Con
240 Mansfield	30.0	11038	Con
249 Leicester South	31.4	13243	Con
257 Derby South	32.2	13855	Con
266 Leicester East	33.1	13442	Con
273 Ashfield	33.7	13268	Con
282 Nottingham East	34.7	10320	Con
323 Nottingham North	40.7	12240	Con
375 Bolsover	49.1	18777	Con
Liberal Democrat seat			
15 Chesterfield	5.8	2586	Lab

EASTERN

Constituency	%maj	maj	2nd
Conservative seats			
7 Bedfordshire South West	1.8	776	Lab
9 Castle Point	2.5	985	Lab
16 Bury St Edmunds	5.0	2503	Lab
22 Brentwood & Ongar	6.5	2821	Ind
26 Norfolk North West	6.8	3485	Lab
30 Suffolk Central & Ipswich North	7.4	3469	Lab
32 Hertfordshire North East	7.7	3444	Lab
37 Suffolk Coastal	8.6	4326	Lab
38 Norfolk Mid	8.7	4562	Lab
44 Suffolk West	10.1	4295	Lab
54 Billericay	11.0	5013	Lab
56 Suffolk South	11.2	5081	Lab
60 Hertsmere	11.8	4902	Lab
61 Hertford & Stortford	11.9	5603	Lab
63 Norfolk South	12.3	6893	LD
65 Chelmsford West	13.0	6261	Lab
69 Cambridgeshire N. E.	13.3	6373	Lab
79 Hitchin & Harpenden	14.8	6663	Lab
89 Essex North	16.0	7186	Lab
98 Bedfordshire Mid	17.3	8066	Lab
99 Hertfordshire South West	17.3	8181	Lab
100 Cambridgeshire S. E.	17.3	8990	LD
101 Cambridgeshire South	17.4	8403	LD
103 Norfolk South West	17.7	9366	Lab
109 Cambridgeshire N.W.	18.4	8101	Lab
110 Rochford & Southend E.	18.8	7034	Lab
111 Bedfordshire North East	19.0	8577	Lab
115 Maldon & Chelmsford E.	19.2	8462	Lab
117 Rayleigh	19.4	8290	Lab
121 Epping Forest	19.9	8426	Lab
129 Southend West	21.2	7941	Lab
142 Broxbourne	23.8	8993	Lab
145 Saffron Walden	24.0	12004	LD
151 Huntingdon	26.1	12792	LD
Labour seats			
2 Braintree	0.7	358	Con
9 Welwyn Hatfield	2.8	1196	Con
24 Harwich	5.4	2596	Con
30 Peterborough	7.2	2854	Con
39 Hemel Hempstead	8.2	3742	Con
59 St Albans	10.2	4466	Con
69 Great Yarmouth	11.3	4564	Con
76 Watford	12.0	5555	Con
88 Norwich North	12.9	5863	Con
89 Harlow	13.0	5228	Con
111 Bedford	15.2	6157	Con
130 Waveney	18.1	8553	Con
135 Basildon	18.9	7738	Con

Contd. /

142 Cambridge	20.0	8579	LD
144 Stevenage	20.2	8566	Con
150 Norwich South	20.7	8816	Con
153 Ipswich	20.8	8081	Con
184 Luton North	25.5	9977	Con
188 Luton South	25.8	10133	Con
207 Thurrock	26.8	9997	Con

Liberal Democrat seats

3 Norfolk North	0.9	483	Con
26 Colchester	12.7	5553	Con

GREATER LONDON

Constituency	%maj	maj	2nd

Conservative seats

3 Orpington	0.5	269	LD
11 Upminster	3.7	1241	Lab
20 Uxbridge	6.3	2098	Lab
21 Chipping Barnet	6.4	2701	Lab
34 Old Bexley & Sidcup	7.9	3345	Lab
53 Beckenham	10.9	4959	Lab
68 Cities of London & Westminster	13.2	4499	Lab
80 Chingford & Woodford Green	14.8	5487	Lab
94 Romford	16.7	5977	Lab
116 Croydon South	19.3	8697	Lab
122 Ruislip Northwood	20.3	7537	Lab
126 Bromley & Chislehurst	20.9	9037	Lab
164 Kensington & Chelsea	31.3	8771	Lab

Labour seats

12 Bexleyheath & Crayford	3.6	1472	Con
14 Hornchurch	4.2	1482	Con
17 Hammersmith & Fulham	4.5	2015	Con
21 Ilford North	5.3	2115	Con
25 Enfield North	6.0	2291	Con
38 Putney	8.1	2771	Con
42 Finchley & Golders Green	8.5	3716	Con
46 Croydon Central	8.7	3984	Con
48 Wimbledon	9.1	3744	Con
92 Harrow West	13.2	6156	Con
93 Enfield Southgate	13.2	5546	Con
98 Battersea	13.7	5053	Con
131 Hendon	18.2	7417	Con
151 Eltham	20.7	6996	Con
161 Hampstead & Highgate	22.2	7876	Con
167 Harrow East	23.1	11124	Con
168 Brentford & Isleworth	23.2	10318	Con
175 Hornsey & Wood Green	24.1	10614	LD
190 Islington S. & Finsbury	25.8	7280	LD
199 Bethnal Green & Bow	26.2	10057	Con
200 Ealing North	26.3	11837	Con
218 Tooting	27.7	10400	Con

219 Regent's Park & Kensington North	27.7	10266	Con
220 Edmonton	28.1	9772	Con
228 Ealing Acton & Shepherd's Bush	29.0	10789	Con
234 Ealing Southall	29.2	13683	Con
239 Lewisham East	29.9	9003	Con
241 Brent North	30.1	10205	Con
251 Dagenham	31.5	8693	Con
258 Dulwich & W. Norwood	32.2	12310	Con
272 Erith & Thamesmead	33.5	11167	Con
274 Ilford South	33.9	13997	Con
285 Feltham & Heston	35.0	12657	Con
294 Holborn & St Pancras	35.9	11175	LD
297 Mitcham & Morden	36.3	13785	Con
305 Barking	37.9	9534	Con
307 Leyton & Wanstead	38.3	12904	Con
310 Lewisham West	38.7	11920	Con
313 Vauxhall	39.0	13018	LD
316 Streatham	39.2	14630	LD
320 Croydon North	40.3	16858	Con
325 Greenwich & Woolwich	41.3	13433	Con
328 Poplar & Canning Town	41.4	14108	Con
330 Hayes & Harlington	41.6	13466	Con
338 Islington North	42.9	12958	LD
347 Walthamstow	44.1	15181	Con
355 Brent East	45.0	13047	Con
358 Hackney North & Stoke Newington	46.1	13651	Con
376 Hackney South & Shoreditch	49.6	15049	LD
387 Lewisham Deptford	52.5	15293	Con
393 West Ham	53.4	15645	Con
394 Tottenham	53.5	16916	Con
401 Camberwell & Peckham	56.3	14123	LD
402 East Ham	56.4	21032	Con
407 Brent South	60.7	17380	Con

Liberal Democrat seats

20 Richmond Park	10.1	4964	Con
22 Sutton & Cheam	10.8	4304	Con
24 Carshalton & Wallington	11.2	4547	Con
29 Twickenham	15.3	7655	Con
49 Southwark North & Bermondsey	26.1	9632	Lab
51 Kingston & Surbiton	31.9	15676	Con

Contd./

NORTH EAST

Constituency	%maj	maj	2nd
Conservative seats			
19 Hexham	6.0	2529	Lab
Labour seats			
140 Tynemouth	19.8	8678	Con
148 Stockton South	20.6	9086	Con
154 Blaydon	21.1	7809	LD
156 Middlesbrough South & Cleveland East	21.3	9351	Con
195 Darlington	26.0	10384	Con
260 City of Durham	32.4	13441	LD
269 Newcastle upon Tyne Central	33.3	11605	LD
286 Wansbeck	35.0	13101	LD
287 Redcar	35.2	13443	Con
288 Blyth Valley	35.3	12188	LD
296 Bishop Auckland	36.1	13926	Con
308 Hartlepool	38.3	14571	Con
318 Newcastle upon Tyne N.	39.7	14450	Con
326 Stockton North	41.3	14647	Con
331 Durham North West	41.6	16333	Con
341 Newcastle upon Tyne East & Wallsend	43.5	14223	LD
344 Sunderland South	43.8	13667	Con
346 Sedgefield	44.0	17713	Con
354 Sunderland North	44.8	13354	Con
361 South Shields	46.3	14090	Con
371 Middlesbrough	48.4	16330	Con
372 Durham North	48.4	18683	Con
383 Jarrow	51.0	17595	LD
391 Gateshead East & Washington West	53.3	17904	LD
399 Tyneside North	54.9	20568	Con
403 Tyne Bridge	57.2	14889	Con
406 Houghton & Washington East	58.9	19818	Con
410 Easington	66.5	21949	Con
Liberal Democrat seat			
46 Berwick-upon-Tweed	23.3	8458	Con

NORTH E ST

Constituency	%maj	maj	2nd
Conservative seats			
23 Westmorland & Lonsdale	6.6	3147	LD
25 Altrincham & Sale West	6.8	2941	Lab
47 Eddisbury	10.3	4568	Lab
86 Macclesfield	15.8	7200	Lab
87 Congleton	15.8	7134	Lab
125 Tatton	20.9	8611	Lab
130 Fylde	21.5	9610	Lab
137 Ribble Valley	22.9	11238	LD
165 Penrith & The Border	33.2	14677	LD
Labour seats			
4 Lancaster & Wyre	0.9	481	Con
26 Oldham E. & Saddleworth	6.0	2726	LD
41 Ribble South	8.2	3802	Con
58 Wirral West	10.0	4035	Con
63 Pendle	10.8	4275	Con
75 Rossendale & Darwen	11.9	4970	Con
79 Morecambe & Lunesdale	12.2	5092	Con
85 Wirral South	12.7	5049	Con
95 Bolton West	13.4	5518	Con
96 Blackpool North & Fleetwood	13.4	5721	Con
103 Copeland	14.3	4964	Con
104 Rochdale	14.3	5655	LD
106 Bury North	14.6	6532	Con
113 City of Chester	15.4	6894	Con
117 Warrington South	16.3	7397	Con
118 Carlisle	16.3	5702	Con
123 Chorley	17.6	8444	Con
157 Blackpool South	21.3	8262	Con
158 Hyndburn	21.5	8219	Con
159 Bolton North East	21.6	8422	Con
163 Lancashire West	22.4	9643	Con
164 Crosby	22.7	8353	Con
166 Blackburn	23.0	9249	Con
174 Crewe & Nantwich	23.8	9906	Con
176 Weaver Vale	24.5	9637	Con
183 Barrow & Furness	25.3	9889	Con
192 Workington	25.9	10850	Con
198 Ellesmere Port & Neston	26.2	10861	Con
206 St Helens South	26.6	8985	LD
217 Stalybridge & Hyde	27.6	8859	Con
225 Burnley	28.5	10498	Con
242 Heywood & Middleton	30.1	11670	Con
259 Bury South	32.3	12772	Con
262 Stockport	32.7	11569	Con
263 Wallasey	32.9	12276	Con
264 Manchester Withington	32.9	11524	LD
270 Worsley	33.3	11787	Con
271 Oldham West & Royton	33.4	13365	Con
275 Stretford & Urmston	34.0	13271	Con

Contd. /

276 Preston	34.0	12268	Con
295 Wythenshawe & Sale East	36.0	12608	Con
302 Bolton South East	37.7	12871	Con
306 Liverpool Garston	38.3	12494	LD
309 Liverpool Wavertree	38.3	12319	LD
312 Warrington North	39.0	15156	Con
324 Wigan	40.9	13743	Con
329 Manchester Gorton	41.5	11304	LD
335 St Helens North	42.3	15901	Con
340 Ashton under Lyne	43.4	15518	Con
343 Eccles	43.8	14528	Con
356 Denton & Reddish	45.6	15330	Con
362 Leigh	46.4	16362	Con
374 Salford	48.9	11012	LD
379 Knowsley N. & Sefton E.	50.4	18927	Con
381 Halton	50.6	17428	Con
382 Makerfield	50.9	17750	Con
384 Liverpool West Derby	51.3	15853	Lib
390 Manchester Central	53.0	13742	LD
396 Birkenhead	53.8	15591	Con
397 Manchester Blackley	54.5	14464	Con
398 Liverpool Riverside	54.7	13950	LD
405 Knowsley South	58.3	21316	Con
409 Liverpool Walton	63.2	17996	LD
412 Bootle	69.0	19043	LD

Liberal Democrat seats

1 Cheadle	0.1	33	Con
18 Southport	7.3	3007	Con
44 Hazel Grove	21.9	8435	Con

SOUTH EAST

Constituency	%maj	maj	2nd

Conservative seats

6 Surrey South West	1.7	861	LD
8 Basingstoke	1.8	880	Lab
13 Isle of Wight	4.5	2826	LD
14 Canterbury	4.6	2069	Lab
15 Eastbourne	4.8	2154	LD
24 Gosport	6.6	2621	Lab
27 Wycombe	7.0	3168	Lab
31 Maidenhead	7.6	3284	LD
33 Spelthorne	7.8	3262	Lab
40 New Forest East	9.1	3829	LD
45 Banbury	10.1	5219	Lab
46 Faversham & Kent Mid	10.2	4183	Lab
48 Havant	10.4	4207	Lab
59 Wantage	11.4	5600	Lab
64 Folkestone & Hythe	12.9	5907	LD
72 Bracknell	13.6	6713	Lab
73 Wokingham	13.7	5994	LD
75 Worthing E. & Shoreham	14.3	6139	Lab
76 Bognor Regis & Littlehampton	14.5	5643	Lab
77 Aldershot	14.6	6594	LD
81 Sussex Mid	15.1	6898	LD
83 Ashford	15.4	7359	Lab
84 Fareham	15.4	7009	Lab
85 Woking	15.8	6759	LD
88 Thanet North	15.9	6650	Lab
91 Witney	16.2	7973	Lab
102 Hampshire East	17.7	8890	LD
112 Henley	19.0	8458	LD
118 Tonbridge & Malling	19.4	8250	Lab
120 Runnymede & Weybridge	19.7	8360	Lab
123 Reigate	20.3	8025	Lab
124 Aylesbury	20.4	10009	LD
127 Worthing West	20.9	9037	LD
128 Windsor	21.1	8889	LD
132 Mole Valley	21.6	10153	LD
133 Epsom & Ewell	21.6	10080	Lab
136 Maidstone & The Weald	22.6	10318	Lab
138 Chichester	22.9	11355	LD
140 Bexhill & Battle	23.5	10503	LD
143 Sevenoaks	23.8	10154	Lab
144 Surrey Heath	24.0	10819	LD
147 Tunbridge Wells	24.2	9730	LD
148 Hampshire North West	24.7	12009	Lab
149 Esher & Walton	25.3	11538	Lab
153 Wealden	26.1	13772	LD
154 Chesham & Amersham	26.2	11882	LD
156 Horsham	26.9	13666	LD
158 Surrey East	28.1	13203	LD
159 Buckingham	29.4	13325	Lab
160 Arundel & South Downs	29.9	13704	LD
161 New Forest West	29.9	13191	LD
162 Hampshire North East	30.2	13257	LD
163 Beaconsfield	31.0	13065	Lab

Labour seats

13 Milton Keynes North East	3.9	1829	Con
18 Thanet South	4.5	1792	Con
23 Gillingham	5.4	2272	Con
32 Dartford	7.4	3306	Con
34 Hove	7.6	3171	Con
51 Sittingbourne & Sheppey	9.3	3509	Con
56 Medway	9.8	3780	Con
62 Hastings & Rye	10.5	4308	Con
65 Chatham & Aylesford	10.9	4340	Con
68 Gravesham	11.1	4862	Con
73 Dover	11.6	5199	Con
84 Brighton Kemptown	12.6	4922	Con
87 Reading East	12.8	5595	Con
100 Portsmouth North	13.9	5134	Con
114 Milton Keynes S.W.	15.4	6978	Con
120 Crawley	17.1	6770	Con
155 Reading West	21.1	8849	Con
173 Brighton Pavilion	23.7	9643	Con
193 Oxford East	26.0	10344	LD
208 Southampton Test	27.0	11207	Con
210 Southampton Itchen	27.1	11223	Con
256 Slough	32.1	12508	Con

Contd. /

Liberal Democrat seats

5 Guildford	1.1	538	Con
11 Newbury	4.8	2415	Con
12 Romsey	4.9	2370	Con
17 Eastleigh	6.4	3058	Con
31 Portsmouth South	15.5	6093	Con
33 Winchester	16.3	9634	Con
35 Oxford West & Abingdon	17.8	9185	Con
42 Lewes	21.4	9710	Con

SOUTH WEST

Constituency	%maj	maj	2nd

Conservative seats

2 Taunton	0.4	235	LD
10 Dorset West	2.9	1414	LD
18 Wells	5.4	2796	LD
28 Totnes	7.3	3597	LD
29 Wiltshire North	7.3	3878	LD
35 Dorset North	7.9	3797	LD
41 Bournemouth East	9.6	3434	LD
49 Bridgwater	10.4	4987	LD
50 Westbury	10.5	5294	LD
57 Tiverton & Honiton	11.3	6284	LD
74 Bournemouth West	14.0	4718	Lab
82 Devon South West	15.2	7144	LD
93 Salisbury	16.5	8703	LD
97 Devon East	17.1	8195	LD
106 Woodspring	18.0	8798	Lab
107 Poole	18.3	7166	Lab
114 Tewkesbury	19.2	8663	Lab
135 Devizes	22.3	11896	Lab
152 Cotswold	26.1	11983	LD
157 Christchurch	27.3	13544	LD

Labour seats

1 Dorset South	0.3	153	Con
19 Forest of Dean	4.6	2049	Con
35 Bristol West	8.0	4426	LD
37 Gloucester	8.0	3880	Con
49 Stroud	9.1	5039	Con
55 Falmouth & Camborne	9.7	4527	Con
70 Wansdyke	11.3	5613	Con
119 Swindon South	16.9	7341	Con
137 Swindon North	19.1	8105	Con
138 Plymouth Sutton	19.2	7517	Con
162 Exeter	22.3	11759	Con
171 Bristol North West	23.4	10887	Con
202 Kingswood	26.5	13962	Con
247 Plymouth Devonport	31.2	13033	Con
267 Bristol East	33.2	13392	Con
281 Bristol South	34.6	14181	Con

Liberal Democrat seats

2 Weston-Super-Mare	0.7	338	Con
4 Dorset Mid & Poole North	0.9	384	Con
6 Somerton & Frome	1.3	668	Con
8 Devon West & Torridge	2.1	1194	Con
13 Teignbridge	5.1	3011	Con
16 Devon North	6.1	2984	Con
19 Yeovil	8.2	3928	Con
21 Cornwall South East	10.4	5375	Con
25 Cheltenham	12.6	5255	Con
28 Torbay	14.1	6708	Con
32 Truro & St Austell	16.0	8065	Con
34 Northavon	17.7	9877	Con
36 Cornwall North	18.2	9832	Con
38 St Ives	20.4	10053	Con
41 Bath	21.4	9894	Con

WEST MIDLANDS

Constituency	%maj	maj	2nd

Conservative seats

36 Meriden	8.5	3784	Lab
43 Aldridge – Brownhills	10.0	3768	Lab
51 Lichfield	10.6	4426	Lab
62 Worcestershire West	12.0	5374	LD
67 Stone	13.2	6036	Lab
70 Shropshire North	13.4	6241	Lab
92 Staffordshire South	16.3	6881	Lab
105 Bromsgrove	17.8	8138	Lab
119 Solihull	19.5	9407	LD
131 Stratford-on-Avon	21.5	11802	LD
134 Leominster	22.2	10367	LD
139 Sutton Coldfield	23.3	10104	Lab
141 Worcestershire Mid	23.7	10627	Lab

KHHC seat

– Wyre Forest	35.9	17630	Lab

Labour seats

22 Rugby & Kenilworth	5.3	2877	Con
29 Redditch	6.7	2484	Con
31 Shrewsbury & Atcham	7.2	3579	Con
43 Wolverhampton S.W.	8.5	3487	Con
44 Birmingham Yardley	8.6	2576	LD
45 The Wrekin	8.6	3587	Con
53 Stourbridge	9.5	3812	Con
61 Burton	10.4	4849	Con
67 Warwick & Leamington	11.1	5953	Con
71 Stafford	11.3	5032	Con
72 Tamworth	11.4	4598	Con
82 Birmingham Edgbaston	12.4	4698	Con
90 Worcester	13.0	5766	Con
97 Staffordshire Moorlands	13.7	5838	Con
121 Nuneaton	17.4	7535	Con
124 Dudley North	17.6	6800	Con

Contd./

	%maj	maj	2nd
132 Halesowen & Rowley Regis	18.7	7359	Con
133 Dudley South	18.8	6817	Con
143 Birmingham Hall Green	20.1	6648	Con
149 Coventry South	20.6	8279	Con
160 Warwickshire North	21.7	9639	Con
170 Birmingham Perry Barr	23.4	8753	Con
185 Coventry North West	25.6	10874	Con
189 Birmingham Selly Oak	25.8	10339	Con
191 Newcastle-under-Lyme	25.8	9986	Con
197 Cannock Chase	26.1	10704	Con
201 Birmingham Northfield	26.4	7798	Con
212 Telford	27.2	8383	Con
224 Walsall South	28.5	9931	Con
230 Walsall North	29.1	9391	Con
233 Stoke-on-Trent South	29.1	10489	Con
238 West Bromwich East	29.9	9763	Con
253 Wolverhampton N.East	31.6	9965	Con
261 Birmingham Erdington	32.6	9962	Con
292 West Bromwich West	35.7	11355	Con
303 Warley	37.7	11850	Con
315 Stoke-on-Trent North	39.1	11784	Con
333 Stoke-on-Trent Central	41.7	11818	Con
334 Coventry North East	42.3	15751	Con
345 Birmingham Hodge Hill	43.9	11618	Con
348 Birmingham Sparkbrook & Small Heath	44.3	16246	LD
357 Wolverhampton South E.	45.7	12464	Con
404 Birmingham Ladywood	57.6	18143	Con

Liberal Democrat seats

	%maj	maj	2nd
9 Hereford	2.2	968	Con
10 Ludlow	3.8	1630	Con

YORKSHIRE & THE HUMBER

Constituency	%maj	maj	2nd

Conservative seats

	%maj	maj	2nd
5 Beverley & Holderness	1.7	781	Lab
12 Haltemprice & Howden	4.3	1903	Lab
52 Yorkshire East	10.8	4682	Lab
55 Ryedale	11.1	4875	LD
150 Vale of York	25.8	12517	Lab
155 Skipton & Ripon	26.3	12930	LD
166 Richmond (Yorks)	37.1	16319	Lab

Labour seats

	%maj	maj	2nd
10 Shipley	3.1	1428	Con
15 Selby	4.3	2138	Con
27 Calder Valley	6.5	3094	Con
33 Scarborough & Whitby	7.5	3585	Con
47 Elmet	9.1	4171	Con
50 Keighley	9.2	4005	Con
54 Brigg & Goole	9.6	3961	Con
57 Colne Valley	9.9	4639	Con
64 Bradford West	10.9	4165	Con
81 Leeds North West	12.3	5236	Con

	%maj	maj	2nd
83 Pudsey	12.5	5626	Con
91 Batley & Spen	13.1	5064	Con
94 Cleethorpes	13.2	5620	Con
112 Halifax	15.2	6129	Con
127 Leeds North East	17.8	7089	Con
139 Wakefield	19.3	7954	Con
145 Dewsbury	20.3	7449	Con
187 Bradford North	25.6	8969	Con
194 Don Valley	26.0	9520	Con
215 Bradford South	27.5	9662	Con
223 Huddersfield	28.4	10046	Con
226 York	28.7	13779	Con
231 Normanton	29.1	9937	Con
245 Scunthorpe	30.8	10372	Con
250 Morley & Rothwell	31.4	12090	Con
277 Sheffield Hillsborough	34.3	14569	LD
278 Sheffield Heeley	34.3	11704	LD
283 Great Grimsby	34.8	11484	Con
290 Doncaster Central	35.4	11999	Con
293 Barnsley West & Penistone	35.7	12352	Con
301 Hull North	37.4	10721	LD
304 Hull West & Hessle	37.9	10951	Con
322 Rother Valley	40.4	14882	Con
332 Sheffield Central	41.7	12544	LD
342 Leeds East	43.5	12643	Con
349 Hemsworth	44.4	15636	Con
351 Rotherham	44.5	13077	Con
363 Leeds West	46.5	14935	Con
370 Doncaster North	48.4	15187	Con
373 Wentworth	48.7	16449	Con
377 Hull East	49.6	15325	LD
385 Barnsley E. & Mexborough	51.6	16789	LD
386 Pontefract & Castleford	52.2	16378	Con
388 Sheffield Attercliffe	52.6	18844	Con
389 Leeds Central	52.7	14381	Con
400 Barnsley Central	54.9	15130	LD
411 Sheffield Brightside	66.7	17049	Con

Liberal Democrat seats

	%maj	maj	2nd
40 Harrogate & Knaresborough	21.0	8845	Con
47 Sheffield Hallam	24.4	9347	Con

Contd. /

SCOTLAND

Constituency	%maj	maj	2nd
Conservative seats			
1 Galloway & Upper Nithsdale	0.2	74	SNP
Labour seats			
16 Edinburgh Pentlands	4.5	1742	Con
28 Ayr	6.6	2545	Con
40 Western Isles	8.2	1074	SNP
66 Inverness East, Nairn & Lochaber	11.1	4716	SNP
74 Aberdeen South	11.9	4388	LD
99 Dundee East	13.8	4466	SNP
107 Aberdeen North	14.7	4449	SNP
108 Edinburgh South	14.8	5499	LD
110 Ochil	15.2	5349	SNP
122 Stirling	17.5	6274	Con
134 Eastwood	18.9	9141	Con
146 Clydesdale	20.4	7794	SNP
152 Dumfries	20.7	8834	Con
169 Dundee West	23.3	6800	SNP
172 Edinburgh Central	23.7	8142	LD
177 Cunninghame North	24.8	8398	SNP
180 Aberdeen Central	25.1	6646	SNP
181 Glasgow Govan	25.3	6400	SNP
182 Cumbernauld & Kilsyth	25.3	7520	SNP
186 Renfrewshire West	25.6	8575	SNP
203 Edinburgh N. & Leith	26.5	8817	LD
209 Glasgow Kelvin	27.1	7260	LD
214 Kilmarnock & Loudoun	27.4	10334	SNP
216 Falkirk West	27.6	8532	SNP
221 Dumbarton	28.2	9575	SNP
222 Strathkelvin & Bearsden	28.2	11717	LD
227 Linlithgow	28.8	9129	SNP
235 East Lothian	29.4	10830	Con
236 Livingston	29.5	10616	SNP
244 East Kilbride	30.6	12755	SNP
246 Fife Central	31.0	10075	SNP
248 Midlothian	31.4	9014	SNP
254 Falkirk East	31.8	10712	SNP
255 Kirkcaldy	31.8	8963	SNP
265 Clydebank & Milngavie	33.0	10724	SNP
279 Paisley North	34.3	9321	SNP
284 Greenock & Inverclyde	34.8	9890	LD
289 Edinburgh East & Musselburgh	35.3	12168	SNP
291 Dunfermline West	35.4	10980	SNP
298 Motherwell & Wishaw	36.9	10956	SNP
299 Carrick, Cumnock & Doon Valley	37.0	14856	Con
311 Airdrie & Shotts	38.9	12340	SNP
314 Paisley South	39.0	11910	SNP
317 Glasgow Cathcart	39.5	10816	SNP
319 Cunninghame South	40.0	11230	SNP
321 Hamilton South	40.3	10775	SNP
327 Glasgow Anniesland	41.4	11054	SNP
336 Glasgow Baillieston	42.3	9839	SNP
339 Glasgow Rutherglen	43.2	12625	SNP
350 Glasgow Maryhill	44.5	9888	SNP
352 Glasgow Pollok	44.6	11268	SNP
353 Hamilton N. & Bellshill	44.6	13561	SNP
366 Glasgow Shettleston	48.0	9818	SNP
378 Dunfermline East	50.1	15063	SNP
380 Coatbridge & Chryston	50.5	15314	SNP
Liberal Democrat seats			
14 Argyll & Bute	5.3	1653	Lab
23 Caithness, Sutherland & Easter Ross	11.0	2744	Lab
27 Aberdeenshire W & Kincardine	12.7	4821	Con
30 Tweeddale, Ettrick & Lauderdale	15.5	5157	Lab
37 Edinburgh West	19.2	7589	Lab
39 Orkney & Shetland	20.8	3475	Lab
45 Gordon	22.5	7879	Con
48 Roxburgh & Berwickshire	26.1	7511	Con
50 Fife North East	28.1	9736	Con
52 Ross, Skye & Inverness W.	37.2	12952	Lab
Scottish National seats			
1 Perth	0.1	48	Con
2 Moray	5.2	1744	Lab
3 Tayside North	8.5	3283	Con
4 Angus	10.3	3611	Con
5 Banff & Buchan	34.1	10503	Con

Contd./

WALES

Constituency	%maj	maj	2nd
Labour seats			
3 Monmouth	0.9	384	Con
7 Cardiff Central	1.9	659	LD
8 Ynys Mon	2.4	800	PC
11 Clwyd West	3.2	1115	Con
36 Preseli Pembrokeshire	8.0	2946	Con
60 Vale of Glamorgan	10.4	4700	Con
80 Carmarthen West &			
Pembrokeshire South	12.3	4538	Con
101 Cardiff North	14.3	6165	Con
125 Llanelli	17.7	6403	PC
126 Vale of Clwyd	17.8	5761	Con
128 Conwy	18.1	6219	Con
141 Gower	19.8	7395	Con
178 Delyn	24.8	8605	Con
196 Alyn & Deeside	26.0	9222	Con
204 Newport West	26.5	9304	Con
205 Clwyd South	26.6	8898	Con
211 Bridgend	27.1	10046	Con
237 Swansea West	29.8	9550	Con
243 Wrexham	30.6	9188	Con
252 Newport East	31.6	9874	Con
268 Cardiff West	33.2	11321	Con
280 Cardiff South & Penarth	34.4	12287	Con
300 Caerphilly	37.1	14425	PC
337 Neath	42.3	14816	PC
359 Pontypridd	46.2	17684	PC
360 Torfaen	46.2	16280	Con
364 Merthyr Tydfil & Rhymney	47.1	14923	PC
365 Rhondda	47.2	16047	PC
367 Ogmore	48.0	14574	PC
368 Cynon Valley	48.2	12998	PC
369 Islwyn	48.3	15309	LD
392 Aberavon	53.4	16108	PC
395 Swansea East	53.7	16148	PC
408 Blaenau Gwent	60.9	19313	PC
Liberal Democrat seats			
7 Brecon & Radnorshire	2.0	751	Con
43 Montgomeryshire	21.5	6234	Con
Plaid Cymru seats			
1 Carmarthen E. & Dinefwr	6.8	2590	Lab
2 Ceredigion	11.4	3944	LD
3 Caernarfon	12.1	3511	Lab
4 Meirionnydd Nant Conwy	27.0	5684	Lab

NORTHERN IRELAND

Constituency	%maj	maj	2nd
Ulster Unionist seats			
1 Antrim East	0.4	128	DUP
2 Antrim South	2.3	1011	DUP
3 Upper Bann	4.0	2058	DUP
4 Belfast South	14.2	5399	SDLP
5 Down North	19.7	7324	UKU
6 Lagan Valley	39.9	18342	APNI
Democratic Unionist seats			
1 Strangford	2.6	1110	UU
2 Londonderry East	4.8	1901	UU
3 Belfast North	15.6	6387	SF
4 Belfast East	19.3	7117	UU
5 Antrim North	28.9	14224	UU
SDLP seats			
1 Newry and Armagh	6.4	3575	SF
2 Foyle	23.6	11550	SF
3 Down South	26.6	13858	SF
Sinn Fein seats			
1 Fermanagh & S. Tyrone	0.1	53	UU
2 Tyrone West	10.4	5040	UU
3 Ulster Mid	19.9	9953	DUP
4 Belfast West	47.2	19342	SDLP

Table 14. Change of Vote Share 1997–2001 in Rank Order and Winning Party

Conservative

Constituency	%change	1st		Constituency	%change	1st
1 Romford	11.4	Con		54 Workington	5.1	Lab
2 Tatton	10.7	Con		55 Cambridgeshire North East	5.1	Con
3 Norfolk South West	10.2	Con		56 Congleton	5.1	Con
4 Richmond (Yorks)	10.1	Con		57 Sherwood	5.1	Lab
5 Christchurch	8.7	Con		58 Rotherham	5.1	Lab
6 Shropshire North	8.4	Con		59 Louth & Horncastle	5.0	Con
7 Yeovil	8.4	LD		60 Hornchurch	5.0	Lab
8 Copeland	8.3	Lab		61 Rother Valley	5.0	Lab
9 Totnes	8.0	Con		62 Hampshire North West	4.9	Con
10 Billericay	7.6	Con		63 Rochford & Southend East	4.8	Con
11 Woking	7.6	Con		64 Poplar & Canning Town	4.8	Lab
12 Southend West	7.6	Con		65 Ribble Valley	4.8	Con
13 Hastings & Rye	7.5	Lab		66 Suffolk Coastal	4.8	Con
14 Penrith & The Border	7.3	Con		67 Westmorland & Lonsdale	4.7	Con
15 Dagenham	7.2	Lab		68 Bromsgrove	4.6	Con
16 Newark	7.1	Con		69 Heywood & Middleton	4.6	Lab
17 Norfolk North West	7.0	Con		70 Rochdale	4.6	Lab
18 Vale of York	6.9	Con		71 Ceredigion	4.6	PC
19 Suffolk West	6.7	Con		72 Castle Point	4.5	Con
20 Blackburn	6.6	Lab		73 Barnsley West & Penistone	4.5	Lab
21 Orkney & Shetland	6.4	LD		74 Bolton South East	4.5	Lab
22 Lichfield	6.2	Con		75 Rossendale & Darwen	4.5	Lab
23 Thanet North	6.2	Con		76 Devizes	4.4	Con
24 South Holland & The Deepings	6.2	Con		77 Dover	4.4	Lab
25 Newcastle-under-Lyme	6.1	Lab		78 Wells	4.4	Con
26 Upminster	6.0	Con		79 Enfield North	4.4	Lab
27 Ashford	6.0	Con		80 Derbyshire South	4.3	Lab
28 Mansfield	6.0	Lab		81 Cornwall North	4.3	LD
29 Folkestone & Hythe	6.0	Con		82 Durham North	4.3	Lab
30 Derbyshire West	5.9	Con		83 Havant	4.2	Con
31 Brecon & Radnorshire	5.9	LD		84 Ashfield	4.2	Lab
32 Skipton & Ripon	5.8	Con		85 Wallasey	4.1	Lab
33 Hexham	5.8	Con		86 Bradford West	4.1	Lab
34 Truro & St Austell	5.8	LD		87 Suffolk South	4.1	Con
35 Carlisle	5.8	Lab		88 Don Valley	4.0	Lab
36 Tiverton & Honiton	5.7	Con		89 Devon East	4.0	Con
37 Isle of Wight	5.7	Con		90 Berwick-upon-Tweed	4.0	LD
38 Sleaford & North Hykeham	5.7	Con		91 Pontefract & Castleford	4.0	Lab
39 Meriden	5.7	Con		92 Sevenoaks	4.0	Con
40 Preseli Pembrokeshire	5.6	Lab		93 Reigate	4.0	Con
41 Newbury	5.6	LD		94 Cotswold	4.0	Con
42 Bedfordshire North East	5.6	Con		95 Wigan	3.9	Lab
43 Erith & Thamesmead	5.6	Lab		96 Huddersfield	3.9	Lab
44 Durham North West	5.6	Lab		97 Devon South West	3.9	Con
45 Dorset South	5.5	Lab		98 Buckingham	3.9	Con
46 Maidstone & The Weald	5.5	Con		99 Welwyn Hatfield	3.9	Lab
47 Barking	5.4	Lab		100 Corby	3.8	Lab
48 Bassetlaw	5.3	Lab		101 Nuneaton	3.8	Lab
49 Norfolk North	5.3	LD		102 Sheffield Hillsborough	3.8	Lab
50 Broxbourne	5.3	Con		103 Wentworth	3.8	Lab
51 New Forest West	5.2	Con		104 Eddisbury	3.8	Con
52 Norfolk Mid	5.2	Con		105 Bosworth	3.8	Con
				106 Harwich	3.7	Lab
				107 Gower	3.7	Lab
				108 Edinburgh Pentlands	3.7	Lab

Contd. /

109 Leominster	3.7	Con
110 Worcestershire Mid	3.7	Con
111 Salisbury	3.7	Con
112 Tunbridge Wells	3.7	Con
113 Epping Forest	3.6	Con
114 Pendle	3.6	Lab
115 Saffron Walden	3.6	Con
116 Torfaen	3.6	Lab
117 Uxbridge	3.6	Con
118 Stockport	3.6	Lab
119 Essex North	3.5	Con
120 Hertsmere	3.5	Con
121 Beaconsfield	3.5	Con
122 Bridgwater	3.5	Con
123 Nottingham North	3.5	Lab
124 Galloway & Upper Nithsdale	3.5	Con
125 Alyn & Deeside	3.5	Lab
126 Dorset West	3.5	Con
127 Great Yarmouth	3.5	Lab
128 Crewe & Nantwich	3.5	Lab
129 Scarborough & Whitby	3.4	Lab
130 Shrewsbury & Atcham	3.4	Lab
131 Hereford	3.4	LD
132 Ryedale	3.4	Con
133 Fylde	3.4	Con
134 Chipping Barnet	3.4	Con
135 Normanton	3.4	Lab
136 Old Bexley & Sidcup	3.4	Con
137 Stalybridge & Hyde	3.3	Lab
138 Caithness, Sutherland & Easter Ross	3.3	LD
139 Orpington	3.3	Con
140 Grantham & Stamford	3.3	Con
141 Stockton North	3.3	Lab
142 Barnsley Central	3.3	Lab
143 Bromley & Chislehurst	3.2	Con
144 Bethnal Green & Bow	3.2	Lab
145 Hemsworth	3.2	Lab
146 Forest of Dean	3.2	Lab
147 Gillingham	3.2	Lab
148 Yorkshire East	3.2	Con
149 Ayr	3.2	Lab
150 Aylesbury	3.1	Con
151 Rushcliffe	3.1	Con
152 Gainsborough	3.1	Con
153 Shipley	3.1	Lab
154 Clwyd West	3.1	Lab
155 Barrow & Furness	3.1	Lab
156 Dudley North	3.1	Lab
157 Sedgefield	3.1	Lab
158 Somerton & Frome	3.1	LD
159 Aldridge - Brownhills	3.0	Con
160 Altrincham & Sale West	3.0	Con
161 Thurrock	3.0	Lab
162 Poole	3.0	Con
163 Taunton	3.0	Con
164 Lancashire West	3.0	Lab
165 Leicestershire North West	3.0	Lab
166 Basildon	3.0	Lab
167 Daventry	2.9	Con
168 Caernarfon	2.9	PC
169 Cannock Chase	2.9	Lab
170 Cleethorpes	2.9	Lab
171 Plymouth Devonport	2.9	Lab
172 Harborough	2.9	Con
173 Western Isles	2.8	Lab
174 Meirionnydd Nant Conwy	2.8	PC
175 Redditch	2.8	Lab
176 Bolsover	2.8	Lab
177 Canterbury	2.8	Con
178 Peterborough	2.8	Lab
179 Beckenham	2.8	Con
180 Staffordshire Moorlands	2.8	Lab
181 Worthing East & Shoreham	2.7	Con
182 Doncaster Central	2.7	Lab
183 Elmet	2.7	Lab
184 Sussex Mid	2.7	Con
185 Carmarthen W. & Pembrokeshire S.	2.7	Lab
186 Monmouth	2.7	Lab
187 Brigg & Goole	2.7	Lab
188 Harlow	2.7	Lab
189 Scunthorpe	2.6	Lab
190 Leigh	2.6	Lab
191 Blyth Valley	2.5	Lab
192 Bridgend	2.5	Lab
193 Mole Valley	2.5	Con
194 Bishop Auckland	2.5	Lab
195 Epsom & Ewell	2.5	Con
196 Wycombe	2.5	Con
197 Hull West & Hessle	2.4	Lab
198 Vale of Clwyd	2.4	Lab
199 Surrey East	2.4	Con
200 Dorset North	2.4	Con
201 Hertfordshire North East	2.4	Con
202 Bolton North East	2.3	Lab
203 Medway	2.3	Lab
204 South Shields	2.3	Lab
205 Hampshire North East	2.3	Con
206 Stoke-on-Trent South	2.3	Lab
207 Banbury	2.3	Con
208 Rutland & Melton	2.3	Con
209 Keighley	2.2	Lab
210 Stone	2.2	Con
211 Amber Valley	2.2	Lab
212 Tyne Bridge	2.2	Lab
213 Cambridgeshire South	2.2	Con
214 Wakefield	2.2	Lab
215 Makerfield	2.2	Lab
216 Stoke-on-Trent Central	2.2	Lab
217 Norwich North	2.1	Lab
218 Hull North	2.1	Lab
219 Glasgow Rutherglen	2.0	Lab
220 Norfolk South	2.0	Con

Contd./

221 St Albans	2.0	Lab
222 Stratford-on-Avon	2.0	Con
223 Darlington	2.0	Lab
224 Gloucester	2.0	Lab
225 Redcar	2.0	Lab
226 Middlesbrough	2.0	Lab
227 Eccles	2.0	Lab
228 Witney	2.0	Con
229 Eastbourne	2.0	Con
230 Hove	1.9	Lab
231 Croydon South	1.9	Con
232 Chelmsford West	1.9	Con
233 Bournemouth East	1.9	Con
234 Suffolk Central & Ipswich N.	1.8	Con
235 High Peak	1.8	Lab
236 Newport West	1.8	Lab
237 Argyll & Bute	1.8	LD
238 Newport East	1.8	Lab
239 Stourbridge	1.8	Lab
240 Blackpool North & Fleetwood	1.8	Lab
241 Easington	1.8	Lab
242 Sheffield Brightside	1.8	Lab
243 Montgomeryshire	1.8	LD
244 Charnwood	1.8	Con
245 Clwyd South	1.8	Lab
246 Selby	1.7	Lab
247 Wiltshire North	1.7	Con
248 Halifax	1.7	Lab
249 Cambridgeshire North West	1.7	Con
250 Dudley South	1.6	Lab
251 Wolverhampton South East	1.6	Lab
252 Lancaster & Wyre	1.6	Lab
253 West Bromwich East	1.6	Lab
254 Birmingham Northfield	1.6	Lab
255 Walsall North	1.5	Lab
256 Bexleyheath & Crayford	1.5	Lab
257 Hitchin & Harpenden	1.5	Con
258 Devon West & Torridge	1.5	LD
259 St Helens North	1.5	Lab
260 Leicester West	1.5	Lab
261 Westbury	1.5	Con
262 Birkenhead	1.5	Lab
263 West Ham	1.4	Lab
264 Birmingham Perry Barr	1.4	Lab
265 Houghton & Washington East	1.4	Lab
266 Bedfordshire South West	1.4	Con
267 Ogmore	1.4	Lab
268 Bedfordshire Mid	1.4	Con
269 Tonbridge & Malling	1.4	Con
270 Halesowen & Rowley Regis	1.4	Lab
271 Derbyshire North East	1.3	Lab
272 Worthing West	1.3	Con
273 Thanet South	1.3	Lab
274 Carrick, Cumnock & Doon Valley	1.3	Lab
275 Hyndburn	1.3	Lab
276 Faversham & Kent Mid	1.3	Con
277 Cambridgeshire South East	1.2	Con
278 Warwickshire North	1.2	Lab
279 Sunderland North	1.2	Lab
280 Plymouth Sutton	1.2	Lab
281 Braintree	1.2	Lab
282 Sunderland South	1.2	Lab
283 Bournemouth West	1.2	Con
284 Cardiff South & Penarth	1.1	Lab
285 Calder Valley	1.1	Lab
286 Birmingham Hall Green	1.1	Lab
287 Norwich South	1.1	Lab
288 Falmouth & Camborne	1.1	Lab
289 Bristol South	1.1	Lab
290 Ynys Mon	1.0	Lab
291 Great Grimsby	1.0	Lab
292 Preston	1.0	Lab
293 Weston-Super-Mare	1.0	LD
294 Barnsley East & Mexborough	1.0	Lab
295 Eltham	1.0	Lab
296 Newcastle upon Tyne North	1.0	Lab
297 Bognor Regis & Littlehampton	1.0	Con
298 Halton	0.9	Lab
299 Blaenau Gwent	0.9	Lab
300 Worcestershire West	0.9	Con
301 Tyneside North	0.9	Lab
302 Carmarthen East & Dinefwr	0.9	PC
303 Tamworth	0.8	Lab
304 Kensington & Chelsea	0.8	Con
305 Cynon Valley	0.8	Lab
306 Swansea East	0.8	Lab
307 Solihull	0.8	Con
308 Derby North	0.8	Lab
309 Rhondda	0.8	Lab
310 Neath	0.8	Lab
311 Merthyr Tydfil & Rhymney	0.8	Lab
312 Nottingham East	0.8	Lab
313 Leeds East	0.8	Lab
314 Wolverhampton North East	0.7	Lab
315 Chingford & Woodford Green	0.7	Con
316 Surrey South West	0.7	Con
317 Horsham	0.7	Con
318 Islington South & Finsbury	0.7	Lab
319 Vale of Glamorgan	0.7	Lab
320 Greenwich & Woolwich	0.7	Lab
321 Milton Keynes South West	0.7	Lab
322 Glasgow Cathcart	0.6	Lab
323 Burnley	0.6	Lab
324 Southwark N. & Bermondsey	0.6	LD
325 Hertford & Stortford	0.6	Con
326 Caerphilly	0.6	Lab
327 Gateshead E. & Washington W.	0.6	Lab
328 Chichester	0.6	Con
329 Morecambe & Lunesdale	0.6	Lab
330 Delyn	0.6	Lab
331 Maldon & Chelmsford East	0.6	Con
332 Eastleigh	0.6	LD
333 Blaby	0.6	Con
334 Edmonton	0.6	Lab

Contd./

335 East Ham	0.6	Lab
336 Leeds Central	0.5	Lab
337 Kettering	0.5	Lab
338 Southport	0.5	LD
339 Ribble South	0.5	Lab
340 Boston & Skegness	0.5	Con
341 Coventry South	0.5	Lab
342 Warrington South	0.5	Lab
343 Leicester East	0.5	Lab
344 Staffordshire South	0.5	Con
345 Hackney South & Shoreditch	0.5	Lab
346 Dorset Mid & Poole North	0.4	LD
347 Pontypridd	0.4	Lab
348 Batley & Spen	0.4	Lab
349 Rayleigh	0.4	Con
350 Crawley	0.4	Lab
351 Tewkesbury	0.3	Con
352 Angus	0.3	SNP
353 Carshalton & Wallington	0.3	LD
354 Dartford	0.3	Lab
355 Bradford South	0.3	Lab
356 Perth	0.3	SNP
357 Fareham	0.2	Con
358 Spelthorne	0.2	Con
359 Wansdyke	0.2	Lab
360 Lincoln	0.2	Lab
361 Beverley & Holderness	0.2	Con
362 Islwyn	0.2	Lab
363 Sittingbourne & Sheppey	0.2	Lab
364 Hammersmith & Fulham	0.1	Lab
365 Ashton under Lyne	0.1	Lab
366 Hull East	0.1	Lab
367 Dumfries	0.1	Lab
368 Teignbridge	0.1	LD
369 Tynemouth	0.1	Lab
370 Dewsbury	0.1	Lab
371 Chesham & Amersham	0.1	Con
372 Sutton & Cheam	0.1	LD
373 Ellesmere Port & Neston	0.1	Lab
374 Runnymede & Weybridge	0.1	Con
375 Wimbledon	0.1	Lab
376 Northampton South	0.0	Lab
377 Telford	0.0	Lab
378 Wealden	0.0	Con
379 Gosport	0.0	Con
380 Bexhill & Battle	0.0	Con
381 St Ives	0.0	LD
382 Chatham & Aylesford	-0.1	Lab
383 Gravesham	-0.1	Lab
384 Croydon Central	-0.1	Lab
385 Doncaster North	-0.1	Lab
386 Swindon North	-0.1	Lab
387 Worcester	-0.2	Lab
388 Wantage	-0.2	Con
389 Cunninghame South	-0.2	Lab
390 Cardiff West	-0.2	Lab
391 Liverpool Garston	-0.2	Lab

392 Belfast East	-0.2	DUP
393 Wolverhampton South West	-0.2	Lab
394 Ilford North	-0.2	Lab
395 City of Durham	-0.2	Lab
396 Glasgow Govan	-0.2	Lab
397 Glasgow Shettleston	-0.2	Lab
398 Jarrow	-0.3	Lab
399 Aberavon	-0.3	Lab
400 Liverpool Walton	-0.3	Lab
401 Cornwall South East	-0.3	LD
402 Henley	-0.3	Con
403 Kilmarnock & Loudoun	-0.3	Lab
404 Motherwell & Wishaw	-0.4	Lab
405 Hampshire East	-0.4	Con
406 Glasgow Pollok	-0.4	Lab
407 Coventry North West	-0.4	Lab
408 Hazel Grove	-0.4	LD
409 Worsley	-0.5	Lab
410 New Forest East	-0.5	Con
411 Hartlepool	-0.5	Lab
412 Stroud	-0.5	Lab
413 Aldershot	-0.5	Con
414 Putney	-0.5	Lab
415 Nottingham South	-0.5	Lab
416 Bootle	-0.5	Lab
417 Conwy	-0.6	Lab
418 Dunfermline East	-0.6	Lab
419 Coventry North East	-0.6	Lab
420 Ipswich	-0.6	Lab
421 Bristol North West	-0.6	Lab
422 Stockton South	-0.6	Lab
423 Weaver Vale	-0.6	Lab
424 Liverpool West Derby	-0.6	Lab
425 Basingstoke	-0.6	Con
426 Hemel Hempstead	-0.6	Lab
427 Glasgow Maryhill	-0.7	Lab
428 Camberwell & Peckham	-0.7	Lab
429 Ealing Acton & Shepherd's Bush	-0.7	Lab
430 Leicester South	-0.7	Lab
431 Tooting	-0.7	Lab
432 Bracknell	-0.7	Con
433 Paisley North	-0.7	Lab
434 Pudsey	-0.7	Lab
435 Macclesfield	-0.7	Con
436 Morley & Rothwell	-0.8	Lab
437 Woodspring	-0.8	Con
438 Haltemprice & Howden	-0.8	Con
439 Broxtowe	-0.8	Lab
440 Burton	-0.8	Lab
441 Manchester Blackley	-0.8	Lab
442 Arundel & South Downs	-0.9	Con
443 Portsmouth North	-0.9	Lab
444 Sheffield Attercliffe	-0.9	Lab
445 Esher & Walton	-0.9	Con
446 Bury North	-0.9	Lab
447 Milton Keynes North East	-0.9	Lab
448 Middlesbrough S. & Cleveland E.	-0.9	Lab

Contd./

449 Bedford	-0.9	Lab
450 Greenock & Inverclyde	-0.9	Lab
451 Derby South	-0.9	Lab
452 Windsor	-0.9	Con
453 Cities of London & Westminster	-0.9	Con
454 Glasgow Baillieston	-1.0	Lab
455 Knowsley South	-1.0	Lab
456 Southampton Itchen	-1.0	Lab
457 Sheffield Central	-1.0	Lab
458 Holborn & St Pancras	-1.0	Lab
459 Knowsley North & Sefton East	-1.0	Lab
460 Wythenshawe & Sale East	-1.1	Lab
461 Cheltenham	-1.1	LD
462 Livingston	-1.1	Lab
463 City of Chester	-1.1	Lab
464 Stevenage	-1.1	Lab
465 Guildford	-1.1	LD
466 Chesterfield	-1.1	LD
467 Paisley South	-1.1	Lab
468 Liverpool Riverside	-1.1	Lab
469 Birmingham Selly Oak	-1.1	Lab
470 St Helens South	-1.1	Lab
471 Liverpool Wavertree	-1.1	Lab
472 Gedling	-1.2	Lab
473 Exeter	-1.2	Lab
474 Roxburgh & Berwickshire	-1.2	LD
475 Wansbeck	-1.2	Lab
476 York	-1.2	Lab
477 Warrington North	-1.2	Lab
478 Warwick & Leamington	-1.2	Lab
479 Walsall South	-1.2	Lab
480 Chorley	-1.2	Lab
481 Warley	-1.3	Lab
482 Devon North	-1.3	LD
483 Stoke-on-Trent North	-1.3	Lab
484 Midlothian	-1.3	Lab
485 Swindon South	-1.4	Lab
486 Coatbridge & Chryston	-1.4	Lab
487 Sheffield Heeley	-1.4	Lab
488 Wrexham	-1.4	Lab
489 Blackpool South	-1.4	Lab
490 Cheadle	-1.4	LD
491 Colchester	-1.5	LD
492 Lewisham West	-1.5	Lab
493 Bradford North	-1.5	Lab
494 Ruislip Northwood	-1.5	Con
495 Dulwich & West Norwood	-1.5	Lab
496 Bolton West	-1.5	Lab
497 Swansea West	-1.5	Lab
498 Watford	-1.5	Lab
499 Glasgow Anniesland	-1.5	Lab
500 Bristol East	-1.6	Lab
501 Kingswood	-1.6	Lab
502 Erewash	-1.6	Lab
503 Wirral South	-1.6	Lab
504 Hamilton South	-1.6	Lab
505 Wellingborough	-1.6	Lab
506 Hertfordshire South West	-1.7	Con
507 Hamilton North & Bellshill	-1.7	Lab
508 Clydebank & Milngavie	-1.7	Lab
509 Denton & Reddish	-1.7	Lab
510 Vauxhall	-1.8	Lab
511 Manchester Gorton	-1.8	Lab
512 Fife Central	-1.8	Lab
513 Tottenham	-1.8	Lab
514 Wirral West	-1.8	Lab
515 Blaydon	-1.8	Lab
516 The Wrekin	-1.8	Lab
517 Sutton Coldfield	-1.8	Con
518 East Kilbride	-1.8	Lab
519 Cumbernauld & Kilsyth	-1.9	Lab
520 Richmond Park	-1.9	LD
521 Waveney	-1.9	Lab
522 Luton South	-1.9	Lab
523 Leeds West	-1.9	Lab
524 Surrey Heath	-1.9	Con
525 Glasgow Kelvin	-1.9	Lab
526 Hackney North & Stoke Newington	-2.0	Lab
527 Finchley & Golders Green	-2.0	Lab
528 Birmingham Edgbaston	-2.0	Lab
529 Regent's Park & Kensington N.	-2.0	Lab
530 Birmingham Ladywood	-2.0	Lab
531 Ross, Skye & Inverness West	-2.0	LD
532 Cardiff North	-2.0	Lab
533 Portsmouth South	-2.1	LD
534 Renfrewshire West	-2.1	Lab
535 Newcastle upon Tyne East & Wallsend	-2.1	Lab
536 Bath	-2.1	LD
537 East Lothian	-2.1	Lab
538 Lewisham East	-2.1	Lab
539 Salford	-2.1	Lab
540 Sheffield Hallam	-2.1	LD
541 Newcastle upon Tyne Central	-2.2	Lab
542 Islington North	-2.2	Lab
543 Colne Valley	-2.2	Lab
544 Walthamstow	-2.2	Lab
545 Lewisham Deptford	-2.3	Lab
546 Crosby	-2.3	Lab
547 Loughborough	-2.4	Lab
548 Dunfermline West	-2.4	Lab
549 Leyton & Wanstead	-2.5	Lab
550 Enfield Southgate	-2.5	Lab
551 Southampton Test	-2.5	Lab
552 Leeds North West	-2.5	Lab
553 Ealing Southall	-2.5	Lab
554 Leeds North East	-2.6	Lab
555 Stafford	-2.6	Lab
556 Rugby & Kenilworth	-2.6	Lab
557 Ochil	-2.6	Lab
558 Hampstead & Highgate	-2.6	Lab
559 Oxford West & Abingdon	-2.6	LD
560 Llanelli	-2.6	Lab

Contd. /

561 Brighton Pavilion	-2.6	Lab
562 Brentford & Isleworth	-2.6	Lab
563 Airdrie & Shotts	-2.7	Lab
564 Hendon	-2.7	Lab
565 Down North	-2.8	UU
566 Feltham & Heston	-2.8	Lab
567 Harrow West	-2.8	Lab
568 Manchester Central	-2.8	Lab
569 Fife North East	-2.9	LD
570 Battersea	-2.9	Lab
571 Cambridge	-3.0	Lab
572 Northampton North	-3.0	Lab
573 Kirkcaldy	-3.0	Lab
574 Ludlow	-3.0	LD
575 Gordon	-3.0	LD
576 Slough	-3.1	Lab
577 Hayes & Harlington	-3.1	Lab
578 Luton North	-3.1	Lab
579 Clydesdale	-3.1	Lab
580 Torbay	-3.2	LD
581 Reading East	-3.2	Lab
582 Harrow East	-3.3	Lab
583 Birmingham Erdington	-3.3	Lab
584 Brent South	-3.3	Lab
585 Oxford East	-3.3	Lab
586 Stretford & Urmston	-3.4	Lab
587 Linlithgow	-3.6	Lab
588 Oldham East & Saddleworth	-3.6	Lab
589 Brighton Kemptown	-3.6	Lab
590 Banff & Buchan	-3.7	SNP
591 Dundee East	-3.7	Lab
592 Cunninghame North	-3.7	Lab
593 Winchester	-3.8	LD
594 Harrogate & Knaresborough	-3.8	LD
595 Croydon North	-3.9	Lab
596 Romsey	-3.9	LD
597 Edinburgh North & Leith	-3.9	Lab
598 Wokingham	-4.0	Con
599 Streatham	-4.0	Lab
600 Dumbarton	-4.0	Lab
601 Bristol West	-4.0	Lab
602 Birmingham Hodge Hill	-4.0	Lab
603 Edinburgh East & Musselburgh	-4.1	Lab
604 Dundee West	-4.1	Lab
605 Aberdeenshire W & Kincardine	-4.1	LD
606 Strathkelvin & Bearsden	-4.1	Lab
607 Manchester Withington	-4.1	Lab
608 Brent East	-4.1	Lab
609 Cardiff Central	-4.2	Lab
610 Tayside North	-4.2	SNP
611 Inverness E., Nairn & Lochaber	-4.2	Lab
612 Northavon	-4.3	LD
613 Falkirk East	-4.3	Lab
614 Twickenham	-4.3	LD
615 Ilford South	-4.4	Lab
616 Moray	-4.5	SNP
617 Antrim East	-4.6	UU

618 Falkirk West	-4.6	Lab
619 Edinburgh South	-4.7	Lab
620 Birmingham Yardley	-4.7	Lab
621 Maidenhead	-4.8	Con
622 Edinburgh Central	-4.8	Lab
623 Eastwood	-4.8	Lab
624 Aberdeen North	-5.0	Lab
625 Aberdeen Central	-5.3	Lab
626 Huntingdon	-5.4	Con
627 Bury South	-5.4	Lab
628 Edinburgh West	-5.4	LD
629 Mitcham & Morden	-5.6	Lab
630 Lewes	-5.6	LD
631 Oldham West & Royton	-5.7	Lab
632 Hornsey & Wood Green	-6.2	Lab
633 Tweeddale, Ettrick & Lauderdale	-6.7	LD
634 Birmingham Sparkbrook & Small Heath	-6.7	Lab
635 Reading West	-6.9	Lab
636 Aberdeen South	-7.1	Lab
637 Brentwood & Ongar	-7.4	Con
638 Stirling	-7.7	Lab
639 Ealing North	-7.9	Lab
640 Kingston & Surbiton	-8.3	LD
641 Brent North	-10.8	Lab
642 Wyre Forest	-17.1	KHHC

Labour

Constituency	%change	1st
1 Hastings & Rye	12.7	Lab
2 Argyll & Bute	8.9	LD
3 Brent North	8.7	Lab
4 East Ham	8.5	Lab
5 Christchurch	8.2	Con
6 Harrow West	8.1	Lab
7 Reading West	8.0	Lab
8 Eastwood	7.9	Lab
9 Angus	7.7	SNP
10 Enfield Southgate	7.6	Lab
11 Shrewsbury & Atcham	7.6	Lab
12 Harwich	6.9	Lab
13 Conwy	6.8	Lab
14 Bradford West	6.4	Lab
15 Gosport	6.4	Con
16 Dorset South	6.0	Lab
17 Windsor	5.8	Con
18 Falmouth & Camborne	5.7	Lab
19 Canterbury	5.6	Con
20 Poole	5.3	Con
21 Moray	5.2	SNP
22 Sittingbourne & Sheppey	5.2	Lab
23 Worthing West	5.2	Con
24 Glasgow Govan	5.2	Lab
25 Chatham & Aylesford	5.2	Lab
26 Worthing East & Shoreham	5.0	Con
27 Woodspring	4.9	Con

Contd. /

28 Hackney South & Shoreditch	4.8	Lab	86 Exeter	2.3	Lab
29 Gillingham	4.7	Lab	87 Bognor Regis & Littlehampton	2.2	Con
30 Fareham	4.7	Con	88 Bristol North West	2.2	Lab
31 Croydon South	4.6	Con	89 Epsom & Ewell	2.1	Con
32 Aberdeen South	4.6	Lab	90 Luton North	2.1	Lab
33 Swindon South	4.5	Lab	91 Isle of Wight	2.1	Con
34 Southport	4.4	LD	92 Mitcham & Morden	2.1	Lab
35 Edinburgh West	4.3	LD	93 Reading East	2.1	Lab
36 Gedling	4.3	Lab	94 Leeds North West	2.0	Lab
37 Hazel Grove	4.3	LD	95 Bridgwater	2.0	Con
38 Warwick & Leamington	4.3	Lab	96 Ealing North	2.0	Lab
39 Bournemouth West	4.3	Con	97 Suffolk Coastal	2.0	Con
40 Chichester	4.2	Con	98 Rugby & Kenilworth	2.0	Lab
41 Ribble Valley	4.2	Con	99 Wythenshawe & Sale East	1.9	Lab
42 Bethnal Green & Bow	4.1	Lab	100 Cheltenham	1.9	LD
43 Crosby	4.1	Lab	101 Weston-Super-Mare	1.9	LD
44 Stroud	3.9	Lab	102 Mole Valley	1.9	Con
45 Galloway & Upper Nithsdale	3.9	Con	103 Louth & Horncastle	1.8	Con
46 Hampshire North East	3.8	Con	104 Hampshire North West	1.8	Con
47 Hayes & Harlington	3.7	Lab	105 Rayleigh	1.8	Con
48 Wolverhampton South East	3.7	Lab	106 Ynys Mon	1.8	Lab
49 Tayside North	3.6	SNP	107 Clwyd West	1.7	Lab
50 Portsmouth North	3.5	Lab	108 Basingstoke	1.7	Con
51 St Albans	3.4	Lab	109 Beaconsfield	1.7	Con
52 Bromley & Chislehurst	3.4	Con	110 Slough	1.6	Lab
53 Sheffield Brightside	3.4	Lab	111 Croydon Central	1.6	Lab
54 Sutton Coldfield	3.3	Con	112 Broxtowe	1.6	Lab
55 Aberdeenshire W & Kincardine	3.2	LD	113 Bristol West	1.6	Lab
56 Bracknell	3.2	Con	114 Scarborough & Whitby	1.6	Lab
57 Gordon	3.2	LD	115 Horsham	1.5	Con
58 Hendon	3.1	Lab	116 Havant	1.5	Con
59 Chelmsford West	3.1	Con	117 Walsall North	1.5	Lab
60 Kilmarnock & Loudoun	3.1	Lab	118 Kettering	1.4	Lab
61 Swindon North	3.1	Lab	119 Newbury	1.4	LD
62 Wealden	3.1	Con	120 Taunton	1.4	Con
63 Wimbledon	3.0	Lab	121 Dumfries	1.4	Lab
64 Congleton	2.9	Con	122 Glasgow Pollok	1.4	Lab
65 Inverness East, Nairn & Lochaber	2.9	Lab	123 Hertford & Stortford	1.4	Con
66 Caernarfon	2.8	PC	124 Croydon North	1.4	Lab
67 Cardiff South & Penarth	2.8	Lab	125 Bexhill & Battle	1.3	Con
68 Harrow East	2.8	Lab	126 Maldon & Chelmsford East	1.3	Con
69 Tunbridge Wells	2.8	Con	127 Cannock Chase	1.3	Lab
70 Wansdyke	2.8	Lab	128 Solihull	1.3	Con
71 Tonbridge & Malling	2.7	Con	129 Hove	1.3	Lab
72 Devon South West	2.7	Con	130 Brighton Kemptown	1.3	Lab
73 Wellingborough	2.6	Lab	131 Jarrow	1.2	Lab
74 Stretford & Urmston	2.6	Lab	132 Suffolk Central & Ipswich N.	1.2	Con
75 Hereford	2.6	LD	133 Loughborough	1.2	Lab
76 Milton Keynes North East	2.5	Lab	134 Kingswood	1.1	Lab
77 Hampshire East	2.5	Con	135 Dewsbury	1.1	Lab
78 Sheffield Attercliffe	2.5	Lab	136 Fife North East	1.1	LD
79 Arundel & South Downs	2.4	Con	137 Ilford South	1.1	Lab
80 Old Bexley & Sidcup	2.4	Con	138 Walsall South	1.1	Lab
81 Banff & Buchan	2.3	SNP	139 Saffron Walden	1.1	Con
82 Wirral West	2.3	Lab	140 Birmingham Hall Green	1.1	Lab
83 Orkney & Shetland	2.3	LD	141 Aldershot	1.0	Con
84 Bury South	2.3	Lab	142 Cambridgeshire North East	1.0	Con
85 Southend West	2.3	Con			

Contd. /

143 Aylesbury	1.0	Con
144 Wolverhampton North East	1.0	Lab
145 Sevenoaks	1.0	Con
146 Beckenham	1.0	Con
147 Liverpool Riverside	0.9	Lab
148 Dorset North	0.9	Con
149 Dudley North	0.9	Lab
150 Hemel Hempstead	0.9	Lab
151 Suffolk South	0.9	Con
152 Paisley South	0.9	Lab
153 Esher & Walton	0.9	Con
154 Eastbourne	0.8	Con
155 Bury St Edmunds	0.8	Con
156 Putney	0.8	Lab
157 Beverley & Holderness	0.8	Con
158 Maidstone & The Weald	0.8	Con
159 Rutland & Melton	0.8	Con
160 Tewkesbury	0.7	Con
161 Perth	0.7	SNP
162 Morecambe & Lunesdale	0.7	Lab
163 Bosworth	0.7	Con
164 Devizes	0.7	Con
165 Roxburgh & Berwickshire	0.7	LD
166 Plymouth Sutton	0.6	Lab
167 Boston & Skegness	0.6	Con
168 Wokingham	0.6	Con
169 Hertfordshire North East	0.6	Con
170 Middlesbrough S. & Cleveland E.	0.6	Lab
171 Shipley	0.6	Lab
172 Kirkcaldy	0.5	Lab
173 Northampton South	0.5	Lab
174 Birmingham Edgbaston	0.5	Lab
175 Batley & Spen	0.5	Lab
176 Stafford	0.4	Lab
177 New Forest West	0.4	Con
178 Devon North	0.4	LD
179 Renfrewshire West	0.4	Lab
180 Hexham	0.4	Con
181 Suffolk West	0.4	Con
182 Ashford	0.4	Con
183 Luton South	0.3	Lab
184 Surrey Heath	0.3	Con
185 Westbury	0.3	Con
186 Ochil	0.3	Lab
187 Sussex Mid	0.3	Con
188 Lancaster & Wyre	0.3	Lab
189 Cornwall North	0.3	LD
190 Brent South	0.3	Lab
191 Banbury	0.2	Con
192 Linlithgow	0.2	Lab
193 Gravesham	0.2	Lab
194 Finchley & Golders Green	0.2	Lab
195 Derby South	0.2	Lab
196 The Wrekin	0.1	Lab
197 Medway	0.1	Lab
198 Liverpool Garston	0.1	Lab
199 Camberwell & Peckham	0.1	Lab
200 Wiltshire North	0.0	Con
201 Heywood & Middleton	0.0	Lab
202 Leeds North East	0.0	Lab
203 Watford	0.0	Lab
204 Sheffield Hillsborough	0.0	Lab
205 Pudsey	0.0	Lab
206 Stourbridge	0.0	Lab
207 Wycombe	-0.1	Con
208 Cambridgeshire South East	-0.1	Con
209 Derbyshire West	-0.1	Con
210 Salisbury	-0.1	Con
211 Bedfordshire South West	-0.1	Con
212 Birmingham Yardley	-0.1	Lab
213 Cotswold	-0.1	Con
214 Glasgow Rutherglen	-0.1	Lab
215 Denton & Reddish	-0.2	Lab
216 Rochdale	-0.2	Lab
217 Yeovil	-0.2	LD
218 Dunfermline West	-0.2	Lab
219 Birkenhead	-0.3	Lab
220 Southampton Itchen	-0.3	Lab
221 Reigate	-0.3	Con
222 Castle Point	-0.3	Con
223 Dorset Mid & Poole North	-0.3	LD
224 Hull West & Hessle	-0.3	Lab
225 Warrington North	-0.4	Lab
226 Meirionnydd Nant Conwy	-0.4	PC
227 Cornwall South East	-0.4	LD
228 Blaby	-0.4	Con
229 Ribble South	-0.4	Lab
230 Battersea	-0.5	Lab
231 Runnymede & Weybridge	-0.5	Con
232 Buckingham	-0.5	Con
233 Faversham & Kent Mid	-0.5	Con
234 Thanet South	-0.5	Lab
235 Feltham & Heston	-0.5	Lab
236 Staffordshire South	-0.5	Con
237 Macclesfield	-0.6	Con
238 Liverpool Walton	-0.6	Lab
239 Bury North	-0.6	Lab
240 Dartford	-0.6	Lab
241 Hitchin & Harpenden	-0.6	Con
242 Huntingdon	-0.6	Con
243 Leominster	-0.6	Con
244 Scunthorpe	-0.6	Lab
245 Vale of York	-0.6	Con
246 Bath	-0.7	LD
247 Tweeddale, Ettrick & Lauderdale	-0.7	LD
248 Woking	-0.7	Con
249 Wantage	-0.7	Con
250 Barnsley West & Penistone	-0.7	Lab
251 Coventry South	-0.7	Lab
252 Braintree	-0.7	Lab
253 Chorley	-0.7	Lab
254 Surrey South West	-0.7	Con
255 Shropshire North	-0.7	Con
256 Midlothian	-0.8	Lab
257 Nottingham South	-0.8	Lab

Contd. /

258 Selby	-0.8	Lab
259 Yorkshire East	-0.8	Con
260 Altrincham & Sale West	-0.8	Con
261 Cambridgeshire South	-0.8	Con
262 Cambridgeshire North West	-0.8	Con
263 Chesham & Amersham	-0.9	Con
264 Fylde	-0.9	Con
265 Chipping Barnet	-0.9	Con
266 Hertfordshire South West	-0.9	Con
267 Lewisham West	-0.9	Lab
268 Spelthorne	-0.9	Con
269 Blackburn	-0.9	Lab
270 Colne Valley	-0.9	Lab
271 Billericay	-0.9	Con
272 Bradford South	-0.9	Lab
273 Hyndburn	-0.9	Lab
274 Tiverton & Honiton	-0.9	Con
275 Uxbridge	-1.0	Con
276 Leicester West	-1.0	Lab
277 Edinburgh North & Leith	-1.0	Lab
278 Walthamstow	-1.0	Lab
279 Edinburgh E. & Musselburgh	-1.0	Lab
280 Devon East	-1.0	Con
281 Lincoln	-1.0	Lab
282 Sheffield Hallam	-1.1	LD
283 Manchester Blackley	-1.1	Lab
284 Halesowen & Rowley Regis	-1.1	Lab
285 Falkirk East	-1.1	Lab
286 Nottingham North	-1.2	Lab
287 Norfolk Mid	-1.2	Con
288 Motherwell & Wishaw	-1.2	Lab
289 Chingford & Woodford Green	-1.2	Con
290 West Bromwich East	-1.3	Lab
291 Bournemouth East	-1.3	Con
292 Brigg & Goole	-1.3	Lab
293 Richmond Park	-1.3	LD
294 Harrogate & Knaresborough	-1.4	LD
295 Ipswich	-1.4	Lab
296 Edmonton	-1.4	Lab
297 Grantham & Stamford	-1.4	Con
298 Blackpool North & Fleetwood	-1.4	Lab
299 Portsmouth South	-1.4	LD
300 Morley & Rothwell	-1.5	Lab
301 Worcestershire Mid	-1.5	Con
302 Aldridge - Brownhills	-1.5	Con
303 Birmingham Northfield	-1.5	Lab
304 Worcester	-1.5	Lab
305 Norfolk South	-1.5	Con
306 Ilford North	-1.6	Lab
307 Hartlepool	-1.6	Lab
308 Henley	-1.6	Con
309 Barrow & Furness	-1.6	Lab
310 Truro & St Austell	-1.6	LD
311 Bedfordshire North East	-1.6	Con
312 Southampton Test	-1.7	Lab
313 Gainsborough	-1.7	Con
314 Devon West & Torridge	-1.7	LD
315 Worcestershire West	-1.7	Con
316 Halton	-1.7	Lab
317 Birmingham Hodge Hill	-1.7	Lab
318 Liverpool Wavertree	-1.7	Lab
319 Essex North	-1.7	Con
320 Eltham	-1.8	Lab
321 Twickenham	-1.8	LD
322 Witney	-1.8	Con
323 Cheadle	-1.8	LD
324 Meriden	-1.8	Con
325 Bolton North East	-1.8	Lab
326 Tottenham	-1.8	Lab
327 St Ives	-1.9	LD
328 Livingston	-1.9	Lab
329 Great Grimsby	-1.9	Lab
330 Bristol East	-1.9	Lab
331 South Holland & The Deepings	-1.9	Con
332 Bexleyheath & Crayford	-1.9	Lab
333 Burton	-2.0	Lab
334 Poplar & Canning Town	-2.0	Lab
335 Cities of London & Westminster	-2.0	Con
336 Newcastle upon Tyne North	-2.0	Lab
337 Birmingham Erdington	-2.0	Lab
338 Dunfermline East	-2.0	Lab
339 Cleethorpes	-2.0	Lab
340 Surrey East	-2.1	Con
341 Dumbarton	-2.1	Lab
342 Norfolk North West	-2.1	Con
343 Clydebank & Milngavie	-2.1	Lab
344 Tynemouth	-2.1	Lab
345 Wolverhampton South West	-2.1	Lab
346 Hertsmere	-2.2	Con
347 Daventry	-2.2	Con
348 Sheffield Central	-2.2	Lab
349 Eccles	-2.2	Lab
350 Sutton & Cheam	-2.2	LD
351 Hamilton North & Bellshill	-2.2	Lab
352 Rushcliffe	-2.2	Con
353 Norwich North	-2.3	Lab
354 Derby North	-2.3	Lab
355 Manchester Central	-2.3	Lab
356 Stockton South	-2.3	Lab
357 Sleaford & North Hykeham	-2.3	Con
358 Fife Central	-2.3	Lab
359 Keighley	-2.4	Lab
360 Bedfordshire Mid	-2.4	Con
361 Edinburgh Pentlands	-2.4	Lab
362 Hammersmith & Fulham	-2.5	Lab
363 Manchester Gorton	-2.5	Lab
364 Erewash	-2.5	Lab
365 Bolton West	-2.5	Lab
366 Caithness, Sutherland & Easter Ross	-2.5	LD
367 Oxford West & Abingdon	-2.5	LD
368 Plymouth Devonport	-2.6	Lab
369 Vale of Clwyd	-2.7	Lab
370 Wells	-2.7	Con
371 Bedford	-2.7	Lab

Contd. /

372 Leeds Central	-2.7	Lab
373 Blackpool South	-2.7	Lab
374 Amber Valley	-2.8	Lab
375 Tamworth	-2.8	Lab
376 Erith & Thamesmead	-2.8	Lab
377 Leyton & Wanstead	-2.8	Lab
378 Warrington South	-2.9	Lab
379 Maidenhead	-2.9	Con
380 Greenwich & Woolwich	-2.9	Lab
381 Newport East	-2.9	Lab
382 Glasgow Cathcart	-3.0	Lab
383 Great Yarmouth	-3.0	Lab
384 Doncaster Central	-3.0	Lab
385 Coatbridge & Chryston	-3.0	Lab
386 West Ham	-3.0	Lab
387 Durham North	-3.1	Lab
388 Oldham East & Saddleworth	-3.1	Lab
389 Newcastle-under-Lyme	-3.1	Lab
390 Bristol South	-3.1	Lab
391 Wrexham	-3.1	Lab
392 New Forest East	-3.1	Con
393 Penrith & The Border	-3.1	Con
394 Basildon	-3.1	Lab
395 Houghton & Washington East	-3.2	Lab
396 Knowsley North & Sefton East	-3.2	Lab
397 Staffordshire Moorlands	-3.2	Lab
398 Ryedale	-3.2	Con
399 Birmingham Selly Oak	-3.2	Lab
400 Dundee West	-3.2	Lab
401 Telford	-3.2	Lab
402 Huddersfield	-3.2	Lab
403 Tyneside North	-3.3	Lab
404 East Kilbride	-3.3	Lab
405 Northampton North	-3.3	Lab
406 Warley	-3.3	Lab
407 Norfolk South West	-3.3	Con
408 Nottingham East	-3.3	Lab
409 Lewes	-3.3	LD
410 Easington	-3.4	Lab
411 Stalybridge & Hyde	-3.4	Lab
412 Stockton North	-3.4	Lab
413 Calder Valley	-3.4	Lab
414 Stevenage	-3.5	Lab
415 Wirral South	-3.5	Lab
416 Leicester South	-3.5	Lab
417 Airdrie & Shotts	-3.6	Lab
418 Greenock & Inverclyde	-3.6	Lab
419 Don Valley	-3.6	Lab
420 Sheffield Heeley	-3.7	Lab
421 Guildford	-3.8	LD
422 Charnwood	-3.8	Con
423 Hornchurch	-3.8	Lab
424 Wallasey	-3.8	Lab
425 Preston	-3.8	Lab
426 St Helens North	-3.8	Lab
427 Stone	-3.8	Con
428 Derbyshire South	-3.8	Lab
429 Stratford-on-Avon	-3.9	Con
430 Middlesbrough	-3.9	Lab
431 Lichfield	-3.9	Con
432 Bromsgrove	-3.9	Con
433 Welwyn Hatfield	-3.9	Lab
434 Salford	-3.9	Lab
435 Weaver Vale	-3.9	Lab
436 Crewe & Nantwich	-3.9	Lab
437 Gateshead E. & Washington W.	-3.9	Lab
438 Pontypridd	-3.9	Lab
439 Enfield North	-4.0	Lab
440 Paisley North	-4.0	Lab
441 Thanet North	-4.0	Con
442 Northavon	-4.1	LD
443 Nuneaton	-4.1	Lab
444 Eddisbury	-4.1	Con
445 Brent East	-4.1	Lab
446 Cynon Valley	-4.1	Lab
447 Dorset West	-4.1	Con
448 Hackney N. & Stoke Newington	-4.1	Lab
449 Redditch	-4.2	Lab
450 Totnes	-4.2	Con
451 Sunderland South	-4.2	Lab
452 Newcastle upon Tyne Central	-4.2	Lab
453 High Peak	-4.2	Lab
454 Gloucester	-4.2	Lab
455 Ealing Acton & Shepherd's Bush	-4.2	Lab
456 Milton Keynes South West	-4.2	Lab
457 Cunninghame North	-4.2	Lab
458 Sherwood	-4.3	Lab
459 Ellesmere Port & Neston	-4.3	Lab
460 Stockport	-4.3	Lab
461 Warwickshire North	-4.3	Lab
462 Cunninghame South	-4.3	Lab
463 Leicestershire North West	-4.3	Lab
464 Aberdeen Central	-4.3	Lab
465 Broxbourne	-4.3	Con
466 Cumbernauld & Kilsyth	-4.3	Lab
467 Upminster	-4.3	Con
468 Ruislip Northwood	-4.4	Con
469 Leigh	-4.4	Lab
470 Elmet	-4.4	Lab
471 Normanton	-4.5	Lab
472 City of Chester	-4.5	Lab
473 Carrick, Cumnock & Doon Valley	-4.5	Lab
474 Blyth Valley	-4.5	Lab
475 Leeds East	-4.5	Lab
476 Aberdeen North	-4.5	Lab
477 Leeds West	-4.5	Lab
478 Cardiff North	-4.6	Lab
479 Glasgow Maryhill	-4.6	Lab
480 Winchester	-4.6	LD
481 Lewisham East	-4.6	Lab
482 Glasgow Baillieston	-4.6	Lab
483 Edinburgh South	-4.7	Lab
484 Folkestone & Hythe	-4.7	Con
485 Vauxhall	-4.7	Lab

Contd./

486 Somerton & Frome	-4.7	LD
487 Kensington & Chelsea	-4.8	Con
488 Derbyshire North East	-4.8	Lab
489 Wentworth	-4.8	Lab
490 Forest of Dean	-4.8	Lab
491 Ayr	-4.9	Lab
492 Rochford & Southend East	-4.9	Con
493 Eastleigh	-4.9	LD
494 Barking	-4.9	Lab
495 Edinburgh Central	-4.9	Lab
496 Monmouth	-5.0	Lab
497 Rossendale & Darwen	-5.0	Lab
498 Liverpool West Derby	-5.0	Lab
499 Skipton & Ripon	-5.0	Con
500 Ashton under Lyne	-5.0	Lab
501 Worsley	-5.1	Lab
502 Makerfield	-5.1	Lab
503 Cardiff Central	-5.1	Lab
504 Blaydon	-5.1	Lab
505 Brentford & Isleworth	-5.2	Lab
506 Peterborough	-5.2	Lab
507 Hemsworth	-5.2	Lab
508 Harborough	-5.2	Con
509 Birmingham Ladywood	-5.2	Lab
510 Stirling	-5.2	Lab
511 Darlington	-5.2	Lab
512 Coventry North East	-5.2	Lab
513 Brecon & Radnorshire	-5.3	LD
514 Regent's Park & Kensington N.	-5.3	Lab
515 Waveney	-5.3	Lab
516 Bootle	-5.3	Lab
517 Halifax	-5.3	Lab
518 Glasgow Anniesland	-5.3	Lab
519 Bolsover	-5.4	Lab
520 Torbay	-5.4	LD
521 Coventry North West	-5.4	Lab
522 Rother Valley	-5.5	Lab
523 East Lothian	-5.5	Lab
524 Streatham	-5.5	Lab
525 Carshalton & Wallington	-5.5	LD
526 Teignbridge	-5.6	LD
527 Sunderland North	-5.6	Lab
528 Bridgend	-5.6	Lab
529 Colchester	-5.6	LD
530 Tooting	-5.6	Lab
531 Stoke-on-Trent Central	-5.6	Lab
532 Barnsley East & Mexborough	-5.6	Lab
533 Dover	-5.7	Lab
534 Delyn	-5.7	Lab
535 Crawley	-5.7	Lab
536 Bassetlaw	-5.7	Lab
537 Cardiff West	-5.8	Lab
538 Lewisham Deptford	-5.8	Lab
539 Knowsley South	-5.9	Lab
540 Lancashire West	-5.9	Lab
541 Brighton Pavilion	-5.9	Lab
542 Dundee East	-5.9	Lab
543 Clydesdale	-5.9	Lab

544 Richmond (Yorks)	-5.9	Con
545 Hamilton South	-5.9	Lab
546 Pontefract & Castleford	-6.0	Lab
547 Dulwich & West Norwood	-6.1	Lab
548 Corby	-6.1	Lab
549 Rhondda	-6.1	Lab
550 Glasgow Kelvin	-6.1	Lab
551 Norwich South	-6.2	Lab
552 Durham North West	-6.2	Lab
553 Carlisle	-6.3	Lab
554 Sedgefield	-6.3	Lab
555 Harlow	-6.3	Lab
556 Bradford North	-6.3	Lab
557 Tyne Bridge	-6.3	Lab
558 Epping Forest	-6.3	Con
559 Copeland	-6.4	Lab
560 Strathkelvin & Bearsden	-6.5	Lab
561 Gower	-6.5	Lab
562 Manchester Withington	-6.7	Lab
563 Doncaster North	-6.7	Lab
564 Birmingham Sparkbrook & Small Heath	-6.7	Lab
565 Hull East	-6.7	Lab
566 Clwyd South	-6.7	Lab
567 Thurrock	-6.8	Lab
568 Dudley South	-6.8	Lab
569 Wigan	-6.8	Lab
570 Romford	-6.9	Con
571 Preseli Pembrokeshire	-6.9	Lab
572 Torfaen	-7.0	Lab
573 Bolton South East	-7.0	Lab
574 Orpington	-7.0	Con
575 Ashfield	-7.0	Lab
576 Redcar	-7.1	Lab
577 Bishop Auckland	-7.1	Lab
578 Stoke-on-Trent North	-7.2	Lab
579 City of Durham	-7.2	Lab
580 Montgomeryshire	-7.3	LD
581 Mansfield	-7.3	Lab
582 Carmarthen East & Dinefwr	-7.3	PC
583 Barnsley Central	-7.4	Lab
584 Islington North	-7.4	Lab
585 Rotherham	-7.4	Lab
586 Blaenau Gwent	-7.4	Lab
587 Oxford East	-7.4	Lab
588 Swansea West	-7.5	Lab
589 Wakefield	-7.5	Lab
590 Falkirk West	-7.5	Lab
591 Carmarthen W. & Pembrokeshire S.	-7.6	Lab
592 Oldham West & Royton	-7.6	Lab
593 York	-7.7	Lab
594 Wansbeck	-7.7	Lab
595 Newark	-7.8	Con
596 Newport West	-7.8	Lab
597 Haltemprice & Howden	-7.9	Con
598 Leicester East	-7.9	Lab

Contd. /

599 Newcastle upon Tyne East & Wallsend	-8.1	Lab
600 Aberavon	-8.2	Lab
601 Stoke-on-Trent South	-8.2	Lab
602 South Shields	-8.3	Lab
603 Cambridge	-8.3	Lab
604 Vale of Glamorgan	-8.5	Lab
605 Dagenham	-8.5	Lab
606 Glasgow Shettleston	-8.5	Lab
607 Berwick-upon-Tweed	-8.5	LD
608 Islington South & Finsbury	-8.6	Lab
609 Burnley	-8.6	Lab
610 Pendle	-8.7	Lab
611 Hull North	-8.7	Lab
612 Workington	-8.7	Lab
613 Chesterfield	-8.8	LD
614 Ceredigion	-8.9	PC
615 Llanelli	-9.3	Lab
616 Southwark N. & Bermondsey	-9.5	LD
617 Brentwood & Ongar	-9.5	Con
618 Alyn & Deeside	-9.6	Lab
619 Caerphilly	-9.6	Lab
620 Westmorland & Lonsdale	-9.7	Con
621 Swansea East	-10.2	Lab
622 Romsey	-10.3	LD
623 Hampstead & Highgate	-10.5	Lab
624 Western Isles	-10.6	Lab
625 Holborn & St Pancras	-11.1	Lab
626 Norfolk North	-11.7	LD
627 Ross, Skye & Inverness West	-11.8	LD
628 Hornsey & Wood Green	-11.9	Lab
629 Ogmore	-11.9	Lab
630 Ludlow	-12.0	LD
631 Ealing Southall	-12.5	Lab
632 Islwyn	-12.6	Lab
633 Neath	-12.8	Lab
634 Kingston & Surbiton	-14.3	LD
635 Merthyr Tydfil & Rhymney	-14.9	Lab
636 Birmingham Perry Barr	-16.5	Lab
637 St Helens South	-18.9	Lab
638 Wyre Forest	-26.6	KHHC

Liberal Democrat

Constituency	%change	1st
1 Kingston & Surbiton	23.5	LD
2 Romsey	17.5	LD
3 Ross, Skye & Inverness West	15.4	LD
4 Hornsey & Wood Green	14.5	Lab
5 Ludlow	13.5	LD
6 Lewes	13.1	LD
7 Birmingham Perry Barr	13.0	Lab
8 Winchester	12.5	LD
9 Cardiff Central	11.8	Lab
10 Maidenhead	11.2	Con
11 Tweeddale, Ettrick & Lauderdale	11.0	LD
12 Torbay	10.9	LD
13 Ceredigion	10.4	PC

14 Haltemprice & Howden	10.1	Con
15 Northavon	10.0	LD
16 Blaydon	10.0	Lab
17 St Helens South	9.7	Lab
18 Edinburgh South	9.7	Lab
19 Huntingdon	9.1	Con
20 Newcastle upon Tyne East & Wallsend	9.0	Lab
21 Cambridge	8.9	Lab
22 Oxford East	8.7	Lab
23 Guildford	8.4	LD
24 Strathkelvin & Bearsden	8.4	Lab
25 City of Durham	8.4	Lab
26 Manchester Withington	8.4	Lab
27 Norfolk North	8.4	LD
28 Southwark N. & Bermondsey	8.3	LD
29 Chesterfield	8.3	LD
30 Colchester	8.2	LD
31 Hampstead & Highgate	8.1	Lab
32 South Shields	8.0	Lab
33 Dumbarton	7.9	Lab
34 Orpington	7.7	Con
35 Bolton West	7.6	Lab
36 Wirral South	7.4	Lab
37 St Ives	7.1	LD
38 East Lothian	7.1	Lab
39 Westmorland & Lonsdale	7.0	Con
40 Carshalton & Wallington	6.8	LD
41 Islington South & Finsbury	6.8	Lab
42 Wansbeck	6.8	Lab
43 Moray	6.8	SNP
44 Newcastle upon Tyne Central	6.7	Lab
45 York	6.6	Lab
46 Sutton & Cheam	6.5	LD
47 Bishop Auckland	6.4	Lab
48 Edinburgh North & Leith	6.4	Lab
49 Berwick-upon-Tweed	5.9	LD
50 Salford	5.9	Lab
51 Ealing Acton & Shepherd's Bush	5.8	Lab
52 Teignbridge	5.7	LD
53 Eastleigh	5.6	LD
54 Bury South	5.5	Lab
55 Barnsley East & Mexborough	5.5	Lab
56 Stirling	5.5	Lab
57 Tooting	5.5	Lab
58 Holborn & St Pancras	5.5	Lab
59 Islington North	5.4	Lab
60 Birmingham Yardley	5.4	Lab
61 Edinburgh Central	5.4	Lab
62 Folkestone & Hythe	5.3	Con
63 Leicester East	5.3	Lab
64 Stevenage	5.3	Lab
65 Bradford North	5.3	Lab
66 Brentford & Isleworth	5.2	Lab
67 Epping Forest	5.2	Con
68 Lewisham East	5.2	Lab

Contd./

69 Glasgow Govan	5.2 Lab	127 Dorset West	4.1 Con
70 Delyn	5.2 Lab	128 Regent's Park & Kensington N.	4.1 Lab
71 City of Chester	5.2 Lab	129 Ochil	4.0 Lab
72 Barnsley Central	5.2 Lab	130 Harrogate & Knaresborough	4.0 LD
73 Hull East	5.1 Lab	131 Dudley South	4.0 Lab
74 Cannock Chase	5.1 Lab	132 Norwich South	4.0 Lab
75 Hull North	5.1 Lab	133 Rossendale & Darwen	4.0 Lab
76 Portsmouth South	5.1 LD	134 Aberdeen Central	4.0 Lab
77 Derby North	5.1 Lab	135 Jarrow	4.0 Lab
78 Northampton North	5.0 Lab	136 Hertfordshire South West	4.0 Con
79 Ilford South	5.0 Lab	137 Harlow	4.0 Lab
80 Derby South	4.9 Lab	138 Warwickshire North	3.9 Lab
81 Coventry South	4.9 Lab	139 Greenock & Inverclyde	3.9 Lab
82 Oxford West & Abingdon	4.9 LD	140 Worsley	3.9 Lab
83 Stockport	4.9 Lab	141 Birmingham Sparkbrook & Small Heath	3.9 Lab
84 Glasgow Anniesland	4.9 Lab	142 Bury North	3.9 Lab
85 Newcastle upon Tyne North	4.9 Lab	143 Wrexham	3.9 Lab
86 Halton	4.9 Lab	144 Galloway & Upper Nithsdale	3.9 Con
87 Angus	4.9 SNP	145 Hackney North & Stoke Newington	3.9 Lab
88 High Peak	4.9 Lab	146 Harborough	3.9 Con
89 Ribble South	4.9 Lab	147 Surrey Heath	3.9 Con
90 St Helens North	4.8 Lab	148 Birkenhead	3.8 Lab
91 Renfrewshire West	4.8 Lab	149 Hamilton South	3.8 Lab
92 Islwyn	4.8 Lab	150 Peterborough	3.8 Lab
93 Houghton & Washington East	4.8 Lab	151 Gloucester	3.8 Lab
94 Perth	4.8 SNP	152 Manchester Gorton	3.8 Lab
95 Wigan	4.8 Lab	153 Surrey South West	3.8 Con
96 Battersea	4.7 Lab	154 Edinburgh East & Musselburgh	3.7 Lab
97 Amber Valley	4.7 Lab	155 Falkirk East	3.7 Lab
98 Cheadle	4.7 LD	156 Darlington	3.7 Lab
99 Knowsley South	4.7 Lab	157 Lewisham West	3.7 Lab
100 Inverness E., Nairn & Lochaber	4.7 Lab	158 Eltham	3.7 Lab
101 Feltham & Heston	4.7 Lab	159 Tamworth	3.7 Lab
102 Mansfield	4.7 Lab	160 Midlothian	3.7 Lab
103 Streatham	4.6 Lab	161 Nottingham South	3.7 Lab
104 Stockton South	4.5 Lab	162 Brighton Pavilion	3.6 Lab
105 Dundee East	4.5 Lab	163 Newport East	3.6 Lab
106 Crawley	4.5 Lab	164 Twickenham	3.6 LD
107 Kilmarnock & Loudoun	4.4 Lab	165 Glasgow Kelvin	3.6 Lab
108 Workington	4.4 Lab	166 Ogmore	3.6 Lab
109 Southampton Test	4.4 Lab	167 Glasgow Maryhill	3.5 Lab
110 Cardiff North	4.4 Lab	168 Doncaster Central	3.5 Lab
111 Dulwich & West Norwood	4.4 Lab	169 Cunninghame North	3.5 Lab
112 Lancashire West	4.4 Lab	170 Montgomeryshire	3.5 LD
113 Tyne Bridge	4.4 Lab	171 Derbyshire North East	3.5 Lab
114 Livingston	4.3 Lab	172 Bedford	3.5 Lab
115 Ynys Mon	4.3 Lab	173 Bethnal Green & Bow	3.5 Lab
116 Harrow East	4.3 Lab	174 Dover	3.5 Lab
117 Ealing North	4.2 Lab	175 Cardiff South & Penarth	3.4 Lab
118 Birmingham Selly Oak	4.2 Lab	176 Liverpool Walton	3.4 Lab
119 Liverpool Garston	4.1 Lab	177 Manchester Central	3.4 Lab
120 Gateshead E. & Washington W.	4.1 Lab	178 Liverpool Riverside	3.4 Lab
121 Durham North West	4.1 Lab	179 Western Isles	3.4 Lab
122 Somerton & Frome	4.1 LD	180 Charnwood	3.4 Con
123 Sheffield Hallam	4.1 LD	181 Leicester South	3.4 Lab
124 Vauxhall	4.1 Lab		
125 Eccles	4.1 Lab		
126 Glasgow Cathcart	4.1 Lab	*Contd. /*	

182 Barrow & Furness	3.3	Lab
183 Airdrie & Shotts	3.3	Lab
184 Southampton Itchen	3.3	Lab
185 Sherwood	3.3	Lab
186 Leeds North West	3.3	Lab
187 Stratford-on-Avon	3.2	Con
188 Warrington South	3.2	Lab
189 Coventry North West	3.2	Lab
190 Alyn & Deeside	3.2	Lab
191 Neath	3.2	Lab
192 Middlesbrough South & Cleveland East	3.2	Lab
193 Brent North	3.2	Lab
194 Leeds East	3.2	Lab
195 Slough	3.2	Lab
196 Tayside North	3.2	SNP
197 Makerfield	3.1	Lab
198 Coventry North East	3.1	Lab
199 Greenwich & Woolwich	3.1	Lab
200 Easington	3.1	Lab
201 Hammersmith & Fulham	3.1	Lab
202 Warrington North	3.1	Lab
203 Ruislip Northwood	3.1	Con
204 Morley & Rothwell	3.1	Lab
205 Brent South	3.1	Lab
206 Cities of London & Westminster	3.1	Con
207 Redcar	3.1	Lab
208 Paisley North	3.0	Lab
209 Stone	3.0	Con
210 Vale of Glamorgan	3.0	Lab
211 Motherwell & Wishaw	3.0	Lab
212 Richmond Park	3.0	LD
213 East Kilbride	3.0	Lab
214 Ipswich	3.0	Lab
215 Banff & Buchan	3.0	SNP
216 Woking	3.0	Con
217 Durham North	3.0	Lab
218 Nottingham East	2.9	Lab
219 Bedfordshire Mid	2.9	Con
220 Stoke-on-Trent South	2.9	Lab
221 Cunninghame South	2.9	Lab
222 Bridgend	2.9	Lab
223 Glasgow Pollok	2.9	Lab
224 Erewash	2.9	Lab
225 Gordon	2.9	LD
226 Wirral West	2.9	Lab
227 Wallasey	2.9	Lab
228 Putney	2.9	Lab
229 Glasgow Baillieston	2.8	Lab
230 Liverpool Wavertree	2.8	Lab
231 Tynemouth	2.8	Lab
232 Bootle	2.8	Lab
233 Lewisham Deptford	2.8	Lab
234 Broxtowe	2.8	Lab
235 Brent East	2.8	Lab
236 Bolton South East	2.8	Lab
237 Dagenham	2.7	Lab
238 Bristol North West	2.7	Lab
239 Ellesmere Port & Neston	2.7	Lab
240 Knowsley North & Sefton East	2.7	Lab
241 Cumbernauld & Kilsyth	2.7	Lab
242 Chorley	2.7	Lab
243 Croydon North	2.7	Lab
244 Hamilton North & Bellshill	2.7	Lab
245 Stoke-on-Trent Central	2.7	Lab
246 Ryedale	2.7	Con
247 Dorset Mid & Poole North	2.7	LD
248 Nottingham North	2.6	Lab
249 Bolsover	2.6	Lab
250 Wolverhampton North East	2.6	Lab
251 Halifax	2.6	Lab
252 Corby	2.6	Lab
253 Sedgefield	2.5	Lab
254 Sheffield Central	2.5	Lab
255 Eddisbury	2.5	Con
256 Mitcham & Morden	2.5	Lab
257 Aberdeenshire W & Kincardine	2.5	LD
258 Bassetlaw	2.5	Lab
259 Blaby	2.5	Con
260 Hemsworth	2.5	Lab
261 Linlithgow	2.4	Lab
262 Waveney	2.4	Lab
263 Clydesdale	2.4	Lab
264 Bristol East	2.4	Lab
265 Hertsmere	2.3	Con
266 Aberdeen North	2.3	Lab
267 Henley	2.3	Con
268 Birmingham Edgbaston	2.3	Lab
269 Totnes	2.3	Con
270 Nuneaton	2.3	Lab
271 Colne Valley	2.3	Lab
272 Roxburgh & Berwickshire	2.3	LD
273 Bournemouth East	2.3	Con
274 Cardiff West	2.2	Lab
275 Elmet	2.2	Lab
276 Pendle	2.2	Lab
277 Normanton	2.2	Lab
278 Norwich North	2.2	Lab
279 Hertford & Stortford	2.2	Con
280 Thurrock	2.2	Lab
281 Doncaster North	2.1	Lab
282 Fife Central	2.1	Lab
283 Bedfordshire North East	2.1	Con
284 Coatbridge & Chryston	2.1	Lab
285 Esher & Walton	2.1	Con
286 Ashton under Lyne	2.1	Lab
287 Camberwell & Peckham	2.1	Lab
288 Blackpool South	2.1	Lab
289 Weaver Vale	2.1	Lab
290 Swansea West	2.0	Lab
291 Leeds North East	2.0	Lab
292 Bath	2.0	LD
293 Falkirk West	2.0	Lab
294 Carrick, Cumnock & Doon Valley	2.0	Lab

Contd. /

295 Dunfermline West	2.0	Lab
296 Blyth Valley	2.0	Lab
297 Newport West	2.0	Lab
298 Leeds Central	2.0	Lab
299 Surrey East	2.0	Con
300 Grantham & Stamford	1.9	Con
301 Kingswood	1.9	Lab
302 Meirionnydd Nant Conwy	1.9	PC
303 Middlesbrough	1.9	Lab
304 Liverpool West Derby	1.9	Lab
305 Halesowen & Rowley Regis	1.9	Lab
306 Monmouth	1.9	Lab
307 Tyneside North	1.9	Lab
308 Hampshire East	1.8	Con
309 Lincoln	1.8	Lab
310 Stretford & Urmston	1.8	Lab
311 Altrincham & Sale West	1.8	Con
312 Staffordshire Moorlands	1.8	Lab
313 Cambridgeshire South East	1.8	Con
314 Newark	1.8	Con
315 Westbury	1.7	Con
316 Crewe & Nantwich	1.7	Lab
317 Leicestershire North West	1.7	Lab
318 Dewsbury	1.7	Lab
319 Bracknell	1.7	Con
320 Sunderland North	1.7	Lab
321 Dunfermline East	1.7	Lab
322 Ashfield	1.6	Lab
323 Birmingham Erdington	1.6	Lab
324 Spelthorne	1.6	Con
325 Norfolk South	1.6	Con
326 Clydebank & Milngavie	1.6	Lab
327 Leigh	1.6	Lab
328 Wentworth	1.6	Lab
329 Batley & Spen	1.5	Lab
330 Newcastle-under-Lyme	1.5	Lab
331 Copeland	1.5	Lab
332 Wantage	1.5	Con
333 Stalybridge & Hyde	1.5	Lab
334 Gravesham	1.5	Lab
335 Kirkcaldy	1.5	Lab
336 Glasgow Shettleston	1.4	Lab
337 Sheffield Heeley	1.4	Lab
338 Don Valley	1.4	Lab
339 Leeds West	1.4	Lab
340 Bristol South	1.4	Lab
341 Northampton South	1.4	Lab
342 Caernarfon	1.4	PC
343 Ilford North	1.4	Lab
344 Luton South	1.3	Lab
345 Dundee West	1.3	Lab
346 Cotswold	1.3	Con
347 Swansea East	1.3	Lab
348 Macclesfield	1.3	Con
349 Calder Valley	1.3	Lab
350 Eastwood	1.2	Lab
351 Chipping Barnet	1.2	Con
352 Carlisle	1.2	Lab

353 Stoke-on-Trent North	1.2	Lab
354 Caerphilly	1.2	Lab
355 Devon East	1.2	Con
356 Daventry	1.2	Con
357 Wakefield	1.2	Lab
358 Burton	1.1	Lab
359 Blackpool North & Fleetwood	1.1	Lab
360 Leicester West	1.1	Lab
361 Reigate	1.1	Con
362 Telford	1.1	Lab
363 Faversham & Kent Mid	1.1	Con
364 New Forest East	1.1	Con
365 Wokingham	1.1	Con
366 Keighley	1.1	Lab
367 Derbyshire South	1.1	Lab
368 Stockton North	1.0	Lab
369 Hyndburn	1.0	Lab
370 Cambridgeshire South	1.0	Con
371 Sleaford & North Hykeham	1.0	Con
372 Paisley South	1.0	Lab
373 Loughborough	1.0	Lab
374 Scunthorpe	1.0	Lab
375 Hartlepool	1.0	Lab
376 Eastbourne	0.9	Con
377 Rother Valley	0.9	Lab
378 Leyton & Wanstead	0.9	Lab
379 Skipton & Ripon	0.9	Con
380 Walthamstow	0.9	Lab
381 Clwyd South	0.9	Lab
382 Bristol West	0.9	Lab
383 Great Grimsby	0.9	Lab
384 Warley	0.8	Lab
385 Edinburgh Pentlands	0.8	Lab
386 Finchley & Golders Green	0.8	Lab
387 Caithness, Sutherland & Easter Ross	0.8	LD
388 Poplar & Canning Town	0.8	Lab
389 Birmingham Northfield	0.8	Lab
390 Hendon	0.7	Lab
391 Vale of Clwyd	0.7	Lab
392 Cambridgeshire North West	0.7	Con
393 Ayr	0.7	Lab
394 Gedling	0.7	Lab
395 Edmonton	0.7	Lab
396 Brighton Kemptown	0.7	Lab
397 Solihull	0.7	Con
398 Watford	0.7	Lab
399 Forest of Dean	0.6	Lab
400 Luton North	0.6	Lab
401 Cleethorpes	0.6	Lab
402 Oldham West & Royton	0.6	Lab
403 Barnsley West & Penistone	0.6	Lab
404 Blaenau Gwent	0.6	Lab
405 Dumfries	0.6	Lab
406 Carmarthen West & Pembrokeshire South	0.6	Lab
407 Welwyn Hatfield	0.5	Lab

Contd. /

408 Walsall South	0.5	Lab
409 Hemel Hempstead	0.5	Lab
410 Sussex Mid	0.5	Con
411 Kensington & Chelsea	0.5	Con
412 Plymouth Sutton	0.5	Lab
413 Witney	0.5	Con
414 Bedfordshire South West	0.5	Con
415 East Ham	0.5	Lab
416 Dudley North	0.5	Lab
417 Fife North East	0.4	LD
418 Chesham & Amersham	0.4	Con
419 Milton Keynes North East	0.4	Lab
420 Bolton North East	0.4	Lab
421 Wiltshire North	0.4	Con
422 Hornchurch	0.4	Lab
423 Croydon Central	0.4	Lab
424 Manchester Blackley	0.4	Lab
425 Basildon	0.3	Lab
426 Devon West & Torridge	0.3	LD
427 Aberdeen South	0.3	Lab
428 Hampshire North East	0.3	Con
429 Beaconsfield	0.3	Con
430 Barking	0.3	Lab
431 Birmingham Ladywood	0.3	Lab
432 Staffordshire South	0.3	Con
433 Sunderland South	0.2	Lab
434 Pudsey	0.2	Lab
435 Rotherham	0.2	Lab
436 Wolverhampton South West	0.2	Lab
437 Worcestershire Mid	0.1	Con
438 Fylde	0.1	Con
439 Reading West	0.1	Lab
440 Romford	0.1	Con
441 Plymouth Devonport	0.1	Lab
442 Worcester	0.1	Lab
443 Merthyr Tydfil & Rhymney	0.1	Lab
444 West Ham	0.0	Lab
445 Runnymede & Weybridge	0.0	Con
446 Chingford & Woodford Green	0.0	Con
447 Pontefract & Castleford	0.0	Lab
448 Bromsgrove	0.0	Con
449 Reading East	0.0	Lab
450 Wellingborough	0.0	Lab
451 Wythenshawe & Sale East	-0.1	Lab
452 Upminster	-0.1	Con
453 Bexleyheath & Crayford	-0.1	Lab
454 Wells	-0.1	Con
455 Carmarthen East & Dinefwr	-0.2	PC
456 Truro & St Austell	-0.2	LD
457 Enfield North	-0.2	Lab
458 Horsham	-0.2	Con
459 Portsmouth North	-0.3	Lab
460 Braintree	-0.3	Lab
461 Mole Valley	-0.3	Con
462 Walsall North	-0.3	Lab
463 Broxbourne	-0.3	Con
464 Sutton Coldfield	-0.3	Con
465 Dorset North	-0.4	Con
466 Birmingham Hodge Hill	-0.4	Lab
467 Thanet North	-0.4	Con
468 Hackney South & Shoreditch	-0.4	Lab
469 Ealing Southall	-0.4	Lab
470 Crosby	-0.4	Lab
471 Rugby & Kenilworth	-0.4	Lab
472 Richmond (Yorks)	-0.5	Con
473 Norfolk Mid	-0.5	Con
474 Kettering	-0.5	Lab
475 Hove	-0.5	Lab
476 Lichfield	-0.6	Con
477 Erith & Thamesmead	-0.6	Lab
478 Weston-Super-Mare	-0.6	LD
479 Uxbridge	-0.6	Con
480 Rushcliffe	-0.7	Con
481 Wolverhampton South East	-0.7	Lab
482 Llanelli	-0.7	Lab
483 Bradford South	-0.7	Lab
484 Warwick & Leamington	-0.7	Lab
485 Falmouth & Camborne	-0.7	Lab
486 Epsom & Ewell	-0.7	Con
487 Redditch	-0.7	Lab
488 Banbury	-0.8	Con
489 Bexhill & Battle	-0.8	Con
490 Brigg & Goole	-0.8	Lab
491 Birmingham Hall Green	-0.8	Lab
492 Medway	-0.8	Lab
493 Edinburgh West	-0.9	LD
494 Fareham	-0.9	Con
495 Dartford	-0.9	Lab
496 Gower	-0.9	Lab
497 Denton & Reddish	-0.9	Lab
498 Cynon Valley	-0.9	Lab
499 Selby	-1.0	Lab
500 Torfaen	-1.0	Lab
501 Leominster	-1.0	Con
502 Hertfordshire North East	-1.0	Con
503 West Bromwich East	-1.1	Lab
504 Stafford	-1.1	Lab
505 Cornwall North	-1.1	LD
506 Rhondda	-1.2	Lab
507 Cornwall South East	-1.2	LD
508 Norfolk North West	-1.2	Con
509 Burnley	-1.2	Lab
510 Tottenham	-1.3	Lab
511 Lancaster & Wyre	-1.3	Lab
512 Tonbridge & Malling	-1.3	Con
513 Milton Keynes South West	-1.3	Lab
514 Swindon North	-1.4	Lab
515 Hayes & Harlington	-1.4	Lab
516 Castle Point	-1.4	Con
517 Rutland & Melton	-1.4	Con
518 The Wrekin	-1.4	Lab
519 Clwyd West	-1.4	Lab
520 Taunton	-1.4	Con
521 Gainsborough	-1.5	Con

Contd./

522 Wycombe	-1.5	Con	580 Vale of York	-3.6	Con
523 Preston	-1.5	Lab	581 Wimbledon	-3.6	Lab
524 Sheffield Attercliffe	-1.5	Lab	582 Bridgwater	-3.6	Con
525 Bosworth	-1.6	Con	583 Enfield Southgate	-3.7	Lab
526 Aberavon	-1.6	Lab	584 Havant	-3.8	Con
527 Cheltenham	-1.7	LD	585 Yorkshire East	-4.0	Con
528 Tewkesbury	-1.8	Con	586 Brecon & Radnorshire	-4.0	LD
529 Derbyshire West	-1.8	Con	587 Sittingbourne & Sheppey	-4.2	Lab
530 Saffron Walden	-1.9	Con	588 Boston & Skegness	-4.2	Con
531 Meriden	-1.9	Con	589 Shipley	-4.2	Lab
532 Glasgow Rutherglen	-1.9	Lab	590 Bury St Edmunds	-4.3	Con
533 Billericay	-1.9	Con	591 Rayleigh	-4.3	Con
534 New Forest West	-2.0	Con	592 Southport	-4.3	LD
535 Rochford & Southend East	-2.0	Con	593 Louth & Horncastle	-4.4	Con
536 Wealden	-2.0	Con	594 Devizes	-4.5	Con
537 Essex North	-2.1	Con	595 Heywood & Middleton	-4.5	Lab
538 Hitchin & Harpenden	-2.1	Con	596 Suffolk Central & Ipswich N.	-4.5	Con
539 Salisbury	-2.1	Con	597 Gosport	-4.5	Con
540 Beckenham	-2.1	Con	598 Stroud	-4.5	Lab
541 Huddersfield	-2.2	Lab	599 Yeovil	-4.6	LD
542 Suffolk West	-2.2	Con	600 Worthing West	-4.6	Con
543 Stourbridge	-2.2	Lab	601 Ashford	-4.6	Con
544 Morecambe & Lunesdale	-2.2	Lab	602 Harwich	-4.6	Lab
545 Thanet South	-2.3	Lab	603 Newbury	-4.7	LD
546 Cambridgeshire North East	-2.4	Con	604 Buckingham	-4.7	Con
547 Old Bexley & Sidcup	-2.4	Con	605 Bromley & Chislehurst	-4.8	Con
548 Hexham	-2.4	Con	606 Chichester	-4.8	Con
549 Blackburn	-2.4	Lab	607 Penrith & The Border	-4.9	Con
550 Wansdyke	-2.4	Lab	608 Tunbridge Wells	-5.0	Con
551 Hazel Grove	-2.5	LD	609 Rochdale	-5.1	Lab
552 Maidstone & The Weald	-2.5	Con	610 Poole	-5.3	Con
553 Sevenoaks	-2.5	Con	611 South Holland & The		
554 Preseli Pembrokeshire	-2.5	Lab	Deepings	-5.3	Con
555 Swindon South	-2.5	Lab	612 Devon South West	-5.4	Con
556 Windsor	-2.5	Con	613 Gillingham	-5.4	Lab
557 Beverley & Holderness	-2.6	Con	614 Exeter	-5.6	Lab
558 Aldridge - Brownhills	-2.6	Con	615 Scarborough & Whitby	-5.8	Lab
559 Pontypridd	-2.6	Lab	616 Dorset South	-5.8	Lab
560 Bournemouth West	-2.6	Con	617 Sheffield Brightside	-5.8	Lab
561 Great Yarmouth	-2.6	Lab	618 Canterbury	-5.9	Con
562 Aylesbury	-2.6	Con	619 Chelmsford West	-5.9	Con
563 Harrow West	-2.6	Lab	620 Woodspring	-6.1	Con
564 Tiverton & Honiton	-2.7	Con	621 Bognor Regis & Littlehampton	-6.4	Con
565 Suffolk South	-2.8	Con	622 Ribble Valley	-6.4	Con
566 Oldham East & Saddleworth	-2.8	Lab	623 Devon North	-6.5	LD
567 Aldershot	-2.8	Con	624 Hereford	-7.1	LD
568 Croydon South	-2.9	Con	625 Isle of Wight	-7.5	Con
569 Hampshire North West	-2.9	Con	626 Shropshire North	-7.6	Con
570 Basingstoke	-3.1	Con	627 Worthing East & Shoreham	-7.6	Con
571 St Albans	-3.1	Lab	628 Congleton	-8.2	Con
572 Hull West & Hessle	-3.1	Lab	629 Southend West	-8.2	Con
573 Suffolk Coastal	-3.2	Con	630 Bradford West	-8.4	Lab
574 Norfolk South West	-3.2	Con	631 Argyll & Bute	-10.3	LD
575 Chatham & Aylesford	-3.2	Lab	632 Orkney & Shetland	-10.6	LD
576 Sheffield Hillsborough	-3.3	Lab	633 Brentwood & Ongar	-10.7	Con
577 Worcestershire West	-3.3	Con	634 Shrewsbury & Atcham	-12.6	Lab
578 Arundel & South Downs	-3.4	Con	*Contd. /*		
579 Maldon & Chelmsford East	-3.5	Con			

635 Conwy	-14.3	Lab
636 Christchurch	-14.8	Con
637 Hastings & Rye	-17.6	Lab

SNP

Constituency	%change	1st
1 Aberdeen North	6.9	Lab
2 Dundee East	4.9	Lab
3 Aberdeen Central	4.2	Lab
4 Clydesdale	4.1	Lab
5 Dundee West	4.1	Lab
6 Western Isles	3.5	Lab
7 Stirling	3.0	Lab
8 Glasgow Springburn	2.9	Spkr
9 Cunninghame North	2.8	Lab
10 Glasgow Shettleston	2.7	Lab
11 Orkney & Shetland	2.1	LD
12 Aberdeen South	1.9	Lab
13 Hamilton South	1.8	Lab
14 East Kilbride	1.8	Lab
15 Edinburgh West	1.4	LD
16 Cumbernauld & Kilsyth	1.2	Lab
17 Falkirk West	0.8	Lab
18 Fife Central	0.3	Lab
19 Strathkelvin & Bearsden	-0.2	Lab
20 Glasgow Baillieston	-0.4	Lab
21 Fife North East	-0.5	LD
22 Ayr	-0.6	Lab
23 Kirkcaldy	-0.7	Lab
24 Falkirk East	-0.7	Lab
25 Paisley North	-0.8	Lab
26 Dunfermline East	-0.8	Lab
27 Aberdeenshire West & Kincardine	-0.9	LD
28 Carrick, Cumnock & Doon Valley	-1.1	Lab
29 Clydebank & Milngavie	-1.1	Lab
30 Glasgow Maryhill	-1.1	Lab
31 Glasgow Rutherglen	-1.1	Lab
32 East Lothian	-1.1	Lab
33 Glasgow Pollok	-1.1	Lab
34 Linlithgow	-1.3	Lab
35 Banff & Buchan	-1.5	SNP
36 Roxburgh & Berwickshire	-1.6	LD
37 Edinburgh Central	-1.7	Lab
38 Dunfermline West	-1.8	Lab
39 Edinburgh East & Musselburgh	-1.8	Lab
40 Caithness, Sutherland & Easter Ross	-1.8	LD
41 Hamilton North & Bellshill	-1.9	Lab
42 Glasgow Anniesland	-2.0	Lab
43 Edinburgh Pentlands	-2.2	Lab
44 Coatbridge & Chryston	-2.2	Lab
45 Cunninghame South	-2.3	Lab
46 Argyll & Bute	-2.4	LD
47 Dumfries	-2.4	Lab

48 Edinburgh South	-3.0	Lab
49 Motherwell & Wishaw	-3.2	Lab
50 Inverness East, Nairn & Lochaber	-3.3	Lab
51 Gordon	-3.5	LD
52 Greenock & Inverclyde	-3.6	Lab
53 Glasgow Cathcart	-3.6	Lab
54 Dumbarton	-3.9	Lab
55 Livingston	-3.9	Lab
56 Paisley South	-4.0	Lab
57 Midlothian	-4.2	Lab
58 Edinburgh North & Leith	-4.2	Lab
59 Ochil	-4.2	Lab
60 Eastwood	-4.5	Lab
61 Glasgow Kelvin	-4.5	Lab
62 Tweeddale, Ettrick & Lauderdale	-4.7	LD
63 Tayside North	-4.8	SNP
64 Airdrie & Shotts	-5.1	Lab
65 Renfrewshire West	-5.2	Lab
66 Ross, Skye & Inverness West	-5.5	LD
67 Perth	-6.7	SNP
68 Kilmarnock & Loudoun	-9.1	Lab
69 Galloway & Upper Nithsdale	-10.1	Con
70 Glasgow Govan	-11.1	Lab
71 Moray	-11.2	SNP
72 Angus	-13.0	SNP

Plaid Cymru

Constituency	%change	1st
1 Llanelli	11.9	Lab
2 Caerphilly	11.4	Lab
3 Neath	10.3	Lab
4 Conwy	9.6	Lab
5 Merthyr Tydfil & Rhymney	8.7	Lab
6 Swansea East	8.1	Lab
7 Rhondda	7.8	Lab
8 Carmarthen East & Dinefwr	7.7	PC
9 Pontypridd	7.3	Lab
10 Ogmore	7.0	Lab
11 Cynon Valley	6.8	Lab
12 Preseli Pembrokeshire	6.3	Lab
13 Carmarthen W. & Pembrokeshire S.	6.0	Lab
14 Blaenau Gwent	5.9	Lab
15 Islwyn	5.6	Lab
16 Newport West	5.5	Lab
17 Clwyd South	5.5	Lab
18 Torfaen	5.3	Lab
19 Gower	5.2	Lab
20 Cardiff West	4.8	Lab
21 Swansea West	4.0	Lab
22 Aberavon	4.0	Lab
23 Vale of Glamorgan	3.8	Lab
24 Bridgend	3.4	Lab
25 Cardiff North	3.2	Lab
26 Newport East	2.9	Lab
27 Wrexham	2.7	Lab
28 Delyn	2.7	Lab

Contd./

	%change	1st
29 Cardiff South & Penarth	2.4	Lab
30 Brecon & Radnorshire	2.0	LD
31 Montgomeryshire	1.8	LD
32 Alyn & Deeside	1.6	Lab
33 Monmouth	1.3	Lab
34 Cardiff Central	1.3	Lab
35 Vale of Clwyd	1.2	Lab
36 Clwyd West	-0.6	Lab
37 Meirionnydd Nant Conwy	-1.1	PC
38 Ceredigion	-3.4	PC
39 Caernarfon	-6.7	PC
40 Ynys Mon	-6.8	Lab

Ulster Unionist

Constituency	%change	1st
1 Down North	24.9	UU
2 Belfast South	8.8	UU
3 Belfast West	2.8	SF
4 Lagan Valley	1.1	UU
5 Belfast East	-2.1	DUP
6 Antrim East	-2.4	UU
7 Antrim North	-2.7	DUP
8 Strangford	-4.0	DUP
9 Tyrone West	-4.1	SF
10 Londonderry East	-8.2	DUP
11 Upper Bann	-10.1	UU
12 Down South	-15.2	SDLP
13 Fermanagh & South Tyrone	-17.5	SF
14 Antrim South	-20.4	UU
15 Newry and Armagh	-21.5	SDLP
16 Belfast North	-39.8	DUP

Democratic Unionist

Constituency	%change	1st
1 Upper Bann	18.0	UU
2 Antrim East	16.6	UU
3 Strangford	12.6	DUP
4 Londonderry East	6.5	DUP
5 Antrim North	3.3	DUP
6 Belfast East	-0.1	DUP
7 Lagan Valley	-0.1	UU
8 Ulster Mid	-5.2	SF
9 Foyle	-6.4	SDLP

APNI

Constituency	%change	1st
1 Foyle	-0.5	SDLP
2 Lagan Valley	-0.6	UU
3 Down South	-2.1	SDLP
4 Londonderry East	-2.3	DUP
5 Antrim North	-3.6	DUP
6 Strangford	-6.4	DUP
7 Antrim South	-7.2	UU
8 Belfast South	-7.6	UU
9 Antrim East	-7.7	UU
10 Belfast East	-8.0	DUP

SDLP

Constituency	%change	1st
1 Belfast South	6.3	UU
2 Antrim East	2.7	UU
3 Antrim North	1.0	DUP
4 Belfast East	0.8	DUP
5 Belfast North	0.6	DUP
6 Lagan Valley	-0.2	UU
7 Strangford	-0.6	DUP
8 Londonderry East	-0.9	DUP
9 Down North	-1.0	UU
10 Foyle	-2.3	SDLP
11 Tyrone West	-3.3	SF
12 Antrim South	-4.1	UU
13 Fermanagh & South Tyrone	-4.2	SF
14 Ulster Mid	-5.3	SF
15 Newry and Armagh	-5.6	SDLP
16 Down South	-6.6	SDLP
17 Upper Bann	-9.3	UU
18 Belfast West	-19.8	SF

SF

Constituency	%change	1st
1 Ulster Mid	11.0	SF
2 Fermanagh & South Tyrone	11.0	SF
3 Belfast West	10.2	SF
4 Tyrone West	10.0	SF
5 Newry and Armagh	9.9	SDLP
6 Down South	9.4	SDLP
7 Upper Bann	9.0	UU
8 Londonderry East	6.5	DUP
9 Belfast North	5.0	DUP
10 Antrim South	3.9	UU
11 Antrim North	3.5	DUP
12 Lagan Valley	3.4	UU
13 Foyle	2.6	SDLP
14 Belfast South	2.5	UU
15 Belfast East	1.3	DUP
16 Strangford	0.9	DUP
17 Antrim East	0.9	UU

Table 15. Seats in Rank Order of Party Highest Share of Vote

Conservative		Labour	
Constituency	**%share**	**Constituency**	**%share**
1 Richmond (Yorks)	58.9	1 Liverpool Walton	77.8
2 New Forest West	55.7	2 Bootle	77.6
3 South Holland & The Deepings	55.4	3 Sheffield Brightside	76.9
4 Christchurch	55.1	4 Easington	76.8
5 Penrith & The Border	54.9	5 Brent South	73.3
6 Kensington & Chelsea	54.5	6 Houghton & Washington East	73.2
7 Broxbourne	54.1	7 East Ham	73.1
8 Buckingham	53.7	8 Blaenau Gwent	72.0
9 Rochford & Southend East	53.6	9 Liverpool Riverside	71.4
10 Hampshire North East	53.2	10 Knowsley South	71.3
11 Romford	53.0	11 Birkenhead	70.5
12 Beaconsfield	52.8	12 Tyne Bridge	70.5
13 Surrey East	52.5	13 West Ham	69.9
14 Skipton & Ripon	52.4	14 Pontefract & Castleford	69.7
15 Fylde	52.3	15 Barnsley Central	69.6
16 Arundel & South Downs	52.2	16 Camberwell & Peckham	69.6
17 Norfolk South West	52.2	17 Tyneside North	69.5
18 Bromsgrove	51.7	18 Halton	69.2
19 Vale of York	51.6	19 Manchester Blackley	68.9
20 Horsham	51.5	20 Birmingham Ladywood	68.9
21 Ribble Valley	51.5	21 Manchester Central	68.7
22 Worcestershire Mid	51.1	22 Bolsover	68.6
23 Mole Valley	50.5	23 Makerfield	68.5
24 Chesham & Amersham	50.5	24 Rhondda	68.3
25 Staffordshire South	50.5	25 Gateshead East & Washington West	68.1
26 Sutton Coldfield	50.4	26 Sheffield Attercliffe	67.8
27 Cotswold	50.3	27 Middlesbrough	67.6
28 Thanet North	50.3	28 Barnsley East & Mexborough	67.5
29 Stratford-on-Avon	50.3	29 Wentworth	67.5
30 Aldridge - Brownhills	50.2	30 Tottenham	67.5
31 Hampshire North West	50.1	31 Wolverhampton South East	67.4
32 Rayleigh	50.1	32 Durham North	67.2
33 Huntingdon	49.9	33 Leeds Central	66.9
34 Bedfordshire North East	49.9	34 Knowsley North & Sefton East	66.7
35 Wealden	49.8	35 Liverpool West Derby	66.2
36 Cambridgeshire North West	49.8	36 Jarrow	66.1
37 Surrey Heath	49.7	37 Hayes & Harlington	65.7
38 Sleaford & North Hykeham	49.7	38 Cynon Valley	65.6
39 Maidstone & The Weald	49.6	39 Hemsworth	65.4
40 Bromley & Chislehurst	49.5	40 Coatbridge & Chryston	65.3
41 Sevenoaks	49.4	41 Denton & Reddish	65.2
42 Tonbridge & Malling	49.4	42 Swansea East	65.2
43 Maldon & Chelmsford East	49.2	43 Salford	65.1
44 Daventry	49.2	44 Lewisham Deptford	65.0
45 Croydon South	49.2	45 Sedgefield	64.9
46 Lichfield	49.1	46 Dunfermline East	64.8
47 Epping Forest	49.1	47 Glasgow Shettleston	64.7
48 Stone	49.1	48 Hull East	64.6
49 Esher & Walton	49.0	49 Nottingham North	64.5
50 Leominster	49.0	50 Leigh	64.5

Contd. /

Liberal Democrat		SNP	
Constituency	%share	Constituency	%share
1 Kingston & Surbiton	60.2	1 Banff & Buchan	54.2
2 Southwark North & Bermondsey	56.9	2 Tayside North	40.1
3 Lewes	56.3	3 Western Isles	36.9
4 Harrogate & Knaresborough	55.6	4 Angus	35.3
5 Sheffield Hallam	55.4	5 Galloway & Upper Nithsdale	33.8
6 Winchester	54.6	6 Dundee East	31.4
7 Ross, Skye & Inverness West	54.1	7 Moray	30.3
8 Northavon	52.4	8 Ochil	30.2
9 Hazel Grove	52.0	9 Perth	29.7
10 Cornwall North	52.0	10 Cumbernauld & Kilsyth	29.0
11 Fife North East	51.7	11 Aberdeen North	28.7
12 St Ives	51.6	12 Dundee West	27.3
13 Berwick-upon-Tweed	51.4	13 Clydesdale	26.2
14 Torbay	50.5	14 Inverness East, Nairn & Lochaber	25.6
15 Bath	50.5	15 Linlithgow	25.5
16 Montgomeryshire	49.4	16 Kilmarnock & Loudoun	25.5
17 Sutton & Cheam	48.8	17 Fife Central	25.3
18 Roxburgh & Berwickshire	48.8	18 Falkirk West	24.2
19 Twickenham	48.7	19 Glasgow Govan	24.0
20 Truro & St Austell	48.3	20 Livingston	23.6
21 Newbury	48.2	21 Falkirk East	23.2
22 Oxford West & Abingdon	47.8	22 East Kilbride	22.7
23 Chesterfield	47.8	23 Kirkcaldy	22.2
24 Cheltenham	47.7	24 Midlothian	21.3
25 Richmond Park	47.7	25 Renfrewshire West	21.3
26 Romsey	47.0	26 Cunninghame North	21.2
27 Cornwall South East	45.9	27 Caithness, Sutherland & Easter Ross	21.2
28 Gordon	45.5	28 Paisley North	21.1
29 Carshalton & Wallington	45.0	29 Argyll & Bute	20.8
30 Portsmouth South	44.6	30 Aberdeen Central	20.4
31 Teignbridge	44.4	31 Clydebank & Milngavie	20.1
32 Devon North	44.2	32 Hamilton South	19.4
33 Yeovil	44.2	33 Glasgow Springburn	19.4
34 Southport	43.8	34 Paisley South	19.4
35 Somerton & Frome	43.6	35 Dumbarton	19.3
36 Surrey South West	43.6	36 Airdrie & Shotts	19.3
37 Aberdeenshire W & Kincardine	43.5	37 Motherwell & Wishaw	19.3
38 Orpington	43.3	38 Glasgow Baillieston	18.7
39 Ludlow	43.2	39 Cunninghame South	18.5
40 Norfolk North	42.7	40 Dunfermline West	17.4
41 Colchester	42.6	41 Edinburgh East & Musselburgh	17.3
42 Guildford	42.6	42 Hamilton North & Bellshill	17.2
43 Cheadle	42.4	43 Glasgow Kelvin	16.8
44 Edinburgh West	42.4	44 Glasgow Pollok	16.7
45 Tweeddale, Ettrick & Lauderdale	42.3	45 Glasgow Shettleston	16.7
46 Devon West & Torridge	42.2	46 Gordon	16.5
47 Dorset Mid & Poole North	42.0	47 Stirling	16.4
48 Dorset West	41.8	48 Strathkelvin & Bearsden	16.1
49 Orkney & Shetland	41.3	49 Edinburgh North & Leith	15.9
50 Taunton	41.3	50 Glasgow Maryhill	15.9

Contd./

Plaid Cymru

Constituency	%share
1 Meirionnydd Nant Conwy	49.6
2 Caernarfon	44.4
3 Carmarthen East & Dinefwr	42.4
4 Ceredigion	38.3
5 Ynys Mon	32.6
6 Llanelli	30.9
7 Rhondda	21.1
8 Caerphilly	21.0
9 Carmarthen West & Pembrokeshire South	18.7
10 Neath	18.4
11 Cynon Valley	17.4
12 Conwy	16.5
13 Merthyr Tydfil & Rhymney	14.7
14 Ogmore	14.0
15 Pontypridd	13.8
16 Clwyd West	12.9
17 Preseli Pembrokeshire	12.7
18 Clwyd South	11.9
19 Islwyn	11.9
20 Swansea East	11.5
21 Blaenau Gwent	11.2
22 Swansea West	10.6
23 Gower	10.3
24 Aberavon	9.8
25 Cardiff West	9.7

Green

Constituency	%share
1 Brighton Pavilion	9.3
2 Leeds West	8.0
3 Hackney North & Stoke Newington	7.4
4 Bradford West	7.0
5 Lewisham Deptford	6.5
6 Islington North	6.2
7 Holborn & St Pancras	6.0
8 Edinburgh Central	5.3
9 Hornsey & Wood Green	5.1
10 Dulwich & West Norwood	5.0
11 Glasgow Kelvin	4.8
12 Brent East	4.7
13 Hampstead & Highgate	4.7
14 Tooting	4.6
15 Tottenham	4.6
16 Ealing Southall	4.5
17 Vauxhall	4.4
18 Streatham	4.4
19 Manchester Withington	4.4
20 Bethnal Green & Bow	4.3
21 Kensington & Chelsea	4.1
22 West Ham	4.1
23 Manchester Central	3.9
24 Cities of London & Westminster	3.9
25 Oxford East	3.8

UKI

Constituency	%share
1 Bexhill & Battle	7.8
2 Totnes	6.1
3 Devon East	5.6
4 Stafford	5.2
5 Harwich	5.1
6 Devon North	5.0
7 Esher & Walton	4.9
8 Devon West & Torridge	4.8
9 Chichester	4.8
10 Arundel & South Downs	4.7
11 Bognor Regis & Littlehampton	4.6
12 Worthing West	4.5
13 Cornwall North	4.4
14 Skipton & Ripon	4.2
15 Hull East	3.9
16 Surrey East	3.9
17 St Ives	3.9
18 Hampshire North East	3.9
19 Beaconsfield	3.9
20 Yorkshire East	3.8
21 Teignbridge	3.8
22 Cornwall South East	3.8
23 Rother Valley	3.7
24 Staffordshire South	3.7
25 New Forest West	3.7
26 Salisbury	3.7
27 Rayleigh	3.7
28 Southend West	3.7
29 Suffolk Coastal	3.7
30 Essex North	3.6
31 Telford	3.6
32 Saffron Walden	3.5
33 Worcestershire West	3.5
34 Suffolk South	3.5
35 Basildon	3.4
36 Ilford South	3.4
37 Woking	3.4
38 Leominster	3.4
39 Thurrock	3.4
40 Redditch	3.4
41 Old Bexley & Sidcup	3.4
42 Huntingdon	3.4
43 Charnwood	3.3
44 Isle of Wight	3.3
45 Epsom & Ewell	3.3
46 Truro & St Austell	3.3
47 Surrey Heath	3.3
48 Tunbridge Wells	3.3
49 Worcester	3.3
50 Morley & Rothwell	3.2

Contd./

Socialist Labour

Constituency	%share
1 Warley	6.2
2 St Helens South	4.4
3 Birmingham Perry Barr	4.1
4 Erith & Thamesmead	3.5
5 Bootle	3.5
6 Knowsley South	2.9
7 Hull East	2.7
8 Hackney North & Stoke Newington	2.6
9 Easington	2.5
10 St Helens North	2.5
11 Bolton South East	2.4
12 Hartlepool	2.4
13 Normanton	2.3
14 Leigh	2.3
15 Hemsworth	2.3
16 Barnsley East & Mexborough	2.2
17 Merthyr Tydfil & Rhymney	2.2
18 East Ham	2.1
19 Newcastle upon Tyne Central	2.1
20 Leicester East	2.1
21 Tyne Bridge	2.0
22 Redcar	2.0
23 Ealing Southall	2.0
24 Sheffield Heeley	2.0
25 Pontefract & Castleford	1.9

Scottish Socialist

Constituency	%share
1 Glasgow Pollok	10.0
2 Glasgow Maryhill	7.8
3 Glasgow Springburn	7.8
4 Glasgow Kelvin	6.9
5 Glasgow Shettleston	6.8
6 Glasgow Baillieston	6.7
7 Glasgow Cathcart	6.3
8 Glasgow Govan	6.1
9 Glasgow Anniesland	5.6
10 Coatbridge & Chryston	5.1
11 Orkney & Shetland	4.6
12 Glasgow Rutherglen	4.5
13 Hamilton South	4.4
14 Cunninghame South	4.4
15 Cumbernauld & Kilsyth	4.3
16 Edinburgh East & Musselburgh	4.3
17 Motherwell & Wishaw	4.2
18 Greenock & Inverclyde	4.2
19 Dundee West	4.1
20 Argyll & Bute	4.0
21 Edinburgh North & Leith	4.0
22 Dumbarton	4.0
23 Clydebank & Milngavie	4.0
24 Hamilton North & Bellshill	3.9
25 Airdrie & Shotts	3.7

Socialist Alliance

Constituency	%share
1 Coventry North East	7.1
2 St Helens South	6.9
3 Hackney South & Shoreditch	4.6
4 Lewisham Deptford	4.3
5 Nottingham East	3.8
6 Coventry South	3.7
7 Tottenham	3.7
8 Liverpool Riverside	3.6
9 Manchester Withington	3.4
10 Holborn & St Pancras	3.1
11 Islington South & Finsbury	2.9
12 Poplar & Canning Town	2.8
13 Leeds Central	2.8
14 Wigan	2.6
15 Vauxhall	2.6
16 Barnsley Central	2.6
17 Hornsey & Wood Green	2.5
18 Sheffield Central	2.5
19 Makerfield	2.5
20 Bootle	2.4
21 Streatham	2.4
22 Dulwich & West Norwood	2.2
23 Birmingham Erdington	2.2
24 Leyton & Wanstead	2.1
25 Camberwell & Peckham	1.9

BNP

Constituency	%share
1 Oldham West & Royton	16.4
2 Burnley	11.3
3 Oldham East & Saddleworth	11.2
4 Barking	6.4
5 Poplar & Canning Town	5.1
6 Dagenham	5.0
7 Pendle	5.0
8 Dudley North	4.7
9 Bradford North	4.6
10 Ashton under Lyne	4.5
11 West Bromwich West	4.5
12 Dewsbury	4.5
13 Stoke-on-Trent South	3.8
14 Bexleyheath & Crayford	3.5
15 Birmingham Hodge Hill	3.4
16 Lewisham East	3.3
17 Bethnal Green & Bow	3.2
18 Chingford & Woodford Green	2.9
19 Blaby	2.8
20 Sunderland North	2.3
21 Broxbourne	2.2
22 Hayes & Harlington	2.2
23 Coventry North East	2.0
24 Leicester East	1.9
25 Sunderland South	1.8

Contd. /

Liberal

Constituency	%share
1 Liverpool West Derby	14.9
2 Exeter	4.9
3 Heywood & Middleton	2.6
4 Southport	1.9
5 Rochford & Southend East	1.6
6 Leeds West	1.4
7 Falmouth & Camborne	1.4
8 Eastbourne	1.3
9 Tweeddale, Ettrick & Lauderdale	1.2
10 Yeovil	1.1

Pro-Life

Constituency	%share
1 Brent East	1.4
2 Birmingham Ladywood	1.2
3 Paisley South	1.1
4 Cardiff South & Penarth	1.0
5 Mole Valley	1.0
6 Chesham & Amersham	1.0
7 Paisley North	1.0
8 Walthamstow	0.8
9 Manchester Central	0.8
10 Solihull	0.8

MRLP

Constituency	%share
1 Wokingham	2.0
2 Sussex Mid	1.3
3 Richmond (Yorks)	1.3
4 Cheltenham	1.2
5 Ochil	1.1
6 Crawley	1.0
7 Sunderland South	0.9
8 Derbyshire West	0.9
9 Croydon Central	0.9
10 Devizes	0.9

LCA

Constituency	%share
1 Workington	2.5
2 Worthing East & Shoreham	2.1
3 Penrith & The Border	2.0
4 Hull North	1.7
5 Carlisle	1.6
6 Braintree	1.5
7 Norwich South	1.5
8 Edinburgh South	1.4
9 Chelmsford West	1.4
10 Calder Valley	1.4

UU

Constituency	%share
1 Lagan Valley	56.5
2 Down North	56.0
3 Belfast South	44.8
4 Strangford	40.3
5 Antrim South	37.1
6 Antrim East	36.4
7 Fermanagh & South Tyrone	34.0
8 Upper Bann	33.5
9 Tyrone West	30.4
10 Londonderry East	27.4
11 Belfast East	23.2
12 Antrim North	21.0
13 Down South	17.6
14 Newry and Armagh	12.3
15 Belfast North	12.0
16 Foyle	6.9
17 Belfast West	6.2

DUP

Constituency	%share
1 Antrim North	49.9
2 Strangford	42.8
3 Belfast East	42.5
4 Belfast North	40.8
5 Antrim East	36.0
6 Antrim South	34.8
7 Londonderry East	32.1
8 Ulster Mid	31.1
9 Upper Bann	29.5
10 Newry and Armagh	19.4
11 Foyle	15.2
12 Down South	15.0
13 Lagan Valley	13.4
14 Belfast West	6.4

APNI

Constituency	%share
1 Lagan Valley	16.6
2 Belfast East	15.8
3 Antrim East	12.5
4 Strangford	6.7
5 Belfast South	5.4
6 Antrim South	4.5
7 Londonderry East	4.1
8 Antrim North	2.6
9 Down South	1.3
10 Foyle	1.2

Contd. /

SDLP

Constituency	%share
1 Foyle	50.2
2 Down South	46.3
3 Newry and Armagh	37.4
4 Belfast South	30.6
5 Tyrone West	28.7
6 Belfast North	21.0
7 Londonderry East	20.8
8 Belfast West	18.9
9 Fermanagh & South Tyrone	18.7
10 Antrim North	16.8
11 Ulster Mid	16.8
12 Upper Bann	14.9
13 Antrim South	12.1
14 Lagan Valley	7.5
15 Antrim East	7.3
16 Strangford	6.1
17 Down North	3.4
18 Belfast East	2.4

SF

Constituency	%share
1 Belfast West	66.1
2 Ulster Mid	51.1
3 Tyrone West	40.8
4 Fermanagh & South Tyrone	34.1
5 Newry and Armagh	30.9
6 Foyle	26.6
7 Belfast North	25.2
8 Upper Bann	21.1
9 Down South	19.7
10 Londonderry East	15.6
11 Antrim North	9.8
12 Antrim South	9.4
13 Belfast South	7.6
14 Lagan Valley	5.9
15 Belfast East	3.4
16 Antrim East	2.5
17 Strangford	2.2
18 Down North	0.8

Table 16. Seats in Rank Order of Winning Party's Share of Vote

Constituency	%share	1st
1 Liverpool Walton	77.8	Lab
2 Bootle	77.6	Lab
3 Sheffield Brightside	76.9	Lab
4 Easington	76.8	Lab
5 Brent South	73.3	Lab
6 Houghton & Washington East	73.2	Lab
7 East Ham	73.1	Lab
8 Blaenau Gwent	72.0	Lab
9 Liverpool Riverside	71.4	Lab
10 Knowsley South	71.3	Lab
11 Birkenhead	70.5	Lab
12 Tyne Bridge	70.5	Lab
13 West Ham	69.9	Lab
14 Pontefract & Castleford	69.7	Lab
15 Barnsley Central	69.6	Lab
16 Camberwell & Peckham	69.6	Lab
17 Tyneside North	69.5	Lab
18 Halton	69.2	Lab
19 Manchester Blackley	68.9	Lab
20 Birmingham Ladywood	68.9	Lab
21 Manchester Central	68.7	Lab
22 Bolsover	68.6	Lab
23 Makerfield	68.5	Lab
24 Rhondda	68.3	Lab
25 Gateshead E. & Washington W.	68.1	Lab
26 Sheffield Attercliffe	67.8	Lab
27 Middlesbrough	67.6	Lab
28 Barnsley East & Mexborough	67.5	Lab
29 Wentworth	67.5	Lab
30 Tottenham	67.5	Lab
31 Wolverhampton South East	67.4	Lab
32 Durham North	67.2	Lab
33 Leeds Central	66.9	Lab
34 Knowsley North & Sefton East	66.7	Lab
35 Glasgow Springburn	66.6	Spkr
36 Liverpool West Derby	66.2	Lab
37 Belfast West	66.1	SF
38 Jarrow	66.1	Lab
39 Hayes & Harlington	65.7	Lab
40 Cynon Valley	65.6	Lab
41 Hemsworth	65.4	Lab
42 Coatbridge & Chryston	65.3	Lab
43 Denton & Reddish	65.2	Lab
44 Swansea East	65.2	Lab
45 Salford	65.1	Lab
46 Lewisham Deptford	65.0	Lab
47 Sedgefield	64.9	Lab
48 Dunfermline East	64.8	Lab
49 Glasgow Shettleston	64.7	Lab
50 Hull East	64.6	Lab
51 Nottingham North	64.5	Lab
52 Leigh	64.5	Lab
53 Eccles	64.5	Lab
54 Hackney South & Shoreditch	64.2	Lab
55 Rotherham	63.9	Lab
56 Sunderland South	63.9	Lab
57 Birmingham Hodge Hill	63.9	Lab
58 Croydon North	63.5	Lab
59 Stockton North	63.4	Lab
60 Brent East	63.2	Lab
61 South Shields	63.2	Lab
62 Aberavon	63.1	Lab
63 Newcastle upon Tyne East & Wallsend	63.1	Lab
64 Doncaster North	63.1	Lab
65 Leeds East	62.9	Lab
66 Manchester Gorton	62.8	Lab
67 Liverpool Wavertree	62.7	Lab
68 Sunderland North	62.7	Lab
69 Durham North West	62.5	Lab
70 Ashton under Lyne	62.5	Lab
71 Walthamstow	62.2	Lab
72 Leeds West	62.1	Lab
73 Torfaen	62.1	Lab
74 Rother Valley	62.1	Lab
75 Ogmore	62.0	Lab
76 Islington North	61.9	Lab
77 Bolton South East	61.9	Lab
78 Hamilton North & Bellshill	61.8	Lab
79 Merthyr Tydfil & Rhymney	61.8	Lab
80 Warrington North	61.7	Lab
81 Wigan	61.7	Lab
82 Islwyn	61.5	Lab
83 Sheffield Central	61.4	Lab
84 Liverpool Garston	61.4	Lab
85 Glasgow Pollok	61.3	Lab
86 Poplar & Canning Town	61.2	Lab
87 Stretford & Urmston	61.1	Lab
88 St Helens North	61.1	Lab
89 Lewisham West	61.1	Lab
90 Glasgow Baillieston	61.0	Lab
91 Hackney North & Stoke Newington	61.0	Lab
92 Coventry North East	61.0	Lab
93 Barking	60.9	Lab
94 Wallasey	60.8	Lab
95 West Bromwich West	60.8	Lab
96 Neath	60.7	Lab
97 Stoke-on-Trent Central	60.6	Lab
98 Greenwich & Woolwich	60.5	Lab
99 Warley	60.5	Lab
100 Mitcham & Morden	60.4	Lab
101 Glasgow Maryhill	60.4	Lab
102 Redcar	60.3	Lab
103 Wolverhampton North East	60.3	Lab
104 Kingston & Surbiton	60.2	LD
105 Newcastle upon Tyne North	60.1	Lab

Contd. /

106 Wythenshawe & Sale East	60.0	Lab
107 Pontypridd	59.9	Lab
108 Scunthorpe	59.8	Lab
109 Blyth Valley	59.7	Lab
110 Hamilton South	59.7	Lab
111 Ilford South	59.6	Lab
112 Brent North	59.4	Lab
113 Erith & Thamesmead	59.3	Lab
114 Bury South	59.2	Lab
115 Feltham & Heston	59.2	Lab
116 Hartlepool	59.1	Lab
117 Vauxhall	59.1	Lab
118 Doncaster Central	59.1	Lab
119 Nottingham East	59.0	Lab
120 Walsall South	59.0	Lab
121 Richmond (Yorks)	58.9	Con
122 Edmonton	58.9	Lab
123 Bishop Auckland	58.8	Lab
124 Stockport	58.6	Lab
125 Barnsley West & Penistone	58.6	Lab
126 Cunninghame South	58.4	Lab
127 Paisley South	58.4	Lab
128 Hull West & Hessle	58.4	Lab
129 Plymouth Devonport	58.3	Lab
130 Slough	58.3	Lab
131 Airdrie & Shotts	58.2	Lab
132 Caerphilly	58.2	Lab
133 Ashfield	58.1	Lab
134 Walsall North	58.1	Lab
135 Wyre Forest	58.1	KHHC
136 Leyton & Wanstead	58.0	Lab
137 Stoke-on-Trent North	58.0	Lab
138 Great Grimsby	57.9	Lab
139 Wansbeck	57.8	Lab
140 Heywood & Middleton	57.7	Lab
141 Leicester East	57.6	Lab
142 Birmingham Sparkbrook & Small Heath	57.5	Lab
143 Glasgow Rutherglen	57.4	Lab
144 Streatham	57.3	Lab
145 Dagenham	57.2	Lab
146 Hull North	57.2	Lab
147 Mansfield	57.1	Lab
148 Worsley	57.1	Lab
149 Morley & Rothwell	57.0	Lab
150 Preston	57.0	Lab
151 Sheffield Heeley	57.0	Lab
152 Southwark North & Bermondsey	56.9	LD
153 Bristol South	56.9	Lab
154 Sheffield Hillsborough	56.8	Lab
155 Birmingham Erdington	56.8	Lab
156 Luton North	56.7	Lab
157 Thurrock	56.5	Lab
158 Lagan Valley	56.5	UU
159 Glasgow Anniesland	56.5	Lab
160 Derby South	56.4	Lab
161 Darlington	56.3	Lab
162 Lewes	56.3	LD
163 Fife Central	56.3	Lab
164 Motherwell & Wishaw	56.2	Lab
165 Cardiff South & Penarth	56.2	Lab
166 Cannock Chase	56.1	Lab
167 Normanton	56.1	Lab
168 City of Durham	56.1	Lab
169 Down North	56.0	UU
170 Birmingham Northfield	56.0	Lab
171 West Bromwich East	55.9	Lab
172 Bradford South	55.8	Lab
173 New Forest West	55.7	Con
174 Barrow & Furness	55.7	Lab
175 Ealing North	55.7	Lab
176 Derbyshire North East	55.6	Lab
177 Harrogate & Knaresborough	55.6	LD
178 Workington	55.5	Lab
179 Stalybridge & Hyde	55.5	Lab
180 Paisley North	55.5	Lab
181 Sheffield Hallam	55.4	LD
182 South Holland & The Deepings	55.4	Con
183 Harrow East	55.3	Lab
184 Ellesmere Port & Neston	55.3	Lab
185 Bassetlaw	55.3	Lab
186 Carrick, Cumnock & Doon Valley	55.3	Lab
187 Middlesbrough South & Cleveland East	55.3	Lab
188 Luton South	55.2	Lab
189 Crosby	55.1	Lab
190 Christchurch	55.1	Con
191 Falkirk East	55.0	Lab
192 Bristol East	55.0	Lab
193 Newcastle upon Tyne Central	55.0	Lab
194 Penrith & The Border	54.9	Con
195 Dulwich & West Norwood	54.9	Lab
196 Manchester Withington	54.9	Lab
197 Kingswood	54.9	Lab
198 Blaydon	54.8	Lab
199 Newport East	54.7	Lab
200 Hyndburn	54.7	Lab
201 Regent's Park & Kensington N.	54.6	Lab
202 Don Valley	54.6	Lab
203 Telford	54.6	Lab
204 Winchester	54.6	LD
205 Birmingham Hall Green	54.6	Lab
206 Cardiff West	54.6	Lab
207 Southampton Itchen	54.5	Lab
208 Nottingham South	54.5	Lab
209 Leicester South	54.5	Lab
210 Lancashire West	54.5	Lab
211 Kensington & Chelsea	54.5	Con
212 Glasgow Cathcart	54.4	Lab

Contd. /

213 Cumbernauld & Kilsyth	54.4	Lab	269 York	52.3	Lab
214 Linlithgow	54.4	Lab	270 Arundel & South Downs	52.2	Con
215 Bolton North East	54.3	Lab	271 Norfolk South West	52.2	Con
216 Crewe & Nantwich	54.3	Lab	272 Bristol North West	52.1	Lab
217 Blackpool South	54.3	Lab	273 Nuneaton	52.1	Lab
218 Sherwood	54.2	Lab	274 Dudley North	52.1	Lab
219 Banff & Buchan	54.2	SNP	275 Leicestershire North West	52.1	Lab
220 Leicester West	54.2	Lab	276 Hazel Grove	52.0	LD
221 Ealing Acton & Shepherd's			277 Cornwall North	52.0	LD
Bush	54.1	Lab	278 Amber Valley	51.9	Lab
222 Blackburn	54.1	Lab	279 Stevenage	51.9	Lab
223 Broxbourne	54.1	Con	280 Falkirk West	51.9	Lab
224 Ross, Skye & Inverness West	54.1	LD	281 Enfield Southgate	51.8	Lab
225 Warwickshire North	54.1	Lab	282 Copeland	51.8	Lab
226 Tooting	54.1	Lab	283 Bromsgrove	51.7	Con
227 Kirkcaldy	54.1	Lab	284 Fife North East	51.7	LD
228 Islington South & Finsbury	53.9	Lab	285 Vale of York	51.6	Con
229 Lincoln	53.9	Lab	286 St Ives	51.6	LD
230 Holborn & St Pancras	53.9	Lab	287 Horsham	51.5	Con
231 Stoke-on-Trent South	53.8	Lab	288 Ribble Valley	51.5	Con
232 Lewisham East	53.7	Lab	289 Delyn	51.5	Lab
233 Buckingham	53.7	Con	290 Coventry North West	51.4	Lab
234 Rochford & Southend East	53.6	Con	291 Clwyd South	51.4	Lab
235 Newcastle-under-Lyme	53.4	Lab	292 Berwick-upon-Tweed	51.4	LD
236 East Kilbride	53.3	Lab	293 Ipswich	51.3	Lab
237 Huddersfield	53.2	Lab	294 Swindon South	51.3	Lab
238 Tynemouth	53.2	Lab	295 Bury North	51.2	Lab
239 Hampshire North East	53.2	Con	296 Oldham West & Royton	51.2	Lab
240 Reading West	53.1	Lab	297 Carlisle	51.2	Lab
241 Clydebank & Milngavie	53.1	Lab	298 Worcestershire Mid	51.1	Con
242 Livingston	53.0	Lab	299 Gedling	51.1	Lab
243 Wrexham	53.0	Lab	300 Ulster Mid	51.1	SF
244 Romford	53.0	Con	301 Derby North	50.9	Lab
245 Halesowen & Rowley Regis	53.0	Lab	302 Blackpool N. & Fleetwood	50.8	Lab
246 Stockton South	53.0	Lab	303 Plymouth Sutton	50.7	Lab
247 Kilmarnock & Loudoun	52.9	Lab	304 Derbyshire South	50.7	Lab
248 Swindon North	52.9	Lab	305 Waveney	50.7	Lab
249 Dunfermline West	52.8	Lab	306 Portsmouth North	50.7	Lab
250 Eltham	52.8	Lab	307 Dundee West	50.6	Lab
251 Beaconsfield	52.8	Con	308 Dewsbury	50.5	Lab
252 Newport West	52.7	Lab	309 Mole Valley	50.5	Con
253 Midlothian	52.7	Lab	310 Chesham & Amersham	50.5	Con
254 Basildon	52.7	Lab	311 Staffordshire South	50.5	Con
255 Edinburgh E. & Musselburgh	52.6	Lab	312 Torbay	50.5	LD
256 Greenock & Inverclyde	52.5	Lab	313 Bath	50.5	LD
257 Surrey East	52.5	Con	314 Bethnal Green & Bow	50.5	Lab
258 Southampton Test	52.5	Lab	315 Sutton Coldfield	50.4	Con
259 Bridgend	52.5	Lab	316 Great Yarmouth	50.4	Lab
260 Weaver Vale	52.5	Lab	317 Cotswold	50.3	Con
261 Hendon	52.5	Lab	318 Thanet North	50.3	Con
262 Birmingham Selly Oak	52.4	Lab	319 Stratford-on-Avon	50.3	Con
263 Northavon	52.4	LD	320 Battersea	50.3	Lab
264 Skipton & Ripon	52.4	Con	321 Foyle	50.2	SDLP
265 Chorley	52.3	Lab	322 Coventry South	50.2	Lab
266 Alyn & Deeside	52.3	Lab	323 Aldridge - Brownhills	50.2	Con
267 Brentford & Isleworth	52.3	Lab	324 Hampshire North West	50.1	Con
268 Fylde	52.3	Con			

Contd. /

325 Rayleigh	50.1	Con
326 Vale of Clwyd	50.0	Lab
327 Huntingdon	49.9	Con
328 Bedfordshire North East	49.9	Con
329 Wakefield	49.9	Lab
330 Gravesham	49.9	Lab
331 Batley & Spen	49.9	Lab
332 Antrim North	49.9	DUP
333 Hornsey & Wood Green	49.9	Lab
334 Dudley South	49.8	Lab
335 Wealden	49.8	Con
336 Cambridgeshire North West	49.8	Con
337 Exeter	49.8	Lab
338 Loughborough	49.7	Lab
339 Bradford North	49.7	Lab
340 St Helens South	49.7	Lab
341 Surrey Heath	49.7	Con
342 Sleaford & North Hykeham	49.7	Con
343 Meirionnydd Nant Conwy	49.6	PC
344 Maidstone & The Weald	49.6	Con
345 Harrow West	49.6	Lab
346 Cleethorpes	49.6	Lab
347 Morecambe & Lunesdale	49.6	Lab
348 Milton Keynes South West	49.5	Lab
349 Bromley & Chislehurst	49.5	Con
350 Northampton North	49.4	Lab
351 Montgomeryshire	49.4	LD
352 Sevenoaks	49.4	Con
353 Oxford East	49.4	Lab
354 Tonbridge & Malling	49.4	Con
355 Burnley	49.3	Lab
356 Crawley	49.3	Lab
357 Corby	49.3	Lab
358 Glasgow Govan	49.3	Lab
359 Warrington South	49.3	Lab
360 Maldon & Chelmsford East	49.2	Con
361 Daventry	49.2	Con
362 Rochdale	49.2	Lab
363 Erewash	49.2	Lab
364 Croydon South	49.2	Con
365 Lichfield	49.1	Con
366 Leeds North East	49.1	Lab
367 Epping Forest	49.1	Con
368 Stone	49.1	Con
369 Birmingham Edgbaston	49.1	Lab
370 Burton	49.0	Lab
371 Halifax	49.0	Lab
372 Staffordshire Moorlands	49.0	Lab
373 Tamworth	49.0	Lab
374 Medway	49.0	Lab
375 Esher & Walton	49.0	Con
376 Leominster	49.0	Con
377 Saffron Walden	48.9	Con
378 Dumfries	48.9	Lab
379 Macclesfield	48.9	Con
380 Brigg & Goole	48.9	Lab
381 Tunbridge Wells	48.9	Con

382 Dover	48.8	Lab
383 Sutton & Cheam	48.8	LD
384 Ruislip Northwood	48.8	Con
385 Roxburgh & Berwickshire	48.8	LD
386 Warwick & Leamington	48.8	Lab
387 Twickenham	48.7	LD
388 Swansea West	48.7	Lab
389 Brighton Pavilion	48.7	Lab
390 Rossendale & Darwen	48.7	Lab
391 Runnymede & Weybridge	48.7	Con
392 Shropshire North	48.6	Con
393 Broxtowe	48.6	Lab
394 Llanelli	48.6	Lab
395 Worcester	48.6	Lab
396 Norfolk North West	48.5	Con
397 City of Chester	48.5	Lab
398 Louth & Horncastle	48.5	Con
399 Truro & St Austell	48.3	LD
400 Chatham & Aylesford	48.3	Lab
401 Wolverhampton South West	48.3	Lab
402 Charnwood	48.2	Con
403 Newbury	48.2	LD
404 Chingford & Woodford Green	48.2	Con
405 Keighley	48.2	Lab
406 Cambridgeshire North East	48.1	Con
407 Bexhill & Battle	48.1	Con
408 Tatton	48.1	Con
409 Epsom & Ewell	48.1	Con
410 Pudsey	48.1	Lab
411 Rutland & Melton	48.1	Con
412 Derbyshire West	48.0	Con
413 Dartford	48.0	Lab
414 Stafford	48.0	Lab
415 Elmet	48.0	Lab
416 Bradford West	48.0	Lab
417 Bedford	47.9	Lab
418 Oxford West & Abingdon	47.8	LD
419 Hertsmere	47.8	Con
420 Reigate	47.8	Con
421 Brighton Kemptown	47.8	Lab
422 Chesterfield	47.8	LD
423 Harlow	47.8	Lab
424 Cheltenham	47.7	LD
425 Richmond Park	47.7	LD
426 Meriden	47.7	Con
427 Eastwood	47.6	Lab
428 Hampshire East	47.6	Con
429 Suffolk West	47.6	Con
430 Rushcliffe	47.5	Con
431 Dumbarton	47.5	Lab
432 Ealing Southall	47.5	Lab
433 Worthing West	47.5	Con
434 Essex North	47.4	Con
435 Wirral South	47.4	Lab
436 Ashford	47.4	Con
437 Devon East	47.4	Con

Contd./

438 Norwich North	47.4	Lab
439 Bedfordshire Mid	47.4	Con
440 Billericay	47.4	Con
441 Hitchin & Harpenden	47.3	Con
442 Aylesbury	47.3	Con
443 Gower	47.3	Lab
444 Windsor	47.3	Con
445 Devizes	47.2	Con
446 East Lothian	47.2	Lab
447 Wirral West	47.2	Lab
448 Croydon Central	47.2	Lab
449 Scarborough & Whitby	47.2	Lab
450 Ryedale	47.2	Con
451 Stourbridge	47.1	Lab
452 Uxbridge	47.1	Con
453 The Wrekin	47.1	Lab
454 Hastings & Rye	47.1	Lab
455 Tiverton & Honiton	47.1	Con
456 Fareham	47.1	Con
457 Chichester	47.0	Con
458 Bolton West	47.0	Lab
459 Romsey	47.0	LD
460 Westmorland & Lonsdale	46.9	Con
461 Renfrewshire West	46.9	Lab
462 Birmingham Yardley	46.9	Lab
463 Hampstead & Highgate	46.9	Lab
464 Devon South West	46.8	Con
465 Wansdyke	46.8	Lab
466 Wellingborough	46.8	Lab
467 Enfield North	46.7	Lab
468 Dorset North	46.7	Con
469 Bracknell	46.6	Con
470 Clydesdale	46.6	Lab
471 Salisbury	46.6	Con
472 High Peak	46.6	Lab
473 Hemel Hempstead	46.6	Lab
474 Stroud	46.6	Lab
475 Birmingham Perry Barr	46.5	Lab
476 Newark	46.5	Con
477 Putney	46.5	Lab
478 Hornchurch	46.4	Lab
479 Chipping Barnet	46.4	Con
480 Strathkelvin & Bearsden	46.4	Lab
481 Blaby	46.4	Con
482 Ribble South	46.4	Lab
483 Down South	46.3	SDLP
484 Southend West	46.3	Con
485 Cities of London & Westminster	46.3	Con
486 Eddisbury	46.3	Con
487 Congleton	46.3	Con
488 Finchley & Golders Green	46.3	Lab
489 Gainsborough	46.2	Con
490 Altrincham & Sale West	46.2	Con
491 Sussex Mid	46.2	Con
492 Wokingham	46.1	Con
493 Henley	46.1	Con
494 Tewkesbury	46.1	Con
495 Grantham & Stamford	46.1	Con
496 Cunninghame North	46.0	Lab
497 Woking	46.0	Con
498 Worcestershire West	46.0	Con
499 Edinburgh North & Leith	45.9	Lab
500 Cornwall South East	45.9	LD
501 Cardiff North	45.9	Lab
502 Hove	45.9	Lab
503 Yorkshire East	45.9	Con
504 Sittingbourne & Sheppey	45.8	Lab
505 Ilford North	45.8	Lab
506 Gloucester	45.8	Lab
507 Wimbledon	45.7	Lab
508 Thanet South	45.7	Lab
509 Faversham & Kent Mid	45.6	Con
510 Redditch	45.6	Lab
511 Harwich	45.6	Lab
512 Upminster	45.5	Con
513 Gordon	45.5	LD
514 Aberdeen Central	45.5	Lab
515 Wiltshire North	45.5	Con
516 Norwich South	45.5	Lab
517 St Albans	45.4	Lab
518 Solihull	45.4	Con
519 Vale of Glamorgan	45.4	Lab
520 Old Bexley & Sidcup	45.4	Con
521 Ochil	45.3	Lab
522 Surrey South West	45.3	Con
523 Watford	45.3	Lab
524 Beckenham	45.3	Con
525 Dundee East	45.2	Lab
526 Banbury	45.2	Con
527 Bognor Regis & Littlehampton	45.2	Con
528 Peterborough	45.1	Lab
529 Poole	45.1	Con
530 Spelthorne	45.1	Con
531 Cambridge	45.1	Lab
532 Selby	45.1	Lab
533 Carshalton & Wallington	45.0	LD
534 Maidenhead	45.0	Con
535 Rugby & Kenilworth	45.0	Lab
536 Witney	45.0	Con
537 Folkestone & Hythe	45.0	Con
538 Western Isles	45.0	Lab
539 Glasgow Kelvin	44.8	Lab
540 Belfast South	44.8	UU
541 Reading East	44.8	Lab
542 Norfolk Mid	44.8	Con
543 Kettering	44.7	Lab
544 Harborough	44.7	Con
545 Hertford & Stortford	44.7	Con
546 Dorset West	44.6	Con
547 Pendle	44.6	Lab
548 Castle Point	44.6	Con
549 Hexham	44.6	Con
550 Portsmouth South	44.6	LD
551 Shrewsbury & Atcham	44.6	Lab

Contd. /

552 Totnes	44.5 Con	607 Norfolk South	42.2 Con
553 Gillingham	44.5 Lab	608 Edinburgh South	42.2 Lab
554 Suffolk Central & Ipswich N.	44.4 Con	609 Devon West & Torridge	42.2 LD
555 Teignbridge	44.4 LD	610 Edinburgh Central	42.1 Lab
556 Bosworth	44.4 Con	611 Bedfordshire South West	42.1 Con
557 Caernarfon	44.4 PC	612 Westbury	42.1 Con
558 Hammersmith & Fulham	44.3 Lab	613 Dorset Mid & Poole North	42.0 LD
559 Hertfordshire South West	44.3 Con	614 Braintree	42.0 Lab
560 Cambridgeshire South	44.2 Con	615 Milton Keynes North East	42.0 Lab
561 Devon North	44.2 LD	616 Dorset South	42.0 Lab
562 Cambridgeshire South East	44.2 Con	617 Leeds North West	41.9 Lab
563 Yeovil	44.2 LD	618 Conwy	41.8 Lab
564 Hertfordshire North East	44.1 Con	619 Taunton	41.7 Con
565 Eastbourne	44.1 Con	620 Carmarthen West &	
566 Shipley	44.0 Lab	Pembrokeshire South	41.6 Lab
567 Havant	43.9 Con	621 Canterbury	41.5 Con
568 Orpington	43.9 Con	622 Suffolk South	41.4 Con
569 Wells	43.8 Con	623 Orkney & Shetland	41.3 LD
570 Southport	43.8 LD	624 Preseli Pembrokeshire	41.3 Lab
571 Woodspring	43.7 Con	625 Beverley & Holderness	41.3 Con
572 Gosport	43.6 Con	626 Hereford	40.9 LD
573 Somerton & Frome	43.6 LD	627 Belfast North	40.8 DUP
574 Ayr	43.6 Lab	628 Tyrone West	40.8 SF
575 Bexleyheath & Crayford	43.6 Lab	629 Eastleigh	40.7 LD
576 Aberdeenshire West &		630 Edinburgh Pentlands	40.6 Lab
Kincardine	43.5 LD	631 Bridgwater	40.4 Con
577 Bury St Edmunds	43.5 Con	632 Colne Valley	40.4 Lab
578 Forest of Dean	43.4 Lab	633 Tayside North	40.1 SNP
579 Suffolk Coastal	43.3 Con	634 Aberdeen South	39.8 Lab
580 Aberdeen North	43.3 Lab	635 Isle of Wight	39.7 Con
581 Bournemouth East	43.3 Con	636 Wantage	39.6 Con
582 Haltemprice & Howden	43.2 Con	637 Falmouth & Camborne	39.6 Lab
583 Worthing East & Shoreham	43.2 Con	638 Weston-Super-Mare	39.5 LD
584 Ludlow	43.2 LD	639 Clwyd West	38.8 Lab
585 Welwyn Hatfield	43.2 Lab	640 Oldham East & Saddleworth	38.6 Lab
586 Lancaster & Wyre	43.1 Lab	641 Cardiff Central	38.6 Lab
587 Boston & Skegness	42.9 Con	642 Ceredigion	38.3 PC
588 Northampton South	42.9 Lab	643 Brentwood & Ongar	38.0 Con
589 Bournemouth West	42.8 Con	644 Newry and Armagh	37.4 SDLP
590 Strangford	42.8 DUP	645 Antrim South	37.1 UU
591 Monmouth	42.8 Lab	646 Brecon & Radnorshire	36.8 LD
592 Basingstoke	42.7 Con	647 Bristol West	36.8 Lab
593 Calder Valley	42.7 Lab	648 Inverness East, Nairn &	
594 Norfolk North	42.7 LD	Lochaber	36.8 Lab
595 Colchester	42.6 LD	649 Antrim East	36.4 UU
596 Guildford	42.6 LD	650 Caithness, Sutherland &	
597 Belfast East	42.5 DUP	Easter Ross	36.4 LD
598 Chelmsford West	42.5 Con	651 Angus	35.3 SNP
599 New Forest East	42.4 Con	652 Ynys Mon	35.0 Lab
600 Wycombe	42.4 Con	653 Fermanagh & South Tyrone	34.1 SF
601 Carmarthen East & Dinefwr	42.4 PC	654 Galloway & Upper Nithsdale	34.0 Con
602 Cheadle	42.4 LD	655 Upper Bann	33.5 UU
603 Edinburgh West	42.4 LD	656 Londonderry East	32.1 DUP
604 Tweeddale, Ettrick &		657 Moray	30.3 SNP
Lauderdale	42.3 LD	658 Argyll & Bute	29.9 LD
605 Stirling	42.2 Lab	659 Perth	29.7 SNP
606 Aldershot	42.2 Con		

Table 17. Seats in Rank Order of Percentage Turnout and Winning Party

Constituency	%turnout	1st
1 Ulster Mid	81.3	SF
2 Tyrone West	79.9	SF
3 Fermanagh & South Tyrone	78.0	SF
4 Newry and Armagh	76.8	SDLP
5 Winchester	72.3	LD
6 Monmouth	71.5	Lab
7 Hexham	70.9	Con
8 Down South	70.8	SDLP
9 Eastwood	70.8	Lab
10 Northavon	70.7	LD
11 Devon West & Torridge	70.5	LD
12 Brecon & Radnorshire	70.5	LD
13 Carmarthen East & Dinefwr	70.4	PC
14 Upper Bann	70.3	UU
15 Surrey South West	70.3	Con
16 Norfolk North	70.2	LD
17 Stroud	70.0	Lab
18 Wansdyke	69.9	Lab
19 Dorset West	69.5	Con
20 Leominster	69.4	Con
21 Buckingham	69.4	Con
22 Somerton & Frome	69.3	LD
23 Teignbridge	69.3	LD
24 Ayr	69.3	Lab
25 Tiverton & Honiton	69.2	Con
26 Wells	69.2	Con
27 Cardiff North	69.0	Lab
28 Mole Valley	68.9	Con
29 Foyle	68.9	SDLP
30 Devon East	68.8	Con
31 Belfast West	68.7	SF
32 Woodspring	68.7	Con
33 Lewes	68.5	LD
34 Devon North	68.3	LD
35 Norfolk Mid	68.1	Con
36 Kettering	68.1	Lab
37 Richmond Park	68.0	LD
38 Wyre Forest	68.0	KHHC
39 Ludlow	67.9	LD
40 Totnes	67.9	Con
41 Westmorland & Lonsdale	67.8	Con
42 Derbyshire West	67.8	Con
43 Preseli Pembrokeshire	67.8	Lab
44 Stirling	67.7	Lab
45 Taunton	67.6	Con
46 Norfolk South	67.6	Con
47 Kingston & Surbiton	67.5	LD
48 Christchurch	67.5	Con
49 Cotswold	67.5	Con
50 Rugby & Kenilworth	67.4	Lab
51 Galloway & Upper Nithsdale	67.4	Con
52 Richmond (Yorks)	67.4	Con
53 Tynemouth	67.4	Lab
54 Wiltshire North	67.3	Con
55 Forest of Dean	67.3	Lab
56 Newbury	67.3	LD
57 Brentwood & Ongar	67.3	Con
58 Romsey	67.2	LD
59 Belfast North	67.2	DUP
60 Worcestershire West	67.1	Con
61 Bromsgrove	67.1	Con
62 Cambridgeshire South	67.1	Con
63 Dumfries	67.0	Lab
64 Hitchin & Harpenden	66.9	Con
65 Vale of Glamorgan	66.7	Lab
66 Shrewsbury & Atcham	66.6	Lab
67 Westbury	66.6	Con
68 Broxtowe	66.5	Lab
69 Rushcliffe	66.5	Con
70 Twickenham	66.4	LD
71 St Ives	66.3	LD
72 Stone	66.3	Con
73 Dorset North	66.3	Con
74 St Albans	66.3	Lab
75 Londonderry East	66.2	DUP
76 Suffolk South	66.2	Con
77 Ribble Valley	66.2	Con
78 Shipley	66.2	Lab
79 Devon South West	66.1	Con
80 Vale of York	66.1	Con
81 Antrim North	66.1	DUP
82 Skipton & Ripon	66.1	Con
83 Bury St Edmunds	66.0	Con
84 Strathkelvin & Bearsden	66.0	Lab
85 Witney	65.9	Con
86 Lichfield	65.9	Con
87 Lancaster & Wyre	65.9	Lab
88 Bedfordshire Mid	65.9	Con
89 Haltemprice & Howden	65.8	Con
90 Leicestershire North West	65.8	Lab
91 Warwick & Leamington	65.8	Lab
92 Ryedale	65.7	Con
93 Wirral South	65.6	Lab
94 Bristol West	65.6	Lab
95 Suffolk Coastal	65.6	Con
96 Elmet	65.6	Lab
97 Dorset Mid & Poole North	65.6	LD
98 Daventry	65.5	Con
99 Montgomeryshire	65.5	LD
100 Dorset South	65.5	Lab
101 Cornwall South East	65.4	LD
102 Salisbury	65.3	Con
103 Carmarthen West & Pembrokeshire South	65.3	Lab
104 Stafford	65.3	Lab
105 Saffron Walden	65.2	Con
106 Stratford-on-Avon	65.2	Con
107 Hereford	65.2	LD
108 High Peak	65.2	Lab
109 Dover	65.1	Lab

Contd. /

110 Crosby	65.1	Lab
111 New Forest West	65.1	Con
112 Norfolk North West	65.1	Con
113 Corby	65.0	Lab
114 Wirral West	65.0	Lab
115 Hertfordshire North East	65.0	Con
116 Selby	65.0	Lab
117 Copeland	64.9	Lab
118 Sleaford & North Hykeham	64.9	Con
119 Bexhill & Battle	64.9	Con
120 Sussex Mid	64.9	Con
121 Bath	64.9	LD
122 Sheffield Hallam	64.8	LD
123 Bedfordshire North East	64.8	Con
124 Arundel & South Downs	64.7	Con
125 Chesham & Amersham	64.7	Con
126 Harrogate & Knaresborough	64.6	LD
127 Milton Keynes North East	64.6	Lab
128 Orpington	64.6	Con
129 Kingswood	64.6	Lab
130 Wantage	64.5	Con
131 Hertfordshire South West	64.5	Con
132 Oxford West & Abingdon	64.5	LD
133 Penrith & The Border	64.5	Con
134 Blaby	64.5	Con
135 Bosworth	64.4	Con
136 Charnwood	64.4	Con
137 Bridgwater	64.4	Con
138 Edinburgh Pentlands	64.4	Lab
139 Bromley & Chislehurst	64.3	Con
140 Tonbridge & Malling	64.3	Con
141 Wimbledon	64.3	Lab
142 Hampshire East	64.3	Con
143 Falmouth & Camborne	64.3	Lab
144 Henley	64.3	Con
145 Gainsborough	64.2	Con
146 Rutland & Melton	64.2	Con
147 Devizes	64.2	Con
148 Exeter	64.2	Lab
149 Yeovil	64.2	LD
150 Eddisbury	64.2	Con
151 Clwyd West	64.1	Lab
152 Wellingborough	64.1	Lab
153 Wokingham	64.1	Con
154 Folkestone & Hythe	64.1	Con
155 Derbyshire South	64.0	Lab
156 Gedling	63.9	Lab
157 Sevenoaks	63.9	Con
158 Thanet South	63.9	Lab
159 Welwyn Hatfield	63.9	Lab
160 Meirionnydd Nant Conwy	63.9	PC
161 Staffordshire Moorlands	63.9	Lab
162 Inverness East, Nairn & Lochaber	63.9	Lab
163 Belfast South	63.9	UU
164 Chichester	63.8	Con
165 Berwick-upon-Tweed	63.8	LD
166 Horsham	63.8	Con
167 Eastleigh	63.8	LD
168 Cornwall North	63.8	LD
169 City of Chester	63.8	Lab
170 Tewkesbury	63.7	Con
171 Ynys Mon	63.7	Lab
172 Vale of Clwyd	63.6	Lab
173 Braintree	63.6	Lab
174 Tatton	63.5	Con
175 Fareham	63.5	Con
176 Enfield Southgate	63.5	Lab
177 Cambridgeshire South East	63.5	Con
178 Newark	63.5	Con
179 Wealden	63.5	Con
180 Bexleyheath & Crayford	63.5	Lab
181 Brigg & Goole	63.5	Lab
182 Truro & St Austell	63.5	LD
183 Suffolk Central & Ipswich N.	63.5	Con
184 Keighley	63.4	Lab
185 Workington	63.4	Lab
186 Gower	63.4	Lab
187 Tweeddale, Ettrick & Lauderdale	63.4	LD
188 Harborough	63.3	Con
189 Renfrewshire West	63.3	Lab
190 Colne Valley	63.3	Lab
191 Surrey East	63.3	Con
192 Delyn	63.3	Lab
193 Solihull	63.3	Con
194 Pudsey	63.3	Lab
195 Lagan Valley	63.2	UU
196 New Forest East	63.2	Con
197 Pendle	63.2	Lab
198 Cheadle	63.2	LD
199 Scarborough & Whitby	63.2	Lab
200 Edinburgh West	63.2	LD
201 Loughborough	63.1	Lab
202 Norfolk South West	63.1	Con
203 Shropshire North	63.1	Con
204 The Wrekin	63.1	Lab
205 Belfast East	63.0	DUP
206 Bury North	63.0	Lab
207 Calder Valley	63.0	Lab
208 Harrow West	63.0	Lab
209 Argyll & Bute	63.0	LD
210 Conwy	62.9	Lab
211 Stockton South	62.9	Lab
212 Weston-Super-Mare	62.8	LD
213 Epsom & Ewell	62.8	Con
214 Maldon & Chelmsford East	62.8	Con
215 Essex North	62.8	Con
216 Gravesham	62.7	Lab
217 Guildford	62.7	LD
218 Congleton	62.7	Con
219 East Kilbride	62.6	Lab
220 Beckenham	62.6	Con
221 Neath	62.5	Lab

Contd./

222 Torbay	62.5	LD		276 Peterborough	61.4	Lab
223 Clydebank & Milngavie	62.5	Lab		277 Aylesbury	61.4	Con
224 East Lothian	62.5	Lab		278 Ochil	61.3	Lab
225 Antrim South	62.5	UU		279 Grantham & Stamford	61.3	Con
226 Ashford	62.5	Con		280 Warrington South	61.2	Lab
227 Aberdeen South	62.5	Lab		281 Watford	61.1	Lab
228 Ribble South	62.5	Lab		282 Morecambe & Lunesdale	61.1	Lab
229 Tayside North	62.5	SNP		283 Huntingdon	61.1	Con
230 Bolton West	62.4	Lab		284 Ruislip Northwood	61.1	Con
231 Sutton & Cheam	62.4	LD		285 Dumbarton	61.1	Lab
232 Clwyd South	62.4	Lab		286 Banbury	61.1	Con
233 Macclesfield	62.3	Con		287 Swindon South	61.0	Lab
234 Hemel Hempstead	62.3	Lab		288 Swindon North	61.0	Lab
235 Milton Keynes South West	62.3	Lab		289 Middlesbrough South &		
236 Hampshire North West	62.3	Con		Cleveland East	61.0	Lab
237 Worcestershire Mid	62.3	Con		290 Aberavon	61.0	Lab
238 Tunbridge Wells	62.3	Con		291 Oldham East & Saddleworth	61.0	Lab
239 Ross, Skye & Inverness West	62.3	LD		292 Ellesmere Port & Neston	60.9	Lab
240 Llanelli	62.3	Lab		293 Fylde	60.9	Con
241 Chorley	62.2	Lab		294 Canterbury	60.9	Con
242 Hertford & Stortford	62.2	Con		295 Spelthorne	60.8	Con
243 Louth & Horncastle	62.1	Con		296 Isle of Wight	60.8	Con
244 South Holland & The				297 Beaconsfield	60.8	Con
Deepings	62.1	Con		298 Waveney	60.8	Lab
245 Old Bexley & Sidcup	62.1	Con		299 Sherwood	60.7	Lab
246 Harwich	62.1	Lab		300 Stevenage	60.7	Lab
247 Bedfordshire South West	62.1	Con		301 Chesterfield	60.7	LD
248 Leicester East	62.1	Lab		302 Poole	60.7	Con
249 Wolverhampton South West	62.1	Lab		303 Bracknell	60.7	Con
250 Beverley & Holderness	62.0	Con		304 Basingstoke	60.7	Con
251 Worcester	62.0	Lab		305 Aldridge - Brownhills	60.6	Con
252 Maidenhead	62.0	Con		306 Western Isles	60.6	Lab
253 Leeds North East	62.0	Lab		307 Cambridge	60.6	Lab
254 Cleethorpes	62.0	Lab		308 Roxburgh & Berwickshire	60.6	LD
255 Caernarfon	62.0	PC		309 Rhondda	60.6	Lab
256 Sedgefield	62.0	Lab		310 Rayleigh	60.5	Con
257 Darlington	62.0	Lab		311 Batley & Spen	60.5	Lab
258 Dartford	61.9	Lab		312 Wycombe	60.5	Con
259 Cheltenham	61.9	LD		313 Suffolk West	60.5	Con
260 Erewash	61.9	Lab		314 Sutton Coldfield	60.5	Con
261 Esher & Walton	61.9	Con		315 Chipping Barnet	60.4	Con
262 Islwyn	61.9	Lab		316 Bristol North West	60.4	Lab
263 Stourbridge	61.8	Lab		317 Meriden	60.4	Con
264 Carrick, Cumnock & Doon				318 Faversham & Kent Mid	60.4	Con
Valley	61.8	Lab		319 Amber Valley	60.3	Lab
265 Aberdeenshire W &				320 Carshalton & Wallington	60.3	LD
Kincardine	61.8	LD		321 Staffordshire South	60.3	Con
266 Burton	61.7	Lab		322 Hertsmere	60.3	Con
267 Kilmarnock & Loudoun	61.7	Lab		323 Altrincham & Sale West	60.3	Con
268 Cambridgeshire North West	61.7	Con		324 Barrow & Furness	60.3	Lab
269 Chelmsford West	61.7	Con		325 Woking	60.2	Con
270 Ceredigion	61.7	PC		326 Caithness, Sutherland &		
271 Hampshire North East	61.6	Con		Easter Ross	60.2	LD
272 Maidstone & The Weald	61.6	Con		327 Crewe & Nantwich	60.2	Lab
273 Perth	61.5	SNP		328 Bridgend	60.2	Lab
274 Cunninghame North	61.5	Lab		329 Reigate	60.2	Con
275 Croydon South	61.4	Con		330 Warwickshire North	60.2	Lab

Contd. /

331 Cambridgeshire North East	60.1	Con	387 Castle Point	58.4	Con
332 Yorkshire East	60.1	Con	388 Great Yarmouth	58.3	Lab
333 Nuneaton	60.1	Lab	389 Boston & Skegness	58.3	Con
334 Strangford	59.9	DUP	390 Hornchurch	58.3	Lab
335 Bedford	59.9	Lab	391 Cardiff Central	58.3	Lab
336 Halesowen & Rowley Regis	59.8	Lab	392 Gordon	58.3	LD
337 Norwich South	59.8	Lab	393 Hastings & Rye	58.3	Lab
338 Worthing East & Shoreham	59.7	Con	394 Bognor Regis &		
339 Cumbernauld & Kilsyth	59.7	Lab	Littlehampton	58.2	Con
340 Harlow	59.7	Lab	395 Leeds North West	58.2	Lab
341 Worthing West	59.7	Con	396 Bournemouth East	58.2	Con
342 Romford	59.6	Con	397 Ogmore	58.2	Lab
343 City of Durham	59.6	Lab	398 Edinburgh E. & Musselburgh	58.2	Lab
344 Upminster	59.6	Con	399 Coatbridge & Chryston	58.1	Lab
345 Northampton South	59.6	Lab	400 Billericay	58.1	Con
346 Eastbourne	59.6	Con	401 Hornsey & Wood Green	58.0	Lab
347 Wrexham	59.5	Lab	402 Ealing North	58.0	Lab
348 Gillingham	59.5	Lab	403 Leicester South	58.0	Lab
349 Blaenau Gwent	59.5	Lab	404 Southend West	58.0	Con
350 Medway	59.5	Lab	405 Linlithgow	58.0	Lab
351 Surrey Heath	59.5	Con	406 Luton North	57.9	Lab
352 Gloucester	59.4	Lab	407 Falkirk East	57.9	Lab
353 Carlisle	59.4	Lab	408 Aldershot	57.9	Con
354 Greenock & Inverclyde	59.3	Lab	409 Tamworth	57.8	Lab
355 Angus	59.3	SNP	410 Halifax	57.8	Lab
356 Clydesdale	59.3	Lab	411 Mitcham & Morden	57.8	Lab
357 Wansbeck	59.3	Lab	412 Derby North	57.8	Lab
358 Redditch	59.2	Lab	413 Brent North	57.7	Lab
359 Croydon Central	59.1	Lab	414 Tyneside North	57.7	Lab
360 Norwich North	59.1	Lab	415 Caerphilly	57.7	Lab
361 Antrim East	59.1	UU	416 Merthyr Tydfil & Rhymney	57.7	Lab
362 Hazel Grove	59.1	LD	417 Edinburgh South	57.7	Lab
363 Newport West	59.1	Lab	418 Torfaen	57.7	Lab
364 Midlothian	59.1	Lab	419 Oldham West & Royton	57.6	Lab
365 Reading West	59.1	Lab	420 Havant	57.6	Con
366 York	59.0	Lab	421 Wallasey	57.6	Lab
367 Thanet North	59.0	Con	422 Weaver Vale	57.6	Lab
368 Derbyshire North East	58.9	Lab	423 Brighton Kemptown	57.6	Lab
369 Hove	58.9	Lab	424 Uxbridge	57.5	Con
370 Down North	58.8	UU	425 Newcastle upon Tyne North	57.5	Lab
371 Newcastle-under-Lyme	58.8	Lab	426 Sittingbourne & Sheppey	57.5	Lab
372 Lancashire West	58.8	Lab	427 Hyndburn	57.5	Lab
373 Dewsbury	58.8	Lab	428 Birmingham Hall Green	57.5	Lab
374 Bury South	58.8	Lab	429 Blaydon	57.4	Lab
375 Eltham	58.7	Lab	430 Aberdeen North	57.4	Lab
376 Rossendale & Darwen	58.7	Lab	431 Bristol East	57.4	Lab
377 Southport	58.6	LD	432 Moray	57.4	SNP
378 Alyn & Deeside	58.6	Lab	433 Portsmouth North	57.4	Lab
379 Brighton Pavilion	58.5	Lab	434 Sheffield Hillsborough	57.3	Lab
380 Durham North West	58.5	Lab	435 Hamilton South	57.3	Lab
381 Chingford & Woodford			436 Finchley & Golders Green	57.3	Lab
Green	58.5	Con	437 Dundee East	57.3	Lab
382 Reading East	58.4	Lab	438 Bishop Auckland	57.2	Lab
383 Harrow East	58.4	Lab	439 Paisley South	57.2	Lab
384 Epping Forest	58.4	Con	440 Birmingham Yardley	57.2	Lab
385 Cardiff West	58.4	Lab	441 Blackpool N. & Fleetwood	57.2	Lab
386 Ilford North	58.4	Lab	442 Gosport	57.1	Con

Contd. /

443 Falkirk West	57.1	Lab	501 Tooting	54.9	Lab
444 Plymouth Sutton	57.1	Lab	502 Don Valley	54.8	Lab
445 Cardiff South & Penarth	57.1	Lab	503 Stockton North	54.8	Lab
446 Dunfermline West	57.1	Lab	504 Leyton & Wanstead	54.8	Lab
447 Enfield North	57.0	Lab	505 Stretford & Urmston	54.8	Lab
448 Windsor	57.0	Con	506 Blyth Valley	54.7	Lab
449 Ipswich	57.0	Lab	507 Newport East	54.7	Lab
450 Dunfermline East	57.0	Lab	508 Kirkcaldy	54.6	Lab
451 Chatham & Aylesford	57.0	Lab	509 Fife Central	54.6	Lab
452 Durham North	56.9	Lab	510 Battersea	54.5	Lab
453 Bassetlaw	56.8	Lab	511 Wakefield	54.5	Lab
454 Ealing Southall	56.8	Lab	512 Dundee West	54.4	Lab
455 Hamilton North & Bellshill	56.8	Lab	513 Airdrie & Shotts	54.4	Lab
456 Rochdale	56.7	Lab	514 Banff & Buchan	54.4	SNP
457 Scunthorpe	56.6	Lab	515 Ilford South	54.3	Lab
458 Plymouth Devonport	56.6	Lab	516 Hampstead & Highgate	54.3	Lab
459 Motherwell & Wishaw	56.6	Lab	517 Greenwich & Woolwich	54.1	Lab
460 Paisley North	56.6	Lab	518 Warley	54.1	Lab
461 Bolsover	56.5	Lab	519 Halton	54.1	Lab
462 Bristol South	56.5	Lab	520 Southampton Itchen	54.0	Lab
463 Putney	56.5	Lab	521 Brentford & Isleworth	53.7	Lab
464 Hammersmith & Fulham	56.4	Lab	522 Warrington North	53.7	Lab
465 Redcar	56.3	Lab	523 Easington	53.6	Lab
466 Glasgow Rutherglen	56.3	Lab	524 Ashfield	53.6	Lab
467 Southampton Test	56.3	Lab	525 Bradford West	53.6	Lab
468 Hayes & Harlington	56.3	Lab	526 Morley & Rothwell	53.5	Lab
469 Birmingham Selly Oak	56.3	Lab	527 Walthamstow	53.5	Lab
470 Edmonton	56.3	Lab	528 Slough	53.4	Lab
471 Cunninghame South	56.2	Lab	529 Dulwich & West Norwood	53.4	Lab
472 Runnymede & Weybridge	56.1	Con	530 West Bromwich East	53.4	Lab
473 Colchester	56.1	LD	531 Pontypridd	53.4	Lab
474 Fife North East	56.0	LD	532 Stockport	53.3	Lab
475 Bolton North East	56.0	Lab	533 Bournemouth West	53.2	Con
476 Birmingham Edgbaston	56.0	Lab	534 Croydon North	53.2	Lab
477 Lincoln	56.0	Lab	535 Rother Valley	53.2	Lab
478 Northampton North	56.0	Lab	536 Newcastle upon Tyne East & Wallsend	53.2	Lab
479 Dudley North	55.9	Lab	537 Heywood & Middleton	53.1	Lab
480 Derby South	55.9	Lab	538 Lewisham East	53.1	Lab
481 Oxford East	55.8	Lab	539 Knowsley N. & Sefton E.	53.0	Lab
482 Swansea West	55.8	Lab	540 Edinburgh North & Leith	53.0	Lab
483 Hartlepool	55.8	Lab	541 Barnsley West & Penistone	52.9	Lab
484 Walsall South	55.7	Lab	542 Sheffield Attercliffe	52.9	Lab
485 Broxbourne	55.7	Con	543 Wolverhampton North East	52.8	Lab
486 Burnley	55.7	Lab	544 Birmingham Northfield	52.8	Lab
487 Livingston	55.6	Lab	545 Wentworth	52.8	Lab
488 Coventry North West	55.5	Lab	546 Rochford & Southend East	52.7	Con
489 Blackburn	55.5	Lab	547 St Helens North	52.7	Lab
490 Cynon Valley	55.4	Lab	548 Bradford North	52.7	Lab
491 Dudley South	55.4	Lab	549 Aberdeen Central	52.7	Lab
492 Cannock Chase	55.4	Lab	550 Ealing Acton & Shepherd's Bush	52.6	Lab
493 Coventry South	55.3	Lab	551 Birmingham Perry Barr	52.6	Lab
494 Mansfield	55.2	Lab	552 Glasgow Cathcart	52.6	Lab
495 Crawley	55.2	Lab	553 Gateshead E. & Washington W.	52.5	Lab
496 Basildon	55.1	Lab	554 Wigan	52.5	Lab
497 Sheffield Heeley	55.1	Lab	555 Orkney & Shetland	52.4	LD
498 Luton South	55.1	Lab			
499 Jarrow	55.1	Lab			
500 Huddersfield	55.0	Lab			

Contd. /

556 East Ham	52.3 Lab	611 Walsall North	49.0 Lab
557 Swansea East	52.3 Lab	612 West Ham	48.9 Lab
558 Great Grimsby	52.3 Lab	613 Regent's Park & Kensington	
559 Hendon	52.2 Lab	North	48.8 Lab
560 Normanton	52.2 Lab	614 Islington North	48.8 Lab
561 Blackpool South	52.2 Lab	615 Wythenshawe & Sale East	48.6 Lab
562 Lewisham West	52.1 Lab	616 Denton & Reddish	48.5 Lab
563 Edinburgh Central	52.0 Lab	617 Stalybridge & Hyde	48.4 Lab
564 Telford	52.0 Lab	618 Sunderland South	48.3 Lab
565 Manchester Withington	51.9 Lab	619 Lewisham Deptford	48.3 Lab
566 Stoke-on-Trent North	51.9 Lab	620 Birkenhead	48.3 Lab
567 Brent East	51.9 Lab	621 Eccles	48.3 Lab
568 Hemsworth	51.8 Lab	622 Tottenham	48.2 Lab
569 Knowsley South	51.8 Lab	623 Birmingham Hodge Hill	47.9 Lab
570 Doncaster Central	51.6 Lab	624 West Bromwich West	47.7 Lab
571 Leeds East	51.5 Lab	625 Hackney S. & Shoreditch	47.4 Lab
572 Stoke-on-Trent South	51.4 Lab	626 Stoke-on-Trent Central	47.4 Lab
573 St Helens South	51.4 Lab	627 Islington South & Finsbury	47.4 Lab
574 Glasgow Pollok	51.4 Lab	628 Cities of London &	
575 Bradford South	51.3 Lab	Westminster	47.2 Con
576 Newcastle upon Tyne Central	51.3 Lab	629 Glasgow Baillieston	47.2 Lab
577 Wolverhampton South East	51.3 Lab	630 Sheffield Brightside	47.2 Lab
578 Brent South	51.2 Lab	631 Glasgow Govan	46.8 Lab
579 Worsley	51.0 Lab	632 Camberwell & Peckham	46.8 Lab
580 Makerfield	50.9 Lab	633 Nottingham North	46.7 Lab
581 Leicester West	50.9 Lab	634 Birmingham Erdington	46.6 Lab
582 Portsmouth South	50.9 LD	635 Hull East	46.5 Lab
583 Rotherham	50.7 Lab	636 Dagenham	46.5 Lab
584 Doncaster North	50.5 Lab	637 Hull West & Hessle	45.9 Lab
585 Coventry North East	50.3 Lab	638 Barnsley Central	45.8 Lab
586 Erith & Thamesmead	50.2 Lab	639 Liverpool West Derby	45.5 Lab
587 Bethnal Green & Bow	50.2 Lab	640 Nottingham East	45.5 Lab
588 Liverpool Garston	50.2 Lab	641 Barking	45.5 Lab
589 Glasgow Anniesland	50.1 Lab	642 Hull North	45.5 Lab
590 Southwark N. & Bermondsey	50.1 LD	643 Manchester Blackley	44.9 Lab
591 Bolton South East	50.1 Lab	644 Poplar & Canning Town	44.9 Lab
592 Nottingham South	50.1 Lab	645 Vauxhall	44.8 Lab
593 Leeds West	50.0 Lab	646 Liverpool Wavertree	44.3 Lab
594 Middlesbrough	49.8 Lab	647 Birmingham Ladywood	44.3 Lab
595 Bootle	49.8 Lab	648 Tyne Bridge	44.2 Lab
596 Pontefract & Castleford	49.7 Lab	649 Glasgow Springburn	43.7 Spkr
597 South Shields	49.7 Lab	650 Glasgow Kelvin	43.6 Lab
598 Leigh	49.7 Lab	651 Kensington & Chelsea	43.3 Con
599 Holborn & St Pancras	49.6 Lab	652 Liverpool Walton	43.0 Lab
600 Barnsley East & Mexborough	49.5 Lab	653 Manchester Gorton	42.7 Lab
601 Houghton & Washington East	49.5 Lab	654 Leeds Central	41.7 Lab
602 Sheffield Central	49.5 Lab	655 Salford	41.6 Lab
603 Birmingham Sparkbrook &		656 Glasgow Maryhill	40.1 Lab
Small Heath	49.3 Lab	657 Glasgow Shettleston	39.7 Lab
604 Feltham & Heston	49.2 Lab	658 Manchester Central	39.1 Lab
605 Preston	49.2 Lab	659 Liverpool Riverside	34.1 Lab
606 Streatham	49.1 Lab		
607 Ashton under Lyne	49.1 Lab		
608 Thurrock	49.0 Lab		
609 Sunderland North	49.0 Lab		
610 Hackney North & Stoke			
Newington	49.0 Lab		

Table 18. Seats in Rank Order of Change in Percentage Turnout 1997-2001

Constituency	%change	1st
1 Antrim South	4.7	UU
2 Fermanagh & South Tyrone	3.4	SF
3 Belfast North	3.0	DUP
4 Upper Bann	2.5	UU
5 Antrim North	2.4	DUP
6 Belfast South	1.8	UU
7 Londonderry East	1.6	DUP
8 Newry and Armagh	1.5	SDLP
9 Lagan Valley	1.1	UU
10 Antrim East	0.9	UU
11 Down North	0.9	UU
12 Tyrone West	0.7	SF
13 Strangford	0.5	DUP
14 Down South	0.1	SDLP
15 Belfast East	-0.1	DUP
16 Foyle	-1.5	SDLP
17 Hackney North & Stoke Newington	-3.0	Lab
18 Sheffield Central	-3.6	Lab
19 Ulster Mid	-4.4	SF
20 Belfast West	-5.4	SF
21 Norfolk North	-5.8	LD
22 Winchester	-6.0	LD
23 Richmond (Yorks)	-6.0	Con
24 Westmorland & Lonsdale	-6.2	Con
25 Dorset West	-6.6	Con
26 Hexham	-6.6	Con
27 West Bromwich West	-6.7	Lab
28 Cities of London & Westminster	-7.0	Con
29 Hackney S. & Shoreditch	-7.0	Lab
30 Leicester East	-7.1	Lab
31 Enfield Southgate	-7.1	Lab
32 Leominster	-7.2	Con
33 Devon East	-7.2	Con
34 Surrey South West	-7.2	Con
35 Teignbridge	-7.3	LD
36 Wyre Forest	-7.3	KHHC
37 Kettering	-7.4	Lab
38 Devon West & Torridge	-7.4	LD
39 Eastwood	-7.4	Lab
40 Sheffield Hallam	-7.5	LD
41 Wiltshire North	-7.6	Con
42 Ludlow	-7.6	LD
43 Thanet South	-7.7	Lab
44 Birmingham Sparkbrook & Small Heath	-7.8	Lab
45 Bristol West	-7.8	Lab
46 Kingston & Surbiton	-7.8	LD
47 Lewes	-7.9	LD
48 Totnes	-7.9	Con
49 Somerton & Frome	-8.0	LD
50 East Ham	-8.0	Lab
51 Carmarthen East & Dinefwr	-8.1	PC
52 Cotswold	-8.2	Con
53 Norfolk Mid	-8.2	Con
54 Milton Keynes North East	-8.2	Lab
55 Harrogate & Knaresborough	-8.2	LD
56 Salisbury	-8.3	Con
57 Leicester South	-8.3	Lab
58 Harwich	-8.4	Lab
59 Northavon	-8.4	LD
60 Scarborough & Whitby	-8.4	Lab
61 Llanelli	-8.4	Lab
62 Dorset South	-8.5	Lab
63 Leyton & Wanstead	-8.5	Lab
64 Tiverton & Honiton	-8.5	Con
65 Yeovil	-8.5	LD
66 Oldham West & Royton	-8.5	Lab
67 Camberwell & Peckham	-8.5	Lab
68 Skipton & Ripon	-8.6	Con
69 Shrewsbury & Atcham	-8.7	Lab
70 Wells	-8.7	Con
71 Folkestone & Hythe	-8.7	Con
72 Tottenham	-8.7	Lab
73 Stroud	-8.8	Lab
74 Inverness East, Nairn & Lochaber	-8.8	Lab
75 Taunton	-8.8	Con
76 St Ives	-8.9	LD
77 Lancaster & Wyre	-8.9	Lab
78 Newbury	-9.0	LD
79 Bury St Edmunds	-9.0	Con
80 Cambridgeshire South	-9.0	Con
81 Monmouth	-9.1	Lab
82 Wansdyke	-9.1	Lab
83 Milton Keynes South West	-9.1	Lab
84 Buckingham	-9.1	Con
85 Penrith & The Border	-9.1	Con
86 Ryedale	-9.1	Con
87 Worcestershire West	-9.1	Con
88 Montgomeryshire	-9.2	LD
89 Romsey	-9.2	LD
90 Cornwall North	-9.3	LD
91 Walthamstow	-9.3	Lab
92 Sleaford & North Hykeham	-9.3	Con
93 Brentwood & Ongar	-9.3	Con
94 Warwick & Leamington	-9.4	Lab
95 Ross, Skye & Inverness West	-9.4	LD
96 Devon North	-9.4	LD
97 Western Isles	-9.5	Lab
98 Blackburn	-9.5	Lab
99 Shropshire North	-9.5	Con
100 Mole Valley	-9.5	Con
101 West Ham	-9.5	Lab
102 Brigg & Goole	-9.5	Lab
103 Bexhill & Battle	-9.6	Con
104 Lewisham Deptford	-9.6	Lab

Contd. /

105 New Forest West	-9.6	Con	160 Bradford North	-10.6	Lab
106 Haltemprice & Howden	-9.6	Con	161 Truro & St Austell	-10.6	LD
107 Westbury	-9.6	Con	162 Wycombe	-10.6	Con
108 Rugby & Kenilworth	-9.6	Lab	163 Boston & Skegness	-10.6	Con
109 Norfolk North West	-9.7	Con	164 Vauxhall	-10.6	Lab
110 Berwick-upon-Tweed	-9.7	LD	165 Holborn & St Pancras	-10.7	Lab
111 Bromley & Chislehurst	-9.7	Con	166 Hove	-10.7	Lab
112 Bradford West	-9.7	Lab	167 Rutland & Melton	-10.7	Con
113 Dorset Mid & Poole North	-9.8	LD	168 Wellingborough	-10.7	Lab
114 Tynemouth	-9.8	Lab	169 Ayr	-10.7	Lab
115 Leeds North East	-9.8	Lab	170 Cardiff West	-10.7	Lab
116 Selby	-9.8	Lab	171 Norfolk South	-10.7	Con
117 Woodspring	-9.8	Con	172 Chichester	-10.7	Con
118 Harrow West	-9.8	Lab	173 Weston-Super-Mare	-10.8	LD
119 Hartlepool	-9.8	Lab	174 Witney	-10.8	Con
120 Vale of York	-9.8	Con	175 Arundel & South Downs	-10.8	Con
121 South Holland & The			176 Cambridgeshire South East	-10.8	Con
Deepings	-9.8	Con	177 Moray	-10.8	SNP
122 Caithness, Sutherland &			178 Newark	-10.8	Con
Easter Ross	-9.8	LD	179 Falmouth & Camborne	-10.8	Lab
123 Sheffield Heeley	-9.9	Lab	180 Cambridge	-10.9	Lab
124 Chesham & Amersham	-9.9	Con	181 Rhondda	-10.9	Lab
125 Birmingham Ladywood	-9.9	Lab	182 Beverley & Holderness	-10.9	Con
126 Thanet North	-9.9	Con	183 Aberavon	-10.9	Lab
127 Argyll & Bute	-10.0	LD	184 Rochford & Southend East	-10.9	Con
128 Bridgwater	-10.0	Con	185 Warley	-10.9	Lab
129 Dorset North	-10.0	Con	186 Daventry	-10.9	Con
130 Norfolk South West	-10.0	Con	187 Stratford-on-Avon	-11.0	Con
131 Ealing Southall	-10.0	Lab	188 Wokingham	-11.0	Con
132 Devon South West	-10.0	Con	189 Suffolk West	-11.0	Con
133 Bromsgrove	-10.0	Con	190 Richmond Park	-11.0	LD
134 Sunderland North	-10.0	Lab	191 Reading West	-11.0	Lab
135 Hereford	-10.0	LD	192 Pudsey	-11.0	Lab
136 Bethnal Green & Bow	-10.1	Lab	193 Vale of Clwyd	-11.0	Lab
137 Shipley	-10.2	Lab	194 Suffolk South	-11.0	Con
138 Islwyn	-10.2	Lab	195 Streatham	-11.0	Lab
139 Wealden	-10.2	Con	196 Christchurch	-11.0	Con
140 Tyneside North	-10.2	Lab	197 Hornsey & Wood Green	-11.1	Lab
141 Suffolk Coastal	-10.2	Con	198 Wimbledon	-11.1	Lab
142 Chesterfield	-10.2	LD	199 Hitchin & Harpenden	-11.1	Con
143 Durham North West	-10.2	Lab	200 Cardiff North	-11.2	Lab
144 Aberdeen South	-10.3	Lab	201 Isle of Wight	-11.2	Con
145 Southwark North &			202 Clwyd West	-11.2	Lab
Bermondsey	-10.3	LD	203 Cardiff South & Penarth	-11.2	Lab
146 Sheffield Brightside	-10.3	Lab	204 City of Durham	-11.2	Lab
147 Sedgefield	-10.3	Lab	205 Morecambe & Lunesdale	-11.2	Lab
148 Cornwall South East	-10.3	LD	206 Epsom & Ewell	-11.2	Con
149 Poole	-10.3	Con	207 Bishop Auckland	-11.2	Lab
150 Gainsborough	-10.3	Con	208 Bath	-11.2	LD
151 Plymouth Sutton	-10.3	Lab	209 Carmarthen West &		
152 Yorkshire East	-10.4	Con	Pembrokeshire South	-11.2	Lab
153 Wolverhampton South West	-10.4	Lab	210 Ynys Mon	-11.2	Lab
154 Louth & Horncastle	-10.4	Con	211 Clwyd South	-11.2	Lab
155 Derbyshire West	-10.5	Con	212 Elmet	-11.2	Lab
156 Sunderland South	-10.5	Lab	213 St Albans	-11.2	Lab
157 Devizes	-10.5	Con	214 Dewsbury	-11.2	Lab
158 Croydon Central	-10.5	Lab	215 Leeds East	-11.3	Lab
159 Preseli Pembrokeshire	-10.6	Lab			

Contd. /

216 Torbay	-11.3	LD
217 Meriden	-11.3	Con
218 Burnley	-11.3	Lab
219 Chipping Barnet	-11.3	Con
220 Aberdeenshire W & Kincardine	-11.3	LD
221 Hampshire East	-11.3	Con
222 Bognor Regis & Littlehampton	-11.3	Con
223 Surrey East	-11.4	Con
224 Solihull	-11.4	Con
225 Pendle	-11.4	Lab
226 Copeland	-11.4	Lab
227 Cleethorpes	-11.4	Lab
228 Kensington & Chelsea	-11.4	Con
229 Forest of Dean	-11.4	Lab
230 New Forest East	-11.4	Con
231 Tonbridge & Malling	-11.4	Con
232 Sevenoaks	-11.4	Con
233 Hastings & Rye	-11.4	Lab
234 Romford	-11.4	Con
235 Peterborough	-11.4	Lab
236 Aylesbury	-11.5	Con
237 Eddisbury	-11.5	Con
238 Hull North	-11.5	Lab
239 Greenock & Inverclyde	-11.5	Lab
240 Orkney & Shetland	-11.5	LD
241 Don Valley	-11.5	Lab
242 Leeds North West	-11.5	Lab
243 Lichfield	-11.5	Con
244 Horsham	-11.5	Con
245 Suffolk Central & Ipswich N.	-11.6	Con
246 Merthyr Tydfil & Rhymney	-11.6	Lab
247 Dulwich & West Norwood	-11.6	Lab
248 Canterbury	-11.6	Con
249 Blaby	-11.6	Con
250 Walsall South	-11.6	Lab
251 Newcastle upon Tyne North	-11.6	Lab
252 Workington	-11.7	Lab
253 Saffron Walden	-11.7	Con
254 Cardiff Central	-11.7	Lab
255 Caernarfon	-11.7	PC
256 Reading East	-11.7	Lab
257 Ashford	-11.7	Con
258 Barrow & Furness	-11.7	Lab
259 Beckenham	-11.7	Con
260 Gower	-11.7	Lab
261 Neath	-11.7	Lab
262 Greenwich & Woolwich	-11.7	Lab
263 Sheffield Attercliffe	-11.7	Lab
264 Orpington	-11.8	Con
265 Broxtowe	-11.8	Lab
266 Tayside North	-11.8	SNP
267 Brecon & Radnorshire	-11.8	LD
268 Swansea West	-11.8	Lab
269 Gedling	-11.8	Lab
270 Tunbridge Wells	-11.8	Con
271 Swindon South	-11.8	Lab
272 Paisley South	-11.9	Lab
273 Birmingham Perry Barr	-11.9	Lab
274 Hampshire North West	-11.9	Con
275 Darlington	-11.9	Lab
276 Southend West	-11.9	Con
277 Dumfries	-11.9	Lab
278 Harborough	-11.9	Con
279 Grantham & Stamford	-11.9	Con
280 Guildford	-11.9	LD
281 Fylde	-12.0	Con
282 Lewisham West	-12.0	Lab
283 Bosworth	-12.0	Con
284 Hampshire North East	-12.0	Con
285 Worcestershire Mid	-12.0	Con
286 West Bromwich East	-12.0	Lab
287 Beaconsfield	-12.0	Con
288 Bournemouth East	-12.0	Con
289 Stone	-12.0	Con
290 Croydon South	-12.0	Con
291 Dundee East	-12.0	Lab
292 Crosby	-12.1	Lab
293 Paisley North	-12.1	Lab
294 Meirionnydd Nant Conwy	-12.1	PC
295 Barnsley West & Penistone	-12.1	Lab
296 Hertfordshire North East	-12.1	Con
297 Northampton South	-12.1	Lab
298 The Wrekin	-12.1	Lab
299 Cheltenham	-12.1	LD
300 Maidstone & The Weald	-12.1	Con
301 Hertfordshire South West	-12.1	Con
302 Bridgend	-12.1	Lab
303 Rotherham	-12.1	Lab
304 Worthing West	-12.1	Con
305 Derby South	-12.2	Lab
306 Leicester West	-12.2	Lab
307 East Kilbride	-12.2	Lab
308 Finchley & Golders Green	-12.2	Lab
309 Chingford & Woodford Green	-12.2	Con
310 Scunthorpe	-12.2	Lab
311 Stafford	-12.2	Lab
312 Galloway & Upper Nithsdale	-12.2	Con
313 Wirral West	-12.2	Lab
314 Wrexham	-12.2	Lab
315 Ceredigion	-12.2	PC
316 Rushcliffe	-12.3	Con
317 Bristol South	-12.3	Lab
318 Clydesdale	-12.3	Lab
319 Dumbarton	-12.3	Lab
320 Dunfermline West	-12.3	Lab
321 Kirkcaldy	-12.3	Lab
322 Durham North	-12.3	Lab
323 Doncaster Central	-12.3	Lab
324 Ribble Valley	-12.3	Con
325 Fareham	-12.3	Con
326 Edinburgh Pentlands	-12.3	Lab

Contd. /

327 Hammersmith & Fulham	-12.3 Lab	383 Blaenau Gwent	-12.8 Lab
328 Wansbeck	-12.3 Lab	384 Wolverhampton South East	-12.8 Lab
329 Bristol East	-12.3 Lab	385 Medway	-12.8 Lab
330 Caerphilly	-12.4 Lab	386 Havant	-12.8 Con
331 Manchester Blackley	-12.4 Lab	387 Strathkelvin & Bearsden	-12.8 Lab
332 Perth	-12.4 SNP	388 South Shields	-12.9 Lab
333 Esher & Walton	-12.4 Con	389 Eastleigh	-12.9 LD
334 Sutton Coldfield	-12.4 Con	390 Tyne Bridge	-12.9 Lab
335 Bedfordshire North East	-12.4 Con	391 Macclesfield	-12.9 Con
336 Calder Valley	-12.4 Lab	392 Manchester Gorton	-12.9 Lab
337 Cambridgeshire North East	-12.4 Con	393 Aldershot	-12.9 Con
338 Edinburgh East &		394 Birmingham Edgbaston	-12.9 Lab
Musselburgh	-12.5 Lab	395 Portsmouth South	-12.9 LD
339 Woking	-12.5 Con	396 Tweeddale, Ettrick &	
340 Tewkesbury	-12.5 Con	Lauderdale	-12.9 LD
341 Gillingham	-12.5 Lab	397 Oldham East & Saddleworth	-13.0 Lab
342 Charnwood	-12.5 Con	398 Bournemouth West	-13.0 Con
343 Leeds Central	-12.5 Lab	399 Carshalton & Wallington	-13.0 LD
344 Cambridgeshire North West	-12.5 Con	400 Birmingham Hodge Hill	-13.0 Lab
345 Worcester	-12.5 Lab	401 Great Yarmouth	-13.0 Lab
346 Clydebank & Milngavie	-12.5 Lab	402 Kingswood	-13.0 Lab
347 Essex North	-12.5 Con	403 East Lothian	-13.0 Lab
348 Braintree	-12.5 Lab	404 Altrincham & Sale West	-13.0 Con
349 Conwy	-12.5 Lab	405 Bedfordshire Mid	-13.1 Con
350 Sutton & Cheam	-12.5 LD	406 Brighton Kemptown	-13.1 Lab
351 Glasgow Kelvin	-12.6 Lab	407 Gosport	-13.1 Con
352 Newcastle upon Tyne East		408 Plymouth Devonport	-13.1 Lab
& Wallsend	-12.6 Lab	409 Stockton South	-13.1 Lab
353 Tatton	-12.6 Ind	410 Worthing East & Shoreham	-13.1 Con
354 Cunninghame North	-12.6 Lab	411 Ruislip Northwood	-13.1 Con
355 Wentworth	-12.6 Lab	412 Keighley	-13.2 Lab
356 Bexleyheath & Crayford	-12.6 Lab	413 Dundee West	-13.2 Lab
357 Houghton & Washington E.	-12.6 Lab	414 Carrick, Cumnock &	
358 Delyn	-12.6 Lab	Doon Valley	-13.2 Lab
359 Oxford East	-12.6 Lab	415 Upminster	-13.2 Con
360 Manchester Central	-12.6 Lab	416 Dunfermline East	-13.2 Lab
361 Batley & Spen	-12.6 Lab	417 Brent South	-13.2 Lab
362 Swindon North	-12.6 Lab	418 Eastbourne	-13.2 Con
363 Corby	-12.6 Lab	419 Rochdale	-13.3 Lab
364 Twickenham	-12.6 LD	420 Roxburgh & Berwickshire	-13.3 LD
365 Renfrewshire West	-12.7 Lab	421 Hertford & Stortford	-13.3 Con
366 Leeds West	-12.7 Lab	422 Aberdeen North	-13.3 Lab
367 Sussex Mid	-12.7 Con	423 Lewisham East	-13.3 Lab
368 Huddersfield	-12.7 Lab	424 Vale of Glamorgan	-13.3 Lab
369 Hull East	-12.7 Lab	425 Burton	-13.3 Lab
370 Dartford	-12.7 Lab	426 Ealing North	-13.3 Lab
371 Halifax	-12.7 Lab	427 Henley	-13.3 Con
372 Brent North	-12.8 Lab	428 Enfield North	-13.3 Lab
373 Spelthorne	-12.8 Con	429 Easington	-13.4 Lab
374 Portsmouth North	-12.8 Lab	430 Hendon	-13.4 Lab
375 Loughborough	-12.8 Lab	431 Old Bexley & Sidcup	-13.4 Con
376 Harrow East	-12.8 Lab	432 Carlisle	-13.4 Lab
377 Angus	-12.8 SNP	433 Stoke-on-Trent North	-13.4 Lab
378 Norwich South	-12.8 Lab	434 Coventry South	-13.4 Lab
379 Doncaster North	-12.8 Lab	435 Southport	-13.5 LD
380 Hull West & Hessle	-12.8 Lab	436 Basingstoke	-13.5 Con
381 Poplar & Canning Town	-12.8 Lab	437 Edinburgh North & Leith	-13.5 Lab
382 Aberdeen Central	-12.8 Lab		

Contd. /

438 Motherwell & Wishaw	-13.5	Lab
439 Colchester	-13.5	LD
440 Dudley North	-13.5	Lab
441 Halesowen & Rowley Regis	-13.5	Lab
442 Oxford West & Abingdon	-13.5	LD
443 Watford	-13.5	Lab
444 Faversham & Kent Mid	-13.5	Con
445 Morley & Rothwell	-13.5	Lab
446 Hampstead & Highgate	-13.5	Lab
447 Blaydon	-13.6	Lab
448 Wantage	-13.6	Con
449 Colne Valley	-13.6	Lab
450 Maidenhead	-13.6	Con
451 Gordon	-13.6	LD
452 Chatham & Aylesford	-13.6	Lab
453 Aldridge - Brownhills	-13.6	Con
454 Bassetlaw	-13.6	Lab
455 Alyn & Deeside	-13.6	Lab
456 Glasgow Anniesland	-13.6	Lab
457 Jarrow	-13.6	Lab
458 Bedford	-13.6	Lab
459 Derbyshire North East	-13.7	Lab
460 Hertsmere	-13.7	Con
461 Telford	-13.7	Lab
462 Birmingham Hall Green	-13.7	Lab
463 Exeter	-13.7	Lab
464 Sheffield Hillsborough	-13.7	Lab
465 Bedfordshire South West	-13.7	Con
466 Castle Point	-13.7	Con
467 High Peak	-13.7	Lab
468 Crewe & Nantwich	-13.7	Lab
469 Hamilton South	-13.7	Lab
470 Islington North	-13.7	Lab
471 Dover	-13.7	Lab
472 Huntingdon	-13.8	Con
473 Glasgow Rutherglen	-13.8	Lab
474 Birmingham Selly Oak	-13.8	Lab
475 Rayleigh	-13.8	Con
476 Cynon Valley	-13.8	Lab
477 Great Grimsby	-13.8	Lab
478 Waveney	-13.8	Lab
479 Barnsley Central	-13.8	Lab
480 Bracknell	-13.8	Con
481 Staffordshire Moorlands	-13.9	Lab
482 Birmingham Yardley	-13.9	Lab
483 Manchester Withington	-13.9	Lab
484 Staffordshire South	-13.9	Con
485 Rother Valley	-14.0	Lab
486 Brent East	-14.0	Lab
487 Torfaen	-14.0	Lab
488 Edmonton	-14.0	Lab
489 Ealing Acton & Shepherd's Bush	-14.1	Lab
490 Gloucester	-14.1	Lab
491 Banbury	-14.1	Con
492 Hamilton North & Bellshill	-14.1	Lab
493 Edinburgh South	-14.1	Lab
494 Blyth Valley	-14.1	Lab
495 Northampton North	-14.1	Lab
496 Barnsley E. & Mexborough	-14.1	Lab
497 Cheadle	-14.1	LD
498 Gravesham	-14.1	Lab
499 Leicestershire North West	-14.2	Lab
500 Stockton North	-14.2	Lab
501 Stirling	-14.2	Lab
502 Coatbridge & Chryston	-14.2	Lab
503 York	-14.2	Lab
504 Birmingham Erdington	-14.2	Lab
505 Halton	-14.2	Lab
506 Reigate	-14.2	Con
507 Derbyshire South	-14.3	Lab
508 Hemel Hempstead	-14.3	Lab
509 Redditch	-14.3	Lab
510 Rossendale & Darwen	-14.3	Lab
511 Nuneaton	-14.3	Lab
512 Wolverhampton North East	-14.3	Lab
513 Banff & Buchan	-14.3	SNP
514 Ilford North	-14.3	Lab
515 Tooting	-14.4	Lab
516 Blackpool North & Fleetwood	-14.4	Lab
517 Stoke-on-Trent South	-14.4	Lab
518 Wakefield	-14.5	Lab
519 Hornchurch	-14.5	Lab
520 Coventry North East	-14.5	Lab
521 Epping Forest	-14.5	Con
522 Slough	-14.5	Lab
523 Bradford South	-14.5	Lab
524 Wythenshawe & Sale East	-14.6	Lab
525 Billericay	-14.6	Con
526 Ribble South	-14.6	Lab
527 Warwickshire North	-14.6	Lab
528 Newcastle upon Tyne Central	-14.6	Lab
529 Broxbourne	-14.6	Con
530 Hyndburn	-14.6	Lab
531 Harlow	-14.6	Lab
532 Redcar	-14.7	Lab
533 City of Chester	-14.7	Lab
534 Surrey Heath	-14.7	Con
535 Welwyn Hatfield	-14.7	Lab
536 Stourbridge	-14.7	Lab
537 Gateshead East & Washington West	-14.7	Lab
538 Salford	-14.7	Lab
539 Bolsover	-14.7	Lab
540 Sittingbourne & Sheppey	-14.7	Lab
541 Edinburgh West	-14.8	LD
542 Sherwood	-14.8	Lab
543 Warrington South	-14.8	Lab
544 Ogmore	-14.8	Lab
545 Uxbridge	-14.8	Con
546 Brighton Pavilion	-14.8	Lab

Contd. /

547 Newcastle-under-Lyme	-14.8	Lab		604 Stevenage	-15.9	Lab
548 Liverpool Garston	-14.9	Lab		605 Linlithgow	-15.9	Lab
549 Bury North	-14.9	Lab		606 Makerfield	-15.9	Lab
550 Bolton West	-14.9	Lab		607 Ilford South	-15.9	Lab
551 Stretford & Urmston	-14.9	Lab		608 Southampton Itchen	-16.0	Lab
552 Congleton	-14.9	Con		609 Leigh	-16.0	Lab
553 Croydon North	-15.0	Lab		610 Erewash	-16.0	Lab
554 Midlothian	-15.0	Lab		611 Glasgow Shettleston	-16.0	Lab
555 Glasgow Cathcart	-15.0	Lab		612 Normanton	-16.0	Lab
556 Lincoln	-15.0	Lab		613 Ochil	-16.1	Lab
557 Glasgow Baillieston	-15.0	Lab		614 Hemsworth	-16.1	Lab
558 Middlesbrough South &				615 Hayes & Harlington	-16.1	Lab
Cleveland East	-15.0	Lab		616 Barking	-16.2	Lab
559 Bolton South East	-15.0	Lab		617 St Helens North	-16.2	Lab
560 Nottingham East	-15.0	Lab		618 Derby North	-16.2	Lab
561 Edinburgh Central	-15.1	Lab		619 Wallasey	-16.2	Lab
562 St Helens South	-15.1	Lab		620 Nottingham North	-16.2	Lab
563 Stoke-on-Trent Central	-15.1	Lab		621 Islington South & Finsbury	-16.3	Lab
564 Chorley	-15.1	Lab		622 Ashton under Lyne	-16.3	Lab
565 Bristol North West	-15.1	Lab		623 Dudley South	-16.3	Lab
566 Walsall North	-15.1	Lab		624 Glasgow Maryhill	-16.3	Lab
567 Fife North East	-15.1	LD		625 Battersea	-16.3	Lab
568 Glasgow Pollok	-15.1	Lab		626 Bolton North East	-16.3	Lab
569 Maldon & Chelmsford East	-15.1	Con		627 Tamworth	-16.3	Lab
570 Swansea East	-15.1	Lab		628 Ashfield	-16.4	Lab
571 Chelmsford West	-15.1	Con		629 Windsor	-16.4	Con
572 Middlesbrough	-15.2	Lab		630 Liverpool Walton	-16.5	Lab
573 Coventry North West	-15.2	Lab		631 Preston	-16.6	Lab
574 Ipswich	-15.2	Lab		632 Norwich North	-16.6	Lab
575 Fife Central	-15.3	Lab		633 Bury South	-16.6	Lab
576 Glasgow Springburn	-15.3	Spkr		634 Pontefract & Castleford	-16.7	Lab
577 Wigan	-15.3	Lab		635 Warrington North	-16.7	Lab
578 Heywood & Middleton	-15.3	Lab		636 Thurrock	-16.7	Lab
579 Cumbernauld & Kilsyth	-15.3	Lab		637 Worsley	-16.8	Lab
580 Cunninghame South	-15.3	Lab		638 Putney	-16.8	Lab
581 Erith & Thamesmead	-15.3	Lab		639 Nottingham South	-16.8	Lab
582 Luton North	-15.3	Lab		640 Ellesmere Port & Neston	-16.8	Lab
583 Falkirk East	-15.3	Lab		641 Basildon	-16.9	Lab
584 Runnymede & Weybridge	-15.3	Con		642 Bootle	-17.0	Lab
585 Luton South	-15.4	Lab		643 Eltham	-17.0	Lab
586 Wirral South	-15.4	Lab		644 Airdrie & Shotts	-17.0	Lab
587 Kilmarnock & Loudoun	-15.4	Lab		645 Knowsley N. & Sefton E.	-17.1	Lab
588 Southampton Test	-15.4	Lab		646 Stalybridge & Hyde	-17.3	Lab
589 Blackpool South	-15.5	Lab		647 Eccles	-17.3	Lab
590 Livingston	-15.5	Lab		648 Liverpool Riverside	-17.5	Lab
591 Newport West	-15.5	Lab		649 Birkenhead	-17.7	Lab
592 Mansfield	-15.5	Lab		650 Crawley	-17.7	Lab
593 Weaver Vale	-15.5	Lab		651 Glasgow Govan	-17.8	Lab
594 Birmingham Northfield	-15.5	Lab		652 Stockport	-18.0	Lab
595 Falkirk West	-15.5	Lab		653 Pontypridd	-18.1	Lab
596 Mitcham & Morden	-15.5	Lab		654 Hazel Grove	-18.2	LD
597 Feltham & Heston	-15.6	Lab		655 Liverpool Wavertree	-18.4	Lab
598 Dagenham	-15.6	Lab		656 Denton & Reddish	-18.4	Lab
599 Amber Valley	-15.6	Lab		657 Cannock Chase	-18.6	Lab
600 Knowsley South	-15.7	Lab		658 Newport East	-18.9	Lab
601 Liverpool West Derby	-15.8	Lab		659 Regent's Park &		
602 Lancashire West	-15.8	Lab		Kensington North	-19.5	Lab
603 Brentford & Isleworth	-15.8	Lab				

Table 19. Seats in Rank Order of Winning Party's Share of the Electorate

Constituency	%share	1st
1 Belfast West	45.5	SF
2 Blaenau Gwent	42.8	Lab
3 Ulster Mid	41.5	SF
4 Rhondda	41.4	Lab
5 Easington	41.2	Lab
6 Kingston & Surbiton	40.6	LD
7 Sedgefield	40.2	Lab
8 Tyneside North	40.1	Lab
9 Richmond (Yorks)	39.7	Con
10 Wyre Forest	39.5	KHHC
11 Winchester	39.5	LD
12 Bolsover	38.8	Lab
13 Bootle	38.6	Lab
14 Lewes	38.6	LD
15 Aberavon	38.5	Lab
16 Durham North	38.3	Lab
17 East Ham	38.2	Lab
18 Islwyn	38.1	Lab
19 Coatbridge & Chryston	38.0	Lab
20 Neath	38.0	Lab
21 Brent South	37.5	Lab
22 Halton	37.4	Lab
23 Buckingham	37.2	Con
24 Christchurch	37.2	Con
25 Northavon	37.1	LD
26 Hayes & Harlington	37.0	Lab
27 Dunfermline East	36.9	Lab
28 Knowsley South	36.9	Lab
29 Durham North West	36.6	Lab
30 Jarrow	36.4	Lab
31 Cynon Valley	36.4	Lab
32 Sheffield Brightside	36.3	Lab
33 New Forest West	36.3	Con
34 Houghton & Washington E.	36.2	Lab
35 Ogmore	36.1	Lab
36 Sheffield Hallam	35.9	LD
37 Harrogate & Knaresborough	35.9	LD
38 Crosby	35.9	Lab
39 Sheffield Attercliffe	35.9	Lab
40 Tynemouth	35.8	Lab
41 Torfaen	35.8	Lab
42 Gateshead East & Washington West	35.8	Lab
43 Lagan Valley	35.7	UU
44 Leicester East	35.7	Lab
45 Merthyr Tydfil & Rhymney	35.6	Lab
46 Wentworth	35.6	Lab
47 Penrith & The Border	35.4	Con
48 Kingswood	35.4	Lab
49 Knowsley N. & Sefton E.	35.4	Lab
50 Workington	35.2	Lab
51 Hamilton N. & Bellshill	35.1	Lab
52 Wallasey	35.0	Lab
53 Darlington	34.9	Lab
54 Mitcham & Morden	34.9	Lab
55 Makerfield	34.9	Lab
56 Mole Valley	34.8	Con
57 Bury South	34.8	Lab
58 Stockton North	34.8	Lab
59 Bromsgrove	34.7	Con
60 Pontefract & Castleford	34.6	Lab
61 Skipton & Ripon	34.6	Con
62 Newcastle upon Tyne N.	34.6	Lab
63 Foyle	34.6	SDLP
64 Wolverhampton South East	34.6	Lab
65 South Holland & The Deepings	34.4	Con
66 Brent North	34.3	Lab
67 Leicestershire North West	34.2	Lab
68 Wansbeck	34.2	Lab
69 St Ives	34.2	LD
70 Hamilton South	34.2	Lab
71 West Ham	34.2	Lab
72 Carrick, Cumnock & Doon Valley	34.2	Lab
73 Vale of York	34.1	Con
74 Swansea East	34.1	Lab
75 Ribble Valley	34.1	Con
76 Birkenhead	34.0	Lab
77 Leominster	34.0	Con
78 Redcar	34.0	Lab
79 Cotswold	33.9	Con
80 Hemsworth	33.9	Lab
81 Scunthorpe	33.9	Lab
82 Croydon North	33.8	Lab
83 Arundel & South Downs	33.8	Con
84 Middlesbrough South & Cleveland East	33.7	Lab
85 Eastwood	33.7	Lab
86 Ellesmere Port & Neston	33.7	Lab
87 Ross, Skye & Inverness W.	33.7	LD
88 Middlesbrough	33.7	Lab
89 Bishop Auckland	33.7	Lab
90 Copeland	33.6	Lab
91 Caerphilly	33.6	Lab
92 Newcastle upon Tyne East & Wallsend	33.6	Lab
93 Barrow & Furness	33.6	Lab
94 Stretford & Urmston	33.5	Lab
95 Liverpool Walton	33.4	Lab
96 Barnsley East & Mexborough	33.4	Lab
97 Paisley South	33.4	Lab
98 City of Durham	33.4	Lab
99 East Kilbride	33.4	Lab
100 Stockton South	33.3	Lab
101 Surrey East	33.2	Con

Contd. /

102 Walthamstow	33.2	Lab
103 Clydebank & Milngavie	33.2	Lab
104 Cornwall North	33.2	LD
105 Warrington North	33.2	Lab
106 Edmonton	33.1	Lab
107 Rother Valley	33.0	Lab
108 Hartlepool	33.0	Lab
109 Plymouth Devonport	33.0	Lab
110 Antrim North	33.0	DUP
111 Down North	33.0	UU
112 Sherwood	33.0	Lab
113 Enfield Southgate	32.9	Lab
114 Norfolk South West	32.9	Con
115 Cunninghame South	32.9	Lab
116 Walsall South	32.9	Lab
117 Luton North	32.8	Lab
118 Horsham	32.8	Con
119 Down South	32.8	SDLP
120 Hampshire North East	32.8	Con
121 Brent East	32.8	Lab
122 Stratford-on-Avon	32.8	Con
123 Berwick-upon-Tweed	32.8	LD
124 Derbyshire North East	32.8	Lab
125 Dumfries	32.8	Lab
126 Greenwich & Woolwich	32.8	Lab
127 Wansdyke	32.8	Lab
128 Bath	32.7	LD
129 Warley	32.7	Lab
130 Crewe & Nantwich	32.7	Lab
131 Gedling	32.7	Lab
132 Chesham & Amersham	32.7	Con
133 Blyth Valley	32.6	Lab
134 Kilmarnock & Loudoun	32.6	Lab
135 Tyrone West	32.6	SF
136 Devon East	32.6	Con
137 Stroud	32.6	Lab
138 Sheffield Hillsborough	32.6	Lab
139 Delyn	32.6	Lab
140 Chorley	32.6	Lab
141 Tiverton & Honiton	32.6	Con
142 Camberwell & Peckham	32.5	Lab
143 Warwickshire North	32.5	Lab
144 Stone	32.5	Con
145 Derbyshire West	32.5	Con
146 Tottenham	32.5	Lab
147 Newbury	32.5	LD
148 Cumbernauld & Kilsyth	32.5	Lab
149 Richmond Park	32.4	LD
150 Derbyshire South	32.4	Lab
151 Leeds East	32.4	Lab
152 Lichfield	32.4	Con
153 Wigan	32.4	Lab
154 Ilford South	32.4	Lab
155 Rotherham	32.4	Lab
156 Montgomeryshire	32.4	LD
157 Twickenham	32.4	LD
158 Broxtowe	32.4	Lab
159 Bedfordshire North East	32.3	Con
160 Glasgow Rutherglen	32.3	Lab
161 Harrow East	32.3	Lab
162 Ealing North	32.3	Lab
163 Bury North	32.3	Lab
164 Daventry	32.3	Con
165 Swindon North	32.3	Lab
166 Sleaford & N. Hykeham	32.2	Con
167 St Helens North	32.2	Lab
168 Bristol South	32.1	Lab
169 Cardiff South & Penarth	32.1	Lab
170 Clwyd South	32.1	Lab
171 Corby	32.1	Lab
172 Warwick & Leamington	32.1	Lab
173 Leigh	32.1	Lab
174 Beaconsfield	32.1	Con
175 Lancashire West	32.0	Lab
176 Pontypridd	32.0	Lab
177 Exeter	32.0	Lab
178 Barnsley Central	31.9	Lab
179 Saffron Walden	31.9	Con
180 Bromley & Chislehurst	31.9	Con
181 Cardiff West	31.9	Lab
182 Doncaster North	31.9	Lab
183 Falkirk East	31.8	Lab
184 Wolverhampton N. E.	31.8	Lab
185 Westmorland & Lonsdale	31.8	Con
186 Worcestershire Mid	31.8	Con
187 Fylde	31.8	Con
188 Surrey South West	31.8	Con
189 Motherwell & Wishaw	31.8	Lab
190 Vale of Clwyd	31.8	Lab
191 Lewisham West	31.8	Lab
192 Dover	31.8	Lab
193 Leyton & Wanstead	31.8	Lab
194 Tonbridge & Malling	31.8	Con
195 Meirionnydd Nant Conwy	31.7	PC
196 Cardiff North	31.7	Lab
197 Halesowen & Rowley Regis	31.7	Lab
198 Airdrie & Shotts	31.7	Lab
199 Hitchin & Harpenden	31.7	Con
200 Denton & Reddish	31.6	Lab
201 Wealden	31.6	Con
202 Hexham	31.6	Con
203 Romford	31.6	Con
204 Rushcliffe	31.6	Con
205 Leicester South	31.6	Lab
206 Sevenoaks	31.6	Con
207 Bridgend	31.6	Lab
208 Wrexham	31.6	Lab
209 Torbay	31.6	LD
210 Norfolk North West	31.6	Con
211 Bristol East	31.6	Lab
212 Romsey	31.5	LD
213 Derby South	31.5	Lab
214 Mansfield	31.5	Lab
215 Bristol North West	31.5	Lab

Contd. /

216 Linlithgow	31.5	Lab
217 Stevenage	31.5	Lab
218 Blaydon	31.5	Lab
219 Glasgow Pollok	31.5	Lab
220 Elmet	31.5	Lab
221 Bassetlaw	31.4	Lab
222 Loughborough	31.4	Lab
223 Hyndburn	31.4	Lab
224 Newcastle-under-Lyme	31.4	Lab
225 Sheffield Heeley	31.4	Lab
226 Lewisham Deptford	31.4	Lab
227 South Shields	31.4	Lab
228 Paisley North	31.4	Lab
229 Reading West	31.4	Lab
230 Birmingham Hall Green	31.4	Lab
231 Stafford	31.3	Lab
232 Swindon South	31.3	Lab
233 Nuneaton	31.3	Lab
234 Staffordshire Moorlands	31.3	Lab
235 Amber Valley	31.3	Lab
236 Gravesham	31.3	Lab
237 Harrow West	31.2	Lab
238 Bexhill & Battle	31.2	Con
239 Hampshire North West	31.2	Con
240 Bedfordshire Mid	31.2	Con
241 Stockport	31.2	Lab
242 Greenock & Inverclyde	31.2	Lab
243 Newport West	31.2	Lab
244 Ashfield	31.2	Lab
245 Midlothian	31.1	Lab
246 Tyne Bridge	31.1	Lab
247 Wirral South	31.1	Lab
248 Slough	31.1	Lab
249 Eccles	31.1	Lab
250 Charnwood	31.1	Con
251 Cannock Chase	31.1	Lab
252 Leeds West	31.1	Lab
253 Brigg & Goole	31.0	Lab
254 Dorset West	31.0	Con
255 Eltham	31.0	Lab
256 Bolton South East	31.0	Lab
257 Barnsley West & Penistone	31.0	Lab
258 Ryedale	31.0	Con
259 Devon South West	31.0	Con
260 Manchester Blackley	30.9	Lab
261 Dorset North	30.9	Con
262 City of Chester	30.9	Lab
263 Maldon & Chelmsford E.	30.9	Con
264 Rutland & Melton	30.9	Con
265 Milton Keynes South West	30.9	Lab
266 Oxford West & Abingdon	30.9	LD
267 Sunderland South	30.8	Lab
268 Worcestershire West	30.8	Con
269 York	30.8	Lab
270 Waveney	30.8	Lab
271 Teignbridge	30.8	LD
272 Liverpool Garston	30.8	Lab
273 Cleethorpes	30.8	Lab

274 Hazel Grove	30.8	LD
275 Cambridgeshire N. W.	30.7	Con
276 Fife Central	30.7	Lab
277 Coventry North East	30.7	Lab
278 Sunderland North	30.7	Lab
279 Shropshire North	30.7	Con
280 Ashton under Lyne	30.7	Lab
281 Truro & St Austell	30.7	LD
282 Wirral West	30.7	Lab
283 Heywood & Middleton	30.7	Lab
284 Wiltshire North	30.6	Con
285 Alyn & Deeside	30.6	Lab
286 Strathkelvin & Bearsden	30.6	Lab
287 Hampshire East	30.6	Con
288 Edinburgh East & Musselburgh	30.6	Lab
289 Birmingham Hodge Hill	30.6	Lab
290 Monmouth	30.6	Lab
291 Tatton	30.6	Con
292 Keighley	30.6	Lab
293 Maidstone & The Weald	30.6	Con
294 Morley & Rothwell	30.5	Lab
295 Birmingham Ladywood	30.5	Lab
296 Huntingdon	30.5	Con
297 Doncaster Central	30.5	Lab
298 Sutton Coldfield	30.5	Con
299 Norfolk Mid	30.5	Con
300 Macclesfield	30.5	Con
301 Leeds North East	30.5	Lab
302 Erewash	30.5	Lab
303 Salisbury	30.5	Con
304 Sutton & Cheam	30.5	LD
305 Bolton North East	30.4	Lab
306 Kettering	30.4	Lab
307 Staffordshire South	30.4	Con
308 Tunbridge Wells	30.4	Con
309 Hackney S. & Shoreditch	30.4	Lab
310 Aldridge - Brownhills	30.4	Con
311 Pudsey	30.4	Lab
312 Sheffield Central	30.4	Lab
313 Luton South	30.4	Lab
314 High Peak	30.4	Lab
315 Rugby & Kenilworth	30.4	Lab
316 Carlisle	30.4	Lab
317 Devizes	30.3	Con
318 Rayleigh	30.3	Con
319 Esher & Walton	30.3	Con
320 Morecambe & Lunesdale	30.3	Lab
321 Vale of Glamorgan	30.3	Lab
322 Wells	30.3	Con
323 Burton	30.3	Lab
324 Great Grimsby	30.3	Lab
325 Somerton & Frome	30.2	LD
326 Llanelli	30.2	Lab
327 Croydon South	30.2	Con
328 Devon North	30.2	LD
329 Totnes	30.2	Con

Contd. /

330 Weaver Vale	30.2	Lab	387 Surrey Heath	29.5	Con	
331 Epsom & Ewell	30.2	Con	388 Newark	29.5	Con	
332 Ayr	30.2	Lab	389 East Lothian	29.5	Lab	
333 Batley & Spen	30.2	Lab	390 Birmingham Selly Oak	29.5	Lab	
334 Warrington South	30.2	Lab	391 Banff & Buchan	29.5	SNP	
335 Islington North	30.2	Lab	392 Livingston	29.5	Lab	
336 Lincoln	30.2	Lab	393 Southampton Itchen	29.5	Lab	
337 Nottingham North	30.2	Lab	394 Oldham West & Royton	29.5	Lab	
338 Dunfermline West	30.2	Lab	395 Wimbledon	29.4	Lab	
339 Worcester	30.1	Lab	396 Great Yarmouth	29.4	Lab	
340 Broxbourne	30.1	Con	397 Derby North	29.4	Lab	
341 St Albans	30.1	Lab	398 Tewkesbury	29.4	Con	
342 Liverpool West Derby	30.1	Lab	399 Bolton West	29.4	Lab	
343 Louth & Horncastle	30.1	Con	400 Dulwich & West Norwood	29.3	Lab	
344 Stoke-on-Trent North	30.1	Lab	401 Ludlow	29.3	LD	
345 Cornwall South East	30.0	LD	402 Normanton	29.3	Lab	
346 Blackburn	30.0	Lab	403 Huddersfield	29.3	Lab	
347 Hull East	30.0	Lab	404 Selby	29.3	Lab	
348 Chichester	30.0	Con	405 Ipswich	29.3	Lab	
349 Wellingborough	30.0	Lab	406 Forest of Dean	29.2	Lab	
350 Gower	30.0	Lab	407 Thanet South	29.2	Lab	
351 Woodspring	30.0	Con	408 Wythenshawe & Sale East	29.2	Lab	
352 Don Valley	30.0	Lab	409 Feltham & Heston	29.1	Lab	
353 Norfolk North	29.9	LD	410 Worsley	29.1	Lab	
354 Sussex Mid	29.9	Con	411 Dudley North	29.1	Lab	
355 Wolverhampton S.W.	29.9	Lab	412 Stourbridge	29.1	Lab	
356 Newport East	29.9	Lab	413 Medway	29.1	Lab	
357 Hackney North & Stoke			414 Shipley	29.1	Lab	
Newington	29.9	Lab	415 Glasgow Springburn	29.1	Spkr	
358 Blaby	29.9	Con	416 Basildon	29.1	Lab	
359 Fareham	29.9	Con	417 Portsmouth North	29.1	Lab	
360 Carmarthen E. & Dinefwr	29.9	PC	418 Hemel Hempstead	29.1	Lab	
361 West Bromwich East	29.8	Lab	419 Aylesbury	29.0	Con	
362 Scarborough & Whitby	29.8	Lab	420 Dumbarton	29.0	Lab	
363 Ruislip Northwood	29.8	Con	421 Blackpool North &			
364 Erith & Thamesmead	29.8	Lab	Fleetwood	29.0	Lab	
365 Essex North	29.8	Con	422 Chesterfield	29.0	LD	
366 Devon West & Torridge	29.7	LD	423 Congleton	29.0	Con	
367 Renfrewshire West	29.7	Lab	424 West Bromwich West	29.0	Lab	
368 Dartford	29.7	Lab	425 Ribble South	29.0	Lab	
369 Eddisbury	29.7	Con	426 Plymouth Sutton	29.0	Lab	
370 Dewsbury	29.7	Lab	427 Fife North East	29.0	LD	
371 Tooting	29.7	Lab	428 Cambridgeshire North East	29.0	Con	
372 The Wrekin	29.7	Lab	429 Hornsey & Wood Green	28.9	Lab	
373 Witney	29.7	Con	430 Folkestone & Hythe	28.8	Con	
374 Gainsborough	29.7	Con	431 Hertsmere	28.8	Con	
375 Shrewsbury & Atcham	29.7	Lab	432 Glasgow Baillieston	28.8	Lab	
376 Cambridgeshire South	29.7	Con	433 Suffolk West	28.8	Con	
377 Ashford	29.6	Con	434 Meriden	28.8	Con	
378 Thanet North	29.6	Con	435 Reigate	28.8	Con	
379 Henley	29.6	Con	436 Solihull	28.7	Con	
380 Falkirk West	29.6	Lab	437 Stoke-on-Trent Central	28.7	Lab	
381 Cheltenham	29.6	LD	438 Bedford	28.7	Lab	
382 Roxburgh & Berwickshire	29.6	LD	439 Epping Forest	28.7	Con	
383 Southampton Test	29.6	Lab	440 Bury St Edmunds	28.7	Con	
384 Birmingham Northfield	29.6	Lab	441 Newry and Armagh	28.7	SDLP	
385 Wokingham	29.5	Con	442 Hertfordshire North East	28.7	Con	
386 Kirkcaldy	29.5	Lab				

Contd./

443 Bradford South	28.6	Lab
444 Bosworth	28.6	Con
445 Belfast South	28.6	UU
446 Glasgow Cathcart	28.6	Lab
447 Stirling	28.6	Lab
448 Hertfordshire South West	28.6	Con
449 Rossendale & Darwen	28.6	Lab
450 Coventry North West	28.6	Lab
451 Southwark North & Bermondsey	28.5	LD
452 Brighton Pavilion	28.5	Lab
453 Harlow	28.5	Lab
454 Lewisham East	28.5	Lab
455 Norfolk South	28.5	Con
456 Manchester Withington	28.5	Lab
457 Ealing Acton & Shepherd's Bush	28.5	Lab
458 Haltemprice & Howden	28.5	Con
459 Walsall North	28.5	Lab
460 Suffolk Coastal	28.4	Con
461 Lancaster & Wyre	28.4	Lab
462 Telford	28.4	Lab
463 Birmingham Sparkbrook & Small Heath	28.4	Lab
464 Yeovil	28.4	LD
465 Blackpool South	28.3	Lab
466 Glasgow Anniesland	28.3	Lab
467 Halifax	28.3	Lab
468 Tamworth	28.3	Lab
469 Beckenham	28.3	Con
470 Orpington	28.3	Con
471 Harwich	28.3	Lab
472 Worthing West	28.3	Con
473 Cunninghame North	28.3	Lab
474 Bracknell	28.3	Con
475 Harborough	28.3	Con
476 Grantham & Stamford	28.3	Con
477 Rochford & Southend E.	28.2	Con
478 Taunton	28.2	Con
479 Newcastle upon Tyne Central	28.2	Lab
480 Suffolk Central & Ipswich North	28.2	Con
481 Pendle	28.2	Lab
482 Old Bexley & Sidcup	28.2	Con
483 Chingford & Woodford Green	28.2	Con
484 Streatham	28.2	Lab
485 Brentford & Isleworth	28.1	Lab
486 Cambridgeshire South East	28.1	Con
487 Chipping Barnet	28.0	Con
488 Norwich North	28.0	Lab
489 Preston	28.0	Lab
490 Preseli Pembrokeshire	28.0	Lab
491 Westbury	28.0	Con
492 Maidenhead	27.9	Con
493 Rochdale	27.9	Lab
494 Leeds Central	27.9	Lab
495 Croydon Central	27.9	Lab
496 Altrincham & Sale West	27.8	Con
497 Ochil	27.8	Lab
498 Hertford & Stortford	27.8	Con
499 Liverpool Wavertree	27.8	Lab
500 Coventry South	27.7	Lab
501 Thurrock	27.7	Lab
502 Woking	27.7	Con
503 Peterborough	27.7	Lab
504 Barking	27.7	Lab
505 Bexleyheath & Crayford	27.7	Lab
506 Watford	27.7	Lab
507 Northampton North	27.7	Lab
508 Clydesdale	27.7	Lab
509 Stoke-on-Trent South	27.7	Lab
510 Dudley South	27.6	Lab
511 Leicester West	27.6	Lab
512 Welwyn Hatfield	27.6	Lab
513 Banbury	27.6	Con
514 Oxford East	27.6	Lab
515 Yorkshire East	27.6	Con
516 Faversham & Kent Mid	27.6	Con
517 Dorset Mid & Poole North	27.5	LD
518 Caernarfon	27.5	PC
519 Brighton Kemptown	27.5	Lab
520 Billericay	27.5	Con
521 Dundee West	27.5	Lab
522 Chatham & Aylesford	27.5	Lab
523 Dorset South	27.5	Lab
524 Birmingham Edgbaston	27.5	Lab
525 Burnley	27.5	Lab
526 Poplar & Canning Town	27.5	Lab
527 Belfast North	27.4	DUP
528 Hastings & Rye	27.4	Lab
529 Spelthorne	27.4	Con
530 Battersea	27.4	Lab
531 Hendon	27.4	Lab
532 Poole	27.4	Con
533 Suffolk South	27.4	Con
534 Cambridge	27.3	Lab
535 Runnymede & Weybridge	27.3	Con
536 Nottingham South	27.3	Lab
537 Western Isles	27.3	Lab
538 Swansea West	27.2	Lab
539 Crawley	27.2	Lab
540 Wakefield	27.2	Lab
541 Gloucester	27.2	Lab
542 Norwich South	27.2	Lab
543 Carshalton & Wallington	27.2	LD
544 Carmarthen West & Pembrokeshire South	27.2	Lab
545 Uxbridge	27.1	Con
546 Upminster	27.1	Con
547 Milton Keynes North East	27.1	Lab
548 Hornchurch	27.1	Lab
549 Salford	27.1	Lab
550 Redditch	27.0	Lab

Contd. /

551 Ealing Southall	27.0 Lab	606 Brentwood & Ongar	25.6 Con
552 Hove	27.0 Lab	607 Wantage	25.6 Con
553 Windsor	26.9 Con	608 Islington South & Finsbury	25.6 Lab
554 Aberdeenshire W &		609 Colne Valley	25.6 Lab
Kincardine	26.9 LD	610 St Helens South	25.6 Lab
555 Calder Valley	26.9 Lab	611 Northampton South	25.5 Lab
556 Manchester Central	26.9 Lab	612 Hampstead & Highgate	25.5 Lab
557 Southend West	26.9 Con	613 Falmouth & Camborne	25.4 Lab
558 Birmingham Yardley	26.9 Lab	614 Bethnal Green & Bow	25.3 Lab
559 Stalybridge & Hyde	26.8 Lab	615 Havant	25.3 Con
560 New Forest East	26.8 Con	616 Canterbury	25.2 Con
561 Nottingham East	26.8 Lab	617 Bournemouth East	25.2 Con
562 Belfast East	26.8 DUP	618 Tayside North	25.0 SNP
563 Manchester Gorton	26.8 Lab	619 Boston & Skegness	25.0 Con
564 Hull West & Hessle	26.8 Lab	620 Hammersmith & Fulham	25.0 Lab
565 Cheadle	26.8 LD	621 Gosport	24.9 Con
566 Tweeddale, Ettrick &		622 Aberdeen South	24.9 Lab
Lauderdale	26.8 LD	623 Aberdeen North	24.9 Lab
567 Edinburgh West	26.7 LD	624 Clwyd West	24.9 Lab
568 Ilford North	26.7 Lab	625 Weston-Super-Mare	24.8 LD
569 Holborn & St Pancras	26.7 Lab	626 Birmingham Perry Barr	24.5 Lab
570 Braintree	26.7 Lab	627 Aldershot	24.4 Con
571 Guildford	26.7 LD	628 Leeds North West	24.4 Lab
572 Regent's Park &		629 Edinburgh North & Leith	24.3 Lab
Kensington North	26.7 Lab	630 Liverpool Riverside	24.3 Lab
573 Hereford	26.6 LD	631 Edinburgh South	24.3 Lab
574 Fermanagh & South Tyrone	26.6 SF	632 Glasgow Maryhill	24.2 Lab
575 Enfield North	26.6 Lab	633 Bristol West	24.2 Lab
576 Dagenham	26.6 Lab	634 Isle of Wight	24.2 Con
577 Finchley & Golders Green	26.5 Lab	635 Aberdeen Central	24.0 Lab
578 Gordon	26.5 LD	636 Colchester	23.9 LD
579 Vauxhall	26.5 Lab	637 Kensington & Chelsea	23.6 Con
580 Gillingham	26.5 Lab	638 Ceredigion	23.6 PC
581 Birmingham Erdington	26.5 Lab	639 Upper Bann	23.6 UU
582 Sittingbourne & Sheppey	26.3 Lab	640 Oldham E. & Saddleworth	23.5 Lab
583 Bognor Regis &		641 Inverness East, Nairn &	
Littlehampton	26.3 Con	Lochaber	23.5 Lab
584 Conwy	26.3 Lab	642 Antrim South	23.2 UU
585 Eastbourne	26.3 Con	643 Glasgow Govan	23.1 Lab
586 Putney	26.2 Lab	644 Galloway & Upper	
587 Bradford North	26.2 Lab	Nithsdale	23.0 Con
588 Chelmsford West	26.2 Con	645 Bournemouth West	22.8 Con
589 Reading East	26.2 Lab	646 Portsmouth South	22.7 LD
590 Bedfordshire South West	26.1 Con	647 Cardiff Central	22.5 Lab
591 Edinburgh Pentlands	26.1 Lab	648 Ynys Mon	22.3 Lab
592 Bridgwater	26.1 Con	649 Edinburgh Central	21.9 Lab
593 Castle Point	26.0 Con	650 Caithness, Sutherland &	
594 Hull North	26.0 Lab	Easter Ross	21.9 LD
595 Brecon & Radnorshire	26.0 LD	651 Cities of London &	
596 Eastleigh	26.0 LD	Westminster	21.9 Con
597 Basingstoke	25.9 Con	652 Orkney & Shetland	21.7 LD
598 Dundee East	25.9 Lab	653 Antrim East	21.5 UU
599 Worthing East & Shoreham	25.8 Con	654 Londonderry East	21.3 DUP
600 Bradford West	25.7 Lab	655 Angus	20.9 SNP
601 Glasgow Shettleston	25.7 Lab	656 Glasgow Kelvin	19.5 Lab
602 Strangford	25.7 DUP	657 Argyll & Bute	18.8 LD
603 Wycombe	25.7 Con	658 Perth	18.3 SNP
604 Southport	25.7 LD	659 Moray	17.4 SNP
605 Beverley & Holderness	25.6 Con		

Table 20. Gender of Candidates by Party

Party	Female	%	Male	%
Lab	149	23.3	491	76.7
LD	139	21.8	500	78.2
Con	92	14.3	551	85.7
UKI	57	13.3	371	86.7
Grn	36	24.8	109	75.2
PL	25	67.6	12	32.4
SSP	24	33.3	48	66.7
SA	18	18.4	80	81.6
SL	18	15.8	96	84.2
SNP	16	22.2	56	77.8
Ind	11	9.3	107	90.7
PC	7	17.5	33	82.5
SDLP	6	33.3	12	66.7
APNI	4	40.0	6	60.0
(No label)	4	21.1	15	78.9
MRLP	4	26.7	11	73.3
SF	3	16.7	15	83.3
Lib	3	21.4	11	78.6
WRP	2	33.3	4	66.7
UU	2	11.8	15	88.2
LCA	2	15.4	11	84.6
BNP	2	6.1	31	93.9
LA	1	100.0	0	0.0
NIWC	1	100.0	0	0.0
WR	1	50.0	1	50.0
WP	1	16.7	5	83.3
MK	1	33.3	2	66.7
Prog U	1	50.0	1	50.0
NF	1	20.0	4	80.0
LP	1	100.0	0	0.0
Tatton	1	100.0	0	0.0
SU	1	50.0	1	50.0
DUP	1	7.1	13	92.9
CD	1	100.0	0	0.0
JWP	0	0.0	1	100.0
JLDP	0	0.0	1	100.0
IOW	0	0.0	1	100.0
JP	0	0.0	1	100.0
Grey	0	0.0	1	100.0
FP	0	0.0	3	100.0
FDP	0	0.0	1	100.0
Elvis	0	0.0	1	100.0
DW	0	0.0	1	100.0
Cust	0	0.0	1	100.0
CPA	0	0.0	1	100.0
Country	0	0.0	1	100.0
Comm	0	0.0	6	100.0
Ch	0	0.0	1	100.0
Bean	0	0.0	1	100.0
AL	0	0.0	1	100.0
EC	0	0.0	1	100.0
RM	0	0.0	1	100.0
Vote	0	0.0	4	100.0
UPP	0	0.0	1	100.0
UKU	0	0.0	1	100.0
UKP	0	0.0	1	100.0
TW	0	0.0	2	100.0
Tr	0	0.0	1	100.0
St	0	0.0	1	100.0
Speaker	0	0.0	1	100.0
Sc Ref	0	0.0	1	100.0
S Alt	0	0.0	2	100.0
NB	0	0.0	1	100.0
RRL	0	0.0	7	100.0
KHHC	0	0.0	1	100.0
Ref	0	0.0	5	100.0
PJP	0	0.0	3	100.0
Pens	0	0.0	1	100.0
PEC	0	0.0	1	100.0
PD	0	0.0	1	100.0
Pac	0	0.0	1	100.0
NIU	0	0.0	2	100.0
AC	0	0.0	1	100.0
Marx	0	0.0	1	100.0
M	0	0.0	4	100.0
LE	0	0.0	1	100.0
RUK	0	0.0	1	100.0
Total	636	19.2	2683	80.8

Contd./

Table 21. Gender of Winning Candidates by Party

Party	Female	%	Male	%
Lab	95	23.1	317	76.9
Con	14	8.4	152	91.6
LD	5	9.6	47	90.4
UU	1	16.7	5	83.3
SNP	1	20.0	4	80.0
SF	1	25.0	3	75.0
DUP	1	20.0	4	80.0
SDLP	0	0.0	3	100.0
PC	0	0.0	4	100.0
KHHC	0	0.0	1	100.0
Speaker	0	0.0	1	100.0

7　Index of General Election Candidates

Candidate name	Party	Const. no.
Anderson, Barry John	Con	357
Anderson, Donald	Lab	565
Anderson, Eleanor	LD	2
Anderson, Janet	Lab	487
Anderson, Norma Catherine	SSP	411
Anderson, Philip Andrew	UKI	486
Andrew, Kenneth	Con	131
Andrews, Peter Michael	SSP	447
Angus, Ian James	SNP	4
Appleton, Tony	–	91
Appleyard, Thomas Michael	SL	432
Approaching, Flash Gordon	MRLP	442
Arbon, Robert	LD	521
Arbuthnot, James Norwich	Con	296
Archer, Gordon	SNP	209
Armstrong, Hilary Jane	Lab	213
Armstrong, Richard Kevin	Grn	473
Armstrong-Braun, Klaus	Grn	10
Arnold, Jacques Arnold	Con	280
Arnold, Stewart David	LD	356
Arnott, Leslie George (commonly known as Les)	UKI	512
Arnott, Pauline Elizabeth	UKI	509
Arnott, Steven	SSP	337
Aron, Roger Joseph	LD	346
Ash, Michael	LD	570
Ashall, Michael Reeves	LD	473
Ashby, Christopher	Grn	340
Ashenden, Peter John	LD	321
Aspis, Simone Florence	Grn	87
Ataman, Erdil	Ref	325
Atherton, Candice Kathleen	Lab	248
Atherton, Michael Roy	SL	546
Athwal, Harpinder	LD	361
Atkins, Charlotte	Lab	534
Atkins, Raymond George	LD	365
Atkinson, David Anthony	Con	79
Atkinson, Peter Landreth	Con	319
Attenborough, Charlotte Nicola (commonly known as Nicky Attenborough)	Con	38
Attwell, Gavin William Hamilton	UKI	607
Attwood, Alex	SDLP	45
Aubel, Felix Franc Elfed	Con	86
Austin, John Eric	Lab	242
Aylett, Brian	UKI	616
Aziz, Abdul	M	61
Aziz, Abdul	SL	602
Azmi, Waqar Uzzaman	Lab	646

Candidate name	Party	Const. no.
Bartlett, David Charles	SA	125
Bartley, Stephen James	Grn	123
Bartrop, David Robert	UKI	440
Basarik, Erol	Ref	233
Bass, John	UKI	461
Bastiman, Philip Duncan	Con	544
Batchelor, William John	Ind	570
Batcup, Madoc Robert	PC	424
Bate, Richard Fields	UKI	658
Bate, Steven	LD	66
Bateman, Bernard Arthur	LD	520
Bateson, John Anthony	Lab	628
Batkin, Steven Reginald	BNP	544
Batten, Gerard Joseph	UKI	625
Battle, John	Lab	360
Baugh, Janet Everall	Lab	9
Baverstock, Paul Antony	Con	329
Bavester, Stuart David	UKI	186
Baxter, Ashley John	Grn	494
Baxter, Dorothy	UKI	65
Bayley, Hugh	Lab	658
Baynes, Arthur Leonard	UKI	116
Beadle, Barry	Ind	637
Beadle, Ronald Walter Alexander Leslie	LD	262
Beaman, Gregory Ronald	UKI	412
Beanse, John Derek	LD	143
Beany, Captain	Bean	1
Beard, Christopher Nigel	Lab	50
Bearder, Catherine Zena	LD	313
Beasley, Janice Joanna	LD	552
Beavis, Ivan	Comm	287
Beckett, Jeremy William Ronald	LD	186
Beckett, Margaret Mary	Lab	183
Beer, Stephen	Lab	609
Beever, Gordon James	LD	155
Begg, Alexander Lawrie	Grn	656
Begg, Anne	Lab	4
Begg, John Lovet	LD	259
Begg, Judith	Lab	146
Beggs, Roy	UU	13
Beirne, John	LD	499
Beith, Alan James	LD	46
Bell, Gordon Alexander	Con	163
Bell, Jacqueline Dianne	LD	404
Bell, Joseph	WP	42
Bell, Mariana	UKI	632
Bell, Martin	Ind	91
Bell, Sarah Teresa Anne	PL	537

Candidate name	Party	Const. no.
Biddulph, Joseph Anthony	PL	460
Bigger, John Edgar	UKI	383
Biggins, Thomas Henry	Con	149
Biggs, Malcolm John	UKI	621
Bignell, Michael Graham	LD	417
Billcliffe, Stephen	Lab	419
Bingham, Bruce Simon	Grn	395
Binns, Robert Davidson	Con	59
Birchall, Grahame George	Lab	250
Bird, Elaine Louise	Lab	77
Bird, Michael Arthur	Con	605
Bishop, David Laurence	Elvis	91
Bissell, Karen Elizabeth	Con	624
Bissett, John	–	343
Black, David Michael	UKI	471
Blackall, Shareen	SSP	292
Blackburn, David	Grn	360
Blackman, Elizabeth Marion	Lab	241
Blair, Anthony Charles Lynton	Lab	506
Blake, Adrian George	UKI	552
Blake, Cynthia Nina	UKI	80
Bleakley, Robert Mark	LD	648
Blears, Hazel Anne	Lab	502
Blizzard, Bob	Lab	616
Bloom, Godfrey William	UKI	94
Blunkett, David	Lab	510
Blunt, Crispin Jeremy Rupert	Con	475
Blunt, John	UKI	185
Boaden, Michael William	Lab	454
Boateng, Paul Yaw	Lab	89
Boddy, Nigel Frederick Harrison	LD	304
Boddy, Stephen Paul	LD	467
Boden, Richard Thomas	Grn	19
Boethe, Nahid	LD	308
Bolderson, Trevor	SL	459
Bolland, David John	Lab	384
Bolton, Robert Ian	WRP	387
Bone, Cora	–	197
Bone, Peter William	Con	619
Bonnar, William	SSP	272
Bonner, Timothy Peter Carleton	Con	586
Booker, Robert Anthony (known as Bob)	LD	295
Boomla, Kambiz	SA	462
Booth, Graham Harry	UKI	582
Booth, Janine Sandra	SA	341
Booth, John Richard	–	304
Booth, Marcus Ashley William	Con	12

Candidate name	Party	Const. no.
Brar, Novjot (known as Joti Brar)	SL	323
Brayshaw, John	BNP	82
Brazier, Julian William Hendy	Con	122
Brazil, Julian Charles Martin	LD	248
Breed, Colin Edward	LD	161
Brelsford, Noelle	Con	511
Brennan, Claire Josephine	Lab	254
Brennan, Dawn	SSP	151
Brennan, Kevin Denis	Lab	126
Brenton, David George	Lab	191
Brewer, Geoffrey Charles (known as Geoff)	LD	568
Bridges, John Richard	LD	551
Bridgwood, Peter John	UKI	524
Brienza, Gerardo (commonly known as Gerry)	PL	415
Brierley, Paul	Con	180
Briginshaw, Jane Rachel	Lab	493
Brinton, Helen Rosemary	Lab	456
Brinton, Sarah Virginia (Sal Brinton)	LD	120
Brisby, Tania Alexandra Teofana Beatrice	Con	92
Britcliffe, Peter	Con	334
Brocklehurst, Andrew	Con	588
Broderick, Hilary Janet	Lab	318
Brodie, Charles Gilchrist	LD	283
Brolly, Francis R.G.	SF	382
Brook, Sharron	LD	27
Brooke, Annette Lesley	LD	196
Brooke, Eric William	LD	460
Brookes, Denis	UKI	651
Brookes, Jane	UKI	652
Brookes, Nicola	UKI	574
Brooks, Jane	Con	391
Brooks, Mark James	Con	242
Brooks-Saxl, David	Grn	609
Brosnan, Terrenia Maria	PL	394
Brown, Colin David	UKI	386
Brown, Hilary Margaret	SNP	221
Brown, Iain	LD	414
Brown, James Gordon	Lab	210
Brown, Jonathan Michael	LD	358
Brown, Keith James	SNP	442
Brown, Keith John	LD	587
Brown, Lesley Frances	UKI	259
Brown, Nicholas Hugh	Lab	422
Brown, Russell Leslie	Lab	207
Brown, William John	UKI	301
Browne, Christopher Alan	UKI	493
Browne, Desmond Henry	Lab	347

Candidate name	Party	Const. no.
Burt, Richard George	LD	203
Burton, Allen Frederick	UKI	34
Bushell, John Gunther	Con	278
Bushill, Christopher Stanley	LD	493
Butcher, Alan Terence	Lab	650
Butcher, Timothy Richard	Con	264
Butler, Christine Margaret	Lab	132
Butler, Paul Anthony	SF	353
Butterfill, John Valentine	Con	80
Butterworth, Simone	LD	331
Buttrey, Richard Granville	UKI	106
Buxton, David Colleton	LD	369
Bye, James George (commonly known as Jamie)	UKI	134
Byers, Stephen John	Lab	592
Byrne, Frank	SSP	455
Byrne, Jim	SNP	273
Byrne, Rosemary	SSP	174
Byron, Josephine Margaret (commonly known as Jo)	LD	523
Cable, John Vincent (commonly known as Vincent)	LD	589
Caborn, Richard George	Lab	511
Cadwallender, Alan	UKI	181
Caffery, James	PL	57
Caiach, Sian Mair	PC	278
Caillard, Peter John	Con	225
Cairns, John David	Lab	283
Calder, Jamie Mackenzie	LD	179
Callan, Justin Patrick	UKI	125
Callison, James Stuart	LD	270
Calton, Patsy	LD	136
Cambridge, Graham (known as King Eddie Vee Minister For Yorkshire Tea Yorkshire Puddings and Elvis Music)	MRLP	658
Cameron, Alistair Ronald	LD	424
Cameron, David William Donald	Con	637
Cameron, Ian John Henry	Ind	304
Campbell, Alan	Lab	591
Campbell, Alasdair	Con	442
Campbell, Amanda Nicole	Lab	51
Campbell, Anne	Lab	116
Campbell, Betty	APNI	202
Campbell, Elizabeth Jennifer	Con	262
Campbell, Gregory Lloyd	DUP	382
Campbell, James Gordon Paul	Ind	113
Campbell, Peter John	Con	219
Campbell, Roderick Alexander McRobie	SNP	490
Campbell, Ronald	Lab	70
Campbell, Scott	Con	350

Candidate name	Party	Const. no.
Challen, Colin Robert	Lab	413
Challis, Stephen Charles	UKI	223
Chamberlain-Webber, James Anthony Amyas Seymour	UKI	95
Chamberlaine, George Frederick John	UKI	79
Chambers, David Ian Reginald	Con	642
Chamings, Richard John	UKI	644
Chandan, Sukant	SL	286
Chandler, Paul Jonathan	LD	644
Chandler-Oatts, Jacqueline Mary	Grn	625
Chapman, James Keith (commonly known as Ben)	Lab	635
Chapman, Keith Anthony	Con	351
Chapman, Martin	SA	1
Chapman, Simon Charles	Con	321
Chapman, Sydney Brooks	Con	144
Charlesworth, Malcolm	UKI	525
Charlesworth, Robert Andrew	LD	182
Charlesworth, Tim Leonard	Con	20
Charleton, Simon Patrick	Lab	475
Charlson, Paul Barry	Con	331
Charlton, Hugo	Grn	147
Charteris, John Anthony	Con	207
Chaudhry, Sultan Mahmood	LD	57
Chaytor, David Michael	Lab	108
Cheema, Surinder	SL	251
Chesters, Pamela Joy	Con	100
Chetwynd, Kevin	SL	277
Cheyne, Lilias Rider Haggard	Grn	71
Cheyney, Guy Rogi Southouse	UKI	436
Chidgey, David William George	LD	223
Chmiel, Ross Michael	LD	173
Chong, Yen-Chit (commonly known as Chit)	Grn	286
Chope, Christopher Robert	Con	146
Choudhry, Mushtaq	Ind	217
Choules, Francis David	SA	245
Christian, Louise	SA	325
Church, David John	SA	604
Church, Richard Wilfrid	LD	433
Clamp, Stephen Joseph	Lab	186
Clapham, Michael	Lab	28
Clappison, William James (known as James)	Con	318
Clare, William Geoffrey	Con	379
Clark, Derek Roland	UKI	434
Clark, Jillian Mary	Con	542
Clark, Lynda Margaret	Lab	230
Clark, Michael John	UKI	417
Clark, Paul	Lab	469
Clark, Paul Gordon	Lab	264

Candidate name	Party	Const. no.
Clark, Timothy Richard	UKI	561
Clarke, Anthony Richard (commonly known as Tony)	Lab	434
Clarke, Charles Rodway	Lab	437
Clarke, Kenneth Harry	Con	494
Clarke, Lloyd	MRLP	389
Clarke, Thomas	Lab	153
Clegg, John Anthony	SA	396
Clelland, David Gordon	Lab	590
Cliff, Janet Mary	Grn	381
Cliff, Michael John William	–	505
Clifford-Jackson, Vivienne Helen	LD	427
Clifton-Brown, Geoffrey	Con	162
Close, Seamus Anthony	APNI	353
Clouston, William Stuart James	Con	213
Clwyd, Ann	Lab	175
Coad, Diana Victoria	Con	522
Coaker, Vernon Rodney	Lab	263
Cochrane, Philip Andrew	Con	533
Cochrane, Robert	SL	174
Cockings, Ronald Ernest (commonly known as Ron)	LD	610
Cockshott, William Paul	SSP	152
Coffey, Ann	Lab	539
Cohen, Elaina	Con	482
Cohen, Harry Michael	Lab	371
Cole, Catherine Helena (known as Helena)	LD	307
Cole, Charles John	UKI	85
Cole, Robert Ian Gawain	Con	192
Coleman, Christopher Francis	LD	544
Coleman, Iain	Lab	294
Coles, Stephen Ralph	UKI	295
Coleshill, Gail Marie	LD	608
Collard, Geoff	Grn	97
Collett, Adrian Paul	LD	7
Collignon, Bernard Michael	UKI	243
Collings, Phillip Maurice MacSherry	UKI	313
Collins, Timothy William George	Con	628
Collins, William Shane Barbor (commonly known as Shane)	Grn	601
Collinson, Robert John	Con	168
Colman, Anthony John (commonly known as Tony)	Lab	468
Colvile, Oliver Newton	Con	458
Commons, John Patrick Bryans	LD	514
Compton, Gareth Francis Thomas	Con	601
Comrie, David	Con	266
Congdon, David Leonard	Con	169
Connarty, Michael	Lab	246
Connell, Stewart McNulty	Con	265
Connett, Alan Michael	LD	458

Candidate name	Party	Const. no.
Conquest, Steven Graham	Lab	570
Conway, Derek Leslie	Con	444
Conway, Patrick Joseph Anthony	Lab	656
Cook, Elaine Dupree	PL	95
Cook, Francis	Lab	540
Cook, James Stuart	Con	590
Cook, Margaret Jane (commonly known as Jane)	Grn	217
Cook, Richard Elliot	Con	267
Cook, Robin	Lab	380
Cook, Stephen Robert (Steve)	SL	340
Cooke, Andrew Simon	Con	344
Cooke, Christopher Worley Radcliffe	UKI	653
Cooke, Daniel Edward	LD	621
Cooksey, Max	Ind	10
Cooksley, Michael John	Ind	618
Coomber, Alan Roy	UKI	306
Coombs, Lawrence William	SA	541
Coombs, Richard	PC	10
Coombs, Simon Christopher	Con	568
Cooper, David Arthur	UKI	193
Cooper, Denis Richard	UKI	389
Cooper, Helen Bridget (known as Maddy Cooper)	SA	298
Cooper, James	UU	252
Cooper, Margaret Kathleen (commonly known as Maggie)	Lab	131
Cooper, Mark Geoffrey	LD	527
Cooper, Yvette	Lab	459
Coote, Mark Steven	Con	306
Cope, John Arthur	BNP	103
Copus, Richard Anthony Argent	LD	245
Corbyn, Jeremy Bernard	Lab	340
Cordon, Simon Robert	LD	561
Cormack, Sir Patrick Thomas	Con	535
Cornelius, Steven	PC	175
Cornforth, John Henry	UKI	332
Cornforth, John William	PL	301
Cornoch, Edward	SSP	374
Cornwell, Andrew	Grn	298
Corston, Jean Ann	Lab	97
Cossar, Andrew James	Con	452
Cotter, Brian Joseph	LD	629
Cotton, Bevis Malory (Known as Bev)	Grn	23
Cotton, Christopher Mark	LD	412
Cotton, John Anthony	Con	65
Course, Richard	–	237
Courtney, Margaret Mary	WRP	116
Cousins, James Anthony	Con	281
Cousins, James Mackay	Lab	421

Candidate name	Party	Const. no.
Cowell, Valerie Lilian	UKI	67
Cowling, Richard	Con	3
Cox, Anthea Jane	Lab	118
Cox, Charles Geoffrey	Con	191
Cox, Gavin Cameron	LD	477
Cox, Michael Francis	LD	492
Cox, Thomas Michael	Lab	581
Crab, Ginger	JWP	345
Crabb, Stephen	Con	465
Craig, Moira	LD	152
Cran, James Douglas	Con	48
Cranston, Kevin David	Grn	552
Cranston, Ross Frederick	Lab	203
Crausby, David Anthony	Lab	73
Crawford, James	Country	486
Crawford, William	UKI	10
Crean, Fraser	UKI	643
Cremer, Iris Mary Jessie	SL	87
Crichton, Donald Finlayson	Lab	486
Cridge, Dennis	SL	56
Crisp, Alan George	UKI	474
Crocker, Henry Frederick	UKI	234
Crompton, Ian Edward	UKI	107
Crompton, Miles	LD	28
Cronin, Helen Dawn (commonly known as Lady Muck)	RRL	374
Cronin, Janice	UKI	444
Crookes, Lance David	Grn	655
Crosbie, Jonathan Craig	UKI	312
Cross, Carl Robert	Con	618
Cross, Timothy Phillip	UKI	650
Croston, Roger Philip	UKI	167
Croucher, Lynn Mary Florence	UKI	580
Croucher, Mark Christopher	UKI	178
Crowther, David	LD	391
Cruddas, Jonathan (known as Jon)	Lab	176
Cryer, Constance Ann (commonly known as Ann)	Lab	344
Cryer, John Robert	Lab	324
Cuell, Timothy James	UKI	307
Cullen, Terence	SL	65
Cumbers, Andrew	SSP	2
Cuming, Richard Andrew	Con	401
Cummings, John Scott	Lab	218
Cunningham, James Dolan	Lab	165
Cunningham, John Anderson	Lab	158
Cunningham, Thomas Anthony	Lab	647
Curran, Frances	SSP	452
Curry, David Maurice	Con	520

Candidate name	Party	Const. no.
Curteis, Henry Malcolm Thomas	UKI	517
Curtis, George Seymour	UKI	244
Curtis-Thomas, Claire	Lab	168
Cuthbertson, Ian Michael	LD	192
Cutts, David	UKI	488
Dailey, Prudence Mary Prior	Con	460
Daisley, Paul Andrew	Lab	87
Dale, Douglas	LD	602
Dale, Graham William	Lab	317
Dale-Mills, Colin	UKI	317
Daley, Wayne	Con	70
Dallat, John James	SDLP	382
Dalyell, Tam	Lab	374
Dandridge, Christopher Ronald	Lab	483
Dardi, Harbhajan Singh	SL	610
Darby, Simon	BNP	203
Darley, Andrew	LD	251
Darling, Alistair Maclean	Lab	227
Darvill, Keith Ernest	Lab	595
Dash, Brian David	LD	416
Date, Andrew Richard	Lab	41
Dauncey, Alexander James (commonly known as Alec)	LD	465
Davenport, Christopher Hugh	Con	291
Davenport, Keith John	FDP	178
Davey, Edward Jonathon	LD	348
Davey, Valerie	Lab	100
David, Wayne	Lab	112
Davidson, Andrew	UU	258
Davidson, Eric Robert Still	UKI	24
Davidson, Ian Graham	Lab	271
Davidson, Michael	BNP	47
Davidson, Norman Alfred	RRL	250
Davidson, Robert Lowington	M	59
Davies, Andrew Robert Tudor	Con	126
Davies, Christopher Gareth	LD	1
Davies, Christopher John	Grn	495
Davies, Clive Winston	UKI	406
Davies, David	LD	415
Davies, David John Denzil	Lab	381
Davies, Geraint Richard	Lab	169
Davies, Glyn	Comm	10
Davies, Harry	LD	537
Davies, Helene Yvette	UKI	119
Davies, John Paul	–	531
Davies, John Quentin	Con	279
Davies, Julia Mary	LD	103
Davies, Michael Edward (known as Mick)	Grn	548

Candidate name	Party	Const. no.
Dingwall, Alexander	SNP	270
Dingwall, Marion	Lab	455
Dismore, Andrew Hartley	Lab	312
Ditta, Allah	PJP	57
Divers, Desmond	SSP	16
Dixon, John Leslie	LD	124
Dixon, Jonathan Mark	Grn	504
Dixon, Michael David	LD	642
Dixon, Simon Neil	Grn	131
Dixon, William James	–	252
Djanogly, Jonathan Simon	Con	333
Dobbie, Joseph	BNP	558
Dobbin, James	Lab	320
Dobbs, Bob	FP	96
Dobbs, Dave	FP	95
Dobbshead, Simon	FP	328
Dobrashian, Thomas	LD	470
Dobson, Frank Gordon	Lab	323
Docherty, Alan Sidney	SA	177
Docherty, Josephine	SNP	267
Docherty, Thomas	Lab	572
Dodds, Nigel Alexander	DUP	43
Doherty, Pat	SF	593
Donald, Nona	Ind	657
Donaldson, Jeffrey Mark	UU	353
Donaldson, Jim	LD	3
Donnelly, Elizabeth Anne	Lab	521
Donnelly, Francis	WP	594
Donnelly, James Alan	Con	208
Donohoe, Brian Harold	Lab	174
Donovan, Nigel Robert	Lib	328
Donovan, Simon Peter	S Alt	606
Doran, Frank	Lab	2
Dorrell, Stephen James	Con	134
Doughty, Rodger William	UKI	373
Doughty, Susan Kathleen	LD	285
Dow, Charles Alistair	LD	56
Dowd, James Patrick	Lab	370
Dowdney, Neil Francis	UKI	631
Downie, Celia Mary	LD	366
Doyle, Michael Paul	LD	344
Drake, Timothy Jason	LD	168
Drew, David Elliott	Lab	552
Driver, Christopher Anthony Peter (commonly known as Screwy Driver)	RRL	506
Driver, Michael Robert	WRP	511
Drown, Julia Kate	Lab	568

Candidate name	Party	Const. no.
Edwards, Jeffrey	Ind	401
Edwards, Judith Caroline	Con	376
Edwards, Paul Anthony	Grn	245
Edwards, Robert Charles	UKI	191
Efford, Clive Stanley	Lab	236
Eldridge, Colin William	LD	643
Elgood, Paul Steven	LD	649
Elliott, Graham James	Grn	616
Ellis, David Brian	Lab	496
Ellis, Jonathan Mark Henry	LD	78
Ellis, Mark Caldor	UKP	508
Ellis, Trevor Keith	LD	244
Ellman, Louise Joyce	Lab	376
Ellwood, Anthony Robin	UKI	619
Ellwood, Tobias	Con	648
Elphick, Felicity Ann Ledgerwood	Con	652
Elphicke, Charles Brett Anthony	Con	498
Elvin, Ann Margaret	LD	553
Emmerson-Peirce, Yvonne Lesley	LD	503
Ennis, Jeffrey	Lab	27
Entwistle, Dorothy Edna	SL	648
Epps, Gareth Daniel	LD	637
Ereira, Mark Alan	Lab	110
Erlam, Andrew Barnes	Lab	138
Ervine, David Walter	Prog U	42
Etheridge, Kevin	LD	342
Etherington, William	Lab	557
Evans, David Doiran	LD	128
Evans, Jason Philip	Con	583
Evans, Kenneth	SL	401
Evans, Malcolm William	PC	652
Evans, Nigel Martin	Con	479
Evans, Richard George	Con	312
Evans, Roger Kenneth	Con	409
Evennett, David Anthony	Con	50
Everest, Roger Joseph	Ind	138
Ewing, Annabelle	SNP	455
Exmouth, Viscount Paul Edward	UKI	573
Eyre, Stephen John Arthur	Con	546
Eyres, George William	Lab	226
Fabricant, Michael Louis David	Con	372
Fagan, John Willoughby Feltrim	UKI	634
Fairburn, Andrew	Con	164
Fairweather, Gwendoline (known as Gwen)	LD	491
Fairweather, Julian Philip	UKI	456
Faith, Daniel Philip (commonly known as Danny)	SA	90

Candidate name	Party	Const. no.
Falkner, Kishwer	LD	345
Fallon, Michael Cathel	Con	508
Fallon, Paul John	Lab	494
Farage, Nigel Paul	UKI	49
Farmer, Graeme William	Grn	227
Farrell, Marietta	SDLP	201
Farrelly, Christopher Paul (known as Paul)	Lab	420
Farren, Ciara	SDLP	42
Farren, Sean	SDLP	14
Farron, Timothy James	LD	628
Faulkner, Michael Patrick	UKI	501
Fawcett, Neil Macgregor	LD	609
Feakes, Alexander David	LD	37
Feaster, Stephen	UKI	496
Featherstone, Edward Harry	LD	317
Featherstone, Lynne Choona	LD	325
Feeley, Robina Lynn (known as Bobby)	LD	150
Fegan, Christopher	Lab	154
Feisenberger, James Rosewell	UKI	169
Fenn, Stephen John	LD	145
Ferguson, Antony David	LD	441
Fernandes, Uma	Con	585
Ferriday, Nicholas Peter (commonly known as Nic)	Grn	90
Field, Carole Ann	LD	212
Field, Frank	Lab	52
Field, Mark Christopher	Con	147
Fildes, Susan Frances Maria	Con	655
Finkelstein, Daniel William	Con	303
Finlay, Darren	LD	360
Finlayson, Roderick	SL	219
Finley, William	UKI	360
Finn, Alexander William Galletly Gonzalez	Con	402
Finnegan-Butler, Anthony Cyril	UKI	305
Finnie, Peter Weldon Llewelyn	Con	228
Firth, Alison Pamela	LD	510
Firth, John Lester	Con	447
Fischer, Brian Bernhard	SL	513
Fisher, Gerald Alexander	SNP	207
Fisher, Mark	Lab	542
Fisher, Paul Simon Luke	Lab	529
Fitchett, Keith	LD	19
Fitton, David Arthur Hayden	Ind	653
Fitzpatrick, James	SL	590
Fitzpatrick, James (commonly known as Jim)	Lab	462
Fitzsimons, Lorna	Lab	482
Flack, John Christopher	Con	238
Flanagan, John Anthony	Lab	156

Candidate name	Party	Const. no.
Fleming, Malcolm Gilchrist	SNP	261
Fletcher, David Alan	LD	107
Fletcher, Kate Anne	LD	20
Fletcher, Roger	LD	181
Fletcher, Suzanne	LD	541
Flight, Howard Emerson	Con	17
Flint, Caroline Louise	Lab	193
Flook, Adrian John	Con	571
Flynn, David	SL	76
Flynn, Francis Michael	LD	388
Flynn, George Stephen	UKI	473
Flynn, John Patrick	UKI	614
Flynn, Michael John	Con	420
Flynn, Paul Phillip	Lab	425
Fogg, Alan David	SL	352
Follett, Daphne Barbara (commonly known as Barbara)	Lab	537
Foote, Celia	LA	358
Foote Wood, Chris	LD	63
Forbes, Jayne Elizabeth	Grn	325
Forbes, Linda Craig	LD	613
Forbes, Ronnie	SL	247
Ford, Belinda Jane	LD	444
Ford, David R.J.	APNI	15
Ford, John Edward	LD	139
Fordham, Katherine Elizabeth	Lab	617
Foreman, Shona	SSP	3
Forgione, Marco Felice	Con	656
Forrest, Paul Ian James	UKI	377
Forsdyke, Richard John	Con	284
Forth, Eric	Con	101
Forth, Thomas Edward (commonly known as Edward)	LD	480
Foster, Derek	Lab	63
Foster, Donald Michael Ellison	LD	33
Foster, John Odell	Comm	268
Foster, Michael Jabez	Lab	306
Foster, Michael John	Lab	644
Foulkes, George	Lab	130
Fox, Albert (commonly known as Albie)	Con	657
Fox, Ashley Peter	Con	33
Fox, Bridget	LD	219
Fox, Colin	SSP	231
Fox, Liam	Con	643
Fox, Paul	LD	625
Frain-Bell, William	Con	292
Frances, Helen	LD	187
Francis, Alan Herbert	Grn	406
Francis, David Hywel	Lab	1

Candidate name	Party	Const. no.
Gascoyne, James Campbell	UKI	250
Gaskell, Christopher Michael	LD	9
Gaskell, Peter Kevin	LD	619
Gasson, Emily Jane	LD	197
Gasson, Jacqueline Anne (known as Jacqui)	LD	126
Gates, Anthony John	PL	138
Gates, Michael Anthony	Lab	428
Gauke, David Michael	Con	87
Gault, Wayne Gordon	SNP	2
Gayler, David Richard	LD	257
Gayler, Mark Adrian	LD	158
Geary, Ian David	Lab	8
Geddes, Keith	Lab	588
Gee-Turner, Adrian John	LD	176
George, Andrew Henry	LD	501
George, Bruce Thomas	Lab	605
George, Kenneth John	MK	161
Gerrard, Neil Francis	Lab	606
Gibb, Nicholas John	Con	71
Gibb, Stewart	SNP	230
Gibbons, Ivan Anthony	Lab	316
Gibson, Brian	SL	506
Gibson, Ian	Lab	436
Gibson, Mark	LCA	454
Gibson, Robert	UKI	628
Gidley, Sandra Julia	LD	485
Gilbert, Paul	UKI	534
Gilbert, Terence Anthony	LD	338
Gilchrist, Phillip Norman	LD	635
Gildernew, Michelle	SF	252
Gill, John	SA	459
Gill, Parmjit Singh	LD	362
Gillam, Anthony John	LD	263
Gillan, Cheryl Elise Kendall	Con	139
Gillard, Christopher Roland (known as Roly)	RRL	568
Gillett, David Bright	Grn	314
Gillman, Ian Francis	UKI	159
Gilman, Charles Edward Lewis	Grn	493
Gilroy, Linda	Lab	458
Gledhill, Bob	Grn	626
Glen, John Philip	Con	457
Glencross, Roger Edmund	CPA	632
Glennon, Steve	SA	537
Glover, Peter	SA	76
Glover, Richard	UKI	497
Goddard, Stephen Howard (known as Steve)	LD	449
Godfrey, Thomas Paul Hicks (known as Paul)	UKI	420
Godsiff, Roger Duncan	Lab	61

Candidate name	Party	Const. no.
Godward, Steven John	SA	54
Goffin, Julia Elaine	PL	317
Goggins, Paul Gerard	Lab	655
Gold, David Stanley	Con	96
Goldie, Ian Roy	SNP	404
Goldspink, Madeline Hermione (known as Mione)	LD	315
Gollins, James Grimsahw	Ind	517
Golton, Barry Stewart	LD	413
Goodall, Brian John	SNP	211
Goodall, Robert	Ind	186
Goodfellow, Alan George William	Lab	416
Goodman, Michael Neil	Lab	160
Goodman, Paul Alexander Cyril	Con	653
Gordon, David Alexander	UKI	194
Gordon, Eileen	Lab	484
Gorn, Linda June	LD	411
Goss, Julian Beresford	SA	123
Gough, Matthew James Charles	Grn	363
Goupillot, Robert Paul	SSP	404
Govier, Andrew James	Lab	571
Grace, David	Lab	133
Graffin, Janette	SF	13
Graham, Andrew James	Ind	236
Graham, Gavin John Elliot	Grn	142
Graham, Kim-Elisabeth Rachel	UKI	31
Graham, Michael	Con	158
Graham, Patricia Margaret	PL	452
Graham, Robert	PL	451
Graham-Leigh, Elaine Amanda	Grn	238
Grainger, Henry Marshall	LD	526
Grant, Catriona Mary	SSP	229
Grant, Nicholas John (commonly known as Nick)	SA	215
Grant, Peter Michael	SA	502
Gratton, Shaun Christopher	SL	338
Gray, Andrew John Plevins	Grn	422
Gray, Ashley	Con	161
Gray, Clive John	LD	508
Gray, James Whiteside	Con	631
Gray-Fisk, Delphine Isabel	UKI	419
Grayling, Christopher Stephen	Con	240
Green, Damian Howard	Con	19
Green, David William	Lib	530
Green, Harold Stephen	RUK	475
Green, John Gorman	SNP	5
Green, Matthew Roger	LD	385
Green, Nathaniel Jacob (known as Nat Green)	LD	323
Green, Simon	LD	199
Greene, William Louis (commonly known as Bill Greene)	LD	334

Candidate name	Party	Const. no.
Greenfield, Christopher John	LD	349
Greenfield, Mark	LD	558
Greenhalgh, Ian	LD	320
Greening, Justine	Con	215
Greenway, John Robert	Con	496
Greenwood, Sarah Frances	Grn	602
Greer, Alan James	Con	13
Gregor MacGregor, Neil Andrew Vincent	Con	241
Gregory, Ian Neil	UKI	102
Gretton, John Collis	PEC	53
Grey, Steven George	UKI	623
Grieve, Dominic Charles Roberts	Con	36
Griffin, Jean	BNP	143
Griffin, Nicholas John	BNP	446
Griffith, Andrew John	Con	159
Griffith, Peter Crichton	UKI	489
Griffiths, Andrew James	Con	203
Griffiths, David Brandon	LD	149
Griffiths, Jane Patricia	Lab	470
Griffiths, Llyr Hughes	PC	129
Griffiths, Michael	SA	602
Griffiths, Nigel	Lab	231
Griffiths, Robert David	Comm	424
Griffiths, Trevor Nigel	LD	618
Griffiths, Winston James (known as Win)	Lab	92
Grigg, Richard Rhys	PC	123
Grogan, John	Lab	507
Guest, George Matthew	UKI	150
Guest, John Michael	LD	127
Gueterbock, Richard Stanley	Con	528
Gulleford, Kenneth Arnold	UKI	91
Gummer, John Selwyn	Con	554
Gunstock, Ashley	Grn	371
Gunter, Luise Victoria Margaretta	Con	569
Guthrie, Peter Coulter	Lab	307
Gutteridge, Philip Gareth Llewellyn	UKI	385
Guynan, David Edward	BNP	557
Hackley, Bryn	LD	108
Hadfield, David	SL	511
Hadley, Michael Peter James	LD	646
Hague, William Jefferson	Con	480
Hail, Ian Stewart	Con	209
Hain, Peter Gerald	Lab	415
Haines, Lila Eilis Maire	PC	125
Haines, Michael Anthony (commonly known as Tony)	Ind	522
Hakewill, James Charles	Con	185

Candidate name	Party	Const. no.
Haley, Martin Arthur	UKI	131
Halfon, Robert Henry	Con	300
Halfpenny, Jim	SSP	451
Hall, Alan Charles (to be known as Charles)	LD	489
Hall, Brian John	UKI	237
Hall, David	Ind	118
Hall, Michael Thomas	Lab	618
Hall, Patrick	Lab	38
Hall, Robert William	Lab	435
Hall, Vanessa	Grn	394
Hall-Matthews, David	LD	359
Hallam, David John Alfred	Lab	314
Hamblen, Clare Alison	LD	476
Hames, Duncan	LD	615
Hames, Michael Denis	RRL	533
Hamilton, Berlyne (known as Bill)	SA	176
Hamilton, David	Lab	404
Hamilton, Fabian	Lab	358
Hammerson, Peter Roy	Ind	470
Hammond, Philip	Con	493
Hammond, Stephen William	Con	632
Hancock, Bleddyn William	PC	460
Hancock, Michael Thomas	LD	464
Hanks, Dancing Ken	MRLP	138
Hansard, Charles Christopher Trevor	Con	98
Hanson, Anders Paul	LD	183
Hanson, Anne Margaret	Lab	431
Hanson, David George	Lab	180
Harasiwka, Frank	LD	74
Harby, Melvin (known as Charlie)	Ind	18
Hardeman, Kenneth George	Con	60
Harding-Price, David	LD	418
Hardy, Alan	UKI	526
Hardy, Mary-Rose	LD	659
Hardy, Stephen Philip	LD	49
Hargreaves, Jeremy Arthur	LD	494
Harley, Patrick Edward	LD	288
Harman, Harriet	Lab	115
Harper, Alastair Douglas	UKI	211
Harper, Justin David	UKI	21
Harper, Margaret Mary	Con	566
Harper, Mark James	Con	257
Harpham, Barbara Anne	Con	403
Harris, David William	Ind	332
Harris, Edward Murray	Lab	24
Harris, Evan Leslie	LD	450
Harris, Geoffrey	UKI	392

Candidate name	Party	Const. no.
Harris, Michael Ross	Con	557
Harris, Nicholas Paul	LD	407
Harris, Peter Richard Bloomfield	LD	515
Harris, Stephen Andrew	UKI	23
Harris, Thomas Oliver Craig (commonly known as Tom)	Con	481
Harris, Tom	Lab	267
Harris, Vicki	LD	455
Harrison, Josephine Kathleen (commonly known as Jo)	LD	535
Harrison, Martin Edmund Ranby	Grn	77
Harrison, William	SL	141
Hart, Stephen James Scott	Lab	366
Harthman, John Paul	Con	512
Hartley, Alan William	LD	26
Hartley, Jon	Lab	31
Hartnell, Joan	SL	213
Hartwell, Gareth Gerard	LD	90
Harvey, Andrew	SSP	261
Harvey, Ian George Hamilton	UKI	139
Harvey, John Stuart	UKI	367
Harvey, Martin	UKI	103
Harvey, Michael James	UKI	638
Harvey, Nicholas Andrew Lawton	Grn	482
Harvey, Nicholas Barton	LD	189
Harvey, Tina Louise	LP	434
Haselhurst, Alan Gordon Barraclough	Con	497
Hassan, Emine	Ref	340
Hastilow, Nigel Graham	Con	53
Hatton, Janet Elizabeth	UKI	148
Haughey, Eilis	SDLP	594
Havard, David Stuart (known as Dai)	Lab	401
Haw, Alistair Macdonald	Con	283
Hawkings, Marilyn Ann	Lab	33
Hawkins, Lisa	UKI	508
Hawkins, Nicholas John	Con	560
Hawkins, Philip Kemplay	Lab	244
Hawkins, Robert James	SL	457
Hawthorn, Ewan Gordon	LD	220
Haxby, Donald Leslie	Ind	418
Hay, William	DUP	258
Hayball, John David	SL	348
Haycock, John Bernard	Ind	366
Hayden, Francis Edward	Grn	608
Hayes, Andrew Robert	Con	633
Hayes, John Henry	Con	525
Hayes, Marcus David	Con	534
Hayes, Simon Alexander	Con	381
Hayman, Judith Lynne	LD	221

Candidate name	Party	Const. no.
Hinchliffe, David Martin	Lab	602
Hirsch, Muriel Josephine	SA	166
Hitchcock, Simon John	Con	141
Hoban, Mark Gerard	Con	249
Hoban, Wayne	LD	238
Hobbins, Peter James	Con	477
Hobbs, John Michael	SA	300
Hobson, Phylip Andrew David (commonly known as Phil Hobson)	LD	394
Hocking, Stephen John	Con	550
Hockney, Nicholas Richard Alexander Damian	UKI	345
Hodge, Linda Jane	PL	449
Hodge, Margaret Eve	Lab	25
Hoey, Catharine Letitia (known as Kate)	Lab	601
Hoey, Thomas Anthony (Tony)	PL	117
Hogg, Rt. Hon. Douglas Martin	Con	521
Hoile, Richard David	Con	362
Holbrook, Simon Andrew	LD	636
Holden, Barrie Leslie	Con	182
Holden, Sean Francis	Con	135
Holden, Terence John Edward	PL	404
Holdsworth, Nancy	UKI	520
Holdsworth, Petrina Alexandra	UKI	562
Hollands, Jason Daniel	Con	325
Hollebone, Raymond Thomas	UKI	589
Holley, Alison Shirley	Con	32
Hollingsworth, James	Con	184
Hollobone, Philip Thomas	Con	346
Holmes, Adrian St. John	Grn	437
Holmes, David Laurence	Ind	339
Holmes, Michael Andrew	SL	527
Holmes, Paul Robert	LD	141
Holmes, Paul Thomas	Lib	248
Holmes, Thomas Frank	NF	576
Holt, Alan Mark	SL	168
Holt, Doreen	LD	67
Homan, Lisa Faith	Lab	563
Hood, Jimmy	Lab	152
Hook, Antony James	LD	200
Hook, Jane	LD	451
Hooker, Sean James	LD	144
Hoon, Geoffrey William	Lab	18
Hope, Alan (commonly known as Howling Lord)	MRLP	7
Hope, James Douglas Sinclair	UKI	642
Hope, Jill Susan	LD	299
Hope, Philip Ian	Lab	159
Hopkins, Kelvin Peter	Lab	386

Candidate name	Party	Const. no.
Hussain, Iftkhar	Con	61
Hussain, Imran	UKI	84
Hussain, Mahmood	M	57
Hussain, Mushtaq	Lab	548
Hussain, Parwez	PJP	56
Hussain, Sabir	Lab	638
Hussain, Shafaq	PJP	61
Hutchens, Kevin John	Lab	5
Hutchin, Stuart James	UKI	96
Hutton, Isabel	SNP	246
Hutton, John Matthew Patrick	Lab	29
Hutton, Lewis	LD	273
Hutton, Steven Robert	Grn	114
Hutty, Philip Andrew	LD	190
Hyde, Richard John	Lab	199
Iddon, Brian	Lab	74
Illsley, Eric Evlyn	Lab	26
Inchley, Andrew Philip	Lab	120
Ingram, Adam	Lab	220
Ingram, Gerald Aleck	UKI	90
Inkin, Susan Lilian (Susie)	Con	599
Ion, Michael Gerard	Lab	518
Iqbal, Zahid	Con	82
Irranca-Davies, Ifor Huw	Lab	86
Isherwood, Mark	Con	10
Ivey, Paul Crago	Con	310
Jack, John Michael	Con	259
Jacks, Kevin Michael	Grn	307
Jackson, Andrew	SSP	210
Jackson, Christian Michael	BNP	453
Jackson, David	LD	272
Jackson, Glenda May	Lab	298
Jackson, Helen Margaret	Lab	514
Jackson, Jane Mary	LD	392
Jackson, Robert Victor	Con	609
Jackson, Stewart James	Con	456
Jacob, John Howard	UKI	504
Jacobsen, David Don	SL	229
Jaffa, Robert Harvey (known as Sam)	Lab	223
James, Brian Norman	UKI	441
James, Paul Simon	Con	275
James, Simon Alexander	LD	581
James, Timothy David Richard (commonly known as Jimmy)	Con	150
Jamieson, David Charles	Lab	457
Jappy, William (commonly known as Bill)	Ind	411
Jardine, Catherine (commonly known as Kate Pickering)	Con	151

Candidate name	Party	Const. no.
Jebb, Henry Walter Gladwyn	LD	543
Jefferys, Michael John	Lab	556
Jeffries, Michael Paul	SA	574
Jemetta, Paul Louis	Con	352
Jenkin, Bernard Christison	Con	244
Jenkin, Conan James Trevenen	MK	586
Jenking, Joyce Lilian	UKI	126
Jenkins, Brian David	Lab	569
Jenkins, Ian Clive	LD	651
Jenkins, Peter	UKI	197
Jenkins, Richard William Arthur Howard	Con	337
Jenkins, Ruth Gudren	Grn	531
Jenkins, Timothy Charles	UKI	565
Jenkinson, Jeanette	UKI	330
Jenner, William John	UKI	280
Jennings, Brian David Timothy	LD	357
Jephcott, Benedict John Alexander	LD	518
Jeremy, Madeleine Elise	PL	123
Jeremy, Sara Hazel	PL	92
Jeremy, William Blair Richard	LD	129
Jethwa, Raj Kumar	Lab	299
Jobbins, Sion Tomos	PC	124
Jobson, Anne Margaret	Con	245
Johal, Satbir Singh	SL	623
John, Helen	Ind	506
Johns, Ramon Paul	BNP	237
Johnson, Alan Arthur	Lab	332
Johnson, Alexander Boris	Con	313
Johnson, Caroline Nicola	SA	59
Johnson, Clare Denise	PL	434
Johnson, Darren Paul	Grn	368
Johnson, Diana Ruth	Lab	91
Johnson, Gareth Alan	Con	370
Johnston, Liam Padraig Martin	SF	547
Johnson, Melanie Jane	Lab	621
Johnson, Peter Frank	UKI	55
Johnson, Sandra	LD	54
Johnston, Stephen	SA	356
Johnstone, Marcus	Lab	479
Jones, Andrew Hanson	Con	301
Jones, Barry	Lab	296
Jones, Barry Mark	UKI	222
Jones, Brendon	LD	536
Jones, Carole Elizabeth	Lab	553
Jones, David Arthur	Ind	351
Jones, David Ian	Con	140
Jones, David Richard	Con	410

Candidate name	Party	Const. no.
Jones, Denise Idris	Lab	399
Jones, Dyfan Rhys	PC	381
Jones, Fiona Elizabeth Ann	Lab	418
Jones, Helen Mary	Lab	611
Jones, Hugh William	UKI	465
Jones, Jenny	Grn	205
Jones, John Tudor	LD	180
Jones, Kevan David	Lab	212
Jones, Laurence Cresswell	Con	530
Jones, Leslie (known as Les)	Con	288
Jones, Lynne Mary	Lab	60
Jones, Malcolm John	SA	391
Jones, Martyn David	Lab	149
Jones, Nigel David	LD	138
Jones, Peter Maxwell	LD	21
Jones, Simon Christopher	UKI	359
Jones, Terence Frederick (commonly known as Terry)	UKI	236
Jouhl, Avtar Singh	SL	59
Jowell, Tessa Jane	Lab	205
Joyce, Eric	Lab	247
Juby, Geoffrey William	LD	398
Jukes, Christopher John	Lab	600
Juned, Susan Aysha	LD	548
Kalinauckas, Paul	Lab	535
Kamall, Syed Salah	Con	625
Kane, Rosie	SSP	273
Kapoor, Anita	Con	195
Karran, Thelma	Con	602
Katz, Michael David	Lab	147
Kaufman, Gerald Bernard	Lab	395
Kawczynski, Daniel Robert	Con	217
Kearney, Peter	SNP	153
Keaveney, Paula Clare	LD	375
Keeble, Sally Curtis	Lab	433
Keen, Alan	Lab	251
Keen, Ann	Lab	90
Keene, Janet Hazel	Lab	81
Keetch, Paul Stuart	LD	314
Kefford, Peter Jonathan	UKI	303
Kelley, Gerald David	UKI	530
Kelley, Joan	UKI	612
Kelly, Anthony	SL	83
Kelly, Brian John	SA	205
Kelly, Dolores	SDLP	596
Kelly, Gerry	SF	43
Kelly, John Joseph	SF	14

Candidate name	Party	Const. no.
Kingman, Alison Elaine	LD	316
Kingsley, Christopher Rupert	UKI	366
Kingsley, Denise Sara	Grn	615
Kinnear, Douglas	SSP	350
Kirk, Gillian	Lab	450
Kirk, Madeleine Anne	LD	235
Kirkbride, Julie	Con	102
Kirkham, John Humphrey (known as Jack)	UKI	611
Kirkpatrick, Shaun Alan	SL	363
Kirkup, Michael Raymond	Ind	607
Kirkwood, Archibald Johnstone	LD	490
Klein, Amos Phillip	–	298
Klepacka, Beata Anna	PL	119
Knapman, Roger Maurice	UKI	189
Knapper, Adrian Mark	Ind	544
Knight, David Edgar	UKI	299
Knight, Gregory	Con	659
Knight, Jim	Lab	198
Knight, Winifred Irene	LD	488
Knopp, Gregory John	UKI	135
Knotts, John Martin	UKI	546
Knowles, Nigel	Lab	385
Koksal, Saim	Ref	287
Kraft, Derek	Lab	629
Kulka, Jane Nicola	LD	475
Kumar, Ashok	Lab	403
Kumar, Suresh	Con	336
Kysow, Jean	SA	369
Labern, Sally Ann	SA	371
Ladwa, Kirti	UKI	362
Ladyman, Stephen John	Lab	577
Laing, Angus Wallace	Con	486
Laing, Eleanor Fulton	Con	239
Laing, James Stewart	Lab	576
Lait, Jacqueline Anne Harkness	Con	37
Lake, Rachael Isabel	Con	607
Laker, John Stephen	Grn	653
Lamb, Norman Peter	LD	428
Lammy, David Lindon	Lab	585
Lancaster, John Mark	Con	441
Landels, David William	SSP	283
Lane, John Watson	UKI	522
Lane, Michael John (known as Mike Lane)	SL	378
Langford, Barry Francis	Lab	481
Langford, Pippa	Lab	48
Langley, Michael Paul	SL	97

Candidate name	Party	Const. no.
Langmaid, Alan	UKI	579
Langston, Jennifer Mary (known as Jenny)	Con	328
Lansley, Andrew David	Con	119
Large, Derrick Graham	LCA	485
Latham, Pauline Elizabeth	Con	104
Latham, Philip Ronald	LD	319
Lathan, John Barry	LD	578
Lathrope, Stephen Michael	Lab	36
Laurence, Christopher George	UKI	39
Lawman, Charles Samuel	UKI	387
Lawman, Sandra Joy	LD	170
Lawrance, Clive Robert	Ind	305
Lawrence, Angela	LD	162
Lawrence, Jacqueline Rita	Lab	465
Lawrence, Stephen Roger	Grn	116
Lawrie, Andrew John George	UKI	215
Lawrie, Raymond Alexander	LD	208
Laws, David Anthony	LD	656
Lawson, Brian	SNP	452
Lawson, Richard Hugh	Grn	643
Laxton, Robert	Lab	182
Layton, Margaret Jean	Grn	362
Lazarowicz, Marek Jerzy	Lab	229
Le Blond, Alan James	Ind	343
Le Page, Nicola Lesley	Con	109
Lea, Sarah	LD	324
Leary, Henry Antrobus	SL	458
Leckie, Carolyn	SSP	274
Ledbury, Matthew	Grn	581
Lee, Adrian Hughes	Con	519
Lee, Anne	LD	430
Lee, George Anderton	Con	487
Lee, Graham John	Grn	492
Lee, John Willis	–	586
Lee, Kim	LD	495
Lee, Richard Brian	UKI	529
Lee, Robert Andrew	LD	439
Leech, Peter John Julian	SA	338
Leeke, Maurice Leonard	LD	282
Legg, Keith	LD	292
Leigh, Edward Julian Egerton	Con	260
Leigh, Julian Charles Thomas	Con	18
Leighter, Hilary Frances	LD	237
Lelliott, Mark Philip	LD	560
Lemon, Tim	UU	42
Lennox, John Anthony	LD	557
Lepper, David	Lab	96

Candidate name	Party	Const. no.
Leslie, Christopher Michael	Lab	516
Lettington, David	LD	135
Letwin, Oliver	Con	199
Levin, Martin	UKI	335
Levitt, Tom	Lab	321
Levy, Martin Richard	Comm	422
Lewis, Anthony	PL	401
Lewis, Brandon Kenneth	Con	515
Lewis, Deborah Anne	Con	56
Lewis, Graham Robert (commonly known as Bob)	UKI	507
Lewis, Ian Rowland	LD	443
Lewis, Ivan	Lab	109
Lewis, Julian Murray	Con	416
Lewis, Richard David	UKI	566
Lewis, Terence	Lab	648
Lewsley, Patricia	SDLP	353
Liddell, Helen	Lab	6
Liddell-Grainger, Ian Richard	Con	93
Lidington, David Roy	Con	21
Lilley, Peter Bruce	Con	322
Lindhurst, Gordon	Con	374
Lindsay, Alison Jean	SNP	6
Lines, Terence (known as Terry)	UKI	275
Link, Maurice Andrew James	UKI	369
Linton, Martin	Lab	35
Lister, John Roger Walter	SA	449
Lit, Avtar	Ind	217
Little, Barbara Ann	UKI	445
Little, Bernard	Grn	511
Liversuch, Paul Amos	SL	185
Llewelyn, Alun	PC	415
Lloyd, Anthony Joseph (known as Tony)	Lab	394
Lloyd, Brian Edward	UKI	567
Lloyd, Ifor Dilwyn	UKI	111
Lloyd, Stephen Anthony Christopher	LD	36
Lloyd-Griffiths, David	LD	156
Llwyd, Elfyn	PC	399
Lo Bianco, Jennifer Bryant	UKI	38
Lo Presti, Jack	Con	97
Lock, David Anthony	Lab	654
Lockhart, Norman Phillip Macdonald	SSP	588
Lockwood, Philip David	LCA	114
Lodge, Oliver Arthur Wynlayne	Con	54
Logan, David Andrew John	Con	157
Logan, Timothy Peter	SL	165
Long, Nicholas (commonly known as Nick)	Ind	370
Longden, Adrian	Lab	137

Candidate name	Party	Const. no.
Machray, Martin Edward	Lab	372
Maciejowska, Judy Sara	Grn	589
Mack, Ian James	LD	429
Mack, Timothy Kenneth Andrew	Con	90
MacKay, Andrew James	Con	81
MacKay, Donald Murdo	UKI	152
Macken, Sarah	PL	87
Mackenzie, Gordon Ferguson	LD	380
Mackie, James Alexander	Con	211
Mackie, Jonathan David	Con	551
Mackinlay, Andrew	Lab	578
Mackinlay, Craig	UKI	584
MacLaren, Marilyne Angela	LD	231
Maclean, David John	Con	454
MacNeil, Angus Brendan	SNP	337
MacShane, Denis	Lab	489
MacStiofain, Tomas	RM	89
Mactaggart, Fiona Margaret	Lab	522
Madgwick, Donald Andrew Edwin (known as Don Madgwick)	SA	170
Mager, Jeff	UKI	196
Maginness, Alban	SDLP	43
Mahmood, Khalid	Lab	59
Mahon, Alice	Lab	289
Mahoney, Barry	UKI	346
Mahoney, Monica Emma	PC	92
Main, Christopher Douglas Roy	Con	472
Main, James Russell	LD	99
Maines, Christopher Stewart	LD	448
Mainland, John MacIver	LD	210
Mair, Hamish John Garrow	Con	221
Maitland, Olga Helen	Con	563
Major, Thomas Stephen	Ind	328
Malakouna, Andrew	Ind	238
Malins, Humfrey Jonathan	Con	638
Mallaber, Judy	Lab	11
Mallin, Rupert	SA	616
Mallon, Francis Michael	UKI	30
Mallon, Seamus	SDLP	426
Mallory, Sue	Lab	503
Mammatt, Hazel Elizabeth (Known as Liz Mammatt)	Con	251
Mandelson, Peter Benjamin	Lab	304
Manley, Alan	SSP	5
Mann, John	Lab	32
Manning, Wendy Suzanne	Con	440
Manningham, Edward David	SA	437
Mansell, Charles John (commonly known as Charlie)	Lab	240
Maples, John Cradock	Con	548

Candidate name	Party	Const. no.
May, Theresa Mary	Con	389
Mayberry, Tamsin	LD	269
Mayer, Gerda Kamilla	UKI	606
Mayes, Stephen	SL	292
Mayo, Jenny Doreen	UKI	604
McAllister, Frank	BNP	484
McAlpine, Mhairi	SSP	247
McAvoy, Tommy	Lab	272
McCabe, Anthony Martin	UKI	485
McCabe, Stephen James	Lab	55
McCabe, William	UKI	463
McCafferty, Christine	Lab	114
McCarthy, Charlie	SSP	265
McCarthy, Danny Thomas	SDLP	547
McCarthy, Donnachadh	LD	115
McCarthy, Kieran	APNI	547
McCarthy, Thomas John	Ind	341
McCartney, Cordelia Emma Julia	Con	368
McCartney, Ian	Lab	391
McCartney, Robert Law	UKU	201
McCartney, Thomas Patterson Gilfillan	UKI	640
McConvey, Eamonn	SF	201
McCord, Ian Alexander	Con	26
McCrea, Robert Thomas William	DUP	15
McCrea, Robert William Ian	DUP	594
McCulloch, James	UKI	649
McCulloch, Margaret	Con	220
McDaid, James	SL	130
McDaid, Louise	SL	173
McDermott, Thomas Brian (known as Brian McDermott)	UKI	298
McDonagh, Siobhain Ann	Lab	407
McDonald, Peter Michael	Lab	102
McDonnell, Alasdair	SDLP	44
McDonnell, John Martin	Lab	308
McDonnell, Michael	SA	89
McEwan, Kenneth	SSP	172
McFall, John	Lab	206
McFarlane, Amanda Jane	SSP	130
McFarlane, James	SSP	209
McFarlane, Ross David John	Con	623
McFatridge, Ian Andrew	Lab	12
McGartland, William	SSP	268
McGavigan, Katharine	SL	265
McGimpsey, Christopher	UU	45
McGinty, Christopher Paul	LD	265
McGlashan, David	SNP	172
McGowan, Joe	Lab	243

Candidate name	Party	Const. no.
Mellon, John Joseph James	SNP	210
Mellstrom, Graham Frederick Charles	UKI	296
Meloy, Kevin John	SL	32
Mennear, Karl Andrew	Con	298
Menzies, Mark Andrew	Con	268
Mercer, Patrick John	Con	418
Merrick, Richard John	Grn	466
Merron, Gillian Joanna	Lab	373
Merryfield, Andrew Philip	Lab	620
Merton, Colin Ralph	UKI	147
Meyer, Nigel Lawrence	LD	484
Michael, Alun Edward	Lab	125
Middleton, Jeremy St. John	UPP	348
Mieville, China	SA	474
Milburn, Alan	Lab	177
Miles, Jeffrey Michael	UKI	358
Miliband, David Wright	Lab	526
Millar, Amanda Jane	SSP	490
Millar, Gordon Forsyth	Con	130
Millard, Andrew Christopher Glanvile	Con	235
Millard, Anthony Paul	Con	635
Miller, Andrew Peter	Lab	234
Miller, Hugh (known as Barney)	Grn	95
Miller, Hugo	UKI	326
Miller, Keith	LD	402
Miller, Lynda	BNP	169
Miller, Maria Frances Lewis	Con	640
Miller, Martin	Lab	309
Miller, Paul Anthony	Grn	474
Millington, Arthur James	UKI	654
Millington, Mary Elizabeth	SL	342
Mills, Tarquin Alexander Graham	UKI	437
Milne, Nanette Lilian Margaret	Con	276
Milne, Wendy Margaret	SSP	380
Miney, Neil Lawrence	UKI	378
Miraj, Mohammad Ali	Con	1
Mirza, Badar Islam	Ind	268
Mirza, Mohammad Salman	SA	61
Mitchell, Andrew John Bower	Con	564
Mitchell, Andrew Michael	Con	507
Mitchell, Austin Vernon	Lab	281
Mitchell, Georgina	SSP	293
Mitchell, Iain Grant	Con	229
Mitchell, Ian Randall	Ind	86
Mitchell, Paul Nigel James	Lab	562
Mitchelson, Michael Robert	Con	127
Mochrie, Robert Irvine	Lab	447

Candidate name	Party	Const. no.
Mugglestone, John Vincent	Con	361
Muir, Colin	SL	358
Muir, Jason	SSP	347
Muir, Kirsty	SL	395
Muir, Linda	SL	330
Muir, Simon David	UKI	100
Mullen, Charles Clarke	SSP	538
Muller, Mark	Lab	634
Mullin, Christopher John	Lab	558
Mulloy, Kevin Joseph Vincent Dominic	LD	440
Mulrenan, John Anthony	SA	115
Mumford, Michael Joseph	Lab	297
Munn, Margaret Patricia (commonly known as Meg)	Lab	513
Munn, Robert MacDougal	SNP	228
Munro, Catriona Mary	Lab	411
Munt, Tessa Jane	LD	555
Murdoch, James Campbell	Con	273
Murdoch, Janice Elizabeth	UKI	293
Murie, Andrew Robert	SNP	283
Murphy, Brendan	Con	598
Murphy, Conor Terence	SF	426
Murphy, Denis	Lab	607
Murphy, Jim	Lab	224
Murphy, John Charles	LD	322
Murphy, Michael Anastasio	Ind	500
Murphy, Mick	SF	202
Murphy, Paul Peter	Lab	583
Murphy, Stephen John	LD	617
Murray, James Peter	LD	76
Murray, Peter Joseph	SSP	224
Murray, Philip	IOW	339
Murray, Simon	Con	247
Murray, Terry Patrick	UKI	595
Murray, Theresa Bernadette	PL	504
Murray-Browne, Kris	SNP	254
Murrison, Andrew William	Con	626
Myers, Jeremy	Con	354
Myles, Andrew	LD	227
Mylvaganam, Pathmanathan Sadchatheswaran	Ind	449
Naish, Bronwen	Con	111
Narang, Harash Kumar	Ind	422
Nation, David John	LD	567
Nattrass, Anneliese	UKI	57
Nattrass, Mark	UKI	54
Nattrass, Mike	UKI	564
Nattrass, Natalya	UKI	59

Candidate name	Party	Const. no.
Nattrass, William Henry	UKI	364
Naylor, Chris	Lab	239
Naysmith, John Douglas	Lab	98
Nazir, Choudry Shahid	Ind	522
Neal, Jon	LD	290
Neal, Joseph William Edward	UKI	430
Neale, Pamela Winwrite	Ind	582
Neary, Karen	SNP	268
Neilson, Peter Thomas	UKI	490
Nellist, David John	SA	163
Nelson, Isabella	LD	271
Nesbitt, Dermot William Gibson	UU	202
Nettleship, Roger	Ind	526
Nettleton, Robert Adcock	Ind	364
Newbound, Kathryn Druscilla	LD	389
Newby, Christopher (known as Chris)	LD	378
Newman, Paul	Con	181
Newmark, Brooks Phillip Victor	Con	85
Newton, Barry	UKI	310
Newton, Kevin	Con	152
Newton, Stephen Charles	LD	483
Newton, William	PL	408
Ng, Rebecca	PL	215
Niblett, Brian William	LD	97
Nichol, Frederick James	SA	65
Nicholls, Geoffrey Lane	Grn	234
Nicholls, Patrick Charles Martyn	Con	573
Nicholson, Alasdair	SNP	627
Nicholson, Paul Matthew	Lab	79
Nicholson, Robert Douglas	Ind	86
Nicoll, Alexander John McDiarmid	Con	581
Nield, Peter Joseph	LD	12
Nielsen, Magnus	UKI	323
Nokes, Caroline Fiona Ellen	Con	527
Nolan, David Patrick	LD	94
Nolan, Mark	Con	414
Nolan, Michael Anthony (commonly known as Buster)	LCA	85
Norman, Archibald John	Con	587
Norman, Derek Arthur	UKI	333
Norman, James Andrew	Lab	560
Norris, Dan	Lab	608
North, Peter	UKI	83
Northgreaves, Raymond	UKI	357
Nowosielski, Noel Andrew Brittain	Lib	360
Noyce, Christopher David	LD	303
Nunn, John David	UKI	114
Nunnery, Arlene	SSP	476
Nuttall, David John	Con	412

Candidate name	Party	Const. no.
O'Brien, Brendan Mark	Lab	523
O'Brien, Mark Terence	SA	378
O'Brien, Michael	Lab	614
O'Brien, Roger	LD	550
O'Brien, Rory	Con	271
O'Brien, Stephen Rothwell	Con	226
O'Brien, William	UKI	249
O'Brien, William	Lab	432
O'Callaghan, Matthew	Lab	495
O'Connor, Danny	SDLP	13
O'Donnell, Hugh	LD	247
O'Donnell, John	LD	172
O'Donnell, Joseph Gerard	SF	42
O'Donnell, Terence Kelly	Ind	452
O'Farrell, John Peter	Lab	389
O'Hagan, Dara Mary	SF	596
O'Hara, Edward	Lab	352
O'Hare, Graham	Con	466
O'Hare, Nicholas	LD	50
O'Malley, Brian	LD	452
O'Neill, George Keith	Lab	71
O'Neill, Martin John	Lab	442
Oakes, Graham John	LD	620
Oakley, Ian	Con	424
Oakley, Robert Nigel	UKI	519
Oaten, Mark	LD	633
Oddy, Christine Margaret	Ind	164
Offord, Matthew James	Con	27
Oliver, Rachel Clare	LD	584
Oliver, William Martin (commonly known as Martin)	LD	374
Olner, William John (known as Bill)	Lab	441
Onuegbu, Crada	Lab	417
Opik, Lembit	LD	410
Oram, Stanley	UKI	297
Ord, Alan Christopher	LD	213
Ord, Christopher James	LD	218
Ord, David	LD	422
Ord-Clarke, John (a.k.a. Viscount Clarkey of Rochdale Canal)	MRLP	306
Organ, Diana Mary	Lab	257
Ormerod, Richard Daniel	LD	327
Ormston, Frank	SA	658
Orr, Alastair	Con	227
Orrell, John Keith	LD	496
Osborne, David	LD	60
Osborne, George Gideon Oliver	Con	570
Osborne, Sandra	Lab	22
Oswald, John	LD	293

Candidate name	Party	Const. no.
Pearce, Simon Nicholas Charles	Con	499
Pearce, Thomas Henry	LD	504
Pearcey, Jacqueline	LD	395
Pearson, Frederick George	UKI	370
Pearson, Ian Phares	Lab	204
Pearson, John Samuel	UKI	46
Pearson, Stephen John	LD	432
Pearson, Trevor John	UKI	659
Pendragon, Arthur Uther (commonly known as King Arthur)	Ind	7
Penlington, Gilbert Napier	LD	164
Penning, Michael Allan	Con	578
Penrose, John David	Con	629
Penycate, Richard William	Grn	489
Pepper, Adrian Norman Spencer	Con	641
Perham, Linda	Lab	335
Perkins, Andrew Mark	Lab	524
Perkins, Timothy James	LD	73
Perrin, Henry Fairfax Robert (commonly known as Robert)	UKI	17
Perrin, Raymond Arthur	Ind	481
Perry, John	Con	509
Perry, Michael Roy	SL	500
Peskett, Pamela Grace	LD	71
Peters, Graem	LD	306
Petrie, David Dick	Con	16
Peverelle, Charles John	Ind	629
Phazey, John Joseph	UKI	372
Philbin, Christopher Simon (commonly known as Herb)	LCA	137
Phillips, David Mervyn	Lab	586
Phillips, Elizabeth Fletcher	UKI	86
Phillips, Ian Robert	UKI	129
Phillips, John Lydon	Grn	329
Phillips, Michael Sheridan	UKI	405
Phillips, Sally	Grn	306
Phillips, William	BNP	606
Pickering, Simon Paul Christopher	Grn	257
Picking, Anne	Lab	221
Pickles, Eric Jack	Con	91
Pickstone, Timothy David	LD	109
Pickthall, Colin	Lab	354
Pidgeon, Caroline Valerie	LD	205
Pierce, Martin Dirk	LD	632
Pike, Peter Leslie	Lab	106
Pinfield, Peter Nicholas (known as Nick)	LD	634
Pinkerton, Jeanne	LD	533
Pinkett, Jennifer	LD	569
Pinnock, Kathryn Mary	LD	34

Candidate name	Party	Const. no.
Pinto, Fiona Karen	PL	621
Pitt, Melvin George	Con	604
Plaskitt, James Andrew	Lab	613
Platt, Craig Charles	Ind	177
Plummer, Michael Ian	LD	296
Plunkett, Richard	Grn	155
Pocock, Robert Leonard	Lab	564
Pollard, Kerry Patrick	Lab	498
Pollock, Jean	Lib	524
Polydorou, Susan Ann	Lab	101
Pond, Christopher Richard	Lab	280
Poole, Bertie Robert	UKI	282
Poorun, Storm	Grn	115
Poots, Edwin Cecil	DUP	353
Pope, Gregory James	Lab	334
Pope, Michael Robert	LD	333
Porter, John Colin	UKI	66
Porter, Sonya Ann	UKI	285
Portillo, Michael Denzil Xavier	Con	345
Potter, Cheryl	Con	449
Potter, Clive	BNP	361
Potter, Donald Richard	Con	167
Potter, Vanessa Ann (known as Long Tall Sally)	MRLP	187
Potts, Gordon Graham	SL	421
Poulsen, Karl	Con	591
Pound, Stephen Pelham	Lab	216
Powell, Aaron James	Con	394
Powell, Raymond	Lab	443
Powell, Richard	Con	489
Powell, William Hugh	LD	614
Prachar, Warwick William	Ind	251
Prasad, Christopher	UKI	99
Pratt, Christopher Norman	UKI	37
Prendergast, David	Lab	103
Prentice, Benjamin Henry	Con	57
Prentice, Bridget	Lab	369
Prentice, Gordon	Lab	453
Prescott, John Leslie	Lab	330
Price, Adam	PC	128
Price, Gerald	UKI	309
Price, Katie (commonly known as Jordan)	Ind	551
Primarolo, Dawn	Lab	99
Prior, Anthony John (Tony)	Lib	656
Prior, David Gifford Leathes	Con	428
Prisk, Mark	Con	315
Pritchard, Adam James	Con	359
Pritchard, Hugh William Lee	LD	249

Candidate name	Party	Const. no.
Pritchard, Mark Andrew	Con	610
Procter, John Michael	Con	467
Proctor, Seth	LD	576
Prosper, Cecilia Isabella	SA	287
Prosser, Gwynfor Mathews (commonly known as Gwyn)	Lab	200
Protz, George Stephen (also known as Steve)	UKI	160
Prout, Allen Gilbert	UKI	257
Pryke, Peter Leonard	Ind	91
Pryor, Andrew Mark	SA	97
Psallidas, Stephen Anthony	LD	421
Pudner, Huw	SA	415
Pugh, John David	LD	530
Pulman, Angela	PC	443
Punyer, Margaret Alison	Con	107
Purchase, Kenneth	Lab	640
Purnell, Christopher Arthur	Lab	448
Purnell, James Mark Dakin	Lab	536
Pursehouse, Jeremy	LD	559
Purser, Nils John	Con	58
Purvis, Dawn	Prog U	44
Puthucheary, Carol	SNP	476
Pym, Hugh Ruthven	LD	631
Pyne, Russell David	LD	284
Pyne, Stephanie Mary	PL	523
Qadar, Ali	LD	511
Quar, Graeme Brian	Con	537
Quarmby, Arthur	UKI	155
Quigley, Kevin Martin	Lab	179
Quin, Joyce Gwendolen	Lab	262
Quinn, Lawrence William (known as Lawrie)	Lab	504
Quinn, Martin	Grn	191
Quintavalle, Josephine Mary	PL	345
Rabone, Barry Maciek	LD	29
Race, Denys Alan Reg	Lab	141
Radcliff, Peter Robert	SA	438
Radford, Stephen Richard	Lib	379
Rajch, Henry	SA	26
Rammell, William Ernest	Lab	300
Ramsay, Peter John	Con	206
Ramsbottom, Marc Steven	LD	446
Randall, Alexander John (known as John)	Con	597
Randall, George Micheal	SL	329
Randall, Stuart Roy	Con	210
Rands, Neil David George	Con	340
Rankin, Davena	Con	269

Candidate name	Party	Const. no.
Richardson, Neil	Con	293
Riches, Elizabeth	LD	253
Richmond, Edward Anthony	Con	177
Richmond, Victoria May	Con	356
Riddle, Keith Alan	UKI	617
Riding, Gary Anthony	LD	393
Rifkind, Malcolm Leslie	Con	230
Rigby, Peter Edward	Ind	322
Rijke, Nicholas David	LD	498
Riley, Nicholas	SA	511
Rimmer, Martin Edward	LD	532
Riseborough, George Frank	DW	83
Rising, Stuart Frederick	UKI	315
Ritchie, David	SNP	271
Ritchie, Heather	SSP	269
Ritchie, Murdo	SL	273
Ritchie, Stuart David	LD	22
Rix, Marion Jennifer	Con	405
Roach, Jennifer	Lib	579
Robathan, Andrew Robert George	Con	64
Roberts, Adrian Kere James	UKI	407
Roberts, Barrie Moelwyn Antony	Con	62
Roberts, Barry John	BNP	369
Roberts, David Paul	SL	361
Roberts, Dominica Mary	PL	81
Roberts, Douglas Charles	Ind	132
Roberts, Gerald	UKI	294
Roberts, John Dominic Wace	PL	107
Roberts, Mike David	Con	622
Roberts, Paul David	LD	226
Roberts, Richard John	LD	351
Roberts, Roger Douglas Clayton	LD	277
Roberts, Stephen John	Lab	485
Robertson, Angus	SNP	411
Robertson, Hugh	Con	250
Robertson, Iain	SNP	206
Robertson, John	Lab	265
Robertson, Julia Margaret	LD	572
Robertson, Julian	Con	201
Robertson, Laurence Anthony	Con	575
Robertson, Les	SSP	206
Robertson, Raymond Scott	Con	224
Robinson, Augustine Alberto	Con	304
Robinson, David	SL	218
Robinson, Geoffrey	Lab	164
Robinson, Ian Raymond	Ind	564
Robinson, Iris	DUP	547
Robinson, Joanne	UKI	290

Candidate name	Party	Const. no.
Rowan, Alice Janette Gilbertson	SSP	24
Rowantree, Robert Iain	Con	113
Rowe, William Patrick	Con	28
Rowen, Paul	LD	482
Rowlands, David John	UKI	409
Rowlands, David William Lloyd	UKI	410
Rowley, Alexandra Margaret	LD	102
Rowlinson, Paul John	PC	180
Roxburgh, William Murray	Con	549
Roy, Frank	Lab	414
Royce, Catherine Margaret	LD	597
Ruane, Christopher Shaun	Lab	598
Ruddock, Joan Mary	Lab	368
Ruff, Aidan Paul	Con	421
Ruffell, Mark Beresford	Con	592
Ruffley, David Laurie	Con	110
Rule, Carlos Joseph Martinez	SL	215
Rule, Eloisa Joan (Ella)	SL	325
Rule, Jonathan Daniel	LD	517
Rumsey, Derek Leonard	UKI	7
Ruskell, Mark Christopher	Grn	538
Russell, Christine Margaret	Lab	140
Russell, Robert Edward (known as Bob)	LD	154
Ruxton, Carrie Helen	Con	435
Ryan, Joan Marie	Lab	237
Ryan, Michael Gerard (commonly known as Gerry)	Lab	171
Rykala, Adam John	PC	68
Saggers, Simon Peter	Grn	119
Sajid, Mohammed	Grn	550
Salim, Mohammed	–	482
Salisbury-Jones, David Newton	Lab	597
Salkeld, Anthony Michael	PC	425
Salmon, Julian Philip	Grn	617
Salmond, Alex Elliot Anderson	SNP	24
Salter, Martin John	Lab	471
Salvage, John Stephen	BNP	624
Sambrook-Marshall, Judith	SL	54
Samuel, Agnes Carmichael	SNP	16
Samuel, Mark Robin Lionel	Ch	171
Samways, Julian Patrick Edward	Con	396
Sandell, Peter Graham	UKI	608
Sanders, Adrian Mark	LD	582
Sanders, Darren	LD	463
Sanderson, Hugh Glen Howard	Con	46
Sandford, James Nicholas (known as Nick)	LD	456
Sangster, John	SSP	276
Sarwar, Mohammad	Lab	268

Candidate name	Party	Const. no.
Serpell, Nicholas John	Con	248
Serrelli, Roseanne	Con	323
Sewards, David	UKI	467
Sewards, Geoffrey Brian	LD	163
Shafique, Chauhdry	Lab	653
Shand, Tim John Cairns	Grn	269
Shapps, Grant V.	Con	621
Sharkey, Margaret Mary	SL	284
Sharma, Baldev Kumar	LD	217
Sharp, John Caley	Con	332
Sharp, Keith	LD	341
Sharp, Pamela Victoria Davies	UKI	568
Sharpe, David John	Con	476
Sharratt, Peter Nicholas	Ind	570
Shaw, Andrew Martin	Lab	532
Shaw, David Lawrence	Con	348
Shaw, Fredrick Bernard	SL	655
Shaw, Gillian Catherine	Con	11
Shaw, John Daniel	LD	528
Shaw, Jonathan Rowland	Lab	135
Shaw, Thomas Christopher Dunkerley	Con	363
Shaw, William Tristram (known as Bill)	Grn	658
Shawcroft, Christine Linda	Lab	400
Sheahan, Sean David	Lab	134
Sheath, Alan	UKI	288
Sheerman, Barry	Lab	329
Shefki, Unver Tuygun	Ref	585
Shephard, Gillian Patricia	Con	431
Shepherd, Richard Charles Scrimgeour	Con	8
Sheppard, Christopher	UKI	578
Sheppard, Edward John	BNP	163
Sheppard, Mark Brian Birch	UKI	570
Sheridan, James	Lab	476
Sheridan, Lynn	SSP	153
Sheridan, Michael Paul	Grn	428
Shersby, Lucinda Caroline Anne (commonly known as Lucy)	Con	35
Sherwin, Christopher Arthur	UKI	498
Shipley, Debra Ann	Lab	546
Shopland, David William	Ind	643
Shore, Lianne	NF	531
Shore, Michael Patrick	NF	54
Short, Clare	Lab	57
Shorter, Giles Barralet	SL	99
Shortt, David John Skey	Ind	576
Shreeve, Sigrid Brigitta	Ind	450
Shrewsbury, Martyn John	Grn	566
Shrewsbury, Sandra Christina (known as Tina)	Grn	278

Candidate name	Party	Const. no.
Sibbald, James Gray Meiklem	SNP	374
Sibley, Leslie Frederick	Lab	23
Sibley, Richard Sydney	Ind	629
Siddique, Ateeq	SA	83
Siggins, Robert John	SL	176
Silcock, Christopher Robin	UKI	105
Silvester, Richard Edward Warner	Ind	274
Simison, Paul Creer	UKI	428
Simmonds, David Timothy	Con	112
Simmonds, Mark Jonathan Mortlock	Con	77
Simon, Sion Llewelyn	Lab	54
Simons, Julie	LD	383
Simpson, Alan John	Lab	440
Simpson, Andrew Stuart John	LD	434
Simpson, David	DUP	596
Simpson, George Mark (commonly known as Mark)	Con	654
Simpson, Jonathan Andrew	LD	298
Simpson, Keith Robert	Con	427
Simpson, Michael Richard Edwards	Con	468
Simpson-Laing, Tracey-Louise	Lab	659
Sinclair, Ronald	SL	394
Sinclaire, Nicole C (commonly known as Nikki)	UKI	398
Singh, Baghwant	SL	624
Singh, Marsha	Lab	84
Singh, Pritam	Grn	449
Singh, Punjab	LD	55
Singleton, Pamela Anne	Con	459
Sinnatt, Simon Peter Randall	Con	367
Sinnett, David Rhys	PC	465
Skaife D'Ingerthorp, Michael John	UKI	371
Skinner, David Edward	SL	332
Skinner, Dennis Edward	Lab	72
Skinner, Rasjid Edward George	Con	453
Slater, Bryan Hilton	UKI	500
Sloan, Thomas Kelly	Lab	261
Smellie, Stephen	SSP	414
Smith, Alan George	UKI	170
Smith, Alyn Edward	SNP	232
Smith, Andrew David	Lab	449
Smith, Andrew George	UKI	239
Smith, Angela Evans	Lab	30
Smith, Barney	Grn	60
Smith, Calum	SNP	549
Smith, Catharine Mary (commonly known as Kate)	LD	11
Smith, Christopher Robert	Lab	341
Smith, Colin	BNP	50
Smith, David	UKI	349

Candidate name	Party	Const. no.
Smith, Dewi Hywel	LD	599
Smith, Elizabeth Jane	Con	455
Smith, Freda	SA	489
Smith, Gail	LD	509
Smith, Geraldine	Lab	412
Smith, Gordon	LD	148
Smith, Graham Paul	Con	432
Smith, Henry Edward Millar	Con	166
Smith, Ian Jonathan	UKI	431
Smith, Jacqueline Jill	Lab	473
Smith, James William Elliot (commonly known as Bill)	LD	18
Smith, John Norman	UKI	29
Smith, John William Patrick	Lab	599
Smith, Joseph William	UKI	22
Smith, Llewellyn Thomas	Lab	68
Smith, Louise	UKI	241
Smith, Peter Edward	SA	605
Smith, Philip Roland	Con	423
Smith, Phillip Ashley	LD	193
Smith, Sir Robert	LD	5
Smith, Roger	SA	331
Smith, Roy Alfred	LD	611
Smith, Russell Alexander	BNP	192
Smith, Sadie Laureina	LD	624
Smith, Stephen Paul	PC	583
Smith, Stephen Philip	UKI	475
Smith, Steven	BNP	106
Smithard, Jane	LD	30
Smithers, Gavin Roderick Nigel	Con	121
Smithson, David Julian Gardner	LD	352
Smithson, Joan Brenda	Grn	192
Smyth, Eric	DUP	45
Smyth, Stewart James Wortley	SA	275
Smyth, William Martin	UU	44
Soames, Arthur Nicholas Winston	Con	562
Socrates, Peter Lee Boswell	−	357
Sole, Michael John	LD	250
Soley, Clive Stafford	Lab	215
Sollitt, Steven Roy	LD	31
Somerville, Shirley-Anne	SNP	350
Sootheran, Paul Balderson	UKI	569
Soult, Graham Andrew	LD	423
Soutar, Hamish Douglas	Grn	503
Southcombe, Michael John	LD	194
Southworth, Helen Mary	Lab	612
Speakman, Lee	UKI	200
Speht, Robert	LD	565

Candidate name	Party	Const. no.
Stevenson, William	Con	246
Stewart, Brian Joseph	Con	52
Stewart, Catherine	SSP	211
Stewart, David John	Lab	337
Stewart, Donald McIntyre	Con	94
Stewart, Iain Aitken	Con	406
Stewart, Ian	Lab	225
Stewart, James Scott	SSP	22
Stewart, John David	LD	347
Stewart, Karl James	SL	166
Stewart, Kaukab	SNP	229
Stewart, Michael Mashud	PD	312
Stewart, Robert	LD	268
Stewart-Mole, Edmund	UKI	615
Still, Joyce Edna	Lab	285
Stinchcombe, Paul David	Lab	619
Stoate, Howard Geoffrey Alvan	Lab	178
Stockton, John Robert	Lab	259
Stoddart, Tim	Con	647
Stokes, David Llewellyn Kelsey	Lab	80
Stokes, Henry Armstrong Allen (commonly known as Harry)	Con	407
Stollar, Gavin Paul	LD	335
Stone, Anthony Bernard	UKI	559
Stone, Gregory Martin	LD	600
Stopps, Jill	UKI	162
Strang, Gavin Steel	Lab	228
Strange, Margaret	UKI	146
Straw, John Whitaker (known as Jack)	Lab	65
Streeter, Gary Nicholas	Con	190
Stride, George Yarver	UKI	71
Stringer, Graham Eric	Lab	393
Stuart, Gisela Gschaider	Lab	53
Stuart, Graham Charles	Con	116
Stuart, John Smeaton	UKI	245
Stuart, Neil	LD	310
Stunell, Andrew	LD	309
Sugarman, Jason Ashley	Con	204
Sugden, Alexandra Elizabeth	LD	462
Sulaiman, Takki Emmanouel	Lab	333
Sully, Janet Christine	Lab	326
Summers, Glyndwr John	Ind	477
Sutcliffe, Gerry	Lab	83
Suter, Mark Anthony	UKI	510
Sutherland, Graham Donald	SNP	380
Sutton, Helen Clare	Con	375
Swain, Marilyn Janice	UKI	279
Swayne, Desmond Angus	Con	417

Candidate name	Party	Const. no.
Teale, Mary Christina Beatrice (known as Mary Chadwick)	PL	298
Teather, Sarah Louise	LD	255
Telfer, Joanne Lindsay	SSP	627
Telfer, William	SSP	549
Tennyson, Graham Stuart Gareth	Con	83
Terry, Janet Anita	SA	194
Tettenborn, Andrew Martin	UKI	33
Thacker, Rajeev Kumar	Grn	632
Theobald, Bernard Andrew	Con	505
Theobald, Geoffrey Trevor	Con	95
Theunissen, Evelyn Edwina	UKI	149
Thomas, David Nicholas	Con	128
Thomas, Gareth	Lab	150
Thomas, Gareth Richard	Lab	303
Thomas, Leigh	PC	342
Thomas, Richard Knight	LD	370
Thomas, Simon	PC	133
Thomas, Wynford Vaughan	SA	264
Thompson, Angela	SA	204
Thompson, Eric	LD	206
Thompson, James Alan (Alan)	LD	607
Thompson, Neil	SA	500
Thompson, Paul Gerard	LD	318
Thompson, Pauline Naplan Coan	SSP	442
Thompson, William John	UU	593
Thoms, Grant Robert	SNP	265
Thomson, Charles Geoffrey	St.	341
Thomson, Ian	SA	418
Thomson, Richard Gordon	SNP	588
Thorn, Ian Leslie	LD	93
Thornber, Peter Michael	UKI	600
Thornberry, Emily Anne	Lab	122
Thornton, Amy Louise	UKI	470
Thornton, Cyril Oscar	Pens	617
Thornton, John Lestock	LD	354
Thorpe, Ellis	Lab	276
Thorpe, James John	Lab	187
Thraves, Alec	SA	566
Thurso, John Archibald	LD	113
Tickell, Oliver Thomas	Grn	313
Timms, Stephen Creswell	Lab	219
Tinch, Robert Ross Templeton	Grn	436
Tinnion, Fay	Lab	480
Tipping, Simon Patrick (commonly known as Paddy)	Lab	515
Titherington, Ian Richard	PC	566
Tod, Martin Paul Niebuhr	LD	215
Todd, Mark Wainwright	Lab	185

Candidate name	Party	Const. no.
Tolman, Mark	BNP	25
Tolstoy, Nicholai	UKI	609
Tombs, Sebastian	LD	229
Tomlin, Deirdre Desiree (known as Dee)	LD	653
Tomlin, John Craig	UKI	334
Tomlinson, William Leonard	LD	605
Tonge, Jennifer Louise	LD	481
Toomer, David	SA	75
Topp, Stuart Leslie	SSP	486
Torbica, Dusan	UKI	433
Tough, Alistair George	LD	153
Touhig, James Donnelly	Lab	342
Towler, Gawain Howard Wilkinson	Con	270
Townsend, Charles Edward	LD	68
Toye, Moira Phyliss	LD	436
Traquair, Robin James	Con	404
Travers, Gillian Mary	Lab	492
Treacy, Michael	BNP	445
Tredinnick, David Arthur Stephen	Con	78
Trend, Michael St. John	Con	634
Tress, Robert David	LD	505
Trevanion, David Hugh	UKI	518
Trickett, Jon Hedley	Lab	311
Trimble, David	UU	596
Troman, Timothy David	Con	422
Truesdale, Peter Jonathan	LD	595
Truss, Elizabeth	Con	311
Truswell, Paul Anthony	Lab	467
Tucker, Gregory	SA	550
Tucker, Vanessa Marie	LD	655
Turek, Paul Walter	SL	311
Turnbull, George Park	Con	490
Turnbull, Lisa	PC	1
Turner, Andrew John	Con	339
Turner, Dennis	Lab	641
Turner, Desmond Stanley (known as Des)	Lab	95
Turner, George	Lab	429
Turner, Martin Marshall	LD	564
Turner, Neil	Lab	630
Turner, Nicholas Robin (known as Nick Turner)	Cust	129
Turner, Peter John Russell	LD	85
Tutton, Andrew James	Ind	1
Twigg, John Derek	Lab	291
Twigg, Stephen	Lab	238
Twigger, Robert Patrick Ingram	EC	450
Tyler, Paul	LD	160
Tynan, Bill	Lab	293

Candidate name	Party	Const. no.
Tyndall, John Hutchyns	BNP	407
Tyrie, Andrew Guy	Con	142
Tyzack, Peter Laurence	LD	98
Udwin, Candy	SA	323
Underwood, Clare Joan Therese	PL	116
Unwin, Robert Dudley (commonly known as Rob)	Grn	513
Urquhart, Jean	SNP	486
Usher, James Robin	Con	611
Utting, Karen	LD	246
Valentine, James Emmanuel	Lab	39
Valentine, Michelle	Grn	396
Vara, Shailesh Lakhman	Con	434
Vaz, Keith	Lab	361
Veasey, Christopher Malcolm	Ind	331
Verma, Sandip	Con	330
Vernall, Charles Delacey	−	575
Vickers, Anthony James Muschamp	LD	287
Victory, Malcolm Gordon	Grn	646
Vigar, Amanda Adele	Con	540
Vigar, David Charles	LD	626
Viggers, Peter John	Con	277
Vincent, Alan Thomas	Con	66
Vincent, Andrew Kenneth (commonly known as Andy)	LD	363
Vincent, John William	LD	240
Vincent, Wayne	UKI	61
Vineall, Nicholas Edward John	Con	205
Vinyard, William Joseph	UKI	338
Vipass, Brenda Muriel	UKI	583
Virdee, Surinder Pal	SL	57
Virgo, Michael Joseph	UKI	316
Vis, Rudi Jan	Lab	255
Vitelli, Siobhan Moyra	LD	35
Vivian, Harvey Bernard	UKI	56
Voizey, Guy Stuart Bennett	LD	577
Von Goetz, Leslie Margaret Campbell	LCA	254
Vowles, Glenn Royston	Grn	99
Wagner, Carl Anthony	LCA	331
Wainman, Allison Joan	LD	390
Wakefield, Cyril	UKI	77
Walder, Clive Richard	SA	58
Waldock, Peter Alan Wayne	SL	241
Wales, Peter Richard	LD	122
Walker, Cecil	UU	43
Walker, Charles Ashley Rupert	Con	216

Candidate name	Party	Const. no.
Watney, Marcus John Andrew	UKI	450
Watson, Alastair	Con	124
Watson, George	SA	18
Watson, Mark Anthony	Con	69
Watson, Thomas Anthony	Lab	623
Watt, Christopher Dean	Con	608
Watt, Claire	SL	414
Watt, David	SSP	4
Watt, David Thomas	Lab	461
Watts, David Kenneth	LD	104
Watts, David Leonard	Lab	499
Watts, Richard Frederick	Lab	37
Waugh, Ronald	SL	351
Waye, Sheila Ramsay	LD	278
Weatherley, Michael Richard	Con	25
Webb, Dorothy Jane	LD	146
Webb, Gavin Geoffrey	LD	542
Webb, Jessica Lilias	Lab	143
Webb, Lawrence James	UKI	324
Webb, Peter	UKI	514
Webb, Steven John	LD	435
Webb, Victor Charles	UKI	587
Webster-Gardiner, Graham Robert	UKI	240
Weddell, Allan Andrew James	UKI	140
Wedon, Kenneth Alfred Ernest	UKI	137
Weir, Anthony	SSP	246
Weir, Michael Fraser	SNP	12
Weiss, Rainbow George	Vote	42,43,44,45
Welfare, Damien Francis John	Lab	144
Weller, John	Con	160
Wellesley, William Valerian	Con	397
Wells, James Henry	DUP	202
Wells, Mark Adrian	Lab	430
Welsh, Geoffrey Lee	LD	64
Wennington, William	Grn	540
West, Christine Maria	CD	320
Westbrook, Nicholas Shawne Edney	LD	461
Weston, Andrew William	LD	350
Weston, Nick Peter	Con	364
Westwood, John Frederick	UKI	204
Whatham, Stephen Benjamin	SL	499
Wheeler, Heather	Con	165
Whelan, John Anthony	Con	433
Whelton, Martin James	Lab	561
Whipp, David Michael Baxter	LD	453
Whitaker, Walter	UKI	516
White, Brian Arthur Robert	Lab	405
White, Christopher Mark Francis	Con	55

Candidate name	Party	Const. no.
White, Derrick	SSP	221
White, Gordon	SA	433
White, Keith Michael	Lab	21
White, Keith Stephen	SSP	254
White, Michael John	Con	176
White, Paul Graham	Con	287
Whitehead, Alan Patrick Vincent	Lab	528
Whitelegg, John	Grn	355
Whitley, Rob	Grn	323
Whittaker, John	UKI	355
Whittingdale, John Flasby Lawrance	Con	392
Whittle, Lindsay Geoffrey	PC	112
Whitton, Alan Derek	UKI	458
Whyte, Iain	Con	232
Whyte, Stewart Norman Gunn	Con	2
Wicks, Malcolm Hunt	Lab	170
Widdecombe, Ann Noreen	Con	390
Wiggin, Sallyann	LD	574
Wiggin, William David (commonly known as Bill)	Con	366
Wilcock, Alexander Iain Matthew Cameron	LD	371
Wilcock, Jeremy David	LD	507
Wilcock, Peter Anthony	LD	305
Wilcox, Paul George	SA	127
Wild, Patricia Ann	UKI	468
Wild, Peter	LD	641
Wild, William Edward (known as Edward)	Con	338
Wilde, Terry	Ind	193
Wildgoose, David Basil	LD	622
Wilding, Peter John	Con	302
Wildy, Thomas Trerise	Lab	584
Wilkins, Irene Lesley	LD	562
Wilkins, Nicholas John Eric	Grn	139
Wilkins, Richard Leslie	Lab	162
Wilkinson, John	UKI	622
Wilkinson, John Arbuthnot Ducane	Con	492
Wilkinson, Richard	Con	173
Willetts, David Lindsay	Con	307
Williams, Alan John	Lab	566
Williams, Alan Richard (known as Richard)	LD	110
Williams, Alan Wynne	Lab	128
Williams, Betty Helena	Lab	157
Williams, Darren James	SA	470
Williams, Eilian Stuart	PC	657
Williams, Gareth David	Con	234
Williams, Geoffrey	LD	469
Williams, Heather	SNP	231
Williams, Huw Benedict	Con	68
Williams, Huw Elfed	PC	150

Candidate name	Party	Const. no.
Williams, Hywel	PC	111
Williams, John Penri	PC	598
Williams, Mark Fraser	LD	133
Williams, Martin	Ind	195
Williams, Richard Francis	Lab	277
Williams, Roger Hugh	LD	86
Williams, Sheila Beryl	UKI	60
Williams, Stephen Roy	LD	100
Williamson, Christine Ann	UKI	214
Williamson, Kevin	SSP	227
Williamson, Maria Theresia	Lib	222
Willie, Brian Stewart (commonly known as Stewart)	LD	48
Willis, David Grant	LD	513
Willis, George Philip (known as Phil)	LD	301
Willock, John	SL	381
Willott, Jennifer Nancy (also known as Jenny)	LD	123
Willoughby, Laura	LD	340
Wills, Michael David	Lab	567
Wilshire, David	Con	532
Wilson, Brian	Lab	173
Wilson, Brian	SA	510
Wilson, Cathy	SA	376
Wilson, Cedric	NIU	547
Wilson, David John	UKI	188
Wilson, Isobel Rosemary	LD	105
Wilson, John Gordon	SNP	293
Wilson, Matthew George	Con	510
Wilson, Peter David	Con	474
Wilson, Robert	Con	129
Wilson, Sammy	DUP	13
Wilson, Stanley William	LD	472
Wilson, Thomas	SNP	130
Wilson Fletcher, Alexander Charles Edward	LD	83
Windridge, Lee	BNP	56
Windsor, Robert Piers	SA	165
Windsor, Yvonne Margaret Clare	PL	468
Winfield, Rif	Lib	37
Winnick, David Julian	Lab	604
Winstanley, Michael William	Con	73
Winterton, Jane Ann	Con	156
Winterton, Nicholas Raymond	Con	388
Winterton, Rosalie (known as Rosie)	Lab	194
Wise, Richard	Ind	542
Wise, Thomas Harold	UKI	41
Wiseman, Andrew David	LD	368
Wishart, Peter	SNP	572
Wonnacott, James Alan	UKI	586
Wood, Alan Stephen	UKI	187